WOMEN'S STUDIES
Essential Readings

3.7 Henrietta Moore Feminism and Anthropology 93

3.8 Akemi Kikumura Childhood (1904–1922) 96

3.9 Barbara Myerhoff Jewish comes up in you from the
roots 99

3.10 Lila Abu-Lughod The Romance of Resistance:
tracing transformations of power through Bedouin
women 102

Further Reading 103

4 **Historical Perspectives on Women's Lives** **105**
Edited and Introduced by Deirdre Beddoe

Introduction 107

4.1 Ivy Pinchbeck Women Workers and the Industrial
Revolution 1750–1850 109

4.2 Catherine Hall Gender Divisions and Class
Formations in the Birmingham Middle Class,
1780–1850 112

4.3 Sheila Rowbotham Hidden from History: three
hundred years of women's oppression and the
fight against it 114

4.4 Angela V. John By the Sweat of their Brow: women
workers at Victorian coal mines 115

4.5 Anna Davin 'Mind that you do as you are told':
reading books for Board School girls, 1870–1902 116

4.6 Margery Spring Rice Working-Class Wives 118

4.7 Jane Lewis The Politics of Motherhood: child and
maternal welfare in England, 1900–1939 121

4.8 Deirdre Beddoe Back to Home and Duty: women
between the wars 1918–1939 122

4.9 Ray Strachey The Cause 124

4.10 Sylvia Pankhurst The Suffragette Movement 127

4.11 Sheila Jeffreys The Spinster and Her Enemies:
feminism and sexuality 1880–1930 127

Further Reading 128

5   **Women, Education and Work**   **131**

Edited and Introduced by Jane Prince

Introduction   133

5.1   Veronica Beechey   Unequal Work   136
5.2   Michèle Barrett   Women's Oppression Today   139
5.3   Lindsay German   Sex, Class and Socialism   141
5.4   Geoffrey de Ste Croix   The Class Struggle in the Ancient Greek World   146
5.5   Valerie Walkerdine   The Mastery of Reason   148
5.6   Robert Hodge and Gunther Kress   Social Semiotics   151
5.7   John McCauley   Academics   155
5.8   Judi Marshall   Women Managers: travellers in a male world   160
5.9   Nigel Fielding   Joining Forces   163
5.10   Marny Hall   Private Experiences in the Public Domain: lesbians in organizations   167
5.11   Heidi Mirza   Young, Female and Black   173

Further Reading   178

6   **Marriage and Motherhood**   **179**

Edited and Introduced by Sue Faulkner and Stevi Jackson

Introduction   181

6.1   Sallie Westwood   Domestic labourers, or stand by your man – while he sits down and has a cup of tea   184
6.2   Sylvia Walby   The Elements of the Patriarchal Mode of Production   187
6.3   Nickie Charles and Marion Kerr   Women, Food and Families   188
6.4   Penny Mansfield and Jean Collard   Solving Problems and Airing Feelings   191
6.5   Haleh Afshar   Gender Roles and the 'Moral Economy of Kin' among Pakistani Women in West Yorkshire   195

WOMEN'S STUDIES
Essential Readings

Edited by

*Stevi Jackson, Karen Atkinson, Deirdre Beddoe, Teri Brewer,
Sue Faulkner, Anthea Hucklesby, Rose Pearson, Helen Power,
Jane Prince, Michele Ryan and Pauline Young*

NEW YORK UNIVERSITY PRESS
Washington Square, New York

For the selection and introductory material copyright is as follows:
Chapter   1 © Stevi Jackson 1993
Chapter   2 © Jane Prince 1993
Chapter   3 © Teri Brewer 1993
Chapter   4 © Deirdre Beddoe 1993
Chapter   5 © Jane Prince 1993
Chapter   6 © Stevi Jackson, Sue Faulkner 1993
Chapter   7 © Stevi Jackson 1993
Chapter   8 © Helen Power 1993
Chapter   9 © Anthea Hucklesby 1993
Chapter 10 © Rose Pearson 1993
Chapter 11 © Stevi Jackson, Jane Prince, Pauline Young 1993
Chapter 12 © Karen Atkinson 1993
Chapter 13 © Pauline Young 1993
Chapter 14 © Michele Ryan 1993

Library of Congress Cataloging-in-Publication Data

Women's studies : essential readings / edited by Stevi Jackson ... [et
al.].
    p. cm.
   Includes index.
   ISBN 0-8147-4214-9 (cloth)   ISBN 0-8147-4215-7 (pbk.)
   1. Feminist theory. 2. Feminist criticism. 3. Women.
I. Jackson, Stevi.
HQ1190.W69 1993
305.4—dc20
                                       93-17832
                                       CIP

CONTENTS

Introduction: About the Reader   xv

1 Feminist Social Theory   1
Edited and Introduced by Stevi Jackson

Introduction   3

1.1   Shulamith Firestone The Dialectic of Sex   7
1.2   Juliet Mitchell Psychoanalysis and Feminism   9
1.3   Michèle Barrett Women's Oppression Today   11
1.4   Heidi Hartmann The Unhappy Marriage of Marxism
      and Feminism   13
1.5   Christine Delphy Sex Classes   16
1.6   Sylvia Walby Forms and Degrees of Patriarchy   18
1.7   Parveen Adams, Rosaline Coward and Elizabeth
      Cowie Editorial, *m/f* 1   19
1.8   Jane Flax Postmodernism and Gender Relations in
      Feminist Theory   20
1.9   Luce Irigaray Women: equal or different   21
1.10 Monique Wittig One is not born a woman   22
1.11 Hazel Carby White Women Listen!   25
1.12 Denise Riley Am I That Name?   26
1.13 Tania Modleski Feminism Without Women   27
1.14 Liz Stanley Recovering 'Women' in History from
      Historical Deconstructionism   28
1.15 Avtar Brah Questions of Difference and
      International Feminism   29

Further Reading   34

2 Women's Minds: psychological and psychoanalytic theory **37**
Edited and Introduced by Jane Prince

Introduction 39

2.1 Jean Grimshaw Autonomy and Identity in Feminist Thinking 42
2.2 Wendy Hollway Male Mind and Female Nature 45
2.3 Corinne Squire Significant Differences: feminism in psychology 50
2.4 Valerie Walkerdine Femininity as Performance 53
2.5 Nancy Chodorow Family Structure and Feminine Personality 58
2.6 Kate Millett Sexual Politics 60
2.7 Juliet Mitchell Psychoanalysis and Feminism 64
2.8 Jacqueline Rose 'Introduction II' to *Feminine Sexuality: Jacques Lacan and the École Freudienne* 67
2.9 David Macey Lacan in Contexts 71

Further Reading 72

3 Cross-cultural Perspectives on Women's Lives **75**
Edited and Introduced by Teri Brewer

Introduction 77

3.1 Margaret Mead Human Fatherhood is a Social Invention 79
3.2 Edward Evans-Pritchard The Position of Women in Primitive Societies and in Our Own 80
3.3 Sherry Ortner Is Female to Male as Nature is to Culture? 82
3.4 Carol McCormack Nature, Culture and Gender: a critique 84
3.5 Peggy Reeves Sanday Female Power and Male Dominance: on the origins of sexual inequality 86
3.6 Michelle Rosaldo The Use and Abuse of Anthropology: reflections on feminism and cross-cultural understanding 90

6.6   Michele Bograd   What are feminist perspectives on
       wife abuse?   197
6.7   Ann Oakley   Becoming a Mother   198
6.8   Ann Oakley   Taking It Like a Woman   202
6.9   Sheila Rowbotham   To be or not to be: the dilemmas
       of mothering   204
6.10   Julia Brannen and Peter Moss   Managing Mothers   207
6.11   Ann Phoenix   Narrow Definitions of Culture: the
       case of early motherhood   211
6.12   Julia Berryman   Perspectives on Later Motherhood   214
6.13   Anne Wollett and Ann Phoenix   Issues Related to
       Motherhood   216
6.14   Lynne Harne   Lesbian Custody and the New Myth
       of the Father   217
6.15   Gemma Tang Nain   Black Women, Sexism and
       Racism   220

       Further Reading   222

7   **Sexuality**   **223**
       Edited and Introduced by Stevi Jackson

       Introduction   225

7.1   Sandra Bartky   Foucault, Femininity and the
       Modernisation of Patriarchal Power   227
7.2   Luce Irigaray   This Sex Which Is Not One   231
7.3   Diane Richardson   The Challenge of AIDS   231
7.4   Diane Scully   Understanding Sexual Violence   234
7.5   Patricia Collins   Black Feminist Thought   236
7.6   Rosemary Pringle   Bureaucracy, Rationality and
       Sexuality   238
7.7   Susan Ardill and Sue O'Sullivan   Difference, Desire and
       Sadomasochism   241
7.8   Sheila Jeffreys   Anticlimax   243
7.9   bell hooks   Ending Female Sexual Oppression   245
7.10   Deborah Cameron   Ten Years On: 'compulsory
       heterosexuality and lesbian existence'   246

       Further Reading   247

8   Women and the Law   **249**

Edited and Introduced by Helen Power

Introduction   251

8.1   Albie Sachs and Joan Hoff Wilson   Sexism and the
       Law   254
8.2   Susan Edwards   Female Sexuality and the Law   265
8.3   Katherine O'Donovan   Sexual Divisions in Law   269
8.4   Catharine MacKinnon   On Collaboration   276
8.5   Wendy Moore   There should be a law against it ...
       shouldn't there?   283
8.6   Gillian Rodgerson and Elizabeth Wilson   Pornography
       and Feminism: the case against censorship   288
8.7   Carol Smart   Feminism and the Power of Law   291

Further Reading   303

9   Women, Crime and Deviance   **305**

Edited and Introduced by Anthea Hucklesby

Introduction   307

9.1   Frances Heidensohn   Crime and Society   309
9.2   Frances Heidensohn   Women and Crime   312
9.3   Pat Carlen   Women, Crime, Feminism and Realism   314
9.4   Jeanne Gregory   Sex, Class and Crime   316
9.5   Pat Carlen   Criminal Women and Criminal Justice:
       the limits to, and potential of, feminist and left
       realist perspectives   317
9.6   Jeanne Gregory   Sex, Class and Crime   319
9.7   Kathryn Chadwick and Catherine Little   The
       Criminalization of Women   321
9.8   Frances Heidensohn   Women and Crime   330
9.9   Pat Carlen   Criminal Women and Criminal Justice:
       the limits to, and potential of, feminist and left
       realist perspectives   333
9.10   Jeanne Gregory   Sex, Class and Crime   336

Further Reading   338

10   Public/Private: women, politics and the state   **339**
Edited and Introduced by Rose Pearson

Introduction   341

10.1   Margaret Stacey and Marion Price   Given the odds, a
       great advance   344
10.2   Susan Edwards   Policing: the under-representation of
       women's interests   346
10.3   Margery Wolf   The Birth Limitation Program:
       family vs state   348
10.4   Peter Squires   Policing the Family   349
10.5   Jill Evans, Clare Hudson and Penny Smith   Women and
       the Strike: it's a whole way of life   351
10.6   Alison Young   Body/Politics: our bodies triumphed   354

Further Reading   359

11   Science, Medicine and Reproductive Technology   **361**
Edited and Introduced by Stevi Jackson, Jane Prince and Pauline Young

Introduction   363

11.1   Anne Fausto-Sterling   Life in the XY Corral   368
11.2   Ruth Herschberger   Society Writes Biology   371
11.3   Ludmilla Jordanova   Natural Facts: an historical
       perspective on science and sexuality   374
11.4   Elaine Showalter   Managing Female Minds   378
11.5   Emily Martin   The Women in the Body   380
11.6   Sophie Laws   Who Needs PMT?   385
11.7   Frances Evans   Managers and Labourers: women's
       attitudes to reproductive technology   388
11.8   Gena Corea   The Reproductive Brothel   389
11.9   Jana Sawicki   Disciplining Mothers: feminism and
       the new reproductive technologies   394
11.10 Christine Delphy   New Reproductive Technologies   396

Further Reading   399

12   Language and Gender   **401**
Edited and Introduced by Karen Atkinson

Introduction   403

12.1   Dale Spender   Language and Reality: who made the
       world?   407
12.2   Susan Ehrlich and Ruth King   Gender-based Language
       Reform and the Social Construction of Meaning   410
12.3   Robin Lakoff   Language and Woman's Place   416
12.4   Nancy M. Henley and Cheris Kramarae   Gender,
       Power and Miscommunication   418
12.5   Deborah Cameron, Fiona McAlinden and Kathy
       O'Leary   Lakoff in Context: the social and
       linguistic functions of tag questions   421
12.6   Jennifer Coates   Gossip Revisited   426

Further Reading   428

13   Feminist Literary Criticism   **431**
Edited and Introduced by Pauline Young

Introduction   433

13.1   Simone de Beauvoir   The Second Sex   438
13.2   Kate Millett   Sexual Politics   439
13.3   Sandra Gilbert and Susan Gubar   The Madwoman in
       the Attic   441
13.4   Adrienne Rich   On Lies, Secrets and Silences   445
13.5   Tillie Olsen   Silences   447
13.6   Elaine Showalter   A Literature of Their Own   448
13.7   Annis Pratt   Archetypal Patterns in Women's
       Fiction   450
13.8   Ann Rosalind Jones   Writing the Body: towards an
       understanding of *l'écriture féminine*   454
13.9   Barbara Smith   Toward a Black Feminist Criticism   458
13.10 Maggie Humm   Feminist Criticism   462
13.11 Patricia Waugh   Feminine Fictions: revisiting the
       postmodern   464

Further Reading   469

14 Representations of Women in the Media   471

Edited and Introduced by Michele Ryan

Introduction   473

14.1 E. Deidre Pribram   Female Spectators   475
14.2 Janice Radway   Reading the Romance   480
14.3 Susanne Kappeler   The Pornography of
      Representation   483
14.4 Annette Kuhn   The Power of the Image   484
14.5 Jeanette Murphy   'A Question of Silence'   486
14.6 Anne Ross Muir   The Status of Women Working in
      Film and Television   489
14.7 Dorothy Hobson   Women Audiences and the
      Workplace   490
14.8 Gillian Dyer   Women and Television: an overview   492
14.9 Christine Geraghty   Women and Soap Opera   494

Further Reading   496

Notes on Contributors   499

List of Sources   501

Acknowledgements   511

Index   517

INTRODUCTION:
about the Reader

This reader is intended for students pursuing women's studies or related courses at undergraduate level. It offers an overview of a range of themes and perspectives in women's studies, while encouraging readers to move beyond this to explore the areas we have covered in greater depth. Each section of the book begins with an introduction mapping out the issues and debates with which it is concerned, and then introduces a selection of short Readings from the work of notable theorists and researchers. We have sought to include writers who have been particularly influential, to offer a cross-section of different feminist perspectives, and to give a flavour of ongoing debates. We hope that this will encourage students to read some of the works extracted in full. Each section ends with additional suggestions for further reading.

Women's studies is now a large and growing interdisciplinary field. No single text can hope to cover all aspects of the subject. Given constraints of space, it is inevitable that there are areas we have not covered and key thinkers who have been excluded. We have, however, tried to give students some insight into a range of issues and debates, and to indicate the diversity of modern feminist thought.

This book is a collaborative project, but one which has developed from our differences as well as our common concerns as teachers of women's studies. All the editors are feminists, but we do not all share the same political perspective, and we work within different academic disciplines. While there has been considerable discussion of the Readings included here, the selections each of us has chosen reflect our particular academic backgrounds and individual theoretical and political preoccupations.

I FEMINIST SOCIAL THEORY

Edited and Introduced by Stevi Jackson

INTRODUCTION

Feminist social theory addresses the broad question of how and why women come to be subordinated, and offers analyses of the social and cultural processes through which that subordination is perpetuated. In seeking to explain women's oppression within Western societies, feminists have addressed three key questions: How is male dominance sustained? How is gender difference constituted? How do we make sense of the diversity of women's experiences arising from differences of class, race or sexuality among us? These interrelated issues of dominance, difference and diversity have been the subject of considerable debate.

The resurgence of feminism in the 1960s and 1970s was based on a shared recognition that women were oppressed, and that we needed to develop a theory and a politics that would further our liberation from this oppression. At this time the major theoretical debates were framed around Marxism. For Marxists, it is class – understood in terms of economic exploitation of the working class by the bourgeoisie – which is the fundamental social divide in capitalist societies. Class struggle provides the central dynamic of history, and will bring about an egalitarian socialist society. Those women who identified themselves as socialist or Marxist feminists sought either to incorporate feminism into a Marxist critique of capitalism, or to extend Marxism to encompass the politics of women's liberation. Others, who were more likely to call themselves radical feminists, argued that theoretical priority should be given to the analysis of patriarchy as a system of male domination. Marxist methods and concepts, however, provided a starting point for many radical feminists as well as Marxist feminists. Conversely, many Marxist feminists made use of the concept of patriarchy.

One of the earliest radical feminist analyses of patriarchy was that of Shulamith Firestone. In *The Dialectic of Sex*, first published in the USA in 1970, she argued that women's reproductive capacities made them vulnerable to male control and that, as a result, they had been subordinated throughout history (Reading 1.1). Firestone's biologism[1] – often wrongly taken as representative of radical feminism – has been rejected by most feminists, but issues of sexuality and reproduction have remained central to the theorisation of male dominance (see Section 7 below).

Throughout the 1970s and early 1980s Marxist feminists found themselves confronting two major problems. First, while they wanted to relate women's subordination to capitalism, they recognised that it predated capitalism. In the second place, Marxism had not originally been developed as a means of exploring gender divisions; it therefore left certain questions unanswered. Women's oppression can be seen as functional for capitalism – for example, by arguing that women provide a cheap and flexible source of labour-power, or that their domestic labour serves to reproduce the labour-power of the male worker. But this, as Heidi Hartmann and others have argued, does not explain why it is women who perform these functions (Reading 1.4). Some Marxist feminists avoided this difficulty by defining patriarchy as an ideological phenomenon rather than one which was explicable in economic terms. Women's oppression was then assumed to be maintained through the cultural construction of masculinity and femininity. This was particularly popular with those, like Juliet Mitchell, who were interested in psychoanalysis (Reading 1.2). Other British Marxist feminists, such as Michèle Barrett, abandoned the concept of patriarchy (Reading 1.3). Barrett argued that explanations for women's subordination within capitalism should be sought in specific historical struggles in which men had often collectively acted against women's interests. Heidi Hartmann shared Barrett's commitment to historical analysis, but argued for a concept of patriarchy as a separate system in articulation with capitalism (Reading 1.4).

Hartmann's position is close to that of Christine Delphy, a materialist radical feminist who applies Marxist methods to the study of patriarchy. Delphy has placed particular emphasis on women's economic exploitation within families, developing the concept of the domestic mode of production.[2] Sylvia Walby has drawn on the work of both Hartmann and Delphy, elaborating further the latter's concept of the domestic mode of production but placing considerable emphasis on patriarchal relations in the workplace. She continues to defend what she calls 'dual systems theory', based upon an analysis of Western society in which capitalism and patriarchy exist as two independent but interacting systems. In her recent work she has attempted to answer the frequent criticism of the concept of patriarchy: that it is ahistorical. While her claim that we are moving from a private to a public form of patriarchy may overstate some of the changes which have occurred, it does none the less constitute an important attempt to demonstrate the historical variability of patriarchy (Reading 1.6).

The question of why men should dominate women has also raised a related one: How are women and men constituted as separate genders? Early attempts to answer this tended to follow Ann Oakley[3] in assuming that gender was culturally and socially constructed, but that it was built upon a foundation of biological sex. This sex–gender distinction left the existence of gender differentiation itself unquestioned. By the early 1980s a current within feminism was emerging, influenced by theoretical developments in France, which sought to 'deconstruct' gender categories, to reveal the ways in which they have been culturally constructed and to demonstrate that they are fictions rather than natural facts.[4] The category 'women' could no longer be regarded as fixed and stable. What it means to be a woman changes over time, varies across cultures, and shifts from one social context to another.

Feminists associated with this tendency identified themselves as poststructuralists or, more recently, as postmodernists.[5] Postmodernists are sceptical about the construction of all-encompassing explanatory theories – what they term 'metanarratives' – and do not consider it possible or desirable to formulate a general theory of women's subordination (Reading 1.8). This is in keeping with their opposition to essentialist conceptualisations of 'women' – that is, to the idea that women exist as a natural category. The charge of essentialism is often levelled against those who have attempted to construct theories of patriarchy. The label essentialist, however, is often used rather too glibly and dismissively as a negative stereotype of other feminisms.[6]

Some feminists, like the French psychoanalyst and philosopher Luce Irigaray, do insist on an essential feminine difference, and argue for a theory and politics based upon that difference (Reading 1.9). For Irigaray, this is a strategy that challenges a patriarchal culture which silences and denies femininity, which defines women negatively, only in relation to men. Most feminists, however, regard gender difference as socially constructed but are none the less wary of taking deconstruction too far. Treating the category 'women' as entirely fictional ignores the material realities that constrain us into membership of that category. It threatens to deprive us of a position from which to speak as women, and a collective basis for struggle. It can also invalidate as essentialist specific political identities such as those of black women or lesbian women. This is something of a paradox, since such differences of identity provide a rationale for problematising the category 'women'.

An alternative anti-essentialist position derives from the work of French materialist feminists such as Christine Delphy and Monique Wittig,[7] who maintain that gender has no natural basis, but differ from postmodernists in claiming that it rests on material foundations. For Delphy and Wittig, sexual difference is the product of – not the basis of – women's oppression. Women exist as a political category (and a class) because of patriarchy. Within this formulation it is possible to retain a conceptualisation of womanhood as a material reality without positing some essential, pre-given femininity. Wittig takes this further in her controversial assertion that lesbians are not women (a position from which Delphy distances herself).[8] Women are defined by their appropriation by men, a condition from which lesbians are fugitives (Reading 1.10).

A major reason why the category 'women' was called into question was that it often served to conceal differences among women. Analyses of the subordination of women had often been framed from the perspective of white,

Western, middle-class heterosexual women. Not all women share a similar position, have similar experiences or similar political priorities. The responses of black feminist writers such as Carby and Brah (Readings 1.11 and 1.15) provide a particularly clear example of the problems posed by this diversity among women. Initially critical of a conceptualisation of 'women' which excluded them, black feminists and women of colour have been at the forefront of debates on the concept of 'women' and the need for political solidarity amongst women to take note of their diversity.

Notes

1. 'Biologism' is the explanation of social phenomena in terms of assumed natural or biological factors; in this case women's ability to bear children is seen as the basis of their subordinate position in society.
2. See particularly 'The main enemy' and 'A materialist feminism is possible', in *Close to Home*, London: Hutchinson, 1984. This work has recently been elaborated further in a book co-authored with D. Leonard – *Familiar Exploitation*, Oxford: Polity, 1992.
3. A. Oakley, *Sex, Gender and Society*, London: Maurice Temple Smith, 1972.
4. The concept of deconstruction derives from the work of the French theorist Jacques Derrida, but it is frequently used without direct reference to his work. In general it means looking closely at any text, argument or assumption in order to reveal the inconsistent and paradoxical use of the concepts which underpin it. It is possible to do this because meaning is never fixed in language. Words and concepts have meaning only in relation to other words and concepts, so their meaning can shift and fluctuate. Hence, in this context, the word 'woman' can change its significance, and statements purporting to define what women are can be shown to contain contradictory assumptions. There is, in the end, no such thing as 'a woman'. See, for example, D. Riley, *Am I That Name?*, London: Macmillan, 1988, from which Reading 1.12 in this section is extracted. For a development of the idea that gender is a fiction, see J. Butler, *Gender Trouble*, London: Routledge, 1990. For an accessible summary of Derrida's work, see M. Sarup, *An Introductory Guide to Post-structuralism and Postmodernism*, 2nd edn, Hemel Hempstead: Harvester Wheatsheaf, 1993; for the applicability of his ideas to feminism, see C. Weedon, *Feminist Practice and Poststructuralist Theory*, Oxford: Basil Blackwell, 1987.
5. These two terms are both used to describe the tendency within social and critical theory which I am outlining here. The structuralism to which it is 'post' – and its theoretical point of departure – is that which looks for structures underlying all human language and culture. This is to be found, for example, in the work of Ferdinand de Saussure (see his *Course in General Linguistics*, London: Fontana, 1974) and Claude Lévi-Strauss (see his *Structural Anthropology*, vols 1 and 2, Harmondsworth: Peregrine, 1977, 1978). The modernism to which it is 'post' – and from which it distances itself – is usually defined in relation to ideas which emerged from the Enlightenment. For example, it has been thought that human beings are possessed of a stable, coherent, rational self, and that rationality applied in the pursuit of science and knowledge will deliver truth. Postmodernists dispute these notions of self, knowledge and truth.

6. For discussions of some of the problems of anti-essentialist arguments, see D. Fuss, *Essentially Speaking*, London: Routledge, 1990; T. de Lauretis, 'Upping the anti [*sic*] in feminist theory', in M. Hirsch and E. Fox Keller (eds), *Conflicts in Feminism*, London: Routledge, 1990. For more general critiques of postmodern feminism, see T. Modleski, *Feminism Without Women*, London: Routledge, 1991; S. Brodribb, *Nothing Mat(t)ers: A feminist critique of postmodernism*, Melbourne: Spinifex, 1992; S. Walby, 'Post-post-modernism? Theorizing social complexity', in M. Barrett and A. Phillips (eds), *Destablizing Theory*, Oxford: Polity, 1992.
7. Delphy and Wittig are the best-known representatives of this theoretical position outside France. Others include Nicole-Claude Mathieu, Colette Guillaumin, Emanuelle de Lesseps and Monique Plaza.
8. For a discussion of the background to this debate, see C. Duchen, *French Connections*, London: Hutchinson, 1987.

1.1 The Dialectic of Sex

Shulamith Firestone

Shulamith Firestone, often taken as the founder of radical feminism, draws on Marxist concepts in arguing that sex class, rather than economic class, is the most basic social division. Although other feminists use a concept of sex class, few share Firestone's view that this is a natural category.

Unlike economic class, sex class sprang directly from a biological reality: men and women were created different, and not equal. Although, as de Beauvoir points out, this difference of itself did not necessitate the development of a class system – the domination of one group by another – the reproductive *functions* of these differences did. The biological family is an inherently unequal power distribution. [...]

The *biological family* – the basic reproductive unit of male/female/infant, in whatever form of social organization – is characterized by these fundamental – if not immutable – facts:

1. That women throughout history before the advent of birth control were at the continual mercy of their biology – menstruation, menopause, and 'female ills', constant painful childbirth, wetnursing and care of infants, all of which made them dependent on males (whether brother, father, husband, lover, or clan, government, community-at-large) for physical survival.
2. That human infants take an even longer time to grow up than animals, and thus are helpless and, for some short period at least, dependent on adults for physical survival.
3. That a basic mother/child interdependency has existed in some form in every society, past or present, and thus has shaped the psychology of every mature female and every infant.

4. That the natural reproductive difference between the sexes led directly to the first division of labour at the origins of class, as well as furnishing the paradigm of caste (discrimination based on biological characteristics).

[...] though it is true that throughout history there have been many variations on this biological family, the contingencies I have described existed in all of them, causing specific psychosexual distortions in the human personality.

But to grant that the sexual imbalance of power is biologically based is not to lose our case. We are no longer just animals. And the kingdom of nature does not reign absolute. [...]

Thus the 'natural' is not necessarily a 'human' value. Humanity has begun to transcend Nature: we can no longer justify the maintenance of a discriminatory sex class system on grounds of its origins in nature. Indeed, for pragmatic reasons alone it is beginning to look as if we *must* get rid of it.

The problem becomes political, demanding more than a comprehensive historical analysis, when one realizes that, though man is increasingly capable of freeing himself from the biological conditions that created his tyranny over women and children, he has little reason to want to give this tyranny up. [...]

Though the sex class system may have originated in fundamental biological conditions, this does not guarantee once the biological basis of their oppression has been swept away that women and children will be freed. On the contrary, the new technology, especially fertility control, may be used against them to reinforce the entrenched system of exploitation.

So that just as to assure elimination of economic classes requires the revolt of the underclass (the proletariat) and, in a temporary dictatorship, their seizure of the means of *production*, so to assure the elimination of sexual classes requires the revolt of the underclass (women) and the seizure of control of *reproduction*: not only the full restoration to women of ownership of their own bodies, but also their (temporary) seizure of control of human fertility – the new population biology as well as all the social institutions of child-bearing and child-rearing. And just as the end goal of socialist revolution was not only the elimination of the economic class *privilege* but of the economic class *distinction* itself, so the end goal of feminist revolution must be, unlike that of the first feminist movement, not just the elimination of male *privilege* but of the sex *distinction* itself: genital differences between human beings would no longer matter culturally. (A reversion to an unobstructed *pansexuality* – Freud's 'polymorphous perversity' – would probably supersede hetero/homo/bi-sexuality.) The reproduction of the species by one sex for the benefit of both would be replaced by (at least the option of) artificial reproduction: children would be born to both sexes equally, or independently of either, however one chooses to look at it; the dependence of the child on the mother (and vice versa) would give way to a greatly shortened dependence on a small group of others in general, and any remaining inferiority to adults in physical strength would be compensated for culturally. The division of labour would be ended by the elimination of labour altogether (through cybernetics). The tyranny of the biological family would be broken.

And with it the psychology of power. As Engels claimed for strictly socialist revolution: 'The existence of not simply this or that ruling class but of any ruling class at all [will have] become an obsolete anachronism.' That socialism has never come near achieving this predicated goal is not only the result of unfulfilled or misfired economic preconditions, but also because the Marxian analysis itself was insufficient: it did not dig deep enough to the psychosexual roots of class. Marx was on to something more profound than he knew when he observed that the family contained within itself in embryo all the antagonisms that later develop on a wide scale within the society and the state. For unless revolution uproots the basic social organization, the biological family – the vinculum through which the psychology of power can always be smuggled – the tapeworm of exploitation will never be annihilated. We shall need a sexual revolution much larger than – inclusive of – a socialist one to truly eradicate all class systems.

1.2 **Psychoanalysis and Feminism**
Juliet Mitchell

Juliet Mitchell also sees patriarchy as a universal feature of human societies, but argues that its origins are cultural rather than biological, and that it is now maintained primarily through the operation of ideology. Here ideology refers to the ideas and beliefs through which we make sense of our lived experience, which can serve to conceal the conditions and contradictions underlying that experience. It is perpetuated through the processes by which subjectivity (our sense of ourselves) is culturally constructed. Hence gendered subjectivity can be seen as constituted ideologically, ensuring the continual reproduction of dominant masculinity and dominated femininity. Mitchell argues that psychoanalysis provides the best means of understanding this process.

The legally controlled exchange of women is the primary factor that distinguishes mankind from all other primates, from a cultural standpoint [...] – the systematic exchange of women is definitional of human society. This act of exogamy transforms 'natural' families into a cultural kinship system.

Within the family both sexes already, so to speak, have each other; they naturally possess their kin in already-formed relationships. A law that merely confirmed this pattern would be futile; marriage laws and the intimately related taboo on incest are set up precisely to prevent any circular fixation at this natural stage. [...] The injunction against incest works two ways: you must *not* sexually possess specified members of your kin group (minimally your sister), you *must* offer them in marriage, exogamously. Society thus being based on the reciprocal exchange of values, sexual laws are therefore the equivalent of inter-human communications and coexistent with society itself. Contrary to popular belief, it is not that there is anything biologically 'wrong' with incest that is important; it is rather that the command to exchange exogamously forbids the cul-de-sac of endogamy. The subjective depth of the taboo indicates social necessity, not biological revulsion; but this is a social necessity so basic (i.e. the very basis of society) that the prohibition is experienced as immutably natural – except, that is, in the testimony of the Oedipal child who is only just learning the law. [...]

The determining feature of Freud'a reconstruction of mankind's history is the murder of the primal father in a prehistorical period. It is this dead father that is the mark of patriarchy. In an imagined pre-social epoch, the father had *all* the power and *all* rights over *all* the women of the clan; a band of sons murdered the father to get at his rights. [...] The brothers identify with the father they have killed, and internalize the guilt which they feel along with the pleasure in his death. The father thus becomes far more powerful in death than in life; it is in death that he institutes human history. The dead, symbolic father is far more crucial than any actual living father who merely transmits his name. This is the story of the origins of patriarchy. It is against this symbolic mark of the dead father that boys and girls find their cultural place within the instance of the Oedipus complex.

In the situation of the Oedipus complex ... the little boy learns his place as the heir to this law of the father and the little girl learns her place within it. [...]

It is the specific feature of patriarchy – the law of the hypothesized prehistoric murdered father – that defines the relative places of men and women in human history. This 'father' and his representatives – all fathers – are the crucial expression of patriarchal society. It is *fathers* not *men* who have the determinate power. And it is a question neither of biology nor of a specific society, but of *human* society itself.

Patriarchy describes the universal culture – however, each specific economic mode of production must express this in different ideological forms. The universal aspects of patriarchy set in motion by 'the death of the father' are the exchange of women and the cultural taboo on incest, but these are rehearsed diversely in the mind of man in different societies. It would seem to me that with capitalist society something new has happened to the culture that is patriarchy.

The complexity of capitalist society makes archaic the kinship structures and incest taboos for the majority of the people, and yet it preserves them through thick and thin. Freud gave the name of the Oedipus complex to the universal law by which men and women learn their place in the world, but the universal law has specific expression in the capitalist family. (Anthropological arguments that make the Oedipus complex general without demarcating its specificity are inadequate; political suggestions that it is only to be found in capitalist societies are incorrect. What Freud was deciphering was our human heritage – but he deciphered it in a particular time and place.) *The capitalist economy implies that for the masses demands of exogamy and the social taboo on incest are irrelevant; but nevertheless it must preserve both these and the patriarchal structure that they imply.* Furthermore, it would seem that the specifically capitalist ideology of a supposedly natural nuclear family would be in harsh contradiction to the kinship structure as it is articulated in the Oedipus complex, which in this instance is expressed within this nuclear family. It is, I believe, this contradiction, which is already being powerfully felt, that must be analysed and then made use of for the overthrow of patriarchy. [...]

Under patriarchal order women are oppressed in their very psychologies of femininity; once this order is retained only in a highly contradictory manner this oppression manifests itself. Women have to organize themselves as a group to effect a change in the basic ideology of human society. To be effective, this can be no righteous challenge to the simple domination of men (though this plays a tactical part), but a struggle based on a theory of the social non-necessity at this stage of development of the laws instituted by patriarchy.

The overthrow of the capitalist economy, and the political challenge that effects this, do not in themselves mean a transformation of patriarchal ideology. This is the implication of the fact that the ideological sphere has a certain autonomy. The change to a socialist economy does not by itself suggest that the end of patriarchy comfortably follows suit. A specific struggle against patriarchy – a cultural revolution – is requisite.

1.3 **Women's Oppression Today**
Michèle Barrett

More representative of mainstream Marxist feminism in Britain, Michèle Barrett initially rejected the concept of patriarchy as ahistorical. In the introduction to the second edition of Women's Oppression Today *she modified her position in a statement included here as a postscript.*

I have argued that it is inadequate to attempt to grasp the character of women's oppression in contemporary capitalism in terms of the supposed needs of capitalism itself. The reasoning in favour of this analysis has tended to be couched in terms of capital's support for a system of the reproduction of labour-power, through domestic labour in the household, that operates at the lowest possible cost and provides a cheap and flexible reserve army of married women workers to lower the price of wages in general. Although these are undoubtedly important points in any explanation of capital's support for a household in which a wife and children are assumed to be dependent upon a male breadwinner, the argument leaves unexplained many aspects of women's oppression. The charge that this argument is a functionalist one is not in my view as important as the fact that it tends towards a reductionist account of women's oppression and denies specific aspects of women's subordination to men in the pre-capitalist period, in socialist societies and within the different classes of contemporary capitalism.

I have argued that this particular form of household, and its accompanying ideology of women's dependence, is not the only possible form for an efficient reproduction of labour-power in capitalist relations of production. It is the product of historical struggles between men and women, both within the working class and the bourgeoisie. Furthermore, the 'reproduction' thesis can deal only in a very mechanistic way with the complexity of the ideological construction of gender as it has developed in capitalism. A consideration of the areas of sexuality and the cultural representation of gender demonstrates a need to understand the force of ideology in the production and reproduction of the categories of masculinity and femininity on which such an analysis implicitly depends, but tends not to explore.

These arguments need not be ruled out altogether, but it is necessary to historicize them. A model of women's dependence has become entrenched in the relations of production of capitalism, in the divisions of labour in wage work and between wage labour and domestic labour. As such, an oppression of women that is not in any essentialist sense pre-given by the logic of capitalist development has become necessary for the ongoing reproduction of the mode of production in its present form. Hence, the oppression of women, although not a functional prerequisite of capitalism, has acquired a material basis in the relations of production and reproduction of capitalism today.

It follows that although important dimensions of women's oppression cannot be accounted for with reference to the categories of Marxism, it is equally impossible to establish the analytic independence of a system of oppression such as the category of 'patriarchy' suggests. The resonance of this concept lies in its recognition of the transhistorical character of women's oppression, but in this very appeal to longevity it deprives us of an adequate grasp of historical change. How useful is it to collapse widow-burning in India with 'the coercion of privacy' in Western Europe, into a concept of such generality? What we need to analyse are precisely the mechanisms by which women's oppression is secured in different contexts, since only then can we confront the problem of how to change it.

Feminists who employ the concept of patriarchy vary in the extent to which they ground it in biological differences between the sexes or in inevitable power structures stemming from these differences. A number of writers have inquired into the historical origins of patriarchy and, related to this, the question of whether these origins are biologically determined. No one would want to deny that there are physiological differences between the sexes, but what is at issue is how these natural differences are constructed as divisions by human social agency. Racists who attempt to provide 'scientific' apologias for the oppression of blacks are treated with the contempt they deserve and we should be equally wary of apologias for gender division, including those emanating from feminist quarters. The valorization of the female principle that a biologistic use of the concept of patriarchy encourages should be rejected at all levels.

I would not, however, want to argue that the concept of patriarchy should be jettisoned. I would favour retaining it for use in context where male domination is expressed through the power of the father over women and over younger men. Clearly some societies have been organized around this principle, although not capitalist ones. In so far as feminist appropriations of psycho-analytic theory have attempted to cast this principle as a primary psychic dynamic of contemporary gender construction, I have dissented from their conclusions. Nevertheless, there remain elements of what might properly be called patriarchal power in the recent history of women's oppression and these can usefully be identified, for instance in some aspects of fascist ideology and the relations of the bourgeois family in the nineteenth century. Hence I would argue for a more precise and specific use of the concept of patriarchy, rather than one which expands it to cover all expressions of male domination and thereby attempts to construe a descriptive term as a systematic explanatory theory.

Postscript

My original, and highly critical, discussion of the concept of patriarchy proved to be one of the most controversial arguments of the book. Many feminists said to me that it was completely wrong to suggest the abandonment of such an eloquent and resonant concept – and one so regularly used in feminist political activism – on rather academic grounds of inconsistent usage and so on. What is at stake here, which I later came to see, was the symbolic status of using the concept of 'patriarchy' as a marker of a position that in general terms I was in fact taking – that we recognize the independent character of women's oppression and avoid explanations that reduced it to other factors.

1.4   The Unhappy Marriage of Marxism and Feminism
Heidi Hartmann

Heidi Hartmann, an American Marxist feminist, shares Barrett's view that women's subordination cannot be reduced to an effect of capitalist relations, but argues for the necessity of a concept of patriarchy to counteract the gender-blindness of traditional Marxism.

Marxism enables us to understand many aspects of capitalist societies: the structure of production, the generation of a particular occupational structure, and the nature of the dominant ideology. Marx's theory of the development of capitalism is a theory of the development of 'empty places'. Marx predicted, for example, the growth of the proletariat and the demise of the petty bourgeoisie. More precisely and in more detail, Braverman among others has explained the creation of the 'places' clerical worker and service worker in advanced capitalist societies.[1] Just as capital creates these places indifferent to the individuals who fill them, the categories of Marxist analysis, class, reserve army of labor, wage-laborer, do not explain why particular people fill particular places. They give no clues about why *women* are subordinate to *men* inside and outside the family and why it is not the other way around. *Marxist categories, like capital itself, are sex-blind*. The categories of Marxism cannot tell us who will fill the empty places. Marxist analysis of the woman question has suffered from this basic problem. [...]

Capitalist development creates the places for a hierarchy of workers, but traditional Marxist categories cannot tell us who will fill which places. Gender and racial hierarchies determine who fills the empty places. *Patriarchy is not simply hierarchical organization*, but hierarchy in which particular people fill *particular* places. It is in studying patriarchy that we learn why it is women who are dominated and how. While we believe that most known societies have been patriarchal, we do not view patriarchy as a universal, unchanging phenomenon. Rather patriarchy, the set of interrelations among men that allow men to dominate women, has changed in form and intensity over time. It is crucial that the hierarchy among men, and their differential access to patriarchal benefits, be examined. Surely, class, race, nationality, and even marital status and sexual orientation, as well as the obvious age, come into play here. And women of different class, race, national, marital status, or sexual orientation groups are subjected to different degrees of patriarchal power. Women may themselves exercise class, race, or national power, or even patriarchal power (through their family connections) over men lower in the patriarchal hierarchy than their own male kin.

We define patriarchy as a set of social relations which has a material base and in which there are hierarchical relations between men and solidarity among them which enable them in turn to dominate women. The material base of patriarchy is men's control over women's labor-power. That control is maintained by excluding women from access to necessary economically productive resources and by restricting women's sexuality. Men exercise their control in receiving personal service work from women, in not having to do housework or rear children, in having access to women's bodies for sex, and in feeling powerful and being powerful. The crucial elements of patriarchy as we *currently* experience them are: heterosexual marriage (and consequent homophobia), female childrearing and housework, women's economic dependence on men (enforced by arrangements in the labor market), the state, and numerous institutions based on social relations among men – clubs, sports, unions, professions, universities, churches, corporations, and armies. All of these elements need to be examined if we are to understand patriarchal capitalism.

Both hierarchy and interdependence among men and the subordination of women are *integral* to the functioning of our society; that is, these relationships are *systemic*. We leave aside the question of the creation of these relations and ask, can we recognize patriarchal relations in capitalist societies? Within capitalist societies we must discover those same bonds between men which both bourgeois and Marxist social scientists claim no longer exist or are, at the most, unimportant leftovers. Can we understand how these relations among men are perpetuated in capitalist societies? Can we identify ways in which patriarchy has shaped the course of capitalist development?

The partnership of patriarchy and capital

How are we to recognize patriarchal social relations in capitalist societies? It appears as if each woman is oppressed by her own man alone; her oppression seems a private affair. Relationships among men and among families seem equally fragmented. It is hard to recognize relationships among men, and between men and women, as *systematically* patriarchal. We argue, however, that patriarchy as a system of relations between men and women exists in capitalism, and that in capitalist societies a healthy and strong partnership exists between patriarchy and capital. Yet if one begins with the concept of patriarchy and an understanding of the capitalist mode of production, one recognizes immediately that the partnership of patriarchy and capital was not inevitable; men and capitalists often have conflicting interests, particularly over the use of women's labor-power. Here is one way in which this conflict might manifest itself: the vast majority of men might want their women at home to personally service them. A smaller number of men, who are capitalists, might want most women (not their own) to work in the wage labor market. In examining the tensions of this conflict over women's labor-power historically, we will be able to identify the material base of patriarchal relations in capitalist societies, as well as the basis for the partnership between capital and patriarchy. [...]

The resolution that developed in the early twentieth century can be seen to benefit capitalist interests as well as patriarchal interests. Capitalists, it is often argued, recognized that in the extreme conditions which prevailed in the early nineteenth century industrialization, working-class families could not adequately reproduce themselves. They realized that housewives produced and maintained healthier workers than wage-working wives and that educated children became better workers than non-educated ones. The bargain, paying family wages to men and keeping women home, suited the capitalists at the time as well as the male workers. Although the terms of the bargain have altered over time, it is still true that the family and women's work in the family serve capital by providing a labor force and serve men as the space in which they exercise their privilege. Women, working to serve men and their families, also serve capital as consumers.[2] The family is also the place where dominance and submission are learned, as Firestone, the Frankfurt School, and many others have explained.[3] Obedient children become obedient workers; girls and boys each learn their proper roles.

The family and the family wage today

The family wage cemented the partnership between patriarchy and capital. Despite women's increased labor force participation, particularly rapid since World War II, the family wage is still, we argue, the cornerstone of the present sexual division of labor – in which women are primarily responsible for housework and men primarily for wage work. Women's lower wages in the labor market (combined with the need for children to be reared by someone) assure the continued existence of the family as a necessary income pooling unit. The family, supported by the family wage, thus allows the control of women's labor by men both within and without the family.

Though women's increased wage work may cause stress for the family ... it would be wrong to think that as a consequence, the concepts and the realities of the family and of the sexual division of labor will soon disappear. The sexual division of labor reappears in the labor market, where women work at women's jobs, often the very jobs they used to do only at home – food preparation and service, cleaning of all kinds, caring for people, and so on. As these jobs are low-status and low-paying patriarchal relations remain intact, though their material base shifts somewhat from the family to the wage differential, from family-based to industrially based patriarchy.[4]

Notes

1. H. Braverman *Labor and Monopoly Capital*, New York: Monthly Review Press, 1975.
2. See B. Weinbaum and A. Bridges 'The other side of the paycheck: monopoly capital and the structure of consumption', *Monthly Review*, vol. 28, no. 3 (1976), pp. 88–103, for a discussion of women's consumption work.
3. For a view of the Frankfurt School, see M. Horkheimer, 'Authority and the family', in *Critical Theory*, New York: Herder & Herder, 1972; Frankfurt Institute of Social research, 'The family', in *Aspects of Sociology*, Boston, MA: Beacon, 1972.
4. Carol Brown argues, for example, that we are moving from 'family-based' to 'industrially based' patriarchy within capitalism, in 'Patriarchal capitalism and the female headed household', *Social Scientist* (India), no. 5 40–41 (1975), pp. 28–39.

1.5   **Sex Classes**

Christine Delphy

Although she defines herself as a radical feminist, Christine Delphy's theoretical position is close to Heidi Hartmann's. Here Delphy argues for the existence of sex classes. Unlike Shulamith Firestone, she sees these classes as the consequence, not the cause, of patriarchal domination.

I use the term 'class' to refer to the division between men and women [...] The concept of class [...] is the only concept I know which at least partially responds to the strict requirements of a *social* explanation. It is perhaps not totally satisfactory, but it is the least unsatisfactory of all the terms used to analyse oppression.

Some talk of men and women as being 'groups', but the term 'groups' says nothing about their mode of constitution. It can be thought that two groups – the dominant and the dominated – each has an origin which is *sui generis*; that having already come into existence, they later enter into a relationship; and that this relationship, at a still later time, becomes characterized by domination. The concept of class, however, inverts this scheme. It implies that each group cannot be considered separately from the other, because they are bound together by a relationship of domination; nor can they even be considered together but independently of this relationship. Characterizing this relationship as one of economic exploitation, the concept of class additionally puts social domination at the heart of the explanation of hierarchy. The motives – material profit in the widest sense – attributed to this domination can be discussed, and even challenged or changed, without the fundamental scheme needing to be changed. Class is a dichotomous concept and it has, because of this, its limitations; but on the other hand, we can see how well it applies to the exhaustive, hierarchical, and precisely dichotomous classifications which are internal to a given society – like the classification into men *or* women (adult/child, white/non-white, etc.). The concept of class starts from the idea of social construction and specifies the implications of it. Groups are no long *sui generis*, constituted before coming into relation with one another. On the contrary, it is their relationship which constitutes them as such. It is therefore a question of discovering the social practices, the social relations, which, in constituting the division of gender, create the groups of gender (called 'of sex').

I have put forward the hypothesis that the domestic relations of production constitute one such class relationship. But family relationships do not account for the whole of the 'gender' system, and they also concern other categorizations (e.g. by age). I would put forward as a second hypothesis that other systems of relationship constitutive of gender division also exist – and these remain to be discovered. If we think of each of these systems as a circle, then the gender division is the zone illuminated by the projection of these circles on one another. Each system of relations, taken separately, is not specific, either to gender division or to another categorization. But these systems of relationships can combine in various different ways, each of which is unique. According to this hypothesis, it is the particular combination of several systems of relationships, of which none is specific, which gives its singularity to division by gender.

Needless to say, much still needs to be done before we reach a complete understanding of the domestic mode of production, and still more before we know about the nature of other systems which oppress women and which articulate with the domestic mode of production to form contemporary patriarchy.

1.6   Forms and Degrees of Patriarchy
Sylvia Walby

Like Christine Delphy, Sylvia Walby does not consider the patriarchal mode of production to be the only basis of patriarchy. Patriarchal structuring of the labour market is of particular importance. The relationship between patriarchal structures determines the historical form which patriarchy takes at any given time, including the shift from private to public patriarchy which she outlines here.

There have been changes in both the degree and form of patriarchy in Britain over the last century, but these changes are analytically distinct. Changes in degree include aspects of gender relations such as the slight reduction in the wages gap between men and women and the closing of the gap in educational qualifications of young men and women. These modifications in degree of patriarchy have led some commentators to suggest that patriarchy has been eliminated. However, other aspects of patriarchal relations have intensified. I want to argue that there have been changes not only in the degree of patriarchy but also in its form. Britain has seen a movement from a private to a public form of patriarchy over the last century.

I am distinguishing two main forms of patriarchy, private and public. Private patriarchy is based upon household production as the main site of women's oppression. Public patriarchy is based principally in public sites such as employment and the state. The household does not cease to be a patriarchal structure in the public form, but it is no longer the chief site. In private patriarchy the expropriation of women's labour takes place primarily by individual patriarchs within the household, while in the public form it is a more collective appropriation. In private patriarchy the principal patriarchal strategy is exclusionary; in the public it is segregationist and subordinating.

The change from private to public patriarchy involves a change both in the relations between the structures and within the structures. In the private form household production is the dominant structure; in the public form it is replaced by employment and the state. In each form all the remaining patriarchal structures are present – there is simply a change in which are dominant. There is also a change in the institutional forms of patriarchy, with the replacement of a primarily individual form of appropriation of women by a collective one. This takes place within each of the six patriarchal structures. (See Table 1.6.1)

Table 1.6.1 Private and public patriarchy

Form of patriarchy	Private	Public
Dominant structure	Household production	Employment/State
Wider patriarchal structures	Employment State Sexuality Violence Culture	Household production Sexuality Violence Culture
Period	C19th	C20th
Mode of expropriation	Individual	Collective
Patriarchal strategy	Exclusionary	Segregationist

1.7   Editorial, *m/f* 1

Parveen Adams, Rosalind Coward and Elizabeth Cowie

A very different direction taken by some feminist theorists from the late 1970s was exemplified in Britain by the journal m/f. Its first editorial provides a clear statement of a move away from materialist analysis towards a focus on gender as a cultural category. While situating the journal within a Marxist tradition, the editorial is critical of forms of Marxism which sought to explain women's subordination in material (economic) terms. Having offered a critique of existing tendencies within Marxist feminism, they go on to outline their own theoretical project.

An examination of these tendencies within Marxist feminism thus produces the necessity to challenge and develop existing theories within Marxism. It also indicates the need for new work which can adequately theorise the production of women's subordinate position in the social formation in relation to and within a theory of class.

It is in the area of this work that *m/f* has placed itself. We are interested in how women are produced as a category; it is *this* which determines the subordinate position of women. Some feminists have taken up psychoanalysis as providing an account of the process of the construction of the sexed subject in society. This is seen as important because it is with the construction of sexual difference and its inscription in the social that feminism is concerned. But psychoanalysis has had little to say on the relationship of this construction to particular historical moments, nor the effect that considering the historical moment might have on psychoanalytic theory itself. Thus psychoanalysis is not a sufficient theory for understanding the construction of women as a category.

The particular historical moment, the institutions and practices within which and through which the category of woman is produced must be addressed. This is not a problem of origins but of the continual production of the sexual division within those institutions and practices.

1.8   **Postmodernism and Gender Relations in Feminist Theory**
Jane Flax

The form of analysis proposed in the previous reading led many feminists to explore poststructuralist and postmodernist theory. Postmodern feminism involves a rejection of any metanarrative (any grand general theory) which purports to identify the basis of women's subordination. The concept of 'women's subordination' is not one which postmodernists would use themselves, since it implies an objective fixed state; they prefer terms such as gender relations, which are suggestive of greater fluidity. Moreover, once gender categories are deconstructed, it is no longer possible to think in terms of women in general. Once we call into question the status of knowledge as objective truth, we can no longer claim that feminist theory can provide a definitive account of gender relations. In the following reading Jane Flax defends this position, arguing that feminism is necessarily postmodern.

As a type of postmodern philosophy, feminist theory reveals and contributes to the growing uncertainty within Western intellectual circles about the appropriate grounding and methods for explaining and interpreting human experience. Contemporary feminists join other postmodern philosophers in raising important metatheoretical questions about the possible nature and status of theorizing itself. Given the increasingly fluid and confused status of Western self-understanding, it is not even clear what would constitute the basis for satisfactory answers to commonly agreed upon questions within feminist (or other forms of social) theory. [...]

Feminist theorists enter into and echo postmodernist discourses as we have begun to reconstruct notions of reason, knowledge, or the self and to reveal the effects of the gender arrangements that lay beneath their neutral and universalizing façades. [...]

It is on the metatheoretical level that postmodern philosophies of knowledge can contribute to a more accurate self-understanding of the nature of our theorizing. We cannot simultaneously claim (1) that the mind, the self, and knowledge are socially constituted and that what we can know depends upon our social practices and contexts and (2) that feminist theory can uncover the truth of the whole once and for all. Such an absolute truth (e.g. the explanation for all gender arrangements at all times is X) would require the existence of an Archimedes point outside of the whole and beyond our embeddedness in it from which we could see (and represent) the whole. What we see and report would also have to be untransformed by the activities of perception and of reporting our vision in language. The object seen (social whole or gender arrangement) would have to be apprehended by an empty (ahistoric) mind and perfectly transcribed by/into a transparent language. The possibility of each of these conditions existing has been rendered extremely doubtful by the deconstructions of postmodern philosophers.

Furthermore, the work of Foucault (among others) should sensitize us to the interconnections between knowledge claims (especially to the claim of absolute or neutral knowledge) and power. Our own search for an Archimedes point may conceal and obscure our entanglement in an episteme in which truth claims may take only certain forms and not others. Any episteme requires the suppression of discourses that threaten to differ with or undermine the authority of the dominant one. Hence, within feminist theory a search for a defining theme of the whole or a feminist viewpoint may require the suppression of the important and discomforting voices of persons with experiences unlike our own. The suppression of these voices seems to be a necessary condition for the (apparent) authority, coherence, and universality of our own.

Thus, the very search for a root or cause of gender relations (or more narrowly, male domination) may partially reflect a mode of thinking that is itself grounded in particular forms of gender (and/or other) relations in which domination is present. Perhaps reality can have 'a' structure only from the falsely universalizing perspective of the dominant group. That is, only to the extent that one person or group can dominate the whole will reality appear to be governed by one set of rules or be constituted by one privileged set of social relations. Criteria of theory construction such as parsimony or simplicity may be attained only by the suppression or denial of the experiences of the other(s).

1.9 Women: equal or different
Luce Irigaray

Luce Irigaray is a French psychoanalyst and philosopher whose work has been primarily concerned with theorising women's difference. Here she defends an essentialist conception of sexual difference and insists that feminism should recognise women's specificity.

Demanding equality, as women, seems to me to be an erroneous expression of a real issue. Demanding to be equal presupposes a term of comparison. Equal to what? What do women want to be equal to? Men? A wage? A public position? Equal to what? Why not to themselves?

Even a vaguely rigorous analysis of claims to equality shows that they are justified at the level of a superficial critique of culture, and utopian as a means to women's liberation. The exploitation of women is based upon sexual difference, and can only be resolved through sexual difference. Certain tendencies of the day, certain contemporary feminists, are noisily demanding the neutralization of sex [*sexe*]. That neutralization, if it were possible, would correspond to the end of the human race. The human race is divided into *two genres* which ensure its production and reproduction. Trying to suppress sexual difference is to invite a genocide more radical than any destruction that has ever existed in History. What is important, on the other hand, is defining the values of belonging to a sex-specific *genre*. What is indispensable is elaborating a culture of the sexual which does not yet exist, whilst respecting both *genres*. Because of the historical time gaps between the gynocratic, matriarchal, patriarchal and phallocratic eras, we are in a sexual position which is bound up with generation and not with *genre* as sex. This means that, within the family, women must be mothers and men must be fathers, but that we have no positive and ethical values that allow two sexes of the same generation to form a creative, and not simply procreative, human couple. One of the major obstacles to the creation and recognition of such values is the more or less covert hold patriarchal and phallocratic roles have had on the whole of our civilization for centuries. It is social justice, pure and simple, to balance out the power of one sex over the other by giving, or restoring, cultural values to female sexuality. [...]

Unless it goes through this stage, feminism may work towards the destruction of women, and, more generally, of all values. Egalitarianism, in fact, sometimes expends a lot of energy on rejecting certain positive values and chasing after nothing. Hence the periodic crises, discouragement and regressions in women's liberation movements, and their fleeting inscription in History.

Equality between men and women cannot be achieved unless we *think of genre as sexuate* [*sexué*] and write the rights and duties of each sex, in so far as they are *different*, into social rights and duties.

Peoples constantly split into secondary but murderous rivalries without realizing that their primary and irreducible division is one between two genres. From that point of view, we are still living in the childhood of culture. It is urgent for women's struggles, for small, popular groups of women, to realize the importance of issues that are specific to them. These are bound up with respect for life and culture, with the constant passage of the natural into the cultural, of the spiritual into the natural.

1.10 **One is not born a woman**
   Monique Wittig

Monique Wittig is fundamentally opposed to essentialist views of 'women' such as those of Irigaray. Her materialist anti-essentialism also differs from postmodernism in that she does consider it possible to speak of women as a category, and argues that women's subordination has a material base. In the reading which follows she defines women as a class but rejects those forms of feminism which essentialise women.

A materialist feminist approach shows that what we take for the cause or origin of oppression is in fact only the *mark*[1] imposed by the oppressor: the 'myth of woman'[2] plus its material effects and manifestations in the appropriated consciousness and bodies of women. Thus, this mark does not predate oppression: Colette Guillaumin has shown that before the socioeconomic reality of black slavery, the concept of race did not exist, at least not in its modern meaning, since it was applied to the lineage of families. However, now, race, exactly like sex, is taken as an 'immediate given', a 'sensible given', 'physical features,' belonging to a natural order. But what we believe to be a physical and direct perception is only a sophisticated and mythic construction, an 'imaginary formation',[3] which reinterprets physical features (in themselves as neutral as any others but marked by the social system) through the network of relationships in which they are perceived. (They are seen as *black*, therefore they *are* black; they are seen as *women*, therefore they *are* women. But before being *seen* that way, they first had to be *made* that way.) Lesbians should always remember and acknowledge how 'unnatural', compelling, totally oppressive, and destructive being 'woman' was for us in the old days before the women's liberation movement. It was a political constraint, and those who resisted it were accused of not being 'real' women. But then we were proud of it, since in the accusation there was already something like a shadow of victory: the avowal by the oppressor that 'woman' is not something that goes without saying, since to be one, one has to be a 'real' one. [...]

The refusal to become (or to remain) heterosexual always meant to refuse to become a man or a woman, consciously or not. For a lesbian this goes further than the refusal of the *role* 'woman'. It is the refusal of the economic, ideological, and political power of a man. This, we lesbians and non-lesbians as well, knew before the beginning of the lesbian and feminist movement. However, as Andrea Dworkin emphasizes, many lesbians recently 'have increasingly tried to transform the very ideology that has enslaved us into a dynamic, religious, psychologically compelling celebration of female biological potential'.[4] Thus, some avenues of the feminist and lesbian movement lead us back to the myth of woman which was created by men especially for us, and with it we sink back into a natural group. Having stood up to fight for a sexless society,[5] we now find ourselves entrapped in the familiar deadlock of 'woman is wonderful'. Simone de Beauvoir underlined particularly the false consciousness which consists of selecting among the features of the myth (that women are different from men) those which look good and using them as a definition for women. What the concept 'woman is wonderful' accomplishes is that it retains for defining women the best features (best according to whom?) which oppression has granted us, and it does not radically question the categories 'man' and 'woman', which are political categories and not natural givens. [...]

The ambiguity of the term 'feminist' sums up the whole situation. What does 'feminist' mean? Feminist is formed with the word 'femme', 'woman', and means: someone who fights for women. For many of us it means someone who fights for women as a class and for the disappearance of this class. For many others it means someone who fights for woman and her defense – for the myth, then, and its re-enforcement. [...]

[...] it is our historical task, and only ours, to define what we call oppression in materialist terms, to make it evident that women are a class, which is to say that the category 'woman' as well as the category 'man' are political and economic categories, not eternal ones. Our fight aims to suppress men as a class, not through a genocidal, but a political struggle. Once the class 'men' disappears, 'women' as a class will disappear as well, for there are no slaves without masters. Our first task, it seems, is to always thoroughly dissociate 'women' (the class within which we fight) and 'woman', the myth. For 'woman' does not exist for us: it is only an imaginary formation, while 'women' is the product of a social relationship.

Furthermore, we have to destroy the myth inside and outside ourselves. 'Woman' is not each one of us, but the political and ideological formation which negates 'women' (the product of a relation of exploitation). 'Woman' is there to confuse us, to hide the reality 'women'. In order to be aware of being a class and to become a class we first have to kill the myth of 'woman' including its most seductive aspects. [...]

To destroy 'woman' does not mean that we aim, short of physical destruction, to destroy lesbianism simultaneously with the categories of sex, because lesbianism provides for the moment the only social form in which we can live freely. Lesbian is the only concept I know of which is beyond the categories of sex (woman and man), because the designated subject (lesbian) is *not* a woman, either economically, or politically, or ideologically. For what makes a woman is a specific social relation to a man, a relation that we have previously called servitude, a relation which implies personal and physical obligation as well as economic obligation ('forced residence',[6] domestic corvée, conjugal duties, unlimited production of children, etc.), a relation which lesbians escape by refusing to become or to stay heterosexual. We are escapees from our class in the same way as the American runaway slaves were when escaping slavery and becoming free. For us this is an absolute necessity; our survival demands that we contribute all our strength to the destruction of the class of women within which men appropriate women. This can be accomplished only by the destruction of heterosexuality as a social system which is based on the oppression of women by men and which produces the doctrine of the difference between the sexes to justify this oppression.

Notes

1. C. Guillaumin, 'Race et nature: système des marques, idée de groupe naturel et rapports sociaux', *Pluriel*, no. 11 (1977). Translated as 'Race and nature: the system of

marks, the idea of a natural group and social relationships', *Feminist Issues*, vol. 8, no. 2 (1988).
2. Simon de Beauvoir, *The Second Sex*, New York: Bantam, 1952.
3. Guillaumin, 'Race et nature'.
4. A. Dworkin, 'Biological superiority: the world's most dangerous and deadly idea', *Heresies*, 6.
5. T. Atkinson, 'If feminism has any logic at all it must be working for a sexless society', *Amazon Odyssey*, New York: Links Books, 1975, p. 6.
6. C. Rochefort, *Les Stances à Sophie*, Paris: Grasset, 1963.

1.11 **White Women Listen!**
Hazel Carby

Taking the category women as unproblematic can effectively silence those women who feel excluded from that category. In one of the first critiques of British feminism from the point of view of black women, Hazel Carby challenges the racism and ethnocentrism implicit in much white feminist theory.

In arguing that most contemporary feminist theory does not begin to adequately account for the experience of black women we ... have to acknowledge that it is not a simple question of their absence, consequently the task is not one of rendering their visibility. On the contrary we will have to argue that the process of accounting for their historical and contemporary position does, in itself, challenge the use of some of the central categories and assumptions of recent mainstream feminist thought. We can point to no single source for our oppression. When white feminists emphasize patriarchy alone, we want to redefine the term and make it a more complex concept. Racism ensures that black men do not have the same relations to patriarchal/capitalist hierarchies as white men. [...]

It is only in the writings by black feminists that we can find attempts to theorize the interconnection of class gender and race as it occurs in our lives and it has only been in the autonomous organizations of black women that we have been able to express and act upon the experiences consequent upon these determinants. Many black women had been alienated by the non-recognition of their lives, experiences and herstories in the WLM. Black feminists have been, and are still, demanding that the existence of racism must be acknowledged as a structuring feature of our relationships with white women. Both white feminist theory and practice have to recognize that white women stand in a power relation as oppressors of black women. This compromises any feminist theory and practice founded on the notion of simple equality. [...]

The way the gender of black women is constructed differs from constructions of white femininity because it is also subject to racism. Black feminists have been explaining this since the last century when Sojourner Truth pointed to the ways in which 'womanhood' was denied the black woman:

> That man over there says women need to be helped into carriages, and lifted over ditches, and to have the best place everywhere. Nobody ever helps me into carriages, and lifted over ditches, or over mud-puddles, or gives me any best place! And ain't I a woman? Look at me! Look at my arm! I have ploughed, and planted, and gathered into barns, and no man could head me! And ain't I a woman? I could work as much and eat as much as a man – when I could get it – and bear the lash as well! And ain't I a woman? I have borne thirteen children, and seen most all sold off to slavery, and when I cried with my mother's grief, none but Jesus heard me! And ain't I a woman?[1]

[...] Black women do not want to be grafted onto 'feminism' in a tokenistic manner as colourful diversions to 'real' problems. Feminism has to be transformed if it is to address us. Neither do we wish our words to be misused in generalities as if what each one of us utters represents the total experience of all black women. [...]

   [...] of white feminists we must ask, what exactly do you mean when you say 'WE'??

Notes

1. J. Lowenberg and R. Bogin (eds), *Black Women in Nineteenth Century American Life*, Pennsylvania State University Press, 1978, p. 235.

1.12 **Am I That Name?**
Denise Riley

Sojourner Truth's speech, quoted by Carby, provides the starting point for Denise Riley's historical deconstruction of the category 'women'. Demonstrating that 'women' has no fixed meaning, she argues that feminism must expose it as a fiction.

The black abolitionist and freed slave, Sojourner Truth, spoke out at the Akron convention in 1851, and named her own toughness in a famous peroration against the notion of woman's disqualifying frailty. She rested her case on her refrain 'Ain't I a woman?' It's my hope to persuade readers that a new Sojourner Truth might well – except for the catastrophic loss of grace in the wording – issue another plea: 'Ain't I a fluctuating identity?' For both a concentration on and a refusal of the identity of 'women' are essential to feminism. This its history makes plain. [...]

I want to ... suggest that not only 'woman' but also 'women' is troublesome – and that this extension of our suspicions is in the interest of feminism. That we can't bracket off either Woman, whose capital letter has long alerted us to her dangers, or the more modest lower-case 'woman', while leaving unexamined the ordinary, innocent-sounding 'women'. [...] 'women' is historically, discursively constructed, and always relatively to other categories which themselves change; 'women' is a volatile collectivity in which female persons can be very differently positioned, so that the apparent continuity of the subject of 'women' isn't to be relied on; 'women' is both synchronically and diachronically erratic as a collectivity, while for the individual, 'being a woman' is also inconstant, and can't provide an ontological foundation. Yet it must be emphasised that these instabilities of the category are the *sine qua non* of feminism, which would otherwise be lost for an object, despoiled of a fight, and, in short, without much life.

1.13 Feminism Without Women
Tania Modleski

Tania Modleski challenges both Riley's reading of Sojourner Truth's speech and her postmodernist project. She suggests that denying that one is a woman is a strategy open only to privileged feminists whose lives are relatively unconstrained by their womanhood.

[...] it is interesting to note that despite the accusations of ethnocentrism and colonialism sometimes leveled at 'essentialists' by anti-essentialists, Denise Riley begins her book by noting the similarity of her title, '*Am I That Name?*' to the words of Sojourner Truth's speech, 'Ain't I a Woman?' Reaching out across racial lines, historical eras, and national boundaries to claim commonality of belief with a black female abolitionist on the nature (or anti-nature) of 'woman', Riley writes, 'It's my hope to persuade readers that a new Sojourner Truth might well – except for the catastrophic loss of grace in the wording – issue another plea: "Ain't I a fluctuating identity?"' (p. 1). How a writer who is concerned to emphasize the historically variable meaning of 'women' can envisage a *new* Sojourner Truth, abolitionist, feminist, ex-slave, is difficult for me to grasp. This caveat aside, I would want to insist on the crucial *difference* between the question posed by Riley and the one posed by the 'real', historically specific Sojourner Truth (whose very name suggests a kind of doubleness – a being at once 'essentialized' and *in process*). Sojourner Truth, employing a negative and a question, invites no simple answer – invites in fact both a yes *and* a no: 'yes', in terms of her 'experience', which in some major respects reduces her to her biology – to being the white man's breeder with little freedom to 'fluctuate' in any way (although in other respects it requires her to possess the physical strength of a man); and 'no' in terms of an ideology based on a notion of frail white Southern womanhood. Given the doubleness of response required by the question as it is posed by a black woman and an ex-slave, it seems to me politically irresponsible for (white) feminism to refuse to grant to Sojourner Truth the status of a woman, for it would then be in complicity with the racist patriarchal system that Sojoumer Truth was protesting and that has denied, and in important ways continues to deny, this status to the black female (in this respect, excluding women from a contested category on the grounds that there *is no category* may well be the latest ruse of white middle-class feminism). On the other hand, to answer the question in the affirmative has, whatever the ontologically correct position, morally and politically devastating consequences to patriarchal values, for it points up the monstrous hypocrisy of a system which could so exploit a woman's body while infantilizing, idealizing, and senti-mentalizing women with its belief in female fragility and spirituality.

In continually repeating the refrain 'And ain't I a woman?' as she recounts her personal history as a slave, Sojourner Truth contests ideology by an appeal to experience, and experience by appeal to ideology, and in the very space of this negation affirms herself *as a woman*. In this respect, the 'loss of grace' resulting from Riley's substitution of the phrase 'fluctuating identity' for the word 'woman' is *in truth* 'catastrophic'. [...]

It is possible, of course, to argue that a nineteenth-century black woman needed to believe in herself as a woman, while in the twentieth century intellectual (white?) women who 'know better' should go a step farther, moving beyond the naiveté of a Sojourner Truth to a point where they are fully conscious of the allegedly fictional status of the term 'woman' – acting when necessary, in Riley's phrase, 'as if' they are women while knowing they are not. But I am very wary of this development within feminism. I worry that the position of female anti-essentialism as it is being theorized by some feminists today is a luxury open only to the most privileged women. [...]

1.14 Recovering 'Women' in History from Historical Deconstructionism

Liz Stanley

Liz Stanley, while accepting the need to expose essentialist conceptions of womanhood, questions the politics of undermining identities which women have constructed for themselves.

Welcoming difference, none the less Denise Riley's feminist deconstructionist argument implicitly portrays as essentialism the differing and sometimes multiple identities painstakingly *constructed* in the very recent past, by lesbians, older women, women of colour, disabled women, and working-class women (to name only some). What must it be like to be a black woman, having gone through much to have named oneself thus and to have recovered something of the history of one's foremothers, to have it implied that this is not only not enough but an intellectual error, an ontological over-simplifcation to have done so? As a working-class lesbian (for so I continue to name myself this different kind of woman), and thus having gone through comparable, if not similar, struggles to name, I sigh another bitter sigh at yet another, although surely unintended, theoretical centrism: the resurgence of Theory from those who were once the certificated namers of other women's experiences and who are now likely to become the certificated deconstructors of the same.

What is needed – and indeed must be insisted upon by those of us who are black, lesbian, aged, disabled, working-class – is that *all* difference must be attended to *equally*. In particular, there must be an end to the now ritual invocation of 'and black women' as the only such difference seen but which actually goes no further than a formula of words that leaves untouched actual relations of power between differently situated groups of black and white women, and which also masks a refusal to see that *black women* is itself no unitary category, but one internally differentiated on grounds of age, class, able-bodiedness, and sexuality.

And yet there is much in Denise Riley's argument about the ontological experience of *women* as shaky, as something we inhabit or are forced into only periodically, as it were at the points, the disjunctures, the fracturings, of ordinary being introduced by actual oppressions in our lives. None the less, oppression and its struggles should be neither denied nor silenced, nor explained away as a momentary and passing necessity transcended by the supposed greater intellectual rigour of deconstructionism.

1.15 Questions of Difference and International Feminism
Avtar Brah

Drawing on recent debates, Avtar Brah discusses the conceptualisation of difference and its political implications. She argues that while 'woman' is not a unitary category, it might none the less – if we can build alliances that recognise our differences – become a unifying category.

The feminist slogan 'sisterhood is global' that was commonly used by the women's movement in the 1970s signalled the centrality of an international dimension to feminist practice but as many critics have since pointed out the slogan failed to acknowledge the heterogeneity of the condition of being a woman. What does it mean to be a Native American or Native Australian woman whose land rights have been appropriated and whose cultures have been systematically denigrated by the state as well as by the dominant ideologies and practices within civil society? What precise meaning do questions of 'domestic labour' hold for peasant women in the poorest areas of Kenya, who not only are responsible for caring work at home but also have to undertake long hours of strenuous work on the land as well as carry water and firewood for long distances to ensure daily survival? What are the realities facing low-paid women workers employed by multinational companies in countries such as the Philippines, Hong Kong and Sri Lanka? What are the similarities and the differences between their life chances and those of women doing similar work in Britain? How do patriarchal ideologies articulate with international relations of power in the formation of sex-tourism as a growing industry? What are the points of convergence and divergence in the lives of black and white women in Britain? Such questions point to major differences in the social circumstances of different groups of women, and this will mean that their interests may often be contradictory. [...]

How may 'difference' be conceptualized? At the most general level 'difference' may be construed as a social relation constructed within systems of power underlying structures of class, racism, gender and sexuality. At this level of abstraction we are concerned with the ways in which our social position is circumscribed by the broad parameters set by the social structures of a given society. [...] It is extremely important to address this level, as it has a crucial bearing on shaping our life chances. Difference may also be conceptualized as experiential diversity. Here the focus is on the many and different manifestations of ideological and institutional practices in our everyday life. These everyday practices constitute the matrix against which we make and remake our group, as well as personal, histories. But we need to make a distinction between 'difference' as representations of the distinctiveness of our collective histories and 'difference' as personal experience, codified in an individual's biography. Although mutually interdependent, the two levels cannot be 'read off' from each other. Our personal experiences arise out of mediated relationships. How we perceive and understand our experience may vary enormously. For example, we may experience subordination without necessarily recognizing it as such. The same social practice may be associated with somewhat different meanings in a different cultural context. There may be psychic and emotional disjunction between how we feel about something and how we believe we ought to feel from the standpoint of our analytical and political perspectives. The group histories that chronicle our shared experience will also contain their own measure of contradictions, but there is no simple one-to-one correspondence between collective experience and personal biography. [...]

Hence we need to make distinctions between, for example, 'black' and 'white' women as historically contingent analytical categories constructed within and referring to specific historical processes of colonialism, imperialism and anti-Black racism, *and* black and white women as individuals. Whilst the former describes a social division, the latter draws our attention to human subjects as complex beings who are sites of multiple contradictions, and whose everyday praxis may reinforce or undermine social divisions.

It is now widely accepted that 'woman' is not a unitary category. The question remains whether it can be a unifying category. I believe that it is possible to develop a feminist politics that is global, but it demands a massive commitment together with a sustained and painstaking effort directed towards developing practices that are informed by understandings of the ways in which various structures of inequality articulate in given contexts, and shape the lives of different groups of women. We need to address how our own position – in terms of class, racism, sexuality, caste, for example – locates us within systems of power *vis-à-vis* other groups of women and men. For example, as an Asian woman living in Britain I am subjected to racism, but as a member of a dominant caste within the specific community from which I originate I also occupy a position of power in relation to lower-caste women. From my standpoint, a feminist politics would demand of me a commitment to opposing racism as much as casteism although I am positioned differently within these social hierarchies, and the strategies required of me in dealing with them may be different.

Similarly, we may take the example of Irish and black women in Britain. Both black and Irish people have a history of being colonized, both occupy predominantly working-class positions within the British class structure and both have been subjected to racism. But anti-Irish racism and anti-Black racism have different histories. We must recognize that as white Europeans Irish women are constructed as a dominant group *vis-à-vis* black women in and through the discourses of anti-Black racism, even when they themselves are in turn subordinated within anti-Irish racism. Alliances that would empower both groups must not only take into account the similarities in their material circumstances but also involve commitment to combating the differing racisms to which the two groups are subjected. Black and Irish women would need to examine the ways in which their 'womanhoods' are both similarly and differently constructed within patriarchal, racial and class relations of power.

As a consequence of the major restructuring of the world economy, the dominance of multinational capital, the impact of the new communications revolution, and the profound political upheavals of recent times, we are witnessing global tendencies that are simultaneously complementary and contradictory. On the one hand, the ever-increasing globalization of cultural industries is leading to homogenization of cultural consumption across transnational boundaries. On the other hand, we are faced with the parallel tendency towards greater fragmentation; the resurgence of local aesthetic, political and ethnic tradition; and the assertion of difference. Under such circumstances it is important to identify when 'difference' is being organized hierarchically rather than laterally. We need to disentangle instances when 'difference' is asserted as a mode of contestation against oppression and exploitation, from those where difference becomes the vehicle for hegemonic entrenchment. In practice this exercise is not clear-cut. For instance, nationalistic discourses may be employed by liberation movements as well as by racist and chauvinistic groups and organizations. Moreover, both sets of discourses may be constituted around, and/or be constitutive of, representations of women which reinforce rather than undermine women's subordination. In these instances feminist practice would require that we pay careful attention to the historical and social circumstances which underpin a given nationalism, and its consequences for different economic groups and for different groups of women.

A distinction between 'difference' as a process of differentiation referring to the particularities of the social experience of a group, from that whereby 'difference' itself becomes the modality in which domination is expressed, is crucial for several reasons. Firstly, it draws our attention to the fact that 'difference' need not invariably lead to divisions amongst different groups of women. Secondly, it reminds us that our experiences are not constituted solely within oppressions. They encompass an immense range of emotional, psychological and social expressions. In this sense, cultural diversity – as expressed, for example, in art, music, literature, science and technology, traditions of political and cultural struggle against domination, and different modes of human subjectivity – may be acknowledged and, depending upon the social perspectives within which these formations are embedded, affirmed and celebrated. But we need to be aware that the notion of 'cultural difference' can be appropriated by social tendencies which seek to construct impervious boundaries between groups. Contemporary racism in Britain provides an instance of such appropriation of 'cultural difference'.

A subordinate group may also mobilize symbols of cultural difference as an expression of pride in its social identity. Such a political assertion of cultural identity could potentially constitute a progressive force, although it too cannot be assumed to be invariably unproblematic simply because it is a form of struggle by a subordinate group. Particular expressions of cultural pride may emerge as a cause for concern if cultural practices are treated as reified symbols of an essentialist historic past. Hence, the meaning of cultural difference – whether inscribed within the specificity of male and female cultures, class cultures, or cultures defined on the basis of ethnicity (and these are overlapping categories) – is contingent not only on the social context, but also upon the extent to which the concept of culture is posited in essentialist or non-essentialist terms.

The issue of essentialism seems to call for conceptual clarification between:

(a) essentialism as referring to a notion of ultimate essence that transcends historical and cultural boundaries;
(b) universalism as commonality derived from historically variable experience and as such remaining subject to historical change; and
(c) the historical specificity of a particular cultural formation.

It should be possible to recognize cultural difference in the sense of (c) and acknowledge commonalities that acquire a universal status through the accumulation of similar (but not identical) experiences in different contexts as in (b) without resorting to essentialism. It is evident that as women we can identify many commonalities of experience across cultures which none the less retain their particularity. In other words, historical specificity and universalism need not be counterposed against each other. [...] I am arguing the case for a non-essentialist universalism; that is, for a concept of universalism as a historical product.

We would be in a better position to address the need for mutual respect for cultural difference without recourse to essentialism if cultures were to be conceived less in terms of reified artefacts and rather more as processes. This may also circumvent the issue of cultural relativism. If cultures are understood as processes instead of fixed products, it would be possible to disapprove of a particular cultural practice from a feminist standpoint without constructing a whole cultural group as being inherently such and such. For example, we may condemn the practice of 'suttee' without following in the tradition of colonial and post-colonial discourses (such as the television film 'Far Pavilions') which seek to represent such practices as the symbols of the inherent barbarism of Indian cultures. This would require that the racialized discourses and practices are challenged equally vehemently and persistently. [...]

A corollary of the above argument is that human subjects are not fixed embodiments of their cultures. Since all cultures are internally differentiated and never static, though the pace of change may be variable, our subjectivities will be formed within the range of heterogeneous discursive practices available to us. Hence, a variety of subject positions will emerge within a single cultural context offering the possibility of political change as we move from one subject position to another – from a non-feminist to a feminist position, for example. But, far from being a smooth transition, a shift in subject position may be accompanied by all manner of emotional and psychic ambivalences and contradictions. These must be addressed if feminist visions that take account of issues of racism, class and sexuality are to make a lasting impact. It is essential to examine the loci of power which produce and sustain specific forms of subjectivity. For instance, we may ask questions about the nature of power that surrounds white subjectivity in a society where non-white people are subjected to racism, or heterosexual subjectivity in a society where lesbian and gay sexuality is subjugated. Critical perspectives developed from such enquiry should enable assessment of the personal implications for us as individuals of adopting anti-racist or anti-heterosexist positions.

A sense of ourselves as located within heterogeneous discursive practices shows not only that we inhabit multiple and changing identities but that these identities are produced and reproduced within social relations of 'race', 'gender', class and sexuality. The degree to which we can work across our 'differences' depends on the conceptual frameworks and political perspectives from which we understand these differences. It is the nature of our political commitments and perspectives that can provide the basis for effective coalition building.

I believe that coalitions are possible through a politics of identification as opposed to a 'politics of identity'. We develop our first sense of community within a neighbourhood, but we soon learn to see ourselves as part of many other 'imagined communities' – imagined in so far as we may never actually meet those people face to face. But we learn to identify with these groups, their experiences, their struggles. These processes of political identification – these processes of formation of 'communities in struggle' – do not erase the diversity of human experience; rather, they enable us to appreciate the particular within the universal, and the universal within the particular. However, this politics of identification is only meaningful, indeed, only possible, if based on under-standings of the material and ideological basis of all oppressions in their global manifestations; of the interconnectedness as well as the specificity of each oppression. And it is only meaningful if we develop a practice to challenge and combat them all. We can work locally in our own groups, organizations, workplaces, and communities, but we need to make connections with wider national and global struggles and movements.

Notes

M. L. Adams, 'There's no place like home: on the place of identity in feminist politics', *Feminist Review*, no. 31 (1989); P. Parmar, 'Other kinds of dreams', *Feminist Review*, no. 31 (1989).

Further Reading

Barrett, M. and Phillips, A. (eds) (1992), *Destabilizing Theory: Contemporary feminist debates*, Cambridge: Polity.
Hill Collins, P. (1990), *Black Feminist Thought*, London: Unwin Hyman.
Delphy, C. and Leonard, D. (1992), *Familiar Exploitation*, Oxford: Polity.
Duchen, C. (1986), *Feminism in France*, London: Routledge.
Duchen, C. (ed.) (1987), *French Connections: Voices from the women's movement in France*, London: Hutchinson.
Fuss, D. (1989), *Essentially Speaking: Feminism, nature and difference*, London: Routledge.
Gunew, S. (ed.) (1990), *Feminist Knowledge: Critique and construct*, London: Routledge.
Gunew, S. (ed.) (1991), *A Reader in Feminist Knowledge*, London: Routledge.
hooks, b. (1984), *Feminist Theory from Margin to Centre*, Boston, MA: South End Press.
Jagger, A. (1983), *Feminist Politics and Human Nature*, Sussex: Harvester.
Nicholson, L. (ed.) (1990), *Feminism/Postmodernism*, London: Routledge.
Ramazanoglu, C. (1989), *Feminism and the Contradictions of Oppression*, London: Routledge.
Stacey, J. (1993), 'Untangling feminist theory', in D. Richardson and V. Robinson (eds), *Introducing Women's Studies*, London: Macmillan.

Sydie, R. A. (1987), *Natural Women, Cultured Men: A feminist perspective on sociological theory*, Milton Keynes: Open University Press.

Tong, R. (1989), *Feminist Thought*, London: Routledge.

Walby, S. (1986), *Patriarchy at Work*, Cambridge: Polity; (especially Chapters 1–4).

Weedon, C. (1987), *Feminist Practice and Poststructuralist Theory*, Oxford: Basil Blackwell.

2 WOMEN'S MINDS
Psychological and Psychoanalytic Theory

Edited and Introduced by Jane Prince

INTRODUCTION

In this Section we are concerned with the ways in which the female mind has been explained theoretically, with a particular focus on psychoanalytic theory and the debates between essentialist, biological determinist and structuralist positions.

While the contribution of psychoanalytic theory to the theorising and understanding of women's minds has been, if always controversial, also often central to debates within women's studies, the position of psychology has been more ambivalent. Within mainstream psychology, gender has been viewed as an independent variable rather than a dependent one; in fact, much research in psychology has ignored gender differences completely, and where they have been researched it has usually been in the context of the feminine being counter-posed against the 'neutral' or 'normal' masculine. The very grouping of psychoanalytic and psychological theory is problematic, since mainstream psychology has, particularly within its scientific discourse, preferred to distance itself from the mentalism of psychoanalysis. Frosh, in a seminal work on the relationship between psychology and psychoanalysis,[1] noted that whilst for psychology the aim of research was to study the subject as object, to offer an account of mental processes which avoided any attempt to encounter the subjectivity or internal dynamics of the person or explain her social positioning, for psychoanalysis this subjectivity is precisely what *is* to be disclosed and explained (see also Readings 2.2 and 2.7, by Hollway and Mitchell).

This has had two consequences. Firstly, until fairly recently, explorations into the implications of psychoanalytic – particularly Freudian – theory have not been located within psychology; secondly, until the last decade gender has been the focus of very little research within psychology. This is not to say that the experiences of women have been totally ignored; rather that the *production* of the category 'women' and the consequences of the category have been ignored. The focus of research has been on descriptions of the female experience and attempts to establish a cause for these experiences within one of psychology's grand narratives – usually worked around theories of individual difference or social learning. The assertion of methodological positions which run counter to the scientific objectivity of orthodox psychology has opened up debates on gender and the position of women; of particular importance has been Wendy Hollway's work in developing an alternative epistemological base for the study of subjectivity and, in particular, gender.

In what way, then, has psychological theory explained 'woman'? During the 1970s it was proposed[2] that stereotyped gender behaviour was a psychological reality for individuals; Sandra Bem developed an inventory (the Bem Sex Role Inventory [BSRI]) which aimed to identify several gender identity options (masculinity, femininity, androgyny), each of which was available to all individuals regardless of biological sex. She concluded that a person who scored high on femininity on the inventory was also *psychologically* feminine – that is, she/he would behave in typically feminine ways. (She also noted that androgyny produced the psychologically healthiest individual.) The feminine/masculine traits in Bem's scale used the relationship/autonomy distinction common to the social psychology of gender; this is viewed as the enduring property of an individual rather than a consequence of a particular intersection of social identities. It is this second aspect of Bem's work which has been rejected by feminist psychology. Nevertheless, to the extent that the BSRI reflected self-categorization and hence, by implication, an understanding and recognition of societal beliefs on gender roles, Bem's work was a development on contemporary explanations of gendered identity and a major recognition of the difference between sex and the gender produced by the interaction between sex and social relations.

In the 1980s, poststructuralist theorists entered the debates within psychology on the nature of the process underlying the production of a gendered subjectivity. At the same time, psychologists in the United Kingdom successfully fought for the recognition of Psychology of Women as a legitimate area of academic concern.[3] Challenges to the methodological basis for earlier research into gender and an insistence that any analysis of gender had to include an analysis of social and political relationships produced writings which were based on the lived experiences of women of all ages, rather than on the experiences and values of the psychologist doing the research. These writings challenged assumptions about the source of 'femininity', locating it in ideological factors rather than in individuals. Behaviour associated with reproductive functions, school performance, career choice, mental health, and sexuality were clearly located in the sociopolitical sphere.[4]

The relevance of psychoanalytic theory to the study of gender is that it allows for theorising the conditions under which a gender-differentiated subjectivity can arise. Within Freudian theory femininity develops through an awareness of lack when little girls compare themselves with little boys; this produces in the female mind a desire to be male; associated with penis envy are the typical 'female' characteristics of weak superego,[5] passivity and masochism. The girl develops a negative attitude towards women, and the ties of affection with the mother as object of desire are loosened. At the same time, for the boy child the recognition of lack in the female becomes, in association with his own libidinal[6] development, a fear of also 'losing' his phallus,[7] as he believes the girl has done. Here we can see why Freud is both attractive to and loathed by different groups of feminists: his writing explains femininity/masculinity as biological and inevitable (and has attracted charges of phallocentrism), while at the same time it offers a social explanation for male derogation of females in terms of anxieties around castration.

Lacan and his followers, who claim to perpetuate and extend the work of Freud, also locate masculinity and femininity in the castration complex; for Lacan, however, this is understood as being consequent on the child entering the world of reality through the acquisition of language and the rules of the symbolic.[8] Entry into the symbolic world produces both prohibition and recognition of the loss associated with prohibition. The signifier of this state is the phallus; the Oedipus and castration complexes involve the recognition of the impossibility of fulfilling the desire. As language is organised around the phallus, the norm being male and the female being signified or defined by 'lack of maleness' (the absence of the female in language is explained clearly by Dale Spender in *Man Made Language*), the subject is split by language and sexuality. Femininity is produced outside the symbolic system – since language is phallocentric and patriarchal, there is no place within its discourses for the feminine. Lacan, too, has been criticised for asserting the power of the biological and, by ascribing to the feminine the qualities of 'absence', for reinforcing negative and stereotypical concepts of femininity.

The third important psychoanalytic approach to evolve is object-relations theory (see Chodorow, Reading 2.5). The drive of human beings is to form relationships, and it is through relationships with objects, and through separations, that the child's identity is produced. This approach locates the critical periods as being prior to the (father-centred) Oedipal stage and on to the earliest stage of the child's life, when it is focused on a relationship with the mother. It has been criticised in that by emphasising the importance of the mother–infant relationship, it reproduces traditional patriarchal discourses of femininity.

In summary, what both psychology and psychoanalytic theory attempt in the context of theorising gender is to locate the origins and continuance of feminine 'performance' – that is, the source of those behaviours and phenomenological experiences which characterise women within society.

Notes

1. S. Frosh, *Psychoanalysis and Psychology: Minding the gap*, London: Macmillan, 1989.
2. S. Bem, 'Measurement of psychological androgyny', *Journal of Consulting and Clinical Psychology*, vol. 42, no. 2 (1974), pp. 155–62.
3. S. Wilkinson, *Feminist Social Psychology*, Milton Keynes: Open University Press, 1986.

4. J. Ussher, *The Psychology of the Female Body*, London: Routledge, 1989; V. Walkerdine, *The Mastery of Reason*, London: Routledge, 1987; C. Griffin, *Typical Girls? Young women from school to the job market*, London: Routledge & Kegan Paul, 1985; C. Kitzinger, *The Social Construction of Lesbianism*, London: Sage, 1987.

5. Superego: the structure in the unconscious built up by early experiences on the basis mainly of relations with parents, which functions as a conscience, causing feelings of guilt and anxiety when the ego gratifies or seeks to gratify desires.

6. Libidinal: orientated at psychosexual desires.

7. Phallus: the male sex organ as a symbol of power.

8. Symbolic: we communicate through signifiers, which refer to a concrete world but are not that world. For example, when I use the word *tree*, that word is referring to something which exists, but is not itself that thing. Language has an arbitrary relationship with the things it symbolises: there is no reason, except social custom and practice, for my choice of the word *tree* rather than the word *dog* to represent that particular concept. Hence language and its meaning is constrained by the social framework within which it is located, but it also reproduces that framework; herein lies its usefulness as a tool for understanding the female condition and subjectivity. A child entering the social world, and its laws and customs, does so through the use of the symbol of language.

2.1   **Autonomy and Identity in Feminist Thinking**
Jean Grimshaw

Jean Grimshaw proposes that to understand 'women's minds' it is necessary to understand that the mind is contained within multiple contradictions for which simple causal explanations are inadequate.

Now any adequate account of self needs to be able, I think, to encompass and try to make intelligible the ways in which women and men experience themselves. And the central reasons for rejecting the 'humanist' paradigm of the self are, firstly, that there may be aspects of the development of self which are not easily accessible to consciousness, and secondly, that there are conscious experiences which are not easy to make intelligible within the humanist paradigm. I want now to look at some aspects of self-experience that I think should be central to any theory of self, and hence to any discussion of women's autonomy. [...]

Fantasy

The dream (on which we may try hard to impose a narrative structure, to make sense of it) is unlike much fantasy in that it often doesn't, of itself, contain any such structure, and the 'story', if it tells one, may be deeply unintelligible to us. Much conscious fantasy is different; we may 'tell a story' to ourselves (or listen to a story and fantasise it as about ourselves); and sometimes we may attempt an imagined resolution, through fantasy, of some aspect of our social situation. One might, thus, fantasise the death of someone seen as a threat, or imagine oneself as possessing enormous fame or wealth. But fantasies, not always in the form of a coherent narrative, may irrupt or intervene; one can be plagued, dominated or obsessed by them. Freud wrote of the way in which fantasies or desires, often seen as evil or dangerous, could come to dominate a person's life. Fantasy may be a threat; it may be inexplicable, bizarre and intrusive. Discovering the fantasies of others, too, may be threatening; the discovery, for example, as Rosalind Coward[1] suggests, that the 'mild' man one lives with is a secret addict of sadomasochistic pornography. Female sexual fantasies can be disturbing as well. Why do many women find *The Story of O* erotic, and why is there a 'split' between sexual fantasy and that which one might find pleasurable or erotic in real life?

Fantasy may be experienced both as pleasurable and as dangerous. But sometimes it can just be pleasurable. Coward discusses, for instance, the importance of the fact that one of the biggest growth areas in publishing in recent years has been women's romantic fiction. Unlike the 'modern' women's novel in which, usually after a series of disastrous sexual misadventures, the female heroine ends up (more or less) 'her own person', romantic fiction is stylised, formulaic and unrealistic. It offers women, Coward argues, the fantasised pleasure (and apotheosis of sexual desire) of finding security in the strong arms of the hard-bitten patriarchal hero, along with the pleasure of having 'tamed' him and domesticated his wild ways by the power one enjoys over him in being a woman.

We have to understand the pleasure there is for women in such fantasies. We have to understand what seems often to attract women more than men to soap operas, or to a passionate interest in the doings of the Royal Family. We need to understand how and why male fantasies may commonly differ from female ones, and why the sorts of fantasies I have mentioned, which may in some ways seem antithetical to feminism, may still have a strong appeal to women who have a feminist allegiance.

The 'Split' between reason and desire

I will suggest, as a first example of this, a book by Suzanne Lowry, on Princess Diana, called *The Princess in the Mirror*.[2] The appearance of the book is at first glance like that of any other glossy book about the Royals . But it sets out, its author says, to deconstruct the image and appeal of the Princess. At the end of the book, Lowry states that the image of the Princess is conformist and reactionary, that it acts as a powerful form of social control, and that Diana is an unwitting agent of that. Yet the presentation of the book, and Lowry's text, often speak of a fascination with the Princess that is more than simply the fascination one can derive from the exercise of deconstructing an image. And this fascination is often in tension with the attempt to articulate a critique.

Or think about the Fonda phenomenon. The text of Fonda's book *Women Coming of Age*[3] exhorts women not to 'think thin', and its theme is mainly that of health. Yet the illustrations are nearly all of women who are pencil-thin enough not to be out of place on the catwalk in a Paris fashion show. The discourse of 'health' is almost inextricably intertwined, in the case of women, with discourse about youth and beauty and sexual attractiveness. The reasons women have for concern about fitness and health are often multiply overdetermined. Notions, for example, of *Ageless Ageing*[4] *slide* between discussions of how to preserve a youthful skin and a young-looking body and how to stave off the ravages of *appearing* older, with discussions of mental vitality and energy, and so forth. A young-looking body is a *sign* of an alert mind.

There is a type of feminist criticism, both in literature and other media (and in fields such as education), which has been called 'Images of Women' criticism. This has supposed that feminist effort should be devoted, first, to showing how the 'images' in question oppress or denigrate women, and second, to offering positive images of women to replace these. One problem with this kind of criticism is that the 'images' in question have often been misinterpreted, since they have been discussed without reference to the context or narrative structure in which they may appear. But there are two other problems with this type of criticism which I want to focus on here. First, what this approach often fails to recognise is the importance of understanding the *appeal* of the 'images' that are criticised; the relations they may have to women's pleasures, desires, fantasies, fears and conceptions of themselves Second, it fails to recognise what is signally obvious in the experience of many women, myself of course included, namely that it is perfectly possible to agree 'in one's head' that certain images of women might be reactionary or damaging or oppressive, while remaining committed to them in emotion and desire. I suspect that this 'split' happens at times in all women, and perhaps particularly in those who have some commitment to feminism. And what it suggests is that structures of desire, emotion and fantasy have deep roots of some sort in the self which are not necessarily amenable in any simple way to processes of conscious rational argument. An adequate theory of subjectivity has to recognise and try to understand these roots.

Notes

1. R. Coward, *Female Desire: Women's sexuality today*, London: Paladin, 1984.
2. S. Lowry, *The Princess in the Mirror*, London: Chatto & Windus, 1985.
3. J. Fonda, *Women Coming of Age*, Harmondsworth: Penguin, 1984.
4. L. Kenton, *Ageless Ageing*, London: Century Arrow, 1986.

2.2 **Male Mind and Female Nature**
Wendy Hollway

Wendy Hollway is concerned with the way in which epistemological[1] assumptions within scientific discourse[2] reconstruct a stereotypical and negative view of women. Hollway analyses the methodological and theoretical issues surrounding the debates on female subjectivity.[3]

The way that modern science emerged was already gendered and this was a condition of the later concepts of masculinity and femininity. Francis Bacon, writing in the early seventeenth century, is commonly acknowledged as the scientist 'who first and most vividly articulated the equation between scientific knowledge and power, who identified the aims of science as the control and domination of nature'.[1] For Bacon the scientist is male (of course) and nature female, and this metaphor for their relationship pervades his writing.[2] The 'coupling' of the two terms (as Keller calls it) varies from 'a chaste and lawful marriage between Mind and Nature' (p. 36) to servitude ('I am come in very truth leading you to Nature with all her children to bind her to your service and make her your slave', p. 39), to something akin to rape ('the power to conquer and subdue her, to shake her to her foundation', p. 36).

This is all very well, but scientists and rationalists will object that metaphor is sheer whimsy and has nothing to do with 'real' meaning, which is characterized by logic. In contrast, the theory of meaning that I have applied is capable of conceptualizing the suppressed significations of nature on the metaphoric axis and theorizing its effects. Moreover, the scientists' objection cannot explain how, during the seventeenth and eighteenth centuries, the conception of nature changed from an active, powerful partner (as in alchemy) to something passive, determined by mechanical laws. Prior to the seventeenth century, knowledge of nature did not involve the principle of difference from nature which dominates in modern science. Knowledge was rather seen as a joining with nature; getting close enough to understand. An account of a historical transformation, whether it is the seventeenth-century one, or the one that I would like to see take place in contemporary psychology, involves huge movements in practices and structures as well as knowledge, but the reproduction and modification of these pass through people, through their actions, understanding and commitments – and people's subjectivities are simultaneously changed by these forces.

Just as I have emphasized throughout this book, how so much of psychology's knowledge hinges on the mistaken assumption of the possibility of transparent language, Keller points out that scientists hold 'the widely shared assumption that the universe they study is directly accessible, represented by concepts shaped, not by language, but only by the demands of logic and experiment' (p. 130). Scientific knowledge is a privileged form 'dissociated from other modes of knowledge which are affectively tinged and hence tainted' (p. 142). The idea of objectivity relies on this view of meaning. Easlea claims, on the contrary, 'that it is precisely through people's rhetoric, and particularly metaphors, that one can gain partial insight into motives and more importantly, unconscious motivation' (p. 7). Until there is a way of theorizing how subjectivity is implicated in producing science, challenges to the principle of objectivity are on weak ground. I have argued in this book that such a theory must incorporate a theory of meaning if it is not to get trapped in dualism.

   To talk about subjectivity in science is to talk about gender, since no subject is non-gendered. However, gender must mean something that is not determined, not homogeneous, not monolithic. This is the idea of gender that I shall apply in what follows. Keller's conclusions regarding the connections between mind and nature are far-reaching:

Psychoanalytic reductionism

According to psychoanalysis, separation from the mother is achieved within the triangular relation of mother–father–child, and is a product of the Oedipus complex. Boys achieve it more traumatically than girls. Separation is thus inevitably gendered. Keller summarizes the implications for science as follows:

> My argument, then, is that the specific kinds of aggression expressed in scientific discourse reflect not simply the absence of a felt connection to the objects one studies but also the subjective feelings many children (and some adults) experience in attempting to secure a sense of self as separate from the more immediate objects of their emotional world.... The need to dominate nature is, in this view, a projection of the need to dominate other human beings; it arises not so much out of empowerment as out of anxiety about impotence. (p. 124)

While there is much of value in Keller's psychoanalytic argument, I believe that the use of psychoanalytic theory in a reductionist way can lead into several blind alleys. One is that a normative theory of development results, in which ego strength is in most cases gradually achieved through development and other cases are seen as pathological. For normal people there is a developmental reduction of projection and other defences. In this view, normal science could still achieve independence from unconscious forces. Second, and linked to the normative account, the reductionist use of psychoanalytic theory can lend itself to an individual-differences view, whereby some classes of individuals retain particular needs – for example, the defensive need of separation – which affect their later choices. Keller tends towards this view concerning scientists. She develops her analysis through using Shapiro's delineation of types related to the (somewhat discredited) psychosexual stages, obsessive–compulsive, neurotic, etc., and finds parallel between his description (see below) and the practices of scientists. She ends up arguing that individuals elect to be scientists because of the match between science's principles and their own proclivities – for domination, maintenance of separateness, and so on (p. 124). What her account does not do is to show up subjectivity as part of a continuous cyclical reproduction and modification of forces which include structures, practices, knowledge and subjectivity. A third danger of using psychoanalysis without an intermediate theory of meaning is specifically related to its theory of gender: a consequence of gender difference being understood as achieved at the Oedipal stage is that differences between women and men then tend to get seen as fixed, with gender equated to sex (I discuss this further below).

I want to introduce a different emphasis in the idea of defensive separation. I still see it as achieved through the defence mechanisms, in which self must be differentiated from other, in order to maintain a fragile and always fearful separation. However, I do not want to reduce this separation simply to a protection against engulfment – though that may be an early dynamic – because that reduces it to process. In my subsequent analysis I distinguish the psychic objects which a position as subject in scientific discourses and practices enables the scientist to keep at arm's length, to render non-threatening, to control.

The suppressed significance of woman and nature

What is the connection between nature and woman? I do not mean nature as it is rationalistically and reductively apprehended, but nature signifying metaphorically, in which, through condensation, significations of woman are contained, though suppressed. There is a close parallel between the meaning of woman and the meaning of nature which suggests the same threat and the same defences. The signifier 'woman' contains an interesting contradiction, between subordinate and powerful, weak and threatening. Below the image of woman as weak and subordinate in dominant Western discourses is an image, often sexualized as in the image of the seductress, of terrifying power, the power to strip a man of his self-control, to awaken in him huge longing. It seems to me fairly obvious that this meaning of woman is achieved through the connection with the suppressed signifier of the mother. Dominant sexist discourses, in which women are positioned as subordinate, act at a cultural level as defence mechanisms, endlessly reproduced by the anxieties and defence mechanisms of individual men. Similarly with nature. Underneath the image of nature in modern science as passive and entirely knowable is a suppressed signifier of nature as the ultimate force, capable of wreaking havoc over mind and culture. It contains intimations of something which always resists being fully known (like woman) and fully controlled (like woman) – else why the emphasis on pursuit and control?

Two more parts to the analysis are necessary to restate Keller's account so that it is fully social: the first makes the connection between signification and scientific discourse and the second establishes the link with scientific practice. I shall discuss both of these in relation to gender.

I have described the way men's anxiety concerning separation would lead to the reproduction of the subject–object split and thus to 'objectivity' in science, but this does not give a complete account of how the difference is achieved between mind and nature – the difference that echoes gender difference. The subject–object split is premissed on distance and in my view distance depends on difference – difference in the meanings of subject and object. I have used the Kleinian concept of splitting to explain that phenomenon whereby good and bad objects in the psyche are separated. In the case of gender identity, the 'bad' objects (the ones produced by gender-differentiated discourses as inappropriate to one's sex) can be projected on to the other of the 'opposite' sex. This account emphasizes these dynamics as they continue to reproduce difference in adult relations. The analysis can equally apply to the relations of scientist to nature. The psychodynamic argument used by Keller can be restated both in terms of the theory of meaning outlined above and the application of the concept of splitting in relation to differentiated positions in the discourse of science.

Women are in a different position in relation to the separation from the mother, since mother is not just 'other' to a woman, but also signifies in 'self', through the metaphoric connection between woman and mother. Her need to separate (and her fear of engulfment) is neither the same nor symmetrical to men's. For a man the difference between himself and the mother comes to signify (at the time of Oedipus?) as the difference between woman and man. The difference between herself and the mother for a girl or woman cannot so signify. Here my use of Kleinian concepts, with the emphasis away from childhood and upon intersubjective defence mechanisms and differentiated positions in discourse, suggests a different direction to Keller's. For a woman, the other does not easily become the vehicle for projections of unwanted parts of the self (but see below). If for men, the other/mother then contains these projections, no wonder she is threatening, and no wonder his defences lure him into taking up differentiated positions in discourses and practices if they confer superiority or control over the other.

But this position also depletes him, because of the parts that he cannot afford to contain, which are projected on to women. The historical connections between masculinity, rationality and science mean that the position of scientist already is a product of projection of these qualities and so prescribes a position and practices which rehearse a male scientist's defences against anxiety without them even having to be activated. Keller (p. 121) quotes Shapiro to describe what I see as the consequent depletion of the scientist's view:

> [For this type of scientist] attention is subject to the same kind of control as is the rest of behaviour, leading to a kind of focus so intensely sharp and restricted that it precludes peripheral vision, the fleeting impression, the, hunch, the over-all feeling of an object. The consequence is loss of conviction: truth is inferred rather than experienced, the basis for judgement and decisions is sought in rules rather than feeling.

As Lacan argued, the Symbolic (what in this context I am referring to as scientific knowledge) is not the product of certainty, but 'produces certainty out of a terror; control or be controlled; master the loss'.[3]

Differences between and among women and men

Now this account is only any good if it can explain several things, which I shall pose in terms of the woman scientist. It must be able to account for the fact that a woman scientist can observe the rules and procedures that derive from the principle of objectivity; that she may do science the same as a man (though she may do it differently). I should stress here that if we can clarify how it is that a woman may do science the same as a man, we also have an explanation for the differences among men in the way they do science. Any theory that implies that all men are destined to do science in a way which is determined purely by the drive to separate and control is at odds with the diversity in actuality.

Let me start by quoting Keller's conclusions about women scientists:

> The metaphor of a marriage between Mind and Nature necessarily does not look the same to (male scientists) as it does to women [scientists].... In a science constructed around the naming of object (nature) as female and the parallel naming of subject (mind) as male, any scientist who happens to be a woman is confronted with an a priori contradiction in terms. This poses a critical problem of identity: any scientist who is not a man walks on a path bounded on one side by inauthenticity and on the other by subversion. Just as surely as inauthenticity is the cost woman suffers by joining men in a misogynistic joke, so it is equally the cost suffered by a woman who identifies with an image of the scientist modeled on the patriarchal husband. (p. 174)

In this argument, because Keller is not using a concept of meaning which understands the links between metaphor and subjectivity, which handles the multiplicity of meanings and recognizes the relation of those suppressed to those expressed, for her the contradiction is an absolute one – between two opposing unities – creating an identity crisis. The woman scientist can only choose between inauthenticity and subversion. The concept of inauthenticity, however much we recognize it from our own experience, cannot help but appeal to a 'real self' (who is the woman) which leaves scientist as the role.

A further conceptual distinction will enable me to escape Keller's conclusions (while profiting from the insights in her analysis): it is the distinction between the meanings (and practices) suggested by a particular position in discourse and the person, whose making of meaning embraces a whole sedimented history of positions in multiple discourses, positions which are often contradictory. Keller's conclusions about women scientists founder in the conflation of these two ideas or, more precisely, in the use of terminology – such as ideology and individuals – which hampers the distinction being made.

Keller is assuming that the woman scientist's self is mirrored in the object of science. My understanding of metaphor makes distinctions between the signifier and signified as different aspects of signification. 'Woman' is signified in the concept of nature continued in the discourse of science, but it is not identical with the signifier 'nature'. More importantly, 'woman' signified in the discourse cannot be equated with any actual woman. The subjectivity of any specific woman is a product of positions in a potentially infinite number of discourses and related practices, many of which confer meanings very different to 'woman' as it is signified in scientific discourse. These meanings all have historical links through metaphoric chains which interconnect; 'signifier replaces signifier, creating complex chains in the move from one discourse to another'. In summary, although these meanings are connected, they do not make up a coherent unitary whole.

Notes to Introduction

1. Epistemological: to do with conceptualisation of knowledge.
2. Scientific discourse: the epistemological approach which understands only certain forms of exploration of knowledge – specifically those based on controlled observation and objective analysis – to be legitimate.
3. Female subjectivity: the positioning of women within the numerous discourses each of which produces gender-appropriate behaviours.

Notes

1. E. Keller, *Reflections on Gender and Science*, New Haven, CT: Yale University Press, 1985, p. 33.
2. B. Easlea, *Science and Sexual Oppression*, London: Weidenfeld & Nicolson, 1981.
3. V. Walkerdine, *The Mastery of Reason: Cognitive development and the production of rationality*, London: Routledge, 1988, p. 200.
4. *Ibid.*, p. 191.

2.3   Significant Differences: feminism in psychology
Corinne Squire

Corinne Squire's writing covers a number of issues relating to the 'problem' of feminism within psychology. In this Reading she examines the role played by essentialist debates in psychological theories of gender, and discusses the problem of women researching women wholly within essentialist paradigms.

The shared concept of the subject also leads woman-centred psychology to repeat, in a clearer form, many of the problems of egalitarian feminist psychology. Although woman-centred psychology revalues traditional psychological discourses of femininity positively, it fails more conspicuously than egalitarian feminist psychology to challenge their contents. Its concern with celebrating femininity encourages it to pass over more of traditional psychology's gender biases than egalitarian feminist psychology does. And because it assumes that gender differences are biologically or culturally fixed, it is especially likely to neglect psychological or social differences between women, to take female subjectivity as defining feminism, and to treat psychology as a form of social action in itself. Eichenbaum and Orbach, for instance,[1] suggest that feminism can start on the inside, with women's individual or group psychological consciousness, and proceed outwards to political campaigning. This chapter will explore how woman-centred psychology reformulates yet repeats different elements of traditional and egalitarian feminist psychologies, beginning from the agent of psychology, the psychologist.

Egalitarian feminist psychologists sometimes argue against the assimilation of feminists into existing psychological professions, and for their separate organization. Walsh emphasizes how this has advanced women's position in US psychology, and suggests that it still provides a needed 'anchor of outrageousness'.[2] But such an argument is reactive rather than affirmative. It implies that if circumstances were less oppressive, women could work with men. Woman-centred psychologists are more convinced of the value of separate working. They claim that female psychologists have something special to contribute by virtue of their sex, and they often see work done by women as feminist simply because women do it. They turn Miller's[3] plea for psychologists to give psychology away into an attempt to give psychology away to all women. They co-opt areas of psychology which rely on female subjects, like early psychoanalysis, for feminism, arguing that these women are the real scientists in these fields, the real psychologists. Alternatively, they view women psychologists as contributing to feminist psychology only when they work in a culturally woman-identified way. In the academic sphere, this might involve working in women's colleges, or, more generally, using female-identified subject matter, method, and theory. An increase in women's numerical representation is therefore given a biological or cultural, rather than an egalitarian, justification. Some woman-centred psychologists think, too, that only a woman should study female subjects, and that she should do so as much as possible, because only she can understand them. Shainess[4] criticizes work on women's psychology done by men for serving male interests, and wants women to do more in this field.

Some aspects of the woman-centred interpretation of female psychologists' place are justified. The single-sex environment of mid-nineteenth-century US women's colleges seems to have provided a uniquely supportive environment for the first women psychologists, for example.[5] But woman-centred psychology's commitment to bringing women into the ranks of psychologists as emblems of femininity has a number of drawbacks. From the perspective of traditional psychology, such psychologists are, even more than egalitarian feminist psychologists, reassuringly marginal. At best, they may be granted a specific validity, as experts in feminine psychology. Many woman-centred psychologists evade this difficulty, because they choose to work outside psychology, in women's studies, or outside academia, in practically orientated women's organizations. But wherever she works, a woman-centred psychologist's sex does not guarantee her feminism, any more than it does for an egalitarian feminist psychologist. As Shainess accepts, female psychologists may collude with male-orientated psychology against their own interests. The possibility that male psychologists might collude, against *their* interests, with a female-orientated psychology, is recognized less. Most woman-centred psychologists doubt men's ability to produce a woman-centred discipline. But a women-identified psychologist, male or female, is in any case still a psychologist, and shows traces of the male-identified authority this position carries.

Woman-centred feminists recognize that feminism's concept of the gendered subject as both a social construct, and an absolute essence, is ambiguous. But their definition of the female subject as a biological or cultural essence leads them to pursue this ambiguity much less than egalitarian feminists. Their essentialism has been the main focus of criticism from other feminists. In psychology, it is intensified by the discipline's own essentialism about the individual subject. It causes woman-centred psychology to be much more restricted to the concept of a purely psychological subject than egalitarian feminist and even some traditional psychologies are. This apolitical essentialism allows many woman-identified psychologists to work in mainstream professional and academic institutions. It lets them operate as egalitarian feminist psychologists at times, too. A psychological conference on women at work can appeal to 'women-centred decision makers and administrators', and at the same time can present an egalitarian feminist agenda, including 'feminist management theory/feminist occupational psychology', 'mobility for career couples', and 'intimacy needs of career women'.[6]

Counting women in among feminist psychologists on the grounds of their biological or cultural femininity also neglects differences between them. This omission has strong precedents in woman-centred feminism generally, as well as in psychology. Morgan's[7] *Sisterhood is Powerful*, for example, recognizes the need to transform feminism so that it addresses the interests of women outside its predominantly white, middle-class constituency, and includes contributions from women outside it. But it remains prone to generalizations: 'we share a common root as *women* ... capitalism, imperialism and racism are *symptoms* of male supremacy − sexism' (pp. xxix, xxxix).

Where woman-centred feminists address class specifically, they often equate femaleness with an oppressed biological 'sex class', set up working-class women as the embodiment of this class, and finger middle-class women as sell-outs to the male sex class. Where woman-centred feminism recognizes 'race' differences, it frequently tries to describe 'race'-specific female essences, and in the process layers on clichés about, for instance, black women's victim or matriarch status, in a way which mythologizes the women and denies difference and change. The only area of difference between women which woman-centred feminists consistently address is that of sexuality. Woman-centred feminism asserts the historical and contemporary ubiquity of lesbians. Often, too, it describes lesbianism as the epitome of the woman-centred approach, as if, by carrying identification with women into the most intimate areas of experience, lesbians crystallize feminist resistance: 'A lesbian is the rage of all women condensed to the point of explosion'.[8] This interest in lesbianism preserves the emphasis dominant discourses of femininity place on women's sexuality. It challenges these discourses, too, by valuing women's active sexuality positively, and by defining lesbianism very broadly, as a matter of political or cultural identity, rather than simply of sexual relations.[9] But this definition ignores the possibility that lesbianism might have different meanings; for some, it might be a matter of object choice but not of political or personal identity. The definition also collapses very different female-identified resistances together. As black, and white working-class lesbians, have pointed out, it tends to reduce lesbianism to the dominant white, middle-class politics and culture of lesbianism.

Notes

1. L. Eichenbaum and S. Orbach, *Outside in, Inside out*, Harmondsworth: Penguin, 1982.
2. M. Walsh, 'Academic women organizing for change: the struggle in psychology', *Journal of Social Issues*, vol. 41, no. 4 (1985), pp. 17–28.
3. G. Miller, 'Psychology as a means of promoting human welfare', *American Psychologist*, 24, (1969), pp. 1063–75.
4. N. Shainess, 'A psychologist's view: images of women – past and present, overt and obscured', in R. Morgan (ed.), *Sisterhood is Powerful*, New York: Vintage, 1970.
5. L. Furumoto and E. Scarsborough, 'Placing women in the history of psychology', *American Psychologist*, 42, (1986), pp. 35–42.
6. National Women at Work Conference, 'Announcement', *Bulletin of the British Psychological Society*, 40, (1987), p. 398.
7. R. Morgan, *Sisterhood is Powerful*, New York: Vintage, 1970.
8. Radicalesbians, 'Women-identified women', in P. Brown (ed.), *Radical Psychology*, New York: Harper & Row, 1973, p. 471.
9. A. Rich, 'Compulsory heterosexuality and lesbian existence', *Signs*, vol. 5, no. 4 (1980), pp. 631–60.

2.4   Femininity as Performance

Valerie Walkerdine

Valerie Walkerdine comments on the cultural construction of femininity within the formal education system, and notes the ways through which girls are produced as gendered subjects.

Performance in school

There is a widespread myth that girls and women perform poorly in school. In the Girls and Mathematics Unit we investigated this issue in relation to mathematics in research, spanning several years and with children aged four to fifteen.[1] The first way in which I want to deal with the issue of performance is to challenge the idea that femininity equals poor performance and to concentrate rather on the ways in which femininity is read. What I am concerned to demonstrate is the discursive production of femininity as antithetical to masculine rationality to such an extent that femininity is *equated* with poor performance, even when the girl or woman in question is performing well. In other words, I am talking not about some essential qualities of femininity, but about the way in which femininity is read as a constellation of signs which mark it off as antithetical to 'proper' performance to an incredible degree. When we first became aware of this, Rosie Walden and I called it 'the just or only phenomenon'.[2] By this, we meant that whenever a positive remark was made about girls' performance in mathematics, particularly the strong sense that girls performed well in school up until the transfer at eleven, a remark would be brought in which suggested that the performance was to be accounted for by 'something which amounted to nothing'. In other words, no matter how well girls were said to perform, their performance was always downgraded or dismissed in one way or another. These pejorative remarks usually related to the idea that girls' performance was based on hard work and rule-following rather than brains or brilliance (in other words, what was supposed to underlie real mathematical performance). This reading of girls' performance was consistent across schools and the age-range. In the younger age-groups it was common for teachers to talk about boys as having 'potential', a term often used to explain their poor performance. Throughout the sample of thirty-nine classrooms, not one teacher mentioned 'potential' within a girl. Quite the contrary, if a girl were performing poorly there was no way she could be considered good – indeed, if she were performing well it was almost impossible for her to escape pejorative evaluations, while boys, it seemed, no matter how poorly they performed, were thought to have hidden qualities:

> Very, very hard worker. Not a particularly bright girl ... her hard work gets her to her standards.

This typical example of a comment about a girl can be compared with the following comment about a boy, of the kind that was never made about girls:

> ... can just about write his own name ... not because he's not clever, because he's not capable, but because he can't sit still, he's got no concentration ... very disruptive ... but quite bright.

Indeed, it was as though boys did indeed in fantasy possess the 'phallus' while girls represented a fictional 'lack' or absence. For whatever was said, again and again, the presence of certain attributes, like good performance, was read as an indication of a lack of something much more fundamental even when, as in the case of many boys, they did not perform well academically (see the quote above).

This led me to point out that in engaging with issues concerning the 'truth about women' it is necessary to avoid being caught in an empiricist trap in which we are led to attempt to prove the mathematical equivalence of girls. For here we are not presented with something as straightforward as 'the evidence of our own eyes'. Here, girls are doing well yet they are said, in one way or another, 'not to have what it takes', while many boys, whose performance is poor, are said to possess something even when it is not visible in their performance. In order to examine and to understand such a situation I believe that we have to move away from a simple empiricism to a position in which we understand fact, fiction and fantasy as interrelated. It is to post-structuralism that I turn for an account which will allow us to examine how it comes about that gender difference is produced in fictional ways which have power in that they are part of the truth-effects of the regulation of children in classrooms. They form a basis of the 'truth about women', in this case the truth that women do not have rational powers of the mind. Such a truth, I shall go on to argue, has to be desperately reasserted for fear that it is not true; only the paranoia of the powerful keeps it in circulation. [...]

Teacher and mother are defined as 'passive' in relation to the child's 'active'. They are nurturant, facilitating, sensitive and supportive, and they know when to intervene but not to interfere.

This opposition is necessary to support the possibility of the illusion of autonomy and control upon which the child-centred pedagogy is founded. In this sense, then, the 'capacity for nurturance' grounded in a naturalized femininity, the object of the scientific gaze, becomes the basis for woman's fitness for the facilitation of knowing and the reproduction of the knower, which is the support for, yet the opposite of, the production of knowledge. The production of knowledge is thereby separated from its reproduction and split along a sexual division which renders production and reproduction the natural capacities of the respective sexes.

The central concepts in the child-centred pedagogy and early mathematics education may themselves be regarded as signifiers – that is, aspects of discourse. That discourse claims to tell the truth about the universal properties of 'the child' which 'has concepts'. In this view, the attempts within psychology and mathematics, for example, may be seen as aspects of the attempt to construct a rationally ordered and controllable universe. We have argued that such an attempt is deeply bound up with the modern form of bourgeois government and the emergence of the modern state. It is also deeply involved with the attempt to describe and therefore regulate 'woman', 'the child', 'the working class', 'blacks' and 'the mad'.

The purpose of examining the conceptualizations which form the bedrock of modern practices is to draw out the key terms to the regime of truth which is constituted in and by the practices. My claim is that the discursive practices themselves – in producing the terms of the pedagogy, and therefore the parameters of practice – produce what it means to be a subject, to be subjected, within these practices. It can be stated that the terms in the discourse, such as *experience, discovery, stage,* etc., are signifiers which take their meaning from their position and function within the discourse itself: they enter as a relation. But this does not mean that there is a simple relation of representation between the material and the discursive. The discourse itself is a point of production and creation. When we say, then, that *experience* is created as a sign within the practice, or the *child* is produced as a subject, what we are talking about is the production of signs. If language does not represent reality, but rather the regulation of a practice itself produces a particular constellation and organization of the material and discursive practices then it can be argued that something is produced. It is in this sense that Foucault's power/knowledge couple can be applied here.

By means of an apparatus of classification and a grading of responses 'the child' becomes a creation, and yet at the same time provides room for a reading of pathology. There are no behaviours which exist outside the practices for producing them, not at any rate in this particular sequence constellation and with these particular effects. The discursive practice becomes a complex sign system in which signs are produced and read and have truth-effects: the truth of children is produced in class-rooms. 'The child' is not coterminous with actual children, just as Cowie[3] argued that the signifier 'woman' is not coterminous with actual women, but central to the argument is the specification of that relation that is between the signifier and signified. If children become subjects through their insertion into a complex network of practices, there are no children who stand outside their orbit. I use the concept of *positioning* to examine further what happens when such readings are produced and how children become *normal* and *pathological*, fast and slow, rote-learning and real understanding, and so forth. In other words, the practices provide systems of signs which are at once systems of classification, regulation and normalization. These produce systematic differences which are then used as classifications of children in the class. It is the meaning of *difference* which is a central feature in the production of any sign system in terms of the relations with other signs within the discourse. Similarity, that is, those signs which are linked within the discourse, also pile or heap together to provide evidence of a related classification. Thus *activity, doing, experience, readiness* and so forth operate in relations of similarity, while *rote-learning* and *real understanding* are signs of contrastive opposition, of difference. I will attempt to demonstrate that these signs are produced and that often one sign may be taken as an indicator of the presence of another (similarity). Thus, for example, *activity* heralds a signal system, a complex discursive practice, whose terms and limits may be specified.

Within this, then, children become embodiments of 'the child', precisely because that is how the practice is set up: they are normal or pathological, and so forth. Their behaviour, therefore, is an aspect of a position, a multifaceted subjectivity, such that 'the child' describes only their insertion into this, as one of many practices. But the behaviours do not precede the practice precisely because their specificity is produced in these practices. This is why discourses of developmental psychology themselves can be understood not simply as providing a distortion of a real object, but may be read as evidence of *real understanding*, while *passivity* may be read as coterminous with, or similar to, *rote-learning*, *rule-following*.

These produce the practices in which 'the child' becomes a sign to be read and a normal is differentiated from a pathological child. 'The child' develops through active manipulation of 'objects' in an 'environment'. Here all the practices become objects existing in a biologized environment. The Plowden Report is full of illustrations, all of which describe the school, the classroom, as an 'environment'. This sets up another aspect of the readings which are to be made. 'The child' is a unique individual, developing at 'his' own pace in an environment. The classroom therefore becomes the site of such development. However many children there are in a classroom, each is an individual – there is no sense of 'a class'. Indeed, it will be remembered that 'the class' forms a signifier in contrastive opposition to 'the child'. In this way, examining both the texts and practices themselves, it is possible to produce a reading of the pedagogy pre-existing object, 'the real child' which they fail to represent or describe adequately. If they are points of production, they have positive and not simply negative effects. In this sense they are our 'raw material'; the 'real' of a child is not something which can be known outside those practices in which its subjectivity is constituted. The signified forms a sign only out of fusion with the signifier. The signifier exists as a relation within a discourse. The material can be known as a relation only within a discursive practice. To say, therefore, that 'the child' is a signifier means that it must be united with a signified. Particular children therefore both become children – but also present behaviours to be read – which may be normal or pathological.

The question remains, of course, what precisely is it that produces these current truths? I have argued that current claims themselves rest upon a constant 'will to truth' which, investing certainty in 'man', constantly seeks to find its Other and opposite in 'woman'. This truth is constantly reproven within classrooms in which the very apparatuses differentiate between success and its posited causes. This has profound material effects upon the life chances of girls.

Notes

1. V. Walkerdine and The Girls and Mathematics Unit, *Counting Girls Out*, London: Virago, 1989.

2. R. Walden and V. Walkerdine, *Girls and Mathematics: The early years*, London: Heinemann, 1982.
3. E. Cowie, 'Woman as sign', *m/f*, no. 1, (1978).

2.5   **Family Structure and Feminine Personality**
Nancy Chodorow

Nancy Chodorow argues that women's mothering role results in women acquiring a relational identity,[1] *while men acquire a positional identity.*[2]

A boy's masculine gender identification must come to replace his early primary identification with his mother. This masculine identification is usually based on identification with a boy's father or other salient adult males. However, a boy's father is relatively more remote than his mother. He rarely plays a major caretaking role even at this period in his son's life. In most societies, his work and social life take place farther from the home than do those of his wife. He is, then, often relatively inaccessible to his son, and performs his male role activities away from where the son spends most of his life. As a result, a boy's male gender identification often becomes a 'positional' identification, with aspects of his father's clearly or not-so-clearly defined male role, rather than a more generalized 'personal' identification – a diffuse identification with his father's personality, values, and behavioural traits – that could grow out of a real relationship to his father. [...]

A boy, in his attempt to gain an elusive masculine identification, often comes to define this masculinity largely in negative terms, as that which is not feminine or involved with women. There is an internal and external aspect to this. Internally, the boy tries to reject his mother and deny his attachment to her and the strong dependence upon her that he still feels. He also tries to deny the deep personal identification with her that has developed during his early years. He does this by repressing whatever he takes to be feminine inside himself, and, importantly, by denigrating and devaluing whatever he considers to be feminine in the outside world. As a societal member, he also appropriates to himself and defines as superior particular social activities and cultural (moral, religious, and creative) spheres – possibly, in fact, 'society' and 'culture' themselves.

Freud's description of the boy's Oedipal crisis speaks to the issues of rejection of the feminine and identification with the father. As his early attachment to his mother takes on phallic-sexual overtones, and his father enters the picture as an obvious rival (who, in the son's fantasy, has apparent power to kill or castrate his son), the boy must radically deny and repress his attachment to his mother. [...]

The development of a girl's gender identity contrasts with that of a boy. Most important, femininity and female role activities are immediately apprehensible in the world of her daily life. Her final role identification is with her mother and women, that is, with the person or people with whom she also has her earliest relationship of infantile dependence. The development of her gender identity does not involve a rejection of this early identification, however. Rather, her later identification with her mother is embedded in and influenced by their ongoing relationship of both primary identification and pre-Oedipal attachment. Because her mother is around, and she has had a genuine relationship to her as a person, a girl's gender and gender role identification are mediated by and depend upon real affective relations. Identification with her mother is not positional – the narrow learning of particular role behaviors – but rather a personal identification with her mother's general traits of character and values. Feminine identification is based not on fantasied or externally defined characteristics and negative identification, but on the gradual learning of a way of being familiar in everyday life, and exemplified by the person (or kind of people – women) with whom she has been most involved. It is continuous with her early childhood identifications and attachments.

The major discontinuity in the development of a girl's sense of gender identity, and one that has led Freud and other early psychoanalysts to see female development as exceedingly difficult and tortuous, is that at some point she must transfer her primary sexual object choice from her mother and females to her father and males, if she is to attain her expected heterosexual adulthood. Briefly, Freud considers that all children feel that mothers give some cause for complaint and unhappiness: they give too little milk; they have a second child; they arouse and then forbid their child's sexual gratification in the process of caring for her/him. A girl receives a final blow, however: her discovery that she lacks a penis. She blames this lack on her mother, rejects her mother, and turns to her father in reaction. [...]

In contrast to males, the female Oedipal crisis is not resolved in the same absolute way. A girl cannot and does not completely reject her mother in favour of men, but continues her relationship of dependence upon and attachment to her. [...]

We might suggest that a girl's internalized and external object relations become and remain more complex, and at the same time more defining of her, than those of a boy. Psychoanalytic preoccupation with constitutionally based libidinal development, and with a normative male model of development, has obscured this fact. Most women are genitally heterosexual. At the same time, their lives always involve other sorts of equally deep and primary relationships, especially with their children, and, importantly, with other women. In these spheres also, even more than in the area of heterosexual relations, a girl imposes the sort of object relations she has internalized in her pre-Oedipal and later relationship to her mother.

Conclusion

Women's universal mothering role has effects both on the development of masculine and feminine personality and on the relative status of the sexes. I have described the development of relational personality in women and of personalities preoccupied with the denial of relation in men. Men, while guaranteeing to themselves sociocultural superiority over women, always remain psychologically defensive and insecure. Women, by contrast, although always of secondary social and cultural status, may in favourable circumstances gain psychological security and a firm sense of worth and importance in spite of this.

Notes to introduction

1. Relational identity: identity defined by relationships with others.
2. Positional identity: identity defined by position (of power) within social structures.

2.6   Sexual Politics
Kate Millett

Kate Millett has articulated the most coherent argument for viewing psychoanalytic theory as anti-feminist and anti-woman. In these three short extracts from Chapter 4 of Sexual Politics *we gain an insight into her claim that Freud can be read only as a proponent of biological determinism in explaining mental phenomena. She explains the ideological imperatives behind the acceptance by (patriarchal) society of biological psychoanalytic accounts of female behaviour, she proposes a reading of Freud which demonstrates an unreasoned, anti-female bias, and summarises Freud's potential for enlightened research, which he spurns in favour of 'the inevitable law of biology'.*

If new ideological support were to come to the patriarchal social order, its sex roles and its differentiated temperaments of masculine and feminine, it could not come from religion, although the decades in question did see a religious revival, particularly in the prestigious and influential quarters of literature and the university. T. S. Eliot's piety and the sanctity of the fashionable neo-orthodoxy at Oxford and in the New Criticism could scarcely serve as a lifeboat for an entire society any more than could the wholesale defection of literary and critical minds from rationality into the caverns of myth. The new formulation of old attitudes had to come from science and particularly from the emerging social sciences of psychology, sociology, and anthropology – the most useful and authoritative branches of social control and manipulation. To be unassailable, there should be some connection, however dubious, with the more readily validated sciences of biology, mathematics, and medicine. To fill the needs of conservative societies and a population too reluctant or too perplexed to carry out revolutionary changes in social life, even to the drastic modification of basic units such as the family, a number of new prophets arrived upon the scene to clothe the old doctrine of the separate spheres in the fashionable language of science.

The most influential of these was Sigmund Freud, beyond question the strongest individual counterrevolutionary force in the ideology of sexual politics during the period. Although popular in England and on the continent in Lawrence's time, the prestige of Freud's sexual theories did not arrive at, still less maintain, such complete ascendancy there as they achieved in the United States. In America, the influence of Freud is almost incalculable, and America, in many ways the first center of the sexual revolution, appears to have need of him. Although generally accepted as a prototype of the liberal urge toward sexual freedom, and a signal contributor toward softening traditional puritanical inhibitions upon sexuality, the effect of Freud's work, that of his followers, and still more that of his popularizers, was to rationalize the invidious relationship between the sexes, to ratify traditional roles, and to validate temperamental differences.

By an irony nearly tragic, the discoveries of a great pioneer, whose theories of the unconscious and of infant sexuality were major contributions to human understanding, were in time invoked to sponsor a point of view essentially conservative. And as regards the sexual revolution's goal of liberating female humanity from its traditional subordination, the Freudian position came to be pressed into the service of a strongly counterrevolutionary attitude. Although the most unfortunate effects of vulgar Freudianism far exceeded the intentions of Freud himself, its anti-feminism was not without foundation in Freud's own work.

In a moment of humble confusion Freud once confessed to his students: 'If you want to know more about femininity, you must interrogate your own experience, or turn to the poets, or else wait until science can give you more coherent information.' On another occasion he admitted to Marie Bonaparte: 'the great question that has never been answered and which I have not been able to answer, despite my thirty years of research into the feminine soul, is "What does a woman want?"' In the face of such basic uncertainty it is most unfortunate that Freud insisted on proceeding so far in constructing a psychology of women. [...]

In reconsidering Freud's theories on women we must ask ourselves not only what conclusions he drew from the evidence at hand but also upon what assumptions he drew them. Freud did not accept his patients' symptoms as evidence of a justified dissatisfaction with the limiting circumstances imposed on them by society, but as symptomatic of an independent and universal feminine tendency. He named this tendency 'penis envy', traced its origin to childhood experience and based his theory of the psychology of women upon it, aligning what he took to be the three corollaries of feminine psychology, passivity, masochism, and narcissism, so that each was dependent upon, or related to, penis envy.

As the Freudian understanding of female personality is based upon the idea of penis envy, it requires an elaborate, and often repetitious, exposition. Beginning with the theory of penis envy, the definition of the female is negative

– what she is is the result of the fact that she is not a male and 'lacks' a penis. Freud assumed that the female's discovery of her sex is, in and of itself, a catastrophe of such vast proportions that it haunts a woman all through life and accounts for most aspects of her temperament. His entire psychology of women, from which all modern psychology and psychoanalysis derives heavily, is built upon an original tragic experience – born female. Purportedly, Freud is here only relaying the information supplied by women themselves, the patients who furnished his clinical data, the basis of his later generalities about all women. It was in this way, Freud believed, he had been permitted to see how women accepted the idea that to be born female is to be born 'castrated':

> As we learn from psycho-analytic work, women regard themselves as wronged from infancy, as undeservedly cut short and set back; and the embitterment of so many daughters against their mothers derives, in the last analysis, from the reproach against her of having brought them into the world as women instead of as men.

Assuming that this were true, the crucial question, manifestly, is to ask why this might be so. Either maleness is indeed an *inherently* superior phenomenon, and in which case its 'betterness' could be empirically proved and demonstrated, or the female misapprehends and reasons erroneously that she is inferior. And again, one must ask why. What forces in her experience, her society and socialization have led her to see herself as an inferior being? The answer would seem to lie in the conditions of patriarchal society and the inferior position of women within this society. But Freud did not choose to pursue such a line of reasoning, preferring instead an etiology of childhood experience based upon the biological fact of anatomical differences.

While it is supremely unfortunate that Freud should prefer to bypass the more likely social hypothesis to concentrate upon the distortions of infantile subjectivity, his analysis might yet have made considerable sense were he sufficiently objective to acknowledge that woman is born female in a masculine-dominated culture which is bent upon extending its values even to anatomy and is therefore capable of investing biological phenomena with symbolic force. In much the same manner we perceive that the traumatizing circumstance of being born black in a white racist society invests skin colour with symbolic value while telling us nothing about racial traits as such.

In dismissing the wider cultural context of feminine dissatisfaction and isolating it in early childhood experience, Freud again ignored the social context of childhood by locating a literal feminine 'castration' complex in the child's discovery of the anatomical differentiation between the sexes. Freud believed he had found the key to feminine experience – in that moment when girls discover they are 'castrated' – a 'momentous discovery which little girls are destined to make':

> They notice the penis of a brother or playmate, strikingly visible and of large

proportions, at once recognize it as the superior counterpart of their own small and inconspicuous organ, and from that time forward fall a victim to envy for the penis.

There are several unexplained assumptions here: why is the girl instantly struck by the proposition that bigger is better? Might she just as easily, reasoning from the naïveté of childish narcissism, imagine the penis is an excrescence and take her own body as norm? Boys clearly do, as Freud makes clear, and in doing so respond to sexual enlightenment not with the reflection that their own bodies are peculiar, but, far otherwise, with a 'horror of the mutilated creature or triumphant contempt for her'. Secondly, the superiority of this 'superior counterpart' which the girl is said to 'recognize at once' in the penis, is assumed to relate to the autoerotic satisfactions of childhood; but here again the child's experience provides no support for such an assumption.

Much of Freudian theory rests upon this moment of discovery and one is struck how, in the case of the female, to recapitulate the peculiar drama of penis envy is to rehearse again the fable of the Fall, a Fall that is Eve's alone. As children, male and female first inhabit a paradisiacal playground where roles are interchangeable, active and passive, masculine and feminine. Until the awesome lapsarian moment when the female discovers her inferiority, her castration, we are asked to believe that she had assumed her clitoris a penis. One wonders why. [...]

A philosophy which assumes that 'the demand for justice is a modification of envy', and informs the dispossessed that the circumstances of their deprivation are organic, therefore unalterable, is capable of condoning a great deal of injustice. One can predict the advice such a philosophy would have in store for other disadvantaged groups displeased with the status quo, and as the social and political effects of such lines of reasoning are fairly clear, it is not difficult to see why Freud finally became so popular a thinker in conservative societies.

Freud had spurned an excellent opportunity to open the door to hundreds of enlightening studies on the effect of male-supremacist culture on the ego development of the young female, preferring instead to sanctify her oppression in terms of the inevitable law of 'biology'. The theory of penis envy has so effectively obfuscated understanding that all psychology has done since has not yet unraveled this matter of social causation. If, as seems unlikely, penis envy can mean anything at all, it is productive only within the total cultural context of sex. And here it would seem that girls are fully cognizant of male supremacy long before they see their brother's penis. It is so much a part of their culture, so entirely present in the favouritism of school and family, in the image of each sex presented to them by all media, religion, and in every model of the adult world they perceive, that to associate it with a boy's distinguishing genital would, since they have learned a thousand other distinguishing sexual marks by now, be either redundant or irrelevant. Confronted with so much concrete evidence of the male's superior status, sensing on all sides the depreciation in which they are held, girls envy not the penis, but only what the penis gives one social pretensions to. Freud appears to have made a major and rather foolish confusion between biology and culture, anatomy and status. It is still more apparent that his audience found such a confusion serviceable.

2.7   **Psychoanalysis and Feminism**
Juliet Mitchell

This extract counterposes Millett's arguments. Juliet Mitchell suggests that Millett's analysis is flawed by her misunderstanding of the symbolism in Freud; she outlines a reading of Freud which produces theory which is potentially feminist and Marxist.

When, as probably in later life, the woman actually comes to have a baby, the emotions she feels will also have attached to them the repressed unconscious penis-wish; the actual baby will therefore satisfy a very deep-seated, unconscious desire, and if it is a baby boy the reality offer will give even greater satisfaction as it will coincide still more pertinently with the unrecognized wish. I know that for the moment we are leaving aside what is for the anti-Freudian feminists the massive stumbling-block of the original wish for the penis – but I think the main problem arises because the suggestion is taken outside the context of the mechanisms of unconscious mental life – the laws of the primary process (the laws that govern the workings of the unconscious) are replaced by these critics by those of the secondary process (conscious decisions and perceptions), and as a result the whole point is missed.

Most hostile critics of Freud implicitly deny the very notion of an aspect of mental life (expressed in its own 'language') that is different from conscious thought-processes. Other psychologies are about consciousness, psychoanalysis is dealing with the unconscious – this was a point on which Freud had to insist even before the first of the important breakaways that came within the psychoanalytic movement. Thus, in 1907, when they were still very much colleagues, we find Freud rebuking Alfred Adler for not realizing the distinction and for offering an analysis of mental life based only on conscious thought-processes. In the light of Adler's penchant for Marxism and future foundation of a school of sociological psychology, it is an interesting rebuke.

Freud's discovery of the unconscious was, of course, completely bound up with his attempts to understand neurotic disturbances, in the early days most particularly the symptoms of hysteria. When he first began to realize that the bodily symptoms of hysteria (paralysis, contortions, and so on) were physical expressions of mental ideas, he started to listen more carefully to what the patients had to say.

Studying hysteria in the late eighties and nineties, Freud was stunned to hear women patients over and over again recount how, in their childhood, their fathers had seduced them. At first he gave an explanation in which the repressed memory of *actual* childhood incest was rewakened at puberty to produce the neurosis. He then realized that the whole thing was a phantasy. And in essence this is the step that, pertinently here, neither Reich nor his feminist critics will take with him, nor allow him to take. Freud found that the incest and seduction that were being claimed never in fact took place. The fact that, as Freud himself was well aware, *actual* paternal seduction or rape occur not infrequently, has nothing to do with the essential concepts of psychoanalysis. Once Freud had acknowledged that he must abandon what he called the 'trauma theory' of actual incest, the notion of phantasy was bound to come in. Whatever the facts and figures of the situation, the desire was far more prevalent than the act. From the notion of unconscious phantasy, Freud's theories moved in one direction to the formulation of unconscious desire and, in another direction, to an understanding of infantile sexuality. Psychoanalysis deals with aspects of the drive: the repression of its psychic representation and its expression in demands, wishes, desires and phantasies – with the interaction of the unconscious, the preconscious and the conscious. Desire, phantasy, the unconscious or even unconsciousness are absent from the social realism of, amongst others, Reichian and feminist critiques. These criticisms are, therefore, in this respect not so much anti-Freudian as pre-Freudian.

In the symptoms of hysteria (and with variations, those of the other two neuroses – obsessionality and anxiety) what is being expressed in another language is the repressed sexual idea which some crisis has re-evoked; a symptom is an alternative representation of a forbidden wish which has broken through from the unconscious, whence it was banished, into consciousness – but in an 'unrecognizable' form. Condensed into the symptom are all the energies of the sexual drive and those that were used originally to repress it; it is both the thoughts attached to the drive and its denial. It can be seen why Freud said that the neuroses were the negative of perversions: perversions are the acting out by the adult of one or other of the undirected, hence polymorphously perverse, sexual drives that the child manifests; neurotic symptoms are the failure of the effort *not* to thus act out such drives and desires. As Freud further pointed out, a man has more opportunity to engage in so-called sexual perversion – a woman, whose sexual activity is more restricted by society, must content herself with a neurotic symptom. As we shall see later, it was because the desires of the child want satisfaction in socially forbidden ways and have to be repressed when, at the time of the Oedipus complex, and the closely connected castration complex, he or she desires either or both parents (incest), that Freud claimed that this moment was 'the nucleus of the neurosis' – it is the resolutions and irresolutions of the Oedipus complex that are re-expressed in the neurotic symptom. (The formation of psychosis is somewhat different.) Because some people resolve the Oedipus complex – the entry into human culture – more thoroughly than others, there is an unequal chance of a later neurosis. (Freud did refer to the possibility of constitutionally determined unequal strength of the drives – but this, he stated firmly, was a question for biology, not psychoanalysis.)

There is, however, obviously, another tenet behind many hostile criticisms of Freud's work. It is claimed that Freud was prescribing a correct 'normal' pattern of behaviour. Yet time and again, during his life, Freud had to point out that so-called 'normality' is only relative and is itself 'neurotic', 'pathogenic', 'psychotic', and so on. Indeed, the very nub of his work was the elimination of an absolute difference between abnormality and normality. Cases of neuroses gave him the clues to normal mental formations, dreams were everybody's everyday, or every night, psychoses: sexual perversions or inversions were both widespread and could constitute a choice. In 1905, Freud wrote in his 'shocking' case-study of a young hysterical girl, Dora: 'The less repellent of the so-called sexual perversions are very widely diffused among the whole population, as everyone knows except medical writers upon the subject', and in 1935, to a mother so overwhelmingly distraught by her son's inversion that she could not bring herself even to mention it:

> Homosexuality is assuredly no advantage, but it is nothing to be ashamed of, no vice, no degradation; it cannot be classified as an illness; we consider it to be a variation of the sexual function. ... Many highly respectable individuals of ancient and modern times have been homosexuals, several of the greatest men among them. ... It is a great injustice to persecute homosexuality as a crime – and a cruelty too ...
>
> By asking me if I can help you, you mean, I suppose, if I can abolish homosexuality and make normal heterosexuality take its place ...
>
> What analysis can do for your son runs in a different line. If he is unhappy, neurotic, torn by conflicts, inhibited in his social life, analysis may bring him harmony, peace of mind, full efficiency, whether he remains homosexual or gets changed ...

'Normality' is a useful marker on a continuum, no more:

> ... a normal ego ... is, like normality in general, an ideal fiction. ... Every normal person, in fact, is only normal on the average. His ego approximates to that of the psychotic in some part or other and to a greater or lesser extent. ...

The notion of normality is neither tenable for psychoanalytic theory, nor is its attainability a desideratum of analytic practice:

> Our aim will not be to rub off every peculiarity of human character for the sake of a schematic 'normality', nor yet to demand that the person who has been 'thoroughly analysed' shall feel no passions and develop no internal conflicts.

It is not just Freud's liberal benevolence speaking through these statements: any other conception would have prevented his foundations of psychoanalysis. Only if we can see that the same mechanisms operate in psychotic, neurotic and normal states (in differing degrees and ways, of course), can we see that normal life, like the other two conditions, is a compromise with reality. Feminist criticisms of Freud claim that he was denying what really happens, and that the women he analysed were simply responding to really oppressive conditions. But there is no such thing as a simple response to reality. External reality has to be 'acquired'. To deny that there is anything other than external reality gets us back to the same proposition: it is a denial of the unconscious. Such a denial also affects the concept of the child. Without the notion of an unconscious mind, there are only three possibilities for a presentation of infancy. The child can be a miniature and perfectly rational adult, correctly appraising social reality. Or it can become the absent centre of a world of other people: it is seen only as others relate to it. Or, finally, the child can simply vanish from the story. In this last case we have an instance at the conceptual level of 'infantile amnesia' – the problem that, as Freud discovered, we forget our early childhood.

2.8 'Introduction II' to *Feminine Sexuality: Jacques Lacan and the École Freudienne*

Jacqueline Rose

The place of Jacques Lacan in the centre of the the debate on the relationship between psychoanalysis and feminism is undeniable. The arguments for Lacan as a positive influence on thinking about women are expressed by Jacqueline Rose: she defends Lacan's position on language, the unconscious and desire and the Law of the Father.

Three points emerge:

1. Anatomy is what figures in the account: 'for me "anatomy is not destiny", but that does not mean that anatomy does not figure',[1] but it *only figures* (it is a sham);
2. The phallus stands at its own expense and any male privilege erected upon it is an imposture: 'what might be called a man, the male speaking being, strictly disappears as an effect of discourse, ... by being inscribed within it solely as castration' [*Seminar* XVIII, 12, p. 4; *Seminars* hereafter abbreviated S];
3. Woman is not inferior, she is *subjected*:

    That the woman should be inscribed in an order of exchange of which she is the object, is what makes for the fundamentally conflictual, and, I would say, insoluble, character of her position: the symbolic order literally submits her, it transcends her. ... There is for her something insurmountable, something unacceptable, in the fact of being placed as an object in a symbolic order to which, at the same time, she is subjected just as much as the man. (SII, pp. 304–5)

It is the strength of the concept of the symbolic that it systematically repudiates any account of sexuality which assumes the pre-given nature of sexual difference – the polemic within psychoanalysis and the challenge to any such 'nature' by feminism appear at their closest here. But a problem remains. Lacan's use of the symbolic at this stage relied heavily on Lévi-Strauss's notion of kinship in which women are defined as objects of exchange. As such it is open to the same objections as Lévi-Strauss's account in that it presupposes the subordination which it is intended to explain. Thus while at first glance these remarks by Lacan seem most critical of the order described, they are in another sense complicit with that order and any argument constructed on their basis is likely to be circular.

I think it is crucial that at the point where Lacan made these remarks he had a concept of full speech, of access to the symbolic order whose subjective equivalent is a successful linguistic exchange.[2] But his work underwent a shift, which totally undercut any such conception of language as mediation in favour of an increasing stress on its fundamental division, and the effects of that division on the level of sexuality itself.

'There is no sexual relation' – this became the emphasis of his account. 'There is no sexual relation' because the unconscious divides subjects to and from each other, and because it is the myth of that relation which acts as a barrier against the division setting up a unity through which this division is persistently disavowed. Hence the related and opposite formula 'There is something of One' (the two formulas should be taken together) which refers to that fantasied unity of relation '*We are as one*. Of course everyone knows that it has never happened for two to make one, but still *we are as one*. That's what the idea of love starts out from ... the problem then being how on earth there could be love for another', (*SXX*, p. 46), to its suppression of division and difference ('Love your neighbour as yourself ... the commandment lays down the abolition of sexual difference', *SXXI*, 4. p. 3), to the very ideology of oneness and completion which, for Lacan, closes off the gap of human desire.

In the earlier texts, the unity was assigned to the imaginary, the symbolic was at least potentially its break. In the later texts, Lacan located the fantasy of 'sameness' within language and the sexual relation at one and the same time. 'There is no sexual relation' because subjects relate through what makes sense in *lalangue*. This 'making sense' is a supplement, a making good of the lack of subjectivity and language, of the subject *in* language, against which lack it is set. Psychoanalysis states meaning to be sexual but it has left behind any notion of a repressed sexuality which it would somehow allow to speak. Meaning can only be described as sexual by taking the limits of meaning into account, for meaning in itself operates *at* the limit, the limits of its own failing: 'Meaning indicates the direction in which it fails', [*Encore*, p. 150; hereafter abbreviated *E*]. The stress, therefore, is on the constant failing within language and sexuality, which meaning attempts to supplement or conceal: 'Everything implied by the analytic engagement with human behaviour indicates not that meaning reflects the sexual but that it makes up for it' (*SXXI*, 15, p. 9). Sexuality is the vanishing-point of meaning. Love, on the other hand, belongs to the *Lust-Ich* or pleasure-ego which disguises that failing in the reflection of like to like (love as the ultimate form of self-recognition).

We could say that Lacan has taken the relationship between the unconscious and sexuality and has pushed it to its furthest extreme, producing an account of sexuality solely in terms of its divisions – the division *of* the subject, division *between* subjects (as opposed to relation). Hence the increasing focus on enunciation, on language's internal division, and also the deliberate formalisation of the account – sexual difference as a divide, something to be laid out (exactly a formality, a question of form [...]). The challenge to the unity of the subject, its seeming coherence, is then addressed to the discourse of sexuality itself: 'instead of one signifier we need to interrogate, we should interrogate the signifier *One*' (*SXX*, p. 23). Thus there is no longer imaginary 'unity' and then symbolic difference or exchange, but rather an indictment of the symbolic for the imaginary unity which its most persistent myths continue to promote.

Within this process, woman is constructed as an absolute category (excluded and elevated at one and the same time), a category which serves to guarantee that unity on the side of the man. The man places the woman at the basis of his fantasy, or constitutes fantasy through the woman. Lacan moved away, therefore, from the idea of a problematic but socially assured process of exchange (women as objects) to the construction of woman as a category within language (woman as *the* object, the fantasy of her definition). What is now exposed in the account is 'a carrying over onto the woman of the difficulty inherent in sexuality' itself ['The phallic phase and the subjective import of the castration complex', p. 118; hereafter abbreviated PP]. [...] Whereas in the earlier texts the emphasis was on the circulation of the phallus in the process of sexual exchange, in these texts it is effectively stated that if it is the phallus that circulates then there is no exchange (or relation). The question then becomes not so much the 'difficulty' of feminine sexuality consequent on phallic division, as what it means, given that division, to speak of the 'woman' at all. It is, as the author of the first article from *Scilicet* hints at the end of the argument, in many ways a more fundamental or 'radical' enquiry:

> whatever can be stated about the constitution of the feminine position in the Oedipus complex or in the sexual 'relation' concerns only a second stage, one in which the rules governing a certain type of exchange based on a common value have already been established. It is at a more radical stage, constitutive of those very rules themselves, that Freud points to one last question by indicating that it is the woman who comes to act as their support. (PP, p. 118–19)

In the later texts, the central term is the *object small a [object a]*, Lacan's formula for the lost object which underpins symbolisation, cause of and 'stand in' for desire. What the man relates to is this object and the 'whole of his realisation in the sexual relation comes down to fantasy' (*E*, p. 157). As the place onto which lack is projected, and through which it is simultaneously disavowed, woman is a 'symptom' for the man.

Defined as such, reduced to being nothing other than this fantasmatic place, the woman does not exist. Lacan's statement 'T̶h̶e̶ women does not exist' is, therefore, the corollary of his accusation, or charge, against sexual fantasy. It means, not that women do not exist, but that her status as an absolute category and guarantor of fantasy (exactly *The* woman) is false (T̶h̶e̶). Lacan sees courtly love as the elevation of the woman into the place where her absence or inaccessibility stands in for male lack ('For the man, whose lady was entirely, in the most servile sense of the term, his female subject, courtly love is the only way of coming off elegantly from the absence of sexual relation', *E*, p. 141), just as he sees her denigration as the precondition for man's belief in his own soul ('For the soul to come into being, she, the woman, is differentiated from it ... called woman and defamed', *E*, p. 156). In relation to the man, woman comes to stand for both difference and loss: 'On the one hand, the woman becomes, or is produced, precisely as what he is not, that is sexual difference, and on the other, as what he has to renounce, that is, *jouissance*' (*SXVIII*, 6, pp. 9–10).

Within the phallic definition, the woman is constituted as 'not all', in so far as the phallic function rests on an exception (the 'not') which is assigned to her. Woman is excluded *by* the nature of words, meaning that the definition poses her as exclusion. Note that this is not the same thing as saying that woman is excluded *from* the nature of words, a misreading which leads to the recasting of the whole problem in terms of woman's place outside language, the idea that women might have of themselves an entirely different speech.

For Lacan, men and women are only ever in language ('Men and women are signifiers bound to the common usage of language', *SXX*, p. 36). All speaking beings must line themselves up on one side or the other of this division, but anyone can cross over and inscribe themselves on the opposite side from that to which they are anatomically destined. It is, we could say, an either/or situation, but one whose fantasmatic nature was endlessly reiterated by Lacan: 'these are not positions able to satisfy us, so much so that we can state the unconscious to be defined by the fact that it has a much clearer idea of what is going on than the truth that man is not woman' (*SXXI*, 6, p. 9).

Notes

1. M. Safouan, *La sexualité féminine dans la doctrine freudienne*, Paris: Seuil, 1976, p. 131; 'Is the Oedipus complex universal?' (transl. B. Brewster), *m/f*, no. 5–6 (1981), pp. 83–90.
2. J. Lacan, 'Fonction et champ de la parole et du langage en psychanalyse', *Écrits*, Paris: Seuil, 1953, pp. 237–322; *Écrits: A selection*, transl. A. Sheridan, London: Tavistock, 1977, pp. 30–113.

2.9 Lacan in Contexts
David Macey

David Macey expresses the views of those who are doubtful of Lacan's contribution to psychoanalytic theory as a whole, and to women's studies in particular; he supplies, if not a refutation of Lacan, serious criticism of the basis for viewing Lacanian theory as an integrated theory.

Arguments from a final state also typify both the anthologies of Lacanian material currently available in English translation. Schneiderman's *Returning to Freud*[1] contains sixteen texts written by eleven authors over a period of almost twenty years, the earliest dating from 1956. They are collectively ascribed to 'The School of Jacques Lacan', even though no such entity has ever existed. Only one of the texts is by Lacan himself. Significantly, it is the only one not to be dated: Lacan, we must assume, exists outside time and space. The papers included in Mitchell and Rose's *Feminine Sexuality* are said to be by 'Jacques Lacan and the École Freudienne'; of the five papers by Lacan himself, three were written long before the foundation of the École Freudienne de Paris in 1964. In purely historical terms, the collection could equally well be ascribed to 'Jacques Lacan and the Société Française de Psychanalyse'. In both these cases, a new final state has been created in the form of writings by an imaginary collective author. To argue that the use of 'school' in these titles is merely a convention or that it is modelled on such hallowed phrases as 'Paintings of the Impressionist School' is surely disingenuous, as it cannot but be overdetermined by an implied reference to the EFP, almost the final institutional state of Lacanian psychoanalysis ('almost' in that it was dissolved by Lacan in 1980).

In *Feminine Sexuality*,[2] a more interesting example of retroaction on the basis of a final state appears at the level of translation practice. Commenting on the length of time over which the texts were written, Jacqueline Rose remarks: 'I have made no attempt to give a false homogeneity to the very different styles which follow from this deliberate selection.' There is one fascinating exception to this self-imposed rule. The collection contains extracts from *Encore*, the transcript of the 1972–73 Seminar (S XX) in which Lacan makes the notorious pronouncement that 'La femme n'existe pas', crossing out or 'barring' the definite article to make his point. As the translator explains: 'It is the central tenet of these chapters that "The Woman" does not exist, in that phallic sexuality assigns her to a position of phantasy. Lacan argues that the sexual relation hangs on a fantasy of oneness, which the woman has classically come to support.' In the *Encore* extract, Rose follows Lacan by 'barring' the definite article ('the Woman') or italicizing it; in her general introduction, she alternates between 'Woman' and 'The Woman' without explaining the shift in usage. Regrettably, this translation is then back-projected into contexts in which

Lacan's use of the definite article is indicative of nothing more than obedience to French grammatical norms. Thus, in 'The Meaning of the Phallus', a paper read to the Max Planck Institute in 1958, we find 'The masculine unconscious ... the unconscious of the woman', the latter being a translation of the banal *l'inconscient de la femme*, which Sheridan renders more prosaically, but so much more acceptably, as 'the unconscious of women'. At the level of translation practice, the retroactive use of a final state results in an unnecessary infelicity of syntax. At the level of theory, it produces a degree of mystification by suggesting that a notion elaborated in 1972–73 was already current in 1958. It is surely significant that in Rose's version, Lacan's *par hypothèse* becomes 'by definition'.

The timeless atmosphere created by the ascription of texts to an imaginary collective author and by the retroactive use of a final state is heightened by slips in textual dating. In both the bibliography and the body of the text, 'The Mirror Stage' is dated '1936'. True, a version of that paper was read to the Marienbad Conference in 1936, but no transcript survives, and the version included in *Écrits* is quite clearly stated to have been read to the 1949 Zurich Conference of the IPA. That it does not date from 1936 is also obvious from internal textual evidence; the transparent allusions to Sartre's *L'Être et le néant* (1943)[3] could not have been made in that year. This is not merely a pedantic point; the inaccurate dating is quite consonant with the anachronisms of the translation and with the construction and reproduction of a final state.

Imaginary constructs typify many English-language presentations of Lacan, as a fundamental assumption of unity and systematicity transforms *Écrits* into a conceptually homogeneous text rather than a collection of papers written over a considerable period of time, with all the shifts and modifications that implies. Thus, the alleged importance of structural linguistics – as opposed to an interest in language – constructs Lacan into the child of Freud and Saussure.

Notes

1. S. Schneiderman, *Returning to Freud: Clinical analysis in the School of Lacan*, New Haven, CT: Yale University Press, 1980.
2. J. Mitchell and J. Rose (eds), *Feminine Sexuality: Jacques Lacan and the École Freudienne*, London: Macmillan, 1982.
3. J.-P. Sartre, *L'Être et le néant*, Paris: Gallimard, 1943.

Further Reading

Brennan, T. (ed.) (1989), *Between Feminism and Psychoanalysis*, London: Routledge.
Butler, J. (1990), *Gender Trouble: Feminism and the subversion of identity*, London: Routledge.
Crawford, J., Kippax, S., Onyx, J., Gault, U. and Benton, P. (1992), *Emotion and Gender: Constructing meaning from memory*, London: Sage.

Frosh, S. (1987), *The Politics of Psychoanalysis: An introduction to Freudian and post-Freudian theory*, London: Macmillan.

Frosh, S. (1989), *Psychoanalysis and Psychology: Minding the gap*, London: Macmillan.

Gallop, J. (1982), *Feminism and Psychoanalysis: The daughter's seduction*, London: Macmillan.

Kitzinger, C. (1987), *The Social Construction of Lesbianism*, London: Sage.

Sayers, J. (1991), *Mothering Psychoanalysis*, London: Hamish Hamilton.

Skevington, S. and Baker, D. (1989), *The Social Identity of Women*, London: Sage.

Ussher, J. (1989), *The Psychology of the Female Body*, London: Routledge.

Wilkinson, S. (1986), *Feminist Social Psychology*, Milton Keynes: Open University Press.

3 CROSS-CULTURAL PERSPECTIVES ON WOMEN'S LIVES

Edited and Introduced by Teri Brewer

INTRODUCTION

In the mid nineteenth century several key works were published which theorised the presumed universal subordination of women by reference to hypothesised events in prehistory. The model of prehistory was based on what was then known about 'primitive' societies.

There was a fascination with non-Western and pre-industrial cultures because it was assumed that in their practices lay the key to understanding the *origins* and *evolution* of human social institutions. A key concept in such studies was the doctrine of *survivals*. Social institutions which appear to be anomalous – that is, to serve no obvious function in the present day – were described as 'survivals', and considered analogous to archaeological remains.

The best-known example of this kind of work is probably the Swiss historian J. J. Bachofen's *Das Mutterrecht* (1861). Bachofen sought an explanation for the range of kinship systems found in other cultures. He assumed that those systems which seemed least complex to him must be more primitive social forms than our own. Tracing descent through the mother seemed the simplest way of reckoning relationships, as he thought that the most ancient and primitive societies must have been sexually promiscuous, consisting of small bands, each dominated by a powerful man; this phase was followed by a stage of rule by women, with descent still traced through the female line.

Bachofen called this the phase of 'mother-right', and attributed the origin of religion to women of this period. He believed that later people transformed religion and cultural forms by intellectualising religion and moving to a period of 'father-right'. His theory that primordial religion was based around the worship of an Earth Mother, as well as many of the other themes in his work, are still with us, and echoes of Bachofen reverberate in aspects of the current Green movement and in 'New Age' spirituality. Bachofen idealised an imagined culture, and saw contemporary cultures with matrilineal kinship systems as examples of survivals.

Bachofen was one of many nineteenth-century writers preoccupied with the need to establish how things began, whether there were predictable historical stages through which all cultures might pass, and why a diversity of social systems could coexist. In the method and style of their analyses they displayed the origins of their subject in the antiquarian studies of the eighteenth century – treating social and behavioural phenomena as though they were objects in the landscape which required archaeological interpretation.

At the same time, many advances were being made in the field of biology – Darwin's theories of natural selection and social evolution being the best known. Towards the end of the nineteenth century these overlapping sociological, biological, antiquarian, archaeological and historical themes contributed to a new discipline of anthropology, which was charged with investigating 'primitive' peoples.

Questions about ascribed gender roles can be seen as central – if sometimes unexamined – preoccupations in the development of anthropology, and understanding this helps us to see why the subject developed as it did in the early twentieth century.

The women's suffrage movement and the opening of educational opportunities to women, particularly in the aftermath of the First World War, encouraged a number of outstanding women to enter a field where issues of personal concern also formed key themes in the theoretical development of their discipline. In the circumstances it is not surprising that the cross-cultural investigation of gender remained an important area of research in anthropology.

Because of the efflorescence of theoretical writing on the subject of gender in the 1960s and early 1970s, it would be easy to assume that these issues were discovered and defined only thirty years ago. In a collection like this there is not the space to sample the range of earlier approaches, but it is worth making the point that the theory-building reflected in the Readings in this Section would not have been possible had it not been for the detailed ethnography and theoretical analysis done by anthropologists over most of the preceding century.

There have been three distinct stages in the development of cross-cultural gender theory.

The first stage has already been discussed; it involved the imaginative re-creation of prehistoric social systems based on what is usually called 'armchair' anthropology – the accounts of Victorian explorers, travellers and missionaries, as well as observations of classical authors such as Herodotus.

The second stage, in part a reaction against the first, involved the collection of systematic first-hand accounts of other cultures by trained observers. The need for descriptive work was also fuelled by a concern that if assumptions about the inevitability of social evolution were correct, the existing 'primitive' cultures were doomed and should therefore be studied before it was too late. This did not preclude theoretical work, but it gave an urgency to fieldwork that resulted in ethnographies which focused in detail on a particular culture without making explicit cross-cultural comparisons.

This intensive ethnologising was done primarily by men, but it is startling how long it took before anyone realised how over-emphasised men's spheres in the cultures studied had become – partly because of problems of differential access, partly because of a tendency to see men's activities as more important than women's. In the period before the 1960s Margaret Mead, Ruth Benedict, Rhoda Metraux, Zora Neale Hurston and Hortense Powdermaker were among those who showed sensitivity to these problems in the United States. In the British tradition Monica Wilson, Phyllis Kaberry, Camilla Wedgwood, Audrey Richards, Hilda Kuper and Mary Douglas produced some of the most interesting ethnography.

The Women's Liberation Movement influenced a review of available data in the late 1960s and early 1970s, and out of this process of review and critique came a consolidation, interrogation and synthesis of earlier work which resulted in a renaissance of cross-cultural gender theory. All except two of the Readings in this Section come from this post-1970 period. Although the styles of analysis vary, the real interest here is in watching how each writer formulates critical questions.

Margaret Mead uses paradox and unexpected analogies to make her reader propose better questions; Edward Evans-Pritchard reconfigures disciplinary history with vivid images which open critical questions. Sherry Ortner and Carol McCormack extend and explore a structural opposition first proposed more than thirty years earlier by Simone de Beauvoir. Peggy Sanday consolidates available data in a well-grounded attempt to develop meaningful cross-cultural generalisations. Michelle Rosaldo and Henrietta Moore reflect on questions asked in the past, which need to be answered or reformulated in the future. The last three Readings demonstrate application of the paradigm shift: Akemi Kikumura and Barbara Myerhoff rejected the academic interpretive hegemony to explore the possibility of a true dialogue through the use of life histories and personal experience narratives. Lila Abu-Lughod goes further to propose a deceptively simple adjustment in perspective which opens a new range of questions.

All these writers are concerned with the dynamic tension between the need to make generalisations, or build theory, and their commitment to rich, personal and particular ethnographic description.

3.1 Human Fatherhood is a Social Invention

Margaret Mead

Margaret Mead (1901–78) was a pioneer in the fieldwork-based study of gender. She played a key part in the 'nature versus nurture' debates which have divided behavioural scientists for most of this century. She was known for introducing anthropological issues into general public debate, and her love of approaching a problem from unusual angles often led to fresh insights. This brief Reading is taken from a book aimed at a general rather than an academic audience.

When we survey all known human societies, we find everywhere some form of the family, some set of permanent arrangements by which males assist females in caring for children while they are young. The distinctively human aspect of the enterprise lies not in the protection the male affords the females and the young – this we share with the primates. Nor does it lie in the lordly possessiveness of the male over females for whose favours he contends with other males – this too we share with the primates. Its distinctiveness lies instead in the nurturing behaviour of the male, who among human beings everywhere helps provide food for women and children. The sentimental figures of speech so common in the modern Western world in which the bees and the ants and the flowers are invoked to illustrate the more suspect aspects of human beings have obscured our recognition of how much of an invention this behaviour of human males is. True, father-birds do feed their young, but men are a long way from birds on the evolutionary tree. Male fighting-fish do make bubble-nests and only capture the female long enough to squeeze her eggs out of her, and then, after driving her away, devote themselves, rather unsuccessfully, to retrieving the eggs that fall out of the bubble-nest, and – when they don't eat up the eggs or the young – some young survive. But these analogies from the world of birds and fish are far from man. Among our structurally closest analogues – the primates – the male does not feed the female. Heavy with young, making her way laboriously along, she fends for herself. He may fight to protect her or to possess her, but he does not nurture her.

Somewhere at the dawn of human history, some social invention was made under which males started nurturing females and their young. We have no reason to believe that the nurturing males had any knowledge of physical paternity, although it is quite possible that being fed was a reward meted out to the female who was not too fickle with her sexual favours. In every known human society, everywhere in the world, the young male learns that when he grows up, one of the things which he must do in order to be a full member of society is to provide food for some female and her young. Even in very simple societies, a few men may shy away from the responsibility, become tramps or ne'er-do-wells or misanthropists who live in the woods by themselves. In complex societies, a large number of men may escape the burden of feeding females and young by entering monasteries – and feeding each other – or by entering some profession that their society will classify as giving them a right to be fed, like the Army and the Navy, or the Buddhist orders of Burma. But in spite of such exceptions, every known human society rests firmly on the learned nurturing behaviour of men ...

3.2   **The Position of Women in Primitive Societies and in Our Own**

Edward Evans-Pritchard

A bemused Edward Evans-Pritchard (1902–73) was asked to give the 1955 Fawcett

*lecture at University College London (honouring Millicent Fawcett, an early feminist).
The suggested topic was English women's progress, a subject on which he felt unable to
contribute much.*

*Instead he offered a lecture which reviewed anthropological thought on the position of
women through history, and across cultural boundaries. An adept historical summary
is only part of the paper. The second half begins with the description of a curious
composite primitive woman whose life consists of features he thought common to the
experience of many women in non-Western societies. This nonexistent sociological
creature is then compared to modern English women in very general terms, with the
conclusion that modern English women were really very little better off in some
fundamental ways, and that he saw little possibility of real change in the future, and
presumed that there are 'deep biological and psychological factors, as well as sociological
factors, involved, and that the relations between the sexes can only be modified ... not
radically altered by them'.*

*Evans-Pritchard's complex determinism and reductionist portraiture has attracted
most critical attention, but it is also worth pursuing the themes he develops in the
theoretical portions of this Reading.*

We have to bear in mind, therefore, that the accounts of the social life of savage
peoples on which the early anthropologists based their conclusions were usually
written by men, and men from middle-class homes and often, especially when
from this country, with an evangelical background.

We have also to bear in mind that anthropologists of this period were strongly
influenced by the writings of Darwin and Huxley. A scheme of social or super-
organic evolution could easily be built on to theories of biological evolution, and
it was, notably by Herbert Spencer; and quite logically, for if there had been the
biological evolution of man postulated, there must also have been social and
cultural evolution; and the status of women had somehow or other to be fitted
into the scheme. This presented no great difficulty to the Victorian anthropologists, and the relation between the sexes was one of their favourite topics, in
fact only religion competed with it for the interest of those puritanical
unbelievers. Obviously, since man had descended from some apelike ancestor
his sex life must at one time have been apelike too, and the task of the
anthropologists was to show how the monkey house stood with regard to the
Victorian drawing-room. There had to be some speculation about the earliest
stages of this development but its general lines were clear since the terminal
points were fixed – the female ape and the Victorian lady. There were the
Akinsonian horde, Bachofen's hetairism, McLennan's infanticidal stock group,
the primitive promiscuity and group marriage of Morgan and Sir John Lubbock,
and so on. To what wild flights of fancy these speculations could reach is well
exemplified in a book, *The Position of Women in Primitive Society* (1914) by a friend
of my youth, C. Gasquoine Hartley, who was the very embodiment of what
early Edwardian progressives were expected to be.

Now, it has become increasingly clear from anthropological research that no
social forms such as those postulated exist. It is equally evident that no amount

of research by prehistorians can ever tell us what were those of earliest man. Moreover, there has been a complete change in the direction of anthropological thinking. Gone are the days, at least for the time being, of such speculative and uncritical evolutionary theorizing. Gone also are the days of vigorous feminism and anti-feminism which formed part of that battle in which the protagonists of all so-called progressive movements and their opponents were mixed up in a general mêlée. Primitive societies, which are vast in number and in variety of forms, provide here a fruitful field of observation. It is as much for that reason as because they are primitive that they are important for anyone interested in the social position of women. Unfortunately, no systematic comparative work on this topic has recently been done; and it is necessary, if one wishes to obtain information about it, to go to the sources, the many ethnographic monographs – laborious undertaking. That no attempt has been made to bring together the results of modern research into a single study may be due, at least to some extent, to lack of interest, woman's status in our own society having ceased to be an acute public issue. However this may be, I beg to submit to you a few reflections on the matter.

It is difficult, if not impossible, to evaluate objectively woman's position in any particular primitive society or in primitive societies in general. In the end any judgement is based on our own opinions and practices, and without prolonged study is, moreover, likely to be superficial, a judgement based on appearances strange to us rather than on the social realities behind them, or, as one might put it, on the cultural expression of relations between the sexes rather than on the psychological and moral content of the relationship. We observe, for example, that in some societies women crawl in the presence of their husbands or that people never eat in the presence of the other sex; but if we were to take these as signs, as we would be inclined to do, of abject female subservience or of a relationship of extreme reserve, or even of hostility, between the sexes, we would draw entirely wrong conclusions.

On the basis of such evidences as were available it was generally accepted by theoretical writers of the Victorian era – Herbert Spencer for example – that in primitive societies women are property to be bought and sold, and are treated as slaves or even animals, enjoying neither sympathy nor respect. Relations between the sexes were thought to be little above those of beasts; marriage, as we understand it, scarcely existing. These judgements rested only too often on quite inadequate accounts and were inclined also to be highly subjective and measured by somewhat arbitrary standards of our own sentiments.

3.3   Is Female to Male as Nature is to Culture?
Sherry Ortner

Sherry Ortner's controversial structuralist analysis was based on ideas proposed initially by Simone de Beauvoir in her book The Second Sex *(1953). It provoked an extensive, long-running debate. Her argument develops with logic and clarity, and is based on accessible theoretical assumptions about the interpretation of symbolic meanings.*

The secondary status of woman in society is one of the true universals, a pan-cultural fact. Yet within that universal fact, the specific cultural conceptions and symbolizations of woman are extraordinarily diverse and even mutually contradictory. Further, the actual treatment of women and their relative power and contribution vary enormously from culture to culture, and over different periods in the history of particular cultural traditions. Both these points – the universal fact and the cultural variation – constitute problems to be explained. [...]

In this paper I try to expose the underlying logic of cultural thinking that assumes the inferiority of women; I try to show the highly persuasive nature of the logic, for if it were not so persuasive, people would not keep subscribing to it. But I also try to show the social and cultural sources of that logic, to indicate wherein lies the potential for change.

It is important to sort out the levels of the problem. The confusion can be staggering. For example, depending on which aspect of Chinese culture we look at, we might extrapolate any of several entirely different guesses concerning the status of women in China. In the ideology of Taoism, *yin*, the female principle, and *yang*, the male principle, are given equal weight; 'the opposition, alternation, and interaction of these two forces give rise to all phenomena in the universe'. Hence we might guess that maleness and femaleness are equally valued in the general ideology of Chinese culture. Looking at the social structure, however, we see the strongly emphasized patrilineal descent principle, the importance of sons, and the absolute authority of the father in the family. Thus we might conclude that China is the archetypal patriarchal society. Next, looking at the actual roles played, power and influence wielded, and material contributions made by women in Chinese society – all of which are, upon observation, quite substantial – we would have to say that women are allotted a great deal of (unspoken) status in the system. Or again, we might focus on the fact that a goddess, Kuan Yin, is the central (most worshipped, most depicted) deity in Chinese Buddhism, and we might be tempted to say, as many have tried to say about goddess-worshiping cultures in prehistoric and early historical societies, that China is actually a sort of matriarchy. In short, we must be absolutely clear about *what* we are trying to explain before explaining it.

We may differentiate three levels of the problem:

1. The universal fact of culturally attributed second-class status of woman in every society. Two questions are important here. First, what do we mean by this; what is our evidence that this is a universal fact? And second, how are we to explain this fact, once having established it?
2. Specific ideologies, symbolizations, and sociostructural arrangements pertaining to women that vary widely from culture to culture. The problem at

this level is to account for any particular cultural complex in terms of factors specific to that group – the standard level of anthropological analysis.

3. Observable on-the-ground details of women's activities, contributions, powers, influence, etc., often at variance with cultural ideology (although always constrained within the assumption that women may never be officially pre-eminent in the total system). This is the level of direct observation, often adopted now by feminist-orientated anthropologists.

3.4   **Nature, Culture and Gender: a critique**
Carol McCormack

The premises and analysis offered in Reading 3.3 are sharply critiqued here, in a brief paper from a volume which responds to the assumed universal opposition of nature and culture as categories of symbolic thought. As the editors say, they offered an opportunity 'simply to reflect upon the manner in which anthropologists especially have used the concepts of nature and culture in the exegesis of other people's gender symbolism'.

Ortner has proceeded in the Lévi-Straussian manner of asking a question about humanity, then setting out to answer it. She asks: how might we account for universal female subordination? Moving quickly to a biological reductionist argument, she sees that 'woman's body seems to doom her to mere reproduction of life; the male in contrast, lacking natural creative functions, must (or has the opportunity to) assert his creativity externally "artificially", through the medium of technology and symbols. In doing so he creates relatively lasting, eternal, transcending objects, while the woman creates only perishables – human beings.' This view, which originates with de Beauvoir, is remarkable for its ethnocentricity. A vast number of societies, and particularly the totemic societies Lévi-Strauss has used for analysis, have lineage systems which exist, by definition, in perpetuity. Each human who is born fits into a great social chain of being, ensuring the immortality of both self and group. Houses rot, villages are moved, empires fall, but the great faith is that the lineage, including the 'real' company of ancestors, will endure for ever.

  Is there anything more intrinsically natural about women's physiology than men's? In most societies men's procreative role is seen as being as essential as women's for the continuity of social groups. Both men and women procreate, eat, defecate and satisfy other survival needs. To do so is natural, but the etiquette of eating, the time, place and position for defecation, and indeed the rules prescribing time, place and position for ejaculation or parturition are cultural. Fertility and birth are guided by definitions of symptoms and technological modifications brought about by chemical and mechanical therapy in virtually all societies and cannot be used as the single characteristic for defining women as 'natural'.

The statement that women are doomed by their biology to be natural, not cultural, is of course a mythic statement, and both Ortner and Lévi-Strauss retreat from it. Of course woman cannot be consigned fully to the category of nature, since [...] she is 'half the human race'[1]. Or, as expressed by Lévi-Strauss, 'women could never become just a sign and nothing more, since even in a man's world she is still a person, and since insofar as she is defined as a sign she must be recognized as a generator of signs.'[2] Thus, Lévi-Strauss's fundamental paradox reappears in metaphoric transformation:

1. Culture transcends nature, but is grounded in the human mind (brain) which is nature.
2. Men transcend nature with their mentality, but are in nature as procreated, procreators, and possessors of human minds.
3. Women transcend nature with their mentality, but are in nature as procreated, procreators, lactators, and possessors of human minds.

Or, 2 and 3 might be combined to read:

4. Men and women transcend nature with their mentality, but are in nature as procreated, procreators, nurturers, and possessors of human minds.

Might we then conclude that both men and women are nature and culture, and there is no logic compelling us to believe that at an unconscious level women, because of their naturalness, are opposed and subordinate to men?

Ideology and the adequacy of models

Ortner states that 'everywhere, in every known culture, women are considered in some degree inferior to men'. But she does not say by whom they are considered to be so. By men? By women? By how many? In fieldwork I have talked with women chiefs, women heads of descent groups, heads of women's secret societies, and women household heads who would not agree with the sweeping thesis as it stands. They would say that women are inferior to men in some ways and men are inferior to women in some ways, giving productive tasks in the division of labour as examples. There would not be the social ferment over gender roles in Western industrial societies today if a substantial number of men and women did not subscribe to the thesis of universal female subordination. The methodological problem is this: can structural models stand without reference to consciously held folk models and actual statistical descriptions? [...]

The link between nature and women is not a 'given'. Gender and its attributes are not pure biology. The meanings attributed to male and female are as arbitrary as are the meanings attributed to nature and culture.

Those who have develop the nature–culture–gender thesis root femaleness in biology and maleness in the social domain. However, if men and women are one species and together constitute human society then, logically, analysis of intrinsic gender attributes must be made with reference to the same domain. Equally in error is the formulation of sociobiologists who root male gender attributes excessively in biology, thus explaining the 'naturalness' of men's political dominance over women.

Notes

1. S. Ortner, Reading 3.3 above.
2. C. Lévi-Strauss, *The Elementary Structures of Kinship*, Boston, MA: Beacon, 1969, p. 496.

3.5   **Female Power and Male Dominance: on the origins of sexual inequality**
Peggy Reeves Sanday

Peggy Reeves Sanday is one of many who began to move beyond the 'nature versus nurture' dichotomy, influenced by the concept of cultural patterning developed by Ruth Benedict in Patterns of Culture *(1934). She started by systematically mapping the spectrum of known power/gender relationships using data on more than 150 societies studied by anthropologists over most of the previous century. With the aid of a range of analytic tables she developed a more fully grounded set of hypotheses than had been previously available.*

In this Reading she pauses to deconstruct the notion of male 'dominance', using her cross-cultural data. Her correlations (between key behavioural traits and the inclusion/exclusion of women from spheres of economic and political control, decision-making and public activity) are modulated by summary historic and environmental characteristics of the societies discussed.

Sex role plans are part of the system of meanings by which a people explain their success, come to terms with their fears, enshrine their past, and stamp themselves with a sense of 'peoplehood'. The unique identity people weave for themselves, the cup they mold from which to drink of life, mediates sexual identities. Hence, sex roles must be viewed as an interdependent part of the logico-meaningful system that defines and gives direction to a people's life. If this system of meanings develops in the absence of forces threatening social survival, women wield economic and political power or authority and the power relationship between the sexes is balanced.

If the system of meanings that defines sexual identities is threatened by internal or external forces, meanings may be recombined, with the result that sexual identities are revised or new ones fabricated. If the whole complex of traditional roles is undermined, people will fight as if they were struggling to hold on to life itself. As the Igbo women said in the aftermath of the women's war, 'we are all dying'.

When the cup of life that defines the male world is broken, men organize to protect their traditional rights, as the Igbo women organized to protect theirs. Sometimes the struggle against hostile forces includes controlling and manipulating women as if they were objects in a game played only by men. The circumstances under which men attempt to make women pawns in their struggle are discussed in this chapter. As will be seen, however, women do not always accept subordination by men. [...]

Male dominance is restricted in this study to ... two general types of behaviors ... . First, there is the exclusion of women from political and economic decision-making. Second, there is male aggression against women, which is measured here by the following five traits: the expectation that males should be tough, brave, and aggressive; the presence of men's houses or specific places where only men may congregate; frequent quarreling, fighting, or wife beating; the institutionalization or regular occurrence of rape; and raiding other groups for wives. The presence of all five traits in a society indicates a high degree of male aggression; the absence of all five indicates that male aggression is weakly developed.[1]

Twenty-eight percent of the societies in which females wield political and economic power or authority are characterized by the extremes of male aggression. Looking at the societies in which females have economic control but no political power, it can be seen that over half (53 percent) are prone to male aggression. The Mundurucu fit into the latter category: Women enjoy economic autonomy and males display aggression against women. Despite efforts by men to control them by force, Mundurucu women neither accept nor agree with the male assessment of their inferior status. The relation between the Mundurucu sexes, Murphy and Murphy say, is 'not, then, one of simple domination and submissiveness, but one of ideological dissonance and real opposition'.[2]

The Mundurucu case illustrates that male aggression against women is not necessarily joined with female passivity. In some societies it is expected that women will fight back. In others, it is assumed that women will adopt the submissive role. The following quote from the Quran, for example, codifies real male dominance and female subordination: 'Men stand superior to women in that God hath preferred the one over the other. ... Those whose perverseness ye fear, admonish them and remove them into bed-chambers and beat them; but if they submit to you then do not seek a way against them.'[3]

The frequency ... with which female economic or political power coexists with male aggression against women shows that the Mundurucu sex-role plan is not unusual. In discussing the bases for male dominance, it is essential to distinguish male aggression against women from the exercise by women of political and economic power. Where the former exists in the presence of the latter, the term *mythical* male dominance will be employed to describe the relationship between the sexes. Where males turn aggression against women and/or women are excluded from economic and political decision-making, the relationship between the sexes will be defined as *unequal*. Finally, where males do not display aggression against women and women exercise political and economic authority or power, the relationship between the sexes will be defined as *equal*. Employing these criteria as guidelines, the relationship between the sexes is classified as equal in 32 percent of the societies of this study and unequal in 28 percent .... The remaining 40 percent of the societies either fit in the criteria expressive of 'mythical' male dominance or represent cases in which women exercise economic but not political power.

The notion of 'mythical' male dominance was adopted from Susan Carol Rogers's discussion of the 'myth of male dominance' in peasant societies. Rogers gives examples of peasant societies in which there is a balance between formal male authority and informal female power. She argues that a non-hierarchical power relationship between the categories 'male' and 'female' is maintained by 'the acting out of a myth of male dominance'. The myth of male dominance, she says, is expressed 'in patterns of public deference toward men, as well as their monopolization of positions of authority and prestige'. She shows, however, that males do not actually dominate, nor do males or females literally believe males to be dominant. The perpetuation of the myth she says, 'is in the interests of both peasant women and men, because it gives the latter the *appearance* of power and control over all sectors of village life, while at the same time giving to the former *actual* power over those sectors of life in the community which may be controlled by villagers.'[4]

A claim for nearly universal sexual asymmetry could be made if mythical male dominance is defined as a form of sexual asymmetry. However, if mythical male dominance is understood as representing a form of balanced sexual opposition, as Rogers argues and as I have argued for societies like that of the Mundurucu, such a claim is unwarranted.

The criteria for classifying societies as sexually equal deserve comment in light of the universal sexual asymmetry argument. Louise Lamphere, who articulates the latter position, defines sexual equality as a situation 'in which all men and women (regardless of social group or strata) could and actually did make decisions over the *same* range of activities and people, that is, exercise the *same* kinds of control' (emphasis mine). Sexual inequality, she says, would be a situation 'where there were some decisions which women could not and did not make, some activities from which they were excluded, and some resources which they did not control'.[5] By this definition, in all human societies men are unequal in some respects and women are unequal in others. There is no society I know of in which the sexes give equal energy to exactly the same activities and decisions. Nor are there many societies in which both sexes have the same access to the same resources.

Male dominance is associated with increasing technological complexity, an animal economy, sexual segregation in work, a symbolic orientation to the male creative principle, and stress. [...]

The sexes are most likely to be equal in gathering, fishing and shifting cultivation economies. The sexes tend to be unequal in animal husbandry societies. The intermediate category of male dominance (which includes mythical male dominance) is prevalent among advanced agriculturalists, hunters, and horticulturalists. [...] Feminine or couple origin symbolism is more frequently found in sexually equal than in sexually unequal societies ... sexual segregration is positively associated with male dominance and sexual integration is negatively associated with male dominance.

Male dominance is significantly associated with environmental and historical conditions, suggesting that the dominance of women is a response to stress. [...]

In favourable environments and in autochthonous cultural conditions, sexual equality (or symmetry) flourishes, whereas in unfavorable environments or in the face of cultural disruption (measured by the experience of recent migration), mythical male dominance or sexual inequality prevails. For nearly three-fourths of the sexually equal societies (71 percent), migration is reported as occurring 'very early', 'long ago', or it is said that the people are 'aboriginal to the area'. Approximately the same proportion of sexually unequal societies (70 percent) are reported as being recent arrivals in their area within the last 100–150 years or the people are said to be expansionist orientated. In support of the importance of a favorable environment (as measured by the nature of the food supply), [...] sexually equal societies are less likely to be faced with periods of famine than sexually unequal societies. Other sources of stress related to male dominance are endemic warfare and chronic hunger [...]

Notes

1. In the book from which this Reading is taken, Sanday backs her discussion with a series of tables summarising the various correlations discussed here with data from many societies. It is not possible to reproduce her tables, owing to space limitations.
2. R. and Y. Murphy, *Women of the Forest*, New York: Columbia University Press, 1974.
3. Sura 4:34. This quote from the Quran was taken from J. Mason, 'Sex and symbol in the treatment of women: the wedding rite in a Libyan oasis community', *American Ethnologist*, vol. 2 (1975), pp. 649–61.
4. S. Rogers, 'Female forms of power and the myth of male dominance', *American Ethnologist*, vol. 2 (1975), p. 729. (See N. Quinn, 'Anthropological studies on women's status', *Annual Review of Anthropology*, vol. 6 (1977), p. 218), for the application of Rogers's concept to a discussion of the relation between the Mundurucu sexes.
5. L. Lamphere, 'Review essay: Anthropology', *Signs*, vol. 2 (1977), pp. 612–27.

3.6   **The Use and Abuse of Anthropology: reflections on feminism and cross-cultural understanding**
Michelle Rosaldo

Michelle Rosaldo's commentary traces recent theoretical developments while at the same time she explores the uses to which outdated anthropological ideas had been put by some feminist authors. She points out the dangers of reasoning about the collective past of humanity based on data collected from contemporary 'pre-industrial' cultures, something which has been very popular among anthropologists and non-anthropologists alike.

Her relentless eye sees grounds for criticism in her own past practice as well as that of other scholars, both in the handling of data and, most importantly, in the formulation of questions about those data.

Much like the nineteenth-century writers who first argued whether mother-right preceded patriarchal social forms, or whether women's difficult primeval lot has been significantly improved in civilized society, feminists differ in their diagnoses of our prehistoric lives, their sense of suffering, of conflict, and of change.

By using anthropology as precedent for modern arguments and claims, the 'primitive' emerges in accounts like these as the bearer of primordial human need. Women elsewhere are, it seems, the image of ourselves undressed, and the historical specificity of their lives and of our own becomes obscured. Their strengths prove that we can be strong. But ironically, and at the same time that we fight to see ourselves as cultural beings who lead socially determined lives, the movement back in evolutionary time brings in inevitable appeal to biological givens and the determining impact of such 'crude' facts as demography and technology. To look for origins is, in the end, to think that what we are today is something other than the product of our history and our present social world, and, more particularly, that our gender systems are primordial, transhistorical, and essentially unchanging in their roots. Quests for origins sustain (since they are predicated upon) a discourse cast in universal terms; and universalism permits us all too quickly to assume – for everyone but ourselves perhaps – the *sociological* significance of what individual people *do* or, even worse, of what, in biological terms, they are. [...]

In short, if the universalizing questions are the ones with which we start, the anthropological record seems to feed our fear that sexual asymmetry is (again, like kinship, and the two, of course, are linked) a deep, primordial sort of truth, in some way bound to functional requirements associated with our sexual phsyiology. Though various, our gender systems *do* appear more basic than our ways of organizing our economies, religious faiths, or courts of law. And so, at much the same time that the evidence of behavioral variation suggests that gender is less a product of our bodies than of social forms and modes of thought, it seems quite difficult to believe that sexual inequalities are not rooted in the dictates of a natural order. Minimally, it would appear that certain biological facts – women's role in reproduction and, perhaps, male strength – have òperated in a non-necessary but universal way to shape and reproduce male dominance.

A common feminist response to the facts that I have outlined here has been, essentially, to deny their weight and argue that the evidence we have itself reflects male bias. By focusing on women's lives, researchers have begun to reinterpret more conventional accounts and school us to be sensitive to female values, goals, and strengths. If formal authority is not something women enjoy, so, this research claims, we ought to learn to understand informal female powers; if women operate in 'domestic' or 'familial' spheres, then we must focus our attention on arenas like these, wherein women can make claims.[1] The value of scholarship of this sort is that it shows that when we measure women against men we fail to grasp important structural facts which may, in fact, give rise to female power. But while this point is an important one – to which I will return – the tendency to ignore imbalances in order to permit a grasp of women's lives has led too many scholars to forget that men and women ultimately live together in the world and, so, that we will never understand the lives that women lead without relating them to men. Ignoring sexual asymmetry strikes me as an essentially romantic move, which only blinds us to the sorts of facts we must attempt to understand and change.

An alternative approach,[2] elaborated in a set of essays by Chodorow, Ortner, and myself[3] has been to argue that even universal facts are not reducible to biology. Our essays tried to show how what appears a 'natural' fact must yet be understood in social terms – a by-product, as it were, of non-necessary institutional arrangements that could be addressed through political struggle and, with effort, undermined. Our argument was, in essence, that in all human societies sexual asymmetry might be seen to correspond to a rough institutional division between domestic and public spheres of activity, the one built around reproduction, affective, and familial bonds, and particularly constraining to women: the other, providing for collectivity, jural order, and social cooperation, organized primarily by men. The domestic/public division as it appeared in any given society was not a necessary, but an 'intelligible', product of the mutual accommodation of human history and human biology; although human societies have differed, all reflected in their organization a characteristic accommodation to the fact that women bear children and lactate and, because of this, find themselves readily designated as 'mothers', who nurture and care for the young.

From these observations, we argued, one could then trace the roots of a pervasive gender inequality: Given an empirical division between domestic and public spheres of activity, a number of factors would interact to enhance both the cultural evaluations and social power and authority available to men. First, it appeared that the psychological effects of being raised by a woman would produce very different emotional dispositions in adults of both sexes; because of the diverging nature of pre-Oedipal ties with *their* mothers, young girls would grow up to be nurturant 'mothers' and boys would achieve an identity that denigrates and rejects women's roles.[4] In cultural terms, a domestic public division corresponded to Ortner's discussion of 'natural' versus 'cultural' valuations, wherein such factors as a women's involvement with young and disorderly children would tend to give here the appearance of less composure, and, therefore, of less 'culture' than men. Finally, sociologically, the views prevalent in our analytical tradition (and at least as old as Plato) that public activities are valued, that authority involves group recognition, and that consciousness and personality are apt to develop most fully through a stance of civic responsibility and an orientation to the collective whole – all argued that men's ability to engage in public activities would give them privileged access to such resources, persons, and symbols as would sustain their claims to precedence, grant them power and disproportionate rewards.

Whatever its difficulties, the account, as it stands, seems suggestive. Certainly, one can find in all human societies some sort of hierarchy of mutually embedded units. Although varying in structure, function, and societal significance, 'domestic groups' which incorporate women and infant children, aspects of child care, commensality, and the preparation of food can always be identified as segments of a larger, overarching social whole. While we know that men are often centrally involved in domestic life and women will, at times, range far beyond it, one can, I think, assert that women, unlike men, lead lives that they themselves construe with reference to responsibilities of recognizably domestic kind.

In short, domestic/public as a general account seems to fit well with some of what we know of sex-linked action systems and of cultural rationales for male prestige, suggesting how 'brute' biological facts have everywhere been shaped by social logics. Reproduction and lactation have provided a functional basis for the definition of a domestic sphere, and sexual asymmetry appears as its intelligible, though non-necessary consequence. Much as, in very simple human groups, the constraints of pregnancy and child care seem easily related to women's exclusion from big-game hunting – and thus from the prestige which comes of bringing in a product requiring extrahousehold distribution[5] – so, in more general terms, domestic obligations and demands appear to help us understand why women everywhere are limited in their access to prestigious male pursuits. Finally, our sense of sexual hierarchy as a deep and primary sort of truth appears compatible with a theory that asserts that mother–child bonds have lasting social and psychological ramifications: sociological constraints appear consistent with psychological orientations that arise through female-dominated patterns of child care.

As should be clear by now, I find much that is compelling in this universalist account: but at the same time I am troubled by some of what appear to be analytical consequences. In probing universal questions, domestic/public is as telling as any explanation yet put forth. Certainly, it seems more than reasonable to assume that marriage and reproduction shape the organization of domestic spheres and link them to more public institutional forms in ways that are particularly consequential for the shape of women's lives. Specifically, if women care for children and child care takes place within the home, and, furthermore, if political life, by definition, extends beyond it, then domestic/public seems to capture in a rough, but telling, set of terms the determinants of women's secondary place in all human societies.

Notes

1. See E. Begler, 'Sex, status and authority in egalitarian society', *American Anthropologist*, vol. 80, no. 3, (1978), pp. 371–88; R. Rohrlich-Leavitt, B. Sykes and E. Weatherford, 'Aboriginal women: male and female anthropological perspectives', in R. Reiter (ed.), *Towards an Anthropology of Women*, New York: Monthly Review Press, 1975, for reasonable attempts to tilt the balance. A juxtaposition of these two articles – which come to radically opposed characterisations of women's lot in Australian aboriginal societies – is informative for what it says about the difficulty of deciding what is, ultimately, an evaluative argument in empirical terms.
2. There is a third approach which situates itself somewhere between the two extremes cited here: that of stressing variation and trying to characterise the factors that make for more or less 'male dominance' or 'female status'. Karen Sacks, 'Engels revisited', in M. Rosaldo and L. Lamphere (eds), *Women, Culture and Society*, Stanford, CA: Stanford University Press, 1974, and Peggy Sanday (in *ibid.*) provide examples, though it is interesting to note that while both forswear universalism, they in fact make use of an analytical separation between domestic and public in organising their variables. M. Whyte, in *The Status of Women in Preindustrial Societies*, Princeton, NJ: Princeton University Press, 1978, argues (most cogently I think) that only by studying variation will we begin to understand any of the processes relevant to the formation or reproduction of sexual inequalities, and therefore that both methodological and political wisdom require us to disaggregate summary characterisations concerning sexual status and their component parts. I agree with him and, further, was pleased to see that his empirical study led towards the recognition that it is virtually impossible to 'rank' societies in terms of women's place. His conclusions agree with mine in that he comes to see more promise in a comparative approach that looks for social structural *configurations* than in one concerned with summary evaluations. Because he is able to show that particular variables mean different things in different social contexts, his results call into question all attempts to talk, cross-culturally, about the components of women's status or their ever-present causes.
3. N. Chodorow, 'Family structure and feminine personality'; S. Ortner, 'Is female to nature as nature is to culture?'; M. Rosaldo, 'Women, culture and society: a theoretical overview', in Rosaldo and Lamphere, *Women, Culture and Society*.
4. N. Chodorow, 'Being and doing', in V. Gornick and B. Moran (eds), *Women in Sexist Society: Studies in power and powerlessness*, New York: Basic Books, 1971.
5. E. Friedl, *Women and Men: An anthropologist's view*, New York: Holt, Rinehart & Winston, 1975, p. 21.

3.7   **Feminism and Anthropology**

Henrietta Moore

The theme of 'difference' is developed here – first in terms of difference between women and among groups of women, and then broadened out to suggest applications of feminist scholarship to a general schematic of sameness and difference that goes beyond discussion of women in isolation from, or relation to, others. This echoes themes raised by Evans-Pritchard in Reading 3.2. Henrietta Moore speculatively maps shifts in practice and perspective as part of her larger project: to explore the possibilities of a feminist anthropology.

Feminist anthropology does not, however, need to be told that women are different. It is the one social science discipline which is actually able to demonstrate from a strongly comparative perspective that what it is to be a woman is culturally and historically variable, and that gender itself is a social construction which always requires specification within any given context. The argument is not, therefore, about whether feminist anthropology acknowledges difference between women, but about what sort of difference it acknowledges. It is true that in the past feminist anthropology was concerned with registering only two forms of difference: gender difference and cultural difference. However [...] feminist anthropology has since developed sustained theoretical positions which specify the interconnections between gender difference, cultural difference, class difference and historical difference. This is most clearly demonstrated in the debates about the penetration of capitalism, the impact of colonial domination and the changing nature of the family. The comparative perspective of feminist anthropology on all these issues, and the way in which it has made gender relations central to any critical understanding of the nature of these processes, provides a challenge to many other areas of social science enquiry. The shift towards class and historical analysis which is evident in feminist anthropology is, of course, part of a wider shift within the discipline of social anthropology itself, but the distinctive contribution of feminist anthropology is the way in which it demonstrates that gender relations are central to any sustained analysis of class and historical relations. It is also worth noting that the debate in feminist anthropology about the changing nature of the family challenges many of the arguments in contemporary sociology and in contemporary feminist debates concerning the relationship between family forms and capitalist relations of production. It also challenges the idea that the teleology of Western development provides a historical model which will be necessarily and beneficially followed elsewhere.

However, it is true that feminist anthropology has only recently turned its attention to studying difference based on race, and to trying to specify how gender, class and race differences intersect in specific historical contexts. This is largely because 'radical' tendencies in social anthropology have generally failed to incorporate arguments about race into their critical revisions of the discipline. For example, during the 1960s and 1970s, a number of anthropologists, both black and white, began to develop a critique of anthropology's colonial past, and suggested that the future of the discipline would have to be one based on a critical awareness of the specific relations of colonial domination, and on an equally critical understanding of the power relations inherent in the ethnographic encounter, that is in the relationship between the anthropologist and the people studied by the anthropologist. Many black anthropologists pointed out that colonial and post-colonial anthropology had been, and continued to be, racist.[1] They based their arguments on the fact that the discipline constructed other cultures as objects of study in such a way that the significant features of the 'other' resided in its relationship to Western culture, and not in terms of its own history and development. It was further argued that anthropology had made no attempt to come to terms with the politics of black–white relations under colonialism, and was continuing to make no attempt to come to terms with these politics in the post-colonial context. The discipline responded to these criticisms in a number of ways, but in the final analysis the blow was a glancing one because anthropology heard these criticisms primarily in terms of a discourse about ethnocentrism and not in terms of a discourse about racism.

However, social anthropology took up the argument about the power relations inherent in the practice of anthropological fieldwork, as well as those concealed in the twin processes of anthropological interpretation and writing. An enormous body of literature exists on these issues, and this 'radical' strand of anthropology has continued into the present. There is currently a lively debate about the way in which anthropology provides written accounts of 'other cultures' and thus monopolizes interpretation and representation. In the process of translating the experience of another in terms of one's own experience, and then representing that experience through the structures of written language, the anthropologist effectively decides to speak *for* others. The current radicalism in anthropology experiments with forms of ethnographic writing in order to try to find some way of letting the people who are being studied speak for themselves. The aim is to produce a 'new' ethnography which would be based on the multiple authorship of anthropological texts, and which would represent both the interlocutory process of fieldwork, and the collaboration between anthropologist and informant on which the practice of social anthropology depends.[2]

A serious critique has yet to be written of this new approach and of its consequences and potentialities for the discipline of social anthropology.[3] However, it is clear that it has strong continuities with the traditional anthropological approach to cultural difference. There has always been a very fruitful tension in the way in which social anthropology handles cultural difference. The tension arises because its maintenance is essential to anthropology's larger comparative project. [...]

The ambiguity surrounding sameness and difference within the overall concept of cultural difference has allowed anthropology to use the idea of ethnocentrism – cultural bias – to sidestep any suggestion that other forms of difference might exist which cannot be subsumed under the heading of cultural difference, and/or that these differences might be irresolvable. The notion that it is possible for anthropologists and for anthropology itself to be ethnocentric is based on the idea that cultures have specific ways of looking at the world, and that they are different one from another. This difference is not, however, absolute, and anthropology acknowledges this by simultaneously emphasizing the similarities and differences between cultures. It is an apparent paradox of anthropological theorizing that the purpose in recognizing ethnocentrism is not to establish absolute cultural differences, but rather to break down the barriers to cultural understanding and to investigate the basis for cultural similarities. This means that, while the critique of ethnocentrism is, in part, about recognizing cultural difference, it is also about trying to overcome or minimize such difference. The critique of ethnocentrism proceeds at a tangent to arguments about racism because the theory of ethnocentrism does not presume the differences it recognizes between cultures to be absolute. Individual anthropologists might argue that differences between cultures are radical, absolute and irreducible, but anthropology as a discourse concerned with interpreting 'other cultures' cannot afford to take such a position. Cultural differences have to be overcome, at least in part, if anthropology is to be successful in translating and interpreting the 'other culture'. The notion of rendering one culture in terms of another, which is at the heart of the anthropological endeavour, can only be achieved by negotiating the inherent tension between sameness and difference, and in so doing it does, of course, run the risk of collapsing differences which should not be collapsed.

Notes

1. See D. Lewis, 'Anthropology and colonialism', *Current Anthropology*, vol. 14, no. 5 (1973), pp. 581–602; B. Magubane, 'A critical look at indices used in the study of social change in colonial Africa', *Current Anthropology*, vol. 12, nos 4–5, (1971), pp. 419–45; M. Owusu, 'Colonial and postcolonial anthropology of Africa: scholarship or sentiment?', in Huizer and Mannheim (eds), *The Politics of Anthropology*, The Hague: Mouton, 1979.
2. See G. Marcus and J. Fischer, *Anthropology and Cultural Critique*, Chicago: University of Chicago Press, 1986; J. Clifford and G. Marcus, *Writing Culture*, Berkeley, CA: University of California Press, 1986; J. Clifford, 'On ethnographic authority', *Representations*, 1 (1983), pp. 118–46.
3. See M. Strathern, 'An awkward relationship: the case of feminism and anthropology', *Signs*, vol. 12, no. 2 (1987), pp. 276–92; 'Out of context: the persuasive fictions of anthropology', *Current Anthropology*, vol. 28, no. 3 (1987), pp. 1–77.

3.8   Childhood (1904–1922)

Akemi Kikumura

This Reading is from the life history of Akemi Kikumura's mother. It is not a simple transcription; over four hundred hours of interviewing (of her mother and other family members in Japan and the United States) lay behind the completed narrative. Most of the book is in her mother's voice, but there are sections where Kikumura provides background or commentary. The interpretation of events and meanings is left largely to the narrator.

One startling thing about this Reading is the contrast between our received ideas about the behaviour of Japanese women and the vivid word portrait of her mother (the anthropologist's grandmother) that Michiko Tanaka gives us.

My parents never disciplined us; they were both busy with business. That's how it was with business people – they thought all they had to do with children was send them to school. From morning until night they would think about making money. People who got a salary were more concerned with disciplining their children than business people, who were more interested in enhancing profits.

My mother was a sharp, shrewd businesswoman. She made the Sato fortune. Not a bit of education ... she couldn't even read or write but she was a genius. She didn't have to use an abacus. She could figure it all up in her head. Wearing black trousers and smoking a long, brown cigarette, Mama ordered everyone around. She was definitely the boss. Businessmen from all around would come to consult with her about their investments. She bought the neighboring stores: the confectionary shop, the blacksmith's, the noodle shop, and a tea shop.

My father was small because Mother was so strong. He was afraid of her; 'How much should I buy? How much should I sell it for?' he would ask. My papa was like a *hotoke* [Buddha]. He never cheated anyone and even if he lost money, he never complained. He was the only one among his brothers who was successful and he shared his good fortune liberally. If his eldest brother went bankrupt, Papa would bankroll him; if his younger brother wanted to open a shop, he would lend him the capital only to find him vacationing in the country. He cried a lot over them.

Papa was a frugal man when it came to himself – never drank or smoked, never spend money to eat out. He would have a lunch made for him as he went to the countryside to collect money from his customers. He delivered sugar to them and collected the money after they sold it. Before, that's how it was. You didn't collect until the merchants sold your products.

During the winter we had twelve people helping in the store. We sold various kinds of sugar, beans, honey, flour, and made *yokan* [sweet jelly of beans], and grape and strawberry syrup. We would sell these syrups as far away as Shimonoseki, well beyond Hiroshima city. We advertised that it was healthy for your body because it didn't contain alcohol.

My mother ... what a *yarite* [a person of ability]! She learned how to make these syrups in Osaka. Her eldest sister lived in Osaka and made syrup so she took the recipe and learned how to make it herself. Our young workers would try to steal the recipe from her but she guarded it with a careful eye. We manufactured the syrup in the back of our workshop, which had a lot of space.

Our place was huge. It was always stocked full with rice that people brought to us. [...] My Papa's youngest sister lived with us. She would get married and keep returning home. The marriages never lasted too long. With the last one she decided never to marry again and she came to live with us. She boiled the rice, made the dinners, and did all the household chores. I would work in the store after school but my mother didn't let me help too often because I gave everything to the customers. It is my nature to be giving. Papa would get mad at me and send me off to Iwakuni and Kuba to collect money from our customers. Since I was young, people gave me extra orders. I went as far as Shimonoseki.

I fought with my sisters and brothers over small matters. But when there are many relatives you do not get along. There were eight of us: three younger brothers and four sisters. I was third from the eldest, I was closest to Haruko, the sister right above me.

Summers I would go with my girlfriends to swim in the river and catch locusts. We often went to Tenji mountain to collect bracken, but the climb was the joy of it: We first crossed a bridge that was only one boad wide, then passed a crematory where they burned the dead bodies and stopped to look at the coffins that were black from human oils.

Most of the time was spent going to school. Since my mother never went to school herself, her only concern was that we get an education. My parents thought that as long as they sent their children to school, they would get smart. I went to a Buddhist school. That's why from when I was young, l was deeply steeped in religion. The schoolmaster was a priest named Nagai Ryujin.

I attended six years of elementary school: two years of *Koto sho gakkō* [middle advanced elementary school], and four years of girls' middle school. We studied English and Japanese, mathematics, literature, writing, and religion. They taught us things of obedience – to obey a person's order. They also taught us womanly things: Women do not stand above men and flaunt their authority; in the house the man is the most important person; a woman must raise her husband up in front of others. But the most important thing that they taught us was religion, for a person who has religion is the happiest. On January 15 through January 16, the day that Shinran Shonin died, I would go by myself to listen to sermons from morning until night.

In those days one could become a teacher after graduating from girls' middle school. Very few were privileged enough to go. I had three best friends: Miyamoto-san, whose father owned a cement factory; Mori-san, whose father owned a prefectural hospital in a quiet place called Kako Machi; and Miyakawa-san. She was from a poor family. She would say to me, 'I talk but you don't understand my stories. All you think about is playing, but I'm thinking of making money when I get out of school.'

Me? She was right ... *tsumaran* [what a waste]! I didn't go to study. I just went to play. She used to say how lucky we were because we didn't have to worry about money. I understand her feelings now, and I often think of what she said to me. I never knew poverty when I was young. It was only after coming to America that I experienced suffering and I began to understand life.

3.9   Jewish comes up in you from the roots
Barbara Myerhoff

Barbara Myerhoff (1935–85) advocated a reflexive and humanistic anthropology. She explored the use of personal narrative and life history in her innovative and distinctive ethnographies and film.

Here she develops a multivocal ethnography. We learn about the people she was studying, a group of elderly Jews who based a sense of community around their common use of a day centre in Venice, California. The Reading opens as she recalls her own grandmother, Sofie Mann, and shares her memories with both the reader and her informants (the women in Basha's living-room). Sofie Mann's voice combines with the anthropologist's ear and eye, as well as with the memories, reactions and reflections, to create a complex descriptive whole.

As a child, I was a notoriously bad eater, and Sofie took this on as a personal challenge. For each bite I took, she gave us entry into one of the houses, and told a different story each day, about the people who lived inside.

These accounts informed my entire life, more than any teacher or book or country I later encountered. Sofie Mann, without her maiden name, without her own birthday, without education, undifferentiated from the stream of her people, Sofie knew and taught me that everyone had some story, every house held a life that could be penetrated and known, if one took the trouble. Stories told to oneself or others could transform the world. Waiting for others to tell their stories, even helping them do so, meant no one could be regarded as completely dull, no place people lived in was without some hope of redemption, achieved by paying attention. The stories carried her through the monotony of her work, the pain of perpetual fatigue, through loneliness, eventually through blindness and crippling. And all this prepared the way for my work at the Center.

What Sofie knew so did some of the Center people. Perhaps her storytelling was part of shtetl kitchen life. Perhaps that is why her maiden name was lost, why no one even called her Sofie – she was 'Ma', or 'bobbe', or to my grandfather, 'Mrs Mann'.

The women in Basha's room listened to my description with great interest. 'You could say I'm not one hundred percent objective,' said Sonya, 'but I am of the opinion that maybe things get better for old women and not so much for the men.' The others generally agreed, and I did, too. In nearly all circumstances, it seemed to me, the Center women as a group were the more capable, active, and authoritative people. There were a number of remarkable and outstanding individual men, but it was clear that their personal characteristics accounted for their distinctiveness. Collectively, most of the men were quieter, vaguer, more sad than angry compared with the vitality and assertiveness of the women. The women effectively ran the Center on a day-by-day basis, and they dominated the community. They seemed, as well, to manage their private lives more successfully.

The scarcity of men could have given them advantage or disadvantage in terms of the leadership in the Center. Their relative rarity might have brought them into prominence. They might have banded together to give each strength and support in dealing with those of their problems not shared by the women. But this was not the case. Instead, the men were isolated from each other and overwhelmed by the women, before whose greater numbers and more intense vitality they paled.

All the old people, men and women, occasionally gave lip service to the notion that men in general were more important than women, but behaviour suggested otherwise. Only two regular Center events brought out the alleged male superiority and female subservience: the Sabbath ceremony and the serving of food. In these areas, the women and men fell into the stereotyped sexual roles. [...]

The roots of the situation lay in the common history of the Center people and their childhood experience with the roles of men and women in the shtetl. Patriarchy was a dominant force in the shtetl, replicated in family and community with perfect consistency. Religion was the concern of everyone, but the specific responsibility and privilege of the men. Women were extremely important, absolutely essential as facilitators of the men's activities. The woman was to bear and socialize the children and provide a harmonious home, conducive to the men's study and prayer. The woman had the exacting job of carrying out the dietary regulations according to the men's instructions and interpretations. Whenever possible, women worked outside the home, enabling their brothers, sons, and husband to spend more time in religious study, providing the support system, the mundane base for the primary undertakings of the men.[1]

In her own right the woman was nothing. Her prayers were not necessary except for her own satisfaction. They did not benefit the community, therefore it was considered a waste to educate women. (Indeed, Rabbi Eliezer said, 'Whoever teaches his daughter Torah teaches her obscenity.'[2]) But to the extent that the woman fulfilled her supportive role, she could achieve great esteem. Folklore extolls a woman who sold her hair for the money that freed her husband for study. Another tale tells of a woman who sold her soul for her husband (but this story may be apocryphal, since there was debate as to whether women actually had souls).[3]

The shtetl woman realized herself through others – children, men, support of the needy. She had only three positive *mitzvoth* to keep (she observed the same negative commandments as men) and their substance illuminates the traditional role of woman's nature and place: She must purify herself in a ritual bath after menstruation so as not to pollute her husband and her community [*mikva*]; she brought her household a taste of Paradise by lighting the Sabbath candles in the home on Friday evenings [*bentching licht*]; she must burn a bit of dough when baking bread ['taking *challah*'], representing a sacrifice to God made in the household oven ever since the destruction of the Temple.[4]

All these commandments pertain to the woman's biology and her position as homemaker and keeper. But it would be a mistake to assume that this ideal picture of the woman's life in the shtetl exhausted her possibilities. In all societies, women and men transcend, change, distort, enlarge, and otherwise make habitable restrictive roles, and as we shall see, the shtetl woman embellished an alternative sex role that was later parlayed into a flexible adaptation, highly suited to the exigencies of old age.

The ideal social role of the woman in the shtetl – performing her household and religious duties in a quiet and self-effacing manner – specified not only her duties but the manner in which they were to be performed, that is, the kind of person she was supposed to be: submissive, docile, decorous, retiring, modest, patient, and utterly devoted to her family, without ambitions or aspirations of her own.[5] In fact, an additional, contrasting sexual stereotype was developed by the women, almost an underground role, generated not by design but out of the practical necessities of her work outside the home, and particularly in the market-place. This role, less overt and not formally vaunted, was nevertheless accepted and admired. It was a *contingent* sexual role, arising in response to and maintained because of its situational appropriateness; within it lay a set of possibilities mined by the Center women in later life.

What were the attributes of this role? First, the shtetl housewife was required by circumstance to be a pragmatist. She needed business acumen and great energy. She needed to know how to deal with government officials and peasants, and as a result often had a superior command over the vernacular languages – usually Russian and Polish – than her pious male relatives. She was the intermediary, often more than the men; she navigated the conflicting, dangerous waters between home, shtetl, and the outside world. She had to manage the household, earn the budget money, regular time, funds, and attention within the family, make countless practical decisions, allocate labor, and organize and integrate family schedules, articulating the familial with the public demands.

In addition to her activities in marketplace and household, the shtetl woman devoted herself with intensity to community work. She attended to the sick, shared home duties and child care with other needy women, collected money for brides without dowries, fed visitors and strangers, raised money for orphans, made clothes for Palestinian refugees, and worked on behalf of poor and needy Jews all over the world.

It was clear that the baleboosteh needed to be purposive, to be robust, intrepid, and efficient. Jokes and stories about this stereotype abound, deriding her as fishwife and shrew. No doubt some of these women were domineering, shrill, and implacable. But this was forgiven, since it was felt that woman's nature inclined her to great vigor and volatility. Naturally she was seen as given to outbursts of emotion and was expected to be more expressive than her male counterpart. She was, after all, closer to natural forces, while men were regarded as more innately spiritual.[6] And because women were viewed as weak and imperfect, their complaints were more acceptable. A woman was fortunate in having at hand explanations for her failures not available to men: After all, what could be expected from a poor, uneducated, sinful woman?

Notes

1. C. Baum, 'What made Yetta Work: the economic role of Eastern European Jewish women in the family', *Response: A Contemporary Jewish Review*, vol. 8, no. 18 (1973), pp. 32–8.
2. Cited by P. Hyman, 'The other half: women in the Jewish Tradition', *Response: A Contemporary Jewish Review*, vol. 8, no. 18 (1973), pp. 67–76.
3. M. Zborowski and E. Herzog, *Life is with People: The culture of the shtetl*, New York: Schocken Books, 1952.
4. P. Hyman, 'The other half'; S. Berman, 'The status of women in Halakhic Judaism', in E. Koltun (ed.), *The Jewish Woman: New perspectives*, New York: Schocken Books, 1976; R. Adler, '*Tumah* and *Taharah*: ends and beginnings'; and 'The Jew who wasn't there: Halacha and the Jewish woman', *Response: A Contemporary Jewish Review*, vol. 8, no. 18 (1973).
5. James Olney, *Metaphors of the Self: The meaning of antobiography*, Princeton, NJ.: Princeton University Press.
6. James Fernandez, 'The mission of metaphor in expressive culture', *Current Anthropology*, vol. 15, no. 2 (1974), pp. 119–33.

3.10 The Romance of Resistance: tracing transformations of power through Bedouin women
Lila Abu-Lughod

The poetry of Bedouin women led Lila Abu-Lughod to an interest in the theory of power and the literature on resistance. Using expressive defiant behaviours, collusions, storytelling events, jokes, songs and the poetic ghinnawas ('little songs') observed during ten years of fieldwork among the Awlad 'Ali Bedouin of Egypt, Abu-Lughod moved beyond the conventional analyses of power.

In this Reading she suggests using the manifestations of resistance to illuminate power structures, but warns against polarising and romanticising subversion. Close observation shows that resistance to and support of prevailing hierarchies are often simultaneous activities.

What are the implications of studies of resistance for our theories of power?

At the heart of this widespread concern with unconventional forms of non-collective, or at least non-organized, resistance is, I would argue, a growing disaffection with previous ways we have understood power, and the most interesting aspect of this work on resistance is a greater sense of the complexity of the nature and forms of domination. For example, work on resistance influenced by Bourdieu and Gramsci recognizes and theorizes the importance of ideological practice in power and resistance and works to undermine distinctions between symbolic and instrumental, behavioral and ideological and cultural, social, and political processes.

Despite the considerable theoretical sophistication of many studies of resistance, within and outside of anthropology, and their contribution to the widening of our definition of the political, it seems to me that because they are ultimately more concerned with finding resistors and explaining resistance than with examining power, they do not explore as fully as they could the implications of the forms of resistance they locate. In some of my own earlier work, like theirs, there is perhaps a tendency to romanticize resistance, to read all forms of resistance as signs of the ineffectiveness of systems of power and of the resilience and creativity of the human spirit in its refusal to be dominated. By reading resistance in this way, we collapse distinctions between forms of resistance and foreclose certain questions about the workings of power.

I want to argue here for a small shift in perspective in the way we look at resistance – a small shift that will have serious analytical consequences. I suggest that we should use resistance as a *diagnostic* of power. In this, I am taking a cue from Foucault, whose theories, or as he prefers to put it, analytics, of power and resistance, although complex and not always consistent, are at least worth exploring. One of his central propositions, advanced in his most sustained discussion of power, in the first volume of *The History of Sexuality*, is the controversial assertion, 'where there is power, there is resistance'. Whatever else this assertion implies, certainly Foucault is using this hyperbole to force us to question our understanding of power as always and essentially repressive. As part of his project of deromanticizing the liberatory discourse of our twentieth-century so-called sexual revolution, he is interested in showing how power is something that works not just negatively, by denying, restricting, prohibiting, or repressing, but also is something productive (of forms of pleasure, systems of knowledge, goods, and discourses). He adds what some have viewed as a pessimistic point about resistance by completing the sentence just quoted as follows: 'Where there is power, there is resistance and yet, or rather consequently, this resistance is never in a position of exteriority in relation to power.'

Further Reading

Abu-Lughod, L. (1986), *Veiled Sentiments: Honor and poetry in a Bedouin Society*, Berkeley, CA: University of California Press.

Altorki, S. and Fawzi El-Solh, C. (1988), *Arab Women in the Field: Studying your own society*, New York: Syracuse University Press.

Ardener, E. (1971), 'Belief and the problem of women', in J. S. La Fontaine (ed.), *The Interpretation of Ritual*, London: Tavistock.

Ardener, S. (1977), *Perceiving Women*, London: Dent.

Asad, T. (1973), *Anthropology and the Colonial Encounter*, London: Ithaca Press.

Bachofen, J. (1967), *Myth, Religion and Mother Right: Selected writings*, transl. R. Mannheim, Princeton, NJ: Bollingen Press.

Bourguignon, E. (1986), *A World of Women*, New York: Praeger.

Briggs, J. (1970), *Never in Anger: Portrait of an Eskimo family*, London: Harvard University Press.

Douglas, M. (1977), *The Lele of the Kasai*, London: International African Institute.

Evans-Pritchard, E. (1965), *The Position of Women in Primitive Society and Other Essays in Social Anthropology*, London: Faber & Faber.

Friedl, E. (1975), *Women and Men: An anthropologist's view*, New York: Holt, Rinehart & Winston.

Gacs, U., Khan, A. *et al.* (1989), *Women Anthropologists: Selected bibliographies*, Champaign, IL: University of Illinois Press.

Gewertz, D. (1988), *Myths of Matriarchy Reconsidered*, Oceania Monograph 33, University of Sydney.

Gmelch, S. (1986), *Nan: The life of an Irish travelling woman*, London: Souvenir Press.

Golde, P. (1970), *Women in the Field: Anthropological experiences*, Chicago: Aldine.

Goodale, J. (1971), *Tiwi Wives*, Seattle: University of Washington Press.

Kaberry, P. (1939), *Aboriginal Women: Sacred and profane*, London: Routledge.

Loizos, P. and Papataxiarchis, E. (1991), *Contested Identities: Gender and kinship in modern Greece*, Princeton, NJ: Princeton University Press.

Marcus, G. and Fischer, M. (1986), *Anthropology as Cultural Critique*, Chicago and London: University of Chicago Press.

Mead, M. (1935), *Sex and Temperament in Three Primitive Societies*, New York: William Morrow.

Morgan, E. (1972), *The Descent of Woman*, London: Souvenir Press.

Morgan, L. (1877), *Ancient Society*, New York: Holt.

The Personal Narratives Group (1989), *Interpreting Women's Lives: Feminist theory and personal narratives*, Indianapolis: Indiana University Press.

Powers, M. (1986), *Oglala Women: Myth, ritual and reality*, Chicago: University of Chicago Press.

Sanday, P. and Goodenough, R. (1990), *Beyond the Second Sex: New directions in the anthropology of gender*, Pittsburgh, PA: University of Pennsylvania Press.

Sanjek, R. (1990), *Fieldnotes: The makings of ethnography*, Ithaca, NY: Cornell University Press.

Shostak, M. (1981), *Nisa: The life and words of a Kung woman*, Cambridge, MA: Harvard University Press.

Whitehead, T. and Conaway, M. (1986), *Self, Sex and Gender in Cross Cultural Fieldwork*, Champaign, IL: University of Illinois Press.

Wolf, M. (1972), *Women and the Family in Rural Taiwan*, Stanford, CA: Stanford University Press.

4 | HISTORICAL PERSPECTIVES ON WOMEN'S LIVES

Edited and Introduced by Deirdre Beddoe

INTRODUCTION

It is no easy task to make a selection of extracts from the ever-growing body of writings on women's history without widely exceeding the space allotted to me. I have had to make some stark choices. The first of these was my decision to limit the extracts to British women's history. Secondly, I had to choose whether to select from primary or secondary sources. Primary sources are letters, diaries, reports, paintings, photographs or anything else which emanates from the period under study; secondary sources, on the other hand, are accounts, usually written much later, by historians who have themselves drawn upon the primary material. In order to fit in with the rest of this reader, and to avoid the lengthy contextualisation which primary sources demand, I have opted, for the most part, to reprint secondary sources. The exception is Reading 4.6, a contemporary account of the daily routine of working-class wives in the 1930s. Other Readings – notably 4.1, 4.5 and 4.8 – quote generously from original sources and speak directly to us from the past. Finally, an obvious way for the historian to impose limits upon herself is to select a minuscule period of time – perhaps just a single year – from the past. This I rejected, as I cannot believe that readers want to know a great deal about a little. The indulgence of this selection is that it covers a wide time span – from the eighteenth century to the mid twentieth – and embraces a wide range of topics – home life, employment, education, politics and sexuality.

The main task facing feminist historians is the rescue and recovery of a women's history which, without our efforts, would be lost. Generations of male historians have ignored women's past, or certainly not considered it to be the stuff of History. Women's history is a product of the women's movement. The first wave of the movement in Britain produced in its wake some superb historical works by such historians as Ivy Pinchbeck, Alice Clarke and Eileen Power. Thereafter the neglect of women's history is a reflection of the decline of feminism. We had to wait for a new women's movement, a second wave in the 1970s, for a revival of women's history. Sheila Rowbotham set the ball rolling again with her aptly named book *Hidden from History*.

Feminist theories have influenced and informed women's history, just as they have other areas of women's studies, and these Readings demonstrate a wide range of perspectives. Sheila Rowbotham and Catherine Hall, for example, present a Marxist feminist viewpoint, while Sheila Jeffreys writes from a radical feminist position. Scholars engaged in researching and writing women's history have given a great deal of thought to – and reached differing conclusions on – what the term itself means. Is it history written by women? Is it history about women? Or is it history written from a feminist viewpoint? Another important question is whether women's history should be written by women about women and for women, or whether it should concentrate on transforming and enriching mainstream history, which has traditionally had so little regard for women. Such issues have long been debated. One contemporary discussion asks whether it is possible to write a history of women or whether we should be considering how the category women has been historically constructed (see Section 1 above, Readings 1.11–1.14). Another related debate is whether feminist historians should focus primarily on one gender – women – or concentrate on relations between the sexes: the two leading British women's history journals, *Women's History Review* and *Gender and History*, reflect these differing theoretical tendencies. But when all is said and done, the rescuing of women's past must remain our primary concern: we owe that not only to the women who have gone before us but to future generations of feminist historians.

These Readings, many from classic texts, provide almost a mini-history of British women from the eighteenth to the mid twentieth century. The apparently diverse topics are all interrelated parts of a unified whole, which comprises women's past.

Ivy Pinchbeck's classic account (Reading 4.1) of the eighteenth-century rural housewife paints a clear picture of her productive role – managing a very large household and taking responsibility for the dairy and poultry. The Industrial Revolution of the late eighteenth and early nineteenth centuries separated work from home, and Catherine Hall shows in Reading 4.2 how middle-class women in one urban centre, Birmingham, were pushed out of the productive process and into the private sphere of the home. Such detailed, local research is essential if we are to give historical substance to the theory of the domestic ideology – which, in turn, must be located historically. Working-class women, on the other hand, were pushed into the production process: they were wanted as cheap labour in factories, mines and workshops (Reading 4.3). It is a contradiction of capitalism, writes Sheila Rowbotham, that women were required both as workers and as the bearers of the next generation of labour. By the 1840s the ruling class discovered the 'problem' of women workers and sought to restore factory wives and pit-women to hearth and home (Reading 4.4). The education provided for working-class girls in the state system, which came into operation in the 1870s, had the primary aim of socialising girls into domesticity: it prepared them for domestic service and for motherhood (Reading 4.5). Reading 4.6, the

only wholly primary source reproduced here, charts the daily routine of
working-class wives in the 1930s: keeping damp and run-down houses – which
lacked even basic amenities – clean, and feeding families on low incomes, was
a demoralising task. Childbearing was another burden on women in a state
which was more concerned with reproducing a healthy workforce and fit armies
than with the health of mothers. In the 1930s maternal mortality rates
deteriorated rather than improved (Reading 4.7). Wars brought temporary
change to women's limited roles as wives and mothers. Women contributed
handsomely to the war effort in the First World War (1914–18) but were
dismissed when it ended and expected to return to the home. A barrage of
propaganda glorified the role of the housewife, and the only fit occupation for
working-class women was deemed to be domestic service. Reading 4.8 shows
the operation of a state policy of compulsory domestic service.

Policies and ideologies *vis-à-vis* women's roles in the home and in the labour
market are mutually reinforcing. Readings 4.9 and 4.10 take us into another area
– politics. In the mid nineteenth century women began to demand the vote. The
history of the suffrage campaign is long and complex, but one key question must
be addressed. After some sixty years of struggle, women over thirty won the
vote in 1918 and women over twenty-one in 1928. But which tactics were more
effective in bringing victory? Was it the constitutional methods of the National
Union of Women's Suffrage Societies, as Ray Strachey would have us believe
in Reading 4.9? Or was it the fear of a revival of militant tactics which made the
government capitulate, as Sylvia Pankhurst argues in Reading 4.10? Both writers
were participants in as well as historians of these events, and their works
straddle the primary/secondary sources divide.

Finally, this Section reflects the emphasis placed in women's history on
married women and on heterosexuality. But not all women married, by any
means, and single women faced different problems. I am also anxious that
lesbian women should be represented. Although the sources for a history of this
hidden group are often hard to locate, it is vitally important. I therefore leave
the last work with Sheila Jeffreys (Reading 4.11), who shows how women's
passionate friendships of earlier ages were reclassified in the twentieth century
as deviant behaviour.

4.1   Women Workers and the Industrial Revolution 1750–1850
Ivy Pinchbeck

*Ivy Pinchbeck, who belonged to the first wave of historians of women, presents us with
a clear picture of the productive role of the housewife in eighteenth-century rural
England.*

Farmers' wives

In the eighteenth century it was still customary for the wife of a large farmer to take an active share in the management of the household, although there were some households in which the mistress had already handed over the main responsibilities to a servant.[1] In such cases a wealthy farmer's wife often took a keen interest in the purely agricultural side. Marshall, in 1782, mentions a large occupier of £17,000 a year, who was able to manage without a steward or bailiff because he had the assistance of 'his lady, who keeps his accounts',[2] and two farmers who went to investigate Coke's agricultural experiments at Holkham, after riding round the estate with Mrs Coke, expressed their 'agreeable surprise in meeting with an amiable lady in high life, so well acquainted with agriculture, and so condescending as to attend two farmers out of Kent and Sussex a whole morning to show them some Norfolk farmeries'.[3]

In the days when almost all the food and a good deal of the clothing were provided at home, the household management of a large farm was no light undertaking. In addition to the purely domestic side, the farmer's wife had also charge of the dairy – including the care of calves and pigs – the poultry, the garden and orchard and all financial dealings connected with them. The butcher, the higler and the cheese factor who came to make purchases at the farm, usually transacted their business with the mistress. In his *Survey of Devonshire*, Vancouver describes a custom which was not confined to that county, by which the wife undertook to support the household out of the profits of her own domain:

> It is a common practice among them on marriage, to give to their wives what is called pin-money; this consists of poultry, pigs, and the whole produce of the dairy; with which supply the wife is expected to clothe and (exclusive of bread, corn, and other vegetables) support the whole household; and here it is but common justice to say, that the industry and attention to business of the farmer's wives and daughters, with the neatness displayed in all their market ware at Exeter, and in other large towns, are subjects deserving the highest praise.[4]

An ability to deal in business matters was as necessary to the farmer's wife in her sphere, as it was for her husband in his, and the well-being of the family depended not a little on the business capacity of the mistress.

Apart from the supervision of the dairy and stock the domestic management of a farm called for a good deal of organisation. A large farm in Oxfordshire in 1768 had living in it seventeen men, five boys and five maids in addition to the family;[5] a household of twenty was common, while day labourers also were sometimes given partial board. On farms such as these one maid was necessary for the brewing and baking alone, another was required for the laundry and the rest divided among them the work of the dairy, milking and the care of stock, household work and winter provisioning. In the evenings all were expected to assist in the sewing and in spinning flax and wool, for every farm provided its own yarn for linen, blankets and a certain amount of clothing for the members of the family. Everything came under the supervision of the mistress and not a little of her time was taken up in training the maids in their respective duties.

On a smaller holding, the farmer's wife, having less assistance, was more actively engaged in manual work. On many farms the entire labour was performed by the members of the family alone, and where this was the case a good deal of outdoor work fell to the lot of the women. A North Country farmer writing in *The Farmer's Magazine* in 1801 speaks of the small occupier's 'necessity of turning out his wife or daughter to drive the plough in the depth of winter'. The wife was obliged to undergo the drudgery of outdoor work as 'upon such farms there is little occasion for day-labourers, except an old woman or two which they employ in harvest'.[6]

In other respects their work was similar to that on a large farm, and since raising the annual rent was a matter which required the utmost industry among smallholders, the greatest care was taken to make the most out of their dairies, poultry and eggs. On a large farm dairy produce was often sold to the badger or higler who collected eggs, poultry and butter at the farm; on a smaller holding the wife or daughter of the farmer was accustomed to take her produce to the market where she retailed it herself. Many housewives and dairy maids rode into market on horseback, their butter, poultry and eggs carefully packed in panniers; and at the Norwich market, which Marshall believed in 1789 to be 'beyond comparison the first in the kingdom', the women also supplied veal, pork and lamb.[7] Norfolk was already celebrated for its turkeys and the skill of the housewives of the county in breeding and rearing poultry: 'Poultry of every species are sold, in the markets, ready picked and skewered fit for the spit; and are in general, so well fatted, and dressed up in such neatness and delicacy, as shew the Norfolk housewives to be mistresses in the art of managing poultry.'[8] The farmers' wives of Sussex bred 'the fattest geese and largest capons' for the London market, and from Suffolk came every year the great droves of turkeys; of Stratford-on-Stour it was said 'that 300 droves of turkies have passed in one season over its bridge towards London, computed at 500 in a drove one with another'.[9]

Notes

1. 'A woman servant that taketh charge of Brewing, Baking, Kitching, Milk-house, or Maulting, that is hired with a Gentleman or a rich Yeoman (whose wife doth not take the pains and charge upon her) shall not take wages by the year with meat and drink above 40 shillings.' *Justices Assessments of 1703.* Thorold Rogers, *History of Agriculture and Prices*, vol. vii, p. 610.
2. Marshall, *Rural Economy of Norfolk*, vol. ii, p. 201.
3. *Annals of Agriculture*, vol. xx, p. 251.
4. Vancouver's *Devonshire* (1808), p. 112.

5. Young, *Northern Tour* (1771 edn), vol. iii, p. 340.
6. *The Farmer's Magazine*, vol. ii, pp. 310, 308.
7. Marshall, *Rural Economy of Norfolk*, vol. i, pp. 195–6.
8. *Ibid.*, p. 375.
9. Postlethwayt's *Dictionary* (1775): Articles on Suffolk and Surrey.

4.2 Gender Divisions and Class Formations in the Birmingham Middle Class, 1780–1850

Catherine Hall

Catherine Hall's work shows how, in the mid nineteenth century middle-class women were pushed out of production, be it on farms or in family businesses. Here she concentrates on this process with regard to businesswomen in one city: Birmingham.

Meanwhile the kinds of businesses which women were running seem to have altered. An examination of the Birmingham Directories reveals women working in surprising trades throughout our period; only in very small numbers it is true, but still they survived. To take a few examples, there were women brass founders at the end of the eighteenth century, a bedscrew maker and a coach maker in 1803, several women engaged in aspects of the gun trade in 1812, an engine cutter and an iron and steel merchant in 1821, plumbers and painters in the 1830s and 1840s, burnishers and brushmakers in the 1850s. There are certain trades in which women never seem to appear as the owners – awl-blade making, for example, or iron founders. But although the percentage of women to men engaged in business goes up rather than down in the early nineteenth century, at least according to the evidence provided by the directories, there seems to be a significant shift towards the concentration of women in certain trades. In the late eighteenth century women were well represented among the button makers, and button making was one of the staple trades of Birmingham. Sketchley's Directory of 1767 described the button trade as:

> very extensive and distinguished under the following heads viz. Gilt, Plated, Silvered, Lacquered, and Pinchback, the beautiful new Manufactures Platina, Inlaid, Glass, Horn, Ivory, and Pearl: Metal Buttons such as Bath, Hard and Soft White etc. there is likewise made Link Buttons in most of the above Metals, as well as of Paste, Stones, etc. in short the vast variety of sorts in both Branches is really amazing, and we may with Truth aver that this is the cheapest Market in the world for these Articles.

But by the 1830s and 1840s women were concentrated in what became traditional women's trades – in dressmaking, millinery, school teaching and the retail trade. Women were no longer engaged as employers in the central productive trades of the town in any number, they were marginalised into the servicing sector, though, of course, it should be clear that many working-class women continued as employers in, for example, the metal trades. G. J. Holyoake described in his own autobiography his mother's disappearance from business:

> In those days horn buttons were made in Birmingham, and my mother had a workshop attached to the house, in which she conducted a business herself, employing several hands. She had the business before her marriage. She received the orders; made the purchases of materials; superintended the making of the goods; made out the accounts; and received the money; besides taking care of her growing family. There were no 'Rights of Women' thought of in her day, but she was an entirely self-acting, managing mistress. ... The button business died out while I was young, and from the remarks which came from merchants, I learned that my mother was the last maker of that kind of button in the town.[1]

It is worth remarking that his mother became a keen attender at Carr's Lane Chapel where, as we shall see, John Angell James taught the domestic subordination of women from the pulpit for fifty years. Women increasingly did not have the necessary forms of knowledge and expertise to enter many businesses – jobs were being redefined as managerial or skilled and, therefore, masculine. For instance, as Michael Ignatieff points out, women gaolers were actually excluded by statute as not fitted to the job.[2] Women could manage the family and the household, but not the workshop or the factory. Furthermore, a whole series of new financial institutions were being developed in this period which also specifically excluded women – trusts, for example, and forms of partnership. Ivy Pinchbeck has argued that women were gradually being excluded from a sphere which they had previously occupied; it appears that in addition they were never allowed into a whole new economic sphere.

The separation of work from home obviously played an important part in this process of demarcation between men's work and women's work. That separation has often been thought of as the material basis of separate spheres. But once the enormous variety of types of middle-class housing has been established, that argument can no longer be maintained. Separating work from home was one way of concretising the division between the sexes, but since it was often not possible it cannot be seen as the crucial factor in establishing domesticity. The many other ways in which the division was established have to be remembered. For doctors there could often be no separation, whereas for ironfounders the separation was almost automatic. In some trades the question of scale was vital – in the Birmingham metal trades some workshops had houses attached, but in many cases they were separated. Sometimes there is a house attached and yet the chief employee lived there rather than the family. James Luckcock, for example, a Birmingham jeweller, when he was just starting up in business on his own, not only lived next to his workshop but also used the labour of his wife and children. As soon as he could afford it he moved out, moved his manager into the house, and his wife stopped working in the business.[3] Shopkeepers moving out from their premises and establishing a separate homes for their families obviously lost the assistance of wives and daughters in the shop – Mrs Cadbury and her daughters all helped in the shop until the family moved out to Edgbaston.

Notes

1. G. S. Holyoake, *Sixty Years of an Agitator's Life*, London, 1900.
2. M. Ignatieff, *A Just Measure of Pain: The penitentiary in the Industrial Revolution 1750–1850*, London, 1978.
3. J. Luckcock, *Sequel to Memoirs in Humble Life*, Birmingham, 1825.

4.3   Hidden from History: three hundred years of women's oppression and the fight against it

Sheila Rowbotham

Working-class women, on the other hand, were pushed into the process of production by the new capitalist industries. This was not without its contradictions, as Sheila Rowbotham points out in her pioneering work of second-wave feminist history.

Capitalism broke down the old forms of social relations both at work and between men and women in the family. The consequences were, however, different for the working class than for the middle class. Middle-class women found themselves cut off from production and economically dependent on a man: working-class women were forced into the factory and became wage-labourers.

So although patriarchal authority was actually strengthened among the dominant class, the economic basis of the working-class man's ownership of his woman was undermined by the wages the woman could earn outside the home. The concern of the middle-class rescuers to protect working-class women frequently ignored the economic and sexual realities of working-class life. The rescuers persisted in seeing the values of their own class as universal and in seeing the state – their state which enforced their class interests – as a neutral body. The working class very often saw the factory inspectors, the housing investigators as alien interfering intruders who would reform their livelihoods away. Also the rebellion against patriarchal authority evoked little immediate response among working-class women, for here capitalist development was undermining such authority in brutal and inhuman ways and many working-class men and women resided what they felt to be a violation of natural bonds between men and women, parents and children.

One of the frequent complaints in the early stages of the Industrial Revolution was that although women and children could find work, the men could not. This had very direct effects on authority in the family. But as Engels points out in his *Conditions of the Working Class in England* of 1844, wage-labour in early-nineteenth-century capitalism brought not freedom, but a reversal of the economic position of men and women. They were still tied not by affection but by economic necessity. Because other social changes had not accompanied the alteration of economic power in the family, the man felt degraded and humiliated and the woman went out to work for less pay, and consequently greater profit for the employer. For although the factory system began to undermine the economic and social hold of the working-class man over the women in his family, patriarchal authority continued in society as a whole. The ruling class could benefit from the assumption − which was still strong − that women belonged to men. Thus the unctuous Ure wrote *The Philosophy of Manufactures*, delighting in the prospect of workers becoming appendages to machines and justifying women's low wages:

> Factory females have in general much lower wages than males, and they have been pitied on this account with perhaps an injudicious sympathy, since the low price of their labour here tends to make household duties their most profitable as well as agreeable occupation and prevents them from being tempted by the mill to abandon the care of their offspring at home. Thus Providence effects its purpose with a wisdom and efficacy which should repress the short-sighted presumption of human devices.[1]

Capitalism in dividing work from home had produced a contradictory need. There was a new demand for female labour in the factory, but somehow children had to be cared for, and families fed. Women were not able to turn this contradiction to their advantage. Instead they were forced to labour both at home and at work.

Notes

1. A. Ure, *The Philosophy of Manufactures*, quoted in W. Neff, *Victorian Working Women*, London, 1966, p. 29.

4.4 By the Sweat of their Brow: women workers at Victorian coal mines

Angela V. John

By the 1830s there was much agitation to get women out of 'unwomanly' work, and in 1842 they were forbidden to work below ground in the mines. However, women continued to perform hard and heavy labour on the surface.

Although by the end of the century the majority of British pit women worked at screening or sorting coal, there were other jobs which they continued to do. Wales had its 'tip girls' who helped to remove cinders from furnaces, unload at the tips and chip bits of iron ore with small picks.[1] Just as the term 'pit brow lass' became extended to cover all forms of female surface work, so too did 'tip girl' become synonymous with female employment at South Wales collieries and ironworks. Women and girls had worked in the Dowlais area since the 1780s, helping prepare mine (iron ore) and pick bits of iron from the furnace cinders. In the nineteenth century they performed many jobs – poll girls took iron ore from trams, sorted out stone and shale, cleaned the ore and piled it ready for the furnaces. Coke girls stacked coal ready for coking and others broke limestone with hammers ready for smelting. Pilers worked in the puddling mills stacking and weighing the heavy iron bars which had been cut to be made into rails.[2] Munby visited South Wales in the 1860s and described women lifting large lumps of coke at Nantyglo, unloading and loading coal and ironstone around Blaenavon and loading bricks at Dowlais.[3] Making refractory bricks for lining furnaces was considered a woman's job at the vast Dowlais Iron Company. Methods were primitive – cold water would be poured on to heated floors in small sheds and the clay had to be worked to an even consistency by treading it with bare feet. Thirty-five pound lumps of clay were also moulded in hot moulding sheds and furnaces which were stoked by women.[4]

Notes

1. Oral testimony from the late Mrs Martha Jane Richards (*née* Waters). Interviewed by Richard Keen on 8 June 1970.
2. *Morning Chronicle*, 21 March 1850; *Ladies*, vol. 1, no. 25 (14 September 1873), *Illustrated London News*, LXII, 18 January 1873.
3. T. A. Owen, *The History of the Dowlais Iron Works*, Risca, 1977, pp. 65–6, 111–19. Welsh women were also employed at tin works as dusters, rubbers and plate openers and wheeled ore at copper works. See transcripts of taped interviews. Coalfied History Project. South Wales Miners' Library, University College, Swansea.
4. Munby MS, Diary 33, 22 September 1865.

4.5   'Mind that you do as you are told': reading books for Board School girls, 1870–1902

Anna Davin

The dominant nineteenth-century ideology declared that a woman's place was in the home. Education for working-class girls was intended to socialise them into the roles of wives, mothers and domestic servants.

In England, state interest in working-class education was established in the middle decades of the nineteenth century, starting with the first grants-in-aid to existing schools ('voluntary' ones run by religious authorities); developing its own system of inspection and partial control administered by a specialized bureaucracy; and consolidated by Forster's Education Act in 1870, which permitted increase of the existing network and also the setting up of a complementary system of 'Board Schools' under local non-denominational administration, both kinds to be funded (one partly, the other entirely) by a combination of local rate and government grants. These developments were justified at the time, and have been discussed since by historians, in social, political and economic terms. I propose here to concentrate on the first, because my starting point is the education of girls. The political explanations relate most directly to the growing labour movement, in which women played no part at this time, and to the 1867 Franchise Act, which created a million or so new voters, none of them women; while the economic context concerns the development of a new skilled and literate workforce (including a whole range of minor technicians significant in the expansion of empire and commerce as well as industry – telegraphists, sappers and signalmen as well as the more obvious draughtsmen, engineers and clerical workers) from which women (to begin with, at least) were again absent. If such political and economic grounds had been the only reasons for introducing general elementary education, one might well ask why girls were included at all. [...]

The following material is based on part of my work on girls' experience of school under the London School Board. The source I have used to explore the ideological content of education is the range of reading textbooks approved for use under the Board. [...]

This particular series specialized in morals about the importance of contentedness in work: Don't count your chickens before they are hatched; All men to their trades; Hard work no misery; The idle man is seldom a happy man; Work to have, to give, and for the happiness there is in work; and so on. The stories preach content, cheerfulness and perseverance. In one story, 'Rich and Poor, or the Discontented Haymaker Reproved', a couple are hay making when a rich and beautiful lady rides past. The wife is envious, but the husband says:

> God knows what is good for all his creatures. Don't let us murmur, Peggy dear, for if many seem to be better off than we are, it is still quite certain that we are better off than many more. ... While I have hands to labour, a good tidy wife to make home comfortable, and dear little children to divert me with their prattle, I am not going to fret because perhaps others have something else that I never feel to want.

Shortly after this admirable declaration the rich lady is thrown from her horse and brought insensible to their humble (but tidy) house. ('Peggy took pride in the thought that she could provide a nice clean pair of sheets and pillow cases'.) The lady dies, so Peggy resolves 'to feel more kindly towards the rich, who, she now saw, were no more free from great sorrows than were the poor'.[1] Like other stories in these books, this one is set in a static, hierarchical world, where fulfilment and content come through keeping one's place and doing one's duty. For a woman this involves listening to one's husband as well as to class superiors, being 'a good tidy wife' and keeping the house clean and comfortable, as well as being generally industrious and content. Other virtues recommended in the readers included patience, humility, modesty, obedience, unselfishness, punctuality, tidiness, and so on. They warn that 'little girls ought to know that it is during childhood that good or bad habits are formed', and set out to make quite clear which habits are to be considered good. 'Don't be envious.' 'To do our duty well in one situation is the best proof we shall discharge it properly in another' is illustrated in a book for Standard IV girls by a story in which a girl who is lazy at home imagines herself in the grand situation of housemaid at the Hall, and again and again girls who are tidy and diligent at home are rewarded with good places in service.[2]

Notes

1. F. Howard and R. M. Conley, *New Code Reader and Speller*, II, London: Longman, 1873.
2. C. Bilton, *Bilton's Reading Books*, IV, London: Longman, 1867–70.

4.6　Working-Class Wives
Margery Spring Rice

This Reading is a primary historical source in itself. Margery Spring Rice describes the daily routine of working-class housewives who took part in the Women's Health Inquiry in the late 1930s.

This is not a question of health. Whatever the condition of fitness, the mother who does the work for a whole family of husband and three or more children has a titanic job under present conditions. If she is fortunate enough to be abnormally strong, she will manage to keep up with it, as long as her daily routine is not checked by some unusual misfortune. But if the ordinary round is harder than her body is strong her health must surely suffer with the result that she will find the course more and more difficult to hold; the less able she is to get through her task, the harder it will become … a circle of peculiar and tragic viciousness.

For the majority of the 1,250 women under review the ordinary routine seems to be as follows. Most of them get up at 6.30. If their husband and/or sons are miners, or bakers, or on any nightshift, they may have to get up at 4 (possibly earlier), make breakfast for those members of the family, and then, if they feel disposed to further sleep, go back to bed for another hour's rest. The same woman who does this has probably got a young child or even a baby, who wakes up early, and sleeping in the same room will in no case give his mother much peace after 6 a.m. If there is a suckling baby as well (and it must be remembered that the woman who has had seven or eight children before the age of 35 has never been without a tiny baby or very young child), she will have had to nurse him at least as late as 10 the night before. There are many complaints of children who for some reason or other disturb the night's rest. Her bed is shared not only by her husband but, in all probability, by one *at least* of her young family. Sleeplessness is not often spoken of in this investigation, because it is not considered an ailment, but it is quite clear that a good night's rest in a well-aired, quiet room and in a comfortable, well-covered bed, is practically unknown to the majority of these mothers. A woman can become accustomed to very little sleep just as she can to very little food.

When once she is up there is no rest at all till after dinner. She is on her legs the whole time. She has to get her husband off to work, the children washed, dressed and fed and sent to school. If she has a large family, even if she has only the average family of this whole group, four or five children, she is probably very poor and therefore lives in a very bad house, or a house extremely inadequately fitted for her needs. Her washing up will not only therefore be heavy, but it may have to be done under the worst conditions. She may have to go down (or up) two or three flights of stairs to get her water, and again to empty it away. She may have to heat it on the open fire, and she may have to be looking after the baby and the toddler at the same time. When this is done, she must clean the house. If she has the average family, the rooms are very 'full of beds' and this will make her cleaning much more difficult than if she had twice the number of rooms with half the amount of furniture in each. She lacks the utensils too; and lacking any means to get hot water except by the kettle on the fire, she will be as careful as possible not to waste a drop. The school-children will be back for their dinner soon after 12, so she must begin her cooking in good time. Great difficulties confront her here. She has not got more than one or two saucepans and a frying pan, and so even if she is fortunate in having some proper sort of cooking stove, it is impossible to cook a dinner as it should be cooked, slowly and with the vegetables separately; hence the ubiquitous stew, with or without the remains of the Sunday meat according to the day of the week. She has nowhere to store food, or if there is cupboard room, it is inevitably in the only living room and probably next to the fireplace. Conditions may be so bad in this respect that she must go out in the middle of her morning's work to buy for dinner. This has the advantage of giving her and the baby a breath of fresh air during the morning; otherwise, unless there is a garden or yard, the baby, like herself, is penned up in the 9 ft square kitchen during the whole morning.

Dinner may last from 12 till 3. Her husband or a child at work may have quite different hours from the school-children, and it is quite usual to hear this comment. Very often she does not sit down herself to meals. The serving of five or six other people demands so much jumping up and down that she finds it easier to take her meals standing. If she is nursing a baby, she will sit down for that, and in this way 'gets more rest'. She does this after the children have returned to school. Sometimes the heat and stuffiness of the kitchen in which she has spent all or most of her morning takes her off her food, and she does not feel inclined to eat at all, or only a bite when the others have all finished and gone away. Then comes the same process of washing up, only a little more difficult because dinner is a greasier meal than breakfast. After that, with luck at 2 or 2.30 but sometimes much later, if dinner for any reason has had to go on longer, she can tidy herself up and REST, or GO OUT, or SIT DOWN.

Leisure is a comparative term. Anything which is slightly less arduous or gives a change of scene or occupation from the active hard work of the eight hours for which she has already been up is leisure. Sometimes, perhaps once a week, perhaps only once a month, the change will be a real one. She may go to the Welfare Centre with baby, or to the recreation ground with the two small children, or to see her sister or friend in the next street, but most times the children don't give her the opportunity for this sort of leisure, for there is sewing and mending and knitting to be done for them; and besides there is always the shopping to be done, and if she possibly can, she does like to rest her legs a bit and sit down. So unless there is some necessity to go out, she would rather on most days stay indoors. And she may not have any clothes to go out in, in which case the school-children will do the shopping after school hours. (Clothes are a great difficulty, 'practically an impossibility'.)

Then comes tea, first the children's and then her husband's, when he comes home from work; and by the time that is all over and washed up it is time the children began to go to bed. If she is a good manager she will get them all into bed by 8, perhaps even earlier, and then at last, at last, 'a little peace and quietude!' She sits down again, after having been twelve or fourteen hours at work, mostly on her feet (and this means *standing* about, not *walking*), and perhaps she then has a 'quiet talk with hubby', or listens to the wireless, 'our one luxury'. Perhaps her husband reads the paper to her. She has got a lot of sewing to do, so she doesn't read much to herself, and she doesn't go out because she can't leave the children unless her husband undertakes to keep house for one evening a week, while she goes to the pictures or for a walk. There is no money to spare anyhow for the pictures, or very seldom. She may or may not have a bite of supper with her husband, cocoa and bread and butter or possibly a bit of fried fish. And so to her share of the bed, mostly at about 10.30 or 11.

4.7   The Politics of Motherhood: child and maternal welfare in England, 1900–1939

Jane Lewis

Women's role was not only to service the needs of the male workforce but also to reproduce the next generation of workers. From the early twentieth century great emphasis was placed first on infant health and then on the health of mothers.

Concern over physical efficiency first arose when attention was drawn to the poor quality of army recruits. The large amount of publicity that was generated led to the appointment of an Inter-departmental Committee on Physical Deterioration. The committee's report, published in 1904, devoted much attention to the welfare of infants and school children, recognising that it was in the national interest to safeguard the next generation and thereby improve the quality of the race.[1] The Education (Provision of Meals) Act of 1906, which provided for meals to be given to school children who needed them, and the Education (Administration Provisions) Act of 1907, which established medical inspection in schools, demonstrated clearly that the welfare of the young had become a matter of national concern rather than an object for private charity,[2] and it was primarily on these grounds that further government intervention in this aspect of family life was justified. In France, where state intervention to secure the physical welfare of school children and voluntary effort on behalf of infants had a much longer history, conscious pronatalism and a concern with the quality of the race had also provided much of the impetus to reform.

Between 1910 and 1916, the Local Government Board issued regular reports on infant, and later maternal, mortality and the scale of local efforts to improve infant welfare during these years increased dramatically. The loss of population during World War I further increased awareness of the importance of infant life, and child and maternal welfare work was extended to include the ante-natal period. Again, state intervention was justified in terms of the national good and racial improvement. When the Ministry of Health was created in 1919, one of its six departments was devoted to maternal and child welfare. During the inter-war period increased emphasis was put on maternal welfare, for while infant mortality declined, maternal mortality actually increased slightly.

Notes

1. PP, 'Report of the Inter-Departmental Committee on Physical Deterioration, Vol. 1', 1904, Cd. 2175, XXXII, p. 1. For more general information on the campaign for physical efficiency, see G. R. Searle, *The Quest for National Efficiency*, Oxford: Oxford University Press, 1971, pp. 59–67. Bernard Semmel, *Imperialism and Social Reform*, London: Allen & Unwin, 1960, and Michael Freeden, *The New Liberalism*, Oxford: Clarendon Press, 1978, also deal with aspects of the efficiency movement.

2. B. B. Gilbert, *The Evolution of National Health Insurance in Great Britain. The Origins of the Welfare State*, London: Michael Joseph, 1966, pp. 102–58, deals with these measures in detail.

4.8   Back to Home and Duty: women between the wars 1918–1939
Deirdre Beddoe

Domestic service was the largest single employment sector for women throughout the nineteenth century and, indeed, until 1939. After the First World War, when many women refused to enter service, it was state policy to coerce them into it.

Official state policy coerced women back into the home – their own or somebody else's: this may be clearly seen by examining how labour exchanges, under government directives, operated the scheme of 'out-of-work donation', to which women war workers were entitled. The press, and the public opinion it purported to represent, were outraged that women wished to hang on to factory work when what the nation needed most was wives, mothers and domestic servants. The operations of the labour exchanges and the angry ravings of the press in the period immediately following the end of the First World War were closely interrelated.

The 'out-of-work donation' scheme came into operation shortly after the Armistice and was designed as an emergency measure to support civilian workers who had lost their employment due to the cessation of hostilities. Civilian workers, especially in munitions, had been laid off many months before the scheme came into effect; previously only women in insured trades, as defined by national insurance legislation, qualified for benefit and that was a meagre 7s. per week. The government dragged its heels in announcing the implementation of out-of-work donations. On 16 November, five days before the Armistice, the *Daily News* warned 'if serious trouble is to be prevented the government must immediately announce the date at which special out-of-work pay will begin, and must undertake to reckon it from the day on which a worker was discharged'.[1]

First payments were made on 6 December 1918 and the rates were more generous than had been mooted even a few weeks earlier.[2] Such an increase was partly due to agitation by the National Federation of Women Workers. Under the scheme, women were entitled to weekly benefit of 25s. for thirteen weeks. In order to qualify, unemployed workers had to attend the labour exchange daily and be available for work. The conflict came over the issue of what sort of work the women were available for. Officialdom viewed domestic service as fit work for practically any woman who signed on: the women had other ideas. Over and over again in these years and later women were denied benefit for refusing posts as domestics. The shortage of domestic servants, labelled by the middle class the 'servant problem', had become acute: middle-class women, who had been prepared to put up with lack of help during the war, were no longer willing to do so. It was considered an outrage that unemployed women would be living it up on their donations whilst mistresses struggled, servantless, at home.

But it was abundantly clear that most working-class women had no intention of submitting to the 'slavery' of service. One woman who had been in munitions for two and a half years, and who reported to the White City employment exchange, said: 'I feel so pleased that the war's over that I'll take any old job that comes along': but when domestic service was suggested she replied (with a laugh), 'except that'.[3] At another employment exchange only one woman out of three thousand entered her name as willing to enter service.[4] At yet another an official entered a room in which forty women were waiting for offers of work and asked, 'Who is for domestic service?'. No one replied. All forty women were immediately handed forms informing them they were not eligible for benefit.[5] The system was one of compulsory domestic service. There are many cases of women being offered domestic work at a mere pittance and, if they refused it, losing their benefit. Dorothy Jewson of the NFWW [National Federation of Women Workers], writing in March 1919 when 650,000 women and girls were out of work, cited the case of a girl offered a live-in domestic post at 8s. 6d. a week for a nine-and-a-half-hour day; because the girl refused this, her benefit was stopped.[6] At Portsmouth labour exchange a woman was struck off the books for refusing work at 8s. a week for a ten-and-a-half-hour day (seven days a week), and another for refusing full-time domestic work at 1s. a day.[7] Even if a woman took one of these jobs and gave it up because she could not live on the money, she lost her benefit. To enter service was to enter an 'uninsured' area of work and therefore to lose further benefits. A London woman, who struggled for three weeks in a laundry at piece rates, found that she could not earn more than 12s. 9d. a week by working as hard as she could; when she give it up, she was denied benefit.[8]

Women did have a right of appeal – first to a local court of referees and beyond that to a government-appointed umpire. The local referees, who rarely included women members, were uncompromising in their attitudes towards women who were not willing to become servants, but the umpire's decisions were more enlightened.[9] Further steps were taken to ensure that women should disappear from the donation lists and enter service: in May 1919 a second registration of unemployed women recorded women by their pre-war and not their war work, and reclassified some 17,000 women as domestics rather than industrial workers.[10]

The press were quick to attack women for even claiming their unemployment benefit when there were jobs available as domestic servants. The *Daily Chronicle* of 6 December 1919, the first day on which out-of-work-payments were made, ran an article headed, 'Unemployed in Fur Coats'. A *Chronicle* reporter went to the Acton exchange, where large numbers of women from the great shell factory at Park Royal and the camp kit and gas mask makers from Shepherds Bush had come to register, and found women in 'well made fur coats' who refused 'to consider posts as "generals" or cooks even at tempting wages'.[11] The *Daily Chronicle*, like other papers, was obsessed by the women's appearance. The next day it reported amongst the crowds at the exchange 'young girls with elaborately curled hair, wearing expensive fur coats'.[12] By 1919 the feminist magazine *The Vote* could somewhat snootily say that to be wearing a fur coat that year had attached to it the stigma of being a munitions worker.[13] The *Evening Standard*, whilst reporting with some glee a crackdown on ex-domestic servants who refused to return to service, painted what was then a familiar picture of well-dressed irresponsible women living it up on out-of-work donation. Under the heading of 'Slackers with state pay' and the sub-heading 'want luxurious days to continue', it informs us:

> Their wages have run up to £2 and £3 per week. Fur coats, high topped kid boots, gramophones, every night off, and Sundays in many cases free, have given them higher moral [e] and not readily, especially with weekly gifts of 25s for walking to the employment exchanges, are they going to take on the shackles of domestic work.[14]

Notes

1. *Daily News*, 16 November 1918.
2. Ministry of Labour, 'Out of Work Donation: summary of scheme', November 1918.
3. *Daily Chronicle*, 7 December 1918.
4. *Daily Telegraph*, 30 December 1918.
5. *Daily Mail*, 23 May 1919.
6. *Reynolds News*, 30 March 1919.
7. *Portsmouth Evening News*, 13 February 1919.
8. Case cited by Madelaine Symons of the NFWW. *Daily Mail*, 23 May 1919.
9. Umpires were granting nine out of ten appeals at this time: *The Times*, 15 December 1919.
10. *The Times*, 9 May 1919.
11. *Daily Chronicle*, 6 December 1918.
12. *Ibid.*, 7 December 1918.
13. *The Vote*, 29 August 1919.
14. *Evening Standard*, 9 January 1919.

4.9   **The Cause**

Ray Strachey

The next two Readings deal with the suffrage movement. The first is by Ray Strachey, who favoured the constitutional methods of the National Union of Women's Suffrage

Societies, led by Millicent Fawcett. Strachey believed that it was the moderate wing of the movement that won the vote.

There were two kinds of effort in the suffrage world, inspired by differing ideals and carried on by rival systems of organisation. The constitutional societies, which were united in the National Union and led by Mrs Fawcett, carried on the regular tradition of the whole movement. They did not regard their work as an attack upon men, but rather as a reform for the good of all, and the next step in human progress. Their newspaper, which existed to promote Women's Suffrage only, was called *The Common Cause*, and it was in these terms that they saw their aim. Their chief effort was the conversion of public opinion, and they felt that this conversion was as important and as much a part of their object as the gaining of the vote itself. Mrs Fawcett, their leader, had seen the whole movement grow; she knew, and she taught her followers to know, that their Cause was part of a development wider even than the change in the position of women itself. Though she watched the progress of the Franchise Bills with the utmost care, and let slip no opportunity to advance them, she was quietly and obstinately convinced that the Cause was bound to triumph, and no set-back, no discouragement, no misfortune perturbed her. When her followers grew too emphatic or too much discouraged, she rebuked them gently enough but very firmly, and the very quietness of her outlook kept them in check. [...]

Under Mrs Fawcett's leadership the numbers of the constitutional suffragists grew rapidly. As the local societies multiplied they became increasingly democratic in their internal organisation, so that their development was governed by their own council meetings, and their constituent societies took a real and highly expert share in the direction of the movement. Within a year or two they had evolved a technique of democracy inside their own ranks which became in itself an absorbing interest, and the surplus energy which the movement was stimulating among its supporters found vent in this direction. The affairs of the National Union during these astonishing years are not now of much moment; the niceties of by-election policy, the adjustments of affiliation fees, the basis of representation, and the devolution into federations are all matters which are dead and gone; but the spirit which caused them to be of such moment, and the energy which was poured into them, prove at once the vitality of the movement and the practical abilities of its supporters. They were not content that their machinery should be less than supremely efficient, and they were prepared to take, and did take, almost unlimited trouble to ensure the perfection of their own organisation.

As the network of societies spread out, and as the number of their members increased, so did the efficiency of the machine improve. It was so planned and so organised as to be capable of almost indefinite expansion, and by 1910 it had grown to be an amazingly powerful and important political instrument.

The militant society was entirely different. Its propaganda, though directed towards the same end as that of the National Union, rang with quite other notes,

with defiance, antagonism and suspicion. 'Deeds not Words' was the motto of
the organisation, and its deliberate policy was to seek sensational achievement
rather than anything else. It leaders did not scruple to brush aside the ordinary
niceties of procedure, and they did not care whom they shocked and
antagonised. They distrusted everyone who was not a militant, and laughed at
all talk of persuasion. What they believed in was moral violence. By this force,
and by the driving power of their own determination, they hoped to turn the
Liberals out of office, and to coerce whoever succeeded them into granting their
demand. The whole atmosphere of their work was thus aggressive and
headlong; it resounded with charges of the treachery and ill faith of their
opponents, and was sharpened by sarcasm, anger, and excitement. Moreover,
since they deliberately put themselves in the position of outlaws dogged by the
police, they were always wrapped round with secrecy and mystification, and
planned surprises alike for their followers and for the public. The policy of
sensational public protest was not one which left much time for the tasks of self-
government, nor was democracy much to their taste. The Women's Social and
Political Union adopted, therefore, a purely autocratic system, and entrusted all
decisions to their leaders – Mrs Pankhurst and her daughter Christabel, and Mr
and Mrs Pethick Lawrence. These people alone decided what was to be done;
the others obeyed, and enjoyed the surrender of their judgement, and the
sensation of marching as an army under discipline.

In course of time divisions of opinion arose within the organisation, and
separate societies were more than once formed from among its members. In 1909
a considerable body, under the leadership of Mrs Despard,[1] broke off and
formed the Women's Freedom League – a society which followed much the
same policy as that of the WSPU though it arrived at it by a different line of
reasoning, and conducted its affairs in a more regular and democratic fashion.
The main body, however, continued on its way, bound together by a loyalty to
its leaders almost more passionate than to its cause, and attracting to its ranks
not only those of extreme opinions but also those whose natural inclination led
them towards drama, hero-worship, and self-surrender. The actual number of
adherents of the society was never known. No attempt was ever made to keep
a record of those who joined it, and no regular subscriptions were paid.
Enormous sums of money passed through the hands of the society, but no full
accounts were ever published, and no audited balance-sheet was ever presented;
for the Women's Social and Political Union spent no time upon 'formalities'. All
was action! action! As fast as money came in it went out again, spent on flags
and banners, leaflets, organisers, meetings, parades, bands, shows, ribbons,
drums or even bombs – anything, everything with which to make a noise and
a stir, and keep enthusiasm burning and the Cause shining in the public eye.

Notes

1. Mrs Despard was one of the early members of the ILP [Independent Labour Party],

and was exceedingly well known both in South London and in Dublin for her work among the poor. She was twice imprisoned. Though she was the sister of General French, she was during the war an extreme pacifist. In 1919 she stood for Parliament unsuccessfully for Battersea, and in 1927 was expelled from the Irish Free State as a dangerous character.

4.10 The Suffragette Movement
Sylvia Pankhurst

Sylvia Pankhurst, on the other hand, believed that it was the fear of renewed outbreaks of violence and the revival of the Women's Social and Political Union's militant tactics which caused the government finally to concede the limited suffrage of 1918.

Undoubtedly the large part taken by women during the War in all branches of social service had proved a tremendous argument for their enfranchisement. Yet the memory of the old militancy, and the certainty of its recurrence if the claims of women were set aside, was a much stronger factor in overcoming the reluctance of those who would again have postponed the settlement. The shock to the foundations of existing social institutions already reverberating from Russia across Europe, made many old opponents desire to enlist the new enthusiasms of women voters to stabilize the Parliamentary machine. Above all, the changed attitude of the large public of all classes towards the position of women, which had grown up in the great militant struggle, made impossible a further postponement of our enfranchisement.

4.11 The Spinster and Her Enemies: feminism and sexuality 1880–1930
Sheila Jeffreys

Many women did not marry. Sheila Jeffreys writes about spinsters, about passionate friendships between women and about lesbians. Here she looks at the turn-of-the-century sexologists and their scientific categorisation of lesbianism.

Lesbianism

As part of their self-imposed task of categorising varieties of human sexual behaviour, the sexologists of the late nineteenth century set about the 'scientific' description of lesbianism. Their description has had a momentous effect on the ways in which we, as women, have seen ourselves and all our relationships with other women up until the present. They codified as 'scientific' wisdom current myths about lesbian sexual practice, a stereotype of the lesbian and the 'pseudohomosexual' woman, categorising women's passionate friendships as female homosexuality and offered explanations for the phenomenon.

Male writers of gay history have tended to see their work as sympathetic and helpful to the development of a homosexual rights movement since they explained male homosexuality in terms of innateness or used psychoanalytic explanations which undermined the view of male homosexuality as criminal behaviour. Female homosexual behaviour was never illegal in Britain, though there were attempts to make it so in 1921, so the sexologists' contribution cannot be seen as positive in that way.

Havelock Ellis provided a classic stereotype of the female homosexual in his *Sexual Inversion* (1897):

> When they still retain female garments, they usually show some traits of masculine simplicity, and there is nearly always a disdain for the petty feminine artifices of the toilet. Even when this is not obvious, there are all sorts of instinctive gestures and habits which may suggest to female acquaintances the remark that such a person 'ought to have been a man'. The brusque energetic movements, the attitude of the arms, the direct speech, the inflexions of the voice, the masculine straightforwardness and sense of honour, and especially the attitude towards men, free from any suggestion either of shyness or audacity, will often suggest the underlying psychic abnormality to a keen observer.
>
> In the habits not only is there frequently a pronounced taste for smoking cigarettes, often found in quite feminine women, but also a decided taste and toleration for cigars. There is also a dislike and sometimes incapacity for needlework and other domestic occupations, while there is some capacity for athletics. [1]

The importance of his description is that it classified as 'homosexual' precisely those forms of behaviour for which spinster feminists, the 'New Women' of the 1890s were criticised by anti-feminists. In the 1890s some women were trying to escape the 'effeminate' stereotype of woman. These feminists were neatly slotted into a picture of lesbian women who were really pseudo-men. Using the accusation of lesbianism to subvert women's attempts at emancipation is a form of attack with which women involved in the contemporary wave of feminism are all too familiar.

Notes

1. Havelock Ellis *Sexual Inversions: Studies in the psychology of sex*, vol. 2, Philadelphia, PA: F. A. Davis, 1927, published 1897; p. 250.

Further Reading

Anderson, B. S. and Zinsser, P. (1988), *A History of Their Own: Women in Europe from prehistory to the present*, 2 vols, Harmondsworth: Penguin.

Hall, C. (1992), *White, Male and Middle Class: Explorations of feminism and history*, Oxford: Polity.

Hufton, O. *et al.*, (1988), 'What is women's history?', in J. Gardiner (ed.), *What is History Today?*, London: Macmillan.

Lesbian History Group (1989), *Not a Passing Phase: Reclaiming lesbians in history 1840–1945*, London: The Women's Press.

Lewis, J. (1984), *Women in England 1870–1950*, Hemel Hempstead: Harvester Wheatsheaf.

5 WOMEN, EDUCATION AND WORK

Edited and Introduced by Jane Prince

INTRODUCTION

This Section is concerned with women's experiences in education and in work. Two distinct strands emerge from these Readings: first, the ways in which 'being female' is theorised have had profound effects on women's lives and material experiences; secondly, that successful attempts to challenge women's oppression in work and in education have been grounded in a base which is both women-centred and explicitly political.

Historically, the study of the female experience in work and education has focused on comparisons (with males) and on the unequal nature of female–male experiences in terms of occupation, pay, promotion, and so on; also on the devaluation of traditional 'female' occupations. This last is best demonstrated in the numerous writings on deskilling associated with the transition of an occupation (for example, secretarial work) from being largely male to largely female. Associated with such approaches is the notion of rationality – that is, the belief that the female experience is a consequence of faulty cognitions *on the part of individuals*, and that in consequence such practices as positive discrimination, anti-sexist education of employers and employees, identifying more female 'role-models', and so on, should change perceptions and lead to a society in which opportunities and experiences were genuinely equal. Counterposed to this is the view that not only is society (rather than individual members of society) sexist, but the negative position of women in society is constantly reproduced through formal social structures – for example, the education system. Within this framework – represented largely, though not exclusively, by radical feminism – it is thought that change will be brought about through challenge to the system rather than through 're-education'.

One challenge has come from those feminists who propose that androcentrism[1] so permeates society that female behaviour is inevitably undervalued. Regardless of whether they take essentialist[2] or social constructionist[3] positions, there is some agreement between researchers[4] that female activity is orientated more to relationality[5] than to competition. Androcentric society values competition; and hence female activity is discounted as irrelevant or inadequate.

John McCauley's study of female academics (see Reading 5.7) illustrates the effects of this on women's work experiences: assumptions about what constitutes good working practices produce an orientation to males' success and females' failure. Changes to androcentric orthodoxy will depend on societal re-evaluation of what constitutes 'success'; for some theorists this will require that women separate from male-dominated organisations to develop economically viable workplaces organised around feminine values.

An alternative perspective is that women's class position within capitalism is the basis for an analysis of the causes of their subordination. To put it simply: Marxists propose that women's (undeniably worse) material experiences compared with those of men are a consequence of their role within the family. The insertion of women within the structure of a family after the transition from feudal society (in which, for the majority of individuals, segregation by gender was not a controlling aspect of their lives) to one organised around industrial production after the Industrial Revolution enabled one set of workers (men) to produce value[6] in the workplace. Whilst women were often not involved in paid work, they nevertheless produced value which was essential for the reproduction of capital.[7] Following the initial exigencies of the capitalist revolution which required women and children to enter into wage–labour relations, ideological, economic and pragmatic imperatives turned towards the reinvention of a family structure which provided a relatively finely tuned mechanism of social control and increased the rate of exploitation of both men and women.

The main distinction between this analysis and that of many 'socialist' feminists lies in the distinction between exploitation and oppression; whilst women, regardless of their class position, may experience sexual oppression, the Marxist analysis holds that the material interests of bourgeois women lies in maintaining exploitative class relations – which, for historical reasons, means maintaining relations of sexual oppression. Thus, women may be oppressed without being economically exploited. It is this economic exploitation which provides the dynamic for the reproduction of capital, and thus the reproduction of relations of oppression. Clearly this does not rule out the possibility of fighting sexual oppression under capitalism; in concrete terms, however, it ties this fight to class struggle.

It could be said that potentially, the most powerful accounts of the relation between education, work and the female condition come from studies which have attempted to identify the processes through which women are classified and their activities are derogated. Within the education system the achievements and activities of female children and adults are shaped and interpreted within a particular framework; activities undertaken by little boys are interpreted in one way, while identical activities undertaken by little girls are classified very differently. Researchers[8] note the difference between the descriptions of achieving children in schools: while boys are described in terms reflecting ingenuity, creativity and general liveliness, achieving girls are described as 'hard-working' and 'careful' – the implication being that academic success requires different characteristics from boys than from girls; moreover, for girls this success is something which requires effort, while for boys it is natural. Walkerdine notes that this difference in terminology is communicated directly to children, via comments on their work and school reports; it therefore reproduces in the recipients of the comments (the children themselves) a specific understanding about the gendering of particular forms of academic performance.

Furthermore, the process of education positions young people according to gender not only with respect to their academic activities and attainments, but also within a wider social context. Through the structuring and content of the formal education system, children are taught which roles and activities, emotions and relationships are appropriate to which sex; where males and females are located in the hierarchies of family, work, play and school – in short, who makes history and who makes tea. Again, McCauley's research demonstrates that even in an undeniably successful (and hence unconventional) group, women academics, the effect of social positioning on work behaviour is profound.

Over the past ten years developments in theorising the position of women in work and in education have been influential in identifying practices which might improve women's experiences in work, education, social relationships and self-fulfilment. The Readings included in this section provide an account of those developments, and reflect the radical changes in theory which have taken place. Nevertheless, there is still a powerful influence from those who argue that women are *by nature* unsuited to success – or, indeed, even to work. The focus by groupings of feminists on essential psychological differences between men and women has been viewed, by socialists and some feminists, as giving a weapon to reactionary forces which will see that very essentialism as a justification for denying women access to those occupations and those niches of power currently occupied by men.

Notes

1. Androcentrism: viewing male characteristics as the norm.
2. Essentialist: viewing gender-differentiated traits and behaviours as having their origins in differences between sexes (rather than differences in experiences/societal values of the sexes).
3. Social constructionist: the view that identity, and so on, is a consequence of social experiences which build up an individual at any one time, and are dynamic.
4. C. Gilligan, 'In a different voice', *Harvard Educational Review*, vol. 47, no. 4 (1977) pp. 481–517; Judi Marshall, *Women Managers: Travellers in a male world* (see Reading 5.8).
5. Relationality: orientation towards and valuing of relations with others.
6. Value: the production of something which can be sold for more than the costs of production (labour costs, raw materials) is the production of value.

7. Capital: if capitalism is to be maintained, the profit derived from surplus-value must be reinvested to create more value.
8. See Reading 5.5.

5.1   Unequal Work
Veronica Beechey

Beechey discusses the gap in theoretical perspectives in researching women's work consciousness; she is critical of the ways in which feminist and Marxist analyses have, at times, established an 'ideal type' of consciousness which, if not overtly expressed by a worker, is assumed to represent reactionary attitudes.

Women's work consciousness

The question of women's consciousness arises in one way or another in each of the texts considered, and all the studies have produced interesting evidence. There are certain similarities between the studies. All represent women's consciousness as being fragmented and contradictory. They all reveal elements of what might be called a work consciousness among the women, but in every study this is shown to coexist with a primarily familial definition of the women's outlook.

Ruth Cavendish,[1] for instance, describes a strong culture operating among the women at UMEC and a strong commitment to the union. This coexists, according to her analysis, with a strongly familial orientation. The Churchmans' women, too, are depicted as having contradictory consciousness, on the one hand hostile to men's privileges within the workplace and resentful at their paternalism, and on the other hand escaping into romance and strongly committed to marriage and domesticity. Similarly the Fakenham women (or at least the full-time ones) seem to have been affected in their work consciousness by their experience in setting up the cooperative but, according to July Wacjman, their consciousness of the sexual division of labour and their wider political consciousness did not seem to have been affected. They, like the Churchmans' women, see to hold contradictory attitudes towards trade unions.

Despite the extremely interesting concrete discussion in each of the texts, none of them has a satisfactory theoretical framework for analysing the women's work consciousness. Furthermore, the theoretical concepts used tend to oversimplify the question, rather than grasping the complexity of the women's consciousness at the level of theory. Thus Ruth Cavendish discounts the role of ideology in structuring the women's experience, since she sees experience as a direct product of the material conditions of the women's work. Anna Pollert[2] does not take cognizance of the women's contradictory consciousness within her broader theoretical framework, and she seems to think that the women's consciousness is somewhat deficient. And despite her endeavours to develop a more sophisticated analysis, Judy Wacjman,[3] too, loses sight of the contradictory nature of the women's outlook in her general theoretical arguments because she places so much weight on the ideology of domesticity.

We have hardly begun to develop an adequate conceptual framework for analysing women's work consciousness. Nevertheless, a number of general observations can be made. The first thing to note is that feminist studies of women's employment, like Marxist studies of employment more generally, have placed a lot of emphasis on the question of consciousness. This is for obvious political reasons, for it is assumed that if women are to act to change their situation they need to understand that the present state of affairs is unsatisfactory, and that things could be different.

Secondly, feminist analysis is in danger of setting up an 'ideal-type' feminist consciousness, and assuming that if women do not express this themselves, then their attitude is somehow reactionary. This is precisely what Anna Pollert does in juxtaposing 'good sense' to 'common sense', but the problem also exists more widely. Just as Marxist studies of class consciousness which set up an 'ideal-type' model often overlook ways in which workers may have a limited and fragmentary awareness of themselves as workers, so feminist studies which adopt a similar approach are in danger of missing important aspects of women's consciousness which may well be positive but which do not fit neatly into the theoretical model which has been constructed.

Third, there exists a tendency in a number of feminist writings to see women's consciousness as entirely separate from men's and to think of it as being rooted in the family while men's awareness is rooted in the labour process. Marilyn Porter's extremely interesting essay in *Work, Women and the Labour Market*[4] is a good example of this tendency. She summarizes her basic argument in the following passage:

> This paper shows how the ideas that women have about work and collective action are currently related both to experience of the material reality of their place in the family. Class consciousness is constructed within the specific context of people's experience. This means, among other things, that we cannot 'read off' women's position ideas or consciousness from men's. Women's experience of work is significantly different to that of men, and I want to suggest that the difference rests upon a sexual division of labour rooted, outside work, in the family.

This simple proposition, however, raises a number of significant questions. What do we understand by consciousness? Is there such a thing as women's consciousness? Is women's consciousness essentially the same as men's or different from it? If different, how can we account for this? How can we develop a framework for analysing consciousness which is appropriate to women?

In the rest of her paper Marilyn Porter analyses the consciousness of a group of married women with dependent children, none of whom had full-time jobs and all of whom were dependent on their husband's wage. She shows how the women's consciousness of themselves as workers is mediated through their role as housewives, and in a particularly interesting passage suggests that women also related to their husbands' work as housewives. I found her analysis extremely interesting. It shows how one group of women experienced both their own and their husband's paid work and it shows how the women's consciousness is rooted in the practicalities of their everyday lives. As a general framework of analysis, however, it is problematic. There are two reasons for this. The first is theoretical. I think it wrong to accept unquestioningly the distinction between the public and private spheres and the association of men with the public and women with the private which is constructed within the dominant ideology. We need instead to allow for the possibility that both women's and men's consciousness of themselves as workers is affected by both their workplace and their familial experiences. This is not to say that women's and men's consciousness is the same. Far from it. But it is to say that we need to use similar concepts to analyse both, and not to use 'familial' concepts to analyse women, and 'workplace' concepts to analyse men. Only then will we have a sound theoretical basis for analysing both the differences and similarities between women's and men's consciousness.

A second objection to Marilyn Porter's analysis is primarily methodological. Marilyn Porter asserts that her group of women constitutes the 'paradigm situation of all women in capitalist society'. Yet it is clear from a footnote that her sample is quite specific. For a start it is part of a sample of couples drawn from a fibreboard factory in Bristol where all the men worked, and is thus drawn from the *men's* place of work. Furthermore, the group of women has quite distinctive characteristics. They are all married, all have dependent children under sixteen, are all dependent on their husband's wage and none of them works full-time. Given the ways in which the sample was drawn and the social and demographic characteristics of the women in question, it is hardly surprising that Marilyn Porter found extensive evidence of domestic ideology. It is quite possible given the evidence from the other studies discussed here that Marilyn Porter's conclusions would have more general validity. It seems equally possible, however, that women's work consciousness varies at different points in the life cycle, as Angela Coyle has suggested.[5] We need to be cautious before making generalizations about women when we are actually studying quite a specific group.

The general methodological point I wish to make is that our studies need to have a much sounder empirical basis. If we wish to analyse the similarities and differences between women's and men's consciousness, we need to study women and men, using the same concepts and asking the same questions. If, on the other hand, we want to look in more detail at women's consciousness, we need to stop thinking about women as a unitary category and to consider the differences among them which the books reviewed here all discuss. Ruth Cavendish, for instance, pays a great deal of attention to ethnic and racial differences, while Anna Pollert distinguishes between young and older women and Judy Wacjman emphasizes the importance of the women's different positions in the life cycle. However, these distinctions are not always carried through satisfactorily in the books' discussions of consciousness. Anna Pollert's theoretical analysis is not informed by the awareness of age and marital differences shown in her more empirical chapters. Since it is clear from aggregate statistical evidence that women's participation in the labour market follows a definite pattern, and that most women have at least one interruption in their working lives, and many women work part-time when they have young children or other dependants to care for, we need to investigate empirically how women's consciousness differs at different points in the life cycle, and to ascertain whether it varies according to different household structures, racial and ethnic groups and social class.

Notes

1. R. Cavendish, *On the Line*, London, 1982.
2. A. Pollert, *Girls, Wives, Factory Lives*, London, 1982.
3. J. Wacjman, *Women in Control*, Milton Keynes, 1983.
4. M. Porter, 'Standing on the edge: working-class housewives and the world of work', in J. West (ed.), *Work, Women and the Labour Market*.
5. A. Coyle, 'Sex and skill in the organisation of the clothing industry', in West (ed.), *Work, Women and the Labour Market*.

5.2 Women's Oppression Today

Michèle Barrett

Michèle Barratt debates the values of theories of patriarchy and theories of class in explaining the experiences of women in education and work. She outlines the position of Marxist feminists.

I want now to consider the attempts made from a Marxist feminist position to reconcile theoretically the arguments about gender division and class structure.

One way of approaching this is to argue that the oppression of women differs significantly from class to class. Engels stressed this point, asserting that the proletarian home in which both husband and wife were engaged in wage-labour was in broad material terms an egalitarian one. Certainly he argued that the situation of the bourgeois wife, where upkeep was provided in return for the production of legitimate heirs, was tantamount to prostitution. This was the basis of his view that the entrance of all women into social production was the precondition for their emancipation. Although Engels's work has been extensively criticized by Marxist feminists, his central insistence on the material factors distinguishing proletarian from bourgeois women has been influential. McDonough and Harrison,[1] for instance, argue that 'patriarchal' control of woman's procreative capacity and sexuality takes different forms for different social classes. For the bourgeoisie this arises from the requirement to produce legitimate heirs, for the proletariat, with the need to reproduce efficiently the next generation of labour-power.

It should be noted that this formulation, although apparently making a useful distinction between the forms of oppression suffered by women of different social classes, results in a collapse of both bourgeois and proletarian patriarchal mechanisms into a model in which both, ultimately, are simply 'functional' for capital. The difference is that the capitalist as posed here is gendered: McDonough and Harrison refer to 'the interests of the male capitalist, ... his need for legitimate heirs and for fresh labour-power'. This is unsatisfactory, for several reasons. First, although it apparently concedes autonomy to patriarchal control, it implicitly withdraws this by posing these mechanisms as functional for the typical capitalist. Second, the entire question of class and gender is evaded by posing the capitalist as male. Some capitalists are female. Third, it incorporates the unmediated functionalism of much work on domestic labour, which has tended to see women's work in the 'home exclusively in terms of its functions for capital – hence failing to explain why it must be women who undertake such work. Finally, if we can doubt the validity of a functionalist explanation of women's oppression in the proletariat, how much more dubious is this view in relation to the bourgeoisie. The reproduction of capital does not necessarily *require* legitimate heirs or, for that matter, many other of the elements of the ideological baggage which has historically accompanied the growth of the bourgeoisie. Unlike the reproduction of labour-power, which *depends* upon the reproduction of the living, human labourer, the reproduction of capital does not depend on individual ownership in the same way. Hence, to incorporate gender division into the structure and definition of 'the capitalist' is a particularly fraught exercise. As Hilary Wainwright[2] notes: 'there is little to be said about sex inequalities as far as ownership of capital is concerned. Primarily for reasons of tax and inheritance women have an almost equal share in the ownership of wealth: they owned about 40 per cent of all private wealth in 1970'.

It is not, in fact, adequate to address the question of class and gender by posing a unity of interest between capitalists and men, since the capitalist class is composed of both men and women. This problem is to some extent avoided by the argument that gender division, and hence women's oppression, is historically constituted as outside the labour/capital relation with which a Marxist analysis of capitalist society is fundamentally concerned. Much of the discussion of the sexual division of labour is directed, ultimately, at the question of women and class. For if women's position in the relations of production in capitalism could be established, then clarification of their class position would follow. Lucy Bland[3] and her co-authors have argued that women's subordination cannot be understood through the categories of capital alone. They argue that 'outside' these economic relations, and historically prior to their emergence, lie the patriarchal relations between men and women which capital has 'taken over' or 'colonized'. A rather similar position is taken by Heidi Hartmann,[4] who argues that the sex-blind categories of Marxism can never in themselves explain why women occupy the situation they do, and must be supplemented by an independent analysis of gender relations as they have developed historically. The most obvious drawback of these arguments is that they run the risk of characterizing Marxism simply as a method for identifying the essential component parts of the capitalist class structure, and stripping it of any ability to explain these in concrete rather than abstract terms. The argument leads to the conclusion that Marxist theory can specify the 'places' which need to be filled, but that feminist theory must be invoked to explain who fills them. This problem of 'dualism', as Veronica Beechey has argued,[5] also arises in attempts to bring Marxist analysis to bear on the question of capitalist *production*, and feminist analysis to bear on the question of the *reproduction* of these relations of production.

Notes

1. R. McDonough and R. Harrison, 'Patriarchy and relations of production', in A. Kuhn and A. Wolpe (eds), *Feminism and Materialism*, London, 1978.
2. H. Wainwright, 'Women and the division of labour', in P. Abrams (ed.), *Work, Urbanisation and Inequality*.
3. L. Bland *et al.*, 'Women inside and outside', in Women's Studies Group of the Centre for Contemporary Studies, *Women Take Issue*, London, 1978.
4. H. Hartmann, 'The unhappy marriage of Marxism and feminism: towards a more progressive union', *Capital and Class*, no. 8 (1979).
5. V. Beechey, 'On patriarchy', *Feminist Review*, no. 3 (1979).

5.3   Sex, Class and Socialism
Lindsay German

The next two extracts present a Marxist view of women's oppression at work in the context of their class position: Lindsay German draws on material from contemporary life, while Geoffrey de Ste Croix concludes that a class analysis was as appropriate to an understanding of women's oppression 2,000 years ago as it is today.

The domestic labour debate

Recognition of the centrality of the family to capitalism was one feature of attempts by Marxists in the late 1960s and early 1970s to theorise women's oppression. The domestic labour debate was about the economic contribution of women's labour in the home to the capitalist system of production. It was characterised by academicism and a level of abstraction. While it was a serious attempt to locate women's oppression in capitalist society and to use Marxist terminology to explain oppression, it was also a concession to feminist ideas. It was a response to the criticism that Marxism only concerned itself with production, and that Marxists always regarded housework as a totally separate sphere.

So while some of the writing on domestic labour produced some valuable insights, there were a number of major flaws in the arguments.

The early domestic labour theorists tended to emphasise the two modes of production and reproduction, and so accepted that housework formed a separate mode of production.[1] Many fell into the functionalist trap of believing that capitalism could not under any circumstances manage to survive without the privatised family. Others argued that the labour of women in the home was productive of surplus-value through the commodity of labour-power. So women constituted a separate class which had an interest in fighting for wages for housework.[2]

The problem with these theories was that both, in their different ways, separated housework off from social production. They first put domestic labour on a par with wage labour performed for the employer, equating it with socialised commodity production. Secondly, they implicitly assumed the continued existence of privatised domestic labour, by claiming that it constituted a separate mode of production.

Several critics of these various positions pointed out that housework could not be equated with wage labour in this way:

> to compare domestic labour with wage labour in a quantitive way is not comparing like with like. However unevenly it operates, the process of value creation within commodity production enables one to talk about quantities of abstract labour in the case of wage labour in a way that is not valid for domestic labour. It is therefore not possible to add together domestic labour-time and wage labour-time in order to calculate the wife's surplus labour because the two are not commensurate.

The housewife has no rigid distinction between work and leisure; she is not directly controlled or supervised; and she is not producing for a market. She is atomised rather than part of a collective. Because market forces do not directly govern her work, the tasks connected with the reproduction of labour-power are performed whether that labour-power is in immediate demand or whether it is not (due to old age, unemployment, and so on).

Nor is the housewife *directly* productive of surplus-value. It is often argued that what the housewife produces are simply use-values:

> Domestic labour is the production of use-values, the physical inputs for the production being commodities bought with part of the husband's wage. The housewife produces directly consumable use-values with them. ... Child-care is the

most time-consuming part of the work of full-time housewives ... it is the most
essential task performed by the housewife for the continuance of capitalism.

To say simply that the housewife is concerned with the production of use-values
implies that she is merely a servant to her husband and children. However,
domestic labour has a social role. The reason that child care is the most essential
task performed for capitalism within the home is that there is a connection
between this work and the production of surplus value. Put succinctly, 'the
relation of domestic labour to the production of surplus-value is simply that the
former makes the latter possible'.

Domestic labour can be seen to be *indirectly productive* of surplus-value,
through being directly productive of labour-power. This feature is important in
order to retain what is central to the domestic labour debate, and to draw the
correct conclusions from it. The two dominant strands of the debate in fact lead
to wrong conclusions: either to the wages-for-housework campaign espoused by
Selma James, or to the idea that the use-values produced by the housewife have
little to do with commodity production or indeed capitalism. This analysis leads
to the view that the reproduction of labour-power takes place outside the
capitalist mode of production. Either theory leads yet again to complete
separatism in terms of struggle and the embracing of patriarchy theory.

The connection of domestic labour with capitalism lies not in the production
of values but in the reproduction of labour-power. The housewife produces only
use-values; but these in turn affect the value of labour-power.

Separatist conclusions may not have been the intention of many of the
domestic labour theorists. They saw their work as a serious attempt to theorise
Marxism and women's oppression. But their attempt to put unpaid work in the
home on a par with the categories of Marx's *Capital* led to a major weakness: the
lack of an understanding of the connection between family and work.

This may appear a contradiction, for after all, one of the central aspects of the
reproduction of labour-power under capitalism is the separation of home and
work. But the two complement and reflect one another as well. Domestic labour
exists in the form it does precisely because of wage labour and commodity
production.

The domestic labour theorists instead saw the family as a separate sphere.
They therefore set out to prove that women's domestic labour was central not
just to the family but to the capitalist system as well. This led away from
attempts to synthesise the two. It similarly failed to take sufficiently into account
the fact that women's labour was increasingly social – outside the home, in the
workplace. Consequently, the theory was only able to give a partial view of
women's oppression.

Male benefits

By the late 1970s, the domestic labour theory was being usurped by more overtly patriarchal theory: in particular the view that men gained some material benefit from women's oppression in the home. Woman's oppression was seen as maintained through men's control of every aspect of her life, including work. So it has been argued that:

> at marriage, the wife gives into the control of her husband both her labour power and her capacity to procreate in exchange for subsistence for a definite period, for life.

Heidi Hartmann,[3] who describes Marxism as 'sex-blind', has attempted a similar materialist, rather than purely idealist, analysis of patriarchy, by arguing that 'the material base upon which patriarchy rests lies most fundamentally in men's control over women's labour power'.

For Hartmann, control does not merely lie within the family but throughout the structures of capitalist society. She too bases her ideas on the two-modes-of-production analysis, and states quite categorically that fledgling capital and men of all classes went into alliance in order to maintain this control over women. Working-class men achieved this through ensuring protective legislation and a family wage. This kept women in the home and gave men a 'higher standard of living than women in terms of luxury consumption, leisure time and personalised services'.

Similar arguments are put by Zillah Eisenstein,[4] who explicitly refers to 'capitalist patriarchy' in her attempt to define women's oppression. The substance of this argument has been dealt with already, but it is worth pointing to a couple of its weaknesses. Firstly it stems from a total misunderstanding of women workers' relationship to the labour market. The woman worker sells her labour-power on the market in exactly the same way that a male worker does. No mediating structure exists between female wage labourers and the capitalist class, preventing her from being able to sell her labour-power. She is employed directly, without reference to her husband.

To pretend that women are somehow in a servile or bond relationship to their husbands with relation to the labour market is simply denying the facts. More important, it leaves patriarchy theorists with no understanding or explanation of the continued preference of the capitalist class for employing cheap female labour.

Protective legislation and the family wage were, as we have seen, the result of *class* interests and part of a class response to the worst ravages of the system, when there seemed little alternative to the awful conditions the working class lived under. Nor were male workers in a powerful position over female ones: only a minority were even in unions; and protective legislation was nowhere near as devastating to women's work as some feminists imply. For example, hardly any such legislation existed in the US until well into the twentieth century, yet the structure of the working-class family in the US was similar to that in Britain.

Johanna Brenner and Maria Ramas[5] make this point in their article 'Rethinking women oppression':

> it is very difficult to make a convincing case that so precarious a socio-political edifice could have played a major role in conditioning the sexual division of labour or the family household system, either in England or the United States.

In Britain, reductions in hours for women and children were often seen as beneficial for the whole working class, since they tended to shorten the working day. Where the unions did act to exclude women from work, they often did so for the most *class-conscious* reasons: to prevent the undercutting of wages and conditions:

> it is entirely unnecessary to resort to ideology to explain why trade unions were particularly adamant in their opposition to female entry into their trades. It is quite clear that when unions were unable to exclude women, a rapid depression of wages and general degradation of work resulted.

Although it may be relatively easy to point to the inconsistencies of Hartmann's historical analysis, it is much harder to defeat the *thrust* of her argument, which does not depend on historical accuracy for its appeal. The idea that men do gain substantial benefits from women's labour in the family is widespread. Most feminists argue that men receive these real benefits – more leisure, more food, more power – and it is this which leads them to support the status quo.

These ideas are powerful precisely because they reflect the appearance of the society in which we live. After all, the 'common sense' of society points to the fact that men get their meals cooked, that they have control over family finances, that they retain control over their wives and children. This is certainly how things would appear and, most feminists would argue, how they actually are.

Yet again, the argument centres on the role of the family under capitalism. Is it for the reproduction of labour-power or is it additionally for the benefit of individual men? If the latter proposition is true, then does this mean that working-class men have a *material* interest in defending the capitalist system?

To argue that men do have such an interest leads away from a class analysis of women's oppression. It is in the overwhelming interest of the working class to fight for the overthrow of the society which exploits them and therefore to fight for – among other things – the liberation of women. It is in the interests of the capitalist class, on the other hand, for labour-power to be reproduced privately as it is at present: for women to labour inside and outside the home, being paid low wages for work outside and nothing for domestic labour; and for the man to see his responsibility in society as providing, however inadequately, for his wife and family.

This situation leads to unequal relationships between the sexes, and within the family. But it does not lead to a situation where the man benefits. On the contrary, all members of the family would benefit from being able to live in a society where relationships were not straitjacketed as they are at present.

Notes

1. J. Harrison, 'The political economy of housework', *Bulletin of the Conference of Socialist Economists*, no. 4 (1974).
2. M. Dallacosta and S. James, *The Power of Women and the Subversion of the Community*, Bristol: 1975.
3. H. Hartmann, 'The unhappy marriage of Marxism and feminism: towards a more progressive union', *Capital and Class*, no. 8 (1979).
4. Z. Eisenstein, *Capitalist Patriarchy and the Case for Socialist Feminism*, New York: 1978.
5. J. Brenner and M. Ramas, 'Rethinking women's oppression', *New Left Review*, no. 144.

5.4 The Class Struggle in the Ancient Greek World
Geoffrey de St Croix

Women

The *production* which is the basis of human life obviously includes, as its most essential constituent part, the *reproduction* of the human species. And for anyone who, admitting this, believes (as I do) that Marx was right in seeing position in the whole system of production (necessarily including *re*production) as the principal factor in deciding class position, the question immediately arises: must we not allow a special *class* role to that half of the human race which, as a result of the earliest and most fundamental of all divisions of labour, specialises in reproduction, the greater part of which is biologically its monopoly? (Under 'reproduction' I of course include in the role of women not merely parturition but also the preceding months of pregnancy, and the subsequent period of lactation which, in any but the advanced societies, necessarily makes the care of the child during the first year and more of its life 'woman's work'.) [...]

Marx and Engels, who were always talking about the division of labour in production, did speak casually, in the *German Ideology* (1845–6) of procreation as involving 'the first division of labour', but for them, 'the division of labour ... was originally nothing but the division of labour *in the sexual act* [*im Geschlechtsakt*]' and this seems to me to miss the main point – as indeed Engels appears later to have realised, for when, two-thirds of the way through the second chapter of *The Origin of the Family*, he quoted this very passage (as appearing in 'an old, unpublished manuscript, the work of Marx and myself in 1846'), he changed the wording slightly, to 'The first division of labour is that between man and woman *for the production of children* [*zur Kinderzeugung*]', and he added, 'The first *class antagonism* [*Klassengegensatz*] which appears in history coincides with the development of the antagonism between man and woman in monogamous marriage, and the first *class oppression* [*Klassenunterdrückung*] with that of the female sex by the male'. And in the same early work from which Engels quoted, Marx and Engels said that 'the nucleus, the first form, of property lies in the family, where wife and children are the slaves of the husband. This latent slavery in the family, though still very crude, is the first form of property; but even at this early stage it corresponds perfectly to the definition of modern economists who call it the power of disposing of the labour-power of others'. Yet Marx and Engels seem hardly to have realised what far-reaching consequences ought to have been drawn from this particular specialisation of role, within their own system of ideas above all. Engels's *Origin of the Family* deals with the subject, to my mind, very inadequately. [...] I propose to take perfectly seriously the characterisation of the role of women, or anyway married women (I leave these alternatives open), *as a class*, which is implied in the *German Ideology*, and for a brief moment, in the passage I have quoted, becomes explicit in the second chapter of *The Origin of the Family*.

Now the effective property rights of women have often been restricted in practice. Sometimes this has applied to all the women of a given society, sometimes particularly to the married women, whose property rights have often been more limited (or even more limited) than those of the rest of their sex, as for example in modern England until the Married Women's Property Acts of 1882 and after began to effect a change. A few years ago the fact suddenly dawned upon me that Athenian women in the fifth and fourth centuries BC – apart perhaps from a handful of expensive prostitutes, like Neaera and her circle and Theodote, who of course were not citizens – were quite remarkably devoid of effective property rights and were apparently worse off in this respect than women in many (perhaps most) other Greek cities of the period, Sparta in particular, or for that matter in Hellenistic and Roman Athens. A suggestion I then made that the question of property rights of Greek women was worth investigating on a much larger scale has already been taken up. [...]

Meanwhile, this is the thesis I propose. In many societies either women in general, or married women (who may be regarded in principle as monopolising the reproductive function), have rights, including above all property rights, markedly inferior to those of men; and they have these inferior rights as a direct result of their reproductive function, which gives them a special role in the productive process and makes men desire to dominate and *possess* them and their offspring. In such societies it is surely necessary, on the premises I have accepted, to see the women, or the wives (as the case may be), as a distinct economic class, in the technical Marxist sense. They are 'exploited', by being kept in a position of legal and economic inferiority, so dependent upon men (their husbands in the first place, with their male kin, so to speak, in reserve) that they have no choice but to perform the tasks allotted to them, the compulsory character of which is not in principle lessened by the fact that they may often find real personal satisfaction in performing them. Aristotle, in a perceptive passage, could speak of the propertyless man (the *aporos*), who could not afford to buy slaves, as using his wife and children in their place.

Needless to say, if we think of women (or married women) as a class, membership of such a class may or may not be the prime criterion of a woman's class position. (It is perfectly possible for many individuals to belong to more than one class, and it may then be necessary to determine the essential one, membership of which is paramount for them.) I suggest that in our present case the relative importance of a woman's membership of the class of women (or wives) will depend to a high degree upon whether her economic and legal condition is very different from that of her menfolk. In Classical Athens I would see the class position of a citizen woman belonging to the highest class as largely determined by her sex, by the fact that she belonged to the class of women, for her father, brothers, husband and sons would all be property owners, while she would be virtually destitute of property rights, and her class position would therefore be greatly inferior to theirs. The humble peasant woman, however, would not in practice be in nearly such an inferior position to the men of her family, who would have very little property; and, partly owing to the fact that she would to some extent participate in their agricultural activities and work alongside them (in so far as her child-bearing and child-rearing permitted), her membership of the class of poor peasants might be a far more important determinant of her class position than her sex. Even less, perhaps, would the class of a non-citizen town-dwelling prostitute or *hetaira* be decided primarily by her sex, for her economic position might be virtually identical with that of a male prostitute or any other non-citizen provider of services in the city. We must of course realise that to place a woman in a separate class from her menfolk would often cut right across the usual criteria of 'social stratification', so far as the property-owning classes are concerned: within a single family the husband might be in the highest class, while his propertyless wife, in respect of the distinction I have just been making, might rate very low indeed; but in life-style she would rank according to the status of her husband. Since those elements in a woman's position which derive from her being virtually the possession of another are very precarious and unstable, I would tend to discount the husband's position as a factor in the real status of the wife, important as it may seem on the surface, and put more emphasis on any dowry which the women can rely on receiving and controlling, in accordance with custom. But this needs a great deal of further thought.

5.5   **The Mastery of Reason**
Valerie Walkerdine

Valerie Walkerdine has conducted a great deal of research into the production of gendered subjectivies within education. Here she explains how classroom practices which have as overt aims the teaching of a formal skill (reading, concept, number) act to reproduce discourses of gender and power.

Later in the same child's session are examples of explicitly pedagogic discourse on my part and of his response to that:

VW: Do you remember what else happened in the story was that they all had bowls of porridge. Do you remember that they all had bowls of porridge? Well I've got three bowls of porridge here, do you think you can give the bears their bowls of porridge?
(*Gives him the bowl cards.*)
CH: Which one's the biggest? (*Touches the biggest bowl.*)
(CH *puts middle-sized bowl by largest bear and large bowl by middle bear.*)
VW: Mm, Mm (*unenthusiastically*). Go on then, can you give the other bears their porridge?
(CH *looks at cards already out and swaps them around.*)
CH: Oh, sorry.
(*Gives small bowl to baby bear.*)
VW: That's it.

I then go on to ask, 'Why do you think the daddy's got the biggest bowl of porridge?', to which he replies 'Cos he eats big ones'. I ask him about the amount eaten by mummy, to which he replies 'Middle-sized one'. I then ask, 'Do you think mummies eat as much as daddies?' to which he replies 'Yeah!' in the tone of, 'of course'. Thus, in this last response, we have the total disjunction of the portions allotted to the bears in the story and what he knows about mothers' and fathers' eating patterns. One might ask, therefore, what is the effectivity of the three bears narrative upon his reading of 'mothers' within the practices of the family.

That is, another effect of the multiplicity of significations is that of the imposition of one reading upon another. Even though this child can articulate that his mother eats as much as his father, he may read her power through those other discursive practices in which women and mothers are positioned. Examples such as these occur throughout the data and are a constant indication that a different kind of analysis is necessary from that to which experimental data is usually subjected.

In order to understand why the children appear to give the wrong answers, when there are other indications that they understand the relationship which the question is aimed at revealing, it is perhaps important to examine what are the parameters of the pseudo-questions asked in this and the teaching situation. The pseudo-questions in this case ask for a yes/no response. The very form of the questions indicates that the child is being tested to elicit knowledge that is already known. It may be for some children that this is what is salient and invokes a wild guessing strategy, or a simple answer in the affirmative as being usually what is required. To understand this it is possible to recall those situations in a conversation where one is not paying attention but realizes that a question has been asked. In these situations we take other cues to work out whether the desired response is in the affirmative or negative. These are usually present in the speaker's intonation and we make a wild guess. The children might also wonder why a question is being asked about such a perfectly obvious matter. These thoughts are speculative, but I suggest that it is in this direction that our analysis should go if we are to understand more fully the responses given by children in experiments.

It is perhaps important to note that when experiments are devised it is usual to attempt to minimize order-effects, though clearly order and the relation of one question to another cannot entirely be removed and may have important effects which deserve study in their own right. Perhaps what is more important is that there exists a level of information given unintentionally by me as experimenter to the children which is entirely outside the techniques for evaluating experimental data. This would be present despite the most stringent attempts to avoid it, since it is axiomatic to interaction and provides an important aspect of the signification to be read.

The most noticeable of these phenomena is the way in which I, as experimenter, mark correct and incorrect responses. Although on a transcript of the test the words appear similar, the manner in which they are conveyed is remarkably different. There are two methods for replying to wrong responses which I use interchangeably. The first is to repeat the child's answer, but in the form of a question:

VW: Is the daddy bear bigger than the mummy bear?
CH: No (*shakes head*).
VW: No?
CH: No ...

What happens on these occasions is that the questioning responses on my part act as a cue for the child either to affirm her/his response, or to change it. The other response pattern is for me to follow the wrong response with a repetition of the child's response, but in a completely flat and unenthusiastic tone, which is in sharp contrast to the tone which follows a correct response. In these cases, while I might not actually say different words, the manner and tone of voice are very different. The words are spoken more loudly and in a markedly enthusiastic tone. For example:

VW: Which one is the smallest one?
CH: That one.
VW: That one!

Despite the information in the words uttered, the mode of conveying the information gives feedback which the children learn to read, just as they read the verbal signs. I will argue that the teacher marks correct and incorrect answers in precisely the same manner. In addition to this I appear frequently to move my body towards, point, or touch the appropriate card for the children to respond to, in a manner of which, during the test, I was completely unaware.

By giving some examples of the children's responses I shall attempt to show how much they are dependent on the kind of interactional information which Cole and Traupmann[1] describe. A very detailed analysis which considered the relations between gesture, word, and facial expression for each child would undoubtedly give a more complex reading.

Notes

1. M. Cole and K. Traupmann, *Learning from a Learning Disabled Child*, Minnesota Symposium of Child Development, 1979 (unpublished).

5.6   **Social Semiotics**
Robert Hodge and Gunther Kress

The authors focus on the pre-school education of children in nurseries and playgroups. They propose that the entry of the child into semiosis is itself gender-specific.

Teeth or pimples: enculturation or resistance

Childhood itself constitutes a broad domain area, in which error is tolerated and forms of resistance can be developed. Even though domains are instituted as strategies for control, they are also sites where real concessions are made to the power or interests of the subordinate. In this section we will look at a text produced in one such sub-domain, the child-care centre as it functions in Australia.

The form of child-care centres is unstable even within Australia, and other closely related cultures such as Britain and America have different forms again. This inconsistency is what is to be expected with sub-domains that are situated on the boundary between two such major domains as home and school, operating with subjects whose classification within the culture is indeterminate (educable or not). The child-minder (usually female) is therefore faced with an ambiguous task. On the one hand 'good' child-care centres are tied in with quite formal educational processes. But the contrary need to relax their prescriptions leads to 'slack' child-care centres where children are allowed 'to run riot' or 'to vegetate'. There is a demand from the culture for action which is controlled and directed, yet the energy and activity of the children is intrinsic to their role as active agents in social life, and it cannot be simply quashed. Children need to be offered (within limits which aren't always fixed) the opportunity to explore the margins of rule systems, or even deliberately contravene them, which may amount to the same thing. The child-minder, then, must have a cultural agenda which shapes or frames activities which do not, however, always arise from within its bounds. The example text which we use to explore this question comes from a pre-school day-care centre. Sarah and Aaron are about $3\frac{1}{2}$ years old.

TEACHER:	Look at this (*pointing to picture of mother and young rhino*)
SARAH:	His mothers a lot of toothes
TEACHER:	How many teeth? How many have they got?
SARAH:	one two three four
TEACHER:	What are they up the top?
SARAH:	One two three four five
TEACHER:	Five at the top and four at the bottom
AARON:	No they're pimples
TEACHER:	Do you think they're pimples?
AARON:	Yeah
TEACHER:	But they're where his teeth should be ... do you think they're just a different colour?
AARON:	Well ... that ... those are pimples cos those are pink
TEACHER:	Um ... could be too ... and what do you call those things there?
SARAH:	Whiskers
TEACHER:	You do too and what's that, Sarah?
SARAH:	A ear
TEACHER:	It's a funny looking ear, isn't it?
AARON:	Yes ... a little ear
SARAH:	That's got two ... one two ... two ears
TEACHER:	Do you think they'd be friendly? ... these rhinoceroses?
AARON: SARAH:	No
TEACHER:	Why not?
AARON:	Cos they'll eat people
TEACHER:	How do you know? What makes them look unfriendly?
AARON:	Their teeth ... they can eat people
TEACHER:	They *are* big ... what about this animal?
SARAH:	That hasn't got any teeth
TEACHER:	Hasn't he?
SARAH:	No
TEACHER:	Do you think he'd be friendly?
SARAH:	Yes
TEACHER: AARON:	Look what he *has* got
SARAH	He's got little claws

TEACHER:	Claws
SARAH:	See ... but that ... but he's still our friendly ...
TEACHER:	He's still friendly even if he's got claws?
SARAH:	Look ... they're not flendry
AARON:	Yes they are
TEACHER:	Do you think lions are friendly, Aaron?
AARON:	Yeah ... because ... if they ... if people hurt them they hurt them back.
TEACHER:	And it's quite safe you think if you don't hurt them?
AARON:	Yes
TEACHER:	I don't know

The child-minder/teacher begins by setting up an agenda of 'difference' between herself and the children. She pins up a poster that shows some African animals. Power and knowledge are entirely fused in that action: the right and ability to put up the poster coincide with the right and ability to determine what area of the cultural domain will be explored. The teacher has control of both. In terms of the logonomic rule system, that (perhaps only momentary) identity of the mimetic and the semiosic planes is crucial. The teacher controls who puts up the poster, and where, and she has control over what is to count as relevant knowledge. Ostensibly what is at issue here is learning about the mimetic plane: about rhinos and lions, and their characteristics. But it quickly becomes apparent that what is really at issue is not so much the teacher's knowledge, but the teacher's power. The teacher's direction to the children to 'Look at this' is reconstructed by Sarah as 'Tell me about this'. Obligingly, she offers the comment that 'His mothers a lot of toothes'. This offers the teacher the substance that she needs and on which she is able to work. Sarah's co-operative mode, attempting to demonstrate solidarity with the teacher, is shattered by Aaron's challenge 'No they're pimples'. Aaron rejects solidarity via a contradiction of Sarah's and the teacher's classification. That is, he uses the mimetic plane to express his challenge to the teacher's power on the semiosic plane. However, Aaron's challenge goes somewhat further, for not only does he challenge the classification, he also challenges the teacher's control of this whole situation. She had signalled the end to this particular conversational sequence by restating/correcting Sarah's last comment. That restatement functions as a signal both of conclusion, closure of one textual episode, and of her intention to initiate a new one. Aaron's challenge is therefore shrewdly timed. Had he chosen to interrupt after Sarah's first comment the teacher would have been entirely unchallenged; had he interrupted after the teacher's 'How many have they got?' his challenge would have been on the mimetic plane alone, as the teacher's closure had not yet been attempted.

In response to this move, the teacher's strategy is to pretend that this is a 'sincere' comment, within the logonomic system that she herself is operating in. She re-labels the challenge as being one about the mimetic plane alone, and indicates that she believes in Aaron's sincerity. 'Do you think they're pimples?'

This then becomes refocused as a difference about classification, where Aaron's 'thinks' is opposed to the teacher's 'knows'. By the simple strategy of 'mishearing' Aaron's challenge, the teacher maintains her power. She could of course have played this differently: 'Aaron, you *are* a naughty boy, always trying to disrupt'. That, however, would simply have acknowledged Aaron's success, and prevented her from scoring the victory in this insurrection.

The teachers closing 'Um ... could be too ... and what do you call ...' goes unchallenged here. Nor is she conceding anything to Aaron's counter-classification. The children will by now have learned to recognize a supportive positively evaluative closure ('Good, right' or 'Yes, good girl') from one which is not supportive. In that context lack of support will signal the teacher's lack of agreement, that is her disagreement. She avoids disagreement, preferring to let the children infer – construct for themselves – her disagreement/disapproval. Other instances of this are her 'How do you know?'; 'They *are* big' (i.e. this could be a relevant criterion but happens not to be in this case); 'Look what he *has* got' (that is, 'Attend to the *relevant* characteristics'); and 'I don't know' (i.e. if it's outside the teacher's range of knowledge it can't be right).

In this text there is a systematic difference between Aaron's and Sarah's responses to the situation. Over the three instances of difference – teeth versus pimples; eating people versus being friendly; dangerous claws versus friendly animal – Aaron opposes the teacher's classification. Sarah twice starts in disagreement with the teacher. On the first occasion she simply leaves it to Aaron to oppose; her perception of the teacher's disagreement ('Why not?') silences her. On the second occasion she again starts on the opposite side to the teacher. However, after three challenges from the teacher – 'Look what he *has* got', 'Claws', 'He's still friendly even if he's got claws?' – she caves in to the pressure. Aaron maintains his opposition on both occasions, each time supporting his challenge with his own set of criteria. Only on one occasion does Aaron go along with the (female) teacher's argument and even here he shifts from the teacher's 'It's a funny looking ear' to 'Yes ... a little ear'. Aaron's overt mode is to reject the possibility of solidarity, which, given that it is solidarity with the powerful, is essentially the possibility of submission and acquiescence. Sarah's overt mode is to seek the possibility of solidarity, and of acquiescence. Of course it is dangerous to speculate from this brief textual example; moreover Sarah's hesitancy, especially her 'See ... but that ... but he's still our friendly ...' suggests that there is more than a residue of disagreement, and some possibility of opposition.

Nevertheless, there is a clear difference which may point, even at this relatively early age, to a difference of gender-specific behaviour. Ultimately, both Sarah and Aaron will enter fully into the semiotic systems of their culture. It does seem, however, as though the paths by which they reach the same end point may be fundamentally different: Sarah by seeking solidarity, Aaron by constant opposition. That difference in routes may indeed leave them differently positioned at the end. While both are fully competent users of the semiotic system, it may be that the possibility of resistance will have quite receded for Sarah, while for Aaron it may remain a possibility. Aaron's opposition/ subversion has the additional advantage of gaining him the attention of the teacher, of the powerful. Just so long as he chooses to remain within the rules of the game, it may be that for him that will always be the reward; whereas for Sarah acquiescence may simply produce the expectation of more acquiescence, delivered ever more readily.

Our point here, sketchily developed at best, is that entry into semiosis seems to have gender-specific aspects. It may be that access to both the mimetic and the semiosic planes tends to be differently structured for male and female children. Of course, the differential treatment by teachers of male and female students has often been commented on, and is well demonstrated. Similarly, the differing curricular paths laid out for children of either gender are also well documented. Our point is that this is a process that is established very early, and proceeds always simultaneously on both of the axes of mimesis and semiosis, of knowledge and power. Further, the differential entry of men and of women into language and into semiosis has a real history, a history of specific experiences in particular social institutions – such as the pre-school day-care centre, or the school – a history which may also be a significantly differentiated one for different individuals from differing social origins. At any rate it is not the pseudo-history posited in asocial, ahistorical psychoanalytic accounts. The entry into semiosis has that institutional specificty, a specificity which attends to class, gender, ethnicity. Children's construction of meaning, their reconstruction of texts, their construction of their semiotic systems always take place in contexts of this kind, not in some decontextualized or contextless fantasy of 'childhood'.

5.7   **Academics**
John McCauley

John McCauley shows that an essentialist view of the female role (nurturing, caring, constructively critical) militates against women achieving at work. He also shows that women's performance and activities are interpreted, even within the 'liberal' workplace of higher education, within the frame of traditional gender roles and essential qualities, and suggests ways of counteracting this at work.

Although the institution is officially highly committed to the teaching activity as providing the basis of its primary mission, other activities are seen as the features that actually define promotion potential. The organizational assumption is that teaching staff are by definition 'good' at the teaching activity – it is a basic prerequisite for appointment to the collectivity – and quality of teaching cannot, therefore, be seen (in the view of the organization) as a sufficient criterion for promotion. In order for there to be promotion from the career grade of senior lecturer to that of principal lecturer, there need to be at least four conditions satisfied. One is that there is available within the 'official establishment' of the department a place for a promotee. If there is, then the would-be promotee must have displayed his/her ability to organize, to research, to be entrepreneurial, or whatever constitutes the requisite task ability for the transition to take place. The third criterion is that the promotee is able to make public that he or she has undertaken these activities. Finally and importantly, there is the discovery of some system of support or sponsorship that will make available a place in the principal lecturer grade.

In the context of their understanding of the sorts of situation that affect women members of staff in higher education, Woodall and her colleagues have written: 'the culture that pervades our higher educational institutions is one that emphasises publishing, dashing around to conferences, competitive debate, scholarly analyses and climbing an academic ladder'.[1] These writers argued that, in their experience, such activities are 'buttressed and cemented' by male patterns of sociability and that the culture in which these activities is located is masculine in its ethos. If we look at the activities which they mention it would seem that, irrespective of gender, at least three of them are entirely appropriate to any higher educational establishment. To undertake work that results in the publication of papers, to attend conferences, and to participate in academic debates are important features of the academic's construction of what it is to be a competent member of the collectivity, both from the point of view of personal development and also in order to generate organizational responsiveness to change. However, what transforms these activities from benign, gender-free endeavours is the ethos within which such activities take place – the general cultural milieu. There is evidence that women see themselves as undertaking these key academic activities in quite a different spirit and in quite different modes from those in which men conduct them.

For example, within the research activity, women claim that, conventionally, little account is taken of gender issues. Indeed, Stanley and Wise[2] characterize their work as coming from a distinctive paradigm of social science, one that always respects the 'data' provided by the subject: in particular, they claim, feminist research is characterized by its essential humanness. Similarly, Maher writes that 'in every scholarly discipline wherein the female experience has been challenged' there is a need to re-evaluate radically 'the research methods by which knowledge of the field was gained in the first place'. The sort of general epistemological shift to which this writer is alluding is that which eschews the 'single objective, rationally derived "right" answer ... for the construction of knowledge from multiple perspectives through cooperative problem-solving'.[3]

Although many men would object to the annexation of this type of research methodology by women (in the sense that many men who are social scientists would see themselves as working out of this paradigm), the important point is that the preferred approach for women undertaking research in the social sciences is not the dominant paradigm within many institutions. Interviews with women (not in the institution) undertaking research in the natural sciences suggest that they do not have this conflict. Even where women do find themselves comfortable with the 'normal' paradigm, they have to confront the structural constraints of the research community. This community, expressed in research validating committees and funding bodies, is predominantly male in its composition. In their major funding operations the concept of 'track record' of applicants for research applies as a rational response when allocating scarce resources. In this situation there is a tendency to give awards to people who are 'known' – and these tend to be men. Furthermore, because women are not, by and large, able to gain access to Reader posts (these are positions which have particular responsibility for research), women are seen as agents of implementation of research rather than agents of creation of research. (A positive aspect of the institution in this case study has been a deliberate policy in at least one faculty to promote women in the research endeavour).

It is clear that women's image of themselves when conducting academic discussions has a very different 'edge' to it from that of men. For example, one of the women interviewed in this research, commenting on the way women typically conduct themselves at conferences and in academic debate, emphasized how women attempt to be supportive of each other in debate. She referred to ways in which comments on each other's papers are designed to be facilitative and constructive, in contrast to the ways in which she saw men as behaving when commenting – that is, essentially, to be destructive, to be individualistic and competitive. She saw the approach of women to intellectual activity as being just as rigorous as that of her male colleagues, but that it came from a different conception of the nature of the pursuit of the scientific debate. Given the dominant paradigm of a male-dominated, individualistically orientated academic culture, a co-operative culture can be seen as institutionally problematic and cause some degree of marginalization and discrediting of people (women) who work in this way, because of men's belief that 'rigour' can only be achieved 'by the cut and thrust of academic debate' – i.e. destructive criticism.

Turning to the core activity of the institution – teaching – there are significant differences in the images that men and women hold about the ways in which this activity is conducted. Interviews with teaching staff indicated that the image that many women have of men (and many men have of themselves) is that the teacher is an expert and that his or her function is largely concerned with the transmission of knowledge: further, that the proper relationship in the classroom is based on the ideas that power is essentially indivisible, that teaching is essentially subject-based, and that it is essentially impersonal with regard to the student population. On the other hand the interviews suggested that the women staff tend to see the teaching situation as one in which there is potential for mutual learning, in which teaching is essentially concerned with the journey towards knowledge, in which attention to process issues may be more important than the subject itself (that is, the process may become the subject), and that teaching is essentially a personal, interactive matter. This approach can be illustrated in the admittedly extreme case of women involved in teaching women's studies courses. Here the underlying personal orientation implied by the model of teaching discussed above may be amplified by the teacher's relationship to the subject itself. Raymond has written that:

> the true aim of the teaching I have been describing [in women's studies] is not to enforce feminist ideology but rather to *empassion* students with feminist knowledge. Inquiry is a profound passion and the teaching of the male academy has most often left its female learners with a passionless knowledge.[4]

(As this author suggests, there may be a boundary issue from time to time in relation to 'passion' becoming 'preaching': her felicitous suggestion is that 'preaching is passion separated from its sources'.)

Both these models of the teaching activity are, in their own ways, positive. They are affirmative of somewhat different ideals about education, but both actually have some sort of grasp of the educational task. However, when teachers are in a bad temper with each other or have not given the matter too much thought, the 'shadow' elements of these models are given transcendency. Men are characterized as 'hard', 'authoritarian' characters, and women as 'emotional', 'unable to control their classes', or 'incapable of actually transmitting any knowledge'. In settings that are male-dominated these images of competence/incompetence become distributed amongst the men. To that extent they are free-floating images in relation to gender. In one department which had been almost exclusively male, two women research staff volunteered to undertake some teaching. The initial assumption made by most of the men was that they would occupy a person-centred position with regard to their teaching. As one of the women observed: 'they, the "liberal" men, took us on because they thought we'd be their natural allies; they were in for a nasty surprise.' Indeed, although the teaching style of these women was student-centred, when it came to assessment of work the women were perceived by themselves and by their male colleagues as being as 'tough' and 'rigorous' as the most 'authoritarian' men. This example illustrates the trite but inescapable difficulty that reality is very complex: both men and women may hold personal ideologies about teaching or research or whatever that are simple in their essence but complicated in their implementation. Behind logics of teaching there may hide sentiments about the activity itself: shadow and substance are actually inextricably intertwined.

Although many women teachers feel that they are ascribed teaching styles and approaches by their male colleagues that tend to be either directly discrediting or else ambivalent in their messages about total competence, the women interviewed did not feel that these ascriptions were inflexible or (even where they were powerful) that they were inescapable. The women saw the roles ascribed to them as potentially or actually negotiable, more in accord with the sort of model of role suggested by Turner[5] – with its emphasis upon the actor's ability to understand and evaluate what is happening in the situation – rather than more deterministic and mechanistic models. The women interviewed felt that, although it was arduous, they could actually negotiate with male colleagues in order to avoid being marginalized (for example, by the demonstration of competence), or being placed into what men considered to be a residual status (by not taking on, for example, an institutionalized 'caring' role).

Some women commented on a continuing difficulty that they encountered in that many men had a negative view about the 'reliability' of women. This was particularly directed towards women with children, but could also be directed towards women generally on the grounds that women are 'less committed' to their careers. This characterization is, of course, undertaken without recourse to 'factual' information, such as data on absence or attendance. Men tend to perceive women as being more tied down by domestic circumstances than are men and therefore more likely to be absent from work. There is a sentient paradox here that operates powerfully to the disadvantage of women. At the heart of the paradox is that members of staff – women and men – are permitted, in the culture of colleagueship, to be absent if they are attending conferences or undertaking consultancy (although staff do operate a rough and ready model of felt equity in this matter). So it is accepted that colleagues can be absent for periods of time. However, there is a transmitted feeling that absence from work for domestic reasons is a source of disapproval from others and of guilt in the self. One of the women interviewed felt that a consequence of her having children was that she had been recategorized into the status 'parent', whereas men with children were not viewed in this sort of way. She went to say:

> 'We have to be really careful to be seen to be doing things. We must not bring children into the department and when things go wrong [at home] we must not show it. Men handle such things covertly – when they have to handle a crisis it is not seen in the same disparaging way!'

More generally, men still created a quite rigid separation between the life of home and the life of the institution and of work. Not only was such a clear distinction seen as 'natural', as a taken-for-granted matter of 'fact', but it was also, for most men, a convenient way of being. (In many settings it can be the cause of some embarrassment if a male colleague brings into work some tale of sadness or evidence of troubles of a domestic sort.) However, there were also women in the institution who practised just as rigid a separation and there were men for whom their domestic and work lives were inextricably intertwined. But one of the consequences of the rigid separation of home and work is that women tend to become lodged in a situation in which they over-compensate. To avoid being seen as not sufficiently 'committed' they throw their resources disproportionately into the teaching activity – a highly visible phenomenon –

at the expense of, for example, research. Although men also experience pressure to take on heavy teaching loads, it seems that women are more likely to succumb to such pressure than are men. Crucially, as I have argued above, teaching is *not of itself* seen as meriting reward in promotion or status terms in the institution. Although this pressure on women (which, it must be emphasized, is generated by themselves as well as by their male colleagues) appears to be widespread, it is not necessarily a binding feature of institutional life. One of the women described the 'existential moment' when she felt able to step a little outside the teaching activity, with the realization that she did not have to undertake *every* possible teaching commitment that came her way. A great sense of release came with the realization that she would have available the sort of time and space that would enable her to undertake research and consultancy activities.

Notes

1. J. Woodall, A. Showstack, B. Towers and C. McNally, 'Never promote a woman if there's a man in sight', *Guardian*, 10 September 1985, p. 22.
2. L. Stanley and S. Wise, *Breaking Out: Feminist consciousness and feminist Research*, London: Routledge & Kegan Paul, 1983.
3. F. Maher, 'Classroom pedagogy and the new scholarship on women', in M. Culley and C. Portuges (eds), *Gendered Subjects*, London: Routledge & Kegan Paul, 1985.
4. J. Raymond, 'Women's studies', in Culley and Portuges, *Gendered Subjects*.
5. R. Turner, 'Role taking: process versus conformity', in A. M. Rose (ed.), *Human Behaviour and the Social Process*, London: Routledge & Kegan Paul, 1962.

5.8   Women Managers: travellers in a male world
Judi Marshall

Judi Marshall's book describes the process of being a woman in management, discussing organisational structures and the ways in which they impede women. Here she outlines the extent to which women feel undervalued in the workplace and deals sympathetically with their strategies – usually indirect – for minimising antagonism. She concludes with a critique (from which these extracts are taken) of methods for increasing female employment, including a proposal for separatism.

I have two interrelated criticisms of the standard proposals for increasing the number of, and opportunities for, women in management jobs. I claim, firstly, that they will have little effect because they repeat, but officially deny, the sexist values of male positive, female negative they supposedly supersede, and that these basic inequalities of power will prevent them achieving their espoused objectives. Secondly, even if they did work, I would criticize their perpetuation of an organization system based on male values. Whilst some women may derive success, growth and satisfaction from following male models of management careers, the underlying pattern that male is the dominant and the desired norm goes unchallenged. Effort is directed at a one-way traffic of socializing women into the prevailing male world, with few, if any, opportunities for women to exert reciprocal influence on that world. Equal opportunities as it is thus officially offered is a sexist interpretation. Women want the right to be women *and* to be valued.

This chapter has constituted a critique of what 'equality' means. I have implicitly been arguing throughout that equality should not be contingent on sameness but should recognize and welcome differences and accord them equal social worth. To move towards valuing women *as women*, which is my definition of full equality, we need:

1. to understand a social system in its complexity and transform it all rather than modify separate parts in isolation;
2. to recognize and be prepared to address the divisions of interest which currently exist between women and men;
3. to accept and cope with the uncertainty, threat and emotions involved.

One of the main reasons why we have not yet achieved this wholehearted movement is that the right and power to assign social worth has remained in the hands of men. By drawing on principles of agency to define current issues and offer solutions, they have further reinforced this power base. At a public level women have largely accepted men's lead and bowed to their valuable capacity for clarity. In private they are tentatively exploring ways to spin new meanings and develop strategies which owe more to communion; women's engagement with choice is impressive and illuminating. Their blending of agency with communion offers an alternative model for change.

Women's development: their relationships with each other and with men

Both theoretically and practically, I believe that women's way forward is to develop and respect their own themes within their own culture before attempting to engage in dialogue with men. Women must become potentially self-sufficient, particularly in terms of assigning worth. Only when they have a solid base of their own can they escape from oppression without seeking to oppress in their turn. I am ambitious about what women can achieve, for themselves and others, if they do develop their own base with thoroughness and courage before attempting to change openly their social relationships with men. Various writers warn of the negative repercussions if this first phase of development is curtailed.[1] The greatest risk is that women will lose their initial energy and direction, and settle for old palliatives instead of creating new options.

The separation of women from men I advocate has indeed happened in many of the early activities of the Women's Movement. An awareness of men's potential to distort and constrain female being prompted the creation of safe spaces defended against men. This was epitomized in the development of consciousness-raising groups and of women-only magazines and newsletters. For most people this phase of self-development was a relatively private affair, perhaps fostered by belonging to a small, secret and exclusive peer group. Whilst there is some guidance available on ground-rules for running a consciousness-raising group (for example, Spender[2]), what they do and how remain relative mysteries to outsiders and the general public. Similarly, individuals have tended to resolve issues about their gender in personalistic terms and many prefer not to share their experiences and solutions, even with people faced by similar circumstances. I find myself both disappointed and heartened by the relative silence and invisibility of women's approaches to these issues. I am disappointed because experiences and gained understandings remain unshared. Each individual must start afresh with their own quest and may feel alone and unique because unaware of and unguided by other travellers. These trends are at the same time heartening because they represent new ways of being and becoming, free from many of the vices of doctrinaire mass movements. No competitive manifestos simplify the issues, or demand loyalty which compromises individuals' capacities for development and judgement.

The process of change through one-by-one personal transformation may seem slow, but it is sure, soundly grounded, authentic and above all continually adaptive. The critical factors for significant impact to be achieved are that numbers should grow, and that the individuals concerned should each act as if they make a difference, thus influencing the sphere in which they operate. This is one meaning for me of the power of 'the personal is political'. In this sense, I see women as the powerful, distributed seeds of a new transformation. Their impacts challenge our stale notions that social change must be large-scale and standardized to be meaningful. They also lead me to revise my conclusion in Chapter 1 that very little is happening to improve women's places in society. I had been looking at the surface, public world and its official statistics. Turning to women's own arena, the private and personal, I find that significant transformations *are* in progress. Women's emerging form of politics provides a critical example. Women made up only 3.5 per cent of the Members of Parliament in the United Kingdom in July 1983. Their representation was the same as in 1974, the year before the Sex Discrimination Act. Some commentators interpret these figures as evidence of women's continuing suppression. On a local scale, however, women are becoming increasingly active to promote causes they believe in through their own considered forms of action. Their resilient demonstration outside Greenham Common air-base, and its ripple effects promoting concordant expressions throughout the country, illustrate their alternative form of politics.

In the near future I see the possibility of taking this social transformation still further. There are signs that a new phase of collaboration between women and men is becoming possible, expanding potential life options. Friedan,[3] one of the founders of the Women's Movement in the United States, suggests that we are now moving to 'The Second Stage', of dialogue and joint development with men. The first stage of separation and opposition was necessary for women to develop their self-understanding and self-respect, but is no longer the only priority.

However welcome this movement forward, women must appreciate and protect against its dangers. Women's delicately developed awareness is vulnerable in the face of the patriarchal forces which have constrained it for so long. Unless dialogue emerges out of female strength and centredness, women cannot engage on equal terms with men. Women must maintain their current channels of self-development to provide the necessary self-affirming balance. Their ability to do so is strengthened by the relatively recent emergence of positive goals within the Women's Movement, which in time can depose original formulations which defined women mainly in terms of their opposition to men. Bardwick describes this changing emphasis:

> The initial feminist analysis was preoccupied with the negative; what women had *not* become. Happily, within feminism and academia we have begun to focus on ourselves. What *have* we become? What are women's strengths, insights, and priorities? What is our history? What are our contributions? What is our tradition? Where have we found our sense of honour? ... When we feel pride in the qualities, values, and accomplishments that have historically been ours, we will have finally given up our psychological minority status.

Notes

1. J. Bardwick, *In Transition*, New York: Holt, Rinehart & Winston, 1979; A. Oakley, *Subject Women*, Oxford: Martin Robertson, 1981.
2. D. Spender, *Made Made Language*, London: Routledge & Kegan Paul, 1980.
3. B. Friedan, *The Second Stage*, London: Michael Joseph, 1982.

5.9   **Joining Forces**
Nigel Fielding

This is an account of attitudes towards female workers in an occupation which is heavily (male)-gendered: police work. Nigel Fielding draws attention to the contradictions between generalised views expressed by officers and their actual experiences of working with women.

Women fell into two sharply divided categories, the rough and the respectable. Respectable women were innocent, ignorant and needed protection. Police-women could be resented because they caused confusion of the categories.

The view that a woman constable's place is in the station house and not the street points to the image of policing carried by the respondent. It is another arena for the preference of crime control over social service as an occupational image. The 'physical' approach to policing underlies comments which otherwise appear only to voice prejudice. Thus:

> 'I've worked with women before. I try not to be biased. I've met one or two good ones. If you get a good woman she is brilliant and she will leave you standing. But the majority are, quite honestly, something to hang a uniform on.'   (3: 5, 3)[1]

It is interesting to compare this with the elaborated answer given a year later by the same respondent. The early views are confirmed but invested with the extra 'credibility' of 'experience', which here seems to pertain more to inhabiting the occupational culture than working with a WPC:

> 'I've walked the beat with one once but I avoid it like the plague. There's three reasons. One, if that woman gets injured I would feel a lot worse than if a bloke gets injured. The second thing I don't like about women is they seem so indecisive and giggly. They frustrate me at work. I don't mind them giggling in bed but I don't like them giggling next to me at work. And, three, a lot of them only join the job to find a husband, and I just haven't got time to tolerate them. A lot of blokes, when they're out working with policewomen, their motivation's not to do the job well, but to impress this female. And I am a male chauvinist pig, no two ways about it.'
> (9: 1, 9)

The point in examining these comments is not to document prejudice, but to examine the way prejudice can be excused in the account by reference to aspects of the police role which are unproblematically defined as desirable. Despite his self-attribution of the label 'chauvinist', the respondent's evaluation is expressed in terms of role requirements. In his conception of the police role, dedication to duty is a signal value:

> 'If my job runs over ... I'll just give the missus a ring, and say, "Hey up, lass, I'm going to be home late." "What, again?" "Look, it's putting food in your belly, don't complain," and put the phone down. But there's girls saying, "Oh, I've got a hair appointment," or they're engaged. I say, "Sod off and leave the file to me to sort out," but it happens so often that it makes you cross. They're not conscientious about the job.'
> (9: 1, 10)

In a final version, the alleged unsuitability of women is presented by two rhetorical devices. The idea of WPCs arises from the 'admin.' who lack a grounding in real policing, and even the WPCs themselves do not wish to work on patrol:

> 'The previous system, the WPCs section, was far better than where they've got this what they call "equality". When I refer to "they" I mean the people who work in admin. I've worked with WPCs who are rubbish, and with WPCs who are better than some men. But as a whole I don't think they feel they should be out on the streets. It's a matter of physical difference and attitude.' (11: 2, 6)

The 'disadvantaged' group is seen as reluctant to accept its own 'advancement'.

The overlap between this perspective and a paternalistic approach is apparent. What the paternalist gains by a denial of prejudice he does not, as it were, lose in the depth of his assumption that women prefer to be treated as delicate and unworldly. Some responses move beyond paternalistic protectiveness to consider the advantage to the benefactor of taking responsibility for a female partner:

> 'They are more or less the weaker sex, aren't they? You can't expect them against most blokes to stand up for themself [sic]. So really it's quite good for them to walk with a bobby. They're a bit more secure. Even the bobby's probably a little bit scared, like. If there's a woman at side of him he's got to put that fear out of his mind.' (1: 2, 4)

The paternalist's answer to the 'violence' problem is to keep the WPC away from such situations:

> 'I find them a bit of a bind sometimes. ... But I'll work with them providing if you get the odd punch-up you can generally leave them in the car or something. ... But the girls I've worked with have done the self-same job as me.' (2: 2, 3)

The lingering pertinence of the assumption that the job is in large part a 'physical' one is so general that the 'physical' aspects must be subdivided; this quality concerns much besides actual fighting. Stamina and psycho–motor co-ordination are as pertinent to success in the physical work of policing as fighting, if not more so. All constables spend some hours walking about in vile weather, need to be able to run, to focus quickly on distant objects, and so on. Not one respondent, male or female, mentioned any physical quality other than those relevant to fighting. Nor were the allusions at all specific; the art of handling fighting drunks probably depends more on holds and hand grips than it does on the pounds force per square inch potential of a particular muscular configuration. But it is precisely the brute force image of the constable which these accounts draw on:

> 'I've worked with them, sometimes a bit temperamental about the work. The only worry I'd have is in a situation where there was going to be some physical violence

offered to me. I've no doubt they can muster a WPC that's six foot tall as well as broad, but there's not many of them knocking around.' (4: 4, 3–4)

The response works towards a dualism whose mutual exclusivity – a thing is either one or the other – obscures the interconnection of things. The WPC belongs to the feminine world of emotion, sensitivity and academic niceties like paperwork; the PC is the man of action and strength.

Locked into this frame of reference, even officers with experience contrary to the stereotype manage to ignore it. Responses like the following suggest the mythic character of the chivalrous/paternal response in fights: 'You tend to look after them a lot more. If it was two bobbies walking around it's all right but if you've got a woman and there's a bit of aggro ... you tend to look after her and you end up getting thumped in the process.' Asked if this had happened, the recruit, who had worked 'a lot' with WPCs over fourteen months, replied, 'It's not happened, no. The ones we've got ... will get stuck in as much as a bobby would if there's fighting. ... They are good policewomen at our place. (But you'd still have some reservations?) You would, yeah' (7: 1, 8). Respondents still orientated to the myth rather than what experience 'taught' them, so that they interpreted experience as 'confirming' initial belief:

'I know I said last time, you do feel slightly protective towards them. They're still a woman when it comes down to it. Even though some of them are very good, better than a man in certain situations, to calm a situation down.' (7: 2, 5)

It matters little if a thing is a myth when it is believed to be factual and a basis for action. The purportedly superior qualities the WPC does have can hardly be tested if, whenever a fight occurs, the 'talkers' are pushed to the rear. The disadvantage of belief in the myth is clear when one considers the sole example offered by a 'paternalism' in support of the 'violence' claim:

'On the whole they are a good thing but ... I've been on football duty with a WPC and we went into a crowd situation and all the time you're looking around, "Where is she, is she all right?" Not thinking about the guy who's about to clobber you. Whereas with a bloke you would never think of this.' (11: 1, 7)

Performance is based on the questionable assumption of a higher prevailing duty – protect the 'defenceless' female – rather than the task at hand.

Reservations about WPCs arise from the 'problem' of physical strength. There were some expressions of concern over female frivolity, lack of commitment, and about female predators hunting for husbands, but these 'problems' would arise from any female presence in the organization. The conception of policing based on physical strength may itself represent an inappropriate occupational image, but the myth is embedded in occupational culture and more than the gender-specific resonances of the operating ideology would have to change to bring about a change in practice. What clinches the view that the myth has a staying power resistant to even direct experience is the attitude to female officers as opposed to female PCs. Female officers are presented as no problem at all; male and female PCs respect them and even become 'gender-blind'. 'I don't mind [a female superior officer]. A superintendent came to some of our informal meetings. I didn't really think anything about it. It was just another police person' (1: 4, 4). A positive cast is put on *la différence*:

> 'You normally find they are more prepared to listen than a man in a senior position. If you've got a point they're more prepared to accept what you've got to say and then throw it out if they don't agree with it. Whereas more often than not a male person in charge will not take notice.'
> (3: 2, 3–4)

The female superior is as intangible as any in the world of officers. A female recruit commented:

> 'I wouldn't find any difference if it was a woman or a man. You wouldn't be able to talk so easily. You wouldn't be able to say what you want to say with a boss, even if it was a woman. You could be a little uneasy in case you did anything wrong.'
> (1: 1, 3)

The responses imply a clash of stereotypes in the recruits. They have little experience of the organization or its officers, bar their immediate supervisors. They do have enormous experience of the resources of cultural meaning which preserve two highly relevant mythic images. One is of the police force as a crime-and-disorder-controlling, mission-orientated, dispassionate and tough body of men. The other is of women as emotional, weak, sympathetic and service-orientated. The nexus of the conflict between these images of women police is the situation of violence; in so far as female officers, like all officers, do not directly experience that situation, the gender of the officer is irrelevant.

Notes

1. Numbers in parentheses refer to interview identification numbers.

5.10 Private Experiences in the Public Domain: lesbians in organizations
Marny Hall

Marny Hall proposes that society's gender expectations of women are violated in the case of lesbian women; this results in hostility, and in painful and often threatening consequences for those lesbians who disclose their sexuality. Hence many lesbians adopt strategies to conceal their sexual orientation from co-workers and employers; these strategies range from selecting non-traditional occupations to simple denial of their sexuality. This means that for lesbian women the choice appears inevitably to lie between either negative outcomes as a consequence of disclosure (i.e. of having one's sexuality identified) or negative outcomes as a consequence of concealment (i.e. of having one's sexuality misunderstood).

The lesbian corporate experience

The danger of disclosure

Constantly occurring in the work setting were experiences that triggered the women's awareness of their lesbianism. Anti-gay jokes, or comments presuming heterosexuality, such as 'Why don't you get married? ... you're almost twenty-eight', stimulated an awareness of being different. Because the revelation of one's lesbianism could have serious consequences, these women were constantly preoccupied with concealing that aspect of their lives. Sometimes concealment occurred as automatically as retinal adjustment to light change. At other times, it was deliberate and felt more stressful. Whether automatic or deliberate, the process of concealment called for constant attention to every nuance of social interaction. The background buzz of assumptions became centrally important for the lesbian because it signalled where vigilance was necessary or where she could relax and 'be herself'. The workplace reality for the lesbian, therefore, was one of heightened awareness and sensitivity toward the usually hidden matrices of behaviour, values and attitudes in self and others.

The respondents had been convinced that disclosure would be dangerous in several ways. Those who had not experienced discrimination directly by losing a job or missing a promotion had experienced it in the homophobic attitudes of co-workers. After the assassination of gay San Francisco City Council member Harvey Milk in 1978, one woman's boss said, 'Good ... things needed to be cleaned up.' One lesbian, not known to be homosexual, was warned by a well-meaning co-worker to stay away from another co-worker who wore a 'dyke' pin. Other respondents experienced direct discrimination against lesbians and gays. One woman knew two lesbians who were fired for being open at work, while another respondent lost a coveted project because the supervisor was told she was lesbian and he refused to work with her.

Dangers of non-disclosure

Accompanying the need for protective secrecy was a 'state-of-siege' mentality, a feeling of 'us and them'. Often the feeling associated with these states was anxiety or anger, or both, sometimes in the form of intellectual distance: 'I don't fit in, and I don't necessarily want to'; They're so ignorant'; 'You just have to see where they're coming from.'

Even if a subject's lesbianism continued to be a well-kept secret, it was perceived as a disadvantage that caused lesbians to receive 'unfair treatment'. No matter how long they had lived with their partners, lesbians couldn't tap corporate benefits, such as 'family' health insurance or travel bonuses which included spouses. One woman, who had lived with her lover for seven years, had earned enough sales points for a company-sponsored trip to Hawaii; however, she had to go alone. There were no family allowances for lesbians who were relocated and whose partners chose to accompany them. Nor could lesbians play the management game, because they would never have the requisite opposite-sexed spouse and a country club membership in the suburbs.

Being secretive created inner conflicts: 'I wanted to come out, but I just couldn't', as well as constant anxiety about discovery: 'If my bosses knew, they'd find a way to get rid of me'; 'In the case of my supervisees, sometimes it gets emotional, and they might hug me. What would go through their minds if they knew I was a lesbian?'

Several women felt that their lesbianism, because it was invisible, was less of a hindrance than their gender, which they could not disguise. Being a woman was seen as a major disadvantage in the corporate world: 'As a woman, I'm generally assumed to be incompetent whereas the men are assumed to be competent unless proven otherwise.'

Their lesbianism reinforced separation between work and leisure. Some respondents contended that this was congruent with their needs: 'I am a private person anyway. Even if I weren't gay, I wouldn't want to mix work with my life outside work.' For the others the discontinuity was a source of frustration and anger: 'These guys go home and their friends are the same people they see all day. For me, coming to work is bowing out of my world completely and going into theirs.'

The respondents felt conflict between the need or expectation to be open and friendly and their realization that if they were to share the ordinary events of their day-to-day lives they would show that they were different from everyone else. One way to avoid this was simply to avoid heterosexual co-workers. Several respondents said they tried to keep out of personal situations: 'I maintain a professional air and shy away from those issues. I never socialize with them.' Another common strategy to cope with this need for deceit was to dissociate oneself from part of one's behaviour. In the same interview, respondents would talk about ways of concealing their lesbianism while stating firmly, 'I don't hide my gayness.' The use of this form of dissociation spared respondents the knowledge – and attendant self-reproach – about their own deceptiveness and, at the same time, protected them from the anxiety and risks of revelation.

Several comments indicated that at times the respondents experienced their lesbianism as a source of strength. 'Because I am gay, I have more confidence'; and 'There's a feeling of camaraderie with other lesbians at work.'

At times, being misapprehended enhanced their status. Because one woman's partner was invisible to management, she was presumed to be unmarried and mobile, and was therefore offered special training in another city. Another woman in a non-traditional job felt that because she was seen as masculine, she was given more challenging job assignments than some of her counterparts who were seen as feminine.

Even though the non-disclosure of their homosexuality was crucial, several respondents felt the secret was not always within their control. For example, one woman was showing a friend from work the plans of the new house she and her lover had bought. Pointing-out the main bedroom, she accidentally said, 'This is where we sleep.' She was appalled to have revealed the intimate nature of her relationship. Other respondents felt they revealed their lesbianism through their physical appearance. A lesbian who wore jeans to a clerical job said, 'The way I dress I was in a way forcing it down their throats.' Another woman said, 'At the time they started suspecting, I made a mistake and cut my hair short. That was the tip-off.'

Many of the interviewees said their homosexuality had been revealed inadvertently. In one instance, a woman was featured in the business section of her home-town newspaper when she became the 300th member to join a local gay business organization. She had been assured, falsely, by the photographer who covered the event that the story would appear only in gay publications. Another woman said her co-workers found out about her when her lover, wearing jeans and short hair, stopped by her office one day to drop something off. These accidental disclosures generated embarrassment and fear and were perceived by respondents as an 'Oh no!' experience. Even when these near-calamities did not trigger the expected dire consequences, the incidents themselves were remembered vividly.

Coping strategies

Karr,[1] McConaghy,[2] and Morin[3] have established experimentally the presence of adverse feelings toward individuals assumed to be homosexual. Additionally, in Karr's experiment, individuals who labelled others as homosexual were frequently regarded positively by observers. Given such a strongly charged atmosphere, we can expect women who define themselves as lesbian in this culture to have developed strategies to manoeuvre in inimical environments in which any deviation from male, heterosexual norms results in less status, less opportunity, loss of co-workers' esteem, ostracism, harassment and/or firing.

A group tends to develop its own strategies. Women, for example, have 'felt constrained to begin in areas of specialization for which they could claim special insight or ability'. Consequently they have been overly represented in personnel departments – the 'relational' sectors of the organization – and under-represented in the technical departments.[4] An additional strategy has been to seek mentors.[5] According to Cheek, a Black strategy has been to 'shine 'em on ... don't let the white man know what you really feel and think'.[6] Similarly, from the analysis of the interviews it can be concluded that lesbian employees have developed strategies for dealing specifically with homophobia in the workplace.

The neuterized/neutralized strategy

Femaleness is the discredited and visible side of one's lesbianism. Consequently if gender can be minimized, lesbianism is less likely to come into focus. Computer-related jobs were particularly popular. One can speculate that, because they combine the masculine aspects of technology with the female tradition of keyboard work, computers effectively de-gender their programmers. Consequently sexuality and sexual preference questions are neutralized.

In a related strategy, women who are perceived as masculine can tap positive qualities attributed to males. In a corporation, the advantages occasioned by such perceptions may outweigh, or at least balance, the disadvantages of being seen as 'unfeminine'.

Non-disclosure strategies

One can infer the pervasive anxiety about disclosure from the extent to which all lesbians, even those who have come out, continue to use non-disclosure as a strategy. The intense observation of details that escape others is part of the non-disclosure strategy. Bateson writes that we are surrounded by an infinitude of detail and possible observations. The differences between a floor tile and a ceiling tile, or two people's hair styles, do not necessarily constitute information. Information, according to Bateson, is 'a difference which makes a difference'.[7]

For most heterosexuals, subtle cues are not as important as they are for the lesbian who feels herself to be in an unsafe environment in which a person's wedding ring, interest in a professional football team, or use of personal pronouns constitute a real difference. From these bits of information the lesbian can construct a hypothesis that will guide her behaviour.

Strategies that balance non-disclosure

All forms of non-disclosure, whether the occasional substitute of 'he' for 'she' when describing a weekend outing with a lover or the complete fabrication of a heterosexual life, leave a lesbian in a difficult moral position. Not only is she denying what she knows to be true, but she is also ignoring the strong exhortations of the lesbian community to come out. [...]

Denial and dissociation Frequently respondents would insist they were not in the closet, and in response to further questioning would contradict themselves, for example, 'No, I haven't actually told anyone I'm gay.' They continued to deny, however, that they were being secretive. Others claimed they felt comfortable in the face of homophobic remarks. Though no respondent said it, I speculate that these respondents were using a dissociative strategy; it was not *they* who were being discussed contemptuously. One respondent distinguished between 'dykey women', and gays who 'handled their gayness discreetly'. The dichotomization between good and bad gays is another dissociative strategy.

Avoidance Several respondents simply avoided personal situations at work. Some regretted the absence of social interactions with co-workers. Others said they did not want to get close to co-workers because they had nothing in common with them.

Distraction Respondents purposefully cultivated images that conveyed differentness – a feminist, a liberal – in order to distract from the more discreditable identification of lesbian. Unfavourable self-assessments about being duplicitous could thus be balanced by principled stand-taking.

Token disclosure While concealing the true nature of their relationships, some respondents let it be known that they had done something with 'a room-mate'. This was a partial disclosure since their room-mates were also their lovers. Similarly, after Harvey Milk's assassination, one woman asked a homophobic job supervisor for time off to go to the funeral of a friend. She did not mention that the 'friend' was Milk. In response to an anti-gay joke, one lesbian said, 'You'd better get yourself some new material', revealing her irritation, but not her gay identity.

   The most common partial-disclosure strategy was simply to disclose their homosexuality only to certain people they felt they could trust. Because this information could leak, such a partial disclosure often set off a new round of strategies to find out if one's secret had been more widely revealed.

   All of these balancing strategies seemed to restore to some degree respondents' threatened sense of integrity.

Implications and conclusions

Rather like a horse that finds itself simultaneously reined in and spurred on, corporate lesbians are caught in a crossfire of conflicting cultural and subcultural imperatives. The strategies lesbians used to manoeuvre their ways through this thicket of contradictions reveal that the old reductionist notion of 'coming out' is not an act, but rather a never-ending and labyrinthine process of decision and indecision, of nuance and calculated presentations as well as impulsive and inadvertent revelations – a process, in short, as shifting as the contexts in which it occurs.

   Is there, one might ask, a position beyond strategy, of simply acting naturally as one respondent claimed she did? Upon examination the 'natural' stance is simply another ploy, an 'as-if' strategy in which the respondent acted as if she were entitled to the same social prerogatives, could count on the same good will assumed by her heterosexual co-workers. According to Goffman, this sort of 'open' strategy thrusts a new career upon the stigmatized person, 'that of representing [her] category. [She] finds [herself] too eminent to avoid being presented by [her] own as an instance of them'.[8] And, one might add, or tokenized by heterosexual co-workers.

And so the final irony for those who are thoroughly, consistently and extensively open at work is that they are effectively shorn of the authenticity and individuality they sought by this 'naturalness'. As Laing writes, 'lonely and painful ... to be misunderstood, but to be correctly understood is also to be in danger of being engulfed, when the "understanding" occurs within a framework that one had hoped to break out of'.[9] And Goffman notes, 'There may be no "authentic" solution at all'.[10]

The rare lesbian who reveals her orientation, and who survives the consequences of violating the gendered expectations which structure the organization succumbs, then, to the organization in another way. Stylized out of existence, she forfeits her private mutinies, cannot mobilize the resistance necessary to shield her individuality from engulfment by the collective purpose of the organization. Homogenized, the token corporate lesbian becomes the consummate 'organization (wo)man'.

Notes

1. R. Karr, 'Homosexual labeling and the male role', *Journal of Social Issues*, vol. 34, no. 3 (1978), pp. 73–83.
2. N. McConaghy, 'Penile volume change to moving pictures of female nudes in heterosexual and homosexual males', *Behaviour Research and Therapy*, 5 (1967), pp. 43–8.
3. S. Morin, 'Attitudes towards homosexuality and social distance', paper presented at a meeting of the American Psychological Association, Chicago, September 1975.
4. P. Warner, P. van Riper, N. Martin and O. Collins, 'Women executives in the federal government', *Public Personnel Review*, October 1982, pp. 227–34.
5. H. McLane, *Selecting, Developing and Retaining Women Executives*, New York: Van Nostrand, 1980.
6. D. Cheek, *Assertive Black ... Puzzled White*, San Luis Obispo, CA: Impact, 1976, p. 16.
7. G. Bateson, *Steps to an Ecology of Mind*, New York: Ballantine, 1972, p. 453.
8. F. Goffman, *Stigma*, Englewood Cliffs, NJ: Prentice Hall, 1964, p. 26.
9. R. D. Laing, *The Divided Self*, New York: Pantheon, 1970, p. 76.
10. Goffman, *Stigma*, p. 124.

5.11 **Young, Female and Black**

Heidi Mirza

Heidi Mirza identifies the two dominant and contradictory ways of theorising the experiences of black women. To put it simply: it has been argued both that the black family is matriarchal and that it is male-centred. This extract provides empirical data as a basis for a re-evaluation of the ideological position of women in black families through an analysis of their economic location; Mirza suggests that black women and white women experience a different cultural construction of femininity.

Studies in America,[1] the Caribbean[2] and in Britain[3] have persistently attributed the relatively high proportion of black women in the economy to the absence of a male provider or his inability to fulfil his role. This pathological explanation of the black family – that has come about from the belief that it is 'culturally stripped', essentially a hybrid of Western culture[4] – has failed to acknowledge that black culture has evolved an essentially egalitarian ideology with regard to work, an ideology that, as Sutton and Makiesky-Barrow observe, 'emphasises the effectiveness of the individual regardless of gender'.[5] This argument is supported by the evidence that the proportion of black women in the labour market relative to their white female counterparts is far greater, a fact that is true for the UK and the USA.

The argument that high black male unemployment determines increased black female labour-market participation cannot be upheld; it is a theory based more on a 'commonsense' assumption than fact. Black male unemployment is no higher than black female unemployment. (In the 25–35 age group in the UK, 17 percent of black women are unemployed, as are 18 percent of black men. In other age ranges the proportion is even greater for black females.[6]) The fact that males and females are concentrated in different sectors of the labour market and so have access to different employment (and educational) prospects is not a consequence of choice but rather due to the dynamics of a sexually segregated labour market.[7]

The study revealed a notable lack of sexual distinctions about work among second-generation West Indian young people. Many girls said that they did not see any difference between themselves and their male counterparts in terms of their capacity to work and the type of work they were capable of:

> 'I think men and women have the same opportunities, it is just up to you to take it.'

> 'Of course women should do the same jobs that men do. If they feel you can't ... them stupid. ... Who's to say anyway, it makes me sick it does.'

> 'Men should do the jobs women do and women the jobs that men do. There's nothing wrong with men midwives, I think all men should find out what it is like to have a child, it's the nearest they can get to it.'

Young black women living in the West Indies expressed a similar point of view with regard to women's work, as one girl illustrated when she stated: 'I think what is good for a woman is good for a man, there's no difference between men and women when it comes to work.'

Further evidence of this trend to refuse to regard certain types of work as the sole preserve of men was shrown in the results of the study. Black girls were far more likely to express their desire to do non-gendered work than their white female peers.

This ideological position regarding work expectations cannot be the outcome of a 'female-orientated' tradition.[8] If it were a female-centred ideology, then it would be difficult to account for the obvious preoccupation many young black girls had for, as one Trinidadian girl explained: 'the need for emotional support and strength from a man, you like to feel he rules, even if he don't'.

The young black women in the study, both in the West Indies and in Britain, often commented on the desire for male companionship. This, and the fact that many women treat men as 'guests in the house',[9] has been interpreted as evidence of a male-centred ideology in the West Indian family structure. The description of the black family as having a male-centred ideology is based largely on the evidence of black male non-participation in the domestic sphere.

It is important to note at this point that there seems to be a contradictory state of affairs with regard to research on the status of the woman in the black family, which can result in a great deal of confusion. On the one hand, it has been argued that what exists is a matrifocal, female-dominated structure;[10] and on the other hand the family ideological orientation is often described as 'male-centred'.[11]

These two fundamentally divergent theoretical interpretations of the ideological dynamics of the black family have evolved as a consequence of the confused interpretation of the two essentially different aspects of family life: relative autonomy between the sexes and male non-participation in domestic affairs. In effect what we are observing in this study is an ideological orientation governed, not by male bias or female bias, but by the notion of relative economic and social autonomy between the sexes.

In home visits to the parents of the girls in the study, the statements by wives and husbands illustrated the existence of a measure of independence between the sexes, as well as joint responsibility towards the family. They frequently related stories and anecdotes that told of their independent, but equal, work roles.

One such example was the case of Mr and Mrs Burgess, who had come to the UK 24 years ago. Between them they had brought up five children, the eldest being the child of a previous relationship of Mrs Burgess. They had both always worked and had an evident pride in their children's achievements (one daughter was a computer programmer, another a social worker, while the others, who were still at school, were doing well). They lived on a bleak, run-down, post-war council estate in Brixton. She enjoyed and got a great deal of satisfaction from her job as a canteen assistant; he found his work 'on the buses' less interesting. Both wages jointly contributed to the family income, although each wage went towards different aspects of family expenditure. He explained in his broad Grenadian accent how he regarded the relationship:

> 'She does she work, she go in every day, come home every day. She do she own ting really. Half de time I ain't know what she get up to, always going out spending she money on Bingo or some ting so. I don't min once she leave me alone. ... I's like to do me own ting too ... ya know.'

Mrs Burgess had her own comments to make: in her equally broad Dominican dialect:

> 'He so lazy, girl. He could sit there all day an' complain. Nothing good enough, well, just sit there then. I does go alone if I want to do anything. ... I does pick up myself ... even go by self to de carnival ... I's have me work, I's like me work, mind.'

The indifference in attitude they now expressed towards each other after many years of marriage should not obscure the relative autonomy each partner enjoyed with regard to their own work and social activities. Despite their disagreements on other matters, neither partner interfered with the other's right to work. For Mrs Burgess her work was and always had been a source of pride and achievement, a realm of experience quite apart from her life at home. She enjoyed talking about her battles and victories in the workplace:

> 'When I first came to England dere was so many jobs. I move from one to another. It took me four weeks to find my first job. I work for Lyons. Two pounds fifty I got. ... I tell you them days a shilling a lot ... now I'm the only coloured face at work, but I put them in their place, I stands up for myself, I ain't gone to leave because of them few. Me an' the Italian woman wer's the only outsiders so they want us out. They don't like me because I'm better than them. I've got better qualifications than them and they's wanted to get rid of me always shouting at me, but now I've got my friends we get on well, laugh and ting, have a good time, like at de Christmas party.'

Considerable independence between the sexes does not presuppose the shedding of social attachments as it can do in other cultural contexts; rather, it necessitates and increases the involvement of both partners in the lives of their families. In spite of their separate economic and social experiences, Mr and Mrs Burgess jointly contributed to the family budget and participated in the upbringing of their children. However, just as each income financed a separate aspect of the household expenditure,[12] so too did each partner perform a different parenting role.

   They both agreed that 'life hard [sic] for the children nowadays', and that it is up to the parents to see that the children do not 'go astray' and were not out roaming the streets, and if they failed and the children were 'bad', then it was the parents who were at fault. They had, especially Mr Burgess, a strong disciplinarian approach towards their children which, it became quite obvious, had alienated the children to some degree.

Conclusion: the cultural context of gender

The evidence presented here suggests that the cultural construction of femininity among African Caribbean women fundamentally differs from the forms of femininity found among their white peers, and indeed their white migrant peers. Thus the theoretical arguments about the way in which gender disadvantage is reproduced become inappropriate in the black context. What the young black women in the study were expressing was essentially an ideology that emphasised the relative autonomy of both the male and female roles.

Ironically, the dynamic that has produced this equality between the sexes within the black social structure has been the external imposition of oppression and brutality. African Caribbean societies in the Caribbean and in industrialised capitalist settings have not simply replicated the Western pattern of sexual stratification.

Like their parents and grandparents, the young black women in the study had not adopted the dominant Eurocentric ideology: an ideology in which gender is regarded as the basis for the opposition of roles and values. These young black women had, instead, a very different concept of masculinity and femininity than their white peers. In the black female definition, as their statements revealed, few distinctions were made between male and female abilities and attributes with regard to work and the labour market. The reason why this particular definition of masculinity and femininity should result in greater female participation in the labour market is explained by Sutton and Makiesky-Barrow, who write:

> the distinct qualities of masculine and feminine sexual and reproductive abilities are not viewed by either sex as a basis for different male and female social capacities. And unlike the self-limiting negative sexual identities the Euro-American women have had to struggle with, female identity in Endeavour [a town in Barbados] is associated with highly valued cultural attributes. Because the women are assumed to be bright, strong and competent, nothing in the definitions of appropriate sex role behaviour systematically excludes them from areas of economic and social achievement.[13]

Notes

1. L. Rainwater and W. Yancey, *The Moynihan Report and the Politics of Controversy*, MIT Press, 1967.
2. M. Smith, *West Indian Family Structure*, University of Washington Press, 1962.

3. N. Foner, *Jamaica Farewell: Jamaican migrants in London*, Routledge & Kegan Paul, 1979.
4. E. Frazier, *The Negro Family in the United States*, University of Chicago Press, 1966; A. Little, *Schools and Race*, Commission for Racial Equality, 1978.
5. C. Sutton and S. Makiesky-Barrow, 'Social inequality and sexual status in Barbados', in A. Schlegel (ed.), *Sexual Stratification: A cross-cultural view*, Columbia University Press, 1977, p. 323.
6. C. Brown, *Black and White in Britain: The third PSI survey*, Heinemann, 1984.
7. R. Farley and S. Bianchi, 'Social class polarisation: is it occurring among the blacks?', in M. Leggon (ed.), *Research in Race and Ethnic Relations*, 4, pp. 1–31.
8. A. Phizacklea, 'In the front line', in A. Phizacklea (ed.), *One Way Ticket*, Routledge & Kegan Paul, 1984.
9. J. Justus, 'Women's role in West Indian society', in F. Steady (ed.), *The Black Woman Cross-culturally*, Schenkman Books, 1985.
10. M. Fuller, 'Young, female and black', in E. Cashmore and B. Troyna (eds), *Black Youth in Crisis*, George Allen & Unwin, 1982.
11. Justus, 'Women's role in West Indian Society'.
12. K. Stone, 'Motherhood and waged work: West Indian, Asian and white mothers compared', in Phizacklea (ed.), *One Way Ticket*.
13. Sutton and Makiesky-Barrow, *Social Inequality*, p. 320.

Further reading

Boston, S. (1989), *Women Workers and the Trade Unions* (2nd edn), London: Lawrence & Wishart.
Bannen, J. and Moss, P. (1991), *Managing Mothers*, London: Unwin Hyman.
Condor, S. (1986), 'Sex role beliefs and "traditional" women: feminist and intergroup perspectives', in S. Wilkinson (ed.), *Feminist Social Psychology*, London: Sage.
Deem, R. (1980), *Schooling for Women's Work*, London: Routledge & Kegan Paul.
Lipman-Blumen, J. (1984), *Gender Roles and Power*, Englewood Cliffs, NJ: Prentice Hall.
Gutek, B. and Larwood, L. (1987), *Women's Career Development*, London: Sage.
Mac an Ghaill, M. (1988), *Young, Gifted and Black: Student–teacher relations in the schooling of black youth*, Milton Keynes: Open University Press.

6 MARRIAGE AND MOTHERHOOD

Edited and Introduced by Sue Faulkner and
Stevi Jackson

INTRODUCTION

Marriage and motherhood have been identified as major sites of women's oppression, but also as relationships which give women's lives meaning and from which they derive a sense of self-worth.

Feminist work on marriage has emphasised the structural inequalities built into marital relationships. This is particularly evident in economic aspects of family life. Most married women are now employed, but the fact that their earning power is considerably less than their husbands' makes them at least partially dependent. Even where women make a considerable financial contribution, husbands are still defined as family breadwinners.[1] Women's increased participation in waged work has not diminished their responsibility for housework; hence women as a whole work much longer hours than men (see Reading 6.1). Feminists have insisted that housework *is* work, but have noted a number of ways in which it differs from waged work. No other job is so intimately bound up with personal ties or so grounded in an ethic of personal service. There is no fixed job description for a domestic labourer, no agreed hours and conditions of work, no clear boundaries or limits, no guaranteed space or time for leisure. Housework is also, of course, unpaid, and performed within social relations very different from those of capitalist production.

During the 1970s many Marxist feminists sought to analyse housework in relation to capitalist production. Since, for Marxists, capital depends upon the exploitation of wage labour, housewives could be seen to make a contribution to the capitalist economy through servicing the existing labour force and rearing future workers. This was the starting point of the 'domestic labour debate', a very complex and technical series of discussions concerning the economic value of housework within capitalism (see Section 5 above).[2] Some participants in the debate argued for wages for housework in recognition of its social and economic importance. Most, however, thought that this would serve only to reinforce women's subordination within the home. Many feminists felt that the whole debate ignored the benefits men gained from their wives' domestic labour. Materialist feminists such as Christine Delphy, Diana Leonard and Sylvia Walby

(Reading 6.2) have advanced an alternative analysis, suggesting that men exploit women's labour within a domestic or patriarchal mode of production.[3]

Men's economic power within families is reflected in the distribution of household resources (Reading 6.3). There is growing evidence that 'while sharing a common address, family members do not necessarily share a common standard of living'.[4] Women often manage household resources, but they do so on behalf of others rather than for their own benefit. Research on money and food indicates that men's needs and desires take precedence over those of their wives and, where money is short, it is women as wives and mothers who go without.[5]

Within marriage, economic relations are often infused with emotional meaning. This is why, for instance, housework is so often seen as a labour of love. Women enter marriage expecting emotional fulfilment and companionship, but here too they often find themselves in an unequal relationship. The portrait of newlywed marriage presented by Penny Mansfield and Jean Collard is one example of research which indicates that women may give more than they receive (Reading 6.4). Marriage on the basis of romantic love clearly does not deliver all it promises: one reason why we should not assume that arranged marriages are necessarily more oppressive than those based on 'love'. Certainly we should not imagine that Asian women want to emulate the marriage practices of white women (Reading 6.5).

The power structure underpinning marriage becomes most overt in the form of violence against wives. Feminist activists and theorists have always insisted that wife abuse should not be seen as an individual aberration on the part of psychologically disturbed men, but should be analysed in terms of the structural inequalities of the marriage contract (Reading 6.6). These inequalities are also bolstered by the state (see Section 10 below).

Becoming a mother is a major event in a woman's life – it has massive implications for her lifestyle, her sense of self and her relation to others. The meanings of childbirth and motherhood are defined by the culture in which they occur, and interlinked with wider social attitudes towards women. In Western industrial societies mothers are perceived as being solely and uniquely responsible for their children. They are expected to behave in a totally selfless way twenty-four hours a day, seven days a week, and this behaviour is held to be 'natural'. Ann Oakley calls this the 'institution of motherhood' (Reading 6.7).

In reality, there is a clash between a mother's needs and those of her child. The relegation of one's own needs to the background in order to respond selflessly to the baby marks a difficult transition for most women. Yet we are expected to accomplish this without difficulty, and to derive personal enrichment and joy from such devotion. Women who do not cope well with the strains this causes are labelled at best inadequate and at worst psychiatrically unbalanced (see Reading 6.8). Not only are the physical demands on the new mother huge, but often the change has an adverse effect on her self-concept as her identity becomes redefined in relation to her child.

Motherhood also has repercussions for her employment prospects and career. Childcare in Britain is among the worst in Europe. Even today childcare is regarded as a private matter: maternal employment is still thought of as – at best – a regrettable necessity, with reliance on a male breadwinner the ideal. There are, of course, many mothers who have no male partner. Growing numbers of women are choosing to have children outside marriage, and high divorce rates swell the ranks of single parents.[6] Lack of childcare and low female wages mean that many lone mothers live in poverty.

Feminist perspectives on motherhood were initially concerned with challenging the myth of motherhood as personal fulfilment. In some respects this implied a denigration of motherhood, and created divisions between mothers and childless women. More recently motherhood has been re-evaluated, with feminists arguing more for social changes which would enhance its positive aspects (Reading 6.9). That there are pleasures as well as penalties associated with motherhood must be restated. Recent feminist work continues, however, to analyse the pressures on women resulting from the professionalisation of motherhood and mother-blaming. In particular feminists have challenged the cultural construction of some mothers (especially young, black or lesbian mothers) as 'deviant'. The right of women to mother outside heterosexual relationships is central to feminist concerns and represents a challenge to patriarchal family structures (Reading 6.14).

Most research and theory on marriage and the family has concerned the experience of white women. This has drawn criticism from black feminists who have argued that in a racist society the family is often a source of resistance to and protection from racism. There are, however, commonalities as well as differences in the family lives of women from different ethnic groups (Readings 6.11, 6.15). For example, women from most communities in Britain are responsible for housework and childcare, and both white and black women can be subject to abuse from their husbands or male partners.

A wider issue here concerns the variability of family forms within modern societies. Less than a third of households in Western industrial nations are traditional nuclear families comprising husbands, wives and dependent children. This has led many writers to caution us against generalisations about 'the family' which treat it as a fixed, unchanging entity. Others, however, point out that most adult women are married or cohabiting with a male partner, and most have children. Hence it can be argued that despite the apparent diversity of family forms, patterns of female subordination within familial relationships can still be discerned.[7]

Notes

1. See, for example, J. Brannen and P. Moss, 'Dual earner households: women's financial contribution after the birth of the first child', in J. Brannen and G. Wilson (eds), *Give and Take in Families*, London: Allen & Unwin, 1987.

2. For critical summaries of this debate, see P. Rushton, 'Marxism, domestic labour and the capitalist economy: a note on recent discussions', in C. Harris *et al.* (eds), *The Sociology of the Family*, Sociological Review Monograph No. 28, University of Keele, 1979; E. Kaluzynska 'Wiping the floor with theory', *Feminist Review*, no. 6, 1980; S. Walby, *Patriarchy at Work*, Oxford: Polity, 1986, chs 2, 3; C. Delphy and D. Leonard, *Familiar Exploitation*, Oxford: Polity, 1992, ch. 2. Many of the key contributions to the debate are reprinted in E. Malos (ed.), *The Politics of Housework*, London: Allison & Busby, 1980.

3. See also C. Delphy, *Close to Home*, London: Hutchinson, 1984; Delphy and Leonard, *Familiar Exploitation*. For an application of these arguments, see S. Jackson, 'Towards a historical sociology of housework: a materialist feminist analysis', *Women's Studies International Forum*, vol. 15, no. 2, 1992.

4. H. Graham, 'Women's poverty and caring', in C. Glendinning and J. Millar (eds), *Women and Poverty in Britain*, Sussex: Wheatsheaf, 1987, p. 221.

5. See Graham, 'Women's poverty and caring'; Jan Pahl, *Money and Marriage*, London: Macmillan, 1989; N. Charles and M. Kerr, *Women, Food and Families*, Manchester: Manchester University Press, 1988; G. Wilson, 'Money: patterns of responsibility and irresponsibility in marriage', in Brannen and Wilson, *Give and Take*.

6. Currently over a quarter of children are born outside wedlock, although most of these have parents living within a heterosexual relationship. Over one-third of marriages end in divorce. For details see Central Statistical Office, *Social Trends*, London: HMSO, 1992; K. Kiernan and M. Wicks, *Family Change and Future Policy*, London: Family Policy Studies Centre, 1990.

7. For examples of opposing views in this issue, see M. Barrett and M. McIntosh, *The Anti-Social Family*, London: Verso, 1982, 1991; Delphy and Leonard, *Familiar Exploitation*.

6.1 Domestic labourers, or stand by your man – while he sits down and has a cup of tea

Sallie Westwood

Sallie Westwood's account of white women factory workers graphically illustrates the unequal distribution of domestic labour and captures the ambivalent feelings women have about their domestic responsibilities. The working routines of Asian women at this factory were similar, but they were less inclined to view housework as a labour of love.

The notion that women were the foundation upon which the whole edifice of social and familial life was based was a common view among the women of StitchCo, and they expressed this in the sentence, 'Men, ah, they don't know they're born, they've got no idea,' which was, of course, very convenient for the men generally. Women, we know, are engaged in the double shift; they work outside the home for wages and within the home for 'love'. It is women who carry the responsibility of organising, managing and executing the work of reproduction in all its aspects. Much has been written on the contribution that this unpaid, and until recently, hidden labour makes to capitalism. Christine Delphy's work also presented us with an analysis of the way in which women's labour is appropriated by husbands in the home and, therefore, how women are economically exploited by the men they live with.

The material oppression to which women are subject is carried on in the hidden world of the family and in isolated households. Yet it was made public in the department at StitchCo because the women who came to work brought these concerns with them, into an environment where the definition of woman as wife and mother was elaborated upon by the culture of the shop floor, thereby reinforcing the view the women held of themselves as wives and mothers first. [...]

Dol, who worked on the portable iron, told me when we were discussing her workload:

> 'Most women spend all their time working. They work at the factory, then they do the shopping and cook and clean. I was hanging out washing before I came to work today. Mind you, I wouldn't be at home all the time; it's too lonely. When you come out to work it's more social, you meet other women and seem more alive, somehow.'

Dol was quite clear that housework was not only irksome and never-ending, but was also carried on in isolation. She, like many women, welcomed the opportunity to work outside the home because it put her in touch with a larger world, with other women, and herself.

The amount of time women spent on housework was apparent from the discussions that they had in their breaks. Not only did this work consume so many of their waking hours, but housework also became a major subject of conversation. [...]

SALLIE: How long do you think you spend on housework?
CHORUS: Hours and hours, at least as long as we spend here, and more ...
FLO: We do two jobs, one here and one in the house. We'd earn a fortune if we ever got paid for both.

The rest of the group agreed. ... Everyone in the group accepted the view that they worked at home unpaid and that the work that they did had a cash value which they never realised because they were servicing the needs of their families. There was no romance surrounding housework and no illusions about the time and effort involved. Yet this knowledge and understanding never seemed to dim the enthusiasm of the younger generation of brides. It seemed to pass over them until they became wives when, in fact, they looked to the models around them and followed them.

FLO: [*continued*]: Housework is a full-time job, let alone coming here all
            week. There's so much to do and you don't do half of it when you're
            working. You've got to have a routine otherwise if you don't do it one
            day you've got two jobs the next.

Everyone murmured their agreement and nodded as they started to tell me
about the routines they followed. [...]
   Flo was a married woman of about 50; she had no children and lived in a flat
that she and her husband were buying. Her week went like this:

'I always do my washing on Sunday and then Monday it's ironing. Tuesday is my
night off and I won't touch a thing. Thursday I do the bathroom and if it's 3 a.m.
I won't go to bed until it's done. I hoover the bedrooms on Wednesday and all the
other rooms Friday. Friday I go up town and pay the bills, do the shopping and
get the 4.40 bus home. I get in and make a cup of tea and, while Les sits and has
his, I unpack the shopping. Then I hoover the hall, lounge (we're in a flat so it's
a bit easier) while I put the dinner in the oven. Every morning I make the bed and
do what's needed for dinner, like cut the potatoes, make the gravy, whatever ...'

Before I had time to interject and marvel at Flo's energy, or ask what was wrong
with Les, the other women came in and supported Flo's account of the week.
Kath intervened quickly with her own routine. She was a woman who looked
older than her 40 years; she was frail and had had pleurisy the previous year.
This had not stopped her working twenty hours a day for her husband and her
children, who were all living at home; one son was working and another son
and her daughter were still at school:

'I'm the same as you, Flo, 'cept we've got a dog so I hoover downstairs every day.
I get up first, but not until 8.30 on a Sunday now. I get the tea on for the first lad
and give him his breakfast because he has to go at 6.30 then, it's me hubby. I make
the lad's bed while the tea's brewing, then it's the other two and then I get meself
ready while I make our bed, cut the sandwiches and I'm off out the door. I wash
about three times a week because me hubby and the lad have overalls. You have
to soak them, they can't go straight in the machine, then I put them in. I do all my
pressing for the whole week on Sunday afternoon and pick up all the washing for
Monday. The whole house gets a clean at the weekend ...' [...]

   Any contribution young men made was at the edges; they expected their new
wives to do the housework, shop, cook, etc., but women like Tessa were already
protesting against their lot:

Carl's bein' really 'orrible to me. I tell him to help and he does nothing. I keep
saying we've got to go and do the washing and he won't bother. He doesn't clean
up, wash up, nothing. I told him I'm not doin' owt for him. I didn't pack his lunch
for 'im today. He should do more, he lives here as well. He just goes out with his
mates, comes in, and flops into bed. Well, it's not good enough, is it?'

Tessa was very unhappy and often alone in the evenings when I went to visit her. I would find her ironing or washing, trying to cook and clean in her small flat. I agreed with her that Carl could do more, but with many of the other women I often had the greatest difficulty in raising questions about their workload at home. Any faint suggestion that I was critical of what they did sent them springing to the defence of husbands and children [...] It was a matter of pride to the women at StitchCo that they cared for their children and their homes as they might have done if they were full-time homemakers. Any criticism seemed cruelly out of place and was interpreted as a criticism of them, not of the men and children in their households and the way that domestic labour was organised. [...] To them, this was women's work, their *proper* work which offered them a place at the centre of family life, and, through that, status and power – which work outside the home did not offer ... it was invested with a special status because it was done for love and was part of the way that women cared for their families. Boring manual work was, therefore, transformed into satisfying, caring work which required both an emotional and an intellectual commitment; that commitment could only be made because the context for this work was the family, with its attendant ideological load.

6.2 The Elements of the Patriarchal Mode of Production
Sylvia Walby

Sylvia Walby argues that men directly exploit and benefit from their wives' domestic labour within a patriarchal mode of production. This patriarchal mode of production, which she describes in this Reading, exists in articulation with the capitalist mode of production.

I would suggest that within the patriarchal mode of production the producing class is composed of housewives or domestic labourers, while the non-producing and exploiting class is composed of husbands. The part of the means of production which can be identified as the objects of labour consists of the exhausted people for whom the domestic labourer works to replenish their labour-power, that is the exhausted husband, and the children, if any. The part of the means of production which can be identified as the instruments of labour consists of the woman's body, especially in the sense of her reproductive capacity, the house and its contents. It is the relationship between these elements which comprises the patriarchal mode of production.

So we see that the work of appropriation of nature, in which the domestic labourer is engaged, is that of the production of labour-power. This is generational production of children, as well as the day-to-pay production of the labour power of her husband.

The exploitation, or expropriation, which is taking place is the expropriation of the surplus labour of the domestic labourer by the husband. As in any other exploitative mode of production this expropriation is made possible because there is a particular way in which the producer does not have complete possession of the means of production. A crucial aspect of the work of the domestic labourer is the labour she performs on the exhausted husband in order to replenish or produce his labour-power. The exhausted husband is one of the objects of the domestic labour and therefore part of the means of production. The domestic labourer does not have possession of the husband who enters the labour process as an exhausted person whose labour-power she replenishes. She thus has no possession of this part of the means of production and as a consequence does not own this part of the product of her labour. She is separated from the product of her labour and has no control over it while the husband always has possession of this labour-power which the wife has produced. She is separated from it on every level: physically; in the ability to use it; legally, ideologically, etc. The husband uses and exchanges that labour-power with an employer as if it were his own, even though the wife laboured to produce it. He sells this labour-power to an employer and receives a wage which is less than the value of the goods he has produced. He gives a portion of this wage to the wife for the maintenance of the family, and retains some for himself. The portion allocated to the wife's use on herself is typically less than the part of the wage allocated for the use of the husband on himself. In addition the housewife typically works longer hours than the man. Thus she performs more labour and receives less than he does. If the wife's level is taken to be the base, then the extra which he has may be regarded as the wife's surplus labour which he has expropriated. He is able to do this because he has control over the labour-power she has produced and hence over the wage he received from the capitalist exchange for it. Therefore the domestic labourer is exploited.

A key characteristic of these relations of production is that they exist as personalized relations between individuals. They are privatized relations involving individual contact with one husband. Thus the forces of production are limited by this situation to a fairly primitive level, relative to productive forces in the other mode of production. Forces of production which would require large-scale co-operation, and socialization of the labour process are ruled out. They must remain on this small-scale, privatized level which involves duplication of these tasks many times over. This is technically inefficient and can be seen as a consequence of these relations of production.

6.3   **Women, Food and Families**
Nickie Charles and Marion Kerr

The way in which women work for others is clear in this Reading, which comes from a study of family food consumption carried out with two hundred Yorkshire women. Nickie Charles and Marion Kerr discuss how and why women defer to men's wishes in the preparation of meals.

[...] women cook for others. This is not a simple statement, for women cooking for others means that they cook to please others. They cook to ensure that people are well fed and well looked after, to ensure that those who they cook for firstly *eat* what is provided and secondly *enjoy* it. The ability to provide food that is good and that is appreciated by a hungry family, particularly a hungry man, is a fundamental part of being a wife and mother. [...]

This need for the end product to be appreciated perhaps goes some way towards explaining the dominance of men's preferences in terms of the food produced. Women felt hurt and rejected, in themselves, if the food they offered to their partners was refused. Children's refusal of food was not usually taken so seriously as they were expected to have changeable tastes and food fads. This partly explains why their preferences are not taken into account to the extent that men's are.

Many women told us of events, usually when they were first married to or living with their partners, which involved a partner's rejection of food. And many referred to a process of trial and error through which they learnt what foods their partners would and would not eat. This process, and the need to provide men with food that they liked, was part of the taken-for-grantedness of most women's lives. [...]

There is concern to cook meals that he will eat and enjoy and discovering his preferences is part of becoming a 'good' wife and showing that you care for him. A corollary of the process of eliminating the foods men dislike from the diet is subordinating your own preferences, and this almost always occurred if conflict was to be avoided. One woman was unable to cook anything other than very plain dishes for her partner:

'My husband is very traditional-minded about food, he does't like anything Chinese or foreign, he doesn't like anything with herbs in it apart from salt and pepper so I tend to stick to the same thing most weeks – I rarely buy anything just for myself ...'

Men had various ways of making their views felt. Some were very cautious, as one woman told us: 'I used to make quite a lot of pizza and after about seven years he told me politely that he didn't like it very much so I didn't make it any more. He didn't say anything for all that time.' This was extremely unusual. Most men were not so accommodating. The woman whose husband would only eat plain food recounted the following experience:

'If I cook something that's got a whiff of herbs in it or something he'll put his knife and fork down and say, "I'm sorry but I'm not eating it". [...] He usually waits

until my parents come and I've prepared something a bit out of the ordinary and
he'll leave it. I'm not happy but there again I'll not make a scene, I'm not one for
rowing – I'll go off and have a little weep to myself.' [...]

It should be said that it was not a majority of the men in the sample who had
at one time or another refused food: 130 (65 per cent) had never refused food
or had only refused it if they had been ill. However, this does not necessarily
mean that they will eat anything they are presented with: it often means that
their partners have very successfully adapted the diet to their preferences, as
this woman told us:

> 'I cook what I know he will like. Even if I cook something different I make sure the
> basic food is what he likes. I mean I don't try things knowing he won't like them.
> Things like pasta I know he won't eat that, so I don't cook it. But he's never actually
> refused anything.' [...]

[...] violent rejection of food was an extreme reaction, but it underlines the
relations of power which underlie the gender division of food provision. Women
within this relation are subservient and subordinate, they are the servers and
providers of food for men. We will quote at length from one of the women's
accounts, as it gives a very clear picture of the power relations governing food
provision. During this interview both husband and wife were present. The
husband began by saying:

HUSBAND: There was once where you made something I didn't like – I
remember that.
WIFE: Oh yes, I forgot about that.
HUSBAND: Yeah – But apart from a broken plate and a rather dirty wall there
was no other damage.
WIFE: I forgot about that altogether.
HUSBAND: Yeah, I threw it at you didn't I? Do you remember?
[Did you?]
HUSBAND: Yeah, Oh dear me, I think I said something like, 'Shove that fucking
muck' – Oh, sorry the tape's on isn't it? I don't want to be rude. That
was when we'd just got married, wasn't it, and you thought that was
an acceptable standard of nourishment.
WIFE: I thought it was nice, it tasted nice.
[That was right at the beginning of your marriage?]
HUSBAND: That's right, yeah. She's never given me any of that rubbish again
so that's all right.

It is hardly surprising, in view of these responses and the hurt experienced by
rejection of food, that women try to cook according to their partner's tastes in
food. One of the single parents had found divorce a liberating experience

because of this and was now free to vary her own and the children's diet. Many of the women reported their husbands as refusing to eat salad, particularly if it was presented to them as a main meal on their return home from work:

> 'If I do a salad it's not a meal to him ... I've just got to do a meal with meat, vegetables and potatoes ... he expects a hot meal and I think he deserves it.'

Men expect a proper meal on their return from work and women seem to feel that this is what they deserve and is appropriate for a working man.

The importance attached by women to the provision of a proper meal for their partners was brought out when we asked them if they would cook differently if they were living on their own. Only twenty-five of them said they would continue to cook the same, the others would all change their diet to a greater or lesser extent. The main changes that would occur seemed to be a reduction in meat [...] balanced by an increase in other foods, foods which are not normally considered to be part of a proper meal such as soup, fruit, cauliflower cheese, and so on. One woman told us: 'Left to my own devices, if I was living on my own I would probably live on soup, milk puddings, muesli and fresh fruit. I'd eat a lot less meat and a lot more fruit and vegetables.' And the main reason for providing proper meals for their families was often men's insistence on meat. 'Well we eat quite a lot of meat and I'm prepared to have say two or three days without it ... I'd be quite happy with cauliflower cheese you see but Michael would regard it as a vegetable, not the main part of the meal.'

[...] women tend to cook food according to their partners' preferences on a daily basis. So that, really, men are pampered, their tastes are catered for in the very way that a family's diet is structured. As one woman, who said she never 'treated' her partner with food, put it: 'I know the things he has more of a liking for and I class a lot of that really as every day but usually, two or three times a week, I'll do the stuff that I know he likes best.'

6.4   **Solving Problems and Airing Feelings**
Penny Mansfield and Jean Collard

This Reading, from a study of sixty-five newlywed couples, reveals the divergent expectations of 'togetherness' held by husbands and wives.

Two views of confiding

[...] several women who admitted that confiding in their spouses was a vital aspect of their marital relationship had been perplexed, and at times disappointed, when they realised that their husbands were not confiding in them. [...] When the newly-weds' own accounts of how and why they did (or did not) disclose their feelings are closely examined, it becomes clear that men and women use the process of self-disclosure in very different ways.

'*Airing feelings*' was an important preoccupation of women and a vital aspect of self-disclosure for them. For some the feelings were aired in the course of general conversation. [...] Husbands quite often regarded this kind of disclosure as 'rabbiting on'. If they gave a hint of affirmation, their wives felt listened to; if they demonstrated their lack of interest by reading the newspaper or walking out, their wives felt unsupported. Husbands who failed to see any point in these monologues of disclosure found them boring:

> 'She talks, it's boring; she goes right into the depths, tells me every single thing, every little detail. I say, "Shut up".'

Another aspect of wives' disclosure was expressing their mood, their feelings of sadness or depression, insecurity or uncertainty:

> 'A lot of the time he'll say, "What's the matter with you?" and I won't really know myself, perhaps going around with a long face or something and I have to delve around for a reason, but there rarely is one.'

> 'Sometimes when I'm moody I'd like to be able to explain how I'm feeling. I find it a bit difficult. I think he understands to some extent but as I can't put it into words, I don't really see how I can expect him to understand, but I wish that I could somehow. Like I say, I don't always understand it myself – there's no real reason behind it – it's just a feeling ... it's the only thing he finds difficult about me, my moods, we've talked about. Otherwise he thinks I'm all right.'

Women expressing their feelings in this way were a threat for many men. Husbands could not understand what their wives meant, or what they could do about it, or what it indicated about their marriage. It was a rare husband who could be confided in successfully. [...]

A few men tried to offer solutions and then withdrew on realising that these 'problems with no name' had no solutions. Most men simply tuned off. 'Rabbiting on' might be boring and 'a pain in the neck' but to some extent it was 'what wives do': it therefore had a place in marriage. 'The problems with no name' were disturbing because they could not be explained. [...]

'*Problem solving*', in contrast, was for most men the main, if not the sole purpose of disclosing to another person. The point of any conversation or talking about feelings was in order to gain advice, information or a knowledgeable opinion. One husband recognised that he 'kept things to himself' and that his wife would like it if he approached her with things that bothered him, but 'though she would like it she can't do anything, she can't solve the problem'. If there were problems at work (and work was a very important part of men's lives), wives were rejected as confidantes because they 'wouldn't understand, they could't do anything':

> 'If it's a problem at work – she don't know what I'm on about half the time, so there's no point.'

Alongside this patronising attitude to disclosing to wives, there was, however, a protective element; some men would shield women from problems to do with work and money because they didn't want to worry them and also in order to protect their own image because it was not manly to admit to such feelings of inadequacy. Wives who challenged their husbands for more information or who probed and dug away were rarely rewarded for their perseverance. Several men were resentful of their wives' attempts to intrude into their world. [...]

The importance of mutual support

'I like being looked after – well, I suppose I am a male chauvinist pig', said Mr Oliver. Few husbands spoke so candidly about the importance of being cared for by their wives, though it was implicit in much of what men said they enjoyed and expected of married life. [...]

[...] for husbands a supportive partner in marriage was someone who kept the home going, and who generally make their life run smoothly.

Wives who were demanding, and those who were 'moody', who sought attention and required expressions of affection (apart from sex), also posed problems for men:

> 'I never say I love her – I don't know why. Sometimes she asks, "Do you love me?" – I say, "I married you" – something like that. She knows she's not going to get a direct answer so she don't bother no more.'
> [Do you think she knows you love her?]
> 'I suppose she does – she wouldn't have married me if she didn't, would she? ... She tells me she loves me, she is affectionate and cuddles up and says, "I love you" – you know that sort of stuff like you see on the telly – she's always moaning that I don't tell her I love her.'

The supportive element in marriage was highly valued by wives and two out of three wives talked about marriage in such a way. They wanted to share their feelings and to be 'understood'; to feel appreciated and cared about by their spouses. Generally, however, wives felt that *they* were the ones who reassured and were understanding and tender towards their husbands (and indeed their spouses recognised this), but they wanted reciprocity. Some wives did have supportive husbands and gladly acknowledged this. [...]

... the newlyweds vividly reveal that as men and women they interpret togetherness very differently. Most (though not all) men seek a *life in common* with their wives, a home life, a physical and psychological base; somewhere and someone to set out from and return to.

But, for nearly all the wives, their desired marriage was a *common life* with an empathetic partner, who was to provide both material and emotional security. Women wanted a close exchange of intimacy which would make them feel valued as a person, not just a wife.

Despite the promise of emotional fulfilment offered by modern marriage, the gender gap of expectation in many of these newly-wed marriages was wide and men seemed either to be unaware of this or unable to accept it. Wives, in contrast, acknowledged the existence of the gap and hoped to bridge it. There is, it seems, 'his' marriage and 'her' marriage existing apart from 'their' marriage. [...]

... the relatively isolated home life of the newly-wed couple ... is an isolation which is at times enjoyed, but at other times endured in the interests of coupleness. When one partner in the couple fails to return, the other partner feels abandoned. It was not surprising that it was wives who felt this more acutely; their social lives had been completely changed by marriage. [...] Many wives who led a restricted social life expected their husbands to be close, attentive companions who returned to them every night to share a common life. However, husbands, as we have already indicated, often had very different ideas; they wanted wives who would create a home, look after it and them, and, most important of all, who would be there when they chose to return. It was rare for husbands to experience 'aloneness' and when they did, their reactions were extreme; their wives were not behaving as 'proper wives'. Wives were becoming resigned to the fact that husbands did behave that way, but they felt it was unfair. They had hoped that in marriage they would find close friendship, and that their husbands would not *want* to be away from them, and so they simply felt let down when their husbands were repeatedly late home.

'Feeling let down'

It became noticeable that in many descriptions of the most recent quarrel, the emotional loading of the issue was often far greater than the apparently trivial trigger. Again it was more frequently wives who felt that way, both according to their own narratives and from their husbands' accounts also (a third of wives and just over a third of husbands). Only two husbands and one wife referred to a husband having felt this way. According to husbands, women were 'more sensitive' and 'take things to heart', but when wives were describing their own feelings it was clear they expected much more of their husbands emotionally than these men were prepared, or felt able, to give.

6.5   Gender Roles and the 'Moral Economy of Kin' among Pakistani Women in West Yorkshire

Haleh Afshar

This Reading gives an account of the rather different meanings marriage has for women of Pakistani descent.

All the women I spoke to saw marriage as an inevitable and desirable part of life and all agreed that their parents should have a say in the arrangements. Even those who were born and brought up in England were somewhat sceptical about romantic love and Western style marriage. On the other hand all the younger generation felt strongly that they should be consulted about the choice of future husbands.

The older generation, who had married without ever meeting their prospective spouses, felt on the whole that the younger generation should be more pliable. Among the second and third generation, however, there was a degree of ambivalence about sight unseen, non-consultative, marriages. In particular, school-girls resented any suggestion that they should leave school in order to be married off. All recognised that parents arranged such marriages in order to get rid of troublesome daughters, who were likely to behave in a way that could lead to a loss of face. The parental ruse of transferring the responsibility for guarding the chastity of young daughters to more able and younger men was clearly observed and generally resented.[1] At the same time such knowledge did play an important role in the self-policing of younger women, who saw their side of the bargain and accepted it. In practice the acquiescence towards arranged marriages was, for daughters, tinged with the fear of having to part from their families and going back to their husband's home.

There was a marked contrast between the wishes of many mothers born and raised in Pakistan, who wished to send at least one daughter back to the homeland to secure close family ties and a home base for the next generation. But the daughters, though they accepted the institution of patrilocal marriages, sought to move next door rather than to another country. The youngest group all expressed the hope of staying close to their mothers and bringing their future husbands home. By contrast the older generation of women, who had been reared almost as guests in their homes and who had been prepared for the move to the mother-in-law's house from the very beginning, felt that their granddaughters were ill-prepared for 'real life' and cooperation with future in-laws.

Mothers found it very difficult to find a middle way. Many, particularly the less well off, had come to depend heavily on the domestic services of their eldest daughter, and when the time came found it extremely difficult to marry them off. The ideal solution was perceived by many to be a double marriage, marrying a daughter away and bringing in a daughter-in-law at the same time. Amongst women I talked to, one had managed to do just this. But although in terms of practicability this seemed a sensible solution, the entire family felt emotionally torn apart by the departure of the eldest daughter.

There was, however, a wide variation in the way marriages were arranged and the degree of consultation that took place with daughters, and sons for that matter. There was a close correlation with parental background. Those who had the closest ties with the rural areas tended to have the least consultation. Those from urban areas, who also tended to be the more affluent, tended to marry their children off later and allow them a greater degree of choice. The introduction of the latest Nationality Act in 1986 made parental decisions considerably harder and caused much heart searching amongst those who had promised their daughters in marriage before the Act and had to go through with the ceremony afterwards in the knowledge that their daughter could not bring her spouse into the country and would have to leave.

Although all the women we talked to approved of the institution of marriage, their views about what it was and the obligations that it entailed varied markedly across the generations. The oldest generation viewed marriage as the beginning of 'real life'. They accepted their mother-in-law as the real authority in charge of their household and some had had their lives mapped out for them by their future in-laws. One grandmother from a rural background had had her marriage arranged with a young educated urban dwelling cousin. Her father-in-law had decided that his son needed an educated wife and had arranged for the future daughter-in-law, accompanied by her sister, to be sent off to a boarding school near Delhi to complete her secondary education. The subsequent marriage and life with the in-laws had been, according to this informant, simple and untraumatic. It may be that the passage of time has made the past seem more agreeable, but this lady was convinced that her early married days were as good as anyone's. She had been trained to cook and sew and her mother-in-law taught her to do so in a way that pleased her husband. When her husband moved to Leeds, she had stayed on with her in-laws until he was ready to receive her, and in many ways she found the parting from her mother-in-law more painful than the move to her marital home from the village. She had hoped that her husband would return and had followed him extremely reluctantly. She found the move to Britain a terrible experience for which she had no mental or emotional preparation. This woman had great sympathy for those young girls who were married off to return to Pakistan and felt very strongly that such a move was emotionally unbearable and should not be imposed on anyone.

Notes

1. Haleh Afshar, 'Khomeini's teachings and their implications for women in Iran', in A. Tabari and N. Yeganeh (eds), *In the Shadow of Islam*, London: Zed Press, 1985.

6.6   What are Feminist Perspectives on Wife Abuse?
Michele Bograd

Michele Bograd outlines the main themes in feminist analyses of wife abuse, the most extreme manifestation of male power in marriage.

Given the wide variety of feminist philosophies, there is no unified feminist perspective on wife abuse. But all feminist researchers, clinicians, and activists address a primary question: 'Why do men beat their wives?' This specific question directs attention to the physical violence occurring in heterosexual relationships that are structured in certain ways within the institution of marriage or partnership as it is currently culturally defined and socially sustained on material and ideological levels. This approach distinguishes feminists from others who ask: 'What psychopathology leads to violence?' or 'Why are people involved in violent interactions in families?' or 'How is violence in the family related to our violent society?' Furthermore, feminists seek answers to their question at the social or group level. Instead of examining why this particular man beats his particular wife, feminists seek to understand why men in general use physical force against their partners and what functions this serves for a given society in a specific historical context. [1]

Gender and power

When a husband uses violence against his wife, people often view this as a random, irrational act. In contrast, feminists define wife abuse as a pattern that becomes understandable only through examination of the social context. Our society is structured along the dimension of gender: Men as a class wield power over women. As the dominant class, men have differential access to important material and symbolic resources, while women are devalued as secondary and inferior. Although important social class and race differences exist among men, all men can potentially use violence as a powerful means of subordinating women. Although there are many ways that men as a group maintain women in oppressed social positions, violence is the most overt and effective means of social control. Even if individual men refrain from employing physical force against their partners, men as a class benefit from how women's lives are restricted and limited because of their fear of violence by husbands and lovers as well as by strangers. Wife abuse or battering reinforces women's passivity and dependence as men exert their rights to authority and control. The reality of domination at the social level is the most crucial factor contributing to and maintaining wife abuse at the personal level.

The family as a social institution

The family as a social institution mediates between oppression at the broadest social level and the personal relationships of intimate adult partners. But the family is not a monolithic universal entity. Its functions, structures, and processes must be examined in their current sociohistorical context. Feminists challenge the cultural ideal of the family as a 'peaceful haven in a heartless world'. Wife abuse is not viewed as a rare and deviant phenomenon that results from the breakdown of family functioning, but as a predictable and common dimension of normal family life as it is currently structured in our society. Feminist theoreticians have cogently argued that wife abuse is closely related to the historical development of the isolated nuclear family in a capitalist society, to division of the public and private/domestic domains, to specialization of 'appropriate' male and female family roles, and to the current position of wives as legally and morally bound to husbands.[2] This is not to deny that wife abuse has existed across the centuries in societies of varying political persuasions and structures. But wife abuse cannot be examined out of its particular sociohistorical context, which shapes its dynamics, its social acceptability, and its meaning. Furthermore, as feminists link wife abuse to the structure of current family life, they draw theoretical and empirical links between the personal and the political, which lead to new understandings of battering: Wife abuse is not a private matter but a social one.

Notes

1. J. Chapman and M. Gates (eds), *The Victimization of Women*, Newbury Park, CA: Sage, 1978; R. E. Dobash and R. Dobash, *Violence Against Wives*, New York: Free Press, 1979; D. Martin, *Battered Wives*, New York: Pocket Books, 1976; M. Pagelow, *Women Battering: Victims and their experiences*, Newbury Park, CA: Sage, 1981; D. Russell, *Rape in Marriage*, New York: Macmillan, 1982; S. Schechter, *Women and Male Violence*, Boston, MA: South End, 1982; L. Walker, *The Battered Woman*, New York: Harper & Row, 1979; L. Walker, *The Battered Woman Syndrone*, New York: Springer, 1984.
2. W. Brienes and L. Gordon, 'The new scholarship on family violence', *Signs: Journal of Women in Culture and Society*, no. 8 (1983), pp. 490–531; Dobash and Dobash, *Violence Against Wives*; Martin, *Battered Wives*; Schechter, *Women and Male Violence*.

6.7   **Becoming a Mother**
Ann Oakley

Ann Oakley's study of sixty-six first-time mothers reveals the massive impact of the transition to motherhood on women's lives.

Throughout human society childbirth is never just one event in a women's life. It is always momentous, but in different ways. For culture, the different cultures that human beings have invented as ways of living, defines the meaning of birth, a biological act.

The meaning of childbirth is interlocked with a society's attitudes towards women. Both reflect its economic system. Capitalism, by concentrating production in places other than the home, altered the status of women: mothers working became The Working Mother. The production of capital requires the production of workers: thus women's role becomes not to produce but to reproduce: 'the mother employed out of the home presents a national problem of the first importance'. [1]

One does not have to be a Marxist to understand these connections between motherhood and the economy. And it is important to appreciate the history of motherhood as it appears to us in industrialised society today, because our sort of motherhood is unique in history [...]

> The institution of motherhood is not identical with bearing and caring for children. ... Institutionalised motherhood demands of women maternal 'instinct' rather than intelligence, selflessness rather than self-realisation, relation to others rather than the creation of self. [2]

The *institution* of motherhood is the way women become mothers in industrialised society today. [...] The industrialised world today insists on certain sex differences while having moved towards an idea of sex equality. Equality and difference are compatible, since equality in this ideology does not mean 'sameness'. It means that women should be allowed to do the same jobs for the same pay as men, that girls should be educated as much as (though differently from?) boys, that a woman should become prime minister if that is what she and the country want. Equality applies to the world outside the home. Inside it, difference flourishes (thereby, of course, rendering external equality more of a mere vision). [...]

First-time motherhood calls for massive changes. Thirty years ago women gave up their jobs on marriage: now the occasion is impending motherhood. The return to work is slow: 20 percent four years after, 52 percent ten years after (and it is likely to be a different sort of work chosen for its compatibility with maternal duties). Becoming a mother is more than a change of job: it involves reorganising one's entire personality. For there is a chasm between mothers' needs and children's needs that mothers have to bridge. In a society where children are reared in small, quite isolated families, babies have an absolute need to be mothered (who else will do it?) but mothers, however 'maternal' they are, only have a relative need for their babies. They have a past identity and a future one in which real children do not feature. [...]

Surveying the mental health of women, research workers in London have found that one in three women have definite psychiatric symptoms of depression and that the likelihood of becoming depressed is crucially related to motherhood. [3] [...] motherhood seems more often to lead to a sense of lowered ('depressed') self-worth: children take the centre of the stage; the mother is merely a supporting player. [...] ... the period spent having and caring for young children is the time when men choose careers and advance in them; by their mid-thirties parenthood has firmly wedged the sexes apart. If mothers want careers outside the home they are at a disadvantage. Responsibility for children is the key factor in the non-employment of female graduates, and it lies behind the phenomenon of part-time work (our generation's panacea for the problems of women's role). In Britain, more than a third of all employed women work part-time. Women under capitalism count as a reserve labour force. The double standard continues to apply: men are the breadwinners, women the housewives; the nuclear family supports the nation. When it suits the nation, women are encouraged to work and it is made easier for them to do so. During the Second World War in Britain, for example, day nursery provision increased enormously as three and three-quarter million more women joined the labour force. But after the war, reaction set in. In the 1950s maternal employment became once again a thorn in the national conscience, a symbol of women's inhumanity, a sign of failing morality and decaying family life.

Having a first baby is a journey into the unknown in more senses than one. Apart from the birth, which is the central drama in the transition to motherhood, three changes have to be accomplished more or less simultaneously: giving up paid work; taking up a totally new occupation – that of mother; becoming a housewife. For a minority of women the break in paid-work career will be short, and the necessary adjustment to domesticity only temporary. But most women stay at home for several years. Some may not 'work' again for a long time.

Unlike other changes of occupation, this transformation of secretary or shop assistant into mother and housewife entails more than small changes in routine: different hours, different workplace, different work-mates, more or less money. The language of capitalism – work (paid) versus housework (unpaid) – masks the actual labour of housework and child care. Cultural images of womanhood have the same effect, inflating the grimy floor and the soiled nappy to the status of personal obligations: an extension of feminine hygiene. But while domesticity may be a theme running through women's lives from birth to death, suddenly having no other occupation to call one's own may seriously injure a women's self-concept, ideas she has cherished for a long while about herself as a person. The housewife–mother's working conditions may pose extra threats to contentment: isolation, monotony, fragmentation, twenty-four-hour-a-day responsibility, lack of money and, for some, poor housing as well. Such occupational hazards of being female may of course have no impact on some women; but in the mind, in anticipation, they hover as grey possibilities on the horizon. To 'work' or not to 'work' is much more than an argument about one versus two incomes; it involves ideas about the needs of babies and ideas about the legitimacy of one's own needs as a person.

This awful dilemma

LOIS MANSON, 29, university, postgraduate training, research work for seven years:

12 weeks pregnant:
I: Do you plan to work after the baby's born?
LOIS: Well, this is the dilemma. I run a large department and in many ways I don't want to give up work and I'd like to go back full time. But I've got terrific problems as to what I would do with the child if I went back full time. I don't fancy the idea of a childminder and my parents don't live near enough to constantly look after it. It's a big problem. So I've come to an agreement to go back part time. [...] Before I became pregnant I didn't think that I'd want to go back to work. I didn't really think about it; I'd assumed that when I became pregnant I would leave and I'd be off for a couple of years – nice – and then I'd go back.
I: So what changed your mind?
LOIS: The actual realisation that I *was* pregnant, I suppose. The awful thought of having to give up the work – the fact that it's been very pleasant ... and I just don't really want to leave. This awful dilemma. There are so many problems. It really is awful. I've been worrying about this ever since I thought there was a possibility that I might be pregnant; it's been uppermost in my mind.

34 weeks pregnant:
I: How did you feel about giving up work?
LOIS: Oh I didn't want to give up – I was very frustrated about it. And I haven't thought about what it's going to be like having a baby to look after. Suddenly yesterday – Dave keeps on at me about having driving lessons for this test that's coming up – and I've been vaguely thinking I've got another ten or twelve weeks till I go back to work, and then yesterday it suddenly occurred to me for the first time that I can't possibly think in terms of ten to twelve weeks, because I'm going to have a baby for the last seven weeks of that. And I'm not going to be able to just ring up and say I want a driving lesson from ten till eleven. And really I was quite – I think I panicked for the first time in my pregnancy. It did really occur to me that I was going to have a responsibility towards something and that it was going to impinge upon my life. I think perhaps I hadn't really thought about that. And suddenly I thought well it's not just going to be a question of getting a nice baby-sitter for a whole evening – that's straightforward; there's no problem there. But it's going to be things like an odd hour or so that you would want. It's very natural now to do what I want, I'm completely my own master; and then I thought Christ, I won't be able to do that: I'd better get on the phone straight away to book up my driving lessons. And then I started thinking: what are all the other things that I should be fitting in these next six weeks? Because it's the last time in my life I'm going to have six weeks free. And I really do get panicky about it, because I actually thought of

it as a child in its own right with demands that were going to make demands on my life.

SOPHY FISHER, 29, a television producer for seven years:
The classic story is that I met somebody – Matthew introduced me to a director he was working with and he didn't take me in, he said how do you do and made a little small talk, and obviously didn't take much interest. Then Matthew had to go away and we were rather unfortunately left together. And he obviously with an enormous effort sort of turned to me and said you're a physiotherapist aren't you? And I said no, no I work in television. And he said who are you – what's your professional name? And I said Sophy Bates, and he knew of me – it's a very small world – and his whole attitude changed, his whole face changed. And suddenly I was a person and somebody it might be interesting to talk to. That was awful and I don't like him for it but it was an absolute indication of how I was not of any interest if I was Matthew's wife. ... It was very alarming. ... I've always said that I want to go on working when I have children: it's very important to me.

Notes

1. T. Ferguson and L. C. Logan, 'Mothers employed out of the home', *Glasgow Medical Journal*, vol. 34 (1953), p. 239.
2. A. Rich, *Of Woman Born*, London: Virago, 1977, p. 42.
3. G. W. Brown and T. Harris, *Social Origins of Depression*, London: Tavistock, 1978.

6.8 Taking It Like a Woman
Ann Oakley

Here Ann Oakley gives us a short autobiographical account of what is commonly labelled and 'treated' as postnatal depression, but it might more usefully be viewed as a normal response to the dramatic change in lifestyle, identity and status associated with motherhood.

There is nothing in my diaries for 1967 and 1968 except clinic appointments, the weights of babies, shopping lists and the beginnings and ends of Robin's terms. We had no holidays and we never went out in the evening together. I can't remember what he did, but I watched old films on television or went to sleep. I do remember – and this is important because it is part of the contradiction, one of the biggest unsolved problems – loving my two bright-eyed children intensely. There were the centre and the purpose of my life.

But none of this served to make me happy. Passionate love, such as the love I felt for my children, doesn't guarantee happiness. It often prevents it, and that is why such love is a major cultural and personal preoccupation. I didn't know this at the time. I didn't understand my own predicament at all. Other people called it depression. If it was postnatal, nobody ventured an opinion as to whose natality it followed. The point was I was ill. It took five or six white pills to make me sleep. It took combinations of little blue and red pills (stelazinc and imipramine – I thought of them as characters in a Shakespearean play) to make me into the mechanical housewife of my daily life. The pills were provided by my GP, a large, energetic, not unkindly man, to whom I took my tears and tales of woe. (Where else could I take them?) He should have given me an analysis of the difference between the experience and the institution of motherhood,[1] and explained how social conditions may provoke distress in women like me, educated for a world outside the home and then confined to life inside it. He should have told me that around four-fifths of women in our society are depressed after birth,[2] about a third most or some of the time.[3] Yet that was (is) too much to expect. Instead, he offered me the traditional remedy of a pharmacological adjustment to my situation, along with weekly appointments in his surgery which did, literally, keep me alive.

Another GP, to whom I went somewhat later, took the distinctly less helpful step of referring all four of us to a psychiatric hospital. We attended once, and a psychiatric social worker had a great time interpreting our family life from Adam and Emily's manipulation of the contents of a doll's house, while a psychoanalyst concentrated so completely on the dynamics of our marital relationship that he failed to notice Emily pouring the dolls' bathwater over his feet. We were offered inpatient treatment for a few months, but they would't tell us what was wrong with us.

However, to say that the medical profession labelled me, along with several million other women, as depressed between 1967 and 1969 is not to explain anything about the way we felt. Personally, I felt exhausted and incapable. I did have every reason to feel exhausted. Two young children have not been one woman's exclusive responsibility and workload throughout most of history. Our own culture's nuclear family arrangement for childrearing is extremely peculiar. My own two children had limitless energy. One of them woke up several times a night for five years. For a total of one year, one or the other had to be fed at night. It was the pills that made me capable of coping with this; at least then I cooked food for the children, washed everyone's clothes and slept for short periods when allowed to do so, even if I had no particular regard for myself. I took the pills self-consciously as a way of coping, and I was not alone in that strategy.[4] I felt that my life, despite its centredness on my beloved children, and a marriage that by anybody's standards was 'good' (few rows, no wife-beating, affection and mutual respect), was simply devoid of meaning. What was it all for? How could I go on?

Antidepressants, tranquillizers, obscurantist psychoanalysts and busy GPs: these represented techniques of adjustment that appeared reasonable because we thought individual adjustment was just exactly what was needed. [...]

When five months pregnant with Emily I put an advertisement in the *New Statesman*: 'Graduate mother of 1½ children needs work to do at home. Anything considered.' I disliked my economic dependence and its connotation of secondariness, of belonging to someone else and not to myself (and we did need more money). To be paid for one's labour is an unhappily mechanical solution to this problem, but it is a solution of a kind. [...]

The years of giving birth and breastfeeding, which should have been years in which I felt fully alive, spelled instead a kind of death. I understand why, now. I did not have the kind of social supports that prevent depression in married women. I had not been prepared properly for the realities of motherhood. I had not been educated for that existence. (What had I been educated for?) I couldn't get away from the fact that by the age of twenty-five I had done the only four things I had wanted to do – viz., get a university degree, a husband, a house and two children. Now I had achieved all this I felt I had achieved nothing except the illness of feeling life over at twenty-five, life meaningless thereafter; no challenge or development anywhere; only the passage of time and the static evolution of the conventional drama of family life.

Notes

1. A. Rich, *Of Woman Born*, London: Virago, 1977.
2. A. Oakley, *Women Confined*, Oxford: Martin Robertson, 1980.
3. G. W. Brown and T. Harris, *Social Origins of Depression*, London: Tavistock, 1978.
4. R. Cooperstock and H. L. Lennard, 'Some social meanings of tranquilizer use', *Sociology of Health and Illness*, vol. 1, no. 3 (1979), pp. 331–47.

6.9   **To Be or not to Be: the dilemmas of mothering**
Sheila Rowbotham

Sheila Rowbotham considers changing perspectives on motherhood within the Women's Liberation Movement.

In the early years of Women's Liberation the emphasis was on challenging the myth that motherhood was woman's inevitable destiny The complaints of young women with children were significant in movement literature.

It has been very important to contest that happiness comes only through motherhood and attack the myth which denies women a range of possibilities. Feminists have maintained that motherhood as we know it carries both oppressive and fulfilling elements. It is far from being a liberatory and enriching experience for all women. Consequently feminists have insisted that motherhood must be freely chosen and socially transformed.

The question of mothering was a powerful influence in the emergence of the women's movement. Many of the earliest meetings discussed childcare. But there remained a gap between those of us who had children and those of us who had not. I was among the have-nots. I can remember in my twenties listening dutifully to tales of the crimes and charms of little Bloggins and feeling secretly restive. Oh if only we could pass on to more exciting stuff like the domestic labour debate or the relevance of Rosa Luxemburg or something. Theoretically I recognized the politics of everyday life. But, not being a mother, I still found the chit-chat exceedingly dull and depressingly dismal. 'How do they put up with it?' I wondered. 'How do they remain relatively sane?' Their lives were not their own at all. Yet I wanted to have a child – but in the future always. In the present there were so many things to do. I was wary about having a baby because I was terrified of the dependence it entailed. The denunciation of motherhood intensified my fears – though it did not make me personally ever imagine I would never conceive. In 1977, breast-feeding a baby at women's meetings, I gazed at the childless feminists in amazement as they intellectually galloped along. How could they think so fast, I wondered, and yearned for the child welfare centre where we were all hypnotized by the micro-world of the babies.

By 1980 Liz Heron was commenting on 'The latterday feminist baby boom'. She noted wryly that many feminists seemed to be 'melting into motherhood'.[1] The shift was noticeable in many other countries. Complaint and denunciation of the mystique of motherhood and the emphasis on choice had put women who wanted children on the defensive. Were they simply the victims of delusion? Was the choice of motherhood an indulgence then? Freewheeling childless feminists could appear to be saying, 'You made your bed, now lie on it'. Writing of the French context, Claire Duchen said this led to 'the ironic equation: enslaved motherhood + voluntary motherhood = voluntary slavery'.[2] There was too, the effect of the biological clock: 'Women have very different attitudes to motherhood when they are 20 and when they are 30.'[3] Readiness to consider why women want to have children without attributing the inclination completely to external media persuasion marked an acceptance of a complexity which had not featured in the earlier literature.

It is not in fact true that in the early days of the Women's Liberation Movement in Britain there was an outright rejection of becoming mothers. The change really was that it became possible to express the negative aspects of mothering, without feeling such a sense of failure. This was not the only response, of course. I can remember in many early discussions women complaining about the practical problems of childcare but expressing happiness in being mothers. Underlying the anger was the impulse to make a life in which there could be a new balance between mothering and a range of other activities for women. We did not see this as an either/or choice. We explicitly rejected the emancipation of the middle-class 'career woman' who was forced to remain childless. Instead we wanted new relationships and conditions in which we could have children and lead fuller lives.

The denial that our only value is as 'reproducers' has not been the only response from feminists. Another approach has been to argue that motherhood is a source of power for women that men seek to control. Linked to this has been an affirmation of 'motherly' values of nurture. As a total political concept this leads to a dead end. It results in an idealization of motherhood which confines women again to a separate sphere as nurturers.[4] As Liz Heron argues: 'To celebrate child bearing and child rearing as "woman power", as one strand of contemporary feminism has done, risks bringing us full circle to another kind of biological determinism.'[5] It undermines women who are sharing childcare, combining mothering with paid work, and disregards the material reality of large numbers of working-class women and black women's daily struggle with low-paid work and childcare. But as a partial acknowledgement of how some women can experience mothering at certain moments it is an important assertion of aspects of experience which are disregarded as a source for alternative social values. [...]

There is a persistent popular stereotype of feminists as curious beings distinct from 'normal' women, immune to contrary emotions. In reality feminists have grappled with the contradictory extremes of female destiny which mothering raises. To dismiss the delights of mothering denies intense and passionate aspects of women's lives. But to elevate these into an alternative ideal is to deny the negative feelings, to return women to the sphere of reproduction and subordinate childless women to a maternalistic hierarchy. [...]

It is too simple to elevate motherhood and represent it as nature. Mary Kelly has argued the psychological ambivalence which exists in the existing symbolic meanings of motherhood:

> 'Mother art', identification with the woman who tends: i.e. the mother who feeds you. She produces milk and therefore all 'good things', patchwork quilts, candles, bread and assorted magic rituals. She is the phallic mother, the uncastrated 'parthenogenator' of the pre-oedipal instance. But there is also the castrated and (unconsciously) despised mother of the Oedipus complex. Her labour of love is signified as 'women's work', a kind of iconography of victimisation ... obsessive activities like scrubbing, ironing and above all preparing food.'[6]

This would suggest that it is not just a matter of challenging how motherhood is portrayed in the external culture. Women bring to the decision whether or not to have a child a psychological image of motherhood as power and submission bound together. The problem for feminists is whether this is a fixed unalterable structure or whether it can be changed. If it can be changed, where should we concentrate our efforts: on psychoanalytic exploration, on attempting to represent mothering differently, on changing the relations in which we mother, or on transforming the social condition of mothering? Not surprisingly, there is no unified strategy. Feminists have busied themselves in all these areas. As the women's movement has become more fragmented it has been harder to consider even how the differing forms of activity and inquiry might interrelate.

It is not just feminists who are confused about motherhood; the received images in a male-defined culture contain their own contradictions! A pregnant women is both weak and powerful, sick and serene within the iconography.

Women have more chance to decide whether to have a baby because both birth control and medical maternal technology are more reliable – if not safe. However, the psychological and social assumptions about motherhood are rooted in the experiences of generations of human beings who did not possess the means of choice. Feminists are thus torn between approaching women's desire to conceive as a socially constructed phenomenon which can be rationally explained and subjected to conscious control, as a psychological structure or as an assertion of women's natural power. There are signs of a more muted quest to dissolve the boundaries and to approach maternity as a continuing interaction between physical growth and mental perception. The implication of such a model for political thought and social change remain unclear.

A generation of women, in Western capitalism, found they had stumbled into uncharted historical territory. The relation between our conscious will and giving birth grew closer, while society's arrangement remained based on the assumption that women as a sex were naturally ordained to be child bearers and rearers. The movement for women's liberation continues to touch nerves which have become raw through the conflicting changes in our predicament. The effort to find a way through has led women to reach out towards contradictory understandings and test these by trial and error.

Notes

1. L. Heron, 'The mystique of motherhood', in Feminist Anthology Collective, *No Turning Back*, London: The Women's Press, 1980, p. 139.
2. C. Duchen, *Feminism in France*, London: Routledge, 1986, p. 60.
3. *Ibid*.
4. For an analysis of these ideas, see H. Eisenstein, *Contemporary Feminist Thought*, London: Unwin Paperbacks, 1984, pp. 65–95; L. Segal, *Is the Future Female?* London: Virago, 1987.
5. Heron, 'The mystique of motherhood', p. 139.
6. M. Kelly, 'Sexual politics, art and politics', in B. Taylor (ed.), *Proceedings of a Conference on Art and Politics*, Winchester: Winchester School of Art Press.

6.10 **Managing Mothers**
Julia Brannen and Peter Moss

This Reading, from a study of women during maternity leave and after their return to work, considers the extent to which women's accounts of motherhood either reflect or challenge dominant ideologies.

Increasing emphasis has been placed on mothers as unfolders of their children's cognitive capacities, with maternal ambition goaded (by a variety of experts and, increasingly, a 'child development' industry of manufacturers, retailers and media) to have the best developed child.[1] However, elements of the preceding phase – namely the importance of mothers in their children's emotional development – have been carried over: mothers are supposed to be instrumental in fostering their child's cognitive and emotional development. [...]

One of the main themes that have constituted the dominant ideology of motherhood in the post-war years [is] that when children are small, 'normal' motherhood is a full-time activity precluding employment, and that the mother has the major responsibility for all aspects of the child's development. This theme has not remained entirely unchanged over the years. We have already noted an increased emphasis on the mother's role in fostering cognitive development. Ideas about mothers' employment have also evolved. For example, the proportion of women who agree with the statement that 'a married woman with children under school age ought to stay at home' has decreased in recent years, from 78 percent in 1965 to 62 percent in 1980 and 45 percent in 1987.[2]

Closer examination shows that this represents an adaptation of existing ideologies, not a fundamental change. Even by the late 1980s, nearly half of all women still opposed maternal employnent without reservation. Moreover, a majority of the remaining women (29 percent out of 55 percent) took the implicitly negative view that going out to work is only acceptable as the lesser of two evils, supporting the statement that a married woman with pre-school children 'should only work if she needs the money'. The remainder held that it was 'up to her whether to go out to work or not'. There continues to be no support for the proposition that women with young children 'ought to work', although it would be regarded as uncontroversial if applied to men with young children.

This evidence suggests a growing, if grudging, acceptance of maternal employment, but not positive approval. [...]

The ideology of motherhood in the 1980s emphasized women's continuing major responsibility for children and their development – and, as a corollary, the male breadwinning role and the unacceptability of full-time maternal employment. Closely related to this was the belief that the care of young children was a private responsibility to be managed within the household, without external social support. This view of childcare as a private issue was given increasing prominence by the Government in the 1980s as a justification for not intervening to support employed parents. It is expressed clearly below by two women – one from our sample, the other a politician and former Minister:

'I feel really we had him, he's really up to us or one of us ... I suppose it's just an old fashioned view really. They are your responsibility and I feel it should be me, not somebody else.' (Health service technician; Contact 1)

'I start off by believing that people should provide for their own children and provide their own childcare – it's not that difficult.' (Edwina Currie, former Department of Health Minister with responsibility for childcare)

The significance of this belief that childcare is a totally private responsibility is brought into relief by the situation in some other societies, for example France or the countries of Scandinavia, where it is accepted that there is some degree of social responsibility for the care of children. [...]

The ideology of the inseparability of the mother–child bond was brought to the fore when women contemplated the return to work. There is a level at which the ideology of mother love parallels the ideology of monogamous love between adults. Both types of love emphasize the desired and desirable situation of one person forming a close, unique relationship with only one other person at a time. Mothers talk about their love for their babies as 'special' and exclusive – as the 'be all and end all'.[3] In describing their search for childcare mothers referred to finding substitutes for, rather than additions to, themselves, as if the child could only be 'properly' attached to one person. Notably, women never alluded to the impact of fathers' separation from the child. Such 'monogamous' notions of the mother–child relationship are likely to induce feelings of conflict as women think about resuming their jobs and putting the child in someone else's care. The language which they drew upon in describing the anticipated separation is highly suggestive – 'breaking the bond', 'abandoning' or 'leaving' the child.

The conflict that women experienced in contemplating the separation did not appear to affect their accounts of the pleasurable aspects of full-time motherhood. Indeed, they largely constructed the rewards of motherhood according to features of 'normal' (i.e. full-time) motherhood, though in response to direct questions, returners were more likely than non-returners to complain about the conditions of full-time motherhood. [...]

The separation of a mother from her child if she returns to work, especially from a very young child and to a full-time job, calls into question the very essence of what it is to be a 'proper' mother in Britain.

Women described a variety of other feelings over the first weeks away from their children, particularly feelings of anxiety, loss and guilt. These feelings were fuelled both by ideologies of motherhood and by their material circumstances. Anxiety manifested itself in a variety of ways. Some women said they had to restrain themselves from continually ringing up the carer in order to check on their children. At the end of the working day many could scarcely contain themselves, rushing off to be reunited with their child. Undoubtedly their anxiety was increased by ideological prescriptions that only mothers' care is 'good enough'. [...]

One of the main preoccupations of working mothers is time and the concern that they may not be giving sufficient time to their children. [...]

Mothers compensated their children for not being there all the time by spending as much time as possible with them when not at work. It was also a way of expiating guilt for not being a 'proper' mother. Setting aside 'special times' for their children was a common strategy (the literature talks about the notion of 'quality time'[4]). Typically, these 'special times' included the period following the mothers' return from work, while some mothers also set aside time at weekends:

> 'Sundays are our day. I try to get everything done so I can have Sunday free with her. We go out together and play a lot.' (Librarian; Contact 4)

[...] Despite the ideological salience of giving time to children, women asserted that working motherhood resulted in a heightened quality of the mother–child relationship because they were not with their children all the time. In some instances women gave the normative notion of 'giving time' a new twist in talking about 'quality time'. [...]

Motherhood continued to be mainly constructed according to the dominant ideology. The mother was regarded as the person responsible for the child's development and for giving the child time and attention. Moreover, in order to be a good mother, it was also necessary to enjoy it.

The continuing power of the ideology of the 'all responsible mother' among full-time working women is not surprising given the political and institutional context concerning childcare and parental employment in Britain. Women's images of motherhood were also influenced by their own mothers' attitudes and experiences. But the mothers of the great majority of women (74 percent) had not been employed when their own children were under school age; of the 26 percent who were said to have been employed at this stage, just over half (only 14 percent of the whole sample) had worked full-time at any time during this period of early parenthood (returners were no more likely than non-returners to have had mothers who had been employed when their children were of pre-school age). In so far as women had identified with their non-employed mothers, they were presented with a problem when they themselves returned to work. Women were also subject to images in the workplace of what it means to be and not to be a mother. In this respect, the following constitutes a critical case – a woman who consciously distances herself from her own mother and the stereotype:

> 'My mother never had anything within her own life. It was totally child oriented. She always had her apron on. There was always at the back of my mind that my mother enjoyed what she did. If only she'd had the opportunity to do something else. I get up, do my hair, put my make-up on. And the reason I do is that it's almost like saying "Look it's all right, I still have time. It's OK. Women can do it. You can still be yourself. You don't have to look bedraggled. You can have a happy home life".' (Worker in a residential home; Contact 4)

In emphasizing the gains for the mother–child relationship, especially the notion of 'quality time', and the reflected benefits for the child of having a happy and fulfilled mother, women began to contribute towards the creation of a new discourse around working motherhood – namely, that if a woman cannot be happy as a full-time mother then it might be better to work, both for herself and her child. These developments, however, should not be exaggerated. The new themes may best be described as emergent, and in many respects modest, not questioning for instance women's primary responsibility for children; notably absent was any developing notion of 'shared parenthood' with fathers, involving an expectation of shared responsibility for children's development and time with children. Similarly, while the possibility of compensating for the absence of full-time motherhood to some extent is recognized the status of full-time motherhood, as the standard against which other 'deviant' types of motherhood should be judged, is not questioned.

Notes

1. Y. Schutze, 'The good mother: the history of the normative model of "mother love"', in *Growing up in a Modern World*, Proceedings of an International Disciplinary Conference on the Life and Development of Children in Modern Society, Trondheim, Norway, 1988, vol. 1.
2. R. Jowell, S. Witherspoon and L. Brook (eds), *British Social Attitudes: The 5th report*, Aldershot: Gower, 1988.
3. A. Oakley, *Women Confined: Towards a sociology of childbirth*, Oxford: Martin Robertson, 1980; A. Oakley, 'Feminism, motherhood and medicine – who cares?', in J. Mitchell and A. Oakley (eds), *What is Feminism?* Oxford: Basil Blackwell, 1986.
4. L. Hoffman, 'The effects of maternal employment on the academic attitudes and performance of school-age children', *Social Psychology Review*, vol. 9 (1980), pp. 319–36.

6.11 Narrow Definitions of Culture: the case of early motherhood

Ann Phoenix

Young motherhood is often seen as problematic, and it is often believed that young black women are more likely to become mothers for 'cultural' reasons. Ann Phoenix challenges this simplistic view of culture. On the basis of a study of women who became mothers between the ages of 16 and 19, she concludes that young black and white women become pregnant for similar reasons because they are subject to similar socioeconomic circumstances.

[The] emphasis on the Caribbean as providing the key to understanding young black British women's behaviour is inappropriate for the following four reasons:

1. It excludes black people from the category 'British'.
2. It oversimplifies Caribbean cultures.
3. It starts from the assumption that all black people are different from all white people.
4. It confuses colour with culture while ignoring issues of power.

... This illustrates Freire's[1] point that it is difficult for people in a position of political dominance to recognize how culture influences their own group's actions. Hence in studies of 'teenage mothers', culture is implicitly accepted as an important influence on young black women, but not on young white women. [...]

Cultures are necessarily dynamic.[2] The culture (as shared systems of meaning) that young black adults now subscribe to has some roots in, but is not precisely that of their parents. Given that [many] young black women [...] were either born in or have lived most of their lives in Britain, their cultural roots are likely to lie at least as much in British society as in the Caribbean (which most have never visited). [...]

Current dominant reproductive ideologies would suggest that women who are under 20 years of age should not become pregnant. This is partly because mothers are meant to be indisputably adult, and it is not clear whether or not teenage women are adult.[3] It is also partly because marriage is expected to precede motherhood, and women who are under 20 years of age are more likely to be single than married when they give birth (63 percent of mothers under 20 years of age who gave birth in 1985 were single[4]). A third reason is that parents are meant to be economically independent of the state, with mothers and children being dependent on the economic provision fathers make for them. Increasing unemployment, however, has meant that young people from the working classes are more likely to be reliant on state provision of money and housing than they were in the past. Young women's position as dependants is not therefore new, since they have long been expected to be dependent on their male partners. However, as their dependence has been increasingly transferred from male partners to the state, mothers who are under 20 years of age have received more public attention as deviants from social norms.

Given this negative social construction it is important to attempt to understand the reasons why about 3 percent of women in this age group have become mothers each year of this decade. If simple 'perpetuation of cultural norms' hypotheses are to be confirmed, then black women and white women should become pregnant for different reasons, with black women having more 'pro-natalist tendencies' and being more desirous of having children early in their life course.[5] However, black women and white women give remarkably similar accounts of reasons for and responses to early pregnancy. The socioeconomic contexts within which they live crucially influence these reasons and responses. These contexts are largely similar for black women and white women who become mothers early in their lives in that the majority come from the working classes. [...]

Most of the women in this study, whether black or white, reported that they thought it better to have children earlier rather than later in life. This is aptly illustrated by considering some quotations from white women:

'If you have a baby when you're older you're tied down ... I'll still be able to do what I want to.'

(Jan, 17 years old)

'Yeah I think I'm young and people say I'm young but I don't think it makes any difference how old you are ... whether you're thirty or sixteen you can still give it as much love. ... She's twenty-six [R's sister] but she's getting on to have a baby when you think of it. The younger you are the more likely that it's going to be healthier.'

(Alice, 17 years old)

[...] It could be argued that since the interviews were conducted in late pregnancy, these women's responses about ideal ages are simply *post hoc* justifications of a situation which is inevitable. However, they illuminate the differences between 'insider' and 'outsider' perceptions of early motherhood.

It is also important to note that early motherhood was common rather than unusual in the women's social networks. Nearly half of the sample's mothers had themselves had their first child before they were 20.

In this study it was not the case that attachment to early motherhood was culturally specific to young black women. White women were similar to black women in wanting to have children early in life, and knowing many other women (including their own mothers) who had done similarly. In addition the mothers in this study, both black and white, generally considered that motherhood conferred high status on women and so felt that having a child would improve their social status. [...]

Women's feelings about the timing of motherhood were influenced by how they anticipated that it would affect other aspects of their lives. Dominant reproductive ideologies suggest a conflictual model of employment and motherhood in which motherhood should be deferred until the employment career is well established. The rationale for this is that mothers ought not to be employed while their children are young. Therefore unless they are well established in their careers, they will be unable to return to the same occupational position.

This deferment of motherhood makes sense only if women have managed to obtain and keep employment which has built-in career progression, and for many women this is not the case. The jobs which women commonly do, in factories, shops, catering, and the health service, give few opportunities for career progression. [...]

For women who are unemployed, childbearing does not threaten the current employment career, and may well appear a welcome alternative to unemployment. [...]

For the majority of the sample it was not possible to be continually employed for the necessary two years in order to qualify for statutory maternity leave. [...]

In summary, the women in this study were clearly not in occupations which had career progression. Their difficulty in finding (and keeping) jobs meant that few were eligible for maternity leave in late pregnancy. Deferring motherhood would have made little difference to this, since the types of employment they were eligible for tended not to be ones which provided career prospects. For these women the intersection of the motherhood career and the employment career does not fit a conflictual model in that childbearing would make little difference to their employment prospects. In the late pregnancy interview it remained to be seen how many women in this group would actually participate in the labour market post-birth. Black women's and white women's experiences of the employment market were largely similar. Differences could more readily be attributed to racial discrimination than narrowly defined cultural differences.

Notes

1. P. Freire, *Pedagogy of the Oppressed*, New York: Herder & Herder, 1971.
2. V. Saifullah Kahn, 'The role of the culture of dominance in structuring the experience of ethnic minorities', in C. Husband (ed.), *'Race' in Britain*, London: Hutchinson, 1982.
3. A. Murcott, 'The social construction of teenage pregnancy', *Sociology of Health and Illness*, vol. 2, no. 1 (1980).
4. Office of Population Censuses and Surveys Monitor, 1986.
5. B. Ineichen, 'Teenage motherhood in Bristol: the contrasting experiences of Afro-Caribbean and white girls', *New Community*, vol. 12, no. 1 (1945/5).

6.12 **Perspectives on Later Motherhood**
Julia Berryman

Older motherhood is also now thought of as a problem, although until recently it was not unusual. Julia Berryman suggests that while the medical literature perceives late motherhood in terms of risks, there are indications from psychological and sociological research that later motherhood may have advantages.

From the medical perspective, later motherhood is seen purely in terms of increased risks, and although much of the research has been strongly criticized, [1] there is now a growing recognition that 'Many doctors deplore trends towards having babies later in life' and 'urge women not to postpone having children'. [2] The increased 'medicalization' of human reproduction has not only made women feel that having babies is an unnatural state, a 'disease' or 'disorder', but it has also undermined their role in reproduction. This is especially the case for those who opt for later motherhood. By defining women of 30 or more as 'elderly' or 'older', it is clear to women that they are viewed as problems from the outset. Indeed, they are even advised by the British Medical Association that they should not view their condition 'through rose-tinted spectacles'. [3] If they had no anxiety about their pregnancies, then comments such as this one may well engender it.

Wendy Savage, who has long campaigned for a woman's right to decide how her pregnancy and delivery should be managed, has stressed that 'if you're surrounded by people who don't expect your body to work, it won't!' [4] This remark was made in a discussion on the trend towards more caesarean section deliveries, but it might equally well apply to a discussion concerned with older mothers. The expectation is, on the basis of their age alone, that such women will have problems, and Savage argues that this becomes a self-fulfilling prophecy.

In the study of older motherhood, whilst most women agreed that there was an ideal age to have a child, there was no consensus on when that age was. Responses ranged from 'it depends' (on personal factors appropriate to the individual woman) to ages in the 20s and 30s and 'every age'. Women's answers to questions such as these were highly influenced by their own experience. One mother, who had at least one child in each decade from her twenties to her forties, felt that she could not give an ideal age because she 'felt OK with all of them'. Perhaps the answer is that the right time is when a woman would welcome a baby whether planned or otherwise. There are no guarantees about parenthood at any age, yet the evidence indicates that older mothers may have skills as a result of their greater maturity which can contribute to their abilities as parents. This view is reinforced by women's reactions. In the perception of women themselves, having a baby later in life is a very positive experience. Whether planned or not, women feel that they have a lot to offer their child, and most are unconcerned about the larger than average generation gap.

The notion that 30 or over is old for a pregnancy is a particularly recent phenomenon. Perhaps if the trend towards later parenting continues then, by sheer force of numbers, the perception of such mothers will change. For the present, I would argue that what is important is that information about the whole experience should be more accessible. In other words, becoming a mother is much more than just becoming pregnant and giving birth, and information on the psychological and sociological aspects of motherhood, at any age and at any stage in the life of the child, needs to be just as widely available as that on the medical aspects of pregnancy and birth. If this were the case, women, and indeed all those concerned with pregnancy, birth and motherhood, would be better able to balance the problem-centred approach to later motherhood with the more positive findings of research in psychology and sociology.

Notes

1. P. K. Mansfield. 'Mid-life childbearing: strategies for informed decision-making', *Psychology of Women Quarterly*, no. 12 (1988), pp. 445–60; C. S. McCauley, *Pregnancy After Thirty-Five*, New York: Dutton, 1976.
2. L. Burke, S. Himmelweit and G. Vines, *Tomorrow's Child: Reproductive technologies in the '90s*, London: Virago, 1990.
3. M. Jeffries (ed.), *You and Your Baby: Pregnancy to infancy*, London: British Medical Association, 1985.
4. Wendy Savage, quoted in V. McKee, 'Childbirth choices: is there a backlash against natural birth?' *Good Housekeeping*, no. 135 (1990), pp. 54–5.

6.13 Issues Related to Motherhood
Anne Woollet and Ann Phoenix

Anne Woollet and Ann Phoenix summarise some of the key issues concerning the professionalisation of motherhood and mother-blaming.

In psychology mothers are seen as essential providers of crucial environmental experiences for their children. This is associated with the 'professionalization' of motherhood and pressures on mothers to perform well. Professionalization is common to many areas of Western life: a glimpse at the magazines on a newsagent's shelves indicates the vast array of 'how to do it' publications, giving advice on everything from decorating and cookery to car maintenance. Mothers respond to (and encourage) expectations that as 'good' mothers their major function is to maximize their children's development and therefore attempt to carry out the tasks of mothering with high degrees of professionalism and expertise by seeking out information about their children's development from a variety of sources, including childcare manuals.

By virtue of the assumption that mothers have major (if not exclusive) responsibility for their children's development and behaviour, psychological writing and childcare manuals (implicitly or explicitly) blame mothers when children demonstrate behavioural or other problems. This 'mother-blaming' is reflected in some feminist analyses of the experience of being mothered which hold mothers responsible for the miseries endured by children in childhood, for any lack of acceptance or disapproval women recall their mothers expressing towards them as well as for many adult miseries. There is, therefore, a consensus that when children have problems or behave in ways considered by society as inappropriate or antisocial, it is mothers, rather than fathers, schools and others who are blamed, as if mothers constituted children's sole environment/environmental influence. Mothers are thus in a 'no win' situation.

Women's experiences as mothers, their insider perspectives, are rarely examined. As a result little is known about how women experience motherhood, how their experiences differ and the factors that account for differences in experience. [...]

One reason why childcare and developmental psychology literature generally romanticize the mother–child relationship is because they ignore what mothering is like for many women in the West. In portraying the reality of motherhood, much feminist literature emphasizes the negative aspects of motherhood without focusing on the pleasures that many women experience. The two sets of literature, therefore, seem dichotomized. Yet there are important overlaps. Firstly, neither fully reflects the reality of motherhood – both the joys and privations – and coming from different directions as they do, they both (including new feminist and 'green' approaches) result in mother-blaming because mothers are ultimately held responsible for the way their children turn out. No new models for how society could or should be changed to give mothers, children (and hence fathers and others) a better deal are provided. In addition, while there are commonalities in mothers' experiences, neither set of literatures fully recognises the differences between mothers, for example of social class, 'race', marital status, or sexuality. While it is important to avoid an essentialist, determinist view of motherhood, failure to theorize these differences helps to maintain the status quo as 'normal mothers' being white, middle-class, married women and other mothers being deviant/aberrant.

6.14 Lesbian Custody and the New Myth of the Father
Lynne Harne

Lesbian mothers have frequently lost custody of their children where ex-husbands have contested it. Lynne Harne describes some of the pressures which lesbian mothers face and warns of threats to the rights of heterosexual mothers. It should be noted that the Children Act 1989 abolishes the concept of custody. Instead a 'residence order' determines the parent with whom children should live, but both father and mother normally retain equal parental rights. Effectively, what was joint custody is now written into the law. This applies where a couple have been married; where there is no formal marriage, the situation is more complex.

Many women have experienced reprisals for daring to be lesbians and removing themselves and the children from male control. It is not uncommon for mothers and their lovers to be physically assaulted, for lovers to be raped or sexually abused, or for lesbian mothers to be accused of being mad, starving their children, being insensitive to their children's needs, or simply being bad mothers.

It is not unusual for such violent behaviour, sexual abuse, and false accusations to be made by an anti-sexist, socialist or liberal man, who may state that he believes in the equality of woman, the swapping of gender roles and the freedom for people to decide their own sexual orientation. He may well take his revenge beyond such harassment and even beyond the courts to, for example, contacting his ex-wife's employers and abusing her to them.

In court he may say that if the children go to the mother, they will be deprived of a 'normal' family background (the normal background that he can supply, as he has usually found a new wife or girlfriend, by this time), that the children will suffer from the lack of a 'father figure' (the mother's lover, if there is one, not being suitable for this role). Alternatively, his liberal façade may crack, and he will say that he doesn't want dirty perverts corrupting his children, and introducing them to a lesbian lifestyle.

Not uncommonly his statements will be backed up by court welfare officers and psychiatrists, who will support the ideology of fatherhood by saying that, without a father figure and male model, the child will suffer a confusion of gender identity and behaviour – boys will not develop along strong masculine lines, girls will learn that they don't have to be available to, and can exist without, men. Further, they will say that children will suffer the social stigma of not growing up in a heterosexual household.

Mothers who win custody through the courts, and a few do, have to show that the transmission of male control (values) will be continued by proxy (that is, without an actual male being present in the household). A mother may be ordered not to advocate lesbian or feminist politics to her children, not to engage in lesbian feminist politics, not to tell her children that she is a lesbian, or to see her lover in the children's presence. All this may be policed by a supervision order (i.e. a social worker visiting the house at intervals to make sure that the mother is complying with the conditions of her having custody). Often the price of getting custody is high.

A new batch of psychological studies (some of them commissioned in support of lesbian mothers) fall over themselves backwards to show that lesbian mothers do not encourage their children to be lesbian or homosexual, that children have many male figures in their lives, including continuing contact with the father (if there is one) – more in fact than single heterosexual mothers – and that children conform to the correct stereotypes of gender behaviour. Here are some sickening examples of such studies:

> At four, Sara asked her mother if girls can marry girls and she was told they could choose a lover of either sex. Mother states she hopes Sara will be heterosexual in

adult life. Sara enjoys dressing up as a princess in mother's high-heeled shoes and
negligee, and plays Mommie in fantasy games. Sara's grandfather, whom she had
visited only twice in her life, was installed in her mind as an '*important and valued
figure*'.

and:

Martin, (aged $6\frac{1}{2}$) dislikes rough play, but shows no *current feminine interests*. He
enjoys building, prefers the company of boys and has a girlfriend who he plans to
marry.
(Taken from an American study called *Lesbian mothers and their children: A
comparative survey*, by Martha Kirkpatrick *et al.*, 1981)

Whilst these studies maybe strategic, in helping to win lesbian custody battles
(the recent British study has yet to prove itself), they take as their basic premiss
that lesbianism is a sickness or abnormality that can only be defined negatively
against heterosexuality, and the heterosexual family. They involve a denial that
lesbian and feminist influence may be good for the children, and that being
brought up without a male may be positively beneficial. They still take the view
that lesbianism has to be explained as some quirk of a faulty and inadequate
personality. [...]

   Until recently the need for male models and the father figure argument has
only been applied to lesbian custody situations. [...] Divorce has, however,
increased, and the number of one-parent families (mainly women) has [also]
increased. Also in the mid-seventies women made some legal gains (on paper
at least) in terms of male violence and being able to get violent men out of the
home ('ouster injunctions'). All this, and the increase in the number of women
choosing not to remarry, has produced a backlash in terms of fathers' rights and
a new ideology of fatherhood.

   The spearhead of such a movement can be seen to be led by Families Need
Fathers (FNF). [...] Since its beginning, FNF has on the one hand argued that
fathers' rights are being eroded, whilst on the other it claims that it only wants
what's best for the children – that children *need* two parents. [...] They have
pushed for joint custody to be made the norm. So far they have been fairly
successful. [...]

   Lesbian mothers are well aware of the effects of joint custody and increased
access orders. Joint custody is often agreed as a strategy in order to keep the case
out of the courts, where the mother would most probably lose. Often the father
does not actually want care and control of the children – this would mean too
much hard graft – but he wants control over what happens to them, the best
access times, and a reason to interfere. Frequent access is often agreed under the
threat that the father will use her lesbianism to contest custody unless she
agrees. Father's access, for lesbian mothers as for other women, is often a huge
time of stress, when he either does not turn up on time, returns the children

late, tired and upset, or does not return them when he says he will, leaving the mother to wonder whether he has 'kidnapped' the children or intends to go to court. He may frequently use access times to harass the mother, as well. Some men go back to court years later, when the hardest of the childrearing years are over, bring up lesbianism, and get care and control of the children.

Of course some may argue that since men are doing more of the childcare they ought to be given more recognition. But there are two points here. One is that there is not much evidence of them actually doing this, and the second is that their involvement in childrearing, since they have the power, can only mean a transmission and reinforcement of those values that as feminists we are working so hard to get rid of.

Those of us who are lesbian mothers, who for one reason or another still have fathers involved with our children, know only too well how these fathers are able to undermine our own relationships with our children, and to put down our own values. Of course they have the backing of a male supremacist and anti-lesbian society in this, so it is not that difficult for them to enforce their values. Fatherhood denotes status and power in our society. Up until the end of the nineteenth century fatherhood meant literally owning women and children as chattels. To act without the father's (male) approval is still very risky. [...]

... as lesbians with children we are continually in the front line for anti-lesbian attacks, either through threats over custody, or from fathers who have access to our children, or from other agencies such as our children's schools, and the social and health services. [...]

As women with children who are stating by our existence and our lifestyle that we don't need and depend on men, either sexually, emotionally, or for protection, the extent of their reaction and revenge is not really very surprising.

6.15 **Black Women, Sexism and Racism**
Gemma Tang Nain

Black feminists have often accused white feminists of Eurocentrism in their accounts of family life. Gemma Tang Nain reviews the debates.

A key source of counter-attack to the feminist critique of the family has come from black feminists who have vocalized their defence of the black family-household as an arena of solidarity and resistance against racism in both Britain and the USA.[1] This view of the black family-household is supported by other writers,[2] who also point to a similar function on the part of the white working-class family in these societies, against the vicissitudes of capitalism.

However, one should not allow this reality – the family-household as a source of resistance to other forms of oppression – to disguise or distort the oppressive elements to women within that very institution. And [...] black feminists [...]

do acknowledge the possibility of such family-based oppression. In adding their support to the view of the family-household as oppressive to women, Arthur Brittan and Mary Maynard point to the mothering, domestic, sexual and emotional services performed by women within the family-household: 'We regard such activities as oppressive ... because they are expected of women, but not of males.'[3] And while women may not perform these tasks to the same degree, given variations in family-household organization in contemporary Britain and the USA, it is arguable that they do perform more of them than men do. But an even more telling point is the ideological expectation that these activities will be performed by women, which means that 'no woman, adolescent, unmarried, lesbian or whatever her status can escape the oppression built into her real or imputed family position'.[4] Additionally, there is the issue of violence against women in the family-household. [...]

Thus it is obvious that the family-household embodies the contradictions of oppression which are characteristic of the wider society.

A further point which needs to be made is that even the white, middle-class, nuclear family which has been the prime focus of the feminist attack, is not without its merits. As Coote and Campbell note: 'Of course, it would be easier to develop a clear political analysis of family life if it were altogether a bad thing ... but ... there are ways in which the family can be a source of care, affection, strength and security.'[5] And this is particularly so given the ideological justification of the family as 'the "haven in a heartless world" of capitalism'.[6]

It is apparent, therefore, that a certain degree of ambivalence has characterized feminism's critique of the family, an ambivalence which has not been acknowledged by black feminists, and hence feminism's consensus on this issue tends to be exaggerated.[7] Further, it is, perhaps, the ambivalent nature of the feminist critique, and its general unpopularity, which at least partly explains why revisionist/pro-family feminists, as well as anti-feminists, have launched their counter-attack in this area, in an attempt to discredit feminism.[8] Elshtain and Friedan, both writing in the early 1980s in defence of the family and in celebration of motherhood, are viewed as the key architects of this revisionist/pro-family backlash within feminism.[9] It is regrettable that the black feminists, in their counter-attack, did not address this alternative trend, either to support it or to distance themselves from it.

Notes

1. See, for example, V. Amos and P. Parmar, 'Challenging imperialist feminism', *Feminist Review*, no. 17 (1984); H. Carby, 'White women listen! Black feminism and the boundaries of sisterhood', in Centre for Contemporary Cultural Studies, *The Empire Strikes Back: Race and racism and 70s Britain*, London: Hutchinson 1982.
2. J. Flax, 'The family in contemporary feminist thought', in J.B. Elshtain (ed.), *The Family in Political Thought*, Sussex: Harvester, 1982; S. Lees, 'Sex, race and culture: feminism and the limits of cultural pluralism', *Feminist Review*, no. 22 (1986).

3. A. Brittan and M. Maynard, *Sexism, Racism and Oppression*, Oxford: Basil Blackwell, 1984, p. 145.
4. *Ibid.*, p. 146.
5. Cited in R. Rowland (ed.), *Women Who Do and Women Who Don't Join the Women's Movement*, London: Routledge, 1984, p. 16.
6. M. Barrett, *Women's Oppression Today*, London: Verso, 1980, p. 212.
7. M. Barrett and M. McIntosh, *The Anti-Social Family*, London: Verso, 1982.
8. For discussions of revisionist/pro-family feminism, see Z. Eisenstein, *Feminism and Sexual Equality*, New York: Monthly Review Press, 1984; J. Stacey, 'Are feminists afraid to leave home? The challenge of conservative pro-family feminism', in J. Mitchell and A. Oakley (eds), *What is Feminism?* Oxford: Basil Blackwell, 1986.
9. Eisenstein, *Feminism and Sexual Equality*; Stacey, 'Are feminists afraid to leave home?'.

Further reading

Barrett, M. and McIntosh, M. (1991), *The Anti-Social Family*, (2nd edn), London: Verso.
Brannen, J. and Wilson, G. (1987), *Give and Take in Families*, London: Allen & Unwin.
Delphy, C. and Leonard, D. (1992), *Familiar Exploitation*, Oxford: Polity.
Finch, J. (1983), *Married to the Job*, London: Allen & Unwin.
Gittins, D. (1985), *The Family in Question*, London: Macmillan.
Graham, H. (1984), *Women, Health and Family*, Hemel Hempstead: Harvester Wheatsheaf.
Jackson, S. 'Women and the family', in D. Richardson and V. Robinson (eds) (1993), *Introducing Women's Studies*, London: Macmillan.
Malos, E. (ed.) (1990), *The Politics of Housework*, London: Allison & Busby.
Oakley, A. (1985), *The Sociology of Housework*, Oxford: Basil Blackwell.
Maclean, M. (1991), *Surviving Divorce: Women's resources after separation*, London: Macmillan.
Nicholson, P. (1993), 'Motherhood and women's lives', in D. Richardson and V. Robinson (eds), *Introducing Women's Studies*, London: Macmillan.
Phoenix, A. (1991), *Young Mothers?*, Oxford: Polity.
Rich, A. (1975), *Of Woman Born*, London: Virago.
Smart, C. (1984), *The Ties that Bind: Law, marriage and the reproduction of patriarchal relations*, London: Routledge.
Smart, C. and Sevenhuijsen, S. (1989), *Child Custody and the Politics of Gender*, London: Routledge.
Smith, D. (1990), *Stepmothering*, Hemel Hempstead: Harvester Wheatsheaf.
Urwin, C. (1985), 'Constructing motherhood: the persuasion of normal development', in C. Steedman, C. Urwin and V. Walkerdine, *Language of Gender and Childhood*, London: Routledge.
Walkerdine, V. and Lucey, H. (1989), *Democracy in the Kitchen: Regulating mothers and socialising daughters*, London: Virago.

7 | **SEXUALITY**

Edited and Introduced by Stevi Jackson

INTRODUCTION

This Section is concerned with the ways in which we experience sexuality in everyday life, and the relationship between sexuality and women's subordination. The term 'sexuality' requires some explanation. Some theorists, especially those influenced by psychoanalysis, use it to mean what others call gender identity or gendered subjectivity: our sense of ourselves as feminine or masculine. Here, however, I am using a narrower definition. Whereas gender refers to culturally constructed femininity and masculinity, the term sexuality covers feelings and actions connected with erotic desire. Sexuality certainly is related to gender, but to conflate the two confuses rather than clarifies their relationship.

Issues concerning sexuality have always been central to the women's movement and to women's studies. Feminists have been concerned with a number of interrelated issues: the ways in which men have historically defined and controlled women's sexuality, the sexual objectification of women, and sexual violence and exploitation. These issues contribute towards a critique of heterosexuality as an institution. Sexuality has been seen as a potential danger to women, a source of oppression and exploitation, but it can also be a major source of pleasure.

One effect of being defined by our sexuality within a patriarchal social and symbolic order[1] is that women develop a relationship to their own bodies which is self-objectifying. Learning that our bodies are the objects of others' gaze (and appraisal) means that we develop a self-consciousness about how we look from childhood.[2] As Sandra Bartky suggests, we subject our bodies to a range of disciplinary practices[3] – such as dieting and depilation – in the production of sexualised femininity (see Reading 7.1).

Many feminists have argued that in a patriarchal society women are in some way alienated from their sexuality, denied their sexual potential. Ever since the publication of Anne Koedt's 'Myth of the vaginal orgasm'[4] we have been aware of the ways in which definitions of what sex is – phallic, penetrative sex – have prioritised male pleasure. There are dangers in an approach which implies that women have some essential pre-given sexuality which male sexual discourse and practice denies them; none the less, a phallocentric definition of sexuality clearly does block alternatives which women might find more pleasurable. Moreover, in the age of AIDS feminists have been quick to point out that non-penetrative sex offers us the best protection against infection with the HIV virus (see Reading 7.3).

Phallocentric sexuality is also potentially coercive. Some feminists have suggested that there is a continuum between 'normal' male sexual practice and sexual violence.[5] This does not mean that men are natural sexual predators, but that elements of masculinity as socially defined and constructed are congruent with aggressive sexuality and the eroticisation of power. The construction of male sexuality as active and dominant, the objectification of women in terms of male desire, the belief that men have rights of sexual access to certain women, all contribute to a social order within which rape, sexual assault and child sexual abuse are endemic. The use of male sexuality as a means of subjugation has, in the course of the history of colonialism and imperialism, become interwoven with racism. Black women's sexuality is defined by racist discourses which construct them as the exotic 'other', legitimate victims of violence and commercial sexual exploitation (see Reading 7.5). Conversely, the construction of black men as potential rapists of white women has been central to racist ideologies and practices.[6]

The eroticisation of power clearly holds dangers for women, but some feminists claim that it is also potentially pleasurable. For example, Rosemary Pringle's analysis of sexuality in the workplace (Reading 7.6) suggests that women can derive pleasure from the interplay of sexuality and power. Issues of pleasure and power are central to feminist debates around pornography (see Sections 8 and 14 below) and sadomasochism (Reading 7.7). For some lesbians, experimenting with power relations is potentially transgressive and liberating: they view those who are critical of such practices as puritanical and moralistic. For many radical and lesbian feminists, as for Sheila Jeffreys (Reading 7.8), patterns of dominance and submission are not to be played with or celebrated: rather, they are evidence of the ways in which our sexuality has been shaped by patriarchal society and culture.

Most feminists do not see male and female sexuality as natural and unchangeable, but rather as socially constructed. Thus heterosexuality cannot be treated as natural, as in some absolute way normal. Adrienne Rich's concept of 'compulsory heterosexuality'[7] captures this sense in which a form of sexuality popularly thought of as natural and normal is in fact imposed upon us. The critique of heterosexuality raises the possibility of lesbianism as a positive alternative. For some this is simply a personal choice, but for others – like Monique Wittig and Sheila Jeffreys[8] – lesbianism is a political choice. Political lesbianism has proved an extremely contentious issue, not least because of its implicit judgement of heterosexual feminists as less than politically correct. If feminism is to address all women, then the critique of heterosexuality should be kept distinct from personal criticism of heterosexual women (see Readings 7.9, 7.10).

Notes

1. The social order can be said to be patriarchal in that major social institutions are male-dominated, and patterns of economic and social reward systematically disadvantage women. The symbolic order is patriarchal in the sense that male dominance is inscribed in language and culture so that, for example, men are defined as more important than women, their view of the world is accorded greater credibility, and theirs is the perspective from which women are defined as 'other'.
2. See, for example, F. Haug *et al.*, *Female Sexualization*, London: Verso, 1987.
3. This concept derives from the work of Michel Foucault. See in particular *Discipline and Punish*, Harmondsworth: Penguin, 1979.
4. A. Koedt, 'The myth of the vaginal orgasm', in A. Koedt *et al.*, *Radical Feminism*, New York: Quadrangle. Reprinted in S. Gunew, *A Reader in Feminist Knowledge*, London: Routledge, 1991.
5. For a full development of this argument, see L. Kelly, *Surviving Sexual Violence*, Cambridge: Polity, 1988.
6. For discussions of these issues, see b. hooks, *Ain't I a Woman?*, London: Pluto, 1982; A. Davies, *Women, Race and Class*, London: The Women's Press, 1980; V. Ware, *Beyond the Pale: white women and racism in history*, London: Verso, 1991.
7. A. Rich, 'Compulsory heterosexuality and lesbian existence', *Signs*, vol. 5, no. 4 (1980), pp. 631–60.
8. M. Wittig, *The Straight Mind and Other Essays*, Hemel Hempstead: Harvester Wheatsheaf, 1992; S. Jeffreys, *Anticlimax*, London: The Women's Press, 1990.

7.1　Foucault, Femininity and the Modernisation of Patriarchal Power
Sandra Bartky

Sandra Bartky draws upon Foucault's analysis of the modernisation of power – which ensures the production of docile bodies through self-surveillance – to explore the ways in which women discipline their bodies in pursuit of ideal femininity. Michel Foucault, a French thinker whose work has been influential in recent feminist theory, originally developed his concept of discipline in the context of his work on penology. The techniques of discipline used in prisons are seen as part of a more general 'mechanics of power' pervading modern society. According to Foucault, 'discipline produces subjected and practised bodies, "docile" bodies'.[1] Our bodies are subjected in the sense that they are dominated, made to conform to particular institutional regimes, and practised in that they are made productive and useful. This is achieved, moreover, not by physical coercion but by a form of surveillance – 'panopticism' – which encourages us to watch ourselves because we imagine ourselves observed by others.[2]

... disciplinary practices ... are part of the process by which the ideal body of femininity – and hence the feminine body-subject – is constructed; in doing this, they produce a 'practiced and subjected' body, i.e. a body on which an inferior status has been inscribed. A woman's face must be made up, that is to say, made over, and so must her body: she is ten pounds overweight; her lips must be made more kissable; her complexion dewier: her eyes more mysterious. The 'art' of make-up is the art of disguise, but this presupposes that a woman's face, unpainted, is defective. [...] The strategy of much beauty-related advertising is to suggest to women that their bodies are deficient, but even without such more or less explicit teaching, the media images of perfect female beauty which bombard us daily leave no doubt in the minds of most women that they fail to measure up. The technologies of femininity are taken up and practiced by women against the background of a pervasive sense of bodily deficiency. [...]

In the regime of institutionalized heterosexuality woman must make herself 'object and prey' for the man: It is for him that these eyes are limpid pools, this cheek baby-smooth.[1] In contemporary patriarchal culture, a panoptical male connoisseur resides within the consciousness of most women: They stand perpetually before his gaze and under his judgement. Woman lives her body as seen by another, by an anonymous patriarchal Other. We are often told that 'women dress for other women'. There is some truth in this: Who but someone engaged in a project similar to my own can appreciate the panache with which I bring it off? But women know for whom this game is played: They know that a pretty young woman is likelier to become a flight attendant than a plain one and that a well-preserved older woman has a better chance of holding on to her husband than one who has 'let herself go'. [...]

... the precise nature of the criteria by which women are judged, not only the inescapability of judgement itself, reflects gross imbalances in the social power of the sexes. [...] An aesthetic of femininity, for example, that mandates fragility and a lack of muscular strength produces female bodies that can offer little resistance to physical abuse, and the physical abuse of women by men, as we know, is widespread. It is true that the current fitness movement has permitted women to develop more muscular strength and endurance than was heretofore allowed; indeed, images of women have begun to appear in the mass media that seem to eroticize this new muscularity. But a woman may by no means develop more muscular strength than her partner; the bride who would tenderly carry her groom across the threshold is a figure of comedy, not romance.[2]

Under the current 'tyranny of slenderness'[3] women are forbidden to become large or massive; they must take up as little space as possible. The very contours a woman's body takes on as she matures – the fuller breasts and rounded hips – have become distasteful. The body by which a woman feels herself judged and which by rigorous discipline she must try to assume is the body of early adolesence, slight and unformed, a body lacking flesh or substance, a body in whose very contours the image of immaturity has been inscribed. The requirement that a woman maintain a smooth and hairless skin carries further the theme of inexperience, for an infantilized face must accompany her infantilized body, a face that never ages or furrows its brow in thought. The face of the ideally feminine woman must never display the marks of character, wisdom, and experience that we so admire in men.

To succeed in the provision of a beautiful or sexy body gains a woman attention and some admiration but little real respect and rarely any social power. A woman's effort to master feminine body discipline [...] partakes of the general depreciation of everything female. In spite of unrelenting pressure to 'make the most of what they have', women are ridiculed and dismissed for the triviality of their interest in ... clothes and make-up. Further, the narrow identification of woman with sexuality and the body in a society that has for centuries displayed profound suspicion toward both does little to raise her status. Even the most adored female bodies complain routinely of their situation in ways that reveal an implicit understanding that there is something demeaning in the kind of attention they receive. Marilyn Monroe, Elizabeth Taylor, and Farrah Fawcett have all wanted passionately to become actresses-artists and not just 'sex objects'.

But it is perhaps in their more restricted motility and comportment that the inferiorization of women's bodies is most evident. [...] Woman's body language speaks eloquently, though silently, of her subordinate status in a hierarchy of gender. [...]

... in so far as the disciplinary practices of femininity produce a 'subjected and practiced', an inferiorized, body, they must be understood as aspects of a far larger discipline, an oppressive and inegalitarian system of sexual sub-ordination. This system aims at turning women into the docile and compliant companions of men just as surely as the army aims to turn its raw recruits into soldiers. [...]

As modern industrial societies change and as women themselves offer resistance to patriarchy, older forms of domination are eroded. But new forms arise, spread, and become consolidated. Women are no longer required to be chaste or modest, to restrict their sphere of activity to the home, or even to realize their properly feminine destiny in maternity: Normative femininity is coming more and more to be centred on woman's body – not its duties and obligations or even its capacity to bear children, but its sexuality, more precisely, its presumed heterosexuality and its appearance. There is, of course, nothing new in women's preoccupation with youth and beauty. What is new is the growing power of the image in a society increasingly orientated toward the visual media. Images of normative femininity, it might be ventured, have replaced the religiously orientated tracts of the past. New too is the spread of this discipline to all classes of women and its deployment throughout the life-cycle. What was formerly the speciality of the aristocrat or courtesan is now the routine obligation of every woman, be she a grandmother or a barely pubescent girl. [...]

The woman who checks her make-up half a dozen times a day to see if her foundation has caked or her mascara run, who worries that the wind or rain may spoil her hairdo, who looks frequently to see if her stockings have bagged at the ankle, or who, feeling fat, monitors everything she eats, has become, just as surely as the inmate of Panopticon, a self-policing subject, a self committed to a relentless self-surveillance. This self-surveillance is a form of obedience to patriarchy. It is also the reflection in woman's consciousness of the fact that *she* is under surveillance in ways that *he* is not, that whatever else she may become, she is importantly a body designed to please or to excite. There has been induced in many women, then, in Foucault's words, 'a state of conscious and permanent visibility that assures the automatic functioning of power'.[4] Since the standards of female bodily acceptability are impossible fully to realize, requiring as they do a virtual transcendence of nature, a woman may live much of her life with a pervasive feeling of bodily deficiency. Hence, a tighter control of the body has gained a new kind of hold over the mind.

Notes to introduction

1. M. Foucault, *Discipline and Punish*, Harmondsworth: Penguin, 1979, p. 138.
2. The concept of the panopticon – in which the inmates are under constant potential surveillance from a central position and can never be sure when they are actually being watched – derives from a design for model prison produced by Jeremy Bentham, a British utilitarian philosopher of the late eighteenth/early nineteenth century (panoptic means all-seeing).

Notes

1. 'It is required of woman that in order to realize her femininity she must make herself object and prey, which is to say that she must renounce her claims as sovereign subject.' S. de Beauvoir, *The Second Sex*, New York: Bantam Books, 1968, p. 642.
2. The film *Pumping Iron II* portrays very clearly the tension for female body-builders (a tension that enters into formal judging of the sport) between muscular development and a properly feminine appearance.
3. K. Chernin, *The Obsession: Reflections on the tyranny of slenderness*, New York: Harper & Row, 1981.
4. M. Foucault, *Discipline and Punish*, New York: Vintage, 1979, p. 201.

7.2   **This Sex Which Is Not One**
Luce Irigaray

The definition of women's bodies as sexual takes place within discourses that define them as objects of male desire, and in which sexuality is itself constructed phallocentrically. This is graphically depicted here by Luce Irigaray, whose critique is framed from within psychoanalysis.

Female sexuality has always been conceptualized on the basis of masculine parameters. Thus the opposition between 'masculine' clitoral activity and 'feminine' vaginal passivity, an opposition which Freud – and many others – saw as stages, or alternatives, in the development of a sexually 'normal' woman, seems rather too clearly required by the practice of male sexuality. For the clitoris is conceived as a little penis pleasant to masturbate so long as castration anxiety does not exist (for the boy child), and the vagina is valued for the 'lodging' it offers the male organ when the forbidden hand has to find a replacement for pleasure-giving.

   In these terms, woman's erogenous zones never amount to anything but a clitoris-sex that is not comparable to the noble phallic organ, or a hole-envelope that serves to sheathe and massage the penis in intercourse: a non-sex, or a masculine organ turned back upon itself, self-embracing.

   About woman and her pleasure, this view of the sexual relation has nothing to say. Her lot is that of 'lack', 'atrophy' (of the sexual organ), and 'penis envy', the penis being the only sexual organ of recognized value.

7.3   **The Challenge of AIDS**
Diane Richardson

The feminist critique of penetrative, male-defined sexuality has gained new urgency with the spread of HIV infection, as Diane Richardson explains.

AIDS could ... bring about enormous changes in how people view sexuality. The notion of safe sex forces us to question many of the assumptions we hold about sex. It demands that we re-evaluate forms of sex that are often considered 'second-best'. It challenges the belief that people, but more especially men, have little voluntary control over their sexual desires (a belief that is frequently reflected in attitudes towards rape, prostitution and pornography). It encourages the development of new meanings for sex and the erotic which are not focused on intercourse, or on necessarily having an orgasm. It could lead to better communication between partners, which may enable women to protect themselves better from other sexual risks such as abusive and unwanted sex. It could enhance intimacy and broaden our enjoyment of sex. It offers an opportunity to talk more openly about sex and to raise issues about sexual choice and control. It could lead to men taking their share of responsibility for making sex safer. It could help break down sexual divisions and stereotypes by emphasising the importance of what you do, rather than how you label yourself. [...] AIDS also challenges what is considered 'natural' or 'normal' about sex. In being advised to practise safer sex we are, in a sense, being urged to be 'unnatural'.

The assumption, very often, is that such changes in sexual attitudes and behaviour will be difficult for most of us. Safe sex will have to be sold to people as fun, exciting and satisfying before they will want to practise it.

This may be more true of men than women. As part of their socialisation, men often come to associate worthwhile sex with intercourse leading to orgasm. One reason, therefore, why men may find it difficult to alter their sexual behaviour in the light of AIDS is that they do not regard safe sex as erotic. Another possible reason is that such changes would represent a threat to their identity and self-esteem. In our society sexual intercourse for men is often a way of achieving status and power over others, and is inextricably linked with being masculine.

There are other reasons why AIDS may be more challenging to male sexuality than to female. With the onset of AIDS many men are experiencing what women have always experienced: an association between sex and danger. Fear of disease is only part of the dangers associated for women with sexuality. Alongside the possibility of sexual pleasure, fear of sexuality is traditionally instilled in women. Fear of being raped. Fear of becoming pregnant. Fear of the health risks associated with using the pill or other forms of contraception. Fear of being humiliated and hurt.

The association of death and desire is also nothing new for women. The physical harm done to victims of sexual violence reminds us of the fatal consequences sex can have for women. The threat of male violence is, however, not the only way in which sex for women has been linked with the possibility of death. Earlier this century it was not uncommon for women to die in childbirth. [...] Women have also died as a result of trying to abort an unwanted pregnancy. [...]

During this century most men have not had to think about the consequences of their sexual behaviour in any serious way, while women have always had to do so – whether in terms of the risk of pregnancy, health risks associated with contraceptive use, or loss of reputation. Now men are being increasingly forced to consider risk and to take responsibility for their actions – or are they?

It seems that it is taken for granted that women will have to take responsibility for safer sex because men won't. [...]

... despite the emphasis in AIDS campaigns to take personal responsibility for our *own* actions, it is women who are frequently responsible for protecting men, as well as themselves, from infection. As the expected gatekeepers of male sexuality, it is they who are landed with the burden of preventing the spread of AIDs, *within* the heterosexual population at least. Yet ironically, what such a view of heterosexual relationships invariably fails to recognise is that in a culture where women are expected to be sexually passive, where sex within marriage is legally defined as a man's right, where rape and sexual abuse are primarily crimes against women, many women will have little if any 'choice' whether safer sex occurs or not.

At the same time, the message now being given to girls and women to carry condoms and encourage their use as part of safer sex raises interesting contradictions. While ignoring practicalities, and the fact that in doing this women are at risk of being labelled an 'easy lay', it challenges the traditional idea that men, not women, should initiate, seek out, and be prepared for sex.

There is also a major contradiction in emphasising the correct use of condoms as the best way of preventing AIDS. You are most at risk of contracting HIV if you engage in anal or vaginal penetration. Yet, despite this, AIDS education campaigns have, by and large, uncritically accepted a view of sex as intercourse. We have the 'condom solution'. Safer sex advice is centred upon fewer sexual partners and being told 'always use a condom'. (Though as a woman I find it difficult to know where I should wear one.) Why do we never hear about non-penetrative sex as a less risky and potentially more pleasurable way of preventing AIDS? Because it's too challenging both to men in general, and to the view of intercourse as 'natural' or 'normal' sex: a view that is enshrined in the law and religious teachings.

To advocate non-penetrative sex would not only transform the meaning of sex from sexual reproduction to sexual pleasure, but also would have positive implications for the majority of women who do not have orgasms through intercourse. It would underline the fact that this is neither abnormal nor a problem, but a valid form of sexual expression. It would also provide an opportunity to discuss lesbian and gay relationships in a more positive light. For instance, when intercourse and penetration are no longer the key words in the language of love, lesbians will hopefully be spared the age-old question 'But what do you *do*?' – which, when translated, means without a penis what can you do?

These are not new issues. Feminists, both earlier this century and more recently, have criticised sexual relationships between men and women, with the emphasis on penetration, as, very often, unsatisfying and dangerous for women. There is consequently a certain irony and not a little anger involved in observing the way in which the government, media and medical profession have responded to the AIDS crisis. It's as if only now, when men's health is at stake, do we need to consider sexual risks and responsibilities. Why wasn't there a campaign for safer sex ten or fifteen years ago? The answer that AIDS is life-threatening is not sufficient. Cervical cancer is the cause of 4,000 deaths every year in British women. Safer sex has a major role to play in the prevention of cervical cancer. Taking birth control pills and other forms of contraceptives can be associated with serious side-effects, which can be fatal. None of these are associated with condom use or non-penetrative sex.

The challenge of AIDS is to create new meanings of sexuality that are not based primarily on heterosexual intercourse, or on men having more control over sexuality than women.

7.4   **Understanding Sexual Violence**
Diane Scully

The association between sexuality and violence is exemplified in the case of rape. On the basis of a study of 114 convicted rapists in the USA, Diane Scully concludes that for men rape is a low-risk, high-reward activity. Rape gives men pleasure through the excitement and sense of power it offers them; it also affords them specifically sexual pleasure.

In an effort to change public attitudes that are damaging to the victims of rape and to reform laws seemingly premised on the assumption that women both ask for and enjoy rape, the feminist position has emphasized the violent and aggressive character of rape. Often these arguments disclaim that sex plays any part in rape at all.[1] This contrasts with the psychopathological position, which emphasizes the sexual nature of rape and ignores the violence. I argue, however, that both positions miss the mark. Rape is a violent act, but it is also a sexual act, and it is this fact that differentiates it from other crimes. Further, it is illogical to argue, on the one hand, that rape is an extension of normative male sexual behaviour and, on the other hand, that rape is not sexual. As MacKinnon[2] correctly observes, rape is not less sexual for being violent, nor is it necessarily true that the violent aspect of rape distinguishes it from legally 'acceptable' intercourse. For example, marital rape is not legally recognized in most of the United States. [...] Emphasizing violence – the victims' experience – is also strategic to the continued avoidance of an association between 'normal' men and sexual violence. Make no mistake, for some men, rape is sex – in fact, for them, sex is rape. The continued rejection of this possibility, threatening though it may be, is counterproductive to understanding the social causes of sexual violence. [...]

Rape as a means of sexual access illuminates the deliberate nature of this act. When a woman is unwilling or seems unavailable for sex, men can use rape to seize what is not offered. In discussing his decision to rape, one man made this clear:

> 'All the guys wanted to fuck her ... a real fox, beautiful shape. She was a beautiful woman and I wanted to see what she had.'

The view of sex as a male entitlement suggests that when a woman says no, rape is a suitable method of conquering the 'offending' object. If, for example, a woman is picked up at a party, in a bar, or while hitchhiking – behavior that a number of these men saw as a signal of sexual availability – and she later resists sexual advances, rape is presumed to be justified. The same justification operates in what is popularly called 'date rape'. The belief that sex was their just compensation compelled a number of rapists to insist they had not raped. In other words, from the perspective of these men, rape depends on whether they, not their victims, perceive a violation. MacKinnon[3] points out that rape laws operate on a similar basis, allowing men's conditioned unconsciousness to counterindicate women's experience of violation. Consider the case of a man who raped and seriously beat his victim when, on their second date, she refused his sexual advances:

> 'I think I was really pissed off at her because it didn't go as planned. I could have been with someone else. She led me on but wouldn't deliver. ... I have a male ego that must be fed.'

His goal was conquest, to seize what was not offered, and, like others, he believed his behaviour was justified. [...]

The idea that rape is impersonal rather than intimate or mutual appealed to a number of rapists, some of whom suggested that it was their preferred form of sex. The fact that rape gave them the power to control and dominate their victims encouraged some to act on this preference. For example, one man explained:

> 'Rape gave me the power to do what I wanted to do without feeling I had to please a partner or respond to a partner. I felt in control, dominant. Rape was the ability to have sex without caring about the woman's response. I was totally dominant.'

Another rapist commented:

> 'Seeing them laying there helpless gave me the confidence that I could do it. ... With rape I felt totally in charge. I'm bashful, timid. When a woman wanted to give in normal sex, I was intimidated. In the rapes, I was totally in command, she totally submissive.'

Although the men were not systematically questioned about their fantasies, one man volunteered that he had been fantasizing about rape for several weeks before committing his offence. He confided that he thought it would be 'an exciting experience – a new high'. Most appealing to him was the idea that he could make his victim 'do it all for him' and that he would be in control. He fantasized that she 'would submit totally and that I could have anything I wanted'. Eventually he decided to act because his older brother told him 'forced sex is great, I wouldn't get caught, and, besides, women love it'. Though now he admits to his crime, he continues to believe his victim 'enjoyed it'.

Notes

1. For an example of this type of bi-polar thinking, see P. Gilmartin-Zena, 'Gender differences in students' attitudes toward rape', *Sociological Focus*, 21 (1988), pp. 279–92.
2. C. A. MacKinnon, 'Feminism, Marxism, method and the State', *Signs*, no. 8 (1983), pp. 635–59.
3. *Ibid*.

7.5 **Black Feminist Thought**

Patricia Collins

Patricia Collins sees pornography, prostitution and rape as key issues for black women. She explores the historical development of forms of sexual exploitation and violence to which black women have been subjected.

Pornographic images are iconographic in that they represent realities in a manner determined by the historical position of the observers, their relationship to their own time, and to the history of the conventions which they employ.[1] The treatment of Black women's bodies in nineteenth-century Europe and the United States may be the foundation upon which contemporary pornography as the representation of women's objectification, domination, and control is based. Icons about the sexuality of Black women's bodies emerged in these contexts. Moreover, as race/gender-specific representations, these icons have implications for the treatment of both African-American and white women in contemporary pornography.

I suggest that African-American women were not included in pornography as an afterthought but instead form a key pillar on which contemporary pornography itself rests. As Alice Walker points out, 'the more ancient roots of modern pornography are to be found in the almost always pornographic treatment of black women who, from the moment they entered slavery ... were subjected to rape as the "logical" convergence of sex and violence. Conquest, in short.'[2]

One key feature about the treatment of Black women in the nineteenth century was how their bodies were objects of display. In the antebellum American South white men did not have to look at pornographic pictures of women because they could become voyeurs of Black women on the auction block. A chilling example of this objectification of the Black female body is provided by the exhibition, in early-nineteenth-century Europe, of Sarah Bartmann, the so-called Hottentot Venus. Her display formed one of the original icons for Black female sexuality. An African woman, Sarah Bartmann was often exhibited at fashionable parties in Paris, generally wearing little clothing, to provide entertainment. To her audience she represented deviant sexuality. At the time European audiences thought that Africans had deviant sexual practices and searched for physiological differences, such as enlarged penises and malformed female genitalia, as indications of this deviant sexuality. Sarah Bartmann's exhibition stimulated these racist and sexist beliefs. After her death in 1815, she was dissected. Her genitalia and buttocks remain on display in Paris.[3]

Sander Gilman explains the impart that Sarah Bartmann's exhibition had on Victorian audiences:

> It is important to note that Sarah Bartmann was exhibited not to show her genitalia – but rather to present another anomaly which the European audience … found riveting. This was the steatopygia, or protruding buttocks, the other physical characteristic of the Hottentot female which captured the eye of early European travelers. … The figure of Sarah Bartmann was reduced to her sexual parts. The audience which had paid to see her buttocks and had fantasized about the uniqueness of her genitalia when she was alive could, after her death and dissection, examine both.[4]

In this passage Gilman unwittingly describes how Bartmann was used as a pornographic object similar to how women are represented in contemporary pornography. She was reduced to her sexual parts, and these parts came to represent a dominant icon applied to Black women throughout the nineteenth century. Moreover, the fact that Sarah Bartmann was both African and a woman underscores the importance of gender in maintaining notions of racial purity. In this case Bartmann symbolized Blacks as a 'race'. Thus the creation of the icon applied to Black women demonstrates that notions of gender, race, and sexuality were linked in overarching structures of political domination and economic exploitation.

The process illustrated by the pornographic treatment of the bodies of enslaved African women and of women like Sarah Bartmann has developed into a full-scale industry encompassing all women objectified differently by racial/ethnic category. […]

Gilman's analysis of the exhibition of Sarah Bartmann as the 'Hottentot Venus' suggests another intriguing connection between race, gender, and sexuality in nineteenth-century Europe – the linking of the icon of the Black woman with the icon of the white prostitute. While the Hottentot woman stood for the essence of Africans as a race, the white prostitute symbolized the sexualized woman. The prostitute represented the embodiment of sexuality and all that European society associated with it: disease as well as passion. As Gilman points out, 'it is this uncleanliness, this disease, which forms the final link between two images of women, the black and the prostitute. Just as the genitalia of the Hottentot were perceived as parallel to the diseased genitalia of the prostitute, so to the power of the idea of corruption links both images'.[5] These connections between the icons of Black women and white prostitutes demonstrate how race, gender, and the social class structure of the European political economy interlock.

In the American antebellum South both of these images were fused in the forced prostitution of enslaved African women. The prostitution of Black women allowed white women to be the opposite; Black 'whores' make white 'virgins' possible. This race/gender nexus fostered a situation whereby white men could then differentiate between the sexualized woman-as-body who is dominated and 'screwed' and the asexual woman-as-pure-spirit who is idealized and brought home to mother.[6] The sexually denigrated woman, whether she was made a victim through her rape or a pet through her seduction, could be used as the yardstick against which the cult of true womanhood was measured.

Notes

1. S. Gilman, 'Black bodies, white bodies: towards an iconography of female sexuality in late nineteenth century art, medicine and literature', *Critical Inquiry*, vol. 12, no. 1 (1985), pp. 205–43.
2. A. Walker, 'Coming apart' in *You Can't Keep a Good Woman Down*, New York: Harcourt Brace Jovanovich, 1981, p. 42.
3. Gilman, 'Black bodies, white bodies'.
4. *Ibid.*, p. 213.
5. *Ibid.*, p. 237.
6. P. Hoch, *White Hero Black Beast: Racism, sexism and the mask of masculinity*, London: Pluto, 1979.

7.6   **Bureaucracy, Rationality and Sexuality**
Rosemary Pringle

Sexuality, including the power relations it currently involves, is very much part of everyday life. Rosemary Pringle discusses sexuality in the workplace in the context of her study of secretaries.

Feminists have insisted that sexual harassment is not only an individual problem but part of an organized expression of male power. Sexual harassment functions particularly to keep women out of non-traditional occupations and to reinforce their secondary status in the workplace. Gutek and Dunwoody[1] have pointed out that even non-harassing sexual behaviour has negative consequences for women. The office affair can have detrimental effects on a woman's credibility as well as her career. Many women say they are not flattered by sexual overtures at work and experience even complimentary remarks as insulting. Men, on the other hand, report virtually no work-related consequences of sexual behaviour and the majority are flattered by sexual overtures from women. Blatant male sexual advances go largely unnoticed because 'organzational man', goal orientated, rational, competitive, is not perceived in explicitly sexual terms. It is ironic that women are perceived as using sex to their advantage, for they are much less likely to initiate sexual encounters and more likely to be hurt by sex at work.

The gender division of labour is mediated by gender constructions that in numerous aspects bear on sexuality. Rich's notion of compulsory hetero-sexuality[2] can be applied here, for the sexual 'normality' of daily life in the office is relentlessly heterosexual. This takes place in concrete social practices ranging from managerial policies through to everyday informal conversations.[3] It involves the domination of men's heterosexuality over women's heterosexuality and the subordination of all other forms of sexuality. [...]

In naming and theorizing sexual harassment feminists have drawn attention to the centrality of sexuality in workplace organization. However, they have largely restricted sexuality to its coercive dimensions. [...] The identification of some activities as 'sexual harassment' may legitimate and obscure other forms of male power. But men control women not only through rape or through forcing them to do what they want to do, but through definitions of pleasure and selfhood.

At this point the argument becomes complicated, for it is not clear where 'male power' begins and ends, whether women are in all cases 'victims' or whether they too can exercise sexual power. It is hard to know what a 'free' choice would be. Rather than being yanked screaming into 'compulsory heterosexuality', most women actively seek it out and find pleasure in it. [...]

Master–slave is an important model for boss–secretary relations, but it is not the only one. Gendered subjectivity is produced on a number of contradictory discourses which make available different positions and different powers for men and women. Following Wendy Hollway's example[4], we might identify three discourses on bosses and secretaries which construct different subject positions. The first, the master–slave discourse, clearly sets up the boss as subject and secretary as object. The latter may take a number of forms including subordinate wife, devoted spinster, attractive mistress. Because these positions are not equally available to men and women, all sorts of difficulties arise when women take up the subject or men the object position. Male bosses fear that if they have a male secretary they will have to give him recognition – and he may then not be a secretary. Secretaries may feel that a female boss is not powerful or prestigious enough to give them the recognition they seek. Even if she is, they may not feel the safety in merging with the powerful that they feel with men, because they cannot trust her to set the boundaries.

Parallel to master–slave is a mother–son discourse which places the secretary in the subject position as mother, dragon or dominating wife, and the man is the object. She insists that he needs her and regards him as a helpless little boy that has to be looked after. He may complain about being mothered or simply deny that it is happening or that he is dependent on her. Often it is not denied so much as trivialized. He may concede he is dependent in a limited way but insist that she is replaceable. [...]

Third there is a discourse of reciprocity–equality. This is supposedly gender neutral with no fixed subject and object positions. The secretary works *with* rather than *for* the boss, and they operate as a 'team'. [...] To the extent that bosses and secretaries are already positioned by the other two discourses it is hard to ignore gender here. While secretaries like to believe in reciprocity, the relation is usually very one way. [...]

In talking about secretaries we are forced to confront the extent to which power relations at work are organized around a particular form of heterosexuality based on sadomasochistic fantasy.

Sexual games are integral to the play of power at work, and success for women depends on how they negotiate their sexuality. It is often assumed they have only two choices. Either they can desexualize themselves and become 'honorary men' (the beige suit syndrome) or they can stay within femininity and be disempowered. In fact women moving into management have a variety of strategies based around power and pleasure. These could include ritualized role reversals where, for example, a woman boss employs a male secretary or has an all-male workforce to nurture her, or narcissistic relations with other powerful women, or various ways of playing off men against each other. Clothes are an important means of empowerment. In wearing suits women are not transgressing gender, becoming 'men', but expressing a more masculine, instrumental relation to the body. To dress in this way is to *feel* like a man does, sexually empowered, an actor rather than an object to be looked at. Secretaries may adopt similar strategies to construct more assertive models of femininity. Since discourses have to be reproduced in specific situations there is always room to challenge and modify them. Rather than treating women as the pathetic victims of sexual harassment, it becomes possible to consider the power and pleasure they currently experience and ask how they can operate more on their own terms. The question then is which pleasures, if any, might threaten masculinity or disrupt rationality?

It makes no sense to banish sexuality from the workplace. What needs to be challenged is the way it is treated as an intruder, for this is the basis of the negative representation of women/sexuality/secretaries. It is by making it visible, exposing the masculinity that lurks behind gender-neutrality, asserting women's rights to be subjects rather than objects of sexual discourses, that bureaucracy can be challenged. The emphasis needs to be on processes of change rather than 'correct' or 'incorrect' practices. It is also important to remember that for women pleasure and danger will go on being in some kind of tension with each other, perhaps impossible to separate.

Notes

1. B. A. Gutek and V. Dunwoody, 'Understanding sex in the workplace', in

A. Stronberg, L. Larwood and B. A. Gutek (eds), *Women and Work: An annual review*, vol. 2, Newbury Hill, CA: Sage, 1987, pp. 249–69.
2. A. Rich, 'Compulsory heterosexuality and lesbian existence', *Signs*, vol. 5, no. 4 (1980), pp. 631–60.
3. J. Hearn and W. Parkin, *Sex at Work*, Sussex: Wheatsheaf, 1987, pp. 94–5.
4. W. Hollway, 'Gender difference and the production of subjectivity', in J. Henriques *et al.*, *Changing the Subject*, London: Methuen, 1984.

7.7 Difference, Desire and Sadomasochism

Susan Ardill and Sue O'Sullivan

Issues of power and sexuality are foregrounded in this Reading, which discusses debates around sadomasochism in London in the mid 1980s. The protagonists identified here are lesbians involved in sadomasochism (SMers) and Lesbians Against Sado-Masochism (LASM).

A simple description of SM might be the sexual dramatization or acting-out of power relations, with its own history of codes and meanings, of ritual and paraphernalia. But is SM a clearly delineated physical practice which only a certain percentage of lesbians will ever be into? Is it therefore of limited relevance to most lesbians? Or is SM the crystallization of the most vital components of *all* erotic tension: teasing, titillation, compulsion and denial, control and struggle, pleasure and pain? Alternatively it could just be that, in the vacuum of lesbians speaking and writing about sex, the language of sexual excitement used in, for example, *Coming to Power: Writings and graphics on lesbian SM*, resonates with a great many women who are not, technically speaking, into SM.[1]

Debates specifically around lesbian SM *have* taken place in the context of a general challenge to feminist sexual orthodoxy. SMers indeed have aligned themselves with other self-defined 'sexual outlaws' – prostitutes, butch and femme lesbians, bisexuals. Several things seem to have been happening at once, and at times it's hard to keep a grasp on exactly what it is at any given moment.

SM lesbians have been engaged in a struggle to 'come out SM', to be open and proud of their sexual practices. Because of the negative connotations of sadism and masochism (linked to actual torture, cruelty and emotional suffering), and the hegemony of political lesbianism, they have been come down on – hard – by large sections of lesbian feminists. Other lesbians, including many socialist lesbians like ourselves, have acted in defence of SM dykes around issues of censorship and exclusion. [...] We do think, though, that a socialist-feminist critique of SM as a political theory and pleasure as a supposedly neutral playground is needed. [...]

Our own political position on SM is that we are all on a continuum. (We refuse the label liberal over this – stuff it.) Is the thrill of deliberate touch on muscle, a pressure on shoulders, done with a sense of dominance, accepted with a sense of submission, any less exciting than tying someone up? We suspect most of our sex lives and sexual histories are very uneven: cuddly sex, bondage, kisses and affection, one-night stands, dressing up – any of these can be what we crave or pursue at any given time. [...]

SM groups saw their rebellion against society's 'norms' and, further, against the 'norms' of what constitutes 'acceptable' sexual practice according to certain groups of lesbians, as a radical act with political significance. In denying that playing out society's power roles in bed had any causal connection to the continuance or development of such relationships in the big wide world, they tended to exclude any discussion about the ways in which sexual relations *are* related to the rest of our lives. For instance, around housing, work, family – as well as state institutions. Lesbian SM literature suggests that organizing around oppositional sexual difference constitutes not just a political practice but a whole political perspective. It's here that SMers come unstuck. By failing to situate themselves as within particular subcultures, linked to certain lifestyle requirements, they inflate their sexual politics with a universality it almost certainly does not have.

The most absurd extension of the SM political position is the implication that if we all played out our SM fantasies in bed, the world would be a better place. The connecting line between this mode of thinking and the LASM one is striking, even if they draw the opposite conclusions.

LASM women claim that they have no real interest in the acts of SM sex except as they represent and become all of the pain, horror and degradation of women, Black people, Jewish people, mothers, disabled people, and so on. Unlike the SMers who deny any harmful reality of sexism, fascism and racism in SM sex roles or rituals, LASM goes to the opposite extreme and claims that things like tying up, spanking, whipping, and wearing collars or belts with studs are in themselves violence against all the oppressed peoples of the world. LASM say they 'do not consent to being terrorised by the presence of the symbols of brutality, which are *just* as threatening as the presence of the real thing' (our emphasis). They deny any possibility of consensual agreement or equality in SM sex, just as the political lesbians do to women in 'ordinary' heterosexual sex. In an unquestioning SM view, we can choose our stage and role. In LASM's view we are acted *upon*; we are permanent victims (or bearers of oppression) except when we refuse the acts, deny the feelings which make us victims. We are implicated in our own victim status if we refuse to do that. This is where morality makes its entrance. (It's a remarkably religious scenario.)

Neither of these views sees the world in movement, in tension, dialectically.

Notes

1. SAMOIS, *Coming to Power*, Alyson Publications, 1981.

7.8 **Anticlimax**
Sheila Jeffreys

Sheila Jeffreys is explicitly critical of libertarian sexual politics. From a radical lesbian feminist perspective, she argues for the eroticisation of equality.

Heterosexual desire is eroticised power difference. Heterosexual desire originates in the power relationship between men and women, but it can also be experienced in same-sex relationships. Heterosexuality as an institution is founded upon the ideology of 'difference'. Though the difference is seen as natural, it is in fact a difference of power. [...]

Once the eroticising of otherness and power difference is learned, then in a same-sex relationship, where another gender is absent, otherness can be reintroduced through differences of age, race, class, the practice of sadomasochism or role playing. So it is possible to construct heterosexual desire within lesbianism and heterosexual desire is plentifully evident in the practice of gay men. The opposite of heterosexual desire is the eroticising of sameness, a sameness of power equality and mutuality. It is homosexual desire.

Under male supremacy, sex consists of the eroticising of women's subordination. Women's subordination is sexy for men and for women too. For years this was a secret within women's liberation. [...]

It should not be a surprise to find that s/m fantasy is significant in women's sex lives. Women may be born free but they are born into a system of subordination. We are not born into equality and do not have equality to eroticise. We are not born into power and do not have power to eroticise. We are born into subordination and it is in subordination that we learn our sexual and emotional responses. It would be surprising indeed if any woman reared under male supremacy was able to escape the forces constructing her into a member of an inferior slave class. [...]

The demolition of heterosexual desire is a necessary step on the route to women's liberation. Freedom is indivisible. It is not possible to keep little bits of unfreedom, such as in the area of sexuality, because they give some people pleasure, if we are serious about wanting women's liberation. Male-supremacist sexuality is constructed from the subordination of women. If women were not subordinate then sex as the eroticised subordination of women would not be thinkable. [...] Feminist revolution is not 'sexy' because it would remove those material power differences between the sexes on which eroticised power difference is based. To retain sadomasochism it is necessary to prevent the progress of women's liberation. [...]

Male sexuality must be reconstructed to sever the link between power and aggression and sexual pleasure. Only then can women be relieved of the restrictions placed upon their lives and opportunities by male sexual objectification and aggression. Men's pleasure in women's subordination is a powerful bulwark of their resistance to women's liberation. [...] Though some are capable of political integrity and of working against their own interests as a class, we cannot expect this to take place on any mass scale.

As women and as lesbians our hope lies only in other women. We must work towards the construction of homosexual desire and practice as a most important part of our struggle for liberation. However important heterosexual desire has been in our lives we will all have some experience of its opposite. We will have experience of sexual desire and practice which does not leave us feeling betrayed, a sexual desire and practice which eroticises mutuality and equality. It is this avenue that we should seek to open up while gradually shutting down those responses and practices which are not about sexual 'pleasure' but the eroticising of our subordination. We need to develop sensitive antennae for evaluating our sexual experience. None of this will be easy. It will take some effort, but then nobody said that the journey to our liberation would be an easy ride. The question we have to ask ourselves is whether we want our freedom or whether we want to retain heterosexual desire. Feminists will choose freedom. [...]

It is heretical in this culture deliberately to avoid the rituals of sadomasochistic sex and to choose to eroticise sameness and equality. Differences of race and class can provide power differences to eroticise even in same-sex relationships. Lesbians committed to the creation of an egalitarian sexuality must be prepared to challenge this too, since same-sex relationships do not automatically ensure a symmetry of power and privilege. [...]

Readers who consider themselves to be heterosexual will probably be wondering whether homosexual desire can fit into an opposite-sex relationship. In a society which was not founded upon the subordination of women there would be no reason why it should not. But we do not live in such a society. We live in a society organised around heterosexual desire, around otherness and power difference. It is difficult to imagine what shape a woman's desire for a man would take in the absence of eroticised power difference since it is precisely this which provides the excitement of heterosexuality today.

Heterosexuality is the institution through which male-supremacist society is organised and as such it must cease to function. It is difficult to imagine at this point what shape any relationship between different sexes would take when such a relationship was a free choice, when it was not privileged in any way over same-sex relationships and when it played no part in organising women's oppression and male power. In such a situation, when heterosexuality was no longer an institution, we cannot yet be sure what women would choose.

7.9   **Ending Female Sexual Oppression**
bell hooks

bell hooks puts the case against political lesbianism as a prescriptive stance.

The suggestion that the truly feminist woman is lesbian (made by heterosexuals and lesbians alike) sets up another sexual standard by which women are to be judged and found wanting. Although it is not common for women in the feminist movement to state that women should be lesbian, the message is transmitted via discussions of heterosexuality that suggest all genital contact between women and men is rape, that the woman who is emotionally and sexually committed to an individual man is necessarily incapable of loyal woman-identified political commitment. Just as the struggle to end sexual oppression aims to eliminate heterosexism, it should not endorse any one sexual choice, celibacy, bi-sexuality, homosexuality, or heterosexuality. Feminist activists need to remember that the political choices we make are not determined by who we choose to have genital sexual contact with. In her introduction to *Home Girls: A Black feminist anthology*, Barbara Smith asserts: 'Black feminism and Black Lesbianism are not interchangeable. Feminism is a political movement and many Lesbians are not feminists.' This is also true for many heterosexual women. It is important for women, especially those who are heterosexual, to know that they can make a radical political commitment to feminist struggle even though they are sexually involved with men (many of us know from experience that political choice will undoubtedly alter the nature of individual relationships). All women need to know that they can be politically committed to feminism regardless of their sexual preference. They need to know that the goal of feminist movement is not to establish codes for a 'politically correct' sexuality. Politically, feminist activists committed to ending sexual oppression must work to eliminate the oppression of lesbians and gay men as part of an overall movement to enable all women (and men) to freely choose sexual partners.

Feminist activists must take care that our legitimate critiques of heterosexism are not attacks on heterosexual *practice*. As feminists, we must confront those women who do in fact believe that women with heterosexual preferences are either traitors or likely to be anti-lesbian. Condemnation of heterosexual practice has led women who desire sexual relationships with men to feel they cannot participate in feminist movement. [...]

Just as feminist movement to end sexual oppression should create a social climate in which lesbians and gay men are no longer oppressed, a climate in which their sexual choices are affirmed, it should also create a climate in which heterosexual practice is freed from the constraints of heterosexism and can also be affirmed.

7.10 **Ten Years On: 'Compulsory Heterosexuality and Lesbian Existence'**
Deborah Cameron

Debates around heterosexuality and lesbianism frequently take as their starting point Rich's classic statement on compulsory heterosexuality. Here Deborah Cameron re-evaluates Rich's arguments in the light of recent developments in feminist sexual politics.

At the core of Rich's complex essay[1] is a startling, yet simple question: why should women be heterosexual? If sex with men is our 'natural' preference, why are we subjected from our earliest years to such intensive propaganda on nature's behalf? Why are we coerced by so many social institutions, from romance to rape, into something we would choose in any case? And what of those who do, in fact, place women at the centre of their sexual and emotional lives? Why should lesbian existence be so repressed and denied?

Rich asserts that heterosexuality is neither natural nor freely chosen: it is itself an institution, to which we are socialised and if necessary compelled. Without it, other institutions crucial to women's subordination, like marriage and the family, could not be maintained in their present forms. Without it, men could not count on guaranteed access to women's sexual and reproductive capacities. The lesbian is a woman who refuses male sexual access and lives outside traditional family structures. Her existence must be marginalised, suppressed and in the last analysis viciously punished, because it challenges the order not of nature but of patriarchy.

Ten years on, I find this argument as provocative and compelling as ever. But the context in which we read it is, alas, rather different. Circumstances have forced many of us, at least in public, to take up less radical positions. The coming of AIDS, and in Britain Section 28, with the attendant intensification of homophobia, finds us retreating to what Rich decries as banal 'lifestyle' or minority politics: please tolerate us, we're just different, we can't help it, of course we won't proselytise. To celebrate lesbianism as a positive, political choice was always subversive; now it could be illegal.

It is also true, though, that Rich's analysis always posed problems for women in the lesbian and feminist communities themselves. Some of these seem to stem from misreadings of 'Compulsory heterosexuality', as when some women ask if Rich is saying only lesbians can be feminists. The answer is clearly no: rather she challenges heterosexual feminists to question the obviousness of their own 'majority' preference, in the interests of freer and more informed sexual choices for all women.

Other problems arise, however, from theoretical debates of the 1980s about the forms of female desire and sexual pleasure. Rich's 'lesbian continuum' includes relationships between women which lack an explicitly sexual component. Many feminists have doubted the wisdom of defining lesbianism in these terms. Doesn't this just reinforce the stereotype of women as emotional or sensual rather than actively sexual? Doesn't it misrepresent the specificity of both sexual and non-sexual relationships between women? Doesn't it deny the authenticity of female heterosexual desire? And doesn't it gloss over differences in the way self-defined lesbians themselves understand the politics of what they do in bed? Some lesbian feminists insist on the absolute centrality of sexual practice to lesbian identity; also, lesbian identity itself historically preceded this wave of feminism, and many lesbians would not call themselves feminist. Ten years on, the question 'What is a lesbian?' seems more complicated than ever.

Rich points out, though, that the answer to this question depends on our posing an even more fundamental one: what is the erotic? In proposing a 'continuum' she implicitly invites us to imagine what sexuality might be like outside of patriarchal structures. This takes us beyond a simple critique of heterosexist institutions, and toward a re-examination of all human relationships that challenges the categories most of us think with.

Notes

1. 'Compulsory Heterosexuality and Lesbian Existence' was first published in *Signs: Journal of Women in Culture and Society*, (1980) vol. 5, no. 4., pp. 631–60.

Further reading

Caplan, P. (1989), *The Cultural Construction of Sexuality*, London: Routledge.

Cartledge, S. and Ryan, J. (eds) (1983), *Sex and Love: New thoughts on old contradictions*, London: The Women's Press.

Coveney, L. *et al.*, (1984), *The Sexuality Papers*, London: Hutchinson.

Coward, R. (1982), *Female Desire*, London: Paladin.

Cameron, D. and Frazer, E. (1987), *The Lust to Kill*, Cambridge, Polity.

Feminist Review Collective (1987), *Sexuality: A reader*, London: Virago.

Foucault, M. (1981), *The History of Sexuality, Volume 1*, Harmondsworth: Pelican.

Fuss, D. (ed.) (1991), *Inside Out: Lesbian theories, gay theories*, London: Routledge.

Haug, F. *et al.* (1987), *Female Sexualization*, London: Verso.

Holland, J. *et al.* (1990), *'Don't Die of Ignorance'. I Nearly Died of Embarrassment: Condoms in context*, London: The Tufnell Press.

Jackson, S. (1982), *Childhood and Sexuality*, Oxford: Basil Blackwell.

Kelly, L. (1988), *Surviving Sexual Violence*, Cambridge: Polity.

Kitzinger, C. (1987), *The Social Construction of Lesbianism*, London: Sage.

Leidholdt, D. and Raymonds, J. (eds) (1990), *The Sexual Liberals and the Attack on Feminism*, New York: Pergamon.

Mitchell, J. and Rose, J. (eds) (1982), *Jacques Lacan and the École Freudienne: Feminine sexuality*, London: Macmillan.

Rich, A. (1980), 'Compulsory sexuality and lesbian existence', *Signs: Journal of women in culture and society*, vol. 5, no. 4, pp. 631–60.

Richardson, D. (1993), 'Sexuality and male dominance', in D. Richardson and V. Robinson, *Introducing Women's Studies*, London: Macmillan.

Stimpson, C. and Spector Person, E. (eds) (1980), *Women, Sex and Sexuality*, Chicago: University of Chicago Press.

Thompson, R. and Scott, S. (1991), *Learning About Sex: Young women and the social construction of sexual identity*, London: The Tufnell Press.

Vance, C. (ed.) (1984), *Pleasure and Danger: Exploring female sexuality*, London: Pandora.

Weeks, J. (1986), *Sexuality*, London: Tavistock.

Wittig, M. (1992), *The Straight Mind and Other Essays*, Hemel Hempstead: Harvester Wheatsheaf.

Feminist Review, no. 11 (1982), (Special issue on sexuality).

Feminist Review, no. 28 (1988), (Family Secrets: Child sexual abuse).

Feminist Review, no. 34 (1990), (Perverse Politics: Lesbian issues).

On psychoanalysis, see Section 2 of this volume.

8 | WOMEN AND THE LAW

Edited and Introduced by Helen Power

INTRODUCTION

Mainstream legal theory or jurisprudence has, like all other fields of study and knowledge, rendered women invisible. Thus, whilst major theorists have wrestled with the concept of Law (as opposed to laws) as a body of rules, as a set of practices, as ideology, as discourse, adopting functionalist, idealist, rationalist, liberal, Marxian and latterly postmodernist perspectives on it, by and large they have not seriously engaged with feminist perspectives. Rather, in so far as women have figured in theorising about Law at all, it has been in terms of specific areas of law and their impact on women.

Specific engagement with feminist issues arising out of the theory and practice of law began with Albie Sachs and Joan Hoff Wilson's account (Reading 8.1) of the nineteenth-century 'persons cases', in which attempts by middle-class British women to gain entry into the professions and politics were consistently blocked by the judiciary until 1929. What marks this account off from previous legal studies of 'women's issues' is its insistence that the judges were not merely applying their prejudices to arrive at their decisions, but applying orthodox legal methodology and assumptions: these enabled them to deal with the women's claims in terms of the meaning of words ('person') rather than in terms of the political issues at stake, thus maintaining the notion of judicial neutrality or impartiality between the parties in court. As Sachs and Wilson suggest, this myth continues to flourish because it masks the reality of an ideologically committed judiciary: '[t]he possessed and the dispossessed are equally entitled to a hearing and equally bound by a judgement; by asserting the principle of equality of access, the courts do not eliminate inequality, they merely render it more tolerable'. The insight here is that it is not merely the substance of law (the content of the legal rules) which oppresses, but the very process of law. This insight is taken further by Susan Edwards (Reading 8.2) in her discussion of the law's contribution to the construction of female sexuality – a process which, she suggests, 'is particularly heinous since law is in itself a symbol of justice and truth'. Legal discourse, she argues, borrows from extra-legal discourses (primarily, in the case of female sexuality, the medical) and transforms their 'truths' into legal truth, a particularly powerful truth in view of the apparently neutral authority with which it is cloaked.

Katherine O'Donovan (Reading 8.3), continuing the theme that legal discourse both draws on and reproduces the differential treatment of women and of men, seeks an explanation in the public/private distinction of liberalism which permeates that discourse. As she puts it elsewhere in the book from which the extract is taken: '[c]entral to liberalism is the concept of privacy as a sphere of behaviour free from public interference, that is, unregulated by law. The interest of an account of traditional usage of the concept of the private is not merely definitional. It is the prelude to an explanation for the divisions between women and men in law.' The explanation offered is that '[c]oncepts of privacy mask patriarchal domination'[1] because it is women who inhabit the private − hence unregulated − sphere where, to all intents and purposes, the man's writ is allowed to run more or less unchecked.[2] The result, as Catharine MacKinnon puts it, is that '[i]n feminist translation, the private is a sphere of battery, marital rape, and women's exploited labour; of the central institutions whereby women are deprived of (as men are granted) identity, autonomy, control and self-determination'.[3]

Readings 8.4, 8.5 and 8.6 deal with the issue of pornography and the legal and feminist responses to it. This issue has been chosen as illustrative of the way legal theory and feminism can interact to produce concrete programmes of action. Catharine MacKinnon is best known for her attempt, with Andrea Dworkin, to formulate a law which would have enabled women in the USA to take direct legal action in dealing with pornography.[4] The 'Minneapolis Ordinance' (as the model law was called) represented an attempt to overcome the public/private distinction which, in relation to pornography, has conceptualised the legal issues in terms of 'freedom of expression and speech' (private right) versus censorship (public regulation). Traditional objections to the public regulation of the private sphere are based on the liberal notion (derived from John Stuart Mill[5]) that the state's coercive powers should be reserved for manifestly harmful conduct; as no causal connection between pornography and manifest harm can be shown, so the argument goes, its public regulation is not justified. MacKinnon's and Dworkin's solution was, firstly, to define pornography itself as a form of harm to justify subjecting it to legal regulation and, secondly, to give the power to regulate directly to women,[6] rather than to the state itself (as is currently the position in the UK, where the police, Customs officials and magistrates have extensive powers to deal with pornographic material). The campaign to get the Ordinance adopted across the USA eventually foundered in the US Supreme Court where it was ruled unconstitutional (being in breach of the right to free speech) − but not before it had provoked a split within American feminist legal circles.[7] Here (Reading 8.4) MacKinnon defends the Ordinance and condemns those feminist lawyers opposed to it as basically 'anti-feminist'. In so doing, Carol Smart argues, MacKinnon falls into the trap of 'grand theorising' about women. Readings 8.5 and 8.6 are taken as representative of the British debate around the legal regulation of pornography which, whilst not so apparently acrimonious as the North American, points up the ambivalence which both first- and second-wave feminists have repeatedly felt in their dealings with the law.

This Section is apparently predicated on an assumption with which many feminists who are also lawyers (whether academic or practising) would disagree – namely, that there is a body of knowledge, of theorising, which can coherently be called feminist jurisprudence or legal theory. For such 'dissidents', there are two basic objections to such theorising, both arising out of a postmodernist mistrust of essentialist thinking. The first objection is quite simply that to theorise about the concept of Law at all (as opposed to particular laws and legal systems) is to embark on a mistaken enterprise, whether it be from a feminist base or not, because it gives law a uniquely powerful role as a determinant of social reality. The second objection is a specifically feminist one common to other areas of feminist study: that the notion of feminist jurisprudence perpetuates the essentialising tendency of all 'grand theorising' about Woman as opposed to 'real' women, whose experiences are marked as much by difference as by commonality. Both these tendencies, Smart argues (Reading 8.7), are implicit in MacKinnon's feminist jurisprudence, in which the category of Woman is a pre-given and the concepts of law, state and society are virtually interchangeable: 'I agree with MacKinnon that law is powerful in silencing the alternative discourse of women, but I see it as far less powerful in transforming society to meet the various needs of all women.' Smart concludes by arguing, as an alternative to feminist jurisprudence, for the decentring of law both as an overwhelming determinant of women's subordination and as a method of seeking change.

Notes

1. K. O'Donovan, *Sexual Divisions in Law*, London: Weidenfeld & Nicolson, 1985, p. 181.
2. This is a play on the legal concept of the King's writ – i.e. the King's law.
3. C. MacKinnon, 'Feminism, Marxism, method and the state: toward feminist jurisprudence', *Signs*, vol. 8, (1983), pp. 635–58 (at 657).
4. For accounts of the Ordinance and the campaign around it, see G. Chester and J. Dickey (eds), *Feminism and Censorship*, Dorset: Prism Press, 1988, *passim*; L. Segal and M. McIntosh (eds), *Sex Exposed: Sexuality and the pornography debate*, London: Virago, 1992, *passim*; the March 1992 issue of the *Harvard Law Review*. A transcript of the Minneapolis City Council hearings on the Ordinance is reproduced as *Pornography and Sexual Violence: Evidence of the links*, London: Everywoman, 1988.
5. J. S. Mill, *On Liberty*, London: Dent, 1910.
6. Had the Ordinance become law, women (and, nominally, men also) would have been entitled to apply for *civil* legal remedies – an injunction to prevent/discontinue dissemination of pornographic materials, and/or compensation (on proof of harm to her/him). The state, in the form of the imposition of *criminal* legal sanctions, would not have been involved. For details, see Appendix 1 in *Feminism and Censorship*, op. cit.
7. See *Feminism and Censorship*, op. cit.

8.1   **Sexism and the Law**
Albie Sachs and Joan Hoff Wilson

Albie Sachs and Joan Hoff Wilson explain the difficulties faced by women in nineteenth-century Britain in trying to gain the legal right of entry to the professions in terms of judicial case law methodology.

The myth of judicial neutrality

The debut of women into person-hood was acknowledged by the judges as an event deserving of special ceremony. Contrary to the usual practice of stating only the conclusion of a judgment, Lord Sankey read out the court's decision in full to the representatives of various women's organisations who crowded the chamber.[1] This little ritual to mark formal sexual emancipation was greeted with celebratory telegrams across the Atlantic while newspaper editorials marked the event with that stiffly gracious prose reserved for congratulating women on the progress they were making. Journals, which for years had equivocated on the question of women's rights, which had suppressed, distorted or jeered at the aims of the suffragette window-breakers and hunger-strikers, greeted the judgment as though it represented the culmination of the smooth and automatic unfolding of an idea. The women were praised for their perseverance, the judges for their adherence to principle, and society as a whole for its possession of such women and such judges. Displayed to the full was the special capacity of writers on the English constitution for healing and hiding the wounds of bitter past battles, not by enveloping them with glory as writers in other countries do, but by pretending they never existed.

The Persons case, as the piece of litigation had become known, brought to an end sixty years of rejection by the judiciary and the legal profession of women's claims. The English common law, which had so often been extolled as being the embodiment of human freedom, had in fact provided the main intellectual justification for the avowed and formal subordination of women; English legal scholars such as A. V. Dicey who had written so influentially on the Rule of Law, had turned their pens to detailed explanations of why women should not have the vote; and English lawyers, who over the centuries had proclaimed their adherence to the principles of justice and had fought against restraints on trade, had consistently refused to allow women into their ranks.

From a technical legal point of view, all that the Canadian Senator's case decided in substance was that it was no longer necessary to assume that participation by women in public life was so startling a concept that only the clearest authorisation by Parliament could permit it. Six decades of precedent stating that women could not be included in the term 'persons' were swept aside by the simple proposition: 'The word "person" may include members of both sexes, and to those who ask why the word should include females, the obvious answer is, why not?' What had suddenly changed to render manifestly correct propositions that had been dismissed as virtually unarguable by earlier judges?

There is nothing in legal logic itself which explains the turn-around of the judges in the Canadian Senator's case. Nor is it likely that in case after case the judges happened by a coincidence of subjective moods arbitrarily to arrive at unanimous decisions against the women, and then by an equally mysterious coincidence happened suddenly to agree that the women were entitled to succeed. The cases thus provide little support for those sceptical realists who emphasise the subjective and erratic character of judicial decision-making. Judicial dyspepsia is not all that rare, and counsel have their own folklore about how judicial behaviour is affected by lunch if not by breakfast, but the chances of all the judges having been afflicted by indigestion at the same time are rather remote, and in any event, the nexus between stomach discomfort and anti-feminism would still have to be established. Sylvia Pankhurst did remark that it was whispered at the Bar that Lord Coleridge's metamorphosis from being counsel for the women in one case to becoming head of the court that rejected their claims in another, was due to his second wife having been more of a Tartar than his first. But the malice that barristers reserve for private discussion is as unreliable a guide to truth as is the concomitant show of solidarity they muster for public display.

In the absence of any other satisfactory explanation, the conclusion becomes inescapable that what had changed was not the meaning of the word 'person', nor the modes of reasoning appropriate to lawyers, but the conception of women and women's position in public life held by the judges.

It should be remembered that political events in Britain had produced changes not only in the climate in which the issues were being decided, but also in the personnel of the judiciary. It could hardly have been coincidence that the first judgment in which women were held in law to be 'persons' was delivered by Lord Sankey, who had been appointed by the Labour Administration as Lord Chancellor in an effort to liberalise the judiciary, and who sat in the Cabinet alongside Margaret Bondfield, the first woman to hold Cabinet office in Britain. [2] Of course, none of these political factors is referred to in the judgment, which is expressed in traditional form with emphasis on questions of linguistics rather than matters of policy. Yet the only inference that can be drawn by a present-day reader from the judgment is that Lord Sankey and a majority, if not all, of his colleagues thought it absurd that women should be debarred from public office solely on grounds of sex, and even more absurd that the word 'person' should be the instrument for achieving this result. Having arrived at that conclusion, or rather, having started off on that premise, it was not difficult for them to write a judgment that paid conventional respect to all the earlier decisions while totally ignoring their effect. In practice, if not in theory, they accepted the view so emphatically denied by their predecessors on the Bench, namely that the law was the instrument of the judges rather than the judges the instrument of the law.

What is so striking is that judicial neutrality was most adamantly asserted precisely during the period of greatest judicial partisanship when the Bench was being packed to the greatest extent, and manoeuvring by the leading judges was being done in the most flagrant fashion. In the period 1832 to 1906 half of judicial appointments went to barristers who had been Members of Parliament in the ranks of the ruling party.[3] Conservatives vied with Liberals to get their appointees on the Bench, with an eye not only to past services rendered in political life but also to future services to be rendered in judicial life. The results of this selection process were manifest in trade union and workmen's compensation cases, where judges tended to divide according to former political allegiance as pro-employer or pro-employee, their decisions having considerable political impact in the country.[4] In the case of the male monopoly litigation, the judicial manoeuvring was found to be unnecessary, since all the judges – whether Conservative or Liberal – accepted the same male-orientated approach. Only in Lady Rhondda's case was there the kind of manoeuvring that had characterised the trade union cases, but by now it represented a belated action by a defeated and aged fraternity, stripped of its power, to retain at least its ethos.

To combat what he regarded as the obstructive influence of past political appointees on the Bench, Lord Sankey encouraged the elevation of career lawyers rather than lawyer-politicians to the judiciary, hoping to reduce the conflict produced by judges of one political generation adjudicating on the legislation of politicians of a later generation. In exchange for loss of influence on public life, the judges were offered greater salaries and additional public esteem. The honour accorded to them was thus inversely proportionate to their political power; the more innocuous they became, the more their majesty was praised.

With the decline in the judges' political influence went a decline in the use of the common law as a means of superimposing the judges' views on those of Parliament. The problem was not simply a constitutional one. Parliament at that time was becoming to some extent responsive to the demands of newly enfranchised working men, while the judiciary on the whole reflected the interests and values of the landed and commercial classes.

The main instrument that the judges had been using to assert the interests of men against women and of employers against workers was the common law. The common law tradition has so frequently been associated with concepts of fundamental right and justice that it is at first startling to find that it was used as the main doctrinal justification for preventing the advancement of working people of both sexes, notably in conspiracy cases, and of women of the middle and upper classes, primarily in the male monopoly cases. In the seventeenth century the common law had been yoked to a principle of the fundamental rights of the people of England as a weapon to challenge the divine rights [sic] of the Kings of England. It drew its doctrinal strength from a claim to have existed since time immemorial, having its roots in an antiquity that predated the prerogative rights of the kings. In order to establish this ancient origin, a history was invented by the judges. This retrospectively created history was almost entirely fictional, but so strong was the need of the judges to assert the supremacy of the common law and the concomitant idea of uninterrupted custom, that contrary facts were simply ignored or treated as irrelevant. Essentially this fictionalised history represented a projection into the past of the current world-view of the judges. Coke was the leading exponent of this asserted antiquity, and it was Coke's manufactured views that were relied upon for the next three centuries as having set out immemorial custom. In the 'persons' cases, it was in fact his pronouncements on the public disabilities of women that were seized upon by the judges to reject the women's claims; yet his assumption of permanent legal subordination of women had as little historical foundation as another claim of his to the effect that Parliament had met before the Norman conquest. In reality Coke was not averse to bending the law to assert his values, and his statements on the legal status of women must be particularly suspect in view of what was by common account his disastrous domestic life. (His second wife wrote after his death: We shall never see his like again, praises be to God).[5] Thus the anti-feminism of one generation of judges was carried by the common law to the anti-feminism of another generation. Attempts by counsel to suggest that Coke's writings on the public rights of women might have been influenced by his personal experiences were peremptorily brushed aside by nineteenth- and twentieth-century judges who essentially agreed with his opinion. In other cases however, statements by early judges with which these judges no longer agreed, to the effect that husbands might castigate insubordinate wives with rods, were held to be manifestly archaic and no longer representative of the common law.[6]

Counsel for the women in the public rights cases laboured assiduously to prove that in reality women in ancient times had voted and had held public office, but the facts that they established turned out to be weaker than the spurious historiography that asserted an inveterate usage to the contrary. The very circumstance that the notion of immemorial usage was based on fiction rather than proof made it a particularly pliable tool in the hands of the judges. In the seventeenth century, the common law judges used the common law to justify challenges to established authority, while in the nineteenth century they used it to resist attempts at reform. What maintained continuity between the idea of the common law over the centuries was that it continued to be the instrument of the judges and to express in a vigorous if indirect form the interests of the social group with whom the judges were associated. The fundamental rights of the English people thus amounted to little more than the fundamental rights of the judges, and chief amongst these was the right to determine how social claims should be legally classified and what procedures should be followed for their enforcement.

This is an appropriate point at which to make a few comments on the English judicial style, which emerged so characteristically in the 'persons' cases. The theory of judicial precedent, in terms of which judges are bound by the decisions of their predecessors, played an important role in giving an appearance of technical propriety to what today we would consider manifestly partisan and oppressive decision-making. In the absence of a written constitution or any fundamental code, the theory is that the judges look only to the words of a particular Act of Parliament and to the decisions of earlier judges when declaring the law. This process is seen as largely deductive, involving the extension by analogy of principles gathered from previous decisions to the circumstances of new cases.[7] It expressly excludes examination of the social or political importance of the issue in hand.

It is adherence to this doctrine that gives to English legal argument its unusually close and tangled character. Where other legal systems promote undue rhetoric, the English legal system engenders extraordinary pedantry. Great forensic battles are fought over the precise meanings of words such as 'building', 'place', 'use' and 'and'. There is little scope for lofty statements or appeals to fundamental concepts of right when the issue in a case is whether the word 'and' only means 'and' or whether it can also mean 'or'. The modes of reasoning employed in the most technical of matters are exactly the same as those used for issues of manifest constitutional importance. Thus, when determining a matter such as whether women should be included in the category of 'persons' for purposes of voting, the judges deployed exactly the same format or argument as they did in deciding whether a wooden hut was a 'building' for purposes of planning permission.

This special emphasis on the word rather than the concept, on the fact rather than the sentiment, on the cited instance rather than the overarching principle, is usually attributed by defenders of the common law to the peculiarly pragmatic character of the English people. The survival of the common law as expressed through a multitude of cases, rather than through a unified code, is said to reflect a native genius for building up doctrine on the basis of concrete responses to the dealings of practical men, and has been seen as an inheritance to be guarded with the utmost care. In other societies, to be rigidly systematic might be regarded as a virtue, but in England it is counted as a serious intellectual fault, inviting the appellation 'doctrinaire'. This self-contained inward-looking character of English lawyers was exemplified by a joke put about in the law journals of the last century, that a jurist was someone who knew something about the laws of all countries except his own.

Yet references to virtues allegedly unique to the English are at best descriptive rather than explanatory. Unless one attributes national character to some biological essence or relies on a crude geographical determinism, one is forced to ask why a certain intellectual style developed amongst lawyers in England, as opposed, say, to those in continental Europe. Max Weber has suggested that the answer lies in the success of the English legal profession in keeping legal education under its control and out of the hands of the Universities.[8] Rather than regarding native genius as an explanation of the character of legal reasoning, he sees the legal profession as the creator of native genius, which it used as a weapon in defence of its group interest. Thus it was in the interests of the legal profession to assert the superiority of their indigenous practical wisdom over the imported speculations of the University professors, and this led to a continuing emphasis on the virtues of English case-law. So successful have the professions been in this respect that not only do they to this day continue to control the qualifications for legal practice, but they have even succeeded in getting the Universities, which they have so frequently humiliated, to extol their virtues.

One consequence of this has been the evolution of a peculiarly aloof judiciary and complacent legal profession, unused to critical debate of their own functioning. Evaluations of the Bench and the profession as institutions are almost invariably construed as attacks on judges, barristers and solicitors as individuals, bringing into question their subjective sincerity. In reality, the question of collective bias, such as that expressed in favour of male monopoly, is totally separate from the question of personal integrity, which will vary from individual to individual. Thus, to accuse the judges of anti-feminist partiality is not to say that they were necessarily hypocritical or corrupt. The days when the judges clandestinely auctioned themselves to the wealthiest litigant had long passed. English law was far too pedantic and the Bar far too disciplined and inward-looking to manifest that gross hypocrisy which characterised the legal professions in some other jurisdictions. Such corruption as there was operated not through bribes but through 'legitimate' patronage and through subtle economic and status pressures. For public officials to have attempted to bribe judges who already shared their way of looking at things would have been a gross waste of taxpayers' money.

If legal academics were not inclined to challenge the judicial posture of neutrality, however, the same could not have been said of the feminist activists. Scores of suffragette women indicated by their conduct in court that, to put it at its politest, they had withdrawn any legitimacy which they might formerly have accorded the judiciary. They shouted till they were hoarse, and some when they could shout no more hurled books, chairs, shoes and ink-bottles at the magistrates. In prison, they refused to abide by the rules, and went on prolonged hunger-strikes. They were deliberately disputing the notion that, where women were challenging the dominion of men, they could expect male judges, lawyers, policemen, prison officers and doctors to function impartially. The women declared in word and action that they would not be bound by a constitution that refused to accord to them the status of being persons in public life. To submit to being tried by a body established by the constitution was to concede its legitimacy in advance. The issue was whether men should decide whether women could decide.

The violence effected and the suffering endured by the suffragettes was largely demonstrative in nature. As young girls they had been brought up to tolerate rather than inflict suffering, and they converted this capacity into a weapon.

They achieved autonomy by courting the violence of the male protectors of the male-dominated state, and then enduring whatever was inflicted on them. Having risked death themselves by extending their daring and endurance to the point of dying, the pro-war section of the movement was later able with special passion to spur on young men to death in the trenches.

The resoluteness with which the women pursued their aims was seen not as proof of consistency but as evidence of hysteria. Modes of struggle that had been determined by their social situation – no guns, no industrial power, no vote – were attributed to their biological condition. The intense feminism represented by Christabel Pankhurst proved peculiarly embarrassing, and neither female nor male historians appear even to this day to have been able to come to terms with it. The feminism expressed by her sister Sylvia was related to male radicalism and socialism, but Christabel's cannot be integrated into any such tradition. This is not because the women's battle, in contrast with that of the workers, has already been won, but because it has hardly got under way; historically the feminist revolt must be regarded as still underdeveloped.

As far as the judges and magistrates were concerned, the suffragettes were merely a particularly annoying set of defendants, whose actions disturbed the dignity of the courts and made it more difficult to plan the list of cases. The major instrument of judicial self-defence against the feminist assaults was to assert judicial neutrality. In case after case, the presiding officers stressed that political questions, including the justice of women's claims, were no concern of the courts, whose function it was merely to uphold the law. In no case does there appear to have been the slightest expression of judicial sympathy for the suffragettes, and the one judicial pronouncement that stands out is the description by a Lord Chief Justice of hunger-striking by women prisoners as 'this wicked folly'.[9] Yet as far as the women defendants and their supporters were concerned, the concept of judicial neutrality was a myth. In their eyes it was impossible for male-exclusive courts applying laws laid down by male-exclusive institutions to be impartial when the very issue at stake was male-exclusiveness. To uphold the law when it was being challenged was necessarily to take sides. Moreover, as the tests cases on male monopoly showed, the judges were not reluctant enforcers of laws they knew to be bad, but dogged defenders of male supremacy. Where they did have a choice on a matter of legal principle, they exercised it against the women, and where they did feel free to make a comment on the women, they did so in terms that were hostile to the claims for equality.

As far as the judges were concerned, land could be apportioned, money distributed, and reputations adjusted, but sex was indivisible. Either women were entitled to vote, or take a seat on a council, or study medicine, or practise as lawyers, or they were not. Male domination could survive the entry of one or two women into the disputed domains, but male-exclusiveness could not. The battle-lines were thus drawn over questions of principle, and the struggle was a political one between bitterly hostile groups whose aims were totally antagonistic. This is not to say that the contestants were identifiable solely by sex. There were men who supported the women's struggles just as there were women who opposed them. But the contest was over gender, and because of the way in which the issue was categorised there could be no compromise, only victory or defeat for one side or the other. Today the essence of the contest remains the same, but the formulation of the issues has changed considerably. As the matter was then projected in terms of a rigid and legally enforced sex bar, the interests could not be adjusted or reconciled. The judges were called upon, within the narrow area of choice permitted them by the English legal system, to support one set of combatants against the other. Writing in her middle age shortly after Lord Sankey's judgment, Sylvia Pankhurst spoke of the efforts that had been made before her birth by her father in his capacity as counsel for the women in the first franchise case:

> If women were to be excluded from the vote by virtue of irremediable defect of mental power, he had argued they were excluded as much by the word 'person' as 'man'. To his hearers his contention perhaps sounded exaggerated; but actually this was the ruling which the Courts were presently to give; women were not to be regarded as *persons* in respect of public rights and functions. It was bad law, but upheld by the prejudices of the time and maintained for half a century. [10]

It is understandable that Sylvia Pankhurst, like all other feminists, should have considered the decisions in the male monopoly cases to be bad law upheld by prejudice, just as their opponents considered it to be good law maintained by neutrality. Rebels are less likely to accept the impartiality of judges than are those whose authority the judges uphold. Members of the women's movement were not inclined to regard as neutral judges who in a series of cases refused to allow women to enrol as lawyers, who failed to uphold the right of women to petition the Prime Minister in person, and who gave their approval to the use of forced-feeding against women hunger-strikers. At the height of the militant campaigns, the courtrooms became battle arenas, in which female defendants created uproar as part of their challenge to the right of the state to prosecute them for demanding the vote. Judges, juries, prosecutors, policemen and prison officers were seen as part and parcel of a single apparatus designed to repress their struggles. The fact that the personnel of the courts were entirely male intensified the feeling of the defendants that they were being judged by men for challenging the institutions of men. Here again the analogy holds with blacks in a white supremacy court. Nelson Mandela, African rebel against white domination in South Africa, challenged the jurisdiction of the court trying him with the following words:

> The white man makes all the laws, he drags us before his courts and accuses us, and he sits in judgment over us. ... I feel oppressed by the atmosphere of white domination that lurks all around in this courtroom. ... I have grave fears that this system of justice may enable the guilty to drag the innocent before the courts. [11]

Deleting the word 'white' where appropriate, this denunciation expressed precisely the opposition of the suffragettes, especially at the height of their campaign, to the male-exclusive courts.

There is no scope for impartiality over questions of power and violence. Women could either vote or not vote, and the violence they did and the violence they had done to them had either to be condoned or punished. The judiciary refused them the vote, penalised them for the violence they committed against property, and sanctioned the violence done to them by prison doctors.

The women correctly perceived that their main battle was a political one directed at Parliament rather than a legal one directed at the judges. And in defence of the judges against present-day criticism, it can be said that the politically sensitive issue of gender discrimination was appropriately one for decision by Parliament rather than the courts. Nevertheless, had the judges favoured the substance of the women's claims, had they attached as much force to the concept of a developing democracy as they did to the idea of an ancient differentiation, they could in good judicial conscience have found for the women. If they had chosen this course, their judgments would have been denounced by some of their contemporaries as being contrary to the spirit of the common law and the constitution of England (Scotland), and hailed by most subsequent commentators as exemplifying the spirit of the common law and the constitution of England (Scotland). The judgment of Lord Mansfield's court outlawing the holding of slaves on English soil is famous, [12] the many judgments rejecting women's claims to equality of treatment are not even known. Posterity too has its biases.

What emerges from a perusal of the male monopoly cases, then, is that the judges serenely ignored not only the natural meaning of the word 'person' but also factual and historical evidence which demonstrated that the legal status of women was one of subordination rather than elevation. One of the characteristics of judicial pronouncement in England, particularly noticeable in these cases, was its lack of self-consciousness or strain. The judges asserted the law with what Karl Mannheim in another context has called a 'somnambulistic certainty with regard to truth'. [13] As Mannheim has pointed out, when a conceptual apparatus is the same for all the members of a group, the presuppositions underlying the individual concepts never become perceptible; human beings do not theorise about the actual situations in which they live as long as they are well adjusted to them. The judges were accordingly content to adopt modes of classification without questioning the assumptions about power, property and sex that underlay them. Mannheim points out that ruling groups can in their thinking become so intensively interest-bound to a situation that they are simply no longer able to see certain facts which would undermine their sense of domination. Collectively and unconsciously certain groups in their thinking obscure the real condition of society both to themselves and to others so as to stabilise that society, just as utopian groups on the other hand hide aspects of reality that would shake their belief or paralyse their desire to change things. The term 'ideology' may thus be used to signify some systematic world-view that describes, explains and justifies a particular form of social ordering. The rationalisation that is implicit in ideology need not be logical; it is enough that it be plausible. Nor need it be expressed systematically or even consciously entertained. In Britain, where it is the height of political insult to accuse an opponent of being ideological, a person's ideology is likely to be an inarticulate conglomerate of opinions held together by what is termed 'common sense'.

Thus we may accept that judges, like other people, are moved more by what they believe than by what they know. Shared beliefs shape reality and explain phenomena, and depend for their credibility not on empirical verification but on antiquity and reiteration. Their tenacity is attributable to the manner in which they serve social needs and not to their capacity to reveal social truths. If an individual's consciousness is at variance with demonstrable reality, he is called mad and locked up. If, however, a whole social group shares a distorted consciousness, they attribute to their consciousness a special virtue and elevate it to a region above ordinary experience.

The function of fallacious truism, then, is precisely to disguise social reality, or rather, to describe the world in terms favourable to the position of a particular group. It helps to explain what would otherwise be non-understandable and to justify what would otherwise be non-acceptable, transmuting hard conflict into soft poetry, sharp fact into hazy metaphor, the unpleasant evident into the palatable self-evident. If the interest it served could be revealed, it would dissolve. But it cannot be disposed of by disputation, since belief structures evidence far more firmly than evidence structures belief. The reality projected by the feminists and sustained by the very fact of the litigation was easily subordinated by the judges to their shared ideology as males.

The expression 'male ideology' should thus not be seen as connoting that the judges viewed women's position in terms of some systematic philosophy traceable to the writings of any particular political philosopher. In the days before the social survey was established as the final authority for any pronouncement, it was usually quotations from the Bible and the Classics that served to validate any significant social statement, but these were used more as ornaments and indicators of cultured dialogue than as sources of doctrine. Nor in suggesting that the judges articulated male ideology is it contended that they were particularly misogynistic, or in any way conspiratorial; those who wielded power normally had no need to resort to deviousness, since they could more easily and safely achieve their purposes by relying on the values and agencies fashioned to sustain their power. On the contrary, the more sincere the judges were in their beliefs, the more effectively could they act upon them.

Male ideology denied the existence of inequity in the treatment by men of women, and rationalised legal disabilities imposed on women in terms of each sex having dominium in its separate sphere. In the context of actual and legal male domination, however, the theory of complementarity was merely a gracious way of explaining female subjection. This rationalisation was not something invented by upper-class Victorian males. There was any amount of literature on which the judges and others could draw to testify to the subordination of women through the ages. The specific contribution they made was to place a halo over domesticity, granting to it a special virtue, and pushing it to an extreme.

The final jurisprudential question that arises from a perusal of the 'persons' cases is whether the issue of judicial bias is really the one around which discussion of the judicial function should revolve. The notion of impartiality is not itself neutral. It is a value-laden concept that presupposes that it is both feasible and desirable for the machinery of state to operate in a neutral manner 'without fear or favour'. In this context the very idea of neutrality presupposes social inequality. To say that judges should be unbiased between rich and poor, white and black, male and female, is to accept that these are enduring social categories. It is the procedural right to a proper hearing in court that then purports to equalise the unequal. In fact, together with the concept of a democratically controlled legislature, the notion of a fair trial is crucial to the legitimation of rule in modern Western states. It is more than simply a mechanism for adjusting disputes between individuals and resolving conflicts of interest between groups. For millions of individuals who never enter a court, the knowledge that the judges are there is what matters. The judiciary stands as a symbol of order in what otherwise might be regarded as a chaotic society.[14] The judges demonstrate that citizens are governed by the rules of the many rather than the ambitions of a few. This is why the principle of equality before the courts is so important. The possessed and the dispossessed are equally entitled to a hearing and equally bound by a judgment; by asserting the principle of equality of access, the courts do not eliminate inequality, they merely render it more tolerable. Thus the myth of judicial neutrality continues to flourish in Britain, and all historical evidence inconsistent with it is either explained away or, more frequently, simply ignored.

Notes

1. For a background to the case, see C. L. Clevedon, *The Women Suffrage Movement in Canada*, Toronto, 1950.
2. J. Kamm, *Rapiers and Battleaxes*, London: Allen & Unwin, 1966.
3. Calculations by Harold Laski, quoted in B. Abel-Smith and R. Stevens, *Lawyers and the Courts*, London: Heinemann, 1967.
4. Cf. K. W. Wedderburn, *The Worker and The Law*, London: Penguin, 2nd edn, 1971; Abel-Smith and Stevens, *Lawyers and the Courts*, n. [3].
5. Quoted in A. Harding, *A Social History of English Law*, London: Penguin, 1966.
6. *R. v. Jackson* (1891) 1 QB 671 (the Clitheroe case); cf. *In re Cochrane* 8 Dowl. 630 (1840).
7. See generally R. Cross, *Precedent in English Law*, Oxford: Clarendon Press, 2nd edn, 1969.
8. M. Weber, *On Law in Economy and Society*, Cambridge, MA: Harvard University Press, 1954.

9. Lord Alverstone, in *Leigh v. Gladstone* (1909) 26 Times Law Reports 139.
10. Pankhurst, *Portrait*.
11. Mandela, application that the judicial officer recuse himself on the grounds of bias.
12. But there were criticisms of his vacillation.
13. K. Mannheim, *Ideology and Utopia*, London: Routledge and Kegan Paul, 1936 and 1946.
14. Cf. T. Arnold, *The Symbols of Government*, New York, 1962.

8.2   Female Sexuality and the Law
Susan Edwards

Susan Edwards argues that it is the unique authority of legal discourse which makes it so powerful — it takes the truths of other discourses and turns them into Truth. Here she argues that the legal construction of female sexuality owes much to the medical discourse of the nineteenth century.

The legal regulation of female sexual behaviour

The regulation of female sexual behaviour finds one of its more resolute expressions in the law as it governs sexual relations.[1]

This is particularly the case in the trial procedure for certain sexual offences where the burden of proof is on the prosecutrix. The system of classification of sex crimes reflects and enshrines certain widely held beliefs and assumptions about the nature of sex-gender asymmetry and appropriate styles of sex-gender conduct. However, the wide diversity of statutes governing sexual expression thwarts any provision of a general theory on the nature of the specific relationship of sex legislation to social or economic forces, although certain particular trends may be observed and their linkages clearly elucidated.

The range of sexual behaviour being regulated has resulted in a series of sex laws that are often contradictory and anomalous. Consider, for instance, the ten-year penalty in cases of homosexual assault as compared with the penalty of up to two years for indecent assault upon a female. This particular disparity finds further expression in the proposals of the Advisory Council on the Penal System for a reduction in certain sentences, for instance that homosexual assault should be punishable with up to five years whilst indecent assault on a woman remains a lesser offence punishable with two years.[2] There are numerous other anomalies too, the most glaring being the definition of certain sex crimes such that a particular sex-gender bias is often institutionalized. The legal definition of rape provides one such example, since it encompasses exclusively the forcible penetration of the vagina by the penis, whilst the forcible insertion of objects and instruments into the vagina, such as curling tongs and broom handles, is considered not nearly so heinous, being processed either as indecent assault or else as grievous bodily harm.[3]

The most productive way of examining sex laws is to observe the principal criteria behind the system of classification. The criterion of consent appears as the key factor, and results in a major division between activities that are illegal although the parties consent and activities that are illegal where the parties do not consent. In the first category there are three sub-divisions: certain kinds of sexual activity between men and women; sexual activity of a heterosexual nature with minors; and ritualistic whipping and related activity. The principle that has guided legal practice in this last context was expressed by Chief Justice Coleridge in the case of *R v. Coney* 1882: 'The consent of the person who sustains the injury is no defence to the person who inflicts the injury.' He continued, 'An individual cannot by such consent destroy the right of the Crown to protect the public and keep the peace.'[4] However, providing that no serious physical harm is done, consent may be offered as a defence in such cases. The distinction between serious and non-serious physical harm has proved a very difficult line to draw, especially since in sexual matters the actual extent of the injury sustained often exceeds that which is initially agreed upon or anticipated. This particular problem lay at the crux of the decision in the *Donovan* case in 1934, where a girl of 12[*] received a severe beating with a cane, which exceeded that which she had initially consented to. Donovan was convicted of common and indecent assault, though this decision was reversed at an appeal hearing since the girl in question had consented.[5]

The second principal category of sex law statutes covers activities where consent is not a feature either in law or in fact. This category enshrines a specific sex-gender bias since it is sex-specific – regulating acts of sexual violence perpetrated against women almost exclusively, as in rape and indecent assault. In the definition and especially the legal management of these crimes are institutionalized certain assumptions about the sexual predilections of women. In this way the negotiation and processing of female victims of rape and indecent assault reveal a particular expression of the control over female sexuality within the legal system, and the linkage between law and the deployment of female sexuality. [...]

Conclusion

The Queen shouted 'No, no! Sentence first – verdict afterwards!' An ironic comment on the workings of the criminal justice system. Certainly such a pronouncement sums up the nature of the double bind that entraps women, reflecting the way *a priori* judgements are pronounced on women in their everyday lives. Understandings of women in our culture have proceeded from conceptions of their sexuality. These so-called analyses have provided nothing more than a series of misunderstandings couched in authoritative rhetoric which has given some element of respectability and soundness to what are essentially fallacies.

---

[*] [Editor's note: Edwards is wrong – the girl was 17.]

Within this book of interdisciplinary endeavour, I have directed the attention of the reader to the key discourses that have individually and collectively provided a contradictory and paradoxical vision of female sexuality. These ideologies, whether of medicology or more specifically gynaecology, have principally turned out to be cul-de-sacs of mythology.

The history of misunderstanding about the nature of female sexually has its origin in antiquity. I have intercepted this seamless web of mystery at a particular historical moment because the changes occurring at that time pointed at least superficially to enlightened thinking on female nature. The beginning of the nineteenth century signalled the development of the medicology of human behaviour and specially of human sexuality. More specifically it announced the development of gynaecology as a science and hence it was supposed that all knowledge must of necessity be enlightened. In this context it marked the growth and emergence of a powerful group of professionals in the field of medicine who developed patriarchalism *par excellence*. From this point onwards and even before, men had access to female patients and thereby power over women, having denied and disinherited female midwives from areas they had controlled, although not altogether wisely, for centuries. Man the gentleman, the protector now became the God of the female sexual organs. Male physicians possessed the mechanisms of control over female sexuality. As scientists, they claimed to offer truth; but they masqueraded with the head of truth and the body of a lie. With the name of science an image was advanced of women as lying hysterical fantasists who were nymphomaniacs and made false accusations against men with greater panache and new credibility.

The medical profession were not alone in their beliefs about womankind. The law in particular, from the nineteenth century onwards reflected the conflicting imagery of women, which became enshrined in legislation and legal practice up until the present. During the nineteenth century, even where statutes avowed that better opportunities and prospects for women lay ahead, the practical application and implementation of law militated against anything other than the most marginal improvement in their status.

The beliefs about female sexuality that arose in this particular climate were readily assimilated into the law. This assimilation and reproduction of such ideas is essentially a dialectical process, in that the law acts as the agent of both production and reproduction. This two-way process is particularly heinous since law is in itself a symbol of justice and truth. Law is also perhaps the greatest symbol and practical enactment of power, and it is within this system that women were to experience profound injustice.

Historical analysis of ideas and legal practices sheds considerable light on contemporary legal practice. Although the position of women has improved considerably, certain laws and legal practices have been founded on the very discourses that have been discussed here. Since the nineteenth century the law has not merely assimilated these various ideas and constructs of the nature of female sexuality; it has supported the discriminatory ideologies in its very institutional practices. But it is not merely the reproduction of ideologies *per se* that has been the chief concern here. The control of female sexuality in its mulifarious guises has much deeper implications.

The oppression of women arises fundamentally from the control over female sexual expression and the patrolling of the boundaries of thought on the nature of the sexuality of women. This control is achieved through a variety of means, one of which is the criminal justice system. It is worth giving some consideration to the statement by Garfinkle, Lefcourt and Schulder:

> In essence, the laws are a formal codification of attitudes toward women that permeate our culture. They are used as a means of coercion to obtain conformity with norms and mores. The law is not then an instrument for altering the unequal male–female relationship; rather, it is an institutional barrier to change.[6]

This statement is a guide to only half the solution. Certain laws have announced substantial changes in the position of women. However, the actual interpretation of law depends on a variety of discourses essentially external to the law, but that have come to have a significant bearing upon it. Garfinkle *et al.* add: 'The change must come, therefore, from outside the law'.[7] Ideologies of female sexuality commonplace in the nineteenth century are still, despite significant improvements in the status of women, being reproduced today in language and in discourse. The Red Queen was right!

Notes

1. See M. Foucault, *The History of Sexuality. Volume 1; An Introduction*, New York: Pantheon, 1978.
2. Since Edwards wrote this, the penalties for the two offences have been standardised at a maximum of 10 years: section 3(3), Sexual Offences Act 1985.
3. For instance, M. Amir, *Patterns in Forcible Rape*, Chicago: University of Chicago Press, 1971, found that 27 per cent of his victims [*sic*] had been subjected to other sexual acts. S. Katz and M. A. Mazur, *Understanding the Rape Victim*, New York and Oxford: John Wiley, 1979, p. 164, observed a similar pattern. Certain individual cases are worthy of consideration: see *R. v. Holdsworth*, *Daily Mail*, 23 June 1977. See also a more recent case at Warwick Crown Court processed as grievous bodily harm: *Birmingham Post and Mail*, 26 February 1980. Other countries are more progressive: in 1979 California introduced a 'rape by instrumentality law', whereby such offenders are punishable with up to 5 years: *Daily Express*, 10 October 1979.
4. *R. v. Coney* [1882] 8 QBD 534 at 537.
5. *R. v. Donovan* [1934] 25 Criminal Appeal Reports 1.
6. A. M. Garfinkle, C. Lefcourt and D. B. Schulder, 'Women's servitude under law', in R. Lefcourt (ed.), *Law Against the People*, New York: Vintage, 1971, pp. 105–22 (at p. 120).
7. *Ibid.*

8.3   Sexual Divisions in Law

Katherine O'Donovan

Katherine O'Donovan locates women's subordination in the liberal public/private distinction which permeates law – 'women's world' is private, and therefore legally unregulated.

[L]aw as regulator or non-regulator is a crucial expression of the limits of state intervention. Law's role in maintaining a boundary between private and public has not always been recognised by philosophers. Yet as Lukes notes: 'liberalism may be said largely to have been an argument about where the boundaries of this private sphere lie, according to what principles they are to be drawn, whence interference derives and how it is to be checked'.[1] This statement might be thought to suggest that law is discounted as a mere boundary divider. [...] [H]owever [...] law is not only central to the concepts of private and public, and to the division between the two, but also plays an important part in the construction of that division. [...]

[D]ifficulties of definition arise because in recent writings the concepts private and public stand for a variety of referents. 'Public' may be used to denote state activity, the values of the marketplace, work, the male domain or that sphere of activity which is regulated by law. 'Private' may denote civil society, the values of family, intimacy, the personal life, home, women's domain or behaviour unregulated by law. The confusion is increased in legal discourse which calls legal relations between state and citizens public and those between individuals private.

If the private is identified as the unregulated zone of life this poses problems which are neither discussed nor recognised in liberal political philosophy. Those areas such as the personal, sexuality, biological reproduction, family, home, which are particularly identified socially as women's domain, are also seen as private. It can be argued that social differentiation between women and men in the gender order has its counterpart in the general social distinction between private and public. A simple summary is: 'the public sphere is that sphere in which "history" is made. But the public sphere is the sphere of male activity. Domestic activity becomes relegated to the private sphere and is mediated to the public sphere by men who move between both. Women have a place only in the private sphere.'[2] This argument raises issues about power in personal relations and in the organisation of the private. [...]

The importance of the distinction between private and public lies in its influence on our perception of the social world and the maintenance of the distinction in law. [...]

Conceptions of privacy

Legal discussions of privacy distinguish between the definition, content and zone of privacy on the one hand, and a notion of the right to that privacy on the other. Lack of agreement about the area to be delimited has prevented a right of privacy from being enacted in English law. However, a leading American authority has shown four areas of interests in privacy that are protected by law. These are intrusion into seclusion or private affairs; public disclosure of embarrassing private facts; false publicity; appropriation of name and likeness.[3] It is noticeable that these areas which are protected concern relations between individuals. The issue of state intervention has hardly been raised yet. This may be because it is open to the state to define what is public and what is private, and the boundary between. [...]

An attempt to arrive at a legal definition of the area of privacy through case analysis is unsatisfactory. There are few cases and they do not make clear where the lines are drawn. Yet the idea of privacy does affect perceptions of the social world and social policy, even if not translated into legal concept. Furthermore the desire for privacy has grown in the recent past, probably as a reaction to market society. As the Younger Committee pointed out:

> The modern middle-class family of two parents and their children, relatively sound-proofed in their semi-detached house, relatively unseen behind their privet hedge and rose trellis, travelling with determined reserve on public transport or insulated in the family car, shopping in the supermarket and entertained by television, are probably more private in the sense of being unnoticed in all their everyday doings than any other sizeable section of the population in any other time or place.[4]

Privacy, then, has various dimensions of which being unnoticed, not having one's seclusion intruded upon, and controlling information and knowledge about oneself are only aspects. Those instances where privacy is regarded as having been violated largely concern individuals. The issue of state intrusion is more difficult. It is for the state to decide how, where, and in what manner it will regulate individuals' lives. Zones can be mapped out as being inside or outside the state's purview. The placement of an aspect of life inside or outside the law is a form of regulation. Legal acknowledgement of its existence defines and constitutes it. So regulation may take a form within or without the law [...]

Where the state recognises the existence of a private zone or behaviour it draws a boundary between what is private and what is to be regulated. In so doing it constitutes both. For instance, prostitution which is off the streets and does not fall within the terms of the Street Offences Act 1959 is unregulated, whereas the same conduct on the streets is a crime. Yet both forms of behaviour are controlled. Control may occur through circumscription of behaviour or through the state's reliance on other agencies, such as the family.

A deliberate policy of non-intervention by the state may mask a passing of control to informal mechanisms. For instance, the legal doctrine of the unity of spouses serves as a justification for state policy of non-intervention in marriage.

As Michael Anderson observes: 'family behaviour has become the most private and personal of all areas of behaviour, almost totally free from external supervision and control.'[5] Who then controls the family? It can be argued that non-intervention by law may result in the state leaving the power with the husband and father, whose authority it legitimates indirectly through public law support for him as breadwinner and household head. A deliberate policy of non-intervention does not necessarily mean that an area of behaviour is uncontrolled.

The distinction between private and public in legal discourse

The idea that private and public can be distinguished is imbued in legal philosophy and informs legal policy. [...]

This division is not confined to distinguishing relations between individual and state from relations between individuals. It also draws a line dividing the law's business from what is called private. Although this boundary between the private and public shifts over time, the existence of the distinction and the notion of boundary are rarely questioned.

The dichotomy between private and public as unregulated and regulated has its origins in liberal philosophy. The seventeenth-century liberal tradition as represented by Locke posits a distinction between reason and passion, knowledge and desire, mind and body. This leads to a split between the public sphere in which individuals prudently calculate their own self-interest and act upon it, and a private sphere of subjectivity and desire. [...]

Nineteenth-century liberal thought, as expressed by John Stuart Mill, continued the tradition of the private/public split. In his feminist work *On the Subjection of Women* the solution for Mill was the grant to women of full equality of formal rights with men in the public sphere. From public equality, he believed, would follow a transformed family, a 'school of sympathy in equality' where the spouses live 'together in love, without power on one side or obedience on the other'. Yet he did not propose the merging of the two spheres but rather sanctioned the division of labour in which women remain in the realm of subjectivity and the private. Thus he argued: 'When the support of the family depends, not on property but on earnings, the common arrangement, by which the wife superintends the domestic expenditure, seems to me in general the most suitable division of labour between the two persons.'[6] Women's role was to remain that of loving and softening men in the domestic realm. Mill's views on household management overlooked the connection between economic power and dominance in the home. Economic inequality leads to an imbalance of power. The division of labour whereby one spouse works for earnings and the other for love encapsulates the public/private split.

The Wolfenden Committee Report on Homosexual Offences and Prostitution provides an excellent example of the implementation in law of the liberal view of the distinction between public and private. The committee accepted as unproblematic the idea of 'private lives of citizens'. It stated that the function of criminal law in relation to homosexuality and prostitution was 'to preserve public order and decency, to protect the citizen from what is offensive and injurious, and to provide sufficient safeguards against exploitation and corruption of others'.[7] [...]

The elaboration in legal discourse of a private domain of subjectivity, morality and the personal as 'not the law's business' has inevitably led to non-intervention in domestic life. Legal ideology views the private as a domain 'in which the King's writ does not seek to run, and to which his officers do not seek to be admitted'.[8] One implication is that those confined to the domestic sphere need not look to law to rectify any power imbalance resulting from the division of labour.

The unregulated family

[I]deas of privacy established in legal decisions preclude intervention in the family. The common law assumption that 'the house of everyone is his castle'[9] is an early and useful bulwark in the defence of civil liberties. But it may also conceal a power struggle within the family. This remains unrecognised and the judicial posture is one of defence of freedom, as the following passage makes clear:

> I for one should deeply regret the day, if it ever came, when Courts of Law or Equity thought themselves justified in interfering more than is strictly necessary with the private affairs of the people of this country. Both as regards the conduct of private affairs, and domestic life, the rule is that Courts of Law should not intervene except upon occasion. It is far better that people should be left free.[10]

Free for what? is the question. In so far as this type of rhetoric involves upholding the values of liberty and the restraint of police powers, it is no doubt admirable. But it also masks physical abuse and other manifestations of power and inequality within the family.

In discussions of the privacy of marital relations or of the boundaries of state intervention, the home, the family and the married couple remain an entity that is taken for granted. The couple is a unit, a black box, into which the law does not purport to peer. What goes on inside the box is not perceived as the law's concern. The belief is that it is for family members to sort out their personal relationships. What this overlooks is the power inequalities inside the family which are of course affected by structures external to it. This ideology of privacy and non-intervention has been articulated by legislators, by the judiciary and by legal scholars.

The reluctance of Parliament to legislate on areas of family life denoted private can be illustrated from a wide variety of materials concerning relations between the spouses and those between parent and child. Twentieth-century debates on equal ownership of the matrimonial home have foundered on Parliament's unwillingness to lay down a legislative principle of equality. In 1980, when a Law Commission Bill on co-ownership of the matrimonial home was introduced in the House of Lords, the Lord Chancellor made it clear that there was no government support.[11] Nineteenth- and early-twentieth-century debates on child protection and incest demonstrated a great reluctance on the part of parliamentarians to legislate on 'that d—d morality' which was regarded as a private, internal and domestic affair.[12]

The judiciary also have repeatedly expressed reluctance to intervene in the private. [...] This legal ideology is described as follows by a legal scholar: 'English practice has been to refrain from formulating general principles as to how families should be managed.'[13] The view is that the ongoing family and marriage should be left alone, so long as conflict does not cause breakdown. But some scholars extend their opinions to prescription:

> The normal behaviour of husband and wife or parents and children towards each other is beyond the law – as long as the family is 'healthy'. The law comes in when things go wrong. More than that, the mere hint by anyone concerned that the law may come in is the surest sign that things are or will soon be going wrong.[14] [...]

The feminist critique of the private

The insistence on the idea that women belong in the private sphere is part of the cultural superstructure which has been built on biological foundations. Identifying these elements and disassembling the whole gave rise to the important insight that gender is socially constructed. Conceptually the distinction between sex and gender brought out the distinction between biological sex and social and cultural expectations and roles based on gender. Feminist analysis, relying on medical research into gender identity, broke the link between biology and culture by showing that one is not necessarily connected to the other.

The focus on the social construction of women's difference from men had an immediate consequence in terms of law. Feminists and liberals were agreed in questioning differential treatment of women and men in legislation. In particular, in the United States, a whole series of challenges to gender-based legislative classifications took place. Each court success – and there were many in the 1960s and 1970s – was regarded as a victory for women.[15] Since social attitudes of employers and those providing such services as credit, housing and education were perceived as denying women equal opportunity, legislation was passed in Britain and the United States making discrimination on grounds of sex illegal.[16] The aim was to eliminate women's differences as a source of subordination so far as possible by opening up the public sphere and assimilating women to men. But in their alliance with liberal reformers feminists seemed to forget that element of the analysis of difference that identified the private sphere as the location of women's oppression.

With the focus on sexual division came the celebration of women's difference. The woman-centred analysis which developed from the mid 1970s studied women's culture, held up by some as a model for all persons. This meant an examination of mothering, of women's virtues, of female sexuality, of female experience as values for the culture as a whole, and a critique of masculinity. Celebrating women's difference as a source of strength rather than of oppression became an accepted mode of analysis. Important and perhaps even essential though this stage in the development of feminist theory was, it seemed to lose contact with the major early feminist dissection of the myths surrounding gender.

There is a curious similarity between the positions of the feminist theorists of the 1960s and early 1970s, who focused on eliminating women's differences, and those from the mid 1970s onwards, who celebrated difference. Both streams accepted the dichotomy between public and private. The first group favoured eliminating the differences between women and men, but not necessarily the division between private and public. The second group celebrated women's private existence.

Yet there is within feminist analysis a slogan, 'the personal is political', which emphasises the falsity of the public/private dichotomy. [...] The meaning of the slogan ... has not been examined in detail in relation to law. Although feminists have produced a literature depicting the relative powerlessness of women as a sex category, this insight has not been documented in relation to law, although some work has begun in the United States. [17] Feminist legal analysis in Britain has been content with the liberal position of opening up access for women to the public sphere through sex-discrimination legislation. [18] The importance of the private has not been recognised, perhaps because lawyers cannot see that not regulating is as significant as regulating. Yet we need a detailed understanding of how the particular gender/social order is constituted by law.

The importance of law

Feminist analysis has largely succeeded in disassembling the structure of current gender arrangements, if not on a universal basis, at least in the West. What has been lacking, however, has been an account of how various social, economic and legal structures combine in creating, ordering and supporting the present system. In particular law has remained resistant to analysis. Because it appears immanent – that is, embedded in the seemingly natural – law's role is difficult to isolate. Understanding how existing legal structures appear natural and necessary is not a process of justification; rather it is essential to a full analysis of the gender order.

Unravelling law's part is not easy. It is not just external and institutional but also has an internal aspect whereby it forms part of individual consciousness.

In its external aspects law may be coercive, but legal institutions also structure, mould and constitute the external world. Law influences the world as well as responding to it. In my view law is historically and culturally contingent. The form it takes depends on the particular conditions in which it occurs. A generally accepted theory is that the law adapts to and reflects shared social values. This ignores the active part played by law in shaping perceptions of these values.

In an essay published in 1971 Professor Robert Summers identified law as a set of techniques for the discharge of social functions. He gave examples of five basic techniques used in modern law. These are the penal, which serves the function of crime prevention; grievance-remedial, which is designed to provide compensation for injury; administrative, which is for regulation; public-benefit-conferral, which is for distributive ends; and private, which is for arranging to facilitate personal choice.[19] Of these only the penal is obviously coercive. Summers's typology enables us to see how law is not merely coercive but takes on a number of different guises in its construction of the social order. The limitation of this account is that it takes a purely instrumental view of law. This ignores the symbolic or ideological aspect, which is also important.

The internal aspect of law is its acceptance by individuals as natural and necessary in the form it takes and the values it expresses. It is internalised and most people are unconscious of its contingency. This helps to explain why the current social/gender order is accepted by those subordinate within that order. Here law as ideology plays an important part. In using the term ideology I am referring to the symbolic statement a particular legal principle or rule makes. In popular consciousness this is generally accepted as a statement of what is fair, or at least what is unchangeable. Teasing out the content of a particular principle or rule is not easy. As the immanent critique of the apparently natural character of law shows, the infusion of law in the social fabric makes isolation difficult. The term ideology stands also for those beliefs that legitimate or justify legal statements of values and perspectives, and consequent practices. Making explicit the implicit content and premises is what the analysis of law as ideology attempts.

How does the immanent critique and the analysis of law as ideology relate to a dissection of current gender arrangements in Britain and the United States? In constructing legal distinctions on biological differences law constitutes both gender and the social order. In relation to the issues explored in this book law rarely shows its coercive side. Yet its external and instrumental techniques, other than coercion, order the regulation of gender categories, sexuality, marriage, taxation, social security and the mapping out of a private zone.

Although I have used the Summers typology to show how law functions, I do not share his instrumental views. For me the great significance of law is that it addresses the ineluctable problems of what people are and how they live, and it prescribes answers.[20] These answers reveal a great deal about the kind of society prescribed. Law is not autonomous. It is part of the social order whose functions it serves. But it is also symbolic. We need to know what it means in people's lives.

Notes

1. S. Lukes, *Individualism*, Oxford: Basil Blackwell, 1973, p. 62.
2. D. Smith, 'Women, the family and corporate capitalism', in M. Stephenson (ed.), *Women in Canada*, Toronto: New Press, 1974, p. 6.
3. W. L. Prosser, 'Privacy', *California Law Review*, vol. 48 (1960), p. 383.
4. *Report of the Committee on Privacy*, Cmnd. 5012, 1972, para. 78.
5. M. Anderson, 'The relevance of family history', in C. Harris (ed.), *The Sociology of the Family*, Keele, Social Review Monograph No. 28, Toronto, 1979, p. 67.
6. J. S. Mill, *On the Subjection of Women*, London: Dent, 1929, p. 263.
7. Cmnd. 247, 1957, para. 13.
8. *Balfour v. Balfour* (1919) 2 King's Bench 571 at 579.
9. *Semayne's Case* (1604) 77 English Reports 194.
10. *In Re Agar-Ellis* (1883) 24 Chancery Division 317 at 335.
11. Hansard (House of Lords), vol. 405 (1980), col. 147.
12. Hansard, vol. 191 (1908), col. 279.
13. J. Eekelaar, *Family Security and Family Breakdown*, Harmondsworth: Penguin, 1971, p. 76.
14. O. Kahn-Freund and K. Wedderburn, 'Editorial foreword' to Eekelaar, *Family Security and Family Breakdown*, n., p. 7.
15. For example, *Reed v. Reed* 404 US 71 (1971); *Frantiero v. Richardson* 411 US 677 (1973).
16. In Britain the Equal Pay Act 1970 and the Sex Discrimination Act 1975 made up an 'equality package'. In the USA the equal protection clause of the Fourteenth Amendment to the Constitution has been the basis for court litigation. Title VII of the Civil Rights Act 1964 and the Equal Pay Act 1963 also form part of American anti-discrimination legislation.
17. See K. Powers, 'Sex segregation and the ambivalent directions of sex discrimination law', *Wisconsin Law Review* (1979), p. 55; F. Olsen, 'The family and the market: a study of ideology and legal reform', *Harvard Law Review*, vol. 96 (1983), p. 1497; N. Taub and E. N. Schneider, 'Perspectives on women's subordination and the role of law', in D. Kairys (ed.), *The Politics of Law*, New York: Pantheon, 1983. I discovered most of this literature when my own work was largely completed.
18. Carol Smart's book *The Ties that Bind* (London: Routledge, 1984), was published after I had finished writing.
19. R. S. Summers, 'The technique element in law', *California Law Review*, vol. 59 (1971), p. 733.
20. See M. Minnow, 'The properties of family and the families of property', *Yale Law Journal*, vol. 92 (1982), p. 376.

8.4   On Collaboration[*]

Catherine MacKinnon

Catharine MacKinnon argues that those North American feminists who opposed the Ordinance on pornography drafted by Andrea Dworkin and herself betrayed women in the name of a misguided, legalistic attachment to liberalism which led them to query the Ordinance as unacceptable censorship.

I am here because I really wanted to talk with you about something.

Over the history of this conference, legal initiatives against rape and battery have been discussed – for instance, the spousal exclusion and the corroboration requirement and the question of disclosure of the victim's sexual history. It was not thought necessary to have someone – a woman, a feminist – represent the rapist or the batterer, although major issues of racism, due process, the horrors of incarceration, police discretion, and the intrusion of the state into the privacy of the bedroom were involved.

Legal initiatives have been taken here to secure equal pay for work of comparable worth, and it was not thought necessary to make sure there was someone – a woman, a feminist – to defend the existing economic distribution of value under the capitalist system because some women have been able to get something out of it, although (to credit the commentators) the entire structure of the American economy is at stake. Legal initiatives against sexual harassment have been discussed at this conference, and those arguing that the sex-for-survival dynamic was *not* the model of women's liberation did not have to be opposed by defenders of men's right to sexual access, calling it 'pro-sex', even though serious issues of privacy and even speech are involved. Nor did women lawyers who identify as feminists worry about how women were ever going to get over, if sleeping our way to the top became legally actionable as sex discrimination. Nor were they concerned that we would lose the source of our power.

Pornography is an eight-billion-dollar-a-year industry of rape and battery and sexual harassment, an industry that both performs these abuses for the production of pornography and targets women for them societywide. Rape is involved when women are coerced into pornography with 'Smile, or I'll kill you'. Sexual harassment is involved when pornography is forced on women with 'Here, you stupid bitch, this is what I want you to do'. Assault and battery are involved when a woman is gang-raped to the tune of 'This is more fun than Custer's Last Stand'. This is also an industry that sets women's value in terms of our sexual accessibility and use. But it took months of argument for me to get even this much access to you, and it was granted only on the condition that someone – a woman, a feminist – be here to speak for the pornographers, although that will not be what she will say she is doing.

---

*This speech was part of a debate at the National Conference on Women and the Law in New York, Mar. 24, 1985. The struggle against pornography has freed many to express themselves in ways that were previously silenced. It freed me to say this.

I want to speak about the civil rights law Andrea Dworkin and I wrote, making pornography actionable as sex discrimination. I have two goals. It is my view that you are being largely lied to; I want you to hear the truth straight, just one time. I also want to consider what it means that women lawyers who identify as feminists oppose this initiative for sex equality.

I have never done anything like this in public before. I also realize that I have been wanting to say it for a very long time.

Women in pornography are bound, battered, tortured, humiliated, and killed. Or, to be fair to the soft core, merely taken and used. This is being done to real women now. It is being done for a reason: it gives sexual pleasure to its consumers and therefore profits to its providers. But to the women and children who are the victims of its making or use, it means being bound, battered, tortured, humiliated, and killed — or merely taken and used, until they are used up or can get out. It is done for a reason: because someone with more power than they have gets pleasure from seeing it, or doing it, or seeing it as a form of doing it.

In the hundreds of magazines and pictures and films and so-called books now available in this country, new ones every month, women's legs are splayed, bodies presented in postures of sexual submission, display, and access. We are pussy, beaver, bitch, chick, cunt — named after parts of our bodies or after animals interchangeably. We are cut up into parts of our bodies or mated with animals interchangeably. We are told this is a natural woman's sexuality, but it is elaborately contrived. The photographs may not be retouched, but the poses are, the bodies are. Children are presented as adult women; adult women are presented as children. Pregnant women are accessible, displayed. Lesbian is a pervasive theme. Lesbian sex is shown as men imagine women touch each other.

Pornography is a major medium for the sexualization of racial hatred. Every racial stereotype is used: Black women presented as violent bitches, struggling against their bonds, bruised and bleeding. The pornography of Asian women is almost entirely one of torture. The women are presented so passive they cannot be said to be alive, so bound they are not recognizably human, hanging from light fixtures and clothes pegs and trees. There are amputees, their stumps and prostheses presented as sexual fetishes. Retarded girls are gratifyingly compliant. In some pornography called 'snuff' films women or children are tortured to death to make a sex film. They exist.

Why do women lawyers who identify as feminists ignore, gloss over, shrug this off? Why do some refuse to discuss the issue of pornography when the pornography is in the room, making it as invisible and nonexistent as its victims have been? How can they ignore even, say, the racism?

You may think snuff is one thing, *Playboy* another. Our law says something very simple: a woman is not a thing to be used, any more than to be abused, and her sexuality isn't either. Why do women lawyers who identify as feminists buy and defend the pornographers' view of what a woman is for, what a woman's sexuality is? Why, when they look in the mirror, do they see the image of themselves the pornographers put there?

Because the medium of pornography is words and pictures, it has been considered speech, even by women lawyers, feminists. Because of the pleasure pornography gives, they have also considered it exempt from scrutiny, repressive to question. This misses what they know best: because pornography is sexual, it is not like the literatures of other inequalities. It is a specific and compelling behavioral stimulus, conditioner, and reinforcer. The way it works is unique: it makes orgasm a response to bigotry. It is a major way that dominance and submission — a daily dynamic of social hierarchy, particularly of gender inequality — are enjoyed and practiced and reinforced and experienced. And fused with male and female. Pornography makes sexism sexy. We live in a society in which intrusion on women is the definition of sex, and the pornographers practice and promote it. Why are there women lawyers, feminists, who defend this, telling us everything is just fine, and the only problem is that 'we' don't have enough of it?

Based on the observation and analysis that everything is not just fine, Andrea Dworkin and I have considered pornography to be a violation of civil rights — the civil rights of women and children primarily, but of everyone who is hurt by it on the basis of their sex. In our view, pornography is a major social force for institutionalizing a subhuman, victimized, and second-class status for women in this country. This is inconsistent with any serious vision or legal mandate of equality and with the reasons speech is protected. Why do women lawyers who identify as feminists not see the insult in a law of the First Amendment that is outweighed by so many other considerations but has looked at pornography for decades, looking for the harm in it, and has never seen anything except sex that men don't want to say they want to see?

Our law defines pornography as the sexually explicit subordination of women through pictures or words that also includes women presented dehumanized as sexual objects who enjoy pain, humiliation, or rape; women bound, mutilated, dismembered, or tortured; women in postures of servility or submission or display; women being penetrated by objects or animals. Men, children, and transsexuals, all of whom are sometimes violated like women through and in pornography, can sue for similar treatment. The term 'sexually explicit' is an existing term with a legal meaning. It has never before, to my knowledge or the knowledge of LEXIS,[1] been considered unclear; it is often used to clarify the meaning of other terms. It refers to something objective in the world, unlike obscenity law's 'prurient interest', yet it captures the active sexual dynamic of the materials.The term 'subordination' refers to materials that, in one way or another, are active in placing women in an unequal position. Presumably, people know that if you are someone's subordinate, you are not their equal. Why do women lawyers seem unable to comprehend the simple statutory requirement that all these elements must be there? Why do they distort the law ludicrously? Can't they get it right and still oppose it? Why do they, feminists, insist that they have no idea what subordination means, what being put down is about or looks like? Why do they say that at most equality in this area should mean that sexual dominance and submission be made available on a gender-neutral basis?

Our civil rights law allows victims of four activities, and four activities only – coercion, force, assault, and trafficking – to sue civilly those who hurt them through pornography. Coercion, force, assault, and trafficking are not ideas; they are not fantasies; they are not, in themselves, speech. Why, when women's agony and pain becomes what pornographers want to say, when our bodies are their media of expression, are women lawyers, feminists, among those who tell us it is only an idea, information, symbolic, a fantasy, just representation? Aren't these women real to them either?

Trafficking in female sexual slavery does not become speech because it is a business, any more than any form of discrimination becomes legalized when it is bought and sold. Nor does it become protected simply because it is only words. A sign that says 'Whites Only' is only words, but it is still an integral act in a system of segregation, which is a system of force. Should it become more protected if it is done on an eight-billion-dollar-a-year scale? Why do women lawyers, feminists, want to require that we reach the acts, not the 'speech' when these acts are done to make the 'speech' or because of the 'speech'? Why can there be a law for every other abuse, but when harmed women want to move against pornographers, women lawyers, calling it feminist, say this is something there should be no law on?

Our hearings in Minneapolis produced overwhelming evidence of the damage done by pornography. Researchers and clinicians documented what women know from life: that pornography increases attitudes and behaviors of aggression and other discrimination, principally by men against women. The relation is causal. It is better than the smoking/cancer correlation and at least as good as the data on drinking and driving. Social studies and other expert and personal testimony documented that the laboratory predictions of increased aggression toward women do occur in real life. There are no contradictions in this evidence. You know, it is fairly frustrating that it takes studies by men of men in laboratories to predict that viewing pornography makes men be sexually more violent and makes them believe we are sexual things, before women are believed when we say that this does happen, and did happen, to us. It's even more frustrating to have women lawyers, feminists, say or act as though it doesn't happen – or, if it does, that it is not as important as the pleasure to be gotten from it.

In *Brown v. Board of Education*, it took one study to show that the harm of segregation was that it affected the hearts and minds of Black children, gave them a sense of their inferiority, and affected their feeling of status in the community in a way that was unlikely ever to be undone.[2] How do you suppose it affects the hearts and minds of women, what does it tell us about our status in the community, that when a woman is hung on a meat hook, a study has to be done to see if there is harm, and then that harm remains constitutionally protected as entertainment and inflicting it is a civil liberty that the ACLU and a woman judge[3] and some women lawyers, identifying as feminists, defend?

Women in our hearings testified to the use of pornography to break their self-esteem, to train them to sexual submission, to season them to forced sex, to intimidate them out of job opportunities, to blackmail them into prostitution and keep them there, to terrorize and humiliate them into sexual compliance, and to silence their dissent. We heard testimony that it takes coercion to make pornography. We heard how pornography is forced on women and children in ways that give them no choice about viewing the pornography or performing the sex. We heard how pornography stimulates and condones rape, battery, sexual harassment, sexual abuse of children, and forced prostitution – all presented in the pornography as sex, sex, sex, sex, and more sex, respectively. Almost none of this had been reported. The most astounding event of all: they were believed. Why don't women lawyers, feminists, believe them? Or, if they do, why don't they act as though they give a goddamn? Why do they tell us it is doing something about pornography that is so risky and endangers our freedom, and talk about *this* status quo as if it has no risks and *is* that freedom?

Under current law, the First Amendment, which guarantees speech against abridgement by government, recognizes exceptions. It is also at times outweighed by other interests. The most common reason is harm: the harm done by the materials outweighs their expressive value, if any. Harm to someone who matters. Why are there women lawyers, feminists, trying to make sure that women don't matter enough?

Our law is not criminal. It places enforcement in the hands of the victim, not the state. It is not protective unless suing organized crime is a form of protection. It does not provide for a ban unless relief for a proven injury is a ban. Its trafficking provision is not a 'prior restraint' – the one thing Judge Barker in Indianapolis, a woman lawyer, not a feminist – got right. The harm is not triggered by any kind of offensiveness. Why do even feminist lawyers repeatedly make this law into what it is not in order to attack it?

Speech interests have been outweighed to some degree when materials are false, obscene, indecent, racist, coercive, threatening, intrusive, inconvenient, commercial, or in aesthetic. Why can't they be civilly actionable if they are coerced? If they are sex discriminatory? What or who are women lawyers who oppose this possibility protecting – and why are they calling their opposition feminism?

The most attacked provision of the ordinance is the trafficking cause of action, which reaches production, sale, exhibition, and distribution. We know that pornography targets women, meaning that so long as the pornography is actively purveyed, saturating our communities, as it does now, women and children will be used and abused to make it, as they are now, and it will be used to abuse them, as it is now. When women lawyers, feminists, tell us to enforce existing law, the question is: why do we have to wait for each act of victimization to occur, confining the work of our lives to cleaning up after the pornographers one body at a time, never noticing that the bodies have a gender, never noticing that the victimization is centrally actualized through words and pictures, never noticing that we encounter the pornography in the laws, in the courts every time we try to prove we are hurt? The pornography sets the real rules of our lives. If we can't reach the traffic, this source of our condition is exempt, off limits, a base of operations outside direct attack through some laws of war we never agreed to. Why do women lawyers, feminists, oppose any avenue of change that might mean we don't have to spend our lives in this mop-up operation?

Pornography is historically defended in the name of freedom of speech. I am here to speak for those, particularly women and children, upon whose silence the law, including the law of the First Amendment, has been built. Their social inequality, which is not just fine, has never been taken into account in its jurisprudence. The First Amendment was written by those who already had the speech; they also had slaves, many of them, and owned women. They made sure to keep their speech safe from what threatened it: the federal government. You have to already have speech before the First Amendment, preventing government from taking it away from you, does you any good. Now the pornographers, who have the so-called speech, with women lawyers, feminists, fronting for them, take as a principled position that what the pornographers do is indistinguishable from what anyone else does, even in the face of our exact description of what they do, which is utterly unlike what anyone else does. Our definition of pornography is, in fact, the pornographers' definition: pornography is created by formula, it does not vary. No pornographer has any trouble knowing what to make. No adult bookstore or theatre has any trouble knowing what to stock. No consumer has any trouble knowing what to buy. We only described what they all already know and do. Yet, knowing this, they and their supporters, including feminist lawyers, who have the speech, have taken the position that the pornographers are the rebels, the disenfranchised, and the hated, rather than the bearers and defenders of a ruling ideology of misogyny and racism and sexualized bigotry – hated to the tune of eight billion dollars a year, some of which they give to the ACLU and some women lawyers who identify as feminists and this conference.

Claiming to represent women, these people have in effect decided that there will continue to exist an entire class of woman who will be treated in these ways so that they can have what they call freedom of speech. Freedom meaning their free access to women. Speech meaning women's bodies saying what they want them to say.

Why are women lawyers, feminists, siding with the pornographers? To be a lawyer orients you to power, probably sexually as well as in every other way. The law has a historical hostility to new ideas, hurt women, and social change. But more than that, we were let into this profession on the implicit condition that we would enforce the real rules: women kept out and down, sexual access to women enforced. These remain the rules whether you are in and up, and whether you practice it or have it practiced on you. It keeps the value of the most exceptional women high to keep other women out and down and on their backs with their legs spread. I may be missing something, but I don't see a lot of women lawyers, feminist or otherwise, selling their asses on the street or looking for a pornographer with a camera in order to fulfil their sexual agency and I don't think it is because they are sexually repressed. What law school does for you is this: it tells you that to become a lawyer means to forget your feelings, forget your community, most of all, if you are a woman, forget your experience. Become a maze-bright rat. Women lawyers as a group have not been much of an exception to this, except that they go dead in the eyes like ghetto children, unlike the men, who come out of law school glowing in the dark. Women who defend the pornographers are defending a source of their relatively high position among women under male supremacy, keeping all women, including them, an inferior class on the basis of sex, enforced by sexual force.

I really want you to stop your lies and misrepresentations of our position. I want you to do something about your thundering ignorance about the way women are treated. I want you to remember your own lives. I also really want you on our side. But, failing that, I want you to stop claiming that your liberalism, with its elitism, and your Freudianism, with its sexualized misogyny, has anything in common with feminism.

Notes

1. LEXIS is a computerised service for legal research that allows random searches of random phrases as well as of concepts and cases.
2. *Brown v. Board of Education*, 347 US 483, 494 (1954) ('… a feeling of inferiority as to their status in the community that may affect their hearts and minds in a way unlikely ever to be undone').
3. *American Booksellers Association v. Hudnut*, 598 F. Supp. 1316 (S.D. Ind. 1984) (Sarah Evans Barker, J.).

8.5   There Should be a Law Against it ... Shouldn't There?

Wendy Moore

Wendy Moore argues for British legislation on pornography, but urges caution and the need to avoid its being hijacked by the anti-feminist lobby as occurred in the McKinnon–Dworkin campaign.

If women are ever to be treated as equal members of society something must be done to change the way they are portrayed in the media. The media shapes our perceptions of each other. It influences our expectations and self-image. It helps create a climate where women are treated as inferior beings and where our needs and desires – whether for freely available childcare or top careers – come second place to men's. It implicitly supports discrimination against women, which in turn is a major determinant in prompting violence against us. But what can be done, since persuasion and education have achieved little success? The most common and often the most effective way of protecting vulnerable people from fear and injury is to introduce legislation. Surely, then, there should be a law in protect women from the harmful effects of degrading images in the media. But such a suggestion is immediately greeted by allegations of censorship. Is this fair?

Censorship, like freedom, is an entirely subjective term (although we can strive for collective agreement on what is acceptable and non-acceptable censorship). All but the most far-right libertarians support 'censorship' when it suits them. All of us protest at attacks on our freedom when we are prevented from doing something we wish to. The arguments are all relative. But in Indianapolis, legislation which, for the first time, restricted the publication of pornographic material was overturned before it could even be used because the pornographers pleaded their right to free speech. Indianapolis city council accepted evidence at a public hearing that pornography could cause violence to women. But the publishers successfully argued that legislation which prevented them printing pornography amounted to censorship, infringing their right to free speech under the First Amendment of the American Constitution. In Britain, moves to bring in similar kinds of legislation which would curb pornography and other discriminatory portrayal of women are now also being attacked as censorship. Such legislation would restrict the so-called freedom of the media, it is said.

Feminists must thoroughly debate whether or not the law could provide some improvement in the way women are portrayed in the media. But we should not be sidetracked by allegations that such a move would be of itself censorship. Legislation might prove ineffectual. It might he rendered useless by the male-dominated and often anti-women judiciary. It might conceivably be used against rather than for us to, for example, prohibit lesbian erotica which poses no threat to women, rather than prohibiting the pornographic and sexist material which poses a daily threat. If legislation were misused in that way, we might justifiably complain of censorship. But the principle of a law which would protect women against the fear and sometimes violence which can result from sexist or pornographic material – a law intended to safeguard the fragile rights of women – should not of itself be described as censorship.

Under British law, unlike in the United States, members of the public are not assigned specific rights. Instead the law lays down what is not allowed. All of British legislation, therefore, is censorious in that it prohibits people from carrying out certain acts. Much of our legal system, although obviously imperfect, is designed to protect the rights and the freedom of individuals, particularly vulnerable individuals. Therefore, it is against the law to murder, to rape, to injure, and to steal. Such laws are inevitably restrictive of individual rights – restricting the 'right' to kill, maim, rape and rob. But such restrictions are, of course, accepted because it is universally recognised that a free and democratic society entails abiding by laws which protect individuals, especially from those with more power, whether through strength, status or economics.

The same principles apply to legislation covering the media. The media do not, by and large, have specific rights under British law. Instead journalists are covered by the same laws as everyone else and work within the confines of those laws. Freedom of the press is a notion which is bounded by the laws which govern all society. The press in this country is 'free' under legislation only inasmuch as it does not contravene the law.

A wide range of legislation already governs what the media – or for that matter anyone else – can publish. Journalists are bound by, among others, laws of defamation; laws preventing the identification of rape victims or defendants, and of juveniles; laws governing the reporting of court cases and criminal charges; by the Official Secrets Act; the Rehabilitation of Offenders Act and by the Race Relations Act. They are restricted too from publishing what is deemed 'blasphemous' or 'obscene' material. In broadcasting specific regulations apply which lay down standards of quality.

Quite clearly, then, legislation is by no means a new phenomenon to the media, and fairly heavy restrictions already govern what can be printed or broadcast. And even the most libertarian of civil rights campaigners would not oppose laws which restrict journalists from printing the names of women who have been raped or children who appear in court. Neither do they call for the repeal of the Race Relations Act, which, for all its ineffectuality, deters journalists or members of the National Front from printing overtly racist material.

Society also clearly accepts the need for laws to limit unproven allegations, despite their curtailment of free speech, because it is accepted that the press should not have unbridled freedom to print whatever it wishes about people, regardless of its inaccuracy or the damage it causes (although sadly the existing libel laws are far from effective in delivering this aim). Indeed a major complaint against the libel laws is that they are currently open only to the wealthy who can afford the huge costs of going to court. Some media campaigners would go further still and are keen to extend the regulations which govern the media, to introduce effective curbs on accuracy and distortion.

It is absurd, therefore, given all the existing restraints, to suggest that introducing one more law, with the aim of protecting the rights of women against attack in the media, is of itself censorship. Significantly, one of the few laws restricting journalists which has been described as censorship is the Race Relations Act, which makes it an offence to publish 'threatening or abusive matter likely to stir up racial hatred'. This protective law has been cited as a possible model for legislation protecting women's rights within the media. It is no coincidence that mainly white, male journalists and lawyers isolate the Race Relations Act and moves to adopt legislation curbing degrading images of women as threats of 'censorship'. They see such legislation in terms of restricting the 'rights' of the media, ignoring the existence of other restrictive laws which they deem as acceptable and denying the rights to protection for vulnerable groups such as black people and women. Laws which protect people's rights are an essential ingredient of a democratic society, whether or not they curtail the rights of the media. Indeed in some instances it is *from* the power of the media that such laws protect.

So, when we discuss the desirability or otherwise of using the legislative system to protect women, we need first of all to reclaim the language. Andrea Dworkin, in her analysis of pornography, *Pornography: Men possessing women,*[1] rightly ascribes the 'power of naming' to men. The male-dominated media use language to make women invisible, to make women possessions, to undermine women and the issues which matter to them and to reduce women to objects of sexual desire. But we must not allow the power of male language to stifle our debate on how to deal with sexism. In America it was the pornographers, the enemies of women, who contorted language to cite 'freedom of speech' as a defence for the publication of pornography. As women, we cannot accept such a definition of free speech. Under any democratic system of law, free speech is necessarily curtailed by restrictions.

As women we have been denied the most basic of civil liberties all of our lives, in the name of men's freedom – freedom to insult, offend, injure and possess. It is time we demanded our own definition of freedom. And in a society which sets down basic freedoms by law – by virtue of prohibiting activities which are accepted as antisocial – we are surely right to demand a law which would protect women from both the offensive existence and the effect of sexist and pornographic material in the media.

The principle of legislation must be a fair one. But before we rush to grab the nearest bill we must think carefully through all of the practicalities. The question we should be asking is not whether the concept of legislation is acceptable, but whether legislation can actually achieve what we want. [...]

Could legislation work?

We can draft our ideal form of legislation, but would it work in practice? In debating whether the law can provide us with some solutions to the way women are portrayed in the media it is important to have realistic expectations. Even the most perfectly drafted legislation could not alone provide the solution. The limitations on legislation and its enforcement are substantial. Legislation may prove to be one element of a range of changes needed to tackle the problem. It may help to achieve concrete changes and it may help to shape attitudes to contribute to other forms of change. But it cannot possibly provide the whole answer. We should ask whether through legislation we can gain more than we would lose. In assessing this it is essential to understand how the legal system works and to learn from past experience of attempting to use laws to improve rights for women.

In her analysis of legislating for equality, *The Politics of Women's Rights*, [2] April Carter details the various problems associated with using the law. Legislation, she points out, cannot change deep-seated attitudes; pitfalls in legislation are exploited by those who wish to avoid its impact; and laws can promote lip-service to equality while failing to bring about any real change. She charts in particular the record of the Sex Discrimination and Equal Pay Acts, for which feminists fought hard but with often disappointing results. But she argues that passing a law instils moral authority, it influences public opinion and it empowers oppressed groups with the knowledge that equality is a right rather than a privilege. British society, she says, is particularly hesitant about using the law, compared to the trend in America, perhaps inspired by the US Bill of Rights, but the mood is slowly changing here with people proving more and more willing to assert their rights through the courts. One reason, she suggests. is the power of the European Court of Justice, which has prompted extensions to equality legislation in this country. She concludes that using the law is a 'slow and frustrating process'. Nevertheless legislation has brought about real improvement for women in employment and even inadequate legislation helps to change general attitudes, influences women's own expectations and encourages them to fight for their rights.

If we aim to campaign for legislation to tackle portrayal in the media we need to acknowledge the likely limitations. We would be certain to encounter technical problems with the legislation itself. But this should not necessarily deter us. Almost all British law has benefited from progressive amendments. Certainly the EPA and SDA both suffered initially from technical pitfalls, but later amendments and changes forced on the government by the EEC have improved their effectiveness. We would be bound to face problems with the offenders devising ways of avoiding prosecution. But again this need not put us off, since the law would still be likely to make their business more difficult, less respectable and, more importantly, more expensive. Perhaps the greatest drawback, however, is the way in which any legislation would be enforced. The issue is who controls the legislation. Obviously there must be major problems in expecting the establishment, which we are trying to change, to bring about alterations on itself.

Indeed it seems particularly curious that Andrea Dworkin ever contemplated using the male-dominated courts, having so brutally condemned all men. Resorting to legislation inevitably means expecting the male-dominated legal profession, government and judiciary to bring about changes which will work against them. This could have several results. It may mean, as in the early days of the EPA and SDA, that decisions will be clearly prejudiced against women. It may mean that the law we devise to improve our rights is used by men against us to limit our rights, by, for example, targeting lesbian erotica rather than anti-women pornography. It may be used by the powerful influences of the Right as a weapon to impose narrow concepts of morality. We must be honest and accept that almost certainly the existing structures of society will conspire to blunt any legislative instrument we can devise. We could therefore do two things. We could abandon all proposals for legislation on the grounds that a perfect world does not exist in which such laws could operate. But the logic of this approach would mean opposing all use of the law, whether general or specifically for women. It is unrealistic to oppose legislation on the grounds of spurious purity. So instead we could campaign for legislation designed as best we can to obviate its limitations. That could mean, for example, ensuring that women are financially and structurally backed in using legislation. It should mean ensuring women play at least an equal role in decision-making, perhaps by calling for equal numbers of women in tribunal hearings. It means avoiding the hierarchical legal system as much as possible by setting up or using an existing commission of appointed or elected members more likely to sympathise with our aims.

It would be foolish to expect miracles. The law is only as good as, and usually much worse than, the rest of society. It would be naive to expect to achieve any of our aims under the current regime. The perfect law has to be seen as a long-term ambition. We must be as sure as possible of the legislation we want to introduce and how it will be controlled. But we must be aware too that legislation would not of itself bring about dramatic and concrete change. And any effect it did have would be slow to emerge. But it would give official state backing to women's right to improve the way they are portrayed in the media. It would almost certainly achieve significant changes in society's attitude towards images of women in media. It would provide women who have campaigned against such images with a new weapon to tackle them. It would give women who have quietly suffered under degrading images a new confidence to oppose such discrimination. And surely, after all, it is these things we are trying to achieve.

Notes

1. A. Dworkin, *Pornography: Men possessing women*, London: The Women's Press, 1981.
2. A. Carter, *The Politics of Women's Rights*, London: Longmans, 1988.

8.6 Pornography and Feminism: the case against censorship

Gillian Rodgerson and Elizabeth Wilson

Members of Feminists Against Censorship take Moore's argument further by suggesting

*that there is no way of avoiding the anti-feminist use of anti-pornography legislation,
which might lead to the 'policing' of diverse sexualities.*

In recent years, the issue of pornography has engendered an intense debate in
the feminist community. Dismissed by some as diversionary, it is a debate
whose stakes, we feel, are high. Will feminism, having achieved some gains,
capitulate to conservative forces, or will it continue to take a stand for the
liberation of women in all domains, including the difficult and contradictory
domain of sexual expression? We are still asking in the mid-eighties what *do*
women want, and the answer is that women have multiple desires and goals.
We want to be valued equally with men as earners, but we don't want to
contribute to the pollution of the planet and the exploitation of other human
beings. We want to be safe from attack and abuse, in our private lives as well
as in the public sphere, but we don't want that safety at the cost of challenge,
risk, exploration and pleasure. Safety and adventure represent conflicting
demands: the relationship between the two, and how to negotiate it, is a key
issue in the current debate[1] (Caught Looking: *Feminism, Pornography and
Censorship*).

What divided the American feminist community in the mid-eighties divides
us in Britain today. Attempts are being made, in the name of feminism, to whip
up public feeling against pornography and add to the laws that restrict its
production and distribution. The other sides of feminism are in danger of being
submerged. The exploration of sexual possibilities, which has been at times
painful but at times immensely liberating, is condemned as a luxury that we are
too embattled to afford. The grand project of changing basic structures of power
gives way to the short-sighted expedient of clapping handcuffs on what anti-
pornography feminists regard as the most excessive manifestations of male
power. The long efforts to understand the complexities of patriarchal culture and
then to challenge and change it get short-circuited by an approach that simply
takes up one side of a polarized argument within and outside feminism – a side
which has allies among reactionary forces, and which has lost sight of the wider
aims of feminism. [...] It is clear, then, from a glance at the history of
pornography that, until feminism entered the debate, pornography and
censoriousness were an inseparable couple. All our definitions of pornography
depended upon this; an essential ingredient of pornography was the desire to
shock, to cross the boundaries, to explore forbidden zones. Repressive sexual
morality always tends to foster and feed its own 'worst enemies' in this way.

Into this traditional ritual of laws and law-breakers, feminism has tried to
intrude with completely new considerations. Feminism has wanted to sidestep
the question of the boundaries of sexual decency and focus on the fact that most
pornography is produced for heterosexual men, that it consists of masculine
sexual fantasies, mainly about women. Some feminist writers have gone so far
as to claim that pornography lies at the very heart of women's oppression, either
because, as Robin Morgan put it, 'pornography is the theory – rape is the

practice' of male domination, or because 'pornography *is* violence against women', as Andrea Dworkin says. Such writers have tended to paint a very lurid picture of pornography, as if it were all images of rape, sadism and degradation in which women are the victims.

Anyone can see that much pornography represents a sexuality in which women are passive and men active, and women are desired and men desire. Pornography does contain stereotypes of women which feminism wishes to challenge. In this respect it is similar to many other genres, from Renaissance painting to *Vogue* magazine, which have been subjected to feminist critiques. This is not to say that pornography is good, simply that most of it is no worse than a great deal of the rest of the patriarchal and misogynist culture which it reflects.

If pornography is defined, as the Williams Committee defined it, as representations that are both sexually explicit and have as their function the sexual arousal of their audience, then it is not *necessarily* oppressive to women. Indeed, many feminists have wanted to challenge the old taboos about sexual material, to talk more frankly about women's bodies – and men's – and to explore what we find arousing. It is certainly possible to imagine a pornography *for* women, though no one could guarantee that it would never be used by men in a misogynist way.

Those feminists who recently have been arguing in favour of censorship have done so on the basis of a new definition of pornography which identifies it with sexually explicit images of degradation and violence against women. This was the approach used in the Minneapolis Ordinance in the United States and it was adopted in 1990 by Dawn Primarolo MP, for her Location of Pornographic Materials Bill. Clause 3 of this bill reads:

> 3(1) Pornographic material means film and video and any printed matter which, for the purposes of sexual arousal or titillation, depicts women, or parts of women's bodies, as objects, things or commodities, or in sexually humiliating or degrading poses or being subjected to violence.
>
> 3(2) The reference to women in sub-section (1) above includes men.

The justification for such formulations is the belief that sexually arousing images have a special efficacy in producing violence against women. (Sub-section 3(2) was added only from a concern, misguided in this context, for gender equality.) As we shall show later, there is no evidence for this belief. Is there an unacknowledged reason why these campaigners have focused on *sexually* degrading images and ignored the myriad forms of non-sexual degradation? Is the underlying reason that they themselves feel revulsion at the more sexually explicit images, or is it that they believe that a campaign against pornography can gain wider support in a way that no other recent feminist cause has done? The problem is that many women feel very ambivalent about pornography, welcoming images we find erotic but being quite disturbed by others. In a society where sex is so freighted with implications of nonconformity and disorder, it is difficult for women to express our pro-sex feelings in public. It is much easier to express the other side of the ambivalence: the disapproval. This has traditional respectability on its side and so is more likely to find a public voice and public support. Pornography is an area where there will be widespread support for further control, but for reasons that are very foreign to feminism.

The pro-censorship, anti-pornography feminists are plugging into a pre-feminist debate, although they claim to have gone beyond it. They are against *degrading* images of women, or images they consider to be degrading. But their allies are against *sexually explicit* images of any kind and against any material that aims to be sexually arousing. As Feminists Against Censorship we wish to challenge and to question this equation of the sexually arousing with the degrading. Otherwise the alliance of the anti-pornography feminists with the traditional moralists may succeed in reversing many of the gains that have been made during the twentieth century.

Notes

1. Caught Looking, Inc. (eds), *Feminism, Pornography and Censorship*, Seattle, WA: The Real Comet Press, 1986.

8.7 Feminism and the Power of Law
Carol Smart

Carol Smart argues that implicit in the very notion of a feminist jurisprudence is a twofold essentialising tendency of 'grand theory' – Woman and Law are taken as unproblematic, with the net result that the power of law as a determinant of women's subordination is exaggerated.

The problem of legal method

By drawing on other disciplines we are now asking if not only the practice of law silences women's aspirations and needs, and conversely privileges those of men, but whether the very construction not only of the legal discourse, but representations of the discourse in the academy (the construction of our understanding and knowledge of law), is the product of patriarchal relations at the root of society.[1]

Anne Bottomley is here raising the question of whether the very core of law – the means by which law is differentiated from other forms of knowledge – is gendered. We are now familiar with other forms of feminist criticism – for example, the criticism of law for excluding women,[2] or the criticism of the content of legislation,[3] or the criticism of the specific practices of law.[4] It is a fairly recent innovation for feminists to start to criticize the very tools of legal method which have been presumed to be neutral.

As Bottomley suggests, this form of critique is not new in other disciplines. Sociology, for example, has long been reflexive about its methodology and methods, and there is a large feminist literature available in this field. As early as 1974 Dorothy Smith, in an article of major importance,[5] argued that it was not sufficient to add women to the subject matter of the social sciences without radically altering the perspective and method of these disciplines. In law this critique has taken longer to materialize. This is undoubtedly linked to the status of law and its claims to Truth. Sociology's claim to truth has always been shaky, not so law's. But in all areas of academe, radical (i.e. at root) dissent from the dominant paradigm of knowledge production causes problems for the dissenter. As Lahey has argued, to follow radically different ways of thinking can amount to professional suicide.[6]

In the discipline of law there is almost a double suicide involved. Not only does the dissenter challenge academic standards, but also the standards of law as a profession. Inasmuch as law has a direct practical application, the dissenter in law is more subversive than in a discipline like sociology. The former challenges the standing of judges, barristers, and solicitors as well as academic lawyers. Little wonder, then, that feminism has such a hard time taking root in law.

Mary Jane Mossman[7] has suggested that law (at least legal method) is probably impervious to the feminist challenge. It is perhaps worth considering her view in some detail. In her article 'Feminism and legal method: the difference it makes' Mossman identifies three main elements to traditional legal method. These are boundary definition, defining 'relevance', and case analysis. The first element, boundary definition, is the process whereby certain matters are identified as outside the realm of law. Hence some issues may be identified as political or moral. It is of course important to recognize that these boundaries may move and that they are little more than a convenience. For example, in the UK prostitution is defined as a moral issue, not a matter for law. However, soliciting for the purposes of prostitution which, by definition, causes a nuisance, is a legal matter. The point that Mossman makes, however, is that boundary definition is important not as a consequence of where the boundaries are drawn, but as a consequence of the neutrality that it confers on the law. So when lawyers and judges maintain that it is the job of the legally trained mind to interpret the law, and not to pass judgement on issues outside the law, they gain credibility. They assert a terrain within which legal method is entirely appropriate, but they also appear to keep out of subjective areas like moral evaluations, or political bias.

The second element or method is the defining of relevance. So, for example, the student of law learns that it is relevant in cases of rape to know the 'victim's' sexual history. If she has had a sexual relationship with the accused this must be made known, and even where it is not with the accused it may be deemed relevant. The sexual history of the accused is, of course, never relevant. In learning this the student of law learns how to defend a rape case successfully, and he or she also learns another technique of oppressing women. Yet law is impervious to this critique because the formulation of the rules guiding rape cases is shrouded in the mists of time – and by the myths of neutrality. The student who argues that this should not be relevant will never make a 'good' lawyer.

The third element is case analysis. This is where the legally trained mind searches out cases which may constitute the precedent of a judicial decision. Some cases become 'good' law, i.e. should be followed; others mysteriously become 'bad' law and are ignored. But even among cases that lawyers call 'good' law there is a vast choice. This raises the question of how they know which ones are relevant. Sumner[8] has argued that judges merely make their decisions and select the cases accordingly. In other words the cases are decided in a *post hoc* fashion, logic does not inexorably lead the judge to the *right* decision. This, of course, is heresy to the legal positivists, yet the observation that cases heard on appeal can overturn previous decisions – several times – should be enough to product scepticism about the infallibility of the case analysis method.

In all of these areas, Mossman argues that it is possible for law to evade the feminist challenge, indeed to identity it as irrelevant nonsense. Women lawyers are faced with the choice of being good feminists and bad lawyers, or the converse. However, whilst accepting the strength of Mossman and Lahey's argument, it may be that they both take law too seriously. Legal method can be deconstructed, and it is well known that law in law schools is quite different to the practices of lawyers 'outside'. It is important to recognize the power that accrues to law through its claim to truth, but law is both more and less than this in practice. It is more than this because the focus on legal method is narrowly 'judge-oriented' and a lot of law in practice never gets near a judge; it is less than this because although law makes a claim to Truth, many lawyers do not, and they too deflate this view of law in their daily practice. The extension of law's domain to which I referred above is not necessarily regarded by everyone as legitimate. It is, for example, fairly common to hear the utterance that more law simply means more money lining the pockets of lawyers. Such utterances indicate that not everyone accepts law's image of itself, nor welcomes the extension of legal terrain; they may even mark the beginnings of a resistance to the power of law.

I would like to return to the point about the focus on legal method being narrowly judge-oriented. In her book *Women's Law*, Stang Dahl describes in detail how the new discipline of Women's Law began in the Law School of the University of Oslo, and what its orientation is. I cannot do justice to her pioneering work here, but I wish to highlight some of the important points she makes about challenging traditional law and legal method (or doctrine, as she calls it). Stang Dahl accepts the idea that law should retain its own method; she states:

> Legal doctrine, i.e. the interpretation of law according to prescribed methodology, should remain the core area of legal science because it is there that lawyers have their own tools and a distinct craft.[9]

This is surprising given the drift of most feminist work in North America and the UK. However, it becomes clear that Stang Dahl does not include in her idea of doctrine all the elements that Mossman includes. So, for example, she points out how Women's Law challenges the usual direction of law by encouraging 'the use of legal sources "from below"'. By this she means that greater reliance should be placed on custom and public opinion of what law ought to be. This, she argues, allows empirical evidence about women's lives greater influence on the law. So law would become more responsive to the 'real' rather than its own internal imperatives. In this way she envisages law and the social sciences coming closer together and a greater role for the women's movement in influencing law.[10]

Stang Dahl's next challenge to traditional law is to emphasize government administration rather than formal law. She argues that legislation (and also the major legal cases of the day) rarely have anything to do with women. In fact she goes so far as to say that even sex discrimination legislation has little to do with women. She argues (rightly, in my view):

> That a law is gender-specific in its formulation need not, however, mean that it is significant for women's position in law or society. The same applies to the directives found in sex discrimination legislation. Even though its express objective gives it an automatic relevance to women's law, and even though the act's enforcement measures are many and comprehensive, this in itself is not tantamount to the law's consequences having special significance for women's lives and rights, either generally or in decisions in individual cases.[11]

In her view the 'law' that affects women's lives is more likely to be the administration of welfare benefits, the operation of the private law of maintenance, and the formulation of guidelines and decision-making at the level of bureaucratic operation.[12] Hence she proposes simply to demote the importance of formal law in feminist work. But she does not suggest that this be done by fiat, she argues that it is a development which is already occurring within law. High status may still be in the realms of formal law, but the routine and necessary work is elsewhere. This point, in turn, is linked to the point about the narrowness of legal method – and therefore feminist concentration on this method. Stang Dahl argues that legal reasoning which applies abstract norms to the facts of an individual case is only relevant where a judge is the addressee.

Hence this method is judge-dominated because, in order to persuade a judge of a particular point, it is necessary to reason in this rigidly legal way. However, such law has little relevance to the lives of women, so Women's Law in Oslo addresses itself to a different audience. Stang Dahl does not promote this as a way of overcoming law's hegemony; however, I think she says more than she realizes here. Whilst it is true that all law is in some way in the shadow of the judges, it is perhaps important to recognize how little law in practice is ever subjected to legal method. The strategy that seems to come from Stang Dahl's work is therefore not to challenge legal method so much as to ignore it and to focus on law in practice. If Mossman is correct that legal method is impervious to feminist critique, then Stang Dahl's option seems more sensible than continuing to push fruitlessly against such an immovable object.

This strategy does not overcome all the problems identified in this chapter, of course. Yet it does overcome the problem of colluding with law's overinflated view of itself. Part of the power that law can exercise resides in the authority we accord it. By stressing how powerless feminism is in the face of law and legal method, we simply add to its power. The strategy available to Stang Dahl in Oslo is not, of course, universally available. There are no law schools in the UK that would contemplate such a radical move as to introduce Women's Law as part of a compulsory syllabus. Yet at least this provides a useful model which indicates how the power of formal law can be decentred. But feminism itself is a source of power and resistance even where we do not have the means radically to change law schools and law itself. Weedon has argued that:

> even where feminist discourses lack the social power to realize their versions of knowledge in institutional practices, they can offer discursive space from which the individual can resist dominant subject positions. [13]

It is therefore important for feminism to sustain its challenge to the power of law to define women in law's terms. Feminism has the power to challenge subjectivity and to alter women's consciousness. It also has the means to expose how law operates in all its most detailed mechanisms. In doing this it can increase the resistance to law and may effect a shift in power. Whilst it is important that feminism should recognize the power that law can exercise, it is axiomatic that feminists do not regard themselves as powerless. [...]

The quest for a feminist jurisprudence

Where MacKinnon is most persuasive in her work on feminist jurisprudence is in her critique of laws as a universal, objective system of adjudication. It is here that she comes closest to Gilligan in the recognition that law's neutrality is in fact the expression of gendered interests. She argues:

> I propose that the state is male in the feminist sense. The law sees and treats women the way men see and treat women. [14]

> When [the state] is most ruthlessly neutral, it will be most male; when it is most
> sex blind, it will be most blind to the sex of the standard being applied. ... Once
> masculinity appears as a specific position, not just the way things are, its judgments
> will be revealed in process and procedure, as well as adjudication and legislation.
> ... However autonomous of class the liberal state may appear, it is not autonomous
> of sex. [15]

The basic insight of these passages lies in the argument that all social
relationships are gendered. There is no neutral terrain, and law least of all can
be said to occupy that mythical space. This may seem self-evident to feminists,
but it remains a heresy to traditional lawyers. But MacKinnon goes beyond this
to argue that the gender order is one of domination, in fact one of
totalitarianism. I would agree that the gender order is indeed a site of power and
resistance, but I am less certain that women are so powerless in a general sense.
The problem is that MacKinnon sees no division between law, the state, and
society. For her these are virtually interchangeable concepts – they are all
manifestations of male power. I would argue that the law occupies a specific
place in the politics of gender which ensures that law is exceptionally powerful
and oppressive of women, but I would not generalize from this in a blanket
fashion as if law were the barometer of the social world. In doing this
MacKinnon gives too much authority to law, it becomes the central plank to her
political analysis and strategy even against her wishes. She states:

> In point of fact, I would prefer not to have to spend all this energy getting the law
> to recognize wrongs to women as wrong. But it seems to be necessary to legitimize
> our injuries as injuries in order to delegitimize our victimization by them, without
> which it is difficult to move in more positive way. [16]

In this passage MacKinnon concedes a great deal to law. She argues that
it is law that can legitimize women's aims, without which they remain
unrecognized. Yet I doubt that law does this. The history of law reforms in the
areas of rape, equal pay, domestic violence must surely reveal the failure of law
to legitimate women's claims. There are other ways of challenging popular
consciousness other than through law, even though law may on occasions
provide a catalyst. But it is also mistaken to imply that once legitimized by law,
women's claims will not be de-legitimized by law at a later stage. The case of
access to legal abortions in the USA and in the UK, and the constant threat to
the notion that women should decide their own reproductive careers, reveals
how vulnerable change, based on law reform, can be. I agree with MacKinnon
that law is powerful in silencing the alternative discourse of women, but I see
it as far less powerful in transforming society to meet the various needs of all
women.

MacKinnon has been very active in using the law to try to challenge gender
oppression. She has, however, been very critical of the dilemma that feminist

lawyers have fallen into of whether to follow the principle of equality or the principle of difference. It is to this debate I shall now turn.

Equality v. difference

The search for a feminist jurisprudence has, to a large extent, been engendered by the equality/difference problem. These competing principles have dogged feminist politics since the nineteenth century, the basic question being whether women should be given special treatment by the state and the law on the basis of their uniquely female capacities and supposed characteristics, or whether justice would be better served by treating women as equal to men, with equal rights and responsibilities. The claim for special treatment (or the difference approach) has focused almost exclusively on pregnancy and maternity, these being biological functions that men cannot perform. At various moments in history the significance of these biological differences has been extended to include psychological differences too (e.g. Sachs and Wilson[17]). This biological difference has been held to mean that women operate under different constraints to men, and that to treat them as the same as men would in fact be to severely disadvantage them. The equality approach, however, has argued that more could be gained for women as a whole if difference was ignored, and women were allowed to bring themselves 'up' to the level of men in every respect.

As MacKinnon[18] and Kenney and others (e.g. Thornton[19]) have shown, both of these approaches presume that men are the norm against which women-as-different or women-as-equal are measured. It is women's reproductive capacity that creates a problem for the male norm inherent in law, not, for example, men's abdication of the caring role. In this respect neither the difference nor the equality approach begins to tackle the problem of the power of law to proclaim its neutrality. Basically these approaches leave law as it is, but seek to find the most successful way of squeezing the interests of women past the legislators and judiciary.

The problem with the debate between these two approaches is that it has the consequence of narrowing the focus of feminist work on law. It incorporates feminism into law's own paradigm. Now, it is not easy to avoid this incorporation when, in terms of legal reform, equality and difference have been constructed as the only two ways forward. But they have also been constructed as mutually exclusive. Hence it appears impossible to apply one principle in one set of circumstances and the other in another. To promote one within the legal system as it stands means that we inevitably undermine the other.

A good example of the impossibility of exercising both principles is the treatment of pregnancy under the Sex Discrimination Act 1975 in the UK. Similar problems have arisen in the USA, where a trend towards the equality principle has also rendered women's reproductive capacities legally problematic.[20] The problem in the UK has been outlined by Kenney.[21] She refers to a case in which a pregnant woman was dismissed where neither the industrial tribunal nor the Employment Appeal Tribunal (EAT) would allow the woman's claim that she had been discriminated against on the grounds of sex. This was because she would not compare herself with a man who had been treated better under the same circumstances (*Turley v. Allders Department Store* 1980 IRLR 4). Only if she could find a male norm against which to compare her treatment could her dismissal have been regarded as discriminatory. Clearly biological difference precluded this possibility. However, the EAT overruled its own decision in Turley in a later case (*Hayes v. Malleable Working Men's Club*, EAT 188/84). In this case it was decided that pregnancy could be treated as a temporary medical condition and hence, that women who were pregnant could compare themselves with men who were suffering from temporary ailments. Then, if it was found that these men were treated better than the pregnant woman concerned, discrimination would have occurred. The tortuousness of this logic defies belief, but it reveals the extraordinary lengths to which a legal system which has staked its policy on the equality approach will go to prove that difference is sameness.

Since the way forward for women in legal terms has been limited to one of two mutually exclusive avenues, it is little wonder that great angst has been created that, in making the wrong choice, we might jeopardize a major breakthrough for women. It should also be realized that this debate is linked to an operationalizable set of policy programmes. We can actually envisage what needs to be done. For example, taking the equality approach we can construct new laws that extend considerably the scope of sex discrimination legislation. It could be extended to cover sexual harassment and pornography, it could be applied to rules of evidence or procedure in criminal trials (especially rape), it could even be extended to cover the provision of public services like transport (i.e. it should be equally safe for women and men to use public transport). Of course we have no guarantee that such extensions to the law would be any more effective than existing law. Nor do we have any guarantee that such legislation would not be used disproportionately by men to enhance their superordinate position.

We can also envisage the extension of the difference approach. For example, extending access to public welfare for women who are engaged in caring work; improving employment protection in relation to pregnancy and also in relation to child care. We could also construct courses on Women's Law, as has happened in university departments in Norway.[22] These are all policies that are, or might quite easily be, envisaged on an agenda for legal and policy reform. Hence they are very attractive because they hold the promise of action and quantifiable 'success' or 'progress'. If quantifying the amount of legislation passed to improve the position of women was the empirical reflection of a reduction in women's oppression, then there would be no need for a feminist movement now. Indeed it has become fashionable to argue that we are now in a phase of post-feminism (using this term in its superficial meaning) either because so much has been achieved that no more is necessary, or because the inability of feminism to alter substantially the subordination of women has been revealed. The equality/difference debate nourishes both of these arguments.

Feminist work which challenges the epistemological neutrality of the legal system (especially if it does not have a blueprint for a feminist alternative) is necessarily less attractive to those who equate politics with institutional forms of change. The production of ideas is seen as a very inadequate substitute – even when we know the old methods of law reform have been tried and failed. Yet we must escape from this interminable debate which has us going round in circles (see *International Journal of the Sociology of Law*, Special Double Edition on Feminist Perspectives on Law 1986; also Scales.[23]) Neither approach can guarantee that it will not ultimately be deleterious for women. The difference approach ultimately nourishes a crude sociobiology; the equality approach can be used as easily by men as by women, and often to the detriment of women.

Sevenhuijsen[24] has argued that we should avoid the difference approach at all costs. She argues that not only is it based on a problematic essentialism which invokes a reactionary politics, but also that, given the current political context of law in 'developed' countries, the equality approach has more purchase for women in many areas. However, she does argue that equality is not appropriate as a blanket solution; most especially she points to the problems of using it in the legal regulation of domestic relations. So, for example, she identifies the move to joint custody in law as a way of celebrating equality as, in fact, a way of increasing men's regulation of women in the post-divorce situation. This, however, tends to ignore the possibility that in opting for equality it will be imposed in all areas. In other words, it is not up to feminists to choose when it should or should not be applied. She also suggests that feminists make the mistake of resorting to law, when in fact *less* regulation would allow greater latitude to create alternative relationships not closely defined by legislation and the courts. While I agree with this, it seems that we must recognize that it is not only feminists who are resorting to law. Increasingly it is men who are using equality legislation and who are extending its scope (e.g. to give greater rights to the biological fathers of illegitimate children).[25]

The point that feminists should not be so anxious to turn to law is an important one, however. Law not only represents itself as a solution, it also defines how we can think about women. For example, MacKinnon, who is most scathing about the futility of the equality/difference debate, none the less speaks constantly of women's inequality. This is a term which infests feminist consciousness to our detriment. If we talk of inequality we necessarily invoke two things. First the idea that we should be equal to *men*, and second that there are institutional means to achieve this. From that point we find we are back into the narrow confines of 'how do we achieve this equality, which laws need changing, how do we incorporate difference, and so on?' Unfortunately, the quest for a feminist jurisprudence when it appears in this narrow (and liberal) form prevents us from redefining the issues and the role that law may have in addressing these issues.

Law as a site of power

In this book I have discussed law's claim to truth and its power to disqualify alternative discourse, and elaborated upon the vision of law as a discursive field which disqualifies women's accounts and experiences. Both of these visions implicate law with masculinity. This is not a simple reductive statement akin to 'all law is man-made'; rather it is intended to draw upon an understanding of how the constitution of law and the constitution of masculinity may overlap and share mutual resonances. The notion of pallogocentric discourse makes this overlap clear. By phallogocentric I mean the combination of phallocentric, which is the masculine heterosexual imperative, and logocentric, which is the term appropriated by feminists to identify the fact that knowledge is not neutral but produced under conditions of patriarchy. The elision of these two concepts into phallogocentric allows for a recognition that these two fields of sexuality and knowledge are interwoven.[26] It is this overlapping that I wish to explore in this final section.

It is often remarked that the adversarial style of many legal systems in which two opposing barristers, in their archaic dress, test the truth of witnesses' accounts according to set rules of argument and logic, replicate masculine aggressive verbosity and machismo. Law is constituted as a masculine profession, not simply on the empirical grounds that there are few women lawyers and judges, but on the grounds that doing law and being identified as masculine are congruous. As Thornton has pointed out:

> feminist scholars have shown how the entire corpus of liberal thought is structured around a series of sexualised, hierarchised dualisms ... men are identified with one side of the dualisms, namely, thought, rationality, reason, culture, power, objectivity and abstract and principled activity. ... Predictably, law is associated with the male side of the dualism, in that it is supposed to be rational, objective, abstract and principled.[27]

It is important to recognize that this is not an argument based on naturalistic assumptions. Most emphatically I am not arguing that somehow men are most suited to law because of their biological constitution. Nor am I saying that in some natural state men are aggressive. Rather the point is that both law and masculinity are constituted in discourse and there are significant overlaps in these. If, for a moment, we consider the historical development of the two professions of nursing and lawyering, we can see immediately that there are overlays of discourses of femity with nursing and of masculinity with lawyering. So law is not rational because men *are* rational, but law is constituted as rational as are men, and men as the subjects of the discourse of masculinity come to experience themselves as rational – hence suited to a career in law.

In attempting to transform law, feminists are not simply challenging legal discourse but also naturalistic assumptions about masculinity. The struggle therefore goes far beyond law. It is not rape law that needs to be the exclusive focus of concern so much as heterosexism. Equally, tackling family law means tackling constructions of fatherhood, masculine authority, and economic power. As Weedon has argued in relation to literary criticism:

> The decentring of liberal-humanism, with its claim to full subjectivity and knowing rationality, in which *man* is the author of his thoughts and speech, is perhaps even more important in the deconstruction of masculinity than it is for women, who have never been fully included in this discourse. [28]

Basically Weedon is arguing that a dominant form of knowledge, namely liberal humanism, in which men are construed as 'naturally' responsible authors of their own actions and fate, incorporates many elements of the discourse of masculinity. Men as masculine subjects (not as biological entities) have a lot invested in many of the dominant discourses such as law and medicine, not simply because they may operate to serve their interests more than others' interests, but because masculinity is part of that world-view. Little wonder then that law is so resistant to more radical forms of feminism but quite comfortable when it is presented in terms of equality, equal opportunity, or difference. The equality claim rests upon an assumption that individuals will be tested (by comparison with the male norm), and if found equal those few individuals will be allowed equality in some insignificant and discrete area of employment or training. Difference, on the other hand, simply confirms the difference (and dominance) of masculinity. The law has had little trouble with this concept in the past (only with the introduction of the principle of equality has it become troublesome). Again Weedon states:

> For instance, the principle of equality of opportunity for women and men in education and work (and law), once established, has not proved any great threat to the balance of power in a society where patriarchal relations inform the very production and regulation of female and male subject. [29]

It is the work of feminism to deconstruct the naturalistic, gender-blind discourse of law by constantly revealing the context in which it has been constituted and drawing parallels with other areas of social life. Law is not a free-floating entity, it is grounded in patriarchy, as well as in class and ethnic divisions. I am uncertain that we should be searching for a feminist jurisprudence which we could substitute for this totality. Rather we should seek to shift the understanding of, for example, rape into a critical deconstruction of naturalist heterosexuality. Rape should not be isolated in 'law', it must be contextualized in the domain of sexuality. Equally, child sexual abuse is not a problem of law, except inasmuch as both sexual abuse and law are exercises of power. But they are both exercised in the masculine mode, so one is not the solution to the other. Finally women's low pay is not a matter of equality but of segregated labour markets, racism, the division of private and public, and the underevaluation of women's work. Law cannot resolve these structures of power, least of all when we recognize that its history and the history of these divisions coincide.

Yet law remains a site of struggle. While it is the case that law does not hold the key to unlock patriarchy, it provides the forum for articulating alternative visions and accounts. Each case of rape, sexual abuse, domestic violence, equal pay, and so on provides the opportunity for an alternative account to emerge. This account may not emerge in court (indeed it would be silenced there), nor in the media, nor in the formulation of reformed legislation, but it can and does emerge in women's writing and feminist groups (e.g. Rape Crisis Groups, Incest Survivors Groups). These resistant discourses are growing in power, and it is often law that provides a focal point for the voice to be heard. This implies a different use of law than the strategy of law reform. [...] I want to imply that the problem of attempting to construct a feminist jurisprudence is that it does not decentre law. On the contrary, it may attempt to change its values and procedures, but it preserves law's place in the hierarchy of discourses which maintains that law has access to truth and justice. It encourages a 'turning to law' for solutions, it fetishizes law rather than deconstructing it. The search for a feminist jurisprudence is generated by a feminist challenge to the power of law as it is presently constituted, but it ends with a celebration of positivistic, scientific feminism which seeks to replace one hierarchy of truth with another.

Notes

1. A. Bottomley, 'Feminism in law schools', in S. McLaughlin (ed.), *Women and the Law*, University College London, Faculty of Law, Working Paper No. 5, 1987, p. 12.
2. A. Sachs and J. Wilson, *Sexism and the Law*, Oxford: Martin Robertson, 1978.
3. S. Atkins and B. Hoggett, *Women and the Law*, Oxford: Basil Blackwell, 1984.
4. Z. Adler, *Rape on Trial*, London: Routledge & Kegan Paul, 1987.
5. D. Smith, 'Women's perspective as a radical critique of sociology', *Sociological Inquiry*, vol. 44, no. 1 (1974), pp. 7–14.
6. K. Lahey, "'... until women themselves have told all that they have to tell ...'", *Osgoode Hall Law Journal*, vol. 23, no. 3 (1985), pp. 519–41. Feminist legal scholars are expected to think and write using the approaches of legal method: defining the issues, analysing relevant precedents and recommending conclusions according to defined and accepted standards of legal method. A feminist scholar who chooses instead to ask different questions or to conceptualise the problem in different ways risks a reputation for incompetence in her method as well as lack of recognition of her scholarly (feminist) accomplishment: M. J. Mossman, 'Feminism and legal method: the difference it makes', *Australian Journal of Law and Society*, vol. 3 (1986), pp. 30–52 at 46.
7. 'Feminism and legal method', op. cit. n. 6.
8. C. Sumner, *Reading Ideologies: An investigation into the Marxist theory of ideology and law*, London: Academic Press, 1979.

9. T. Stang Dahl, *Women's Law: An introduction to feminist jurisprudence*, Oxford: Oxford University Press, 1987, p. 32.
10. The idea of social scientific or academic work influencing legal judgments does not have as much purchase in the UK as it does in the continental European legal tradition, which has a more scholarly base. Indeed, it would require a major shift in the English legal system to achieve this basic premise, which Stang Dahl is able to take almost for granted.
11. Stang Dahl, *Women's Law*, p. 29.
12. Stang Dahl is right that the kind of law which is most likely to affect women's daily lives is administrative law. However, law has an influence beyond those it actually touches. Hence every rape trial is significant, even if few women find themselves involved in such events. For this reason I do not think we can simply ignore law as it operates in these other forums.
13. C. Weedon, *Feminist Practice and Post-Structuralistic Theory*, Oxford: Basil Blackwell, 1987, pp. 110–11.
14. C. MacKinnon, 'Feminism, Marxism, method and the state: toward feminist jurisprudence', *Signs*, vol. 8 (1983), pp. 635–58 at 644.
15. *Ibid.*, p. 658.
16. C. MacKinnon, *Feminism Unmodified: Discourses on life and law*, London: Harvard University Press, 1987, p. 104.
17. Sachs and Wilson, *Sexism and the Law*, see extract in Reading 8.1 above.
18. C. MacKinnon, *Feminism Unmodified*.
19. S. J. Kenney, 'Reproductive hazards in the workplace: the law and sexual difference', *International Journal of the Sociology of Law*, vol. 14 (1986), pp. 393–414; M. Thornton, 'Feminist jurisprudence: illusion or reality?', *Australian Journal of Law and Society*, vol. 3 (1986), pp. 5–29.
20. A. Scales, 'Towards a feminist jurisprudence', *Indiana Law Journal*, vol. 36 (1980), pp. 375–444.
21. Kenney, 'Reproductive hazards'.
22. See generally Stang Dahl, *Women's Law*.
23. Scales, 'Towards a feminist jurisprudence'.
24. S. Sevenhuijsen, 'Fatherhood and the political theory of right: theoretical perspectives of feminism', *International Journal of the Sociology of Law*, vol. 14 (1986), pp. 329–40.
25. C. Smart, '"There is of course the distinction dictated by nature": the law and the problem of paternity', in M. Stanworth (ed.), *Reproductive Technologies*, Cambridge: Polity Press, 1987.
26. C. Duchen, *Feminism in France*, London: Routledge & Kegan Paul, 1986.
27. Thornton, 'Feminist jurisprudence', p. 7.
28. Weedon, *Feminist Practice*, p. 173.
29. *Ibid.*, p. 111.

Further Reading

Atkins, S. and Hoggett, B. (1984), *Women and the Law*, Oxford: Basil Blackwell.
Brophy, J. and Smart, C. (eds) (1985), *Women in Law*, London: Routledge & Kegan Paul.
Dahl, T. S. (1987), *Women's Law*, Oxford: Oxford University Press.

Edwards, S. S. M. (ed.) (1985), *Gender, Sex and the Law*, London: Croom Helm.

Jackson, E. (1992), 'Catharine MacKinnon and feminist jurisprudence: A critical appraisal', *Journal of Law and Society*, vol. 19, no. 2, p. 195.

MacKinnon, C. (1983), 'Feminism, Marxism, method and the state: toward feminist jurisprudence', *Signs*, vol. 8, no. 2, pp. 635–58.

McLaughlin, S. (ed.) (1987), *Women and the Law*, University College London, Faculty of Law, Working Papers No. 5.

Mossman, M. J. (1986), 'Feminism and legal method: the difference it makes', *Australian Journal of Law and Society*, vol. 3, pp. 30–52.

Segal, L. and McIntosh, M. (eds) (1992), *Sex Exposed: Sexuality and the pornography debate*, London: Virago.

Smart, C. (1989), *Feminism and the Power of Law*, London: Routledge & Kegan Paul.

Thornton, M. (1986), 'Feminist jurisprudence: illusion or reality?', *Australian Journal of Law and Society*, vol. 3, pp. 5–29.

9 | WOMEN, CRIME AND DEVIANCE

Edited and Introduced by Anthea Hucklesby

INTRODUCTION

Gender has become a legitimate concern of criminology. It is now an accepted part of both criminological teaching and research. This mirrors developments in the other social science disciplines. Although gender issues have permeated all areas of the criminological agenda, in this Section I will be concentrating on theoretical criminology: the study of why people commit crime. Having said this, it is worth noting that the inclusion of gender has resulted in the widening of the criminological agenda: from its traditional concerns of why people (males in particular) commit crime, and therefore how to address the problem, to include areas such as victimology.

Until the 1970s, few theories took gender into account; criminology was almost exclusively the study of male criminality. As Kathryn Chadwick and Catherine Little[1] point out, the contrasting social worlds and experiences of men and women were not analysed; as a result, criminology failed to address the different criminal careers of women and the different treatment they received from the criminal justice system.

Women have not, however, been rendered totally invisible within traditional criminology. Women were included in some early criminological theories (see for example, those of Lombroso[2]), but these theories relied on sex-stereotyped physiological and psychological explanations of their criminal activities. In short, women's criminality was determined by their inherent nature – their biology and physiology (particularly their sexuality), to the exclusion of social and economic factors. This emphasis has persisted, despite a shift in explanations of male criminality from biological and psychological factors towards social, economic and environmental factors. Furthermore, as Carol Smart points out,[3] this emphasis has had long-term and harmful effects on both the study of female crime and the treatment of female offenders. She goes on to argue that one consequence has been inappropriate and expensive facilities for female offenders in penal establishments, which perpetuate and reinforce the typical feminine role.

Another trend in traditional criminology which is worth noting is the dichotomy between 'good' and 'bad' women. The distinction is drawn between those women who conform to society's prescribed feminine role and adhere to the moral and social code, and those who deviate from that role by contravening the social or moral code, and are thus labelled as deviant.

Traditional criminology's lack of reference to female crime may not at first sight seem surprising when you look at the criminal statistics. They show that over long periods of time, in many different countries, women consistently have a much lower crime rate than men, so that women have traditionally been seen as law-abiding. The statistics for the number and types of crime committed by women make it easy to dismiss its incidence as unproblematic and not worthy of study, as crimes committed by men are much more numerous and of a more serious nature and are, therefore, perceived as a greater social problem. However, the importance of this disparity between male and female criminal participation rates for criminology as a whole cannot be underestimated. The important questions that must be addressed are: Why is there such a huge disparity in criminal participation rates for men and women? What differences are there between men and women that result in this disparity? As I mentioned above, criminology – historically, at least – has been the search for the cause(s) of crime. This endeavour has been rather fruitless to date: no one factor or group of factors has been conclusively identified as a cause of crime. Some mileage may be gained, however, by focusing on the reasons for women's relatively low criminal participation rate. Frances Heidensohn discusses these points in greater depth in Reading 9.1.

Gender seems, therefore, to be an important – if not the most important – predictor of criminal involvement. In Reading 9.2 Heidensohn analyses why criminology has ignored this fact.

In Reading 9.3, Pat Carlen provides a summary of the major areas within criminology that have been focused upon; she describes them as 'contributing to a demolition of certain sexist myths concerning women's lawbreaking and calling into question the more discriminatory and oppressive forms of social control and regulation of women'.[4]

Although gender has become firmly established as an integral part of criminology this exercise has not been without its own problems. In Reading 9.4 Jeanne Gregory discusses one of the problems that has arisen: focusing on women's involvement in crime has highlighted the issue and given rise to the 'liberation thesis'. This asserts that the growth of the women's movement and the perceived liberation of women is linked to the increasing level of female crime. The liberation thesis assumes that 'as women acquire the same legal rights as men they will cast off their chains ... and commit crimes like men'.[5]

Another potentially harmful debate has been the dispute over whether we should talk about feminist criminology or feminist criminologies. Lorraine Gelsthorpe and Alison Morris[6] argue that this debate is of no importance and deflects from the task in hand: 'remedying the wrongs done to women criminals by criminologists, police, courts and prisons'.[7] However, the more fundamental debate over whether there should be a distinct feminist criminology at all raises important issues. Firstly, the danger of the creation of an academic ghetto where the work that has been undertaken to put women on the agenda has little or no impact on mainstream criminology. Secondly, gender is only one of the multiplicity of factors affecting individuals within society, and the study of women and crime must draw on issues that have been raised outside feminism, particularly in relation to class divisions and race, otherwise there is a danger that the interrelationships between these factors may be ignored. This issue is explored further by Pat Carlen in Reading 9.5.

In the space available, it is impossible to do justice to the contributions that have been made to criminology in general and theoretical criminology in particular by the inclusion of feminist ideas. This task is made more difficult by the fact that neither criminology nor feminism is a homogeneous discipline; both encompass a broad spectrum of perspectives. The exercise of including women on the criminological agenda is still in the relatively early stages of development. In Readings 9.6 to 9.10, however, I have tried to represent the main directions that are being pursued.

Notes

1. K. Chadwick and C. Little, 'The criminalization of women', in P. Scraton, *Law, Order and the Authoritarian State*, Milton Keynes: Open University Press, 1987, pp. 255–78.
2. Cesare Lombroso (1836–1909).
3. C. Smart, *Women, Crime and Criminology*, London: Routledge & Kegan Paul, 1976.
4. P. Carlen, 'Women, crime, feminism and realism', *Social Justice*, vol. 17, no. 4 (1990), pp. 107–8.
5. P. Carlen, *Criminal Women*, Oxford: Polity, 1985, p. 6.
6. L. Gelsthorpe and A. Morris (eds), *Feminist Perspectives in Criminology*, Milton Keynes: Open University Press, 1990.
7. P. Carlen, 'Women, crime, feminism and realism', p. 107.

9.1 Crime and Society

Frances Heidensohn

Frances Heidensohn analyses the criminal statistics to argue that gender should be an important – if not the most important – consideration in the pursuit of the causes of crime.

The incidence of recorded crime is strongly linked to sex and to age. So are the rates of self-reported crime and of victim- or observer-recorded offences. All strongly suggest that crime is an activity carried out by young, and young adult, males. Sex crime ratios (that is, the proportions of men and women offending) vary by offence, but of convictions for serious offences in England and Wales in recent years, over 80 per cent have been of males. Shoplifting, often thought of as a 'typically' female crime, is one of which more males than females are convicted in Britain. The most dramatic differences, however, occur in more serious crimes such as robbery, and in recidivism rates. Women tend to commit less serious crimes and to do so less often. In consequence, there are far fewer women and girls in custody than there are males: of an incarcerated population of nearly 50,000 in Britain, fewer than 1,500 are female. This pattern, while it varies somewhat over time and place, is remarkably stable. In the USA, as in England and Wales, about 80 per cent of court referrals of delinquency cases are of boys,[1] and a survey showed that males constituted 97 per cent of all inmates in state correctional institutions – a proportion very close to that in Britain.

Figures from other countries, although they always have to be treated carefully and critically, are consistent with male predominance in crime. They vary only in the degree of that predominance. In India and in Sri Lanka in the 1970s, males made up over 95 per cent of convicted offenders, whereas the male share in many Western countries is closer to 80 per cent.[2] While the female share of criminality has risen slightly in some Western countries in the later twentieth century, this share is still very small.

Attempts to correct this apparently stubbornly stable ratio in recorded crimes by revealing the hidden and secret crimes of women have not been successful. Self-report studies, victim surveys, observational and other studies tend broadly to confirm the picture of crime as a largely male activity.[3] Many critics of criminal records have, of course, pointed out that they are not just an *inadequate* and *incomplete* account of all criminal activity, much of which must inevitably remain unobserved and uncounted. They are also fundamentally flawed, since they mark police (and public) concern with only certain kinds of deviant acts or actors and not others. Armed robberies, which may net only hundreds of pounds, are carefully logged, publicised and pursued. Perpetrators are given long sentences, as are purveyors of illicit drugs. Yet these, it can be argued, are the crimes of the poor and the powerless. Depredations wrought by white-collar criminals – huge embezzlements, elaborate computer frauds, etc. – are often concealed or only lightly punished.[4] Undoubtedly, corporate crime is literally big business today, and criminal law is selectively shaped and selectively enforced. Exposing these sections of the submerged 'iceberg' of crime would not, however, increase women's contribution to recorded criminality. On the contrary, as Box points out, if anything, it would *reduce* their share, since they play little or no part in the hierarchy of organised crime syndicates, nor indeed in the higher echelons of finance where such coups are possible.

One further point about concealed crime needs to be made at this point. There is little or no evidence of a vast shadowy underworld of female deviance hidden in our midst like the sewers below the city streets. As we have become increasingly aware in modern times, quite the opposite is true. There is a great deal of crime which is carefully hidden from the police, from families, friends and neighbours. Much of this takes the form of domestic violence, the abuse of children both physically and sexually, incest and marital rape. The overwhelming majority of such cases involve men, usually fathers, and husbands injuring or abusing their wives and children. As Young puts it:

> professional criminals engaged in violent crime [are] a quantitatively minor problem when compared to domestic violence ... the one most likely to commit violence is the man of the house against his wife.[5]

Mothers do harm their own children and sometimes even collude in their sexual abuse: nevertheless, 'private' crime seems to be even more male-dominated than public street crime. No doubt this is because it is so crucial to male dominance (Stanko, 1984; Walby, 1986). Among the observations made when criminal records were first kept was that women were far less criminal than men This is still true. As a classic text has it:

> Sex status is of greater statistical significance in differentiating criminals from non-criminals than any other trait. If you were asked to use a single trait to predict which children in a town of 10,000 people would become criminals, you would make fewer mistakes if you chose sex status as the trait and predicted criminality for the males and non-criminality for the females.[6]

Sex is therefore a crucial variable – indeed, *the* crucial variable – in predicting criminality. You might expect, then, that students of crime, its causes, consequences and remedies, would have used this observation frequently in their work of explaining criminality; that it provides an obvious touchstone for all theories of criminal behaviour, a vital litmus test for the validity and reliability of all types of studies; that the remarkable conformity of females, as well as the sex differences, would stimulate considerable research. You might reasonably suppose these things but, at least until the late 1960s, you would have been wrong. Some attention had been paid to sex differences in recorded crime during the twentieth century, but it was slight, intermittent and profoundly unilluminating.

Notes

1. D. R. Cressey and E. H. Sutherland, *Criminology* (10th edn), Philadelphia, PA: Lippincott, 1978, p. 130.
2. *Ibid.*, p. 131.
3. F. Heidensohn, *Women and Crime*, London: Macmillan, 1985, ch. 1.
4. S. Box, *Power, Crime and Mystification*, London: Tavistock, 1983.
5. J. Young, 'The failure of criminology: the need for a radical realism', in R. Matthews and J. Young (eds), *Confronting Crime*, London: Sage, 1986, p. 22.
6. Cressey and Sutherland, *Criminology*, p. 130.

9.2   **Women and Crime**

Frances Heidensohn

Frances Heidensohn argues that there are four important reasons for the invisibility of gender in traditional criminology.

[...] First there is the delinquent machismo tradition in criminology which has treated male working-class delinquency as heroic and romantic; Thrasher and Whyte were early examples, but the tendency is clear in subcultural theory and is shared too in the 'new' sociology of deviance which often becomes 'a *celebration* rather than an analysis of the deviant form with which the deviant theorist could *vicariously identify* – an identification by *powerless intellectuals* with deviants who appeared *more successful* in controlling events'.[1] For Stan Cohen there is 'obvious fascination with these spectacular subcultures'.[2] Morgan, not himself a sociologist of deviance, catches the 'image of the male sociologist bringing back news from the fringes of society, the lower depths, the mean streets, areas traditionally off limits to women investigators'.[3] In short, it seems that the 'college boys' became fascinated by the 'corner boys'.

One cannot possibly criticise a perfectly legitimate intellectual interest of this kind. What is of concern to feminist social scientists is the second 'strand' in this particular pattern, that of male dominance in academic life. Oakley distinguished three crucial aspects of the male hegemony found in sociology.[4] These are first the 'founding *fathers*' origins of the discipline, with their emphasis on male interests; second, the numerical and hierarchical preponderence of men in the academic profession, especially at the top; and finally she referred to what she called the 'ideology of gender': a value system which involves constructing reality in sexually stereotyped ways – looking at delinquent boys and away from girls. As Oakley puts it: 'a way of seeing is a way of not seeing'. Thus at least until recently, it has been quite acceptable to study certain topics and not others and, more crucially, to present that viewpoint as the only or the total perspective. Whyte, for example, called his book *Street Corner Society*,[5] suggesting a fuller view than the study contained. With the exception of Cohen's *Delinquent Boys*,[6] nearly every major work which deals with crime and delinquency is exclusively about males but implies a wider relevance – *Outsiders, The Other Side, Delinquency and Drift, Becoming Deviant, The Delinquent Solution, The Gang*, and so on.

There were also, I believe, important situational factors which were peculiar to the study of crime. Girls and women do undoubtedly have lower recorded crime rates. Moreover, their official delinquencies tend to be of a relatively minor kind, lacking social threat and damaging their nearest and dearest rather than society at large.[7] Female crime has therefore had a low public profile; it has not seemed to be an acute social problem, needing solution, for which research funds might be forthcoming and upon which careers might be built. From the researcher's point of view these features have also meant that girl subjects have been more elusive, more thinly scattered; girls are located elsewhere than on the street corners or in the gangs. They are 'negotiating a difference space', and this seems to be characterised by its privacy, as McRobbie and Garber feelingly put it:

> Girl culture ... is so well insulated as to operate to effectively exclude not only other 'undesirable' girls – but also boys, adults, teachers and researchers.[8]

Perhaps the most crucial factor explaining the Cinderella role which females played for so long in criminology concerns the central theories of the discipline. Most recent accounts of research on sex differences rightly stress that, on most measures, men and women are more alike than unlike in their behaviour.[9] But recorded criminal behaviour remains – certain changes notwithstanding – a stubborn exception to this rule. Ironically, self-report studies which were originally seen as providing a truer picture of participation in crime on the whole confirm the sex differential.[10] For every hundred males convicted of serious offences there are only eighteen females so convicted. Age and sex remain the best predictors for crime and delinquency – better than class, race or employment status. It follows that any adequate theory of crime and delinquency must include an explanation of sex differences in crime rates. Most theorists take the sex differential for granted and do not develop adequate analysis. Thus theorists who locate crime causation in the social environment of the city, the structure of the society or the interaction process between public, police, courts and offenders need to make clear why these factors operate so much more effectively on males than females.

I believe they did not do so because they were able (as I have tried to show) to pursue an exclusive interest in male criminality in a comfortable world of academic machismo. There was for a long time no intellectual critique of this approach nor any strong social pressure because of political issues. Feminist criticisms of academic sexism were almost unheard of before the late 1960s. Theories of sex roles and sexual divisions were little more than assertions of stereotypes. Including the gender dimension, then, would have been uncongenial to masculinist scholars and could seriously have undermined key approaches:

> Sexist domain assumptions, in whatever specialized field of enquiry, do have consequences for the outcome of investigations and in many cases the final outcome would have been very different had the investigation taken account of questions of gender.[11]

Moreover, the theoretical tools were lacking. [...] To understand female criminality fully we have to turn not to the formulations of sociologists of deviance but to the understanding of the control and oppression of women in family, work and public space which feminist analysis offer us. [...]

[...] I have tried to show that both the paradigms of deviant behaviour and the methods of study of modern sociologists led to the exclusion of women as a central topic. Choice clearly played its part, as is strikingly shown in the romanticisation and celebration of young male delinquents. Women are but shadows in these accounts, but they are vital shadows. Their social roles and positions are essential to all these explanations of crime, since these depend on assumptions about 'masculine' and 'feminine' behaviour, on the nature of the family and women's role in it and even on variations on the Victorian doctrine of separate spheres for men and women. Where female deviance is discussed within a sociological framework it is only, and most significantly, prostitution which is examined. What is so striking about all these accounts is how little they examine the assumptions about sex and gender on which they base so much theorising. Definitions of deviance and normality may be problematic, as are the processes by which these definitions occur, but definitions of male and female, masculine and feminine are not challenged or examined. Within these terms female crime could simply not be studied nor understood. [...]

Notes

1. I. Taylor *et al.*, *Critical Criminology*, London: Routledge & Kegan Paul, 1975, emphasis added.
2. S. Cohen, *Folk Devils and Moral Panics*, Oxford: Martin Robertson, 1980.
3. D. Morgan, 'Men, masculinity and the process of sociological enquiry', in H. Roberts (ed.), *Doing Feminist Research*, London: Routledge & Kegan Paul, 1981, p. 87.
4. A. Oakley, *Subject Women*, Oxford: Martin Robertson, 1981.
5. W. F. Whyte, *Street Corner Society*, 2nd edn, Chicago: University of Chicago Press, 1955.
6. A. K. Cohen, *Delinquent Boys*, London: Free Press, 1955.
7. F. Heidensohn, 'Sex, crime and society', in G. A. Harrison (ed.), *Biosocial Aspects of Sex*, Oxford: Basil Blackwell, 1970.
8. A. McRobbie and J. Garber, 'Girls and subcultures', in S. Hall and T. Jefferson (eds), *Resistance through Ritual*, London: Hutchinson, 1976.
9. E. Maccoby and C. Jacklin, *The Psychology of Sex Differences*, Stanford, CA: Stanford University Press, 1974; J. Nicholson, J. *Men and Women*, Oxford: Oxford University Press, 1984.
10. D. A. Smith and A. C. Visher, (1980) 'Sex and involvement in deviance/crime: a quantitative literature of the empirical literature', *American Sociology Review*, vol. 45.
11. D. Morgan, 'Men, masculinity and the process of sociological enquiry', p. 87.

9.3   Women, Crime, Feminism and Realism
Pat Carlen

Pat Carlen describes the major areas of the work that has so far been undertaken to include gender in criminology.

One of the first concerns of the new wave of writers on women and crime was to put 'women' on the criminological agenda, to demonstrate that most previous explanations of crime had in fact been explanations of *male* crime, and to argue that when women break the law they do so in circumstances that are often very different from those in which men become lawbreakers.[1] A constant theme in these analyses has been that women's crimes are pre-eminently the crimes of the powerless.[2]

A second concern has been to demonstrate how essentialized and sexualized typifications of womanhood, gender, and femininity have fashioned not only criminological explanations of women's lawbreaking, but also the treatment of deviant women by the welfare, criminal justice, and penal systems.[3]

Third, some writers have joined with campaigning organizations and/or women ex-prisoners to campaign for a better deal for women in trouble, before the courts, or in prison[4] and some of these latter have not disdained an explicit policy orientation.[5]

Finally, some writers (usually, but not always, explicitly eschewing empirical and policy-orientated work altogether) have been concerned to debate (variously): (1) whether the development of a feminist criminology is a possible theoretical project;[6] (2) whether the focus on women lawbreakers is a 'proper' concern of 'feminism';[7] and (3) the desirability (or not) of a feminist jurisprudence.[8] [...]

Notes

1. A. McRobbie and J. Garber, 'Girls and subcultures', in S. Hall and T. Jefferson (eds), *Resistance through Ritual*, London: Hutchinson, 1976.
2. S. Box, *Power, Crime and Mystification*, London: Tavistock, 1983; J. Messerschmidt, *Capitalism, Patriarchy and Crime: towards a socialist feminist criminology*, Totowa, NJ: Rowan & Littlefied, 1986; P. Carlen, *Women, Crime and Poverty*, Milton Keynes: Open University Press, 1988.
3. P. Carlen, *Women's Imprisonment: A study in social control*, London: Routledge & Kegan Paul, 1983; S. Edwards, *Women on Trial*, Manchester: Manchester University Press, 1984; M. Eaton, *Justice for Women?*, Milton Keynes: Open University Press, 1986; A. Worrall, *Offending Women*, London: Routledge & Kegan Paul, 1990.
4. P. Carlen, *Criminal Women*, Cambridge: Polity, 1985; N. Seear and E. Player, *Women in the Penal System*, London: Howard League for Penal Reform, 1986; U. Padell and P. Stevenson, *Insiders*, London: Virago, 1988; S. Casale, *Women Inside*, London: Civil Liberties Trust, 1989.
5. Seear and Player, *Women in the Penal System*; Carlen, *Women, Crime and Poverty*; P. Carlen, *Alternatives to Women's Imprisonment*, Milton Keynes: Open University Press, 1990; Casale, *Women Inside*.
6. M. Cousins, 'Men's rea: a note on sexual difference, criminology and the law', in P. Carlen and M. Collinson (eds), *Radical Issues in Criminology*, Oxford: Martin Robertson, 1980; Carlen, *Criminal Women*.
7. J. Allen, 'The masculinity of criminality and criminology: interrogating some impasses', in M. Findley and R. Hogg (eds), *Understanding Crime and Criminal Justice*,

Sydney: The Law Book Company, 1988, pp. 1–23; C. Smart, 'Review of *Women, Crime and Poverty*, by Pat Carlen', *Journal of Law and Society*, vol. 16, no. 4 (1990), pp. 521–4.
8. C. MacKinnon 'Feminism, Marxism, method and the state: toward feminist jurisprudence', in S. Harding (ed.), *Feminism and Methodology*, Milton Keynes: Open University Press, 1987; C. Smart, *Feminism and the Power of the Law*, London: Routledge & Kegan Paul, 1989.

9.4   **Sex, Class and Crime**

Jeanne Gregory

Jeanne Gregory argues that the 'liberation thesis' has no statistical or theoretical basis, and can therefore be dismissed as a moral panic.

Carol Smart, in launching her attack on criminology for neglecting women, recognized the danger that if the question of female crime became a visible instead of an invisible social problem, a moral panic might well ensue.[1] If the media became sensitized to a new issue, an escalation of reports of female crime could well result in an increased diligence on the part of law enforcement agencies which would in turn appear in the statistics as a rise in the rate of female crime. Criminal activity is then equated with liberation and the women's movement is blamed for the growth in female crime, along with the increase in divorce rates and the incidence of female lung cancer. Freda Adler falls into precisely this trap when she writes of the phenomenon of female criminality as 'but one wave in [the] rising tide of female assertiveness' and claims that crimes of violence are for women increasing at rates six or seven times as great as those for men.[2] These staggering claims have prompted a response from various quarters, so that just about every statement on which the thesis is based has been discredited. To begin with, the assumption that liberation is an accomplished fact of women's lives is challenged by demonstrating the extent to which the male monopoly of social economic power persists.[3] More specifically, the women who commit crimes can in no sense be regarded as liberated.[4] It cannot be denied that female crime rates are rising, but as the initial figures are small, quite small numerical increases will seem large when expressed in percentage terms.[5] Far from providing proof of liberation, these increases can be understood as a response to deteriorating economic conditions, as they occur mainly in non-occupational areas such as welfare fraud and minor property offences. Contrary to Adler's claims, women have not made a major entry into the masculine world of violent crime; the male rate in these areas continues to rise faster than the female rate.[6] As Steven Box argues, sex-role stereotyping still prevails in the world of organized crime, which could hardly be described as an equal opportunity employer![7] Women continue to play subordinate roles in the world of crime as much as in the legitimate world of business.

Notes

1. C. Smart, *Women, Crime and Criminology*, London: Routledge & Kegan Paul, 1976, p. xiv.
2. F. Adler, *Sisters in Crime*, New York: McGraw-Hill, 1975.
3. E. B. Leonard, *Women, Crime and Society*, Harlow: Longman, 1982; L. Crites (ed.), *The Female Offender*, Lexington: D. C. Heath, 1976.
4. J. G. Weis, 'Liberation and crime: the invention of the new female criminal', *Crime and Social Justice*, 6 (1976), pp. 17–21.
5. C. Smart, 'The new female criminal: reality or myth?', *British Journal of Criminology*, vol. 19, no. 1 (1979), pp. 50–59; S. A. Mukherjee and R. W. Fitzgerald, 'The myth of rising female crime', in S. A. Mukherjee and A. Scutt (eds), *Women and Crime*, Australian Institute of Criminology in Association with George Allen & Unwin, 1982.
6. D. J. and R. H. Steffensmeier, 'Trends in female delinquency', *Criminology*, 18 (1980); Mukherjee and Fitzgerald, 'The myth of rising female crime'.
7. S. Box, *Power, Crime and Mystification*, London: Tavistock, 1983, ch. 5.

9.5 Criminal Women and Criminal Justice: the limits to, and potential of, feminist and left realist perspectives
Pat Carlen

Pat Carlen describes and evaluates the debate over whether feminist criminology is 'desirable or possible'.

[...] I find it difficult to attribute any meaning to the term 'feminist criminology' which would be either desirable or possible. It would not be *desirable* because any universalizing theories of a taken-for-granted criminality inherring in biological female subjects must be as reductionist and essentializing as the much maligned biological ones. It is not possible for three reasons. First, present knowledge about criminal women and criminal justice has not developed via explanatory concepts which could be called distinctly 'feminist' – unless one counts as explanatory the usually descriptive use of the word 'patriarchy';[1] secondly, once the historically and socially specific discourses and practices within which women's lawbreaking and criminalization occur in Britain, the United States, Canada and Australia are investigated, a concern with gender constructions rapidly merges with questions concerning class, racism and imperialism. Thirdly, no single theory (feminist or otherwise) can adequately explain three major features of women's lawbreaking and imprisonment: that women's crimes are, in the main, the crimes of the powerless; that women in prison are disproportionately from ethnic minority groups; and that a majority of women in prison have been in poverty for the greater part of their lives.

Yet although I do not believe that a 'feminist criminology' is either desirable or possible, I take issue with writers who (ironically, given the overall thrust of their writing) do not believe that feminists should study 'women and crime' at all. Two major arguments are advanced by such writers: one I call 'anti-criminology', the other 'deconstructionalist libertarian'.

The anti-criminology position on women and crime argues against the discipline of 'criminology' *per se*. It implies that specification of empirical referents at the outset of an enquiry must inevitably entail investigations forever trapped in essentialist categories obstructing the production of new knowledge.[2] This is not such a new insight as anti-criminologists and deconstructionists have claimed. It was an awareness that the empirical referents of social scientific discourses are already endowed with more taken-for-granted and ideological meanings that always-already have discursive effects than are discourses in the physical sciences that led earlier sociologists to develop the notorious 'sociological jargon' (or 'sociologese') so particularly sneered at by their traditionalist opponents.

Yet deconstructionists have access to modes of thought which should diminish the radical theorist's perennial fear of the ideological power of the empirical referent. In particular they can adopt the methodological protocol of Bachelard[3] that systems of thought must say 'No' to their own conventions and conditions of existence. Additionally, they can take comfort from Saussurian linguistics, which demonstrate that individual words themselves have no essential meaning but only acquire meaning with syntagma which through differentiation assign the value of a specific sign. If then, in taking the assumptions of Bachelard and Saussure[4] as prescriptive and working on the contradiction that the already-known has to be both recognized and denied, deconstructionists use a 'bricolage' of concepts from other disciplines,[5] there is no reason why they should not *both* take seriously (that is, recognize) *and* deny the empirical referent's material and ideological effects.[6] Thereafter whether such investigations are pursued under the political sign of 'feminism' or the academic sign of 'criminology' is important only in so far as such signifiers provide the author with a support group or a salary! From a deconstructionist perspective labels such as 'feminist', 'criminological' (or 'left realist') are irrelevant; none can guarantee the 'truth' of the arguments.

The 'deconstructionist libertarian' stance on 'women and crime' is one sometimes implicit (though not always held to[7]) in the work of Carol Smart.[8] It implies a denial that a reduction in women's crime is a proper concern of criminologists and that therefore criminologists should not seek to justify policy proposals on the grounds that they might help criminal women keep out of trouble in future. (Though according to Allen,[9] who on this takes a line similar to Smart's it's OK to seek to reduce *men's* lawbreaking!) This is a position very close to that which Jock Young[10] has called 'left idealist', and together with the 'anti-criminology' reluctance to engage with the empirical reality of women's lawbreaking and criminalization, could result in policy on 'women and crime' being abandoned either to what Smart[11] has referred to as the 'macho left' (realists?) or to the realists of the right. To my mind, neither alternative would be acceptable.

Notes

1. M. Cousins, 'Material arguments and feminism', m/f, no. 2 (1978).
2. M. Cousins, 'Men's rea: a note on sexual difference, criminology and the law', in P. Carlen and M. Collinson (eds), *Radical Issues in Criminology*, Oxford: Martin Robertson, 1980; B. Brown, 'Women and crime: the dark figures of criminology', *Economy and Society*, vol. 15, no. 3 (1986), pp. 355–402; J. Allen, 'The masculinity of criminality and criminology: interrogating some impasses', in M. Findley and R. Hogg (eds), *Understanding Crime and Criminal Justice*, Sydney: The Law Book Company, 1988; M. Cain, *Growing Up Good*, London: Sage, 1989; 'Towards transgression: new directions in feminist criminology', *International Journal of the Sociology of Law*, vol. 18, no. 1 (1990), pp. 1–18.
3. G. Bachelard, *The Philosophy of No* (transl. G. L. Waterson), London: Orion Press, 1940.
4. F. Saussure, *Course in General Linguistics*, London: Fontana, 1974.
5. J. Derrida, *Of Grammatology* (transl. G. C. Spivak), London: Johns Hopkins University Press, 1976.
6. F. Burton and P. Carlen, *Official Discourse*, London: Routledge & Kegan Paul, 1979.
7. C. Smart, *Feminism and the Power of the Law*, London: Routledge & Kegan Paul, 1989.
8. C. Smart, 'Feminist approaches to criminology, or postmodern women meet atavistic man', in L. Gelsthorpe and A. Morris (eds), *Feminist Perspectives in Criminology*, Milton Keynes: Open University Press, 1990.
9. J. Allen, 'The masculinity of criminality and criminology'.
10. J. Young, (1986) 'The failure of criminology: the need for a radical realism', in R. Matthews and J. Young (eds) (1986) *Confronting Crime*, London: Sage.
11. C. Smart, 'Review of *Women, Crime and Poverty* by Pat Carlen', *Journal of Law and Society*, vol. 16, no. 4 (1990), pp. 521–4.

9.6   Sex, Class and Crime

Jeanne Gregory

Jeanne Gregory critically discusses the contrasting directions that have been taken by different branches of feminism within criminology.

Within feminist criminology, there is a tendency for the three strands of feminism to become entangled; although the critique of existing theories and policies is clearly articulated, the way forward often remains obscure. Bourgeois feminists are the easiest to identify; they have drawn attention to the denial of civil liberties that occurs within the criminal justice system whenever those who come under its scrutiny are treated differently on the basis of sex. Their goal is sexual equality (women catching up with men); their strategy is to eliminate sexual ideology from the legal system. For American feminists, the campaign for the Equal Rights Amendment provided the focal point of this strategy for a number of years.[1] The failure of this campaign was a severe setback for the equal rights lobby. It also reduced the chances that the long-term limitations of its strategy would be recognized. Erasing sexual ideology from the legal system becomes a symbolic gesture unless we simultaneously attack the structural inqualities that underpin this ideology. Catching up with the men is a vital first step but it should be the beginning and not the final goal of the political struggle. Gains secured under the equal rights banner are inherently fragile as individuals or groups with competing rights claim equal legitimacy. A woman's right to choose an abortion is challenged in terms of the rights of the unborn foetus. Father compete with mothers for an extension of rights in relation to their children. Such divisions cannot be resolved within the framework of competitive individualism that capitalism breeds.[2]

Although radical feminists are more strident in their critique of the existing political and economic system than bourgeois feminists, their analysis is even more divisive in its implications. Their major intervention in criminology is on the issue of how to protect women from the more extreme manifestations of male power, particularly domestic violence, rape and pornography. Several thoughtful and well-documented studies in these areas provide a vivid demonstration of the ways in which men oppress women and also reveal the deeply entrenched sexual bias exhibited at all stages of the law enforcement process. The radical feminist interpretation of this evidence is unequivocal: extreme forms of abuse merit an extreme response. The writers of the studies themselves, although they are by no means unanimous in their conclusions and would by and large resist the radical feminist label, also lean heavily towards the introduction of more punitive measures against the perpetrators of these particular crimes.[3] It is impossible to resolve this dilemma without relocating the issue of what to do about violent men within the general debate about penal policy. Radical feminists have no interest in such an enterprise. Their analysis of crime is partial and often reactionary; if the criminal justice system is merely an expression of patriarchal power and nothing else, then men cannot be oppressed by it. A feminist criminology informed by radical feminism would simply replace the sex-blindness of Marxism with its own class-blindness.

A socialist-feminist criminology would seek to avoid the pitfalls of both Marxist and feminist criminology by combining the insights of both. At the theoretical level, the obstacles that confront such an enterprise often seem insurmountable; capitalism and patriarchy are presented as two competing and mutually exclusive frames of reference. At the substantive level, however, the prospect becomes less daunting. The difficulties begin to recede as the analysis uncovers the ways in which men and women are both oppressed by gender and class relations. Once this is recognized, an analysis of one without the other becomes unthinkable. For example, the ways in which poor, black women are treated within the criminal justice system can only be fully understood in terms of the material and ideological realities of both class and gender.[4]

Notes

1. See, for example, M. Eastwood, 'The double standard of American justice', *Valparaise University Law Review*, vol. 5, no. 2 (1971); C. E. Temin, 'Discriminatory sentencing of women offenders: the arguments for E.R.A. in a nutshell', *American Criminal Law Review*, vol. 11, no. 2 (1973); L. Frankel, 'Sex discrimination in the criminal law: the effect of the Equal Rights Amendment', *American Law Review*, vol. 11, no. 2 (1973); Symposium in the *Harvard Law Review*, March 1971.

　　The proposed Equal Rights Amendment stated: 'Equality of rights under the law shall not be denied or abridged by the United States or by any state on the account of sex.' It was approved by Senate in 1972 but failed to obtained the necessary ratification by individual states, despite an extension of the time limit (thirty-five states ratified the amendment, three short of the required number).
2. M. Cousins, 'Men's rea: a note on sexual difference, criminology and the law', in P. Carlen and M. Collinson (eds), *Radical Issues in Criminology*, Oxford: Martin Robertson, 1980; J. Eekelaar, *Family Law and Social Policy*, London: Weidenfeld & Nicholson, 1978; A. Bottomley *et al.*, *The Cohabitation Handbook*, London: Pluto, 1984.
3. A. Dworkin, *Pornography: Men possessing women*, London: The Women's Press, 1981; S. Griffin, *Pornography and Silence*, London: The Women's Press, 1981.
4. H. M. Hacker, 'Class and race: differences in gender roles', in L. Duberman (ed.), *Gender and Sex in Society*, New York: Praeger, 1975; D. Klein and J. Kress, 'Any women's blues: a critical overview of women, crime and the criminal justice system', *Crime and Social Justice*, 5 (1976), pp. 34–47; J. Young, 'Thinking seriously about crime', in M. Fitzgerald *et al.*, *Crime and Society: Readings in history and theory*, London: Routledge & Kegan Paul, 1980; J. Box-Grainger, 'Sentencing rapists', in R. Matthews and J. Young (1986), op. cit.

9.7　**The Criminalization of Women**
Kathryn Chadwick and Catherine Little

Kathryn Chadwick and Catherine Little argue that to understand the criminalisation of women we must study its social, economic and political context, focusing particularly on the power relations that exist within society.

It is the criminalization of women's behaviour, and in particular the perceived sexuality of women, which will be our focus. Although our overall analysis will be from a feminist perspective the analysis incorporates themes first developed within the labelling perspective, in terms of the defining of behaviour and criminalization, and from within earlier critical criminology, in terms of the significance of social, political, economic and ideological contexts and constructions. Through the feminist critique we challenge the traditional academic and common-sense biological assumptions about the natural role of women as mothers and carers. Dorothy Smith[1] and Carol Smart[2] refer to this as the 'reconstruction of patriarchal ideologies' around women. A negative picture, very often related to their biologies, has always been painted of women, and feminist criminology sets out to replace these negative patriarchal ideologies with research that locates the issues into a wider structural context. This means considering women not only in relation to the family, but also in relation to the state and criminal justice process. This raises further the issue of the impact of patriarchal ideologies, and their institutionalized presence within the criminal justice process, on women's lives.

Following on from a theoretical analysis of the process of criminalization, beginning with the work of labelling theorists through to more recent debates within critical criminology, we consider how the social control of women leads to state control,[3] thus consolidating the process by which women are criminalized. Also, it is important to consider the position of women in relation to the nuclear family and the relationship between women's paid and unpaid work and the function of domestic work in the home, as the economic marginalization of women is also central to criminalization [...].

The process of criminalization

Hall and Scraton[4] define the process of criminalization as 'the application of the criminal label to a particular social category'. Derived from the work of social interactionists such as Becker and Lemert,[5] an act is not perceived as a crime until it has been defined as such. The significant areas of debate within this process focus on: how certain acts are labelled, who has the power to label, and how police and judicial control is legitimated as the application of justice within the criminal justice process. Where the analysis has moved beyond the formative work of social interactionists is in its critical and rigorous examination of the construction and significance of the 'power of the definers'.[6] It has achieved this objective by locating political, economic and patriarchal relations as central to an analysis of the rule of law and the process by which certain behaviours become criminalized.

Theoretically, then, the process of criminalization has its roots in the labelling perspective which focused on the social construction of crime as a means of 'social control'. In contrast critical criminologists have adopted the concept of 'state control',[7] suggesting that criminal labels were applied not only to activities perceived as illegal by the majority but, more importantly, to activities which are identified as being threatening to the political stability and established order of the state.

The criminalization of specific acts, then, not only legitimates the control of such activities within the criminal justice process, but also captures the consent of the people who are more likely to support state action against political or social movements linked to criminal activities. Evidence to support this can be found in three recent examples. First, the criminalization of those involved in recent industrial disputes such as the 1984–5 coal dispute and the 1986–7 print workers' dispute at Wapping, both of which have been portrayed as constituting a violent threat to democracy and the maintenance of law and order.[8] Secondly, in June 1985, the police response to the Peace Convoy which was perceived as a threat to established family life and conventional forms of living.[9] Finally the Greenham women are portrayed as having stepped outside and rejected the role ascribed to all women: the 'natural' role in which domesticity, femininity, sexuality, housewifery and caring are central.[10] Like so many groups of women in similar situations, asserting their independence from male control threatens the established order of patriarchal relations within society.[11]

As Hall and Scraton state:

> Some criminal groups have sometimes been singled out by the media and treated repressively for social and political reasons. Though it is their crimes which appear to attract attention, they may in fact, be the victims of wider attitudes of social hostility, which find a conveniently displaced expression through the focusing on the criminal aspect.[12]

What recent critical research in criminology has shown is that the process of criminalization, a process by which political acts can be redefined as unlawful, is used to protect and reinforce the interests of an established order, be they primarily political or economic. The process is intricate, as not only does it demand state institutional responses from the police, the courts, the mental institutions and the prisons, it also relies on the winning of popular consent for state policies and legal shifts which are essentially authoritarian.[13] The role of the media in the creation of social and political concern, the most extreme form being that of 'moral panics',[14] is central to this process. Criminalization is a political response to political and social protest – a political response which uses the legal form to regulate and put down social and political unrest. The derivation of this response often lies within inherent economic contradictions, be they related to the processes of advanced capitalism or patriarchy. The state institutional response, however, relies heavily on winning 'hearts and minds' by establishing ideological appeals to popular consent.[15] Political, economic and ideological forces, then, work together to facilitate the criminalization process. It is in relation to popular ideologies of sexism that we prioritize women and social welfare. Using the examples of women who cohabit rather than marry, women who work as prostitutes, and women involved in political protest, we examine the proposal that through sexist ideology the criminalization of women is different to that of men.

The social and state control of women

In order to understand why certain acts are criminalized and, specifically, the way in which women are treated and regulated by state power, it is important to consider the broader contexts in which women and women's behaviour is socially defined and controlled. Recent feminist research shows overwhelmingly that gender divisions and women's regulation begin with the process of primary socialization in the family and, secondly, socialization in the peer groups, school and the media.[16] Socialization acts to:

> reinforce the ways of acting, thinking and feeling 'characteristic' of the female role, femininity and womanhood, to the more formal processes of institutional intervention through legislation by the state, the implementation of the law, the penal system and the criminal process.[17]

Smart and Smart state that social control takes many different forms and is evident in both 'public' and 'private' domains. It is acknowledged that certain dimensions of social control relate only to women. These include the reproductive cycle, a double standard of morality, a subordinate and legal status in the family, and the separation of 'home' and 'work' coupled with the ideology of women's place.[18]

It is 'in their place' – in the home with the family – that Jill Radford suggests women are most closely controlled. She states: 'The prime agency for the controlling, watching, supervising, segregating and changing the behaviour of women is the family'.[19] Within the privacy of the traditional nuclear family in patriarchal societies, the authority, dominance and responsibility for this regulation lies with men. Women who move outside 'their place' – into the public sphere – are met with controls and policies. Controls in the public sphere work at two different levels; in the workplace women are constrained and controlled by the types of work available to them and by sexual harassment.[20] Second, women are controlled by their lack of access to social space and recreation, such as in pubs and on the streets.[21] Women's rational fear of abuse, attack and sexual assault controls access to all forms of social space.[22] Likewise, fear of loss of status and reputation relating to respectability and sexuality[23] controls women's responses and opportunities.

This range of controls on women's social and personal lives within and outside the family has many consequences. Clearly it creates isolation, with little confidence and self-esteem. As Mary Eaton suggests,[24] women are so 'effectively controlled by their socialization and the conditions of their existence' that this must be seen as a major factor in explaining why so few women become involved in criminal activities. The regulation and surveillance of young girls' and women's behaviour and movements gives them little opportunity to indulge in criminal activities.[25]

What, however, happens to those women who do not conform to these processes of regulation – women who cohabit rather than enter into the marriage contract; women who are forced into prostitution in order to make a living; women who do not fit into the neat category of white, middle-class respectable heterosexuality; women who exert their independence to fight social and political issues – women who do not fit into the image or the acceptable way of behaviour? Invariably women who do not subscribe to living within the nuclear family or who attempt to exercise control over their own lives are labelled and treated as deviant. In short, they have stepped outside their prescribed role and have challenged 'their' definers, thereby challenging established 'power relations'.

[...] [W]e are concerned with the criminalization of those women who exert control over their own sexual activities and/or their own sexuality. There is a connection between the marginalization of women through their economic dependence and the control of women's sexuality. [...]

Women, the family and work

Given the strength of biological explanations and expectations around sexuality, motherhood and childbirth, the family role and functions prescribed for women not only form a strong economic and ideological construction but permeate throughout state institutions and create the foundations upon which the political management and regulation of women is institutionalized. In advanced capitalist societies, as with other patriarchal societies, the family has developed as an oppressive and constraining institution for women.[26] Women's fundamental function within the family is to reproduce and care for the paid workforce and the future wage-labourers. Beveridge demonstrated that this primary role should be reinforced by the Welfare State. He stated:

> Maternity is the principal object of marriage. The attitude of the housewife to gainful employment outside the home is not and should not be the same as that of a single woman. She has other duties.[27]

Elizabeth Wilson[28] suggests that the Welfare State maintains the regulation of women by creating ideologies of the 'natural'. If women established independence through paid work in the labour market they are inhibited from meeting the demands and expectations of the established nuclear family.[29]

In the justification of these social arrangements a biological determinist argument is inevitable. This ensures that women remain literally housewives. The post-war period provided clear evidence of this position in the policy of returning women back to the home following their brief period in paid employment as part of the 'war effort'. Bowlby's work on maternal deprivation,[30] which reinforced the ideology of women as 'natural' carers because of their reproductive capacity and thus suiting them to domestic duties,[31] was particularly significant at this time. It is important to emphasize the persistence of the notion of 'naturalness'. For it is women's genetic constitution, the existence of the womb, which makes them better carers. That this role might be learned through years of preparation as girls and young women was not part of the appeal to 'common sense'. This position constructs the family as an alternative location to full state welfare provision. It assumes that women as 'natural' carers will look after the aged, the sick, and the disabled under the laudable banner of 'community care'.

Because women are defined in terms of unpaid domestic work within the family they are made financially dependent on men in that the male wage is constructed as a 'family wage'. The principle inherent in social welfare policy is that the man's wage is a family wage and is sufficient to support 'his' wife and 'his' children. Michèle Barrett and Mary McIntosh[32] trace the historical development of the 'family wage' and consider that as capitalism developed women became 'marginalized' in the labour market and children excluded. This forced women to become dependent on men and the 'family-wage'. However, a 'family wage' system never operated effectively in Britain because, with few exceptions, working-class wages have never been adequate in providing for a family. Consequently women have been forced into badly paid, part-time and unprotected work in order to establish a minimum standing of living. It can be seen from a cursory glance at the nineteenth-century provision of poor relief that this societal commitment to the 'male breadwinner' has a long history in the practice and principle of state policy.

The 'family wage' system is based on the 'average typical household' of two parents and two children; yet there are few so-called 'average' households.[33] Further, this system does not account for households in which married women work, or where there is a single woman heading the family. Hilary Land[34] examines this 'myth of the male breadwinner'. She quotes a Minister of State for the Department of Health and Social Security as saying: 'The widespread view is that a husband who is capable of work has a duty to society, as well as to his wife, to provide the primary support for his family.'[35] She indicates that this views the 'wife's' wages as of secondary importance or, as widely described, as 'pin money'. The woman's primary responsibility remains that of domestic work, caring for children, the elderly and disabled. This idea is clearly inherent in welfare policy, where women are seen to be economically inactive.

Clearly, then, the implications for women of state policy and practices are the perpetuation of their financial dependence on men and, consequently, the structural inequalities of patriarchal relations. Despite the 1975 Equal Pay Act and the 1975 Sex Discrimination Act, little has been done effectively to challenge these inequalities.[36]

This is not to argue that women do not participate in the labour market, but clearly women's paid work is considered secondary to that of men. Women are not classed as part of the 'core' workforce because the historical nature of their work has been predominantly part-time, unskilled, manual, casual and non-unionized.[37] Jenny Somerville[38] argues that women are central to the labour market not only as workers, but as reproducers of the labour force. Women reproduce, care for and turn out the past, present and future paid and unpaid labour force. Significant here is Marx's theory of the 'industrial reserve army of labour', of which women have constituted a significant part. According to Marx, the reserve army of labour is central to the development of the accumulation of capital. In times of periodic crises, structurally inherent in capitalist growth, an easily disposable workforce is necessary to protect and maintain 'core' jobs. Women have continued to provide capital with such a workforce. The 'peripheral' status of women's paid labour together with restricted opportunities in paid employment have served to emphasize women's dependence on the 'male breadwinner'. Collectively women have remained an easily exploitable reserve ever adaptable to the ebb and flow of capital accumulation. The ideological construction of women's role justifies this secondary role in the labour market. In order that female labour can be disposed easily the ideology of women's 'natural' place in the home is used to remove women from the labour market and to 'return' them to the home. Moral panics are created over 'latchkey kids', and it is seen to be desirable for women to devote their entire time to their children and domestic duties. That, however, is not to say that when women are active in the labour market their domestic duties are alleviated; rather they still hold full responsibility for the organization and management of the household.

The structure of the capitalist-patriarchy in its advanced political-economic form leaves women with restricted choices. If they are to gain some degree of independent status, by necessity they must take choices that will benefit them. [...]

Conclusion

We have argued that criminalization is a power relation in which certain individuals or groups are labelled and their activities outlawed by those with access to power. Criminalization, then, is inherently a structural, political process. Marginalization is specifically economic [...]. The political and ideological relations of patriarchy serve to maximize and justify the dimensions of marginalization. As we have seen, women are on the margins of employment;[39] they are peripheral to the main paid workforce and many suffer from structured and long-term unemployment. Black women are not only subjected by their gender and, often, class, but owing to their position in a white racist society experience an added dimension to their oppression.[40] Politically, women endure discrimination on the grounds of sex in many of the institutions they encounter; the family, work and state agencies. In experiencing the administration of criminal justice women are subjected to discrimination as a consequence of the patriarchal relations within the police and the courts. Institutionalized attitudes and responses effectively serve to politically marginalize women. Reputations and stereotyped images are not only constructed but also are transmitted through patriarchal ideologies. This provides a consistency and permanence at a structural institutional level which is beyond the potential of small-scale reforms or legal adjustment. Through the transmission and perpetuation of common-sense images and ideologies women learn the role, the place and the acceptable forms of behaviour to which they must adhere in order to gain status, respectability and protection. The strength of ideology is that it becomes internalized and, therefore, manifested in and through the daily lives of the people it categorizes.

When women react to this control and regulation of their sexuality, which is central to the criminalization of women, they are defined as deviant. When women protest against the control and regulation of their lives, for example in protests against violence against women, they are perceived as a real threat and are treated as such. In addition to this, women increasingly are perceived as a threat to the established order, and this has been most evident in the media and state response to the women's protest at Greenham Common. While the social and state control of women is powerful, women have established strategies of resistance both in direct and in personal ways. [...]

Notes

1. D. Smith, 'An analysis of ideological structures and how women are excluded', *Canadian Review of Sociology and Anthropology*, vol. 12, no. 4 (1975), Part 1.
2. C. Smart, *Women, Crime and Criminology*, London: Routledge & Kegan Paul, 1976.
3. See C. Smart and B. Smart (eds), *Women, Sexuality and Social Control*, London: Routledge & Kegan Paul, 1978.
4. S. Hall and P. Scraton, 'Law, class and control', in M. Fitzgerald *et al.*, *Crime and Society*, Milton Keynes: Open University Press, 1981, p. 488.
5. H. S. Becker, *Outsiders*, New York: Free Press, 1963; 'Whose side are we on?', *Social Problems*, vol. 14, 1967; E. Lemert, *Social Pathology*, New York: McGraw-Hill, 1951; E. Lemert, *Human Deviance, Social Problems and Social Control*, Englewood Cliffs, NJ: Prentice Hall, 1967.
6. Becker, 'Who's side are we on?' *Social Problems*, vol. 14, 1967.
7. See the discussion of the contribution of N. Poulantzas in Hall and Scraton, 'Law, class and control'.
8. See E. Wade, 'The miners and the media: themes of newspaper reporting', in P. Scraton and P. Thomas (eds), *The State v The People: Lessons from the coal dispute*, Oxford: Basil Blackwell, 1985.
9. See P. Hillyard, in *Working Papers in European Criminology*, No. 8 (1987) European Group for the Study of Deviance and Social Control.
10. For further discussion of these ascribed roles, see P. Carlen, *Women's Imprisonment*, London: Routledge & Kegan Paul, 1983; F. Heidensohn, *Women and Crime*, London: Macmillan, 1985.
11. Patriarchy refers to a structure of societal and social reproduction based on the material and cultural dominance of men over women. For further discussions of patriarchy, see V. Beechey, 'In patriarchy', *Feminist Review*, no. 3, (1979); S. Rowbotham, *Dreams and Dilemmas*, London: Virago, 1983, Section 5 on Patriarchy.
12. Hall and Scraton, 'Law, class and control', p. 487.
13. See S. Hall, *Culture, Media, Language*, Centre for Contemporary Cultural Studies, 1980; *Drifting into a Law and Order Society*, Cobden Trust, 1982.

14. See S. Hall *et al.*, *Policing the Crisis: Mugging, the state and law and order*, London: Macmillan, 1978; S. Cohen, *Folk Devils and Moral Panics* (2nd edn) Oxford: Martin Robertson, 1980; P. Golding and S. Middleton, *Images of Welfare*, Oxford: Martin Robertson, 1982; L. Curtis, *Ireland: The propaganda war*, London: Pluto, 1984.

15. Popular ideologies exist around crime, criminality, family life, nationalism, patriotism, race and gender. See Hall, *Culture, Media, Language*; *Drifting*.

16. See A. McRobbie and J. Garber, 'Girls and subcultures: an exploration', in S. Hall and T. Jefferson (eds), *Resistance Through Rituals*, London: Hutchinson, 1977; A. Oakley, *Sex, Gender and Society* (revised), Aldershot, Hants.: Gower, 1985; S. Sharpe, *Just like a Girl: How girls learn to be women*, Harmondsworth: Penguin, 1976.

17. C. Smart and B. Smart (eds), *Women, Sexuality and Social Control*, London: Routledge & Kegan Paul, 1978, p. 2.

18. See H. Roberts (eds), *Women, Health and Reproduction*, London: Routledge & Kegan Paul, 1981; C. Smart, *Women, Crime and Criminology*; C. Smart and J. Brophy, *Women-in-Law*, London: Routledge & Kegan Paul, 1985; A. Oakley, *The Sociology of Housework*, London: Martin Robertson, 1974; *Housewife*, Harmondsworth: Penguin, 1976; *Women Confined*, Oxford: Martin Robertson, 1980; *Subject Women*, Oxford: Martin Robertson, 1982.

19. J. Radford, *Women, Crime and Criminology*, unpublished, Open University, 1983, p. 79.

20. See M. Benn *et al.*, *Sexual Harassment*, London: NCCL, 1982.

21. See V. Hey, *Pubs and Patriarchy*, Milton Keynes: Open University Press, 1986; R. Deem, *All Work and No Play: The sociology of women and leisure*, Milton Keynes: Open University Press, 1986.

22. See R. Hall *et al.*, *Ask Any Woman*, Bristol: Falling Wall Press, 1985; J. Radford, 'Policing male violence – policing women', unpublished paper, 1985.

23. Women who step out of line are frequently defined as whores and slags. See J. Radford and S. Jeffreys, 'Contributing negligence of being a woman?', in P. Scraton and P. Gordon (eds), *Causes for Concern*, Harmondsworth: Penguin, 1984; P. Pattullo, *Judging Women*, London: NCCL, 1983.

24. M. Eaton, *Women, Criminology and Social Control*, Milton Keynes: Open University Press 1986, D310 Block 4.

25. Women's opportunities to commit crime are often seen to be related to their powerlessness. Young girls and women are socialized into accepting a passive role, and this is often suggested as a partial explanation for their lack of criminal activity. See E. Leonard, *Women, Crime and Society*, London: Longman, 1982; S. Box, *Power, Crime and Mystification*, London: Tavistock, 1983; F. Heidensohn, *Women and Crime*, London: Macmillan, 1985.

26. See M. Barrett and M. McIntosh, *The Anti-Social Family*, London: Verso, 1982; E. Zaretsky, *Capitalism, The Family and Personal Life*, London: Pluto, 1976.

27. W. Beveridge, *Social Insurance and Allied Services*, London: HMSO, 1942.

28. E. Wilson, *Women and the Welfare State*, London: Tavistock, 1977.

29. See J. Somerville, 'Women: a reserve army of labour', *m/f* no. 7 (1982); V. Beechey, 'Some notes on female wage labour in capitalist production', in M. Evans, *The Woman Question: Readings on the subordination of women*, London: Fontana, 1982.

30. J. Bowlby, *Child Care and the Growth of Love* (2nd edn), Harmondsworth: Penguin, 1965.

31. A. Oakley, *The Sociology of Housework*, London: Martin Robertson, 1982.

32. M. Barrett and M. McIntosh, 'The family wage', in E. Whitelegg (ed.), *The Changing Experience of Women*, Milton Keynes: Open University Press and Oxford: Martin Robertson, 1982.
33. It has been estimated that there are only 20 per cent of households which fit into this category. See J. Root, *Pictures of Women: Sexuality*, London: Pandora, 1984.
34. H. Land, 'The myth of the male breadwinner', *New Society*, October 1975; 'The family wage', *Feminist Review*, no. 6 (1980).
35. Land, 'The family wage', p. 71.
36. For an examination of the effectiveness of the Equal Pay and Sex Discrimination Acts, see J. Lewis, *Women's Welfare, Women's Rights*, London: Croom Helm, 1983; S. Atkins and B. Hoggett, *Women and the Law*, Oxford: Basil Blackwell, 1984.
37. See J. Beale, *Getting it Together: Women as trade unionists*, London: Pluto, 1982.
38. Somerville, 'Women: a reserve army of labour'.
39. *Ibid.*
40. H. Carby, 'White women listen! Black feminism and the boundaries of sisterhood', in Centre for Contemporary Cultural Studies, *The Empire Strikes Back*, London: Hutchinson, 1982; B. Bryan *et al.*, *The Heart of the Race*, London: Virago, 1985; A. Davis, *Women, Race and Class*, New York: Random House, 1982; b. hooks, *Ain't I a Woman?*, London: Pluto, 1982.

9.8   Women and Crime
Frances Heidensohn

Frances Heidensohn draws on 'control theories' of criminality and argues that the additional social control mechanisms that exist for women in society can explain the discrepancy between male and female involvement in crime. Therefore, we must look to the wider structural context of social control for an explanation of crime.

In both the widely expressed values of our society and in the structure of that society are embodied particular notions of normal women and controls to ensure their production and conformity. This all works very 'successfully' despite many inherent contradictions and the very considerable costs to individual women. That is why understanding the control of women is so important to our appreciation of their criminality. Obviously since women are, in Hagan's term, 'over-controlled' they commit less crime and fewer serious and repeated offences. Even when they do deviate they do so within a particular man-made framework of controls. Some women may correspond to conventional stereotypes of female crime – wicked, evil and beyond reason: the witch of myth and legend. Others may be sexually deviant: the harlot of ancient tradition. Even if women are not in fact conforming to stereotypes, the chances are that their behaviour will be so defined by the media, by the agents of control and perhaps even by the women themselves. That most criminal women are, in fact, trivial property offenders whose crimes, as Box pointed out, appear to be related to their powerlessness and economic marginalisation is hardly recognised at all.[1] Of course, if there were a simple equation that 'poverty and powerlessness equals criminality', girls and women would be the leaders in crime waves. That they are not leads us to consider the highly effective system of controls and bonds which make criminality a damaging and difficult course for women to take. Barbara Wootton pointed out many years ago that if men behaved like women the courts and prisons would be empty. Strictly speaking, that is not true, but it is very interesting to speculate on the reversal of the present system of social order. Could boys and men be contained as comprehensively as women have been? I have not dealt with the ways in which some women have begun to circumvent those constraints and tried to loosen some of the knots on the silken bonds. If nothing else, the analysis that has been engendered helps us look at women in public and in private, the normal and the deviant, and to see how these interact. It is a considerable and formidable enterprise to try to understand, let alone to change, the system. As Hutter and Williams put it:

> The pervasiveness of controls over women suggest that, as a group their attempts to free themselves from their unequal position in society offer a particularly strong threat to existing social arrangements.[2] [...]

Towards a theory

Involvement in crime must be the outcome of a variety of social, economic and other pressures. 'Crime' is itself a social construct, and a fairly wobbly construct at that. Most contemporary crime consists of offences concerning motor vehicles, or thefts from self-service stores: acts which have only been made possible by modern developments in technology and retailing. There are no *a priori* reasons for believing that female crime should be very different from male and indeed it is clear that women can and do emulate men in committing all types of crime. But the sexes differ markedly in the frequency and seriousness of their offences and in the respective social consequences of being labelled an offender.

After recent contributions to the study of crime commission,[3] we can say that carrying out deviant acts which break the law must be related to:

1. opportunity
2. time
3. space
4. scope
5. available role models
6. deviant images and stigma.

Being observed, caught, cautioned or convicted will in turn depend on how agencies of control operate and use:

1. values and ideology
2. agency practices
3. formal rules and laws
4. conventional behavioural stereotypes (of race, sex, etc.).

I should like to suggest that women face distinctively different opportunity situations and to some extent with agencies of control, the main point with the latter being that women face an additional series of controls. They are the one section of society whose policing has already been 'privatised', even though they have not ceased to be publicly controlled as well. [...]

These are just some of the reasons which seem to me to justify a considerable shift in perspective in the study of female crime. If we start from the broader issues of conformity and control and observe and analyse how these affect *all* women to some degree and *some* groups of women more than others, we can then learn rather more about those who become involved in crime as compared with other kinds of activities which might be available to them. This would, I think, show that female crime is not a particularly homogeneous category: thus some groups of women have deliberately broken the law to expose the contradictions in the social and legal position of their sex and to make political statements. Others, constrained by socioeconomic pressures, commit crimes because alternative sources of income for them and their dependants are poor. For others, especially young girls, there will be subcultural pressures to conform to group or gang norms. Whatever the respective controls and constraints on roles and actions, the arena in which women's behaviour occurs will be similar for most groups of women and affect the outcomes in terms of their criminal careers.

In short, I am arguing for a perspective that is not primarily criminologically based, nor even one located in the sociology of deviance (which has proved still more disappointing as an approach) but one which uses the interesting and challenging analyses of family life, male dominance and separate spheres which feminist theory and studies have to offer.

Notes

1. S. Box, *Power, Crime and Mystification*, London: Tavistock, 1983, p. 199.
2. B. Hutter and G. Williams, *Controlling Women*, London: Croom Helm, 1981, p. 11.
3. *R v. Clarke*, 'Opportunity-based crime rates', *British Journal of Criminology*, vol. 24, no. 1 (1984).

9.9   Criminal Women and Criminal Justice: the limits to, and potential of, feminist and left realist perspectives
Pat Carlen

Pat Carlen argues that some aspects of left realist criminology have important contributions to make to the study of women and crime.

Criminal women and criminal justice: the potential of left realist criminology

One of the most notable features of the writing of feminists who take up an anti-criminology position is the extent to which their concerns are reminiscent of some identical concerns of left-wing criminologists of the early 1970s. Fears that radical critique will be neutralized by incorporation into state repressive apparatuses, together with an apprehensiveness that any engagement in policy debate will contaminate them with a conservative reformism, seems today to be atrophying some British academic feminists' capacity is engaged in penal politics in much the same way that twenty years ago the new criminologists temporarily distanced themselves from penal debate for similar reasons. By contrast, today's left realists recognize that such a stance was in part responsible for the hijacking of law and order issues by the radical right and, as a consequence, their major injunction is to take crime and its effects seriously. This is not only because of the need to regain some of the ground predominantly occupied by the new realists on questions of crime control, but also because of a recognition that crime is a real problem and especially to working-class people who suffer disproportionately both as victims of crime and as apprehended lawbreakers.[1] In tirelessly confronting the challenge of right-wing administrative criminology,[2] Young and his associates[3] have developed the following tenets:

Theoretical

1. 'The basic triangle of relations which is the proper subject-matter of criminology [is] – the offender, the state and the victim.'[4]
2. Theoretical explanations must be symmetrical – there must be the same explanation for social action and social reaction.
3. 'Man [sic] is a creator of human nature';[5] and therefore explanations of crime should not be deterministic and people should be seen as being responsible for their actions.

Political

1. Crime is a real problem and especially to working-class people who suffer disproportionately from personal crime, such as robbery, assault, burglary, rape.
2. The 'left' should attempt to develop a credible (populist?) approach to crime control in order to prevent the 'right' from having a monopoly of the 'crime problem'.
3. The purpose of theorizing should be to make practical interventions into law and order issues.
4. In order to reduce crime there is a need to achieve a higher level of cooperation between police and public, and this will be best achieved by a democratization of local control of the police.

A vast body of critique of left realist criminology has been developed during the last ten years.[6] [...] I shall only discuss its potential for informing theoretical and political work on women's lawbreaking and criminalization.

Taking crime seriously – left realism as a politics

As I said above, one of the most important aspects of left realism in criminology is that it explicitly identifies the criminal justice arena as a site of political struggle. Because of the deconstructionist theoretical programme which I have advocated, I myself see no reason why feminists should be wary of engaging in theoretical debate about the possible meanings of the peculiar mix of ideological, political and economic conditions in which 'women as a status group' break the law, are criminalized and, in a minority of cases, are imprisoned.

Realism's advocacy of empirical investigation is an essential prerequisite of theoretical relevance and political interventions

In talking of theoretical relevance I am not intending to imply that theoretical concepts have essential relationships with empirical referents. Rather, I am assuming that, because the effects of racism, class exploitation and gender discrimination require different explanations, and because also the discourses and practices of women's lawbreaking and criminalization vary across time and between places, it can never be assumed that discourses and practices of gender differentiation *necessarily* play primary parts in the conditioning of that lawbreaking and criminalization. Close observation and investigation of the empirical phenomenon has a part to play in the shaping of the questions to be asked and the concepts to be used – even though the theoretical system constructed to answer them should also lead to their displacement and the requirement of further theoretical and/or empirical work. Such strategies of investigation and theorizing might or might not involve the use of concepts having claims to be labelled 'feminist'. But, almost certainly, they will often draw on political theories and jurisprudential concepts not primarily concerned with the rights and wrongs of *women* and where political intervention on women and crime issues is premissed primarily on concerns about racism or class injustice.

The starting point for realism is the strategy of democratization

It is in left realism's emphasis[7] on a democratization of the criminal justice system that I see a major (formal, if not substantive) convergence with feminist concerns. For realists not only take lawbreaking seriously, they also take seriously people's experiences of it as *victims*. Indeed, the realists' work on women as victims of crime has been one of their major contributions to both feminist struggle and criminology.[8] What they have not taken so seriously are people's experiences of crime as suspects, lawbreakers, defendants and prisoners (see below for criticisms of those parts of the 'taking crime seriously' programme which have frequently substituted populism for analysis, and moralism for theory). Yet an understanding of crime and criminal justice from the offender's standpoint is a necessary prerequisite to the reduction of crime[9] and to a diminution of the increased oppression which women incur as a result of their lawbreaking.[10] And this is the main justification for pursuing qualitative investigations which take seriously women's (and men's) own perceptions and experiences of their offences and the state's responses to them. It is not because of any distinctly 'feminist method' which 'allows women to speak for themselves'.[11] Such a procedure would be rampant (populist) empiricism rather than theoretical investigation. Rather, it is in the symbolic interactionist (realist) tradition which assumes that if people perceive things as real they will be real in their effects.[12] Taking seriously women's views of their lawbreaking might lead to: political demands for a diminution of the oppressive conditions in which much of women's lawbreaking is committed; the democratic construction of feasible interventionary programmes in relation to the drug-taking, thieving and other crimes which often cause misery to women other than the offender, as well as aggravating the existing problems of the woman lawbreaker itself; and the democratic management of housing and other schemes for women in trouble.

Notes

1. J. Young, (1986) 'The failure of criminology: the need for a radical realism', in R. Matthews and J. Young (eds), *Confronting Crime*, London: Sage.
2. J. Wilson, *Thinking about Crime*, New York: Basic Books, 1975.
3. J. Lea and J. Young, *What is to be Done about Law and Order?*, Harmondsworth, Penguin, 1984; R. Kinsey *et al.*, *Losing the Fight Against Crime*, Oxford: Basil Blackwell, 1986; J. Young, 'The tasks of a realist criminology', *Contemporary Crisis*, vol. 2, no. 4 (1987); J. Lea, 'Left realism: a defence', *Contemporary Crisis*, vol. 2,

no. 4 (1987), pp. 357–70; R. Matthews, 'Taking realist criminology seriously', *Contemporary Crisis*, vol. 2, no. 4 (1987), pp. 371–401.

4. Young, 'The failure of criminology'.
5. Young, 'The tasks of a realist criminology'.
6. Middlesex Polytechnic, *Realism: A selective bibliography*, London: Middlesex Polytechnic Centre for Criminology, 1989.
7. Lea, 'Left realism', p. 368.
8. T. Jones *et al.*, *The Islington Crime Survey*, Aldershot, Hants: Gower, 1986.
9. S. Box, *Recession, Crime and Punishment*, London: Tavistock, 1987, p. 29.
10. P. Carlen, *Women, Crime and Poverty*, Milton Keynes: Open University Press, 1985.
11. V. Jupp, *Methods in Criminological Research*, London: Unwin Hyman, 1989.
12. W. I. Thomas, *Social Behaviour and Personality*, New York: Social Science Research Council, 1951.

9.10 Sex, Class and Crime

Jeanne Gregory

Jeanne Gregory argues that what is required is a non-sexist criminology that recognises the importance of gender distinctions and their consequences.

Towards a non-sexist critical criminology

This paper does not advocate an androgynous criminology that would seek to explain male and female criminality in identical terms, but rather a criminology which has the explanatory power to encompass within its framework an understanding of both. This distinction is important, because 'non-sexist' is not used here to mean that gender relations are to be ignored. On the contrary, the analysis of such relations is a crucial component of the approach advocated. A non-sexist criminology would be firmly rooted in the distinction between sex and gender, insisting that gender is socially constructed and not biologically given, recognizing that the ideas of masculinity and femininity are extremely powerful in their consequences but refusing to share the assumptions on which they are based. Having successfully challenged those theories which conflate sex and gender in the direction of biological determinism, it is just as important not to collapse them in the other direction, by denying that there are any biological differences at all. The consequences of such an over-reaction are superbly illustrated in the recurring controversy over the relationship between pre-menstrual tension and female criminality.

Menstrual taboos have a long and varied history but are particularly pronounced in societies which have a clear-cut division of labour between the sexes. When women begin to exert pressure to improve their social position, there often seems to be a resurgence of interest in ideas about the harmful effects of menstruation, so that an emphasis on biological difference becomes a vindication of traditional sex role patterns.[1] Hence the hostile reaction of certain groups within the women's movement in Britain recently when the judiciary accepted pre-menstrual tension as the basis for pleas of diminished responsibility.[2] The data suggesting a relationship between the menstrual cycle and crime were not new, so why were the courts suddenly so receptive? Were they not simply providing additional ammunition for those who wished to exclude women from positions of power and responsibility? The prevailing social meanings attributed to the biological phenomenon of pre-menstrual tension are so powerful, and so patently damaging to the cause of female equality, that the temptation to deny the existence of the biological phenomenon is overwhelming. There is however, evidence that some women do experience considerable pain and distress at certain times of the month. The problem is how to recognize this and respond to it humanely, while resisting the connotations of social inferiority normally associated with this response. This is not an easy position to sustain in a culture which exhibits a general tendency to regard women who step outside the feminine stereotype as requiring medical attention: it is, however, vital.

Our efforts to demystify notions of femininity and masculinity will be placed in jeopardy if the distinction between sex and gender is not retained. They will also be placed in jeopardy if we fail to recognize that the impact of gender is mediated by class. The medicalization of 'deviant' behaviour is particularly oppressive in its consequences for working-class women, both as a diversion from the realities of economic and social deprivation and in terms of the forms of social control which it produces.[3] Interventionist policies derived from a partial analysis could well make matters worse. To demand formal equality for women while the substantive inequalities remain may in the short run increase the oppression of the most vulnerable groups. If equality means the disappearance of leniency and hence the separation of more female offenders from their children, or even if it means taking drugs away from women who cannot face the misery of their daily routine without them, then such 'reforms' can only be part of a more radical programme of change.[4]

Notes

1. J. Sayers, *Biological Politics*, London: Tavistock, 1982.
2. In November 1981 there were two cases that attracted a great deal of publicity. In the first, a barmaid was given three years' probation after being convicted of threatening to kill a policeman and possessing an offensive weapon. In the second, a woman pleading guilty to manslaughter (she killed her lover by driving a car at him) was given a conditional discharge. In both cases, judges accepted pleas of diminished responsibility after hearing medical evidence that the crimes were provoked by pre-menstrual tension. Representatives from Women's Health Concern expressed strong objections to the verdicts, believing that they would have damaging consequences for women in general (*The Standard*, London, 12 November 1981).

3. B. Hutter and G. Williams, *Controlling Women*, London: Croom Helm, 1981; V. Greenwood, 'The role and future of female imprisonment', Middlesex Polytechnic Mimeo, 1983.

4. For an even more striking example of what happens when middle-class feminists assume that particular changes will liberate all women equally, see the 'protective legislation' debate. Although it is true that legislation restricting the hours and conditions of work for women has been used to impede their employment and promotion prospects, simply to remove such legislation and thereby free women to work the night shift without making any other changes will not be experienced as liberating! See J. Coussins, *The Shift Work Swindle*, London: National Council for Civil Liberties, 1979; J. Gregory, 'The future of protective legislation', Occasional Paper No. 3, Middlesex Polytechnic, 1981.

Further Reading

Gelsthorpe, L. and Morris, A. (eds) (1990), *Feminist Perspectives in Criminology*, Milton Keynes: Open University Press.

Heidensohn, F. (1985), *Women and Crime*, London: Macmillan.

Carlen, P. (1985), *Criminal Women*, Cambridge: Polity Press.

Carlen, P. (1988), *Women, Crime and Poverty*, Milton Keynes: Open University Press.

Carlen, P. and Worrall, A. (eds) (1987), *Gender, Crime and Justice*, Milton Keynes: Open University Press.

Eaton, M. (1986) *Justice for Women?*, Milton Keynes: Open University Press.

Smart, C. (1976), *Women, Crime and Criminology*, London: Routledge & Kegan Paul.

Worrall, A. (1990), *Offending Women*, London: Routledge & Kegan Paul.

10 PUBLIC/PRIVATE: WOMEN, POLITICS AND THE STATE

Edited and Introduced by Rose Pearson

INTRODUCTION: Women and the State: a new form of patriarchy?

The nation-state is the major form of social organisation in the modern world, so we need to start by defining 'the state', and saying a little about how it came into being and what its functions are, before looking at how it impinges upon women's lives today.

When we talk about the state, we are referring to a political organisation in a particular geographical territory. The form of political organisation varies, but some person or body of persons makes laws, and there is a legal system with courts or tribunals backed up by a system of coercion and punishment. Force is at the heart of state organisation, in that those who are in control of the state police their territory internally, and can command armed forces to defend the external boundaries. The state has sometimes been defined as 'the monopoly of force over a given geographical area', because in theory *only* those acting on behalf of the state are permitted to exercise violence and coercion within the law, and the territory becomes internally pacified. (State organisations are, of course, paid for by taxes levied within the given territory.) This has particular implications for women, for the power of the private male-headed household diminished as the state became the major authority. In theory, women could look to the courts for protection from the tyranny of male kin and the random violence of marauding men, but in practice this was not a reality, since women continued to be regarded as male property until the advent of first-wave feminism in the late nineteenth century challenged such attitudes.

The modern state, or nation-state, has emerged in the last one hundred and fifty years, and goes beyond internal pacification. Governments have increasingly developed policies to deal with the mass populations under their control, frequently in order to regulate groups who may be seen as potentially

dangerous to the established order, such as the poor, but also to promote
particular kinds of lifestyles considered to be desirable. The modern state
regulates both work and leisure activities, and oversees the provision of the
economic infrastructure of energy and transport. Of particular significance for
women is the provision of education and the many ways in which the state
regulates the family. All this, along with a plethora of other functions, has
required the development of complex civil service and local government
apparatus.

The state has become stronger and more intrusive in its influence on the lives
of both women and men in the twentieth century, and despite the stated
intentions of governments of the New Right in Britain, America and elsewhere
to 'push back the frontiers of the state', this trend is accelerating. It is a global
phenomenon, with female populations throughout the world being subjected to
control by the modern state over areas of their lives previously regulated by
custom, religion and the immediate (male-dominated) social group. For women
this has sometimes had positive effects, for the state often intervenes to prevent
some of the cruellest abuses of patriarchy – physical mutilations such as
footbinding or clitoridectomy, or forced marriage. But such protection is by no
means universal and is often ineffectual, and the benefits may well be cancelled
out by the restructuring of regulatory frameworks which perpetuate the
disadvantaged and unequal status of women. State population policies, whether
restrictive or pro-natalist, are a case in point.

Let us begin by considering the notion of the patriarchal state. Women now
have the vote in most countries, although they are still disenfranchised in some,
such as Saudi Arabia and Kuwait, as a gender; or in others – South Africa or
Hong Kong – as a result of race or property restrictions. Yet they hardly ever
comprise as much as a quarter of elected representatives, and are virtually
absent from ruling bodies of military regimes. The demise of European
Communist regimes has removed a number of governments in which female
representation was better than the norm, though not at the very highest levels.

The argument for describing the state as a patriarchal institution, however, is
based not upon who fills the positions, but rather upon what the state does, and
its effects on women. Norway, for example, is a country where half the MPs and
the Prime Minister are women, but the status of women there is not significantly
higher than it is in other similar countries. The patriarchal state can be defined
as one which promotes and maintains institutions and practices which
systematically oppress women: these have been identified as family and
household structures, and employment and welfare policies, which perpetuate
women's status as economic dependants. Such subjection may be the result of
discriminatory policies – for instance, denying social security payments to
married or cohabiting women; or of inaction: failure to provide decent public
childcare, or to bring forward effective equal pay legislation. What is important
here is that the state and the accepted model of the family, acting in unison,
reinforce the female role.

Sylvia Walby[1] has distinguished 'private' from 'public' patriarchy, suggesting that the private patriarchal structures of family and household, which regulated women's sexuality and economic activities, have to some extent been replaced by a form of public patriarchy, in which the state and other public bodies, such as employers, increasingly define the lives of individual women through legal, employment and welfare policies. Walby suggests that it may be easier for women to mount challenges to public policies than to confront the private, though it is crucial, as Stacey advocates, that women organise politically to do so.

The arrival of the welfare state in Britain in the late 1940s under the Labour government headed by Clement Attlee (building upon earlier policies of Liberal governments in the period preceding the First World War) has been a major focus for feminist debates concerning the role of the state. Aspects of the welfare state helped women as mothers enormously – better schooling, the National Health Service, the council house building programme, and various cash benefits such as Family Allowance (precursor of Child Benefit) and the maternity grant. Lord Beveridge's aim – to provide freedom from poverty and unemployment – seemed to be realised in the post-war years, and this was of considerable advantage to women. Yet the welfare state and its provisions were constructed on the principle that women should be primarily mothers and housewives, and the whole National Insurance system reflected this, denying married women most benefits in their own right. Where women did gain, the intended beneficiary was often her child rather than the woman herself.

The welfare state, then, poses a number of contradictions. It has made it possible, through the social security system, for women to bring up children on their own, and has thus provided a space for some autonomy, and the ability to reject the alternatives of shotgun wedding, adoption, or the continuation of an unhappy marriage. This same system, of course, perpetuates the poverty and dependence of the single mother, and state 'benevolence' is problematic: it involves continual monitoring, regulation and snooping by bureaucrats, epitomised in the cohabitation rule. It is also something of a precarious space, as the lowering standard of living of state dependants under the Conservative governments of the 1980s demonstrated. Strenuous efforts have been made to use financial pressure to bring women back into dependence on individual men, justified by the familial ideologies of the New Right.

The welfare state of the New Right has institutionalised women as carers – unpaid except for token allowances. Individualised childcare places enormous physical and emotional burdens upon women, yet alternatives are portrayed in terms of dystopic images of collective state batch-rearing. The 'Care in the Community' policy, introduced following the Griffiths Report,[2] is causing many more women to lead isolated and poverty-stricken lives as carers for the long-term sick, the disabled, the physically handicapped and the mentally ill.

The question posed is whether the state can become a vehicle for introducing a more communal kind of care, involving both women and men, and providing a comprehensive range of support mechanisms. This is theoretically possible, but it would involve a reprioritising of funding, and a restructuring of working hours and domestic roles for both sexes. It is a political agenda of radical transformation, in stark opposition to the current global capitalist restructuring, which stresses profit and consumerism and has a special role for women as a cheap, flexible workforce. For many women, building a fully welfarist state is a programme worth fighting for.

Other feminists, however, reject any form of state intervention. They argue that the state is active in and central to the maintenance of gendered inequality, and will implement measures which appear to raise the status of women either because this serves other ends – providing women workers at a time of labour shortage, for instance – or as cosmetic gestures to dissipate feminist demands. According to this argument, state intervention means that women surrender control to state officials, and public money should not be accepted as a potential source of support or funding. Refuge groups in Germany and Denmark have taken such a stance, relying on their own resources of donations, legacies and fund-raising. Women's Aid in Britain has viewed the public allocation of funding as a political issue, but the crisis caused by the cutbacks of the 1980s and 1990s may well vindicate the antistatist perspective. The welfare state may appear helpful at one juncture, only to re-establish its underlying ethos of control, whilst placing issues to do with protecting women very low on the agenda.

Women's relationship to the state is changing. New kinds of action have grown out of the ideas and organisations of the feminist movement – beginning with the suffragettes, but becoming far more extensive and radical in the issues they raise and the manner in which they often challenge traditional images of femininity. Innovative forms of public protest have emerged which relate directly to the concerns of women and those they love, and do so in creative ways which transform both the nature of popular collective action and the lives of those who are involved.

Notes

1. S. Walby, *Theorizing Patriarchy*, Oxford: Basil Blackwell, 1990.
2. Sir R. Griffiths, *Community Care: Agenda for action*, London: HMSO, 1988.

10.1 **Given the Odds, a Great Advance**
Margaret Stacey and Marion Price

This Reading is optimistic about women's progress over the last two hundred years, but points out that many of the traditional sites of female power have been eroded, so that if women wish to influence society they must become involved in the public political sphere.

If we replace the slogan 'liberty, equality, and fraternity' by the more acceptable one of 'liberty, equality, and comradeship', what stance should women take in relation to formal political power? How can we achieve liberation at the same time as we retain and extend the valuable qualities of caring, of mutuality, of long-term attachment and loyalty that have been the best features of the family, patriarchal though it has been for aeons of history in the Western world?

To do this we have to recognize, first of all, that women are not equally and universally oppressed and, most importantly, that some women oppress other women. The oppressions of patriarchy, of capitalism, and of state power interlock and are mutually sustained, and all have to be opposed. There is no doubt that sections of the working-class movement have been subverted to the maintenance of capitalism. Working-class leaders have not been able, so far, to use the positions of power they have achieved to make life more free and equal for all, either across classes or between sexes. This may be because socialist parties in now relatively minor states like Britain are not able to overcome the forces of international capitalism. It is also because those who achieve power are ambivalent about equality and comradeship. Whether women or men, they are people who want to get on and do well and who are thus readily subverted. If a strategy of increasing the involvement of women in politics is to be followed, it is important, in our view, that the successful women should be kept closely in touch with a well-organized women's movement. Furthermore, we would agree with Rowbotham that such a movement must have a majority of working-class women.[1] Rowbotham is clear about the importance of organization for the liberation of women, and in an extended essay[2] she argues that the Women's Liberation Movement has contributed towards socialist as well as feminist liberation by creating ways of organizing in which leadership is much more widely dispersed than in left-wing organizations. [...] In reviewing this work Elizabeth Wilson has drawn attention to the ambiguity in the feminist movement where some have wished for state power or the access to resources that power would give, while at the same time feminists have presented a radical critique of power relations. She asks: 'What sort of power do [feminists] seek? In what way do we wish to make our mark on the world? Do we want to share in the world or do we simply want "women's sphere" to be given greater value? Or do we want to break out of these dichotomies altogether?'[3]

These questions have to be answered. Yet it would seem to us that if women wish to make changes in the societies they live in, they must seek and achieve power positions. It is essential that women should enter the political arena, since the societies are all male-dominated, for men certainly cannot be relied upon to initiate or carry through the necessary changes. State socialist societies, communes, reformist and revolutionary societies have remained male-dominated. In advanced capitalist societies the older forms of women's power have been so far eroded and their private domain so utterly invaded by husband–father and state advisers that women have no choice left to them but to seize an equal share of political power, notwithstanding all the odds which we have seen are stacked against us.

Participating in male-dominated capitalist states is a risky business, hence the importance of organizational backing. Furthermore, the strategy of encouraging women to gain power positions must clearly be linked with continuing discussions as to how we can achieve liberty, equality, and comradeship as concrete, not abstract, values and link individual autonomy with collective action. Otherwise, in pursuance of this strategy, the sisterly and comradely goals of the women's movement will be subverted. In terms of its implications for women in relation to political institutions this discussion has been too long neglected. Socialists and feminists should put it high on their agenda.

Notes

1. S. Rowbotham, *Woman's Consciousness, Man's World*, Harmondsworth: Penguin, 1973, p. 126.
2. S. Rowbotham, L. Segal and H. Wainwright, *Beyond the Fragments: Feminism and the making of socialism*, London: Merlin Press, 1979, p. 81.
3. E. Wilson, 'Beyond the ghetto: thoughts on *Beyond the fragments: Feminism and the making of socialism* by Sheila Rowbotham, Hilary Wainwright and Lynne Segal', *Feminist Review*, no. 4 (1980), pp. 28–44 (42–3).

10.2 **Policing: the under-representation of women's interests**
Susan Edwards

Susan Edwards argues that violence against women is under-policed, but this is the result of the patriarchal nature of the law, which also results in a disproportionate number of women being prosecuted for prostitution and allied offences.

Chief Superintendent Roger Street of Streatham Police Station in south London, in a paper presented to the 1988 Annual Conference of the Howard League for Penal Reform on the subject of 'Women and policing', recognized the under-representation of women's interests in policing issues. He said:

> So far as domestic violence was concerned, women who participated in the determination of eventual policy, indicated dominantly that they felt that it was not treated seriously in the Criminal Justice System. Police practice had always been based on the assumption that, other than in extreme circumstances, what happened in a male–female relationship was essentially a private matter between the parties concerned. What clearly emerged from the exercise was that women had

a right to expect the protection of the law, whether or not they had a close relationship with the offender. The new policy therefore was based on this fundamental tenet and included a number of strategies which sought to achieve this. [1]

Despite the endeavours of senior police officers, it remains the case that women's interests are under-represented in policing, as in the public and political arena. The all-pervasiveness of patriarchal attitudes in society, in law and in policing has had certain fundamental consequences for what is policed and who are protected. Violence in the home is accorded a low priority because it happens behind closed doors, has a low visibility, occurs within a sphere traditionally considered private and is perpetrated against women by male partners. It is also the case that the police treatment of rape victims and prostitute women and their response to the sale and distribution of pornography, all of which involve violence against or exploitation of women, are matters accorded a low priority and sometimes insensitively handled. Much of the criticism of policing by left-wing women's pressure groups is concerned with precisely these issues, where rape victims are treated unsympathetically and charges dropped, prostitutes are subject to constant surveillance and arrested while ponces, pimps and punters are rarely prosecuted, and women are exploited in pornography while sellers and distributors are rarely prosecuted and even more rarely convicted. Police priorities depend on the visibility of the illegality, and the pressure from public opinion. For 'public opinion' read, as Dicey acknowledged, 'those citizens who have at a given time taken an effective part in public life ... and made legislation in accordance with their interests'. [2]

It is no accident that the man who beats his wife on the street is more likely to be prosecuted than the man who behaves in exactly the same way in his own home. The visibility of their behaviour is one of the reasons police regularly arrest and prosecute prostitutes for street soliciting, whilst the organizer, producer and controller of prostitution, who organizes behind closed doors in saunas, clubs and massage parlours, goes unseen and relatively untouched. Again, in the pornography trade it is the visibility that creates the 'offence'. In these as in other cases, such as the policing of domestic violence, rape, prostitution and pornography, the police response has been antipathetical to women's interests. But to blame the police for the legal and evidential requirements in a rape trial which put the victim on trial, to blame the police for the drafting of a law relating to prostitution that penalizes women only and not their clients, and to blame the police for unworkable obscene publications legislation which leads to an apparent under-enforcement of law relating to the seizure of pornographic material would be to miss the point raised at the outset. The law in its form and content, and in its application, mirrors particular interests. In a society which is organized around the control of women by men, the laws, as well as the application of those laws, reflect patriarchal interests.

Any consideration of the application of law and the question of police accountability must recognize that the law is the basis for much of what police do. These laws affect women, often denying their interests. One barometer of the implementation of law is provided by examining official statistics on the incidence of certain crimes and on their prosecution and conviction. While we have no reliable criminal statistics on the extent of violence against wives, figures for prostitution and allied offences, and obscene publications, indicate a disproportionate number of prosecutions of men for offences of violence against women, pornography and controlling prostitution, compared with the number of women prosecuted for offences relating to prostitution, considering what is involved in each offence. Do these variations in prosecution reflect differences in crimes committed, or do they reflect instead the amount of police time and effort spent in the control of women prostitutes on the streets, and the amount of police time spent in the control of men who manage prostitutes, and men who sell and distribute pornography? In 1982, for example, there were 308 prosecutions for obscene publications (including possession and distribution). In 1983, this figure had risen to 523; by 1984 it had risen still further to 623; by 1985 it had fallen dramatically to 320; and in 1986 there were only 161 prosecutions. The setting up of the Crown Prosecution Service in 1986 can account for the fall in prosecutions for obscene publications, because of the overwhelmingly high acquittal rate in previous years (47 per cent). Yet there seems to have been no similar moratorium for prostitute women.

Notes

1. R. Street, 'Women and policing', Address to the Howard League for Penal Reform, September 1988, p. 4.
2. A. V. Dicey, 'Law and public opinion in England', in V. Aubert (ed.), *The Sociology of Law*, Harmondsworth: Penguin, 1969, pp. 71–9 (72).

10.3 **The Birth Limitation Program: family vs state**
Margery Wolf

Margery Wolf argues that the birth control programme in China in the 1980s was carried out at the expense of women; they were held responsible for conception, sanctions were directed only against women, and women without sons continued to suffer socially and economically.

It is, of course, on women that the burden of the birth limitation program falls most heavily and most painfully. In rural areas, women who bear girls are sometimes scorned and even beaten by their husbands and parents-in-law. Even those who should know better let the mothers take the blame. We see massive posters and miles of characters saying that girl babies are just as precious as boy babies, but little is said about how the sex of a child is determined. If that basic fact were well established in farmers' minds, it would save women a lot of grief. But the major question, to comply or not to comply with the state's 'call' for a single child, catches women in an impossible situation. If a woman's husband and his family decide that it is worth the economic risk, it is her body that must conceal the illegal pregnancy, her body that will be the target of the cadre's anger if his quota is exceeded, her body that will endure a forced abortion perhaps too late to be entirely safe. She will be treated as if she had made the decision to have this illegal child even though the same cadre who is condemning her may also have 'guided' his own sons and daughter-in-law in their reproductive decisions.

In sum, the birth planning program that promises so much for women is also run at their expense. They must take responsibility for the contraceptive devices that they may or may not wish to make use of. An urban factory worker whom I asked what would happen if someone who had a one-child certificate got pregnant told me, 'She would be encouraged to have an abortion.' What if she refused? 'She would lose her bonus and at the next wage increase she would be left out and lose her extra points. And her fellow workers would scorn her.' The child is in her body, so she must be to blame. I asked, to the point of being a nuisance, about male sterilization. The usual answer was that men were not willing, but many said vasectomies 'weakened' men, and since they must work for the family it was better to have the women sterilized. The weakening is nonsense, and although the failure rate is somewhat higher with vasectomies, the Chinese have made remarkable breakthroughs in other areas of contraception. Why not in vasectomies? They perfected the vacuum aspiration technique for abortions and have devised many safer and more effective IUDs, as well as a host of new, less dangerous oral contraceptives. One can only assume that the government agrees with the male farmer who told me that women were expendable, men were not, and that was why vasectomies were rarely performed.

10.4 **Policing the Family**
Peter Squires

Peter Squires charts the way in which the British state since the war has attempted to discourage and financially penalise single parenthood, and to prescribe, where possible, the payment of private maintenance by a 'liable relative', forcing a woman into economic dependence.

Although the Beveridge Report had declared a firm commitment to the principles of the patriarchal family, two problematic issues began to emerge. As the post-war decades wore on, 'failure to maintain dependants' and 'undisclosed cohabitation' generated more and more attention. In 1948, the National Assistance Board had assumed responsibility for some 41,600 single women and their children. In the 1950s and 1960s the number rose markedly, but despite the increasing incidence of illegitimacy and family break-up, a concern about the phenomenon of 'fictitious desertion' seemed to motivate attempts to apply financial pressure on single parents through the medium of social security.

In 1948, the problem of the 'absent liable relative' seemed only a peripheral concern, but by the following year, following a 100 per cent increase in the number of claims made by separated wives and unmarried mothers, 'enforcement of liability' assumed the status of a problem. In particular, the loss to public funds resulting from this 'abuse' led the Board to consider what further action it might take to tackle the issue. By 1950 the Board was pleased to report that, 'with increasing experience ... officers had more success in tracing defaulting liable relatives'.[1] Subsequent years reveal a steadily rising number of prosecutions for 'failure to maintain' and also the emergence of an apparent 'hard core' who seemed 'so set in their determination never to support their wives that they will go to prison, if need be over and over again, rather than pay'.[2] Such developments reflect similar processes occurring with respect to the patrolling of the labour market.

In the following year, 1952, the law was changed to enable wives to give evidence against husbands charged with the offence of 'failure to maintain'. The effect of the change was to return the law to the position it had occupied under the Poor Law. Although enacted as a means by which to pursue deserting husbands, the new regulation applied a lever primarily against the wife. Deserted wives and single parents were 'encouraged' to divulge information to enable the administration to trace former partners so that it (or the women themselves) might prosecute or take action to recover maintenance due from 'alleged fathers'. Women who were reluctant to co-operate with 'liable-relative officers' might prejudice their entitlement to benefit. The Board was adamant that women and children could not be left to starve, 'in the hope of effecting a reconciliation'.[3] But the language used is not wholly convincing. Only when the Board's officers were convinced that 'the separation looks like continuing' did they appear to 'feel obliged' to grant sufficient assistance. In its actions in such cases the NAB manifested a tendency to take a particularly harsh line with those who failed to conform to certain established behavioural norms. Indeed, in a more general sense, social policy has shown itself especially susceptible to scandalous relationships. In particular the myth of 'fictitious desertion' has played no small part in legitimating a more intensive 'policing' of single parents. Of course, such remarks apply with equal weight to the phenomenon of 'undisclosed cohabitation', a scandalous relationship which has prompted some of the most intrusive and stigmatising interventions adopted by social security investigators.[4]

The number of individuals against whom liable-relative proceedings were instituted continued to rise throughout the second half of the 1950s and the whole of the 1960s, although the practice of subjecting women to a testing interview drew increasing criticism. In 1974, evidence from the Health Visitors' Association, corroborated by evidence from the Women's National Commission, presented to the Finer Commission on One-Parent Families, stated that, 'undue pressure is brought to bear at a time when the mother is already under considerable stress'.[5] Such criticisms led to the adoption of new rules designed to protect mothers from harassment by liable-relative officers but, by 1981, these rules were apparently being ignored. The pressure on single parents was maintained, seemingly because 'it is officially suspected that this is the area in which there is most fraud'.[6] As if to confirm this impression, a government statement on 'fraud savings' in 1981 suggested that liable-relative work was the most cost-effective of all the government's initiatives against social security 'abuse'.[7] Subsequent guidelines issued for the use of liable-relative investigators when conducting interviews with single parents suggest that the patriarchal commitments of the British social security system have spawned a powerful disciplinary legacy policing the family with an intensity not dissimilar to that focused upon the labour market.[8]

Notes

1. National Assistance Board *Annual Reports*, (1948–65), London: HMSO, 1950, p. 18.
2. *Ibid.*, 1951, p. 19.
3. *Ibid.*, 1953, p. 20.
4. F. Field and M. Grieve, *Abuse and the Abused: CPAG evidence to the Fisher Inquiry*, London: Child Poverty Action Group, 1971; P. Clayton, *The Cohabitation Guide*, London: Wildwood Press, 1981; P. Squires, 'Studies in the criminalisation of poverty: pauperism, pathology and policing', PhD Thesis, University of Bristol, 2 vols, 1984.
5. *Report of the Committee on One-Parent Families* (The Finer Report), Cmnd. 5228, London: HMSO, 1974, vol. 1, pp. 138–41.
6. P. Healy, 'Liable lore', *New Society*, April 1981, p. 61.
7. P. Jenkin, *Hansard*, vol. 4, 6 May 1981, vols 79–80.
8. For a fuller analysis, see Squires, 'Studies in the criminalisation of poverty'.

10.5 Women and the Strike: it's a whole way of life

Jill Evans, Clare Hudson and Penny Smith

The final two Readings in this Section concern two major political movements of women in the 1980s: Women Against Pit Closures, and the anti-nuclear protesters at Greenham Common.

> *This Reading describes the involvement of women in South Wales in the miners' strike of 1984–5. It is suggested that collections of money and food by Women Against Pit Closures and the support systems provided constituted an 'alternative welfare state'. Women's participation in picketing, and male opposition, are also described.*

> 'My attitudes have changed through the strike. I thought I was a socialist before. Now I know what socialism is – it's a whole way of life, and we're living it in our valley right now'. (Neath and Dulais Valley)

In the tradition of their foremothers, women living in the South Wales mining communities have, from the very start of the 1984 strike, taken up the struggle as their own. That has meant battling on two fronts: standing up for their communities, their menfolk and their children's future; but also claiming their right to take an active part, to define the struggle as being as much theirs as their menfolk's and the NUM's:

> 'If I want to go, I'll go picketing. After all it's my money. If he doesn't have a job to go to ... we're not taking that lying down.' (Mardy)

There is an understandable reticence on the part of the women in the strike to voice at this time their anger and frustration at attempts by some individual miners and certain union officials to undermine their independence and muffle their voices. The women are dealing with it as they have to – speaking out against some of it, keeping quiet about the rest. When many of the women speak about this strike they may be treading a tightrope between their solidarity with and their grievances against the men in their communities. Union officials who in public applaud these 'heroines' sometimes in private do their damnedest to prevent them gaining any political ground. The women are often gagged by their loyalty and their entirely justifiable fear of dividing communities and households which are already up against a rich, powerful and sometimes violent enemy. But many of the women believe that their part in this strike is changing attitudes in the union:

> 'We're overcoming the problem slowly, but it is slow because the NUM is a male dominated industry. But attitudes are changing. The younger miners are better than the older ones. But there are a lot of older miners in the group and we do get a bit of hassle, but in the end they give in.' (Treherbert)

Food collection

Women's groups in most areas became involved initially through organising food collection and distribution, fund-raising events, such as galas, and sponsored walks. That was, and is, vital work – not just because of what was collected, but because food collection and fund-raising are the first points of contact between those on strike and the rest of the community. The most fundamental act of solidarity is to give food or money to a family on strike – and fund-raising events have become an important focal point for communities to show their support for the struggle.

Food collection and distribution is a full-time operation for many women and men involved in the strike. Mardy Lodge, for instance, distributes 700 food parcels a week to miners' families all the way down the valley as far as Porth. The support group pays £600 a week, which it has to collect itself, to the NUM headquarters at Pontypridd. After a food-buying run to a cash and carry store, £1,400 worth of food is then delivered to Mardy. There, volunteers divide it into parcels.

'We can only afford to put in the basics: eight pounds of potatoes, a tin of corned beef, a tin of veg, rice pudding, fruit, sometimes sugar, tea bags, tins of beans or spaghetti and so on. We have to raise the money ourselves through raffles and socials, and going away to speak at meetings. We did well last week – from meetings in Birmingham and Oxford we brought back £1,000. If someone's in real need, they can ask us for more food – single men are the worst off. They're never turned away if they come and ask.'

For some women, the full horror of what was happening on the picket line was brought home to them when their husbands returned home from Orgreave:

'The string vest was ripped to pieces, the strap of the watch was broken, the glass watch was stepped on and crushed to pieces, his gym shoes were split all the way round where the dogs had caught him, his jeans were ripped at the bottom and he had a big mark where the shield had caught him. He was covered in bruises, and all marks and cuts. And he was only doing his duty.' (Ammanford)

After going on picket lines themselves, many of the women said they began to understand how easily anger can flare up:

'We hadn't been on the picket line before. Our men had come back with all these stories of police violence and provocation, and we thought maybe it was an exaggeration. But we found out that it wasn't. You see a convoy coming out and you're seething with rage. I did a V sign at one of the drivers and a policeman told me I could be taken away for that. So I just turned my fingers round the other way. But the drivers made signs like that at us – and no one threatens to arrest them.' (Neath and Dulais Valley)

'I was surprised at how aggressive I felt that day. Your fuse is shorter than usual. I could feel it bubbling up inside me.' (Neath and Dulais Valley)

'I'm beginning to see how the violence happens. Coming back from Birmingham we were on the motorway and we ended up in the middle of the coke convoy from Port Talbot. Lots of the drivers saw us and made rude signs at us, they showed us their union cards and waved money at us. It drove us mad in the back of our bus. We regard ourselves as law-abiding people but we were really furious. I can see why our boys get so angry on the picket line and sometimes lose their self-control. When you've been out for nearly five months and someone taunts you like that, it drives you wild.' (Ferndale)

Now many of the women see picketing as an integral part of their involvement in the strike:

'... the women in our valley would go on any picket line anywhere they were needed. Not at the beginning of the strike – we wouldn't. Now it's all changed.' (Neath and Dulais Valley)

10.6 **Body/Politics: our bodies triumphed**
Alison Young

Alison Young draws on poststructuralist and postmodernist ideas to explore the political activity of the women protesters at Greenham Common. Here, she discusses the employment of the 'protesting body' , and suggests that in recuperating the repressed body, and redefining the meaning of the female body, a 'truly transformative' form of political protest has been discovered.

One of the most striking aspects of the Greenham protest has concerned the modes of employment of 'the protesting body'. Here I am using 'body' in a number of senses. It can signify a large number of people, as in 'the social body'. At Greenham, protest has often been carried out in this way (a common characteristic of mass political movements). At the December demonstrations, when women are solicited in their thousands, the aim is to constitute a mass dissenting body: the organising factor of the particular demonstration is size. At these occasions, there is, in contrast to the proffered spontaneity, a 'regulation' dress (warm clothes, often rainbow patterned, jewellery which employs the symbols of the dove or the anatomical denotation of the woman); a repertoire of action (joining hands, shouting slogans, singing songs, holding candles, 'keening') . This constitutes a mass writing. Such a large-scale 'organisation in opposition' will always cause the 'failure' of the protest. The protesters in their thousands chant and sing their cause (which is the subject of the action), a gesture which seeks to install this subject as valid or worthy, while, more hopefully or more honestly, the song would claim only that the protesters are in dissent, are going to blockade, to march. The Greenham women incorporate these simple declarations in their songs: 'You can't kill the spirit, she is like a mountain. Old and strong, she goes on and on and on'. This expresses simply the intention and continuation of dissent, the object of protest is given no place in the opposition. It is external. The protest is independent of it.

There are other levels than this of the mass body of the Greenham protest. Such massive demonstrations as these are rare events in comparison with the predominant means of protest: constant physical presence. To this extent the protest shares similarities with the 'vigil', an occurrence in which what takes place is secondary to the fact of its happening. Thus the Greenham women often simply 'live' at the peace camp, not engaging in any overt form of protest, except for the fact that their living there is an endless protest. Recognition of this aspect of continual mute protest through persistent presence is provided in the 1985 End of Year Report of the United States Air Force stationed at Greenham Common. Listed under 'the many accomplishments of the unit' we find 'four hundred arrests of peace women' and also 'hitting one peace woman with a vehicle'. (I note that a protester, Helen Thomas, was killed in a collision with a police vehicle in August 1989: the *Observer* and the *Guardian*, on 6 and 7 August, carried extremely brief reports of this event.) The Greenham Common protest, therefore, unlike those which conventionally involve intermittent demonstrations usually on a large scale (for example, CND) is continuous, bearing witness through the physical presence of the women outside the base.

The body is brought to the fore at Greenham in other ways. Women who went there discovered that they could express their emotional reactions to the possibility of nuclear war, whereas other groups in the peace movement tended towards disapprobation of this. Fears and terrors can be voiced at Greenham through writing poetry, recounting dreams or simply weeping at meetings. The body that is so important to the protest is therefore also an *emotional* body. This can be contrasted with the body that is constructed as actor in the debates of the pro-nuclear campaigners. Emotion or feeling is there denigrated in favour of a faith in reason, that is, a rationalism which seeks to expel emotion. At Greenham Common, the protesters seek to retrieve the lost emotional body as a valid, perhaps essential part of dissent. This does not imply that reasoned arguments play no part in the Greenham protest. The Greenham women, as their writings and their speeches in court demonstrate, can provide extremely articulate and coherent rationales for their protest. (Such a retention of rationality is necessary to resist the erosion of argument by reaction [Nietzsche].) The elevation and affirmation of emotion in the Greenham protest is not meant to construct an irresolvable divide between feeling and thought.

The search for means to express these emotional responses to the possibilities of nuclear war has led the Greenham women to present their arguments and aims in extremely innovative ways, often with a strong emphasis on the 'carnivalesque'. An event can be likened to carnival if it is populist, involving a shifting multitude of people, of heteroglot exuberance, hybrid, excessive, coarse and derisive. In many senses, the Greenham protest conforms to this description: all women from all cultures and nations are seen as being welcome participants, it involves a considerably diverse mix of activities with every idea a potential action. The women's peace camp deals always in excess, transgressing boundaries and subverting categories, it derides the comforting assumptions of pro-nuclear policies and brings disrepute to the ordered and regulated world of the opposing culture.

To this extent, two different value systems are in confrontation across the perimeter fence. On one side, the world of the base, with its miles of barbed and razor wire, grey concrete, watch towers, a hierarchy of uniformed soldiers. On the other side lies the encampment, a haphazard collection of tents, polythene, a disorganised chaos, colourful posters, diversely dressed women. At another, less immediately corporeal, level there is another opposition across the fence, which is to do with the abstract representation of the cultural body: the corpus represented by the base is the classical one, smooth, hairless, bland, elevated on high, idealised. Outside the base, there exists an altogether different image: of corporeal physicality and functionalism, a body with orifices exposed, where idealised beauty is irrelevant, replaced with grotesque realism, where the cerebral functions accede to bodily reaction.

This conceptualisation of the Greenham protest, comparing it to the riotous carnivalesque, should include the notion that carnival can exist not just as a physical phenomenon but also as a mode of understanding, a cultural analytic. This dimension can be understood to permeate the Greenham protest at all levels: decision-making (unhierarchical, based on individual wants and ideas), symbolism (an element of ritual, a restoration of ancient symbols and meanings), action (troublemaking, ingenious, bawdy, musical, humorous). However, it is important not to idealise the revolutionary potential inhering to the carnivalesque: there are obvious limitations to the subversions available to the carnival as cultural form. The most important is that carnival was a licensed phenomenon; it was assimilated into bourgeois high culture and contained.

A pessimistic analysis of the Greenham protest would have to allow that this possibility does exist: as the years have passed, the carnival of dissent expressed at Greenham has become a routine part of state and local control problems. Various strategies have been taken up as the most efficient means of policing the protesters (evictions by the council, aggression from the police, harassment from local residents). These representatives of the dominant culture (police, residents, councillors) would prefer that the protest did not exist, but while it persists, they have evolved means that defuse its revolutionary promises. For this reason, the potential of the Greenham peace camp as carnival to break down the high/low cultural barrier is constrained by its relative powerlessness in comparison with the institutions of the opposed order.

One way in which the Greenham protest has been immensely successful is through symbolism. Here the protesting body becomes an entity which reacts at various levels to symbols offered as meaning. At the peace camp, the protesters have retrieved from disuse many symbols or meanings of symbols and re-presented them as relevant to the contemporary situation. In this respect, the image of the snake is an important one. Choosing to play up certain forgotten or lesser known aspects of the snake as symbol, for the women it represents psychological renewal, shedding constricting attitudes and beliefs with its old skin. It can also represent eternity, endless life and wisdom in its unclosing eyes. One journalist, Caroline Blackwood, who visited Greenham, criticised the 'choice' of the snake as a 'stupidly frightening and poisonous symbol'.[1] She felt that soldiers or ordinary people would be unable to understand such subtle imagery as was wrapped up in the myth of the snake; however, this is a very closed view to take: it is true that the image of the snake is a multi-vocal one (as all images are), but its very ambiguity is a source of power and potential for resistance to the dichotomy which presumes images to either possess or lack meaning.

As well as their investigations into snake mythology, the Greenham women have developed and explored the meanings and themes surrounding the image of the spider spinning its web. Blackwood calls the spider's web 'a very unfortunate peace symbol: for many people are scared of spiders and webs are cunning traps for the unwary'.[2] This, however, misses most of the symbolic point through concentrating on the reaction to the creature which is spinning rather than effect or achievement. It is correct that the Greenham women deliberately use identification with the spider:

> Like the spider-goddess, I will weave with you the threads of our existence, human, animal and plant together. I will bind them with truth and love and gentleness. Together ... we will build again a web of life.[3]

The tone and import of these words involves no image of the spider as predator or as objects of phobia. Instead, the emphasis is all on sharing, connection and creation. For the Greenham women, the *web* is the most important aspect of this imagery: the web represents creativity, strength and growth; it shows connections between women or between ideas; it can be begun at any point or at any time; each single strand is weak and fragile, yet when interwoven it is strong, beautiful and efficient, baffling to policemen and court officials. To revalorise the image of the spider, the spinner, is also a gesture of irony. Spinning is traditionally the work of women, done in the home, but it became devalued after the Industrial Revolution, and a woman spinner was seen as a failure. Daly[4] rejects the modern pejorative use of the term 'spinster' in favour of a positive evaluation of a spinster as a woman not defined by her lack of a husband but rather as a woman with a trade, an independent woman; similarly the Greenham women have sought to redeploy the spinner as an image of strength.

Spinning has also come to represent a way of thinking. It opposes itself to the regimented mental organisation that is seen as underlying the policy of nuclear deterrence. Instead, there is a commitment to visualising the 'whole', to the discovery of interconnections. In 1985, the theme of the December demonstrations was 'Widening the Web'. The themes which were organised included: animal liberation, veganism, anarchism, nuclear dumping, food mountains, aid and development, women in prison, violence against women, racism and apartheid. The Greenham women have also taken their philosophy and style of protest further than the geographical area around the base. Jones writes:

> Cruise is only one symptom of a much more complex problem. That problem is our complete lack of control over our own lives. Action at Greenham becomes for some of us a metaphor for action in other areas where we lack control. The kind of action we take, and the symbols we use, illuminate the connections between those areas.[5]

Many at Greenham have been involved in 'widening the web'. An example of this is the campaign carried out by them against the multinational company Rio Tinto Zinc (RTZ) which is involved in uranium mining in Namibia, Australia and Canada, without concern for the deaths and injuries sustained by their employees as a result of nuclear pollution. Other links have been made: with black struggles in South Africa, with the rights of dissidents in the Soviet Union, with the work of women in Northern Ireland, with the miners' strike and the occupation of a hospital in London in protest at the atrophying of the health service while defence spending increases.

Two specific demonstrations by the women show how these disparate uses of the political dissenting body can be effective and powerful. The first concerns a 'die-in' outside the Stock Exchange in London. The women lay down and 'died' across five roads around the Stock Exchange, blocking all the traffic going through the City. 'The Stock Exchange ... was chosen to highlight the connection between the vast sums of money spent on nuclear weapons and the consequences in human lives.'[6] Some women lay in the street, some handed out leaflets, explaining the reasons for the action: that the women represented the millions who would be killed in a nuclear strike on London, in an attempt to confront people going to work with the terror behind the day-to-day world of money, the city, work. This use of the body allowed for stark images and strong impact, hoping to shock and provoke positive connection and rejection of the investment in weapons of destruction.

The second demonstration I wish to cite seems to me to be exemplary of body politics. On 9 August 1984 (Nagasaki Day), women stripped naked, covered themselves and the ground with ashes and formed a blockade at the main gate. The army personnel were filled with horror and seemed reluctant to touch the women (which was necessary to remove them). Eventually, protective clothing was worn to do so. The immediate, most obvious connection was with the victims and survivors of the bombing of Nagasaki, but the women were also presenting a challenge to the stereotype of the naked woman (that of pornography) in which the woman is conventionally attractive to men, disposable by them and powerless. These horrifying yet naked and vulnerable women were stating a right to self-determination and self-definition at the same time as they demonstrated the effects of nuclear warfare. In this, the power and strength of the Greenham politics shows most strikingly: in their recuperation of the repressed body, and, specifically, in their redefinitions of the meaning of the *female* body, the Greenham protesters have found a form of political protest which is truly transformative.

Notes

1. C. Blackwood, *On the Perimeter*, London: Fontana, 1984, p. 21.
2. *Ibid.*, p. 21.
3. B. Harford and S. Hopkins, (eds), *Greenham Common: Women at the wire*, London: The Women's Press, 1984.
4. M. Daly, *Gyn/Ecology*, London: The Women's Press, 1984.
5. L. Jones, 'Perceptions of "peace women" at Greenham Common, 1981–5', in S. MacDonald *et al.* (eds), *Images of Women in Peace and War*, London: Macmillan, 1987, pp. 200–1.
6. A. Cook and G. Kirk, *Greenham Women Everywhere*, London: Pluto, 1983.

Further Reading

Baker, J. 'Family policy as an anti-poverty measure', in M. Hardy and G. Crowe (eds) (1991) *Lone Parenthood: Coping with constraints and making opportunities*, Hemel Hempstead: Harvester Wheatsheaf.

Dobash, R. and Dobash, R. (1991), *Women, Violence and Social Change*, London: Routledge (ch. 4).

Hardy, M. and Glover, J. 'Income, employment, daycare and lone parenthood', in M. Hardy and G. Crowe (eds) (1991), *Lone Parenthood: Coping with constraints and making opportunities*, Hemel Hempstead: Harvester Wheatsheaf.

Hicks, C. (1988), *Who Cares? Looking after people at home*, London: Virago.

Land, H. 'The introduction of family allowance: an act of historic justice?' in C. Ungerson (ed.) (1985), *Women and Social Policy: A reader*, London: Macmillan.

Loney, M. *et al.* (eds) (1991), *The State or the Market?* (2nd edn), Milton Keynes: Open University Press, esp. Part II, 'Public Policy and the Family'.

McClean, M. and Groves, D. (1991), *Women's Issues in Social Policy*, London: Routledge.

McIntosh, M. 'The state and the oppression of women', in A. Kuhn and A. Wolpe (eds) (1978), *Feminism and Materialism*, London: Routledge & Kegan Paul.

West, G. and Blumberg, R. L. (1990), *Women and Social Protest*, Milton Keynes: Open University Press.

11 | SCIENCE, MEDICINE AND REPRODUCTIVE TECHNOLOGY

Edited and Introduced by Stevi Jackson, Jane Prince and Pauline Young

INTRODUCTION

In this Section we will be examining scientific and medical ideas about women's bodies and minds, how these ideas are implemented in medical and psychiatric practice, and how they affect women's experience of our own bodies. Because science has so often been used to justify women's subordination, to define us as 'naturally' different from or inferior to men, it is important to challenge it, to expose its presuppositions and biases (Readings 11.1, 11.2). Scientific knowledge is framed in language which lays claim to rationality and objectivity. Scientists, we are told, make 'discoveries'; they deal with 'evidence' and 'facts' which contribute to 'advances' in our understanding of the natural order. Science is thus mythologised as revelatory truth. The apparent neutral authority with which it speaks conceals its gendered assumptions (see Reading 11.2).

Science, like all knowledge, is culturally constructed, produced under particular social and historical conditions. Since medical and scientific institutions have long been male-dominated, women have more often been objects of scientific knowledge than producers of it. Women are identified as 'other' in relation to men; as 'the sex'; as somehow deviant when measured by the yardstick of masculine normality.[1] As Ludmilla Jordanova points out (Reading 11.3), women have often been identified with 'nature', which has been conceptualised in opposition to masculine 'culture'; while scientific theory and practice is concerned with knowledge of and mastery over nature. The objectification of women through scientific discourse can thus be seen as a means of defining and controlling our bodies and minds. Science also objectifies women in that it constructs unicausal, universal explanations which supposedly hold true for all women irrespective of the diversity of female experience.

A key aspect of women's 'otherness' from the perspective of masculine scientific discourse is our reproductive capacity. Women have historically been defined in terms of reproductive biology in a way that men are not. For example, 'hysteria' was used to explain women's deviant behaviour in the nineteenth century, just as the 'pre-menstrual syndrome' is today. Hence women's bodies are pathologised and we are represented as victims of our unruly organs and hormones. Men, too, have reproductive organs, they too have hormones, but while their anatomy and physiology is sometimes used to account for general masculine proclivities (such as aggression) only rarely is any individual man's behaviour explained in these terms. When a man loses his temper we seldom hear anyone say 'It's just an excess of androgens', yet think how often women's anger is explained in terms of 'the time of the month'. Reproductive biology itself is understood through the language of male dominance and female submission. For example, the process of conception is generally represented through the imagery of heroic sperm swimming determinedly upstream to the waiting, passive egg. This imagery persists even though it is now known that the ovum is more active in the process and the sperm far less purposeful than was once supposed.[2]

Women's bodies are also specific sites of medical knowledge and practice. There is no medical specialism, equivalent to gynaecology, focused on the male body. The medicalisation of women's bodies means that any changes or variations we experience become constructed as disease states ripe for medical or even surgical intervention. The menstrual cycle, the processes of growth and ageing from menarche to menopause, conception, pregnancy and childbirth are all definable as illnesses requiring treatment. As Jane Ussher says of the so-called pre-menstrual syndrome:

> The medicalisation, renaming and general mystification of cyclical phenomena have served to isolate women from their own experiences, placing control in the hands of self-proclaimed experts – the doctors and drug companies – who attempt to define reality.[3]

Women by no means always concur with medical definitions of their reality, but the privileged status accorded to medical knowledge and the institutionalised power of the medical profession often undermine alternative versions of women's experience. Moreover, as privileged knowledge, medical discourse also affects the ways in which women are defined and controlled through a range of social settings – in legal, educational, familial and occupational contexts as well as medical ones.

We need to trace the origins of these ideas and practices which have such a profound impact on women's lives, and to understand the ways in which science and medicine became established as sites of patriarchal knowledge and power. The modern medical profession did not become organised as such until the nineteenth century.[4] Before that, separate healing traditions had existed side by side, although they were differentiated by status. Midwifery was an exclusively female occupation, and midwives frequently practised more general healing skills. Within the private sphere of the home, healing was considered part of the more general skills of housewifery. Other branches of medicine were male dominated. There is some evidence of women acting as physicians, surgeons and apothecaries in their own right, but from the fifteenth century onwards there had been attempts to exclude women from these occupations. None the less, the wives of medical men were often active participants in their husbands' businesses until the separation of work and home in the early nineteenth century (see Section 4 above).

The same social changes which excluded women from their husbands' work also fostered the growth of public, market-orientated medicine at the expense of women's domestic healing skills.[5] Apothecaries, surgeons and physicians sought to professionalise medicine, to raise its status and then to preserve its exclusivity and hierarchy. Male doctors also began to take over the traditional female preserve of midwifery, eventually establishing obstetrics as a specialist branch of medicine.[6] In Britain the Medical Registration Act of 1858 effectively established a male monopoly. Women were excluded not by the Act itself, but because they did not have access to the education and training necessary to qualify for registration. They subsequently had to fight for reinclusion in the profession or were reincorporated in a supporting role as nurses or midwives.

It is important to note that the professionalisation of medicine preceded the advances in medical science which were later used to justify it. The knowledge produced by this masculine profession – not surprisingly – reflected and contributed to historically specific definitions of womanhood (Readings 11.3, 11.4). Women's bodies had long been considered inferior to those of men, but it was in the nineteenth century that they became thoroughly pathologised, regarded as intrinsically diseased and malfunctional.[7] The nineteenth century was a period of increasing faith in scientific knowledge, so that pronouncements on women's nature acquired the status of scientific fact. Science was then used to legitimate women's exclusion from medical training and other forms of education. It was argued, for example, that intensive education would place intolerable strain on women's reproductive organs, or conversely that women could not be trusted in responsible occupations because menstruation, childbirth and the menopause rendered them mentally unstable. Once science and medicine had become established as masculine institutions and as masculine modes of knowledge, ever more sophisticated accounts of women's 'otherness' were produced. Even today we are told that our hormones dominate our cognitive and emotional functioning (Reading 11.6).

The establishment of modern science and medicine created a male monopoly over what had once been women's own sphere of influence: pregnancy and childbirth. These processes have become medicalised, defined as illness, and subject to increasing technological intervention. This is of concern to feminists because control over our own fertility and reproductive capacities is seen as essential to women's liberation. Women's feelings about the medical management of pregnancy and childbirth are often mixed (Reading 11.7). On the one hand it offers the possibility of safer and less painful delivery; but on the other it can be experienced as dehumanising, as a loss of control over one's own body, reducing pregnant and labouring women to the status of prize sows.

Medical technologies which affect conception are potentially very significant for women. At first feminists focused on what are often known as 'old' reproductive technologies – those which prevented pregnancy – and demanded access to safe, reliable contraception and abortion. There have also been campaigns against the experimental use of contraceptive techniques on poor and Third World women. More recently, 'new' reproductive technologies which offer assisted conception and genetic engineering have become a major cause for concern. In the early 1970s Shulamith Firestone[8] envisaged the possibility of women being freed from childbirth by these technologies. Now, however, feminists are more likely to see their application as intensifying male power over women's bodies. Technologies are not developed in a social vacuum. What is at issue here is how and why certain technologies are developed, who controls them, and their probable consequences for women.

In the first place there are worries about the effects of technologies on the women who make use of or are subjected to them. For example, *in vitro* fertilisation (IVF) is presented as a miracle cure for infertility, but equal attention is not given to its high risks and low success rate. Clearly, this raises questions about informed choice and the way in which the medical profession in general restricts access to knowledge. There are also issues here about the availability of such techniques: only relatively privileged women will be able to make use of them. The provisions of the 1990 Human Fertilisation and Embryology Act effectively deny IVF to lesbians, and there have been suggestions that Artificial Insemination by Donor (AID) should be subject to similar restrictions. Both old and new reproductive technologies have been deployed in such a way as to discourage the 'unfit' (poor women, black women and lesbians) from breeding.

The concepts of rights and choices are themselves problematic. We obviously exercise rights and make choices within given social constraints and in terms of particular alternatives available to us. Opening up new alternatives for some infertile women may not be in the interests of all women. The existence of IVF, for example, may help to foster a climate of pro-natalism and the idea that women are not fulfilled until they have given birth. Childless women are frequently seen as incomplete individuals; this makes it more difficult for infertile women to accept their situation. Moreover, the money spent on research into high-technology assisted conception might be better used investigating and remedying the many environmental hazards that cause infertility in the first place. A counter-argument here is that few feminists challenge the right of women to have children by natural means, yet there is a vocal critique of the use of IVF.

The possible consequences for women of technologies controlled by male-dominated professions are potentially extremely negative. Some feminist visions of the future use of such technologies are truly apocalyptic. There are two main fears here. First, there is the danger of femicide: reducing the number of female children born. This is already possible through selective abortion of female fetuses identified as such through ultrasound scans and amniocentesis.

There is evidence that it is happening, despite the fact that it is medically unethical.[9] The possibility of femicide is enhanced by the development of genetic engineering techniques.[10] The second major worry is that techniques already in use on farm animals could, if applied to women, result in what Andrea Dworkin and Gena Corea have called 'the reproductive brothel', a system in which only some women would be regarded as genetically fit to reproduce, while others would be used merely to gestate their offspring (Reading 11.8). It might even be possible in the future to bring pregnancies to term in artificial wombs, and thus do away with women altogether. These fears led radical feminists to form an international organisation to combat the development of reproductive technologies. FINNRAGE (Feminist International Network of Resistance to Reproductive and Genetic Engineering) was founded in 1985.

Other feminists have been more cautious in their approach, suggesting that we should focus attention on control over these technologies rather than outright opposition to them.[11] While most feminists are certainly wary of the potential dangers identified by FINNRAGE, some have suggested that they misjudge the impact of reproductive technologies. Jana Sawicki, for example, has suggested that their impact has been to make women more productive rather than rendering them redundant (Reading 11.9). Christine Delphy suggests that apocalyptic visions of femicide and artificial wombs ignore the non-reproductive ways in which men find women useful to them. She also questions the appeal to 'nature' underpinning many feminist analyses of reproductive technology (Reading 11.10).

Feminist opposition to the new reproductive technologies does indeed tend to emphasise their unnaturalness. These technologies are seen as interfering with women's natural reproductive capacities, as an instance of male science seeking to control female nature. This discourse of 'naturalness' is problematic. In the first place, there are times when we are glad of science and medicine's interference with natural processes: few of us would say no, for example, to a life-saving operation. More fundamentally, we should remember that the concept of 'nature' has long been used to justify women's subordination. A feminist concept of nature is no less essentialist than its patriarchal version and risks leading us to accept sexual difference as natural, as biologically determined. We should be wary of embracing the very dualism between masculine culture/science and feminine nature which was so fundamental to the development of patriarchal scientific discourse.

Notes

1. On women as 'other', see S. de Beauvoir, *The Second Sex*, Harmondsworth: Penguin, 1972. For a discussion of the way in which women are identified as 'the sex' in language, see M. Black and R. Coward, 'Linguistic social and sexual relations: a review of Dale Spender's *Man Made Language*', in *Screen Education*, no. 39 (1981),

reprinted in D. Cameron (ed.), *The Feminist Critique of Language*, London: Routledge, 1990.

2. See E. Martin, 'The egg and the sperm: how science has constructed a romance based on stereotypical male–female roles', *Signs*, vol. 16, no. 3 (1991). See also Martin's 'Body narratives, body boundaries', in L. Grossberg *et al.* (eds), *Cultural Studies*, London: Routledge, 1992.

3. J. Ussher, *The Psychology of the Female Body*, London: Routledge, 1989, p. 46.

4. For histories of women's participation in medicine, see B. Ehrenreich and D. English, *Witches, Midwives and Nurses*, London: Writers and Readers Co-operative, 1973; J. Leeson and J. Gray, *Women and Medicine*, London: Tavistock, 1978; A. Witz, *Professions and Patriarchy*, London: Routledge 1992.

5. See Witz, *Professions and Patriarchy*.

6. In addition to references given in Note 4, see A. Rich, *Of Woman Born*, London: Virago, 1977; A. Oakley, *The Captured Womb*, Oxford: Basil Blackwell, 1984.

7. See S. Edwards, *Female Sexuality and the Law*, Oxford: Martin Robertson, 1981; B. Ehrenreich and D. English, *For Her Own Good*; London: Pluto, 1979; L. Jordanova, *Sexual Visions*, Hemel Hempstead: Harvester Wheatsheaf, 1989; E. Martin, *The Woman in the Body*, Milton Keynes: Open University Press, 1989; C. E. Russett, *Sexual Science*, Cambridge, MA: Harvard University Press, 1989; Sally Shuttleworth, 'Female circulation: medical discourse and popular advertising in the mid-Victorian era', in M. Jacobus *et al.* (eds), *Body/Politics*, London: Routledge, 1990; E. Showalter, *The Female Malady*, London: Virago, 1987; E. and E. Showalter, 'Victorian women and menstruation', in M. Vicinus (ed.), *Suffer and be Still: women in the Victorian age*, London: Methuen, 1980.

8. S. Firestone, *The Dialectic of Sex*, London: Paladin, 1972.

9. For a discussion of this in the context of Indian society, see M. Kishwar, 'The continuing deficit of women in India and the impact of amniocentesis', in G. Corea *et al.*, *Man-Made Women*, London: Hutchinson, 1985.

10. For discussions of this issue, see Corea, *Man-Made Women*; P. Spallone, *Beyond Conception*, London: Macmillan, 1989.

11. For arguments from this perspective, see M. Stanworth (ed.), *Reproductive Technologies*, Oxford: Polity, 1987; L. Birke *et al.*, *Tomorrow's Child*, London: Virago, 1990.

11.1   Life in the XY Corral
Anne Fausto-Sterling

Anne Fausto-Sterling describes how a scientific attempt to explain the origins of sex differentiation in the human embryo has, in the end, to revert to classic gender stereotypes of 'male = active and female = passive' to describe DNA action. She also notes that definitions of male and female in the scientific community are arbitrary and rely on cultural rather than putatively objective referents.

In December, 1987, we were treated to a memorable media blast. Scientists at

MIT, we learned, had discovered the secret of sex determination; the secret, they said, consisted of a master gene on the Y chromosome. In the TV and newspaper interviews, Dr David Page, the researcher in question, suggested that his discovery had fundamental and new importance for all of developmental biology. Had Page, who calls his laboratory at MIT's Whitehead Institute the XY Corral, [1] really uncovered the secrets of sex?

In analyzing the work of Page and others on mammalian sex determination three intersecting issues arise. The first is the use of the universal language of man; in much of the literature discoveries billed as the key to sex determination are in fact only keys to male development. The second concerns the representations of male as presence and female as absence. This representation has been widely written about in psychoanalytic and linguistic feminist analyses, but it also extends into the heart of biological theories about male and female. The third is the treatment of 'sex' as something clear cut and unambiguous. Feminist theorists have critically examined the categories of sex and gender, [2] but despite the 'data' at their finger tips, biologists continue to write about sex as if it were an uncomplicated dualism. [...]

Presence and absence

In the opening sentence of [an article in] *Cell* [...], Page *et al.* write: 'The presence or absence of the Y chromosome determines whether a mammalian embryo develops as male or female'. [3] In the introduction, they restate the theme: 'The mammalian Y chromosome, by its presence or absence, constitutes a binary switch upon which hinge all sexually dimorphic characteristics' (p. 1091). And again in the conclusion they open with: 'Our studies suggest that the sex of an individual is determined by the presence or absence of a very small portion of the human Y chromosome … female WHT1013 carries 99.8% of the Y chromosome; she lacks only the 160 kb that comprise intervals 1A2 and 1B – yet she is a female' (p. 1099). Usually, development of specific tissue types is understood to involve the activation of specific genes or gene sequences. Yet the generally accepted theory of sex determination claims that female differentiation is determined by the *absence* of something, that a female develops when something is lacking. I suggest that the pervasiveness of our cultural construction of female as absence, seen in everything from Freudian theory to the non-equivalence of the words male and female in our language (the opposite of male is not female, but non-male), has also insinuated itself into biological theories about male and female development. The process by which this has happened is completely unconscious, and it has gone unnoticed until feminists, by focusing an alternate prism on the subject, became able to 'see' what had previously appeared invisible. [...]

The complications of sex

David Page investigated sex determination using the following tactic. He obtained DNA samples from unusual clinical cases in which individuals with two X chromosomes had been designated as males (XX males) and ones with an XY chromosomal constitution had been designated as females (XY females). He and his co-workers reasoned that if there is a male-determining gene on the Y chromosome, then what must be going on in these unusual cases is that the gene, that is, a small stretch of DNA not visible under the microscope, had been translocated from the Y chromosome to some other chromosome. If this were the case then even though an XX male had no microscopically detectable Y chromosome, he must have the key piece of DNA responsible for maleness present on one of his other chromosomes. Similarly, even though the XY females appeared to have a normal Y chromosome, they must have lost a key submicroscopic portion of the Y, the so-called testis determining factor. By collecting DNA samples from a number of different XX males and XY females, and by examining them with the most modern of molecular techniques, Page *et al.* confirmed that a small stretch of Y chromosome DNA was indeed present in the genome of XX males and missing from that of XY females.

But then came the puzzling result. This same stretch of DNA, or at least one very similar to it in base sequence, is also present on the X chromosomes of normal females. If this Y-chromosome DNA sequence is the 'master sex-determining locus' and if its presence means male and its absence means female, then what is it doing on both X and Y chromosomes? Page and co-authors offer several hypotheses. The first, and least satisfactory, is that although the gene is on the X chromosome, it does nothing when there: i.e., it is passive in a female but active in a male. The other models, while somewhat more plausible, fall short because these researchers understand the word 'sex' in too simple a fashion. In fact the subjects from whom they obtained DNA samples present a more complex story.

In the *Cell* paper, Page *et al.* give no hint that the XX males and XY females from whom they obtained DNA samples were anything other than fully normal representatives of their sex. But this is not the case. (If it were they would probably never have been discovered, since it was clinical symptoms which brought them to attention in the first place.) For example, the four XX males whom they studied were all sterile (no sperm production), had small testes which totally lacked germ cells, that is, the precursor cells for sperms, high follicle stimulating hormone levels and low testosterone levels. Presumably they were classified as males because of their external genitalia and the presence of testes. But clearly their development had not been fully normal.[4] Similarly, the development of the XY females were [sic] abnormal. Although both of these patients' external genitalia were normal, their ovaries lacked germ cells. In both XX males and XY females, then, what does the notion of a sex-determining gene mean? Is maleness decided on the basis of external genital structure? Often not, since sometimes physicians decide that an individual with female genitalia is really male and surgically correct the external structures so that they match the chromosomal and hormonal sex. Is it the presence of an ovary or testis that decides the matter? If so, oughtn't the gonad to have germ cells in it to 'count'? Or is it enough to be in the right place and have the right superficial histological structure? There are no good answers to these questions because even biologically speaking sex is not such an either/or construct. Page and co-workers choose to leave some of the messy facts out of their account, which makes the story look much cleaner than it actually is. What is called for here is to develop an account of sexual differentiation which permits the existence of intermediate states.

Notes

1. L. Roberts, 'Zeroing in on the sex switch', *Science*, 239, (1988), pp. 21–2.
2. J. Flax, 'Postmodernism and gender relations in feminist theory', *Signs*, 12, (1987), pp. 621–43.
3. D. Page *et al.* 'The sex-determining region of the human Y chromosome encodes a finger protein', *Cell*, 51 (1987), pp. 1091–1104.
4. G. Guellan *et al.* 'Human XX males with Y single-cop DNA fragment', *Nature*, 307 (1984), pp. 172–3.

11.2 Society Writes Biology
Ruth Herschberger

Ruth Herschberger, writing in the 1940s, was one of the first feminists to challenge patriarchal scientific discourses. She engages in an ironic rewriting of orthodox science's descriptions of male and female reproductive organs and sexual functioning; she presents an alternative in which the female *organs and functioning is the norm and those of the male are deviant and abnormal. This change in perspective enables a clearer understanding of the extent to which scientific discourses distort concepts of women's sexuality.*

> well, here's looking at ourselves
> (E. E. Cummings)

There is a prevalent belief that scientists are unprejudiced. It is true that they of all citizens make the most stirring attempt at objectivity, but in realms close to the social structure, as in the biological sciences, it is easy for the scientist and popularizer of science to slip into hidden evaluations in their reports on organic fact. If we like their bias, we contentedly ignore it. In accounts of sexual processes, however, there is a painfully persistent tendency to award the female a derogatory role. [...]

A patriarchal society writes biology

Embryology

Male.   The human embryo first passes through an indifferent or asexual stage in which it is not possible to distinguish male from female. In the second month, however, nature prepares for the great differentiation which is to come.

The genital projection, later the penis, is joined by a large genital fold, a sort of collar. This collar later becomes the scrotum.

Along the genital projection is a cleft, a median slit which leads to the kidneys and internal genital glands.

As development proceeds, the penis grows rapidly, and the genital cleft closes to form the urethra, which opens temporarily at the base of the glans.

In the third month the glans splits and forms a groove which recloses, continuing the urethra to its proper place at the tip of the penis.

Just before or after birth the testes progress from their position within the pelvic region to their definitive place in the scrotum. [...]

A matriarchal society writes biology

Embryology

Female.   The human embryo first passes through an indifferent or asexual stage in which it is not possible to distinguish female from male. In the second month, however, nature prepares for the great differentiation that is to come.

The genital projection, later the clitoris, is joined by a large genital fold, a sort of collar. This collar later becomes the outer lips of the vulva.

Along the genital projection is a cleft, a median slit which leads to the kidneys and internal genital glands. This cleft widens to form the inner lips of the vulva.

As development proceeds, the vestigial human tail, which projects from the body just as the genital tubercle does, begins to recede, taking its proper place at the base of the spine.

In like manner – but only in the female – the genital tubercle also progresses to its proper place at the head of the labia minora, or inner lips of the vulva. This interesting development of the clitoris is accompanied in the female by an extensive development of the genital fold, which becomes the pubis and outer lips of the vulva.

Thus the female human being utilizes the asexual embryonic projection (or genital tubercle) to develop the distinctive organs of clitoris and vulva.

Male.   The male, we find, does not develop in any important way from the asexual or early embryonic state. His sexual organs remain in an infantile condition, displaying an early arrest of development.

Whereas in the female the genital tubercle becomes the complex and highly differentiated organ, the clitoris, in the male the infantile genital projection remains, merely thickening and growing larger. The penis is best described as a vestigial clitoris which has lost much of its sensitivity. [...]

It is clear that the sperm plays a very small and hesitant part in this larger panorama of the creation of life. We must not assume, however, that the sperm is any less essential than the egg; it is a difference in function. There is no question of superiority or inferiority.

The female system differs from that of the male in that the female egg is produced once each month with timely regularity and therefore with greater chance of being fertilized, while a margin of several million sperm is required for the fertilization of one mature egg.

Reproduction and the sex act are more closely allied in the female than in the male, because no matter how many male sperm are present, unless the female provides an ovum the set act cannot result in fertilization. Only once each month, when the female egg is present, does intercourse have any reproductive significance for the male.

The male reproductive function. The coordinated system of the male is merely the negative reflection of the positive features of the female. The male functions to produce sperm to give to the female.

The sperm are manufactured by the testes and stored away. At this time they have wispy thread-like projections but are totally incapable of any motion. When the female induces a sexual response in the male, passive sperm are forced up the tubes and receive a milky secretion from the prostate. It is this secretion which gives the sperm a limited capacity for self-locomotion.

The motility of the sperm should not be exaggerated. It is the contractions of muscular tissues which force the semen from the penis. The sperm have no capacity for motion until they are supplied with the milky fluid from the prostate during ejaculation; under this influence they move jerkily about. So abortive are their movements, however, that it is no wonder millions of spare sperm are necessary.

The movement of the sperm is neither swift nor certain. Not all sperm have effective tails, and if the prostatic secretion is deficient, there may be no movement whatever. Those sperm which do move cover about one millimetre in three minutes or one centimetre in a half hour.

The mature female egg is obliged to bide its time, not without impatience, until one of the tiny snail-like cells manages to reach it. No wonder the complicated sexual system of the female undertakes as one of its principal tasks the helpful encouragement of the dependent male cell. The fatal acids of the vagina are neutralized as much as possible by sexually stimulated glands. Active moistures supply a milieu without which the sperm would soon dry up and die.

Nature, in order to induce the male to consent to sexual union, has provided him with a sensitive pleasure-producing zone. This zone is the penis, especially the glans. The male differs from the female in that his source of pleasure is only outside the body, while the female's is both outside and inside.

Many men say that they do not experience pleasure during orgasm, and some have come to regard pleasure as a luxury.

From the point of view of function, it may be said that they are right; pleasure for men is indeed a luxury. No woman in a matriarchal society will consent to intercourse unless pleasure is involved, and therefore there can be no conception without female pleasure and satisfaction. But for the male function of supplying sperm, an emission, whether accompanied by pleasure or not, will serve to supply the egg with its needed fertilization.

Frigidity.   Frigidity is a condition in males in which sexual desire or the ability to reach a climax is lacking. This is very frequent, and the theory may be advanced that the cause of this, more frequently than usually realized, is an actual organic inadequacy in the human male, perhaps resulting from the rigors of evolution. The frigidity of a husband should not interfere any more than necessary with the normal gratification of the woman's sexual impulse.

Impotence.   Impotence is the occasional inability of a woman to obtain erection or to enjoy intercourse, either because of revulsion to the man, indifference, or because of a psychological barrier.

11.3   Natural Facts: an historical perspective on science and sexuality

Ludmilla Jordanova

Ludmilla Jordanova explores the ways in which oppositions between nature and culture, woman and man, have been deployed within scientific discourse since the Enlightenment, and how women have come to be identified with 'nature'.

The distinction between women as natural and men as cultural appeals to a set of ideas – with a long history – about the biological foundations of womanhood. To understand the historical dimensions of these interrelated pairs of dichotomies, it is necessary to consider the close relationships between natural knowledge and notions of sexuality. Although I shall focus here on the biomedical sciences in eighteenth- and nineteenth-century France and Britain, the links between nature/culture, woman/man, are both ancient and widespread; they may be found in numerous other domains besides science and medicine. However, sex roles have long been discussed in terms of what is deemed natural and authoritatively uncovered by systematic, that is scientific, study. Equally, the natural sciences have found sexuality appealing not just as a subject for intensive investigation but as a source of images, metaphors and symbols. The distinction between nature and culture, like that between women and men, is one of value. However, the term that is given greater value can shift dramatically in both cases, hence it is not surprising to find that the two dichotomies have been combined in different ways and given a variety of meanings. In what follows I explore the association between women and nature because it has been one of the most pervasive historically, not because there are essential connections between them.

Perhaps we should dispel a common misapprehension right at the beginning. Associations made in the past between women and nature did not arise out of attempts to capture social life in abstract terms. The associations have always existed as representations, not as descriptions. There is no longer any doubt about the diversity of female social and economic roles in the past, a diversity that coexisted with inflexible contemporary ideas about those roles.[1] It is now frequently suggested that during the eighteenth century a process of hardening began whereby gender polarities were understood as firmer, less flexible than they had been previously. This stiffening inspired numerous attempts to bring social life into line. Such a dramatic and persistent lack of fit between ideas and experience clearly points to the ideological function of the nature/culture dichotomy as applied to gender.[2] It was in the domain of medicine above all that these ideological matters were canvassed in eighteenth- and nineteenth-century Europe.

In our attempts to understand the deployment of symbols and metaphors, we must recognize the fact that one of their most powerful forms in our culture has been the dichotomy, where two opposed terms mutually define each other. It is not just male/female and nature/culture but also town/country, matter/spirit, mind/body, public/private, capitalist/worker, and so on. Our entire philosophical set presents natural and social phenomena in terms of oppositional characteristics.[3] [...]

The power of dichotomies such as man/woman, nature/culture, city/country, does not just consist in the apparent clarity of definition by contrast. There can also be a dialectical relationship between the members of each pair. The fact that there are a number of related pairs, connected in complex ways, demonstrates the point that we are not speaking of simple linear hierarchies. Especially since varied values could be assigned to individual terms, to pairs and whole clusters of dichotomies, a single, continuous scale was never at issue. Frequently, it was precisely the degree of fuzziness between the two sides that was most attended to. For example, debates about sex and sex roles, especially during the nineteenth century, hinged on the ways in which sexual boundaries had become blurred. It was as if the maintenance of the social order depended on clarifying certain key distinctions whose symbolic meanings spread far beyond their explicit context. At certain times, perhaps those of perceived rapid change, medical practitioners were at the forefront of serious concerns about the feminization of men, for which homosexuality could be adduced as evidence and the masculinization of women, which was believed to result from excessive physical and mental work. [...]

There are strong reasons for beginning a consideration of nature, culture and gender with the Enlightenment. Shifts in the meaning and usage of words such as 'culture', 'civil', 'civilize', 'nature' and 'life' indicate far-reaching changes in the way human society and its relations with the natural world were conceived. 'The Enlightenment' is, of course, no easier to define than notions of nature and culture are.[4] In the very term we see an appeal to light as a symbol of a certain form of knowledge, which had the potential for improving human existence, and which was based on first-hand observation whenever possible. Rational knowledge rooted in empirical information derived from the senses was accordingly deemed the best foundation for secure knowledge. Starting with a sensualist epistemology and a number of assumptions about the potential social application of an understanding of natural laws, many Enlightenment writers critically examined forms of social organization. They employed a language rich in sexual metaphors and systematically examined the natural facts of sexuality as integral parts of their programme.[5]

Science and medicine were fundamental to Enlightenment investigations of sexuality in three different ways. First, natural philosophers and medical writers addressed themselves to phenomena in the natural world such as reproduction, sexual behaviour and sex-related diseases. Second, science and medicine held a privileged epistemological position because their methods appeared to be the only ones which would lead away from dogma and superstition towards a secular empirically based knowledge of the natural and social worlds. Third, as activities, science and medicine were understood through sexual metaphors, for example by designating nature as a woman to be unveiled, unclothed and penetrated by masculine science. [...]

As we well know, nature was endowed with a remarkable range of meanings during the period of the Enlightenment.[6] However, one common theme stands out. Nature was taken to be that realm upon which mankind acts, not just to intervene in or manipulate directly, but also to understand and render intelligible, where 'nature' includes people and the societies they construct. Such an interpretation of nature led to two distinct positions: nature could be taken to be that part of the world which human beings have understood, mastered and made their own. Through the unravelling of laws of motion, for example, the inner recesses of nature were revealed to the human mind. Nature was also that which had not yet been penetrated (either literally or metaphorically): the wilderness and deserts, unmediated and dangerous nature.

To these two positions correspond two radically different senses in which women are identified with nature. According to the first, they stand as repositories of natural laws to be revealed and understood. This was the point Michelet made when he denied that women were unpredictable but fully subject to nature's rhythms and laws – as the menstrual cycle, which enabled their states of mind and body to be read off, amply demonstrated. According to the second, women's emotions and uncontrolled passions, including those of a sexual kind, gave them special qualities. Women, being endowed with less reason than men, even with less need for reason, since their social lives required of them more feeling than thought, were more easily dominated by their sentiments. It was then quite easy to conceptualize women as wild and dangerous because less amenable to the guiding light of reason.[7] According to this second perspective, moves to contain women's disruptive potential were required; scientific scrutiny – a prelude to control – was but one route by which the wild was rendered tame. Women's potential for disorder could be minimized by drawing and maintaining strong boundaries around them, using the full range of social, cultural, political and economic practices. Such a situation, far from giving the male/female dichotomy a fixed quality, made it constantly in flux. Furthermore, these two positions gave rise to a variety of moral evaluations of womanhood.

The nature, culture and gender matrix in the history of our own society has served to express the desire for clarity in profoundly unstable and inherently problematic areas. The historical interrelatedness of these ideas shows how apparently distinct domains are linked through sets of symbols and metaphors, which at some times persist for generations and at others shift over shorter periods. Although the terms 'man' and 'woman', 'masculine/feminine', 'sexuality' and 'sex roles' pertain to phenomena of different kinds and of different degrees of abstraction, they are none the less linked through imagery. Science and medicine have acted as major mediators of ideas of nature, culture and gender, with verbal and visual images as the tools of that mediation. One of the most powerful aspects of scientific and medical constructions of sexuality is the way in which apparently universal categories were set up. These implied that there were profound similarities among all women; to a much lesser extent among men. The precise characteristics thereby attributed to the two sexes – the constituent elements of gender imagery – were thus composed both of those given currency in the immediate historical setting and of those more abstract ones of mythic proportions.

Notes

1. The historical literature on women's work has been especially successful in revealing the diversity of women's activities. See, for example, Tilly and Scott, *Women, Work and Family*, New York: 1978; Pinchbeck, *Women Workers in the Industrial Revolution*, London: 1969; and Prior (ed.), *Women in English Society*, London: 1985, especially the chapter by Prior.
2. The relationships between ideas about and experiences of gender have been explored by Davidoff and Hall, *Family Fortunes*, London: 1987; they also mention other work on this subject.
3. There are now well-developed philosophical debates on these matters. A useful synthesis that considers themes close to this book is Lloyd, *The Man of Reason: 'Male' and 'female' in Western philosophy*, London: 1984.

4. The literature on the Enlightenment is, of course, massive. Of relevance for our concerns in this chapter are Hankins, *Science and the Enlightenment*, Cambridge: 1985; Gay, *The Enlightenment: An interpretation*, New York: 1966, 1970. Also useful is Porter and Teich (eds), *The Enlightenment in National Context*, Cambridge: 1981, because it comes at the issues from a different and unusual angle.
5. Sexuality in this period is now receiving more attention. Samples of recent approaches may be found in Bouce (ed.), *Sexuality in Eighteenth Century England*, Manchester: 1982; *Dix-huitième siècle* (special issue on sexuality in 1980); and Rousseau and Porter (eds), *Sexual Underworlds of the Enlightenment*, Cambridge: 1980.
6. Lovejoy, '"Nature" as an aesthetic norm', in *Essays in the History of Ideas*, New York: 1960, pp. 69–77; Charlton, *New Images of the Natural*, Cambridge: 1984; Ehrard, *L'Idée de Nature*, Paris: 1963.
7. This wildness is best exemplified in the widespread preoccupation with women's madness, especially during the nineteenth century: Gilbert and Gubar, *The Madwoman in the Attic*, New Haven, CT: 1979; Showalter, *The Female Malady*, London: 1987; Shuttleworth, '"The surveillance of the sleepless eye"', in Levine (ed.), *One Culture*, Madison, WI: 1987, pp. 313–35.

11.4 **Managing Female Minds**
Elaine Showalter

The idea of women as wild and dangerous is evident in nineteenth-century attitudes to women's madness. Elaine Showalter discusses the moral and practical management of the Victorian female lunatic, so diagnosed because her behaviour deviated from that associated with the decorous stereotype of the perfect lady; she was subjected to a rigid regime which was intended to rehabilitate her into her 'proper' domestic role.

Since women were accustomed to being ordered to submit to the authority of their fathers, brothers, husbands, doctors anticipated few problems in managing female lunatics. Yet rebellion was in fact frequent. Victorian madwomen were not easily silenced, and one often has the impression that their talkativeness, violation of conventions of feminine speech, and insistence on self-expression was the kind of behavior that had led to their being labeled 'mad' to begin with. Conolly noted that it was the female side of the asylum 'where the greatest daily amount of excitement and refractoriness was to be met and managed'. Mortimer Granville was concerned that female lunatics were always 'chattering about their grievances' or else involved in 'an excess of vehement declaration and quarreling'. He recommended that the women be set to work that would keep them too busy to talk.[1] The commissioners visiting Colney Hatch 'regularly remarked that the female department, as is usually the case in all asylums, was the most noisy'. And even a male patient at the Glasgow Royal Asylum felt qualified to complain that 'female lunatics are less susceptible to control than male. They are more troublesome, more noisy, and more abusive in their language.'[2]

Women's deviations from ladylike behaviour were severely punished. At Bethlem, for example, women patients were put in solitary confinement in the basement 'on account of being violent, mischievous, dirty, and using bad language'. At Colney Hatch, they were sedated, given cold baths, and secluded in padded cells, up to five times as frequently as male patients.[3]

The excessive confinement that replicated the feminine role outside the asylum may have contributed to the excitability and restlessness of asylum women. They simply had fewer opportunities than male patients for outdoor activity, physical recreation, or even movement within the building. While physical exercise and manual labour seemed more necessary therapies for male patients, social activities and social decorum were regarded as more important for women. In one large asylum in 1862, only 50 out of 866 female patients ever went from their ward to the day room. At Colney Hatch, women left the asylum for fewer walks or excursions than male patients. Although Dr D. F. Tyerman, who headed the male department, believed physical exercise was essential to mental health and so had a 'properly prepared and level Cricket-ground' constructed in the 1850s where male patients could play, women were only allowed to watch the games from a 'specially fenced-off enclosure'.[4] Ideally, women patients contented themselves with genteel, improving, and passive activities, as in Bethlem, where they might admire the Landseer prints on the walls, feed the birds in the avaries, sew, and make use of the library.

Women's work within the asylum was also more rigidly circumscribed than that of men. Women's occupations were intended to reinforce conventional sex-role behaviour; in Conolly's scheme for a model asylum, the domestic traits he thought healthy for women patients were reflected in his optimistic vision of their happy hours making puddings in the asylum's 'busy and cheerful and scrupulously clean kitchen'.[5] While male patients worked at a variety of jobs in workshops and on the asylum farms, women patients had little choice in their employment, which took place indoors and in some cases was meaningless fancy-work or make-work, such as sorting coloured beans into separate piles that were dumped together again at night.[6] That task uncannily resembles the mythic labors of Psyche, who was ordered by Aphrodite to sort a huge pile of barley, millet, poppy seeds, peas, lentils and beans. This motif, echoed in many fairy tales and folk tales, has been interpreted by Erich Neumann to mean that the woman is being assigned to bring order into the 'disordered welter of fruitful predispositions ... that are present in the feminine nature'.[7]

A more prosaic view of feminine nature was suggested by the primary tasks of women in the asylum: cleaning, laundry, and sewing. Female patients supplied the asylum with thousands of dresses, shirts, aprons, chemises, petticoats, and caps. Isaac Ray, a visiting asylum superintendent from Rhode Island, noted that the piles of fancy clothing produced by female patients at Wakefield and Hanwell were enough 'to set up a respectable shop on

Broadway'.[8] The women's work most highly touted by the Victorians for its therapeutic effects was laundry. Andrew Wynter proudly noted as a sign of progress that in Bethlem the old manacles had been converted into stands for flatirons, an ironically efficient transformation of restraint into domestic work.[9] [...]

Finally, but most tellingly, Victorian madwomen became subject to the moral management of their appearance. Victorian psychiatrists had strong views about the way their women patients should look. Female lunatics were expected to care more about their appearance than males, and indeed, their sanity was often judged according to their compliance with middle-class standards of fashion. Conolly worried about bareheaded female patients, believing that 'it is not *natural* to the woman to neglect the dress of her head'. This natural tendency could be encouraged or restored, he thought, by presenting each female inmate with 'a neat or even pretty cap' for Sunday wear. In his own biweekly rounds of Hanwell Asylum, he noted and commended women who had 'hair more carefully arranged, a neater cap, a new riband'.[10] Inmates who wished to impress the staff with their improvement could do so by conforming to the notion of appropriate feminine grooming. Asylum superintendents were especially urged to use clothing as a weapon in managing women patients: 'Dress is women's weakness, and in the treatment of lunacy it should be an instrument of control, and therefore of recovery'.[11]

Notes

1. J. Conolly, 'Treatment of the insane', in J. M. Granville, *The Care and Cure of The Insane*, vol. 1, Hardwick and Bogue, 1877, p. 107.
2. Hunter and Macalpine, *Psychiatry for the Poor*, Colney Hatch Asylum 1851, Friern Hospital 1973, London: Dawsons, 1974, p. 113.
3. Hunter and Macalpine, *Psychiatry for the Poor*, p. 91.
4. A. T. Scull, 'Museums of madness', Ph.D dissertation, Princeton University, 1976; and Hunter and Macalpine, *Psychiatry for the Poor*, pp. 45, 76, 88.
5. Conolly, 'Treatment of the insane', p. 58.
6. Granville, *Care and Cure*, vol. 2, p. 177.
7. E. Neumann, *Amor and Psyche: The Psychic Development of the Feminine*, Princeton: Princeton University Press, 1956, pp. 41, 94–6.
8. I. Ray, 'Observations of the principal hospitals for the insane in Gt Britain, France and Germany', *American Journal of Insanity*, 2 (1846), pp. 309–10.
9. A. Wynter, *The Borderlands of Insanity*, 2nd edn, London: Robert Hardwick, 1875, p. 353.
10. J. Conolly, *The Construction and Government of Lunatic Asylums and Hospitals for the Insane* [1847], London: Dawsons, 1968, p. 61.
11. Granville, *Care and Cure*, vol. 1, p. 53.

11.5 **The Woman in the Body**
Emily Martin

Emily Martin explains the ways in which menstruation has been represented as debilitating and controlling of women's behaviour. She describes the metaphors of control used in medical textbooks.

Nineteenth-century writers were extremely prone to stress the debilitating nature of menstruation and its adverse impact on the lives and activities of women. Medical images of menstruation as pathological were remarkably vivid by the end of the century. For Walter Heape, the militant anti-suffragist and Cambridge zoologist, in menstruation the entire epithelium was torn away,

> leaving behind a ragged wreck of tissue, torn glands, ruptured vessels, jagged edges of stroma, and masses of blood corpuscles, which it would seem hardly possible to heal satisfactorily without the aid of surgical treatment.

A few years later, Havelock Ellis could see women as being 'periodically wounded' in their most sensitive spot and 'emphasize the fact that even in the healthiest woman, a worm however harmless and unperceived, gnaws periodically at the roots of life'.[1]

If menstruation was consistently seen as pathological, menopause, another function which by this time was regarded as without analogue in men, often was too: many nineteenth-century medical accounts of menopause saw it as a crisis likely to bring on an increase of disease.[2] Sometimes the metaphor of the body as a small business that is either winning or losing was applied to menopause too. A late-nineteenth-century account specifically argued against Tilt's earlier adjustment model: 'When the period of fruitfulness is ended the activity of the tissues has reached its culmination, the secreting power of the glandular organs begins to diminish, the epithelium becomes less sensitive and less susceptible to infectious influences, and atrophy and degeneration take the place of the active up-building processes.'[3] But there were other sides to the picture. Most practitioners felt the 'climacteric disease', a more general disease of old age, was far worse for men than for women.[4] And some regarded the period after menopause far more positively than it is being seen medically in our century, as the '"Indian summer of a woman's life – a period of increased vigor, optimism, and even of physical beauty"'.[5]

Metaphors in descriptions of female reproduction

In overall descriptions of female reproduction, the dominant image is that of a signaling system. Lein, in a textbook designed for junior colleges, spells it out in detail:

> Hormones are chemical signals to which distant tissues or organs are able to respond. Whereas the nervous system has characteristics in common with a telephone network, the endocrine glands perform in a manner somewhat analogous to radio transmission. A radio transmitter may blanket an entire region

with its signal, but a response occurs only if a radio receiver is turned on and tuned to the proper frequency ... the radio receiver in biological systems is a tissue whose cells possess active receptor sites for a particular hormone or hormones.[6]

The signal–response metaphor is found almost universally in current texts for pre-medical and medical students (emphasis in the following quotes is added):

The hypothalamus *receives signals* from almost all possible sources in the nervous system.[7]

The endometrium *responds directly* to stimulation or withdrawal of estrogen and progesterone. In turn, regulation of the secretion of these steroids involves a well-integrated, highly structured series of activities by the hypothalamus and the anterior lobe of the pituitary. Although the ovaries do not function autonomously, they *influence*, through *feedback* mechanisms, the level of performance *programmed* by the hypothalamic–pituitary axis.[8]

As a result of strong stimulation of FSH, a number of follicles *respond* with growth.[9]

And the same idea is found, more obviously, in popular health books:

Each month from menarch on, [the hypothalamus] acts as elegant interpreter of the body's rhythms, *transmitting messages* to the pituitary gland that set the menstrual cycle in motion.[10]

Each month, *in response to a message* from the pituitary gland, one of the unripe egg cells develops inside a tiny microscopic ring of cells, which gradually increases to form a little balloon or cyst called the Graafian follicle.[11]

Although most accounts stress signals or stimuli traveling in a 'loop' from hypothalamus to pituitary to ovary and back again, carrying positive or negative feedback, one element in the loop, the hypothalamus, a part of the brain, is often seen as predominant. Just as in the general model of the central nervous system the female brain–hormone–ovary system is usually described not as a feedback loop like a thermostat system, but as a hierarchy, in which the 'directions' or 'orders' of one element dominate (emphasis in the following quotes from medical texts is added):

Both positive and negative feedback control must be invoked, together with *superimposition* of control by the CNS through neurotransmitters released into the hypophyseal portal circulation.[12]

Almost all secretion by the pituitary is *controlled* by either hormonal or nervous signals from the hypothalamus.[13]

The hypothalamus is a collecting center for information concerned with the internal well-being of the body and in turn much of this information is used *to control* secretions of the many globally important pituitary hormones.[14]

As Lein puts it into ordinary language:

> The cerebrum, that part of the brain that provides awareness and mood, can play a significant role in the control of the menstrual cycle. As explained before, it seems evident that these higher regions of the brain exert their influence by modifying the actions of the hypothalamus. So even though the hypothalamus is a kind of master gland dominating the anterior pituitary, and through it the ovaries also, it does not act with complete independence or without influence from outside itself ... there are also pathways of control from the higher centers of the brain.[15]

So this is a communication system organized hierarchically, not a committee reaching decisions by mutual influence. [...]

Menstruation not only carries with it the connotation of a productive system that has failed to produce, it also carries the idea of production gone awry, making products of no use, not to specification, unsaleable, wasted, scrap. However disgusting it may be, menstrual blood will come out. Production gone awry is also an image that fills us with dismay and horror. Amid the glorification of machinery common in the nineteenth century were also fears of what machines could do if they went out of control. Capturing this fear, one satirist wrote of a steam-operated shaving machine that 'sliced the noses off too many customers'.[16] This image is close to the one Melville created in 'The Bell-Tower', in which an inventor, who can be seen as an allegory of America, is killed by his mechanical slave,[17] as well as to Mumford's sorcerer's apprentice applied to modern machinery:[18]

> Our civilization has cleverly found a magic formula for setting both industrial and academic brooms and pails of water to work by themselves, in ever-increasing quantities at an ever-increasing speed. But we have lost the Master Magician's spell for altering the tempo of this process, or halting it when it ceases to serve human functions and purposes.[19]

Of course, how much one is gripped by the need to produce goods efficiently and properly depends on one's relationship to those goods. While packing pickles on an assembly line, I remember the foreman often holding up improperly packed bottles to us workers and trying to elicit shame at the bad job we were doing. But his job depended on efficient production, which meant many bottles filled right the first time. This factory did not yet have any effective method of quality control, and as soon as our supervisor was out of sight, our efforts went toward filling as few bottles as we could while still concealing who had filled which bottle. In other factories, workers seem to express a certain grim pleasure when they can register objections to company policy by enacting imagery of machinery out of control. Noble reports an incident in which workers resented a supervisor's order to 'shut down their machines, pick up brooms, and get to work cleaning the area. But he forgot to tell them to stop. So, like the sorcerer's apprentice, diligently and obediently working to rule, they continued sweeping up all day long'.[20]

Perhaps one reason the negative image of failed production is attached to menstruation is precisely that women are in some sinister sense out of control when they menstruate. They are not reproducing, not continuing the species, not preparing to stay at home with the baby, not providing a safe, warm womb to nurture a man's sperm.

Notes

1. Quoted in T. Laqueur, 'Female orgasm, generation and the politics of reproductive biology', *Representations*, 14 (1986), pp. 1–82 (p. 32).
2. C. Smith-Rosenberg, 'Puberty to menopause: the cycle of femininity in nineteenth century America', in M. Hartman and L. W. Banner (eds), *Clio's Consciousness Raised*, New York: Harper & Row, 1974; Joel Wilbush, 'What's in a name? Some linguistic aspects of the climacteric', *Maturitas*, 3 (1981), pp. 1–9.
3. A. F. Currier, *The Menopause*, New York: Appleton, 1897.
4. C. Haber, *Beyond Sixty-Five: The dilemma of old age in America's past*, Cambridge: Cambridge University Press, 1983, p. 69. See J. M. Good, *The Study of Medicine*, New York: Harper & Bros, 1843, pp. 23–5, for an explanation of why the climacteric affects men more severely than women.
5. Smith-Rosenberg, 'Puberty to menopause', p. 30.
6. A. Lein, *The Cycling Female: Her menstrual rhythm*, San Francisco: W. H. Freeman, 1979, p. 14.
7. A. C. Guyton, *Textbook of Medical Physiology* (7th edn), Philadelphia, PA: W. B. Saunders, 1986, p. 885.
8. R. C. Benson, *Current Obstetric and Gynecologic Diagnosis and Treatment*, Los Altos, CA: Lange Medical Publishers, 1982, p. 129.
9. F. H. Netter, *A Compilation of Paintings on the Normal and Pathologic Anatomy of the Reproductive System*, Summit, NJ: CIBA, 1965, p. 115.
10. R. V. Norris, *PMS: Premenstrual syndrome*, New York: Berkeley Books, 1984, p. 6.
11. K. Dalton and R. Greene, 'The premenstrual syndrome', *British Medical Journal* May 1983, p. 6.
12. V. B. Mountcastle, *Medical Physiology* (14th edn), St Louis, MO: C. V. Mosby, 1980, p. 1615.
13. Guyton, *Textbook of Medical Physiology*, p. 885.
14. *Ibid*.
15. Lein, *The Cycling Female*, p. 84.
16. M. Fisher, *Workshops in the Wilderness*, New York: Oxford University Press, 1967, p. 152.
17. *Ibid.*, M. Fisher, 'Melville's "Bell-Tower": a double thrust', *American Quarterly*, 18 (1966), pp. 200–7.
18. L. Mumford, *The Myth of the Machine: Technics and human development*, New York: Harcourt, Brace & World, 1967, p. 282.
19. L. Mumford, *The Myth of the Machine: the pentagon of power*, New York: Harcourt, Brace & World, 1970, p. 180.
20. D. Noble, *The Forces of Production*, New York: Knopf, 1984, p. 312.

11.6 **Who Needs PMT?**
Sophie Laws

A major way in which women's menstrual cycles are pathologised is through the concept of pre-menstrual tension (PMT) or the pre-menstrual syndrome (PMS). Drawing on parallels with nineteenth-century medical attitudes to women, Sophie Laws warns that it is politically dangerous to understand cyclical changes in our bodies in terms of illness. She argues that PMT is used to invalidate women's feelings and to put us in our place.

Feminists have always recognized the political importance of the health and control of women's bodies. However, is not always at all obvious which approaches to women's health will turn out to be most positive for women. There seems to be a deep conflict between the need for us to control our bodies, especially our fertility, and the need of our bodies to be left alone. While we remain in many ways dependent on the medical profession and bound by existing medical knowledge it is extremely difficult to work out where our control of our bodies ends, and their control of us begins. Many of us have found ourselves longing for freedom from our bodies (an aspiration which is encouraged by the male view of women as defective men), and unable to conceive of women becoming free *in* our bodies. [...]

In recent years men seem to have taken to using PMT as a weapon for putting women in their place. A woman who expresses anger or admits to feeling under stress will often be asked, pityingly or aggressively, if it is 'that' time of the month.

PMT is only one of the many ways in which women's learnt hatred of their bodies is expressed: others are slimming, self-starvation, obsession with appearance, plastic surgery including breast surgery ... the list goes on and on. I feel that for women to act in the world on their own behalf, we need also to free ourselves from the undermining effects of this body-hatred. Women are debilitated, it is true, by more than their fair share of actual ill health, but it is also debilitating for a human being to live in constant doubt as to whether or not she is 'normal'. It seems to me that women are being encouraged to search themselves regularly, rather as police search suspects, for signs of wrongness, disease. The new attention to 'women's health' will certainly have backfired on us if it turns out to mean that women have to be more rather than less worried about their health.

The menstrual cycle has now been transformed by the medical profession into something only experts can tell us about. Women are supposed to be at the mercy of it, and our hopes for release depend upon doctors gaining a full understanding and finally control of it. The medical description of the menstrual cycle is taught to women, rather than women's own versions of their experiences being listened to: if you deviate from their norm, you need treatment. PMT is part of this medical model, not an idea which came from women.

PMT is not only an imposed category. It provides a survival strategy for women. If unacceptable parts of one's personality can be labelled PMT and regarded as the results of a pitiable hormonal imbalance, one can retain one's hold on a self-definition as a good woman. [...]

PMT can be used to completely invalidate a woman's feelings. Dalton cites with sympathy a marriage guidance counsellor who 'arranges to see both partners eight days after they quarrel: in this way he hopes that the woman will have safely passed through both her premenstruum and her menstruation before the time of the interview'.[1] This man, then, simply refuses to contemplate women's feelings at this time – he declares them invalid and places them outside the range of what must be dealt with in repairing the marital relationship.

I think that many women will recognize this situation, where a man feels that he can ignore what you say if you are premenstrual at the time you say it. A man who is spoken to angrily by a woman can at any time quietly comfort himself with the idea that she's only upset because of her hormones. PMT, of course, only covers women who menstruate: anger in older women can be put down to the menopause, in pregnant women to their state of pregnancy, in adolescent women to their adolescence, in women who don't have periods or whose periods are irregular to their hormonal peculiarity. It's a pretty complete system, and each part of it supports all the others! [...]

Reading modern writings about PMT, I was strongly reminded of discussions among feminist historians about the 'female complaints' from which nineteenth-century women were said to suffer. In the second half of the nineteenth century in Britain and the USA there was great public concern about invalidism among middle- and upper-class women. It is difficult for us to know what those women were experiencing. The medical descriptions are often very clearly descriptions of a rebellious woman. All women's thoughts and deeds tended to be put down to something wrong with their reproductive organs. Dr Isaac Ray wrote in the 1860s that all women should be seen as hovering on the verge of hysteria, insanity and crime:

> With women it is but a step from extreme nervous susceptibility to downright hysteria, and from that to overt insanity. In the sexual evolution, in pregnancy, in the parturient period, in lactation, strange thoughts, extraordinary feelings, unseasonable appetites, criminal impulses, may haunt a mind at other times innocent and pure.[2]

Besides these dangers of the normal female body, any gynaecological disorder was widely thought to lead to insanity. [...]

All menstruating women experience cyclic change of many kinds – Southam and Gonzaga[3] describe changes in nearly every system of the body. It is clear that some women feel these changes more intensely than others, but these changes still constitute part of a woman's being, and are not signs of sickness. Women do not have times of normality (mid-cycle) followed by times of illness (PMT and menstruation), when their hormones suddenly overcome them – the menstrual cycle forms a continuum of change, physical, mental and social. If these changes are to be examined, one must look at the positive as well as the negative changes. Looking at bias in the interpretation of study results, an editorial in the *Lancet* points out that:

> With some exceptions, the data seem equally consistent with the hypothesis of a mid-cycle syndrome of lowered crime, fewer epileptic seizures, increased self-esteem and elation, and increased sexual desire and activity. It would be incomplete to say only that women perform worse at certain times in the cycle than others; their performance may at all times be better than the average performance of males on the task in question.[4]

There is no reason why change as such should be assumed to be a bad thing.

There is no denying that many women feel worse premenstrually than they do during the rest of their cycles. Could it not be that 'PMT sufferers' should be seen as saving up the bad feelings of the whole month and feeling them intensely during the premenstrual period, rather than as having extra misery directly created by their hormones? This seems to be a more acceptable view of the menstrual cycle than one which implies that if it did not exist women would be calm, cheerful and placid at all times. [...]

Many women's lives are very difficult. The word 'stress' seems totally inadequate to describe the circumstances in which women are expected to live. And women's pain is rarely taken seriously by those who are supposed to 'help'. PMT has seemed to offer a way of getting one's troubles listened to; it enables a medical solution to be found which avoids us being labelled as neurotic or inadequate. But ultimately it dehumanizes us to be forever looking inside ourselves for the cause of our problems. [...]

And what sort of control does a medical solution give us? Accepting the medical model of PMT implies that women cannot live their lives without medical help. We are disabled when our ability to allow for our own physical changes is denied.

PMT is a political construct. When a woman is said to have PMT, her distress or anger is invalidated. It is part of our oppression as women that if we are feeling bad we are encouraged to blame that feeling on our female bodies. The way some people use it, PMT has become a word which describes female badness, unreliability, inferiority. PMT is a medical invention and will not be useful to us in attempting to find new, positive ways of seeing our bodies.

Notes

1. K. Dalton, *The Menstrual Cycle*, Harmondsworth: Penguin, 1969, p. 112.

2. I. Ray, *Mental Hygiene*, New York: Hafner Publishing Co., 1968 (facsimile of the 1863 edn).
3. A. L. Southam and F. P. Gonzaga, 'Systematic changes during the menstrual cycle', *American Journal of Obstetrics and Gynecology*, vol. 19, no. 2 (1965), pp. 142–65.
4. Editorial: 'Premenstrual syndrome', *Lancet*, December 1981, pp. 1393–4.

11.7 Managers and Labourers: women's attitudes to reproductive technology

Frances Evans

Feminists have generally been critical of medical intervention in pregnancy and labour. On the basis of a study of two hundred women carried out in 1981, Frances Evans suggests that most women are more ambivalent in their attitudes. Here she explains why, despite being critical of the treatment they receive, women retain their faith in doctors and often welcome the use of medical technology.

At the outset I expected that the use of technology as a routine part of maternity care would emerge as an issue of major importance to the women I met. I felt most would be concerned about its excessive and perhaps unnecessary use, for with the advent of the Women's Liberation Movement feminists have generally assumed that most women do not want technological intervention, and that more natural childbirth techniques should be promoted. [...]

I felt sure that the research would show ... that there was widespread dissatisfaction with the technology encountered in pregnancy and childbirth. In fact, the mothers in the survey did not fit my preconceived model. They were not particularly concerned about an excessive use of technology. Indeed, many women would have liked it used more often, seeing it as a *basic right* of the pregnant and labouring woman. Just as men with heart attacks are not left to die a 'natural' death, the women felt their pregnancies should not be left completely to 'nature'. There were two main arguments for putting forward this view. The first was that technology should be used as an interventionist measure to relieve difficult pregnancies and labours. [...] The second was that technology should be available as a routine service to detect fetal abnormality. [...]

It was striking that mothers who had been referred to a London teaching hospital because of complications were very impressed with the advanced machinery they saw there, saying admiringly that it was like something from *Tomorrow's World*. This had made them confident that the best possible care would be given to them, and many commented that it was unfair that this level of technology was not available at every hospital in the UK.

Complaints about too little technology, and demands for its greater use, should not be taken in isolation. Their context is the total lack of control which women felt over their pregnancy and birth. Indeed, the absence of explanation about, or control over, the pregnancy was the most common complaint. Women felt humiliated and indignant about the way they were ordered around and refused any opportunity to ask questions or to be involved in the decisions about their care. [...]

Generally, women did not mention the public controversy about the appropriateness of some of the techniques used on them. Only a very small number suggested that the use of technology might actually carry risk. It is interesting that so little of the debate inside and outside the medical profession has filtered through to pregnant women themselves.

Finally, women in the survey displayed a great trust in doctors, despite strong dissatisfaction with the service in the clinics they attended, which are often compared to a meat market. [...]

Women's continued belief in the abilities of doctors, despite deep resentment about their actual behaviour ... seems now to be a product both of the history of struggle over childbirth in which men assumed the role of managers, and of the confused and confusing picture of pregnancy and motherhood which accompanied that change. It is also consistent with the socialized respect for professionals, and for men, in an area of the health service where 'consumers' are exclusively female.

In this context, the ambivalence women felt about the use of technology appears less surprising. The use of techniques designed to detect abnormalities, for example, can be seen as a palliative for the confused mother-to-be who feels neglected by the doctors in whom she is expected to place so much trust. [...]

Many women seemed to express a contradictory wish for more control over their pregnancies, as well as a wish for more use of technology, which implies a loss of control to the technicians. It now seems that this is not so much a contradiction as two sides of the same coin: that of women's uncertainty and ignorance, fostered by the male monopoly of medical knowledge and decision-making. The technology which was asked for can be seen to be wanted not so much as an end in itself, but rather as a means of achieving a feeling of confidence about the pregnancy and its outcome in the absence of sufficient information or reassurance from doctors.

11.8 **The Reproductive Brothel**
Gena Corea

Gena Corea's vision of the 'reproductive brothel' is based upon speculation about what could happen if techniques currently used on farm animals were applied to human reproduction. This is a classic expression of the fears many feminists have about reproductive technologies. Gina Corea is a member of FINNRAGE.

As I envision it, most women in a reproductive brothel would be defined as 'non-valuable' and sterilized and, in this way, their progeny culled. This vision came to me after repeatedly seeing reproductive engineers link their new technologies – *in vitro* fertilization, embryo transfer, egg banks – with sterilization. [1] They invariably suggest that the sterilization will benefit those operated upon. Women could be sterilized knowing that if they later want a child, they can have one through use of the new technologies. In this way, women would be able to avoid modern steroidal contraception.

In the United States, women of colour probably would be labelled 'non-valuable', sterilized and used as breeders for the embryos of 'valuable' women. The white women judged genetically superior and selected as egg donors would be turned into machines for producing embryos. Through superovulation, 'valuable' females as young as 2 years and some as old as 50 or 60 could be induced to produce eggs.

Reproductive engineers would engage in three major activities in the brothel: (1) getting eggs; (2) manipulating them; (3) transferring embryos.

Getting eggs

There are a number of ways engineers might recover or, as they term it, 'capture' eggs from women. They could flush them out of women using the technique developed by Drs Richard and Randolph Seed with the medical team at the Harbor-UCLA Medical Center. (The Seed brothers worked on egg flushing and embryo transfer for six years in cows before moving on to women. They had their first human success in 1983 when they established pregnancies through embryo transfer in two women in Torrance, California.) However, the Seeds' flushing procedure would probably not yield the necessary quantity of eggs. It is also unlikely that engineers would use two techniques employed experimentally in animals: placing tubular instruments inside the women's reproductive tracts and keeping them there permanently so that eggs would pass into the instruments and out of the bodies; and relocating women's ovaries to make it easier to get at it the eggs. These techniques had been 'found wanting' in animals and abandoned. [2]

Eggs are far more likely to be obtained by extracting them directly from the ovaries, a procedure which requires control over the female cycle. In *Farm Journal* in 1976, Earl Ainsworth, identifying the factor which prevented farmers from treating sows totally as machines, wrote: 'Estrus control will open the doors to factory hog production. Control of female cycles is the missing link to the assembly-line approach.' [3] The 'missing link' to the assembly-line, brothel approach to human reproduction is being forged in *in vitro* fertilization clinics around the world where teams are working intensively to control the cycles of women.

In the brothel, on the appropriate days of their cycles, women would line up for Pergonal shots which will stimulate their ovaries. Engineers would superovulate only the top 10 to 20 per cent of the female population in the brothel. Then, after following the development of the eggs through ultrasound and blood tests, they would operate on the women to extract the eggs. Perhaps they would allow the women to heal from the operation every other month so that women would only be subjected to surgery six times per year.

To obtain eggs, engineers could also do what they now do with certain cows. When the championship cow Sabine 2A died in 1982 during a Caesarean section, embryologists from the firm Genetic Engineering Inc. removed her ovaries, obtained thirty-six eggs from them, and froze the eggs. During her lifetime, Sabine's embryos had been fetching $10,000 or more on the embryo transfer market and when the eggs from the dead Sabine are thawed and fertilized *in vitro*, they may fetch the same.[4] In the reproductive brothel, as a valuable woman dies, engineers could operate on her, remove her ovaries and salvage eggs from those ovaries, perhaps by using enzymes to eat away the connective tissue and release hundreds of thousands of eggs. They could then freeze the eggs for future *in vitro* fertilization and transfer into a 'non-valuable' female. A woman could be used for reproduction long after she is dead.

Not only could dead women be used in reproductive brothels. So could women who were never even born. A female embryo could be developed just to the point where an ovary emerges and then the ovary could be cultured so that engineers could get eggs from it. The full woman would never be allowed to develop. Just her ovary.

Partial ectogenesis – culturing organ rudiments from their earliest appearance to a mature state – is already well established as a technique used in certain biological studies. If various fragmented procedures reported by different scientists could be brought together and, in combination, used in one species, mature organs might soon be produced externally from a fertilized egg, embryologist Dr Clifford Grobstein has predicted. One of the organs men have extensively investigated is the ovary. By maturing the ovary externally, Grobstein wrote, a supply of eggs for *in vitro* fertilization could be provided without surgical intervention in a woman's body.[5]

Manipulating eggs

Once the eggs have been recovered, reproductive engineers along the assembly line could manipulate them in a number of ways:

Twin the embryos, producing two humans out of one embryo.

Use the eggs of 'non-valuable' women for clones, destroying the egg nuclei with lasers and injecting the nuclei of valuable men.

Remove the female genetic component from the egg and inject two sperm into the egg, producing a child with two fathers and no mother.

Genetically engineer the embryo for various qualities. If ever partial or total ectogenesis were applied to humans, it would be 'no more than a game for the "manfarming biologist" to change the subject's sex, the colour of its eyes, the general proportions of body and limbs, and perhaps the facial features', wrote biologist Jean Rostand, over-confidently.[6]

Fertilize the eggs in the laboratory using a culture media concocted from bits and pieces of women. 'We made our culture fluids resemble the female reproductive tract by adding very small pieces of human uterus or Fallopian tube ... ' wrote *in vitro* fertilization pioneers Patrick Steptoe and R. G. Edwards.[7] Another reproductive engineer used 'minced fragments of [women's] fallopian tubal mucosa'.[8]

Select the sex of the embryo by fertilizing the egg with either gynosperm (female-engendering) or androsperm (male-engendering). Researchers are hard at work now trying to separate these two types of sperm. Should they fail, there is another way to predetermine the child's sex. Engineers could snip a few cells off the fertilized egg to check its gender. Most female embryos could simply be discarded. The brothel administration would decide how many would be needed.

Transferring embryos

Once the embryo has been manufactured, reproductive engineers would have several options.

They could freeze the embryo in the bank for later use. Or they could immediately transfer the embryo into a woman in the lower 80 to 90 per cent of the female population. These would be the breeders, the women who had been called 'surrogate mothers' in the early stage of the reproduction revolution when engineers had been conscious of the need for good public relations.

The transferred embryo might gestate in the breeder for the entire nine-month pregnancy. When delivery time approached, the breeder would find no cosy 'birthing rooms' in the brothel, but rather an assembly line. The description women gave of their obstetrical experiences in American hospitals in the 1950s are likely to be as apt for the brothel of the future: 'They give you drugs, whether you want them or not, strap you down like an animal.' 'Women are herded like sheep through an obstetrical assembly line, are drugged and strapped on tables while their babies are forceps-delivered.' 'I felt exactly like a trapped animal ... '[9]

Alternatively, engineers could transfer the embryo into a breeder, allow it to gestate for a certain number of months, and then remove the foetus by Caesarean section at whatever point at which their incubators could take over. (Today that point is twenty one weeks' gestation.) In the incubator, they would perform surgery on the foetus, inoculate it or undertake whatever alterations they deemed desirable.

The breeder into whom an embryo is placed need not be alive. This possibility is suggested by several recent cases in which the bodies of brain-dead pregnant women were kept functioning until the foetus had developed enough to be delivered. In one case, a 27-year-old woman suffered a fatal seizure when she was twenty-two weeks pregnant. Her husband and other family members wanted the woman's body kept in operation until the foetus became viable. Physicians put her on a life-support system. Their most difficult medical challenges during the nine weeks they maintained the dead woman, they report, were keeping control of the woman's many failing body functions and combating infection. The woman developed diabetes insipidus and Addison's disease and, periodically, a blood infection throughout the body. Doctors did blood studies on the dead woman every two hours. They performed a Caesarean section on her more than two months after she had been declared dead, extracted a healthy baby and then removed the life-support apparatus. She stopped breathing. Relatives reportedly expressed 'a great deal of pleasure' at the birth. [10]

'The experience left me with real confidence that this can be done without any great difficulties. ... In the future, I'll suggest to family members that the option is there', Dr Russell K. Laros Jr of the Department of Obstetrics, Gynecology and Reproductive Sciences at the University of California School of Medicine in San Francisco, said. [11]

(Immediately over the Newark *Star-Ledger's* account of the birth – 'Brain Dead Woman Gives Birth' – appeared a photograph of smiling parents holding their infants, the nation's first test-tube twins.)

Perhaps in the distant future, few women, dead or alive, will be required. If reproductive engineers have developed an artificial womb, they might place the cultured embryo directly into The Mother Machine.

The reproductive brothel is one possible institution within which men might control women, or various groups of women, in the future. Other scenarios involving use of the new technologies are also conceiveable.

Notes

1. H. J. Muller, 'Human evolution by voluntary choice of germ plasma', *Science*, 134 (1961); J. Fletcher, *The Ethics of Genetic Control: Ending reproductive roulette*, New York: Anchor/Doubleday, 1974; J. Fletcher, 'Ethical aspects of genetic controls', in T. Shannon (ed.), *Bioethics*, New York: Paulist Press, 1976; R. W. Seed and R. C. Seed, Statement before the Ethics Advisory Board of the Department of Health, Education and Welfare, October 1978; C. Djerassi, *The Politics of Contraception*, New York: Norton, 1979; R. G. Edwards, 5 January 1979, Letter to the US Ethics Advisory Board in *Appendix: HEW support of research involving human in vitro fertilization and embryo transfer*, Washington, DC: US Government Printing Office, 4 May 1979.
2. K. J. Betteridge, 'An historical look at embryo transfer', *Journal of Reproductive Fertility*, 62 (1981), pp. 1–13 (p. 8).
3. In J. Mason and P. Singer, *Animal Factories*, New York: Crown Publishers, 1980.
4. H. Brotman, 'Engineering the birth of cattle', *New York Times Magazine*, 15 May 1983.
5. C. Grobstein, *From Chance to Purpose: An appraisal of external human fertilization*, Reading, MA: Addison-Wesley, 1981.
6. J. Rostand, *Can Man be Modified?* New York: Basic Books 1959.

7. R. G. Edwards and P. Steptoe, *A Matter of Life*, New York: William Morrow, 1980.
8. L. P. Shettles, 'A morula stage of human ovum developed in vitro', *Fertility and Sterility*, vol. 6, no. 4 (1955), pp. 287–9.
9. G. D. Shultz, 'Journal mothers report on cruelty in maternity wards', *Ladies House Journal*, May 1959.
10. 'Brain dead woman gives birth', *Star Ledger* (Newark, NJ), 31 March 1983.
11. OGN, 'Maintenance of brain-dead gravida held viable course', *Ob. Gyn. News*, 18, 11 (1983), p. 2.

11.9 **Disciplining Mothers: feminism and the new reproductive technologies**

Jana Sawicki

Jana Sawicki is critical of the stance taken by FINNRAGE activists. Drawing on Foucault's concept of 'disciplinary technologies',[1] she suggests an alternative perspective on reproductive technology.

... new reproductive technologies represent the most recent of a set of discourses (systems of knowledge, classification, measurement, testing, treatment and so forth) that constitute a disciplinary technology of sex. [...] Disciplinary technologies are not primarily repressive mechanisms. In other words, they do not operate primarily through violence against or seizure of women's bodies or bodily processes, but rather by producing new objects and subjects of knowledge, by inciting and channeling desires, generating and focusing individual and group energies, and establishing bodily norms and techniques for observing, monitoring, and controlling bodily movements, processes, and capacities. Disciplinary technologies control the body through techniques that simultaneously render it more useful, more powerful and more docile.

New reproductive technologies represent one of a series of types of body management that have emerged over the past two decades rendering women's bodies more mobilizable in the service of changing utilities of dominant agencies.[1] Their aim is less to eliminate the need for women than to make their bodies even more useful. They enhance the utility of women's bodies for multiple shifting needs. As Linda Singer aptly noted:

> The well managed body of the 80s is constructed so as to be even more multifunctional than its predecessors. It is a body that can be used for wage, labor, sex, reproduction, mothering, spectacle, exercise, or even invisibility, as the situation demands.[2]

Singer points out that fertility technologies can be used either for purposes of consolidating race and class privilege or for eliminating competition in the labor market from white, upper-middle-class women who have delayed pregnancy for careers.

New reproductive technologies clearly fit the model of disciplinary power. They involve sophisticated techniques of surveillance and examination (for instance, ultrasound, fetal monitors, amniocentesis, antenatal testing procedures) that make both female bodies and fetuses visible to anonymous agents in ways that facilitate the creation of new objects and subjects of medical as well as legal and state intervention. Among the individuals created by these new technologies are infertile, surrogate and genetically impaired mothers, mothers whose bodies are not fit for pregnancy (either biologically or socially), mothers who are psychologically unfit for fertility treatments, mothers whose wombs are hostile environments to fetuses, mothers who are deemed 'negligent' for not choosing to undergo tests, abort genetically 'deficient' fetuses, or consent to Caesarean sections. As these medical disciplines isolate specific types of abnormality or deviancy, they contract new norms of healthy and responsible motherhood. Additionally, in so far as the new technologies locate the problem of infertility within individuals, they deflect attention and energy that could be used to address the environmental causes of infertility. Hence, they tend to depoliticize infertility. They link up with the logic of consumerism and commodification by inciting the desire for 'better babies' and by creating a market in reproductive body parts, namely, eggs, wombs, and embryos. Finally, they make women's bodies useful to agencies that regulate and coordinate populations.

At the same time that these new technologies create new subjects – that is, fit mothers, unfit mothers, infertile women, and so forth – they create the possibility of new sites of resistance. Lesbians and single women can challenge these norms by demanding access to infertility treatments. Women who have undergone infertility treatment can share their experiences and demand improvements or expose inadequacies in the model of treatment. The question is not whether these women are victims of false consciousness in so far as they desire to be biological mothers, as much as it is one of devising feminist strategies in struggles over who defines women's needs and how they are satisfied.

To suggest that the new reproductive technologies 'produce' problems and desires and thereby contribute to the further medicalization of mothers' bodies is not to suggest that these problems (for instance, infertility) are not real, that the experts are charlatans, and that those who seek their advice are blinded by the ideology of medical science. It does not imply that things were better before these technologies appeared. It does suggest, however, that part of the attraction of the new technologies is that many women perceive them as enabling. Of course, referring to them as disciplinary technologies does highlight their controlling functions. Yet this control is not secured primarily through violence or coercion, but rather by producing new norms of motherhood, by attaching women to their identities as mothers, and by offering women specific kinds of solutions to problems they face. In fact, there may be better solutions; and there may be better ways of defining the problems. There is the danger that medical solutions will become the only ones and that other ways of defining them will be eclipsed.

Notes to Introduction

1. For further elaboration of the Foucauldian concept of discipline, see Section 7, Reading 7.1 above.

Notes

1. See S. Bordo, 'Anorexia nervosa'; S. Bartky, 'Foucault, femininity and patriarchal power', in Quinby and Diamond (eds), *Feminism and Foucault*, Northeastern University Press, 1988, for two examples of how disciplinary practices produce specifically feminine forms of embodiment through the development of diet and fitness regimes, pathologies related to them, and expert advice on how to walk, talk, dress, wear make-up, and so forth.
2. L. Singer, 'Bodies, pleasures, powers', *differences*, vol. 1 (1989), p. 57.

11.10 New Reproductive Technologies
Christine Delphy

In the final Reading in this Section, Christine Delphy questions the assumptions underlying feminist critiques of reproductive technology. She suggests that these accounts over-emphasise the importance of reproduction to patriarchy, and tend to romanticise and naturalise links between mothers and children.

Many feminists are currently studying the new reproductive technologies, and with few exceptions their attitudes towards them range from fairly negative to apocalyptic. Now, some disquiet about reproductive technology is certainly legitimate. Research suggests those who seek to have their eggs removed by laparoscopy and then reimplanted in their uteruses may not be making a fully informed choice. They may not know the risks involved in the operation nor realise the very low success rate.

But is this something specific to surgical interventions to 'remedy' infertility or doesn't it also apply to many other (if not to the majority of) medical interventions? If so, what is at issue is just another instance of a more general problem – the retention of information and abuse of power by the medical profession, practised to the detriment of people who should be clients but are only patients – which is always serious.

Another line of criticism argues that surrogate motherhood will lead to poor women being exploited for the benefit of rich women, and suggests we should not accept surrogate motherhood in principle, since it involves selling one's biological processes.

However, if the issue is the exploitation of poor women's bodies, then surrogacy is not the most striking instance. Every day hundreds of thousands of prostitutes, three-quarters of whom are not voluntary but were captured or sold by a relative and held in conditions of slavery and torture, sell their bodies – often with no profit to themselves. There are a few hundred surrogate mothers and their 'exploitation' lasts nine months; it is voluntary; and they themselves receive money. If feminist critics were really concerned about the exploitation of women's bodies, how can we explain their being more scandalised by surrogate motherhood than by prostitution? Which leads me to think it is not 'the exploitation of the body' which is their real cause for concern.

In addition, those opposed to reproductive technology often paint apocalyptic pictures of a conspiracy by men to replace women by artificial uteruses. The few feminists who have criticised such scenarios have pointed out that there is really no substance to such prophecies. Macho intellectuals might want to replace women with technology, but there is no evidence to suggest they are actually researching *doing* so. Above all, there is no evidence they have the *means* to do so. The goal attributed to such men when the spectre of 'genocide' is evoked, is the elimination of women thanks to artificial wombs. But the snag is that as yet, not a single artificial womb exists. Such a machine is far from being created, even if men wanted it to exist. The longest anyone has been able to keep an embryo *in vitro* is a few days – which is a far cry from the requisite nine months. And even if men could produce such a machine, imagine what it would cost – and even more how much it would cost to produce millions of them! Can we really imagine the construction of enough such machines to replace three billion women?

But leaving aside the feasibility of the operation, to imagine this is the goal of the masculine half of humanity is to think (a) that men only consider women in so far as we serve them; and (b) that women only serve men through reproduction.

Now although the first proposition is unfortunately true, the second is not. To say that men, who do hold power and do only consider women in an instrumental way, only 'use' us for reproduction, is to fall in the trap of accepting men's own ideology. Men do indeed often say 'women are only good for having babies', but this is their way of minimising how useful we are to them (hence, from their point of view, how useful we are to humanity, since they see humanity as composed only of themselves). It minimises the extent to which they (are seen to) exploit us – for women are not only 'good' for reproduction. We also do more than half of all human work, and three-quarters of the work we do is unpaid and benefits men. So why should they want to eliminate us? Not only our eggs but also our work is free. If they were to eliminate us, they would be killing the geese that lay the golden eggs.

The fear that women will be physically eliminated is therefore both unfounded and in the present circumstances (i.e. given the wide-ranging exploitation to which women are subjected) absurd. It is therefore hard to believe this is really what preoccupies those who oppose the new reproductive technologies. So what is at stake for them? I think one indication is given by their constantly repeated assertion that women's role in biological reproduction is more important than men's.

In studying the theme of 'nature' in discussion of reproductive technology, Marie-Jo Dhavernas found that in order to pass new laws on assisted reproduction, a single, unique form of descent and kinship, the Western married couple and their legitimate children, had been erected as the unchangeable and supposedly natural model. But not only has this form always been a model, an ideal, which has never corresponded to reality (i.e. it has never been the statistical norm), but it is itself in the process of losing even its normative status.

Things are therefore being asked of people who want to use assisted reproduction – that they be heterosexual and married, etc. – which other people not only do not fulfil, but which are not even asked of them any longer. For instance, much more is required of those who want assisted reproduction than is asked of would-be adopters; and more is required of would-be adopters than is asked of ordinary parents. The majority of naturally procreated children live in (what for the model are) non-'natural' families. In sum, parents deemed non-natural are the only ones obliged to follow a supposedly natural model of parenthood; a model which has nothing to do with what natural parents actually do.

Some feminists' views on what should be allowed and what forbidden when reproduction is assisted *also* involve a model based on reference to nature – though theirs is not the same nature as the nature invoked by legislators. In 'feminist' nature:

1. the only biological tie in reproduction is the one between a woman and a child. The role of the biological father is minimised (read ignored);
2. this biological bond between woman and child is considered to be the basis of kinship, i.e. of affiliation or descent.

But this supposedly natural matrilineal descent also does not prevail in either norms or fact. So here it is feminists who in turn are demanding of potential 'non-natural' parents (of those seeking assisted reproduction) that they conform to so-called natural requirements – things they do not require of natural parents, i.e. people who do not need to use reproductive technologies.

Such feminists seem to find the debate on reproductive technology an occasion on which to express their views on what descent *should* be, just as lawyers and politicians find it the occasion to express theirs. But in the case of feminists, their views are expressed indirectly. For whatever form descent may take, it is *always* a social convention. However, instead of attacking the social convention and demanding that, as a social convention, it could and should be changed, most feminist critiques of reproductive technology simply assert that descent exists already – in nature.

Further Reading

Corea, G. (1985), *The Mother Machine*, New York: Harper & Row.

Doyal, L. and Elston, M. (1986), 'Women, health and medicine', in V. Beechey and E. Whitelegg (eds), *Women in Britain Today*, Milton Keynes: Open University Press.

Ehrenreich, B. and English, D. (1973), *Witches, Midwives and Nurses*, London: Readers and Writers Cooperative.

Ehrenreich, B. and English, D. (1979), *For Her Own Good: 150 years of experts' advice to women*, London: Pluto.

Haraway, D. (1989), *Primate Visions*, London: Routledge.

Haraway, D. (1991), *Simians, Cyborgs and Women*, London: Free Association Books.

Jacobus, M., Fox Keller, E. and Shuttleworth, S. (eds) (1990), *Body/Politics: Women and the discourse of science*, London: Routledge.

Laws, S. (1990), *Issues of Blood: The politics of menstruation*, London: Macmillan.

McNeil, M., Varcoe, I. and Yearly, S. (eds) (1987), *The New Reproductive Technologies*, London: Macmillan.

Oakley, A. (1984), *The Captured Womb: A history of the medical care of pregnant women*, Oxford: Basil Blackwell.

Oakley, A. (1991), *From Here to Maternity*, Harmondsworth: Pelican.

Russett, C. E. (1989), *Sexual Science*, Cambridge, MA.: Harvard University Press.

Shelley, M. (1818), *Frankenstein*, Oxford: Oxford University Press, 1992.

Spallone, P. (1989), *Beyond Conception: The new politics of reproduction*, London: Macmillan.

Stanworth, M. (ed.) (1987), *Reproductive Technologies: Gender, motherhood and medicine*, Cambridge: Polity.

Ussher, J. (1989), *The Psychology of the Female Body*, London: Routledge.

Ussher, J. (1991), *Women's Madness*, Hemel Hempstead: Harvester Wheatsheaf.

Wajcman, J. (1991), *Feminism Confronts Technology*, Cambridge: Polity.

Witz, A. (1992), *Professions and Patriarchy*, London: Routledge.

12 | LANGUAGE AND GENDER

Edited and Introduced by Karen Atkinson

INTRODUCTION

Language is part of the fabric of our everyday lives, and its interrelationship with gender has been at the centre of feminist discussions for some time now. The Readings in this Section, being located within a predominantly sociolinguistic framework, provide only a small and selective sample of the general area overall. They divide into two broad areas, Sexist Terminology (Readings 12.1, 12.2) and Women's Talk (Readings 12.2–12.6), but are all concerned with how language users operate in a social context. Across both areas, 'dominance' models of explaining and evaluating language practice are seen as a springboard from which subsequent questions and theories have been developed, particularly those of Jennifer Coates (Reading 12.6), which focus on the diversity and strength of female discourse. Also common to both sub-sections is the issue of extending the debate towards more contextually sensitive analysis, away from earlier broad generalisations.

Sexist Terminology

That linguistic sexism is prevalent has been fairly well documented to date (see Notes 1–4). As a rather broad umbrella term, 'linguistic sexism' covers a wide and diverse range of verbal practices, including not only how we, as women, are labelled and referred to, but also how realised language strategies in mixed-sex interaction may serve to silence or depreciate us as interactants. It is to the former, however, that this sub-section addresses itself.

Building on the work of earlier theorists (see Notes 1–3), Dale Spender, one of the more well-known writers on this subject, identified our language as 'man-made' at the beginning of the 1980s. Following Sapir–Whorfian lines of linguistic determinism[5] for much of the time, Spender's underlying argument is that language not only reflects but also perpetuates and contributes to gender inequality. Women, as the subordinated group in a patriarchal society, are kept in that lowly position, since language and its meanings are invented and controlled by men. More specifically, Spender argues that women are oppressed through sexist labelling, including the semantic asymmetry of oppositions like 'bachelor–spinster', 'master–mistress', 'stud–slag'. In addition (and the linguistic practice upon which her extract here focuses), usage of generic terminology such as 'he' and 'man' (which supposedly incorporates female) renders women invisible, and therefore powerless. While acknowledging that merely changing our linguistic practice would not automatically mean that we are 'liberated' from all modes of patriarchal structure, Spender does advocate the coinage of new words and meanings as a way of breaking male control of language, seemingly contradicting her earlier claims that we, as women, are trapped within a 'man-made' language. Nevertheless, once we have coined new words and meanings, asserts Spender, 'we will not be a muted group'.[6]

At the time, Spender's work was clearly influential in keeping the issue of language at the forefront of gender research and – perhaps more importantly – in providing a controversial thesis against which further debate could take place. One of the most thought-provoking attacks came from feminist linguist Deborah Cameron, who questioned Spender's assumption that language is ultimately so powerful. Accusing her of perpetuating 'the pernicious belief that we can be controlled and oppressed by our language',[7] Cameron asserts that 'male control over meaning is an impossibility', and that 'meanings ... are highly contextualised, dependent on that environment and those people, subject (as the environment is) to variation and change'.[8] Indeed, this necessity of seeing language in context is taken up in Reading 12.2 by Susan Ehrlich and Ruth King, who show how analyses of the various appropriations of meaning need to be understood from particular sociopolitical perspectives. Taking as an example the issue of sexist language reform, they demonstrate how successful linguistic change is dependent on the ideological perspective of the subgroup that is targeted. This may seem an obvious conclusion, but such fine differentiation between subgroups was overlooked by proponents of earlier deterministic generalisations. Quoting Fatemeh Khosroshahi's[9] research, which does distinguish between groups of different political persuasions, Ehrlich and King note how a female speech community which endorsed equality generally was certainly not constrained within a determinist language 'trap'. They go on to report how Khosroshahi's subjects themselves dynamically defined the meaning of so-called 'neutral' generic 'they', and indeed the masculine pronoun 'he', as 'female'. On the other hand, with social groups that embraced sexist values generally, even the generic pronoun 'they' was largely taken as signifying 'male'. Inevitably this questions the grass-roots effectiveness of language reform, and reaffirms Cameron's claim that other factors besides language (for instance, structures of society) also need to change if women are to get a fairer deal.

Women's Talk

The charge of contextual insensitivity is also an accusation justifiably levelled at early (and, quite legitimately, at some later) work on female discourse. Robin Lakoff was one of the first linguists to write on gender, politics and language, and in this sub-section we see how, in her terms, women are once again defined as powerless within the 'dominance theory' framework. Such a subordinated role within our patriarchal society is reflected, argues Lakoff, in the style of language women use. She proceeds to draw up a list of features which supposedly represent typical female discourse, as distinct from male talk. These include, a large degree of 'disfluency' (more hesitations, false starts, pauses); more 'empty' (?) adjectives such as 'divine, charming, cute'; more tag questions such as 'isn't it' and 'aren't they' (evaluated by Lakoff as approval-seeking); and a greater proportion of epistemic modal forms such as 'perhaps', 'sort of' and 'maybe'. Lakoff (Reading 12.3) focuses on these latter two discourse features which, she believes, contribute to female interactional deficit.

Such a thesis – not surprisingly – proved provocative, and almost twenty years later, as subsequent Readings testify, feminist linguists are still engaging with Lakoff's work. Her research received wide-ranging criticisms, including the charge that the data used to draw up such broad generalisations were largely intuitive and ungrounded in any systematic empirical work. Nancy Henley and Cheris Kramarae (Reading 12.4) take issue with the very notion of female deficit theory, articulately outlining the implicit dangers of adopting it to evaluate women's discourse. They claim that since deficit theory sees female language as deviant, the onus is always upon women to change in order to fit in with a male 'norm'. Furthermore, rather than requiring men to change their interactional style, women are required to redefine male communicative incompetence in acceptable terms.

A number of studies have also challenged Lakoff's broad generalisations of what constitutes male/female language – Marjorie Swacker;[10] Betty Lou Dubois and Isobel Crouch;[11] and Geoffrey Beattie[12] present contradictory findings as to what constitutes 'female talk'. In taking up the Labovian discussion on tags, Deborah Cameron, Fiona McAlinden and Kathy O'Leary (Reading 12.5) refer to these studies, arguing for a more context-sensitive analysis of the function of particular linguistic features. They claim that there is no simple correlation between a tag and its function, and that a tag can mean a variety of different things depending on who uses it to whom, in what situation, and for what purpose. It need not automatically signal tentativeness or a request for confirmation of information about which the speaker is uncertain (modal tags) but can be used to mitigate face-threatening talk or to express solidarity, encouraging interlocutors to engage in the discourse (affective tags). They also argue that it is untrue to claim that women generally use tags more often than men, but do concede that women use more affective tags in their frequent role as conversational facilitators. What was initially seen by Lakoff as powerless and weak in female language, then, is now redefined as a valuable interactional skill.

It is precisely this aspect of female discourse which Jennifer Coates takes up in the final Reading in this Section (12.6). To some extent, she also argues for contextuality to be considered, in particular pushing for a distinction to be made between mixed-sex and all-female discourse.[13] Challenging Lakoff's negative evaluation of 'perhaps', 'sort of', and so on, as deficit, Coates argues that within all-female-friend interaction, such epistemic modality is exploited by women to express solidarity and interpersonal sensitivity, especially during discussion of face-threatening topics. Rather than signifying uncertainty, the use of such features between female friends is the same as that of affective tags: a demonstration of interactional 'co-operativity'. Women's speech, Coates concludes, is, in effect, women's strength.

Feminist linguists have come a long way since Lakoff, and the move away from seeing females as passive, helpless victims of discourse, and towards acknowledging conversational dynamics, has been a necessary step in the right direction. Coates's[14] call to look at 'co-operativity' in other all-female contexts where status cannot be so easily categorised as 'symmetrical' is an important one. Against a backdrop which now offers to redefine women's talk as positive, however, we must be wary of jumping on the 'co-operativity' bandwagon: of assuming that the use of epistemic modality, hedges or affective tags constitutes 'co-operativity' on all dimensions. Nina Eliasoph[15] touches on this in her account of female cosmetic sales representatives who reportedly used solidarity markers with female clients, since this stimulated higher sales. My own research on intergenerational communication also begs the question of what all-female discourse 'co-operativity' actually is. Younger carers report using 'co-operative' feedback such as minimal backchannelling ('hm mm', 'yeah', 'right') as a survival technique of weathering the high frequency of 'troubles talk'[16] from their elderly carees while remaining sociopsychologically distant. It is time to appreciate that female discourse 'co-operativity' itself is a multidimensional concept to be unpacked, and the sooner we start doing this, the clearer will be our understanding of the issues surrounding women's talk.

Notes

1. M. Schulz, 'The semantic derogation of women', in B. Thorne and N. Henley (eds), *Language and Sex: Difference and dominance*, Rowley, MA.: Newbury House, 1975.
2. J. Stanley, 'What's in a label: the politics of naming', Symposium on Sexism in Language, Northeastern Illinois University, Chicago, 6 April 1974.
3. C. Miller and K. Swift, *Words and Women: New language in new times*, New York: Anchor/Doubleday, 1976.
4. D. Cameron, *Feminism and Linguistic Theory*, Basingstoke: Macmillan, 1985.
5. E. Sapir and Benjamin Lee Whorf's work is one of the best-known theses on language and reality. 'Linguistic determinism' as a central tenet of their theory rests on the idea that language determines the way we see the world. A good accessible discussion of the Sapir–Whorf argument can be found in R. Anderson, *The Power and the Word: Language, power and change*, London: Paladin, 1988, ch. 5.
6. D. Spender, *Man Made Language*, London: Routledge & Kegan Paul, 1980, p. 190.
7. Cameron, *Feminism and Linguistic Theory*, p. 173.

8. *Ibid.*, pp. 134–44.
9. F. Khosroshahi, 'Penguins don't care, but women do: a social identity analysis of a Whorfian problem', *Language in Society*, 18 (1989), pp. 505–25.
10. M. Swacker, 'The sex of the speaker as a sociolinguistic variable', in B. Thorne and N. Henley (eds), *Language and Sex: Difference and dominance*.
11. B. L. Dubois and I. Crouch, 'The question of tag questions in women's speech: they don't really use more of them, do they?', *Language in Society*, 4 (1975), pp. 289–94.
12. G. W. Beattie, 'Interruption in conversational interaction and its relation to the sex and status of interactants', *Linguistics*, 19 (1981), pp. 15–24.
13. J. Coates, (1989) 'Gossip revisited', in D. Cameron and J. Coates (eds), *Women in Their Speech Communities*, New York: Longman, 1989.
14. *Ibid.*, p. 121.
15. N. Eliasoph, 'Politeness, power and women's language: rethinking study in language and gender', *Berkeley Journal of Sociology: A critical review*, vol. XXXII (1987), pp. 92–3.
16. G. Jefferson, 'On "stepwise transition" from talk about a "trouble" to inappropriately neat-positioned matters', in J. Atkinson and J. Heritage (eds), *Structures of Social Action*, Cambridge: Cambridge University Press, pp. 191–222.

12.1 Language and Reality: who made the world?
Dale Spender

Dale Spender, following the deterministic lines of Sapir–Whorf, argues that language constructs our reality. Controversially, she maintains that women are both trapped by and excluded from a language that is 'man-made'. To illustrate this assertion she here discusses usage of generic 'he/man'. Feminist linguists have since questioned the linguistic determinism implicit in Spender's writings.

'The objects and events of the world do not present themselves to us ready classified', states James Britton. 'The categories into which they are divided are the categories into which *we divide* them.'[1]

My question which arises from this statement is not whether it is an accurate assessment, for I readily accept that language is a powerful determinant of reality, but who is the WE to whom James Britton refers? Who are these people who 'make the world' and what are the principles behind their division, organization and classification?

Although not explicitly stated, Britton is referring to males. It is men who have made the world which women must inhabit, and if women are to begin to make their own world, it is necessary that they understand some of the ways in which such *creation* is accomplished. This means exploring the relationship of language and reality.

Once certain categories are constructed within the language, we proceed to organize the world according to those categories. We even fail to see evidence which is not consistent with those categories.

This makes language a paradox for human beings: it is both a creative and an inhibiting vehicle. On the one hand it offers immense freedom, for it allows us to 'create' the world we live in; that so many different cultures have created so many different 'worlds' is testimony to this enormous and varied capacity (Berger and Luckmann have categorized this aspect of language as 'world openness'[2]). But on the other hand we are restricted by that creation, limited to its confines, and, it appears, we resist, fear and dread any modifications to the structures we have initially created, even though they are 'arbitrary', approximate ones. It is this which constitutes a language *trap*.

Given that language is such an influential force in shaping our world, it is obvious that those who have the power to make the symbols and their meanings are in a privileged and highly advantageous position. They have, at least, the potential to order the world to suit their own ends, the potential to construct a language, a reality, a body of knowledge in which they are the central figures, the potential to legitimate their own primacy and to create a system of beliefs which is beyond challenge (so that their superiority is 'natural' and 'objectively' tested). The group which has the power to ordain the structure of language, thought and reality has the potential to create a world in which they are the central figures, while those who are not of their group are peripheral and therefore may be exploited.

In the patriarchal order this potential has been realized.

Males, as the dominant group, have produced language, thought and reality. Historically it has been the structures, the categories and the meanings which have been invented by males – though not of course by *all* males – and they have then been validated by reference to other males. In this process women have played little or no part. It has been male subjectivity which has been the source of those meanings, including the meaning that their own subjectivity is objectivity. Says Dorothy Smith:[3] 'women have largely been excluded from the work of producing forms of thought and the images and symbols in which thought is expressed and realised', and feminists would state unequivocally that this has been no accident. [...]

Man (and *he*) is in constant use as a term which supposedly includes females, and one of the outcomes of this practice has been to plant *man* uppermost in our minds.

Alleen Pace Nilsen[4] found that young children thought that *man* meant male people in sentences such as 'man needs food'. Linda Harrison[5] found that science students – at least – thought male when discussing the evolution of man; they had little appreciation of the female contribution even when explicitly taught it; J. Schneider and Sally Hacker[6] found that college students also thought male when confronted with such titles as Political Man and Urban Man. Unless students are unrepresentative of our society – an unlikely possibility –

there seems to be considerable empirical evidence to suggest that the use of the symbol *man* is accompanied, not surprisingly, by an image of male.

When the symbol *he/man* disposes us to think male, women who are required to use those symbols are required to think again. This is an extra activity, one which males are not called upon to perform. As members of the dominant group, having ascertained that their male identity is constant, males are not required to modify their understandings: they are never referred to as *she/woman*. But having ascertained their female identity women must constantly be available – again – for clues as to whether or not they are encompassed in a reference, for sometimes they are included in the symbol *he/man*, and sometimes they are not. What the dominant group can take for granted is problematic to the muted group, and this could be another means whereby they are kept muted.

The effects of *he/man* language are considerable – though different – for both sexes. This is literally a man-made product which serves to construct and reinforce the divisions between the dominant and muted groups. Such a small 'device', such a little 'tampering' with the language – but with what enormous ramifications for the inequality of the sexes!

Through the introduction of *he/man*, males were able to take another step in ensuring that in the thought and reality of our society it is the males who become the foreground while females become the blurred and often indecipherable background. *He/man* makes males linguistically visible and females linguistically invisible. It promotes male imagery in everyday life at the expense of female imagery so that it seems reasonable to assume the world is male until proven otherwise. It reinforces the belief of the dominant group that they, males, are the universal, the central, important category so that even those who are not members of the dominant group learn to accept this reality. It predisposes us to see more male in the world we inhabit, so that we can, for example, project male images on to our past and allow females to go unnoticed; we can construct our theories of the past, including evolutionary ones, formulating explanations that are consistent only with male experience. [...]

He/man also makes women outsiders, and not just metaphorically. Through the use of *he/man* women cannot take their existence for granted: they must constantly seek confirmation that they are included in the *human* species. [...]

For women to become visible, it is necessary that they become linguistically visible. This is not such a huge obstacle as it may at first appear: there are no uses of *he/man*, for example, to refer to women in this book. There is no ambiguity here about *man*, for when I use the symbol *man* I use it only in reference to male images. But other changes are also required. New symbols will need to be created and old symbols will need to be recycled and invested with new images if the male hold of language is to be broken. As the language structure which has been devised and legitimated by male grammarians exacts ambiguity, uncertainty, and anomie for females, then in the interests of dismantling the muted nature of females, that language structure and those rules need to be defied.

I do not think the world will end if we deliberately break those rules – but there might be a fissure forged in the foundations of the male supremacist world.

Notes

1. J. Britton, *Language and Learning*, Harmondsworth: Penguin, 1975, p. 23.
2. P. Berger and T. Luckmann, *The Social Construction of Reality*, Harmondsworth: Penguin, 1972, p. 69.
3. D. Smith, 'A peculiar eclipsing: women's exclusion for man's culture', *Women's Studies International Quarterly*, vol. 1, no. 4 (1978), pp. 281–96.
4. A. P. Nilson, (1973) 'Grammatical gender and its relationship to the equal treatment of males and females in children's books', unpublished PhD thesis, University of Iowa.
5. L. Harrison, 'Cro-magnon woman-in eclipse', *Science Teacher*, April 1975, pp. 8–11.
6. J. Schneider and S. Hacker, 'Sex role imagery and the use of generic man', *American Sociologist*, vol. 8, no. 1 (1973), pp. 12–18.

12.2 **Gender-based Language Reform and the Social Construction of Meaning**
Susan Ehrlich and Ruth King

Susan Ehrlich and Ruth King take the debate one step further and opt for a more contextually sensitive analysis of what happens when language reform is attempted. Although their research leads them to the conclusion that success is limited within patriarchal structures, they argue convincingly for the continuation of non-sexist usage.

In November 1989, Queen's University in Kingston, Ontario, Canada, sponsored its annual 'NO MEANS NO' rape awareness campaign. In reaction to the campaign, obscene and violent messages appeared in the windows of men's dormitories: 'NO MEANS HARDER', 'NO MEANS DYKE', 'NO MEANS MORE BEER', 'NO MEANS "TIE ME UP"'. In March 1991, during a nationally televised Ontario university hockey game, two University of Waterloo students held signs saying 'NO MEANS HARDER' and 'STOP MEANS PLEASE'. While these signs are extremely disturbing in terms of their normalizing and justifying of violence against women, they are also a strong illustration of the way in which meanings are socially constructed and constituted: the meaning of the word 'no' in this particular context has been appropriated by the dominant culture. Another example of this phenomenon came in April 1991 when British Columbia

Supreme Court Judge Sherman Hood announced in his judgment of an alleged rape case that 'at times "no" may mean "maybe" or "wait a while"'.[1]

This appropriation of meaning has profound consequences for gender-based language reform. As McConnell-Ginet[2] points out (in connection with women saying 'no' to men's sexual advances), 'meaning is a matter not only of individual will but of social relations embedded in political structures'. Because linguistic meanings are, to a large extent, determined by the dominant culture's social values and attitudes, terms initially introduced to be non-sexist and neutral may lose their neutrality in the 'mouths' of a sexist speech community and/or culture.

While sexist language clearly reflects sexist social structures, the continuing existence of such social structures throws into question the possibility of successful language reform. Graddol and Swann[3] comment:

> Sexist language is not simply a linguistic problem. The existence of unmarked expressions 'in the language' does not mean that these will be used and interpreted in a neutral way. This may lead one to question the value of the linguistic reforms advocated in writers' and publishers' guide-lines.

Cameron[4] makes a similar point:

> Therefore, in the interests of accuracy we should strive to include the female half of the human race by replacing male terms with neutral ones. But the 'reality' to which language relates is a sexist one, and in it there are no neutral terms. ... In the mouths of sexists, language can always be sexist.

Given that language is not a neutral vehicle in the representation of reality and it is necessarily laden with social values, the introduction of neutral and/or non-sexist terms does not guarantee neutral and/or non-sexist usage. In this article, we argue that the relative success of attempts at gender-based language reform is dependent on the social context in which the language reform occurs. When language reform occurs within the context of a larger sociopolitical initiative whose primary goal is the eradication of sexist practices (e.g. employment equity programmes), it is more likely to succeed. By contrast, when language reform occurs within the context of a speech community that embraces sexist values and attitudes, it is less likely to succeed. [...]

The appropriation of meaning by the dominant culture is by no means a phenomenon restricted to innovative forms in a language. Shulz[5] traces the semantic derogation of terms designating women in English, showing that words, such as *hussy* and *spinster*, originally neutral or positive in interpretation took on negative connotations in a way that was unparalleled for words designating men. That is, sexist values also influence the meanings of terms that already exist in a language.

(Mis)interpretation and (mis)use of non-sexist terms

In attempting to characterize the type of social conditions that are conducive to successful language reform, Labov's[6] findings concerning the effect of social factors on linguistic change are relevant. Labov claims that the spread of a particular linguistic innovation is determined by the status of the social subgroup leading the change.[7]

> If the group in which the change originated was not the highest-status group in the speech community, members of the highest-status group eventually stigmatized the changed form through their control of various institutions of the communication network ...[8]

Extrapolating from Labov's observations, we can say that the success of gender-based language reform will be determined by the extent to which high-status subgroups within a speech community adopt non-sexist values. Assuming that non-sexist language reform originates in a social subgroup that is not of the highest status within a given speech community (i.e. it originates among socially conscious women), then Labov's findings predict that, all else being equal, these linguistic innovations will be stigmatized unless the highest-status social group also displays non-sexist values. Indeed, there is much evidence to suggest that innovative, non-sexist linguistic forms do undergo a kind of depreciation. While this does not always manifest itself in overt stigmatization of the innovative forms, it does lead to the misuse and misinterpretation of non-sexist terms.[9] Examples of this misuse and misinterpretation follow.

The title Ms was originally popularized by feminists in the 1970s to replace Miss and Mrs and provide a parallel term to Mr, in that both Ms and Mr designate gender without indicating marital status. Miller and Swift[10] see the elimination of Mrs and Miss in favour of Ms as a way of allowing women to be seen as people in their own right, rather than in relation to someone else. Unfortunately, while Ms was intended to parallel Mr, considerable evidence suggests that its use is often resisted, or it is not used and/or interpreted in the intended way. Fasold,[11] in a survey of news organizations' style guides, reports that the *Washington Post*'s manual disallows Ms 'except in direct quotations, in discussing the term itself, or "for special effect"'. The Associated Press 1987 style guide[12] recommends Ms *only* if known to be the preference of the individual woman.

Examples of 'misuses' of the term Ms abound. Frank and Treichler[13] cite the following directive, sent to public information officers in the state of Pennsylvania: 'If you use Ms. for a female, please indicate in parentheses after the Ms. whether it's Miss or Mrs.' In a similar way, Graddol and Swann[14] explain that Ms is not a neutral title for women in Britain: 'in some contexts it seems to have coalesced with Miss (official forms sometimes distinguish only

Mrs. and Ms)'. Atkinson[15] in a Canadian study of attitudes towards the use of Ms and birthname retention among women, found that many of her respondents had a three-way distinction: they used Mrs for married women, Miss for women who had never been married and Ms for divorced women. All three usages described here demonstrate the high premium placed on identifying women by their relationship (current or otherwise) to men, in spite of the intended neutrality associated with Ms.[16]

In a similar way, neutral terms such as *chairperson* and *spokesperson*, introduced to replace masculine generics such as *chairman* and *spokesman*, seem to have lost their neutrality in that they are often only used for women. The following example containing announcements of academics' changing jobs, cited by Dubois and Crouch[17] (from the *Chronicle of Higher Education*, 1977), demonstrates that a woman is a *chairperson*, but a man is a *chairman*:

> Margarette P. Eby, *Chairperson* of Humanities at U. of Michigan at Dearborn, to Dean of the College of Humanities and Fine Arts and Professor of Music at U. of Northern Iowa.
> David W. Hamilton, Assoc. Professor of Anatomy at Harvard, to *Chairman* of Anatomy at U. of Minnesota.
> Eileen T. Handelman, *Chairperson* of Science at Sinon's Rock Early College, to Dean of Academic Affairs.
> Elaine B. Harvey, Acting *Chairperson* of Graduate Pediatrics at Indiana U. to Dean of the School of Nursing at Fort Hays Kansas State U.
> Philip E. Hicks, Professor of Industrial Engineering at New Mexico State U., to *Chairman* of Industrial Engineering at North Carolina A & T State U.

From this example, we can see that the attempt to replace a masculine generic with a neutral one has been somewhat unsuccessful in that neutral terms like *chairperson*, *spokesperson*, etc., are functioning to designate only female referents. Rather than ridding the language of a masculine generic, the introduction of neutral generic *person* forms has (in some situations, at least) led to a sex-based distinction between forms such as *chairperson* vs *chairman*.

Much research has demonstrated that *he/man* generics do not function generically (even though they may be intended generically) to the extent that they readily evoke images of males rather than of males and females. Other studies have shown that the use of *he/man* language has detrimental effects on individuals' beliefs in females' ability to perform a job, and on females' own feelings of pride, importance and power. The use of neutral generic pronouns such as *he or she*, *she or he* or singular *they* is thus advocated by supporters of language reform, given the negative effects, both symbolic and practical, of *he/man* language.

A recent study by Khosroshahi[18] attempts to investigate the effects of neutral generics vs masculine generics in terms of the mental imagery evoked. Her subjects included both males and females with both reformed and traditional language usage (i.e. four groups of subjects). Khosroshahi summarizes her results:

> All groups were androcentric except the women who had reformed their language; androcentric in the sense that when they read a paragraph that was ambiguous with respect to gender, they were more likely to interpret it as referring to a male than to a female character. Even if the paragraph used he or she or they, feminine referents did not become more salient than masculine ones.[19]

Thus, these results demonstrate that for most of the subjects in this experiment the use of masculine vs neutral generics had no significant effect on the image evoked: male referents were always more salient than female ones. Khrosroshahi explains her results:

> Given the repeatedly documented fact that women are significantly under-represented in a variety of literatures, the finding that the masculine tends to be read as representative is not very surprising. ... In a literature dominated by male characters, initially sex-indefinite words must quickly develop masculine connotations.[20]

Thus, like the misuse of Ms described above, this research shows that neutral generic terms are not readily interpreted as neutral. Again, we see that it is the prevailing values and attitudes of a culture that determine, to a large extent, how these innovative, non-sexist terms get used and interpreted, in spite of their intended neutrality. It is interesting to note here that the exceptional group in Khosroshahi's study, the reformed language women, not only interpreted neutral generics in terms of female referents but also interpreted the masculine generic mostly in terms of female referents. In other words, they displayed the opposite pattern to the three other groups: female (as opposed to male) referents were evoked regardless of the type of generic pronoun used. Again, we see that the interpretation of terms (neutral or not) seems to be heavily influenced by the ideologies of an individual or speech community rather than by the particular pronoun used in a given context.

While the evidence presented above is meant to demonstrate the way in which non-sexist meanings and usages can be socially constituted by a sexist speech community, we are not suggesting that language reform is always or ever futile. First, it should be noted that even if gender-based language reform is not immediately and/or completely successful, it does sensitize individuals to ways in which language is discriminatory towards women: language has become one of the many arenas in which social inequalities are elucidated. Penelope[21] maintains that becoming aware of linguistic choices forces us to monitor our thought processes and 'will gradually enable us to unlearn patriarchal ways of thinking'. Second, language reform can be a source of empowerment for members of disadvantaged groups. Finally, by considering 'unsuccessful' cases of language reform, we can better understand the social mechanisms at work in cases of successful language reform.

Notes

1. 'Judge Rules "No" May Mean "Maybe" in Sex Assault Case', *Toronto Star*, 25 April 1991.
2. S. McConnell-Ginet, 'The sexual (re)production of meaning', in F. Frank and P. Treichler (eds), *Language, Gender and Professional Writing*, New York: Modern Language Association, 1989, p. 47.
3. D. Graddol and J. Swann, *Gender Voices*, New York: Blackwell, 1989.
4. D. Cameron, *Feminism and Linguistic Theory*, London: Macmillan, 1985.
5. M. R. Shulz, 'The semantic derogation of women', in B. Thorne and N. Henley (eds), *Language and Sex: Difference and dominance*, Rowley, MA.: Newbury House.
6. W. Labov, *Sociolinguistic Patterns*, 1975, Philadelphia, PA: University of Philadelphia Press, 1972.
7. This is not to say that linguistic innovations will always begin with the highest-status subgroup; the relative prestige associated with a particular subgroup and its linguistic innovations may be based on factors other than the socioeconomic ones typically associated with high prestige, e.g. ethnic identity, class loyalty, etc. may play a role. See Labov, *Sociolinguistic Patterns*, for discussion.
8. Labov, *Sociolinguistic Patterns*, p. 179.
9. Henley makes a similar point regarding the possibility of successful language reform. However, Henley focuses on the way in which non-sexist forms are stigmatized and stereotyped because women, a lower-prestige group, are the innovators: N. Henley, 'This new species that seeks a new language: on sexism in language and language change', in J. Penfield (ed.), *Women and Language in Transition*, New York: State University of New York, 1987.
10. C. Miller and K. Swift, *Words and Women: New language new- times*, New York: Doubleday, 1976.
11. R. Fasold, 'Language policy and change: sexist language in the periodical news media', in P. Lowenberg (ed.), *Language Spread and Language Policy*, Washington, DC: Georgetown University Press.
12. C. W. French (ed.), *The Associated Press Stylebook and Libel Manual* (rev. edn), Reading, MA: Addison-Wesley, 1987.
13. F. Frank and P. Treichler (eds), *Language, Gender and Professional Writing*, New York: Modern Language Association, 1989.
14. Graddol and Swann, *Gender Voices*.
15. D. Atkinson, 'Names and titles: maiden name retention and the use of Ms', *Journal of the Atlantic Provinces Linguistic Association* (JAPLA), 9 (1987), pp. 56–83.
16. There is also some evidence to suggest that Ms has been overtly stigmatized, as Labov predicts of linguistic innovations that are not introduced by the highest-status group within a speech community. Pierre Berton, in a column in the *Toronto Star*, 15 June 1991, reports that a *Star* copyeditor would not allow him to use Ms before a woman's name because it was 'demeaning'.
17. B. L. Dubois and I. Crouch, 'Linguistic disruption: he/she, s/he, he or she, he-she', in J. Penfield (ed.), *Women and Language in Transition*.

18. F. Khosroshahi, 'Penguins don't care, but women do: a social identity analysis of a Whorfian problem', *Language in Society*, 18 (1989), pp. 505–25.
19. *Ibid.*, p. 517.
20. *Ibid.*
21. J. Penelope, *Speaking Freely*, New York: Pergamon, 1990.

12.3 **Language and Woman's Place**
Robin Lakoff

Robin Lakoff controversially evaluates women's language as deficit, sparking off a long-running debate. Here she focuses on tags and epistemic modality (labelled 'hedges') as characteristic of what she perceives to be a typically weak and powerless female discourse style.

It will be found that the overall effect of 'women's language' [...] is this: it submerges a woman's personal identity, by denying her the means of expressing herself strongly, on the one hand, and encouraging expressions that suggest triviality in subject matter and uncertainty about it.

When we leave the lexicon and venture into syntax, we find that syntactically too women's speech is peculiar. To my knowledge, there is no syntactic rule in English that only women may use. But there is at least one rule that a woman will use in more conversational situations than a man. (This fact indicates, of course, that the applicability of syntactic rules is governed partly by social context – the positions in society of the speaker and addressee, with respect to each other, and the impression one seeks to make on the other.) This is the rule of tag-question formation.

A tag, in its usage as well as its syntactic shape (in English), is midway between an outright statement and a yes–no question: it is less assertive than the former, but more confident than the latter. Therefore it is usable under certain contextual situations: not those in which a statement would be appropriate, nor those in which a yes–no question is generally used, but in situations intermediate between these.

One makes a statement when one has confidence in his knowledge and is pretty certain that his statement will be believed; one asks a question when one lacks knowledge on some point and has reason to believe that this gap can and will be remedied by an answer by the addressee. A tag question, being intermediate between these, is used when the speaker is stating a claim, but lacks full confidence in the truth of that claim. So if I say:

1. Is John here?

I will probably not be surprised if my respondent answers 'no'; but if I say:

2. John is here, isn't he?

instead, chances are I am already biased in favor of a positive answer, wanting only confirmation by the addressee. I still want a response from him, as I do with a yes–no question; but I have enough knowledge (or think I have) to predict that response, much as with a declarative statement. A tag question, then, might be thought of as a declarative statement without the assumption that the statement is to be believed by the addressee: one has an out, as with a question. A tag gives the addressee leeway, not forcing him to go along with the views of the speaker.

There are situations in which a tag is legitimate, in fact the only legitimate sentence form. So, for example, if I have seen something only indistinctly, and have reason to believe my addressee had a better view, I can say:

3. I had my glasses off. He was out at third, wasn't he?

Sometimes we find a tag question used in cases in which the speaker knows as well as the addressee what the answer must be, and does't need confirmation. One such situation is when the speaker is making 'small talk', trying to elicit conversation from the addressee:

4. Sure is hot here, isn't it?

In discussing personal feelings or opinions, only the speaker normally has any way of knowing the correct answer. Strictly speaking, questioning one's own opinions is futile. Sentences like (5) are usually ridiculous:

5. *I have a headache, don't I?

But similar cases do, apparently, exist, in which it is the speaker's opinions, rather than perceptions, for which corroboration is sought, as in (6):

6. The way prices are rising is horrendous, isn't it?

While there are, of course, other possible interpretations of a sentence like this, one possibility is that the speaker has a particular answer in mind – 'yes' or 'no' – but is reluctant to state it baldly. It is my impression, though I do not have precise statistical evidence, that this sort of tag question is much more apt to be used by women than by men. If this is indeed true, why is it true?

These sentence types provide a means whereby a speaker can avoid committing himself, and thereby avoid coming into conflict with the addressee. The problem is that, by so doing, a speaker may also give the impression of not being really sure of himself, of looking to the addressee for confirmation, even of having no views of his own. This last criticism is, of course, one often leveled at women. One wonders how much of it reflects a use of language that has been imposed on women from their earliest years. [...]

Women's speech seems in general to contain more instances of 'well', 'y'know', 'kinda', and so forth: words that convey the sense that the speaker is uncertain about what he (or she) is saying, or cannot vouch for the accuracy of the statement. These words are fully legitimate when, in fact, this is the case (for example, if one says, 'John is sorta tall', meaning he's neither really impressively tall nor actually short, but rather middling, though toward the tall side: 5 feet 9 rather than 6 feet 5, say). There is another justifiable use in which the hedge mitigates the possible unfriendliness or unkindness of a statement – that is, where it's used for the sake of politeness. Thus, 'John is sorta short', where I mean: He's 5 feet 2 and you're 5 feet 8, Mary, so how will it look if you go out with him? Here, I know exactly how short he is, and it is very short, but I blunt the force of a rather painful assertion by using the hedge. What I mean is the class of cases in which neither of these facts pertains, and a hedge shows up anyway: the speaker is perfectly certain of the truth of the assertion, and there's no danger of offense, but the tag appears anyway as an apology for making an assertion at all. Anyone may do this if he lacks self-confidence, as everyone does in some situations; but my impression is that women do it more, precisely because they are socialized to believe that asserting themselves strongly isn't nice or ladylike, or even feminine. Another manifestation of the same thing is the use of 'I guess' and 'I think' prefacing declarations or 'I wonder' prefacing questions, which themselves are hedges on the speech-acts of saying and asking. 'I guess' means something like: I would like to say ... to you, but I'm not sure I can (because I don't know if it's right, because I don't know if I have the right, because I don't know how you'd take it, and so on), so I'll merely put it forth as a suggestion. Thus, if I say, 'It will rain this afternoon,' and it doesn't, you can later take me to task for a misleading or inaccurate prediction. But if I say, 'I guess it will rain this afternoon,' then I am far less vulnerable to such an attack. So these hedges do have their uses when one really has legitimate need for protection, or for deference (if we are afraid that by making a certain statement we are overstepping our rights), but used to excess, hedges, like question intonation, give the impression that the speaker lacks authority or does't know what he's talking about. Again, these are familiar misogynistic criticisms, but the use of these hedges arises out of a fear of seeming too masculine by being assertive and saying things directly.

12.4 **Gender, Power and Miscommunication**

Nancy M. Henley and Cheris Kramarae

Nancy Henley and Cheris Kramarae attack the general assumptions underpinning the 'deficit theory', claiming that its implications are dangerous and unfair. That this debate is still ongoing gives some indication of the influence of Lakoff's book Language and Woman's Place.

Consequences and implications of female deficit theory

Theories of female deficit, along with those of cultural difference (see below), have probably had the most consequence in our daily lives. A primary consequence of female deficit theory is the expansion of notions of male normativeness. By this we mean a view that sees female/male difference as female deviation from what is often called 'the' norm, but is actually the male cultural form. The male normativeness is manifested in several ways.

1 *There is a focus on female forms and female 'difference'.* This is obvious in the many recent writings on language and gender that emphasize female speech, such as *Language and Woman's Place*,[1] *The Way Women Write*,[2] *Women's Language and Style*,[3] and 'How and why women are more polite'.[4] Although most writing about language and speech is tacitly based on men's actions, very little is written on men's language and speech forms *per se*, which should merit as much attention as female ones, as distinctive cultural forms. This focus on the female is found not only in recent writings, but has earlier origins in, for example, the chapter on 'The Woman' in Jespersen's *Language: Its nature, development and origin*[5] and the early writings of anthropologists who observed in far-away cultures what they often called 'women's languages'.[6]

The focus on female difference, of course, emphasizes the underlying assumption that the female is a deviant[7] while the male is 'normal' and speaks 'the language'. The ultimate conclusion of this view defines women as puzzling or unknowable, remaining for linguists 'one of the mysteries of the universe'.[8]

2 *There is pressure on women to use 'men's' language.* Lakoff takes for granted that women will want to use men's language, though she does not always call it that:

> most women who get as far as college learn to switch from women's to neutral language under appropriate situations (in class, talking to professors, at job interviews, and such) ... if a girl knows that a professor will be receptive to comments that sound scholarly, objective, unemotional, she will of course be tempted to use neutral language in class or in conference.[9]

In the late 1970s and early 1980s, the general problem with communication between women and men was presented as women's hesitancy in stating their interests and wishes. The basic solution presented by many 'experts' was (especially in the US) assertiveness training, which was to help women change their behaviour and be more assertive. That is, both the blame and the potential solution were located within the woman experiencing trouble in making others understand her.[10]

3 *There is an expectation that females should (re-)interpret male expressions.* Lakoff suggests that girls and women have to be bilingual, to speak both women's and men's languages. But there is no suggestion that boys or men have to be bilingual, even though she claims that young boys learn women's language as their first language, and have to unlearn it by around the age of 10.[11] Why are not men already bilingual, or why are they not too required to become bilingual?

Evaluation of female deficit theory

This requirement of bilingualism, or bidialectalism, if it is true (we know of no empirical research directly on the question), would be more invidious than it might at first appear. We believe there is an implicit deficit theory underlying dominant US culture, which requires (and teaches, through popular magazines) females, not males, to learn to read the silence, lack of emotional expression, or brutality of the other sex as not only other than, but more benign than, it appears. From a young girl's reframing of a boy's insults and hits as signs that he likes her, to a woman's reframing of her husband's battering as a perverse demonstration of caring, females are encouraged to use their greater knowledge of males' communication to interpret men's assaultive behavior, to make it in an almost magical way 'not so'.[12] [...]

Although Jespersen's[13] romp through examples of female deficit had many hearings in bibliographies, his statements and evidence are no longer given official credence. Nevertheless, the newer theories have had strong effect; a belief in women's 'inferior talk' is undoubtedly still the basis for many stereotypes affecting women's lives. Lakoff's suggestions and recommendations have led to many written papers that treat her hypotheses as fact or as the most important communication factors to study; this legacy persists in advice books that caution women to, for example, avoid 'weak, feminine' tag questions. These simplistic critiques too often ignore context and within-gender variation, and treat women's expressions as feeble deviations from men's stronger expressions.

We reject much in the theories of female deficit because of their biased evaluation of female and male speech styles, and we reject biologically based theories as ignoring the large and complex contributions of culture and psychology to speech differences. However, the point made by Lakoff that society differentially evaluates women's and men's speech is largely true and must be taken into account in any theory of difference and miscommunication.

Notes

1. R. Lakoff, *Language and Woman's Place*, New York: Harper Colophon, 1975.
2. M. Hiatt, *The Way Women Write*, New York: Teachers College Press, 1977.
3. D. Butturf and E. Epstein (eds), *Women's Language and Style*, Acron, OH: (L & S Books), 1978.

4. P. Brown, 'How and why women are more polite: some evidence from a Mayan community', in S. McConnell-Ginet, R. Borker and N. Furman (eds), *Women and Languages in Literature and Society*, New York: Praeger, 1980.

5. O. Jespersen, 'The woman', in *Language: Its nature, development, and origins*, London: Allen & Unwin, 1922.

6. D. Blood, 'Women's speech characteristics in Cham', *Asian Culture*, 3 (1962), pp. 139–43; A. Chamberlain, 'Women's language', *American Anthropologist*, 14 (1912), pp. 579–81.

7. E. Schur, *Labelling Women Deviant: Gender, stigma and social control*, Philadelphia, PA: Temple University Press, 1983.

8. R. Shuy, 'Sociolinguistic research at the Centre for Applied Linguistics: the correlation of language and sex', in *Industrial Days of Sociolinguistics*, Rome: Istituto Luigi Sturzo, 1970.

9. Lakoff, *Language and Woman's Place*, pp. 6–7.

10. J. Baer, *How to be an Assertive (Not Aggressive) Woman in Life, in Love, and on the Job: A total guide to self-assertiveness*, New York: New American Library, 1976; P. E. Butler, *Self-Assertion for Women: A guide to becoming androgynous*, New York: Cornfield, 1976; N. M. Henley, 'Assertiveness training in the social context', *Assert*, 30 (1980), pp. 1–2.

11. Lakoff, *Language and Woman's Place*.

12. L. Baughman, Graduate Paper, Department of Speech Communication, University of Illinois, Urbana-Champaign, 1988.

13. Jespersen, 'The woman'.

12.5 Lakoff in Context: the social and linguistic functions of tag questions

Deborah Cameron, Fiona McAlinden and Kathy O'Leary

Deborah Cameron, Fiona McAlinden and Kathy O'Leary accuse Lakoff of naivety in assuming that one linguistic form correlates with one function. Specifically challenging Lakoff's evaluation of tags, they argue for a finer contextually sensitive analysis of female discourse.

The tag question

The linguistic feature chosen here as a case study is one which has really got into the bones of the debate on language and sex since it was originally discussed by Lakoff, and we have had occasion to allude to it several times already in our theoretical discussion: the tag question. The idea that women use more tag questions than men because tags in many contexts indicate tentativeness and approval-seeking has passed out of the domain of academic speculation and into folklinguistic common sense, not excluding the folklinguistic common sense of feminists.

Tag questions in casual conversation

Aims of the study

The first study is based on a corpus of nine texts of 5,000 words each from the Survey of English Usage (SEU) conversational corpus based at University College, London. Three texts involved male speakers only, three female speakers only, and three speakers of both sexes. Some 25 speakers were sampled altogether, the constraints of the SEU (which set out to collect examples of 'educated' British English usage, i.e. middle-class, mostly southern and overwhelmingly white English speech) ensuring a relatively homogeneous group in terms of social status. The aim of the study was to discover what sex differences, if any, existed in this group's use of tag questions.

Tag questions were defined formally as grammatical structures in which a declarative is followed by an attached interrogative clause or 'tag' where the first element of the declarative's AUX component (or dummy DO), usually with its original polarity reversed, and a pronoun coreferential with the original subject NP are 'copied out' — as in, for instance:

1. *You were missing last week/weren't you* (SEU)

or, with polarity constant rather than reversed:

2. *Thorpe's away/is he* (SEU)

Examples of tag questions from the 45,000 words sampled were further coded for variation on a number of formal features: position (utterance-initial vs utterance-medial), polarity (constant vs reversed) and intonation (rising ($/$) vs falling ($\backslash$) tone).

In addition to this formal analysis we attempted a functional classification of the tag questions in our data. Given our criticisms of mindless quantification, we were anxious to avoid merely comparing women's total usage of tags with men's without first ascertaining that they were using the structure in comparable ways; we were also interested in challenging Lakoff's very cut-and-dried, restrictive view of tag questions' functions: that unless they request information unknown to the speaker they should be treated as 'illegitimate', markers of tentativeness, a sign that the speaker has 'no views of his [*sic*] own'.[1] This view has recently also been challenged by the New Zealand linguist Janet Holmes.

Analysing tag questions: the work of Holmes

Holmes is very much aware of what we have labelled the 'form and function' problem. She notes that in discussions of sex differences in speech style:

> Most investigators have simply counted linguistic forms and compared the totals for women vs. men with very little discussion of the functions of the forms in the context of the discourse in which they occur.[2]

In elucidating these functions, Holmes suggests:

> at least two interrelated contextual factors need to be taken into account, namely the function of the speech act in the developing discourse, and the relationship between the participants in the context of utterance.[3]

Holmes's own analysis distinguishes two main functions of tag questions which she calls *modal* and *affective*. Modal tags are those which request information or confirmation of information of which the speaker is uncertain; in Holmes's terms they are 'speaker-orientated', i.e. designed to meet the speaker's need for information. Examples of this type from the Survey data include:

3. *You were missing last week/weren't you* (SEU)
4. *But you've been in Reading longer than that/haven't you* (SEU).

'Affective tags', by contrast, are addressee-orientated: that is, they are used not to signal uncertainty on the part of the speaker, but to indicate concern for the addressee. This concern can take two distinct forms. On one hand, it can exemplify what Brown and Levinson[4] call 'negative politeness': a speaker may use a tag to 'soften' or mitigate a face-threatening act. Holmes gives the example:

5. *Open the door for me, could you*

where the baldness of the directive is mitigated by the tag, and the face-threat to the addressee correspondingly reduced. Tags used in this way are referred to by Holmes as 'softeners'. On the other hand, concern can be directed to the addressee's positive face: rather than merely reducing possible offence, a tag may be used to indicate a positive interest in or solidarity with the addressee, and especially to offer her or him a way into the discourse, signalling, in effect, 'OK, your turn now'. Holmes labels this kind of tag 'facilitative'. Examples from the Survey data include:

6. *His portraits are quite static by comparison\aren't they* (SEU)
7. *Quite a nice room to sit in actually\isn't it* (SEU)

It is precisely this kind of 'facilitative' tag which Lakoff would read as 'illegitimate', a covert request for approval. The speakers of (6) and (7) express personal opinions and value-judgements which in no way require confirmation from anyone else. Indeed, for an addressee to disagree or withhold agreement here would be markedly and noticeably uncooperative. Thus Lakoff would hold that the tag is uncalled-for and overly deferential. But Holmes finds this reading unsubtle and unhelpful. Facilitative tags may have no informational function, but they do have an important *interactional* function, that of drawing other participants into an exchange. To call this 'illegitimate' begs the question.

Holmes's analysis of the functions of tag questions allows her to modify the Lakoff hypothesis. As we know from studies like Dubois and Crouch's,[5] it is not invariably true that women use more tags overall than men. But it might be plausible to suggest that they use more tags with affective meaning, especially facilitative tags. Women, after all, are allegedly 'co-operative' conversationalists who express frequent concern for other participants in talk; in mixed interaction it has been suggested that women are expected to do what Pamela Fishman[6] has called 'interactional shitwork', – essentially a talk-facilitation task.

Holmes's own data support this modified hypothesis. She found that in her sample, 59 per cent of women's tags were facilitative compared to 35 per cent which were modal; for men these proportions were more or less reversed, at 25 per cent facilitative tags and 61 per cent modals (the remaining percentage for both sexes is accounted for by softeners, of which men in fact use a higher proportion. For actual values see Table 12.5.1 below).

In our own study we set out to investigate two questions: first, where the modal/affective distinction could fruitfully be applied to data from the SEU; and second, whether the application of the distinction would yield findings on sex difference similar to those reported by Holmes.

Sex-difference findings

The 45,000 words sampled from the SEU gave us a database of 96 tag questions,

Table 12.5.1 Tag questions in casual conversation

	Holmes 1984		SEU	
	F	M	F	M
Modal	18 (35%)	24 (61%)	9 (25%)	24 (40%)
Affective				
Facilitative	30 (59%)	10 (25%)	27 (75%)	36 (60%)
Softeners	3 (6%)	5 (13%)	—	—
Total tags	51	39	36	60

of which 36 were produced by women and 60 by men. When these 96 tags were analysed as either modal or affective, subject, of course, to the reservations outlined above, the expected sex difference did appear (see Table 12.5.1) It is noticeable that while our findings for women are more decisive than Holmes's – that is, the women in the SEU sample lean even more firmly towards facilitative rather than modal tags – our findings for men's speech are less decisive. Men in the SEU sample used far more facilitative tags than those whose speech was sampled by Holmes. On examination, we discovered an interesting factor which may have skewed the scores for the SEU men: three speakers in our sample texts had been aware that recording was taking place, and these speakers – two of whom were men – had abnormally high scores for facilitative tags. It may be that their speech reflected a concern to elicit as much talk as possible from other participants, in order to generate as much data as possible for the Survey. In other words, these speakers had either consciously or unconsciously taken on the role of conversational 'facilitator'. If their contribution were discounted altogether, the incidence of facilitative tags among men would fall by around 6 per cent (though this is not enough to account for the considerable difference between our results and Holmes's).

What, if anything, do our findings suggest? One hypothesis which they seem to point towards (though obviously it would need to be more rigorously tested) is that the use of facilitative tags correlates with conversational role, rather than with gender *per se*. Where men take on a facilitating role they are able to produce large numbers of facilitative tags.

Both Holmes[7] and Fishman[8] have claimed that the role of facilitator in conversation is taken on (at least in casual conversation) more frequently and markedly by women than by men. The SEU findings do not necessarily lead us to dispute the validity of that claim. Nevertheless, future research must take very seriously the possibility of an intervening variable between gender and language use.

Notes

1. R. Lakoff, *Language and Woman's Place*, New York: Harper Colophon, 1975, p. 17.
2. J. Holmes, 'Hedging your bets and sitting on the fence: some evidence for hedges as support structures', *Te Reo*, 27 (1984), pp. 47–52 (p. 52).
3. *Ibid.*
4. P. Brown and S. Levinson, 'Universals in language usage: politeness phenomena', in E. Goody (ed.), *Questions and Politeness*, Cambridge: Cambridge University Press, 1978, pp. 56–310.
5. B. L. Dubois and I. Crouch, 'The question of tag questions in women's speech: they don't really use more of them, do they?', *Language in Society*, 4 (1975), pp. 289–94.
6. P. M. Fishman, 'Conversational insecurity', in H. Giles, W. P. Robinson and P. Smith (eds), *Language: Social psychology perspectives*, Oxford: Pergamon, 1980.
7. Holmes, 'Hedging your bets'.

8. P. Fishman, 'Conversational insecurity'; P. Fishman, 'Interaction: the work women do', in B. Thorne, C. Kramarae and N. Henley (eds), *Language, Gender and Society*, Newbury, MA: Rowley House, 1983.

12.6 Gossip Revisited

Jennifer Coates

Jennifer Coates builds on the redefinition of female discourse. Positively re-evaluating the epistemic modal forms that Lakoff had seen as weak and powerless, she moves the debate one step further by empirically showing female friends using hedges in an interactionally 'co-operative' way. In doing so, she also lays the foundation on which subsequent research can now build, in its unpacking of the very complex notion of female discourse 'co-operativity'.

Epistemic modality

Epistemic modal forms are defined semantically as those linguistic forms which are used to indicate the speaker's confidence or lack of confidence in the truth of the proposition expressed in the utterance. If someone says *Perhaps she missed the train*, the use of the word *perhaps* indicates lack of confidence in the proposition 'she missed the train'. Lexical items such as *perhaps, I think, sort of, probably*, as well as certain prosodic and paralinguistic features, are used in English to express epistemic modality.

Such forms, however, are used by speakers not just to indicate their lack of commitment to the truth of propositions, but also to hedge assertions in order to protect both their own and addressees' face (for a full account of the role of epistemic modality in spoken discourse, see Coates[1]). It is my impression (based on an admittedly small corpus of data) that women in single-sex groups exploit these forms more than men. Table 12.6.1 gives the totals for the most commonly used forms in two parallel texts, each lasting about 40 minutes.

Table 12.6.1 Sex differences in the use of epistemic modal forms

	Women	Men
I mean	77	20
well	65	45
just	57	48
I think	36	12
sort of	35	10

Utterances such as those in Examples 1 and 2 below are typical of the discussion sections of the all-women conversations recorded (epistemic modal forms in italics).

Example I

[funeral discussion] *I mean I think it really* depends on the attitude of the survivors who are '*there* +

Example 2

[speaker describes old friend she'd recently bumped into] she looks very *sort of* um (−) *kind of* matronly *really* +

It is my contention that women exploit the polypragmatic nature of epistemic modal forms. They use them to mitigate the force of an utterance in order to respect addressees' face needs. Thus, the italicised forms in Example 2 hedge the assertion *she looks matronly* not because the speaker doubts its truth but because she does not want to offend her addressees by assuming their agreement (describing a friend in unflattering terms is controversial). Such forms also protect the speaker's face: the speaker in Example 2 can retreat from the proposition expressed there if it turns out to be unacceptable. Where sensitive topics are discussed (as in Examples 1 and 2), epistemic modal forms are used frequently. This seems to provide an explanation for women's greater use of such forms (see Table 12.6.1). The women's conversations I have analysed involve topics related to people and feelings; in the parallel all-male conversation I have analysed, the men talk about *things* – home beer-making, hi-fi systems, etc. Presumably such topics do not trigger the use of epistemic modal forms because they are not so face-threatening.

Epistemic modal forms are used to respect the face needs of all participants, to negotiate sensitive topics, and to encourage the participation of others; the chief effect of using epistemic modal forms is that the speaker does not take a hard line. Where a group rather than an individual overview is the aim of discussion, then linguistic forms which mitigate the force of individual contributions are a valuable resource. [...]

It seems that in conversations between women friends in an informal context, the notion of co-operativeness is not a myth.

Notes

1. J. Coates, 'Epistemic modality and spoken discourse', *Transactions of the Philological Society*, 1987, pp. 110–31.

Further Reading

Anderson, R. (1988), *The Power and the Word: Language, power and change*, London: Paladin.

Aries, E. (1976), 'Interaction patterns and themes of male, female, and mixed groups', *Small Group Behaviour*, vol. 7, no. 1, pp. 7–18.

Cameron, D. (1985, 1990), *Feminism and Linguistic Theory*, Basingstoke: Macmillan.

Cameron, D., McAlinden, F. and O'Leary, K. (1989), 'Lakoff in context: the social and linguistic functions of tag questions', in J. Coates and D. Cameron (eds), *Women in Their Speech Communities*, New York: Longman.

Coates, J. (1986), *Women, Men and Language*, London: Longman.

Coates, J. (1989), 'Gossip revisited', in J. Coates and D. Cameron (eds), *Women in Their Speech Communities*, New York: Longman.

Coates, J. (1989), 'Women's speech, women's strength?', *York Papers in Linguistics*, 13, pp. 65–76.

Coates, J. and Cameron, D. (eds) (1989), *Women in Their Speech Communities*, London: Longman.

Coupland, N., Giles, H. and Wiemann, J. (eds) (1991), *Miscommunication and Problematic Talk*, Newbury Park, CA: Sage.

Crosby, F. and Nyquist, L. (1977), 'The female register: an empirical study of Lakoff's Hypothesis', *Language in Society*, 6, pp. 313–22.

Edelsky, C. (1981), 'Who's got the floor?' *Language in Society*, 10, pp. 383–421.

Ehrlich, S. and King, R. (1992), 'Gender-based language and reform and the social construction of meaning', *Discourse and Society*, vol. 3,(2) no. 2, pp. 138–62.

Fishman, P. (1977), 'Interactional shitwork', *Heresies*, 2, pp. 99–101.

Henley, N. and Kramarae, C. (1991), 'Gender, power and miscommunication', in N. Coupland, H. Giles and J. Wiemann (eds), *Miscommunication and Problematic Talk*, Newbury Park, CA: Sage.

Johnson, F. and Aries, E. (1983), 'The talk of women friends', *Women's Studies International Forum*, vol. 6, no. 4, pp. 353–61.

Jones, D. (1980), 'Gossip: notes on women's oral culture', in C. Kramarae (ed.), *The Voices and Words of Women and Men*, Oxford: Pergamon.

Khosroshahi, F. (1989), 'Penguins don't care, but women do: a social identity analysis of a Whorfian problem', *Language in Society*, vol. 18, pp. 505–25.

Lakoff, R. (1975), *Language and Woman's Place*, New York: Harper Colophon.

Leet-Pellegrini, H. M. (1980), 'Conversational dominance as a function of gender and expertise', in H. Giles, W. P. Robinson and P. Smith (eds), *Language: Social psychological perspectives*, Oxford: Pergamon.

O'Barr, W. and Atkins, B. (1980), '"Women's language" or "powerless language"?' in S. McConnell-Ginet, R. Borker and N. Furman (eds), *Women and Language in Literature and Society*, New York: Praeger.

Spender, D. (1985), 'Language and reality: who made the world?', in *Man Made Language*, (2nd edn), New York: Routledge & Kegan Paul.

Todd, A. D. and Fisher, S. (eds) (1988), *Gender and Discourse: The power of talk*, Advances in Discourse Processes Series, vol. XXX, New York: Ablex.

West, C. and Zimmerman, D. (1983), 'Small insults: a study of interruptions in cross-sex conversations between unacquainted persons', in B. Thorne, C. Kramarae and N. Henley (eds), *Language, Gender and Society*, Rowley, MA: Newbury House.

Wodak, R. (1981), 'Women relate: men report: sex differences in language behaviour in a therapeutic group', *Journal of Pragmatics*, 5, pp. 261–85.

13 | FEMINIST LITERARY CRITICISM

Edited and Introduced by Pauline Young

INTRODUCTION

> This is an important book, the critic assumes, because
> it deals with war. This is an insignificant book
> because it deals with the feelings of women in the
> drawing room. [1]

The 'critic' in the above quotation is, of course, assumed to be male. In fact he is probably a white, middle-class, well-educated male. All of which indicates, as does the quotation, that you can't separate feminist literary criticism from politics.

'Women and literature' is a problematic correlation. Women are products of a culture which values the activities of men, and literature both shapes and responds to this, perpetuating patriarchal ideals through representations of women which omit reference to the reality of female experience.

The position of the woman writer is equally difficult to locate. Constructed within society as 'other' or 'the opposite sex', she lacks an autonomous identity and is pressurised to respond negatively to the prescriptive roles imposed upon her:

> A woman who is trying to come to terms with a world and with values where she
> is object and not subject, an outsider, regarded as an inferior dependant with no
> voice of her own, must at all costs avoid the subjective voice if she is to conform
> to standard morality. [2]

The problem of the female subject – fragmented, dislocated, frequently absent – is a significant concern of those writers and critics whose work is reproduced here. For several – Simone de Beauvoir, Tillie Olsen, Kate Millett – their recognition of the alien nature of the dominant discourse is a starting point from which they can begin to address the essential definition of female subjectivity; a critique of patriarchal society and its institutionalised structures providing the basis for an alternative, female-centred critical approach. Thus Olsen (see Reading 13.5) speaks personally of her experience as a female writer, of the circumstances which delayed her own definition as a writer and the cost of a lifetime's habit of meeting domestic needs. The woman writer is, she says, 'a survivor'; she writes knowing that she is 'one in twelve', and that many of the other eleven are excluded not by talent but by circumstances which have defined and determined their role and so circumscribed their talent that it never emerges. 'We who write are survivors, only's.'

Kate Millett's is a distinctive voice in the history of feminism (see Reading 13.2). Focusing on male writers, she documents the oppressive nature of sexual politics characterised in the literature of the period 1830–1930 by a deeply rooted misogyny. She discerns three distinct responses to what she terms the sexual revolution in these years: the most optimistic is a recognition of the need for social and cultural reform; the second emanates from a sentimental paradigm of the good and virtuous woman whose elevated status rests upon her function as moral exemplum in the roles of wife and mother; in the third, the unconscious masculine fear of unbridled female sexuality leads to a projection of woman as demon – sensual, intemperate, and with a powerful ability to subvert and corrupt the patriarchal culture.

Sandra Gilbert and Susan Gubar (Reading 13.3) invoke psychoanalysis, and Freud in particular, in discussing a model of literary history which is essentially male, and to which women are alien. The reduction of women to the stereotypical angel and monster by the male literary culture clearly excludes whatever sense of self the female writer may have as definition of her own gender. Differentiated from her male counterparts by her loneliness, and her need to contradict and isolate herself from the patriarchal authority of her art, she has to find an independent female model for herself as woman and writer to legitimise her autonomous rebellious existence. The positive aspect of this is that the woman writer is literally writing a 'blank page', helping to create both her subjective self and her tradition; and complementary to the almost inevitable 'anxiety of authorship' is the unanimity of purpose and sense of sisterhood which unites all women writers.

Within a patriarchal culture, women have learned to lie well and convincingly, for dishonesty has sometimes been the price of our physical survival. Adrienne Rich (Reading 13.4) argues that lying is endemic to definitions of the female as constructed and promoted in the dominant ideology. In lying, to ourselves and to others, we collude with those definitions, isolate ourselves from one another and facilitate the manipulation which continues to confine us. Rich suggests that our future as women depends upon our making known our versions of reality, so that the false power gained through lying can be replaced by truth to experience. Only through repudiating the imposition of subject definitions which encourage them to police their own oppression can women gain full control over their lives.

Elaine Showalter, in *A Literature of Their Own* (see Reading 13.6), writes of the institutionalisation of literature and the exclusion of all but a few privileged women writers from the literary 'canon'. Her book charts the development of women's fiction from the early adoption – perforce – of masculine models and structures, through to the subversive strategies of the concealed writer in the late nineteenth century, to the openly developed considerations of a female consciousness in the twentieth century. She discusses the problem, for the feminist literary critic, of dealing with the tension between the very act of creating fiction and the novelist's validation of cultural norms through stereotypical representations of women. There is, she argues, a need to revisit and redefine female self-awareness, to reclaim those works excluded from the literary canon, and to re-establish historical links, so that the tradition of female authorship can be validated and, in its affirmation, offer security to both reader and writer.

Many nineteenth-century novelists were well aware of the ideological function of literature. Trollope, in his autobiography, refers to the influence a good novel could have in instilling a proper understanding of love and duty in its impressionable female readers. The novel thus became an agent of state control, defining the limits of women's sexual and emotional subjectivity and confining them to the proper domestic sphere, where they would function effectively as wives and mothers. In *Archetypal Patterns in Women's Fiction*, Annis Pratt (see Reading 13.7) comments: 'even the most conservative women authors create narratives manifesting an acute tension between what any normal human being might desire and what a woman must become.'[3] This tension, she argues, is most acutely represented in the novel of marriage, where marriage is both inscribed within the text as a woman's proper goal, and also describes its narrative structure. In Reading 13.7 the 'proper' narrative structure of romantic heterosexual love and marriage is examined for its proscriptiveness, its implications of closure and enclosure both in terms of representations of female experience and in terms of fictional strategy.

The common ground for the three French critics dealt with by Ann Jones (Reading 13.8) lies in their opposition to what they see as the essentially phallogocentric nature of Western culture – phallocentrism denoting a system which assigns primary power to the phallus, and logocentrism indicating the privileging of the 'Word' in Western thinking. Phallogocentrism is a patriarchal model which generates meaning by placing terms such as nature and culture in opposition within the binary system. Hélène Cixous, writer and psychoanalyst, focuses attention on the patriarchal value system which, in dealing with sexual difference, validates a hierarchical construction of binary oppositions. The biological opposition male/female is used to construct a series of negative female values which are then imposed as definitions of the female. Where 'male' equates with activity and power, 'female' equates with passivity and powerlessness. For meaning to be acquired by one term it must destroy the other; and as signifying supremacy is attached to the male, the battle is one in which the female must always lose. Cixous, denouncing the equation of femininity with passivity and death, calls for a recognition of the relationship between the female body and feminine writing, or *écriture féminine*, liberated through *jouissance* (orgasmic ecstasy), which responds to and emanates from the forceful creativity of women's sexual drives. The female unconscious is, she argues, shaped by the body, and must acknowledge the power of physical creativity:

> Write your self. Your body must be heard. Only then will the immense resources of the unconscious spring forth. ...
> To write. An act which will not only 'realize' the decensored relation of a woman to her sexuality, to her womanly being, giving her access to native strength; it will give her back her goods, her pleasures, her organs, her immense bodily territories which have been kept under seal.[4]

Luce Irigaray also challenges phallocentric definitions of woman. Repudiating Freudian definitions of woman as 'other' because she lacks the positive power of the phallus, she argues for a transformation through an assertion of difference. In contrast to male sexuality, based on the penis, Irigaray locates female sexuality in the totality of the female body:

> Women's desire does not speak the same language as men's desire, and it probably has been covered over by the logic that has dominated the West since the Greeks. ... Woman has sex organs just about everywhere. ... The geography of her pleasure is much more diversified, more multiple in its differences, more complex, more subtle than is imagined – in an imaginary centred too much on one and the same.
> 'She' is indefinitely other in herself. That is undoubtedly the reason she is called temperamental, incomprehensible, perturbed, capricious – not to mention her language in which 'she' goes off in all directions and in which 'he' is unable to discern the coherence of any meaning.[5]

The exclusion of women as sign/symbol has led both to their imprisonment within the symbolic order and to their exclusion from powerful public discourse. Women speaking and writing operate a form of resistance to the oppression of patriarchal logic, but Irigaray's attempt to affirm that woman and her language are undefinable, fluid and multiple abandons them to a position of permanent opposition. In effect, her theoretical position is one of a biological essentialism which neither addresses the problem of woman as product of that patriarchal logic nor allows for the transformation of those power structures (which she regards as male obsession) in order that the very nature of that power might be changed.

Julia Kristeva adopts a less woman-centred position than either Cixous or Irigaray. She has refused to define woman, though she recognises the political necessity of accepting definitions in the fight against patriarchal supremacy. Kristeva accepts that that which is woman remains outside naming and ideologies – a theory which in some measure relates her to Cixous and Irigaray. The difference is that Kristeva regards the definition of woman as other in relational and strategic terms, utilising marginality in order to challenge and subvert the phallocentric order. Subject definition is a matter not of biology but of choice, dependent on gender-relationships formed early in a child's development. Femininity, defined as marginal to the symbolic order, is – in terms of Kristeva's theoretical constructs – open to both men and women. Though femininity and womanhood are not the same, patriarchy has rendered them identical, and women marginalised from the supremacy of phallocentric order have occupied a position allied to unreason, madness and chaos. For Kristeva, feminism embodies different attitudes to the symbolic: liberal feminism addresses the problem of female inequality within the symbolic order; radical feminism abolishes that order and the value system which it represents.

Barbara Smith's classic essay 'Toward a black feminist criticism' (see Reading 13.9) clearly outlines the relationship between definitions of female subjectivity and their cultural construction. Black feminist critics begin, she argues, 'with a primary commitment to exploring how both racial and sexual politics and black and female identity are inextricable elements in black women's writings'.[6] The tradition of black women's writing essentially emanates from a black political movement, and black women recount their own cultural experiences and utilise their own language, black female subjectivity is quite literally defined in the process of writing the text. While she acknowledges the need to signify the specific differences of black and lesbian literature, Maggie Humm, in *Feminist Criticism* (Reading 13.10), cautions against an exclusive separatist approach. The establishment of a distinct black literary canon is clearly important, but feminist criticism remains incomplete without the creation of contextual strategies which make a black critical approach accessible to white feminist readers.

Finally, Patricia Waugh, in *Feminine Fictions: revisiting the postmodern* (Reading 13.11), engages in a contemporary literary debate concerning the dislocation of the subject in postmodernist texts. She argues that in the postmodernist deconstruction of subjectivity there might be grounds for common concern with feminist theorists, since where the postmodernists take issue with the notion of a historically validated representation of reality through a unified subject, feminist critics argue that there *is* no unified subject in literature, art and culture that accurately reflects any acceptable female 'reality'. Yet postmodernist critics frequently omit reference to women's writing, and to feminist literary criticism. Waugh indicates that many twentieth-century women writers, from Virginia Woolf to Anita Brookner, have attempted to break down traditional structures and dislocate narrative strategies in order to re-examine subject identity and to demonstrate the complexity of female experience, but that the institutionalisation of literary criticism has acknowledged neither their position within the debate nor their potential radicalism.

Notes

1. Virginia Woolf, *A Room of One's Own*, London: Hogarth, 1967, p. 111.
2. Eva Figes, *Sex and Subterfuge*, London: Macmillan, 1972, p. 17.

3. Annis Pratt, *Archetypal Patterns in Women's Fiction*, Sussex: Harvester, 1982, p. 6.
4. Hélène Cixous, 'Le rire de la méduse', in E. Marks and I. de Courtivron (eds), *New French Feminisms*, Hemel Hempstead: Harvester Wheatsheaf, 1981, p. 250.
5. Luce Irigaray, *Ce sexe qui n'en est pas un* (1977), transl. C. Porter as *This Sex Which Is Not One*, Ithaca, NY: Cornell University Press, 1985.
6. Barbara Smith, 'Toward a black feminist criticism', in J. Newton and D. Rosenfelt (eds), *Feminism and Social Change*, London: Methuen, 1985, p. 8.

13.1 **The Second Sex**
Simone de Beauvoir

In this brief Reading from the Introduction to Simone de Beauvor's classic text The Second Sex, *she poses questions about the nature and definition of woman perceived as relative to man.*

If her functioning as a female is not enough to define woman, if we decline also to explain her through 'the eternal feminine', and if nevertheless we admit, provisionally, that women do exist, then we must face the question: what is a woman?

To state the question is, to me, to suggest, at once, a preliminary answer. The fact that I ask it is in itself significant. A man would never set out to write a book on the peculiar situation of the human male. But if I wish to define myself, I must first of all say: 'I am a woman'; on this truth must be based all further discussion. A man never begins by presenting himself as an individual of a certain sex; it goes without saying that he is a man. The terms *masculine* and *feminine* are used symmetrically only as a matter of form, as on legal papers. In actuality the relation of the two sexes is not quite like that of two electrical poles, for man represents both the positive and the neutral, as is indicated by the common use of *man* to designate human beings in general; whereas woman represents only the negative, defined by limiting criteria, without reciprocity. In the midst of an abstract discussion it is vexing to hear a man say: 'You think thus and so because you are a woman'; but I know that my only defence is to reply: 'I think thus and so because it is true', thereby removing my subjective self from the argument. It would be out of the question to reply: 'And you think the contrary because you are a man', for it is understood that the fact of being a man is no peculiarity. A man is in the right in being a man; it is the woman who is in the wrong. It amounts to this: just as for the ancients there was an absolute vertical with reference to which the oblique was defined, so there is an absolute human type, the masculine. Woman has ovaries, a uterus: these peculiarities imprison her in her subjectivity, circumscribe her within the limits of her own nature. It is often said that she thinks with her glands. Man superbly ignores the fact that his anatomy also includes glands, such as the testicles, and that they secrete hormones. He thinks of his body as a direct and normal connection with the world, which he believes he apprehends objectively, whereas he regards the body of woman as a hindrance, a prison, weighed down by everything peculiar to it. 'The female is a female by virtue of a certain *lack* of qualities,' said Aristotle; 'we should regard the female nature as afflicted with a natural defectiveness.' And St Thomas for his part pronounced woman to be an 'imperfect man', and 'incidental' being. This is symbolized in Genesis, where Eve is depicted as made from what Bossuet called 'a supernumerary bone' of Adam.

Thus humanity is male and man defines woman not in herself but as relative to him; she is not regarded as an autonomous being. Michelet writes: 'Woman, the relative being ...' And Benda is most positive in his *Rapport d'Uriel*: 'The body of man makes sense in itself quite apart from that of woman, whereas the latter seems wanting in significance by itself. ... Man can think of himself without woman. She cannot think of herself without man.' And she is simply what man decrees; thus she is called 'the sex', by which is meant that she appears essentially to the male as a sexual being. For him she is sex – absolute sex, no less. She is defined and differentiated with reference to man and not he with reference to her; she is the incidental, the inessential as opposed to the essential. He is the Subject, he is the Absolute – she is the Other. [1]

Notes

1. Emmanuel Lévinas expresses this idea most explicitly in his essay *Temps et l'Autre*: 'Is there not a case in which otherness, alterity [*altérité*], unquestionably marks the nature of a being, as its essence, an instance of otherness not consisting purely and simply in the opposition of two species of the same genus? I think that the feminine represents the contrary in its absolute sense, this contrariness being in no wise affected by any relation between it and its correlative and thus remaining absolutely other. Sex is not a certain specific difference ... no more is the sexual difference a mere contradiction. ... Nor does this difference lie in the duality of two complementary terms, for two complementary terms imply a pre-existing whole. ... Otherness reaches its full flowering in the feminine, a term of the same rank as consciousness but of opposite meaning.'
   I suppose that Lévinas does not forget that woman, too, is aware of her own consciousness, or ego. But it is striking that he deliberately takes a man's point of view, disregarding the reciprocity of subject and object. When he writes that woman is mystery, he implies that she is mystery for man. Thus his description, which is intended to be objective, is in fact an assertion of masculine privilege.

13.2 Sexual Politics

Kate Millett

This Reading from Kate Millett's Sexual Politics *documents three different responses to the sexual revolution in the literature of the period from 1830 to 1930: realistic/ revolutionary; sentimental/chivalrous, and what she terms the 'school of fantasy'.*

One can locate three different responses to the sexual revolution in the literature of the period (1830–1930). The first is the realistic or revolutionary. It took in a wide spectrum of radical analysis from Engels to Mill, to the critics and reformers such as Ibsen and Shaw, to the moderates such as Dickens and Meredith. If a critical attitude toward the sexual politics of patriarchy precedes reform, reform itself precedes revolution. The first school expressed themselves either deliberately in theory or polemic, or indirectly in the fictive situations of the theatre or the novel.

The second response belongs to the sentimental and chivalrous school of which Ruskin's 'Of Queen's Gardens' is the best and most complete example. It operates through an appeal to propriety and protestation of its good intentions, rather than through any specific recommendations for change. In fact, its general intention is to forestall change of any kind by proclaiming the status quo both good and natural. It presupposes an ideal state of awed reverence toward virtuous womanhood while it temporizes hypocritically on the issue of status, idly pretending an eagerness to award a superior position to a group whom in fact it begrudges egalitarian place, for it is designed specifically to meet the challenge of 'levelers'. Loath to make any economic concessions, it sentimentalizes the monogamous family, which it refuses to see as an economic unit and would defend to the death. At its most generous moments it might regretfully permit a few legal reforms; but on the whole it finds even these unnecessary, for since all good men cherish their good wives, the fact that they legally own them is not sufficiently important to deserve mention. Even education is a disagreeable subject with the chivalrous because a decorative and slender instruction is not only feminine and aesthetic, it also complements masculine higher learning. Serious education for women is perceived, consciously or unconsciously, as a threat to patriarchal marriage, domestic sentiment, and ultimately to male supremacy – economic, social, and psychological. The phenomena of prostitution or of poverty, the plight of many women at the time, can, under this benign sentimentality, only be deplored. Poverty may be glossed over as a problem to be dealt with through the trivial offices of charity assigned to the female sphere. As to prostitution, it is better ignored as unfit for discussion, especially in polite or literary contexts, or in circles where it might cause a 'blush' to arise. Most Victorian poetry is deliberately escapist, resolutely shunning the contemporary world as the verse of probably no other period before had dared to do. Poetry itself has nearly always been identified with the ruling class, its views, values, and interests. Only in the novel did the real world openly intrude. And for all the decorous disguises it assumed in the Victorian novel, the actual contemporary world did intrude very often; the ugly facts of sexual politics and the upsetting facts of the sexual revolution along with it. Yet here too the chivalrous mentality exerted itself and infested candid discussion.

The third school, which we shall call the school of fantasy, involves itself with a point of view nearly exclusively masculine. It often expresses the unconscious emotions of male response to what it perceives as feminine evil, namely, sexuality. However much this may resemble the old myth of feminine evil, there is something new about it – it is painfully self-conscious. Finding that there was much in its culture it could no longer take for granted, the Victorian period tends to exaggerate and be ill at ease in traditional gestures. In its fantasies of feminine evil there is something so uneasily self-aware that a number of tensions and overtones appear which one had not usually met with before in this convention. The disparity between the good and the evil, chaste and sensuous woman, figures older than Christianity, becomes far more overt than it had ever been previously, partly because the cover of religious sanction afforded by the figures of Eve and Mary had pretty well collapsed. Earlier periods had also cherished two separate and contradictory versions of woman – one vicious, one adulatory. But in no period of Western literature had the question of the sexual politics or of woman's experience within it grown so vexing and insistent as it did in this. The myth of feminine evil appears more in the poetry of the age than in other literary forms. In the novel feminine evil is too likely to wear the recognizable social and economic garments of prostitution or penury; in prose fiction the sexuality projected upon the female demands the more honest explanation of the whore, the 'fallen woman', the servant seduced: Nancy, Tess, Esther Waters. The more accommodating vehicle of myth which is proper to poetry deals actually – and rather transparently – with a sexuality the male has perceived in himself, and despising it, casts upon the woman. In the poetry of Tennyson, the myth combines with the other period legend of chivalry, and masculine sensibility weighs the virtuous woman against the vicious woman. We are told that it is the first of whom the poet approves, even if he fails to demonstrate it. Later on in Victorian poetry, there is less and less resort to chivalrous palliation. And with Rossetti and Swinburne, even the eternal need to vent disapproval on the malefic woman begins to disappear. It does so with a curious and highly significant novelty; what was once simply evil and terrifying remains all this, perhaps even more so, but it is now wonderfully attractive as well. The bitch goddess whom Mailer's Rojack righteously strangles is transformed by *fin de siècle* into a dazzling apparition before whom a poet like Swinburne is willing to prostrate himself in paroxysms of masochistic ecstasy, and a playwright like Wilde is even willing to go so far as to identify *himself* with.

13.3 **The Madwoman in the Attic**
Sandra Gilbert and Susan Gubar

Using a Freudian model of literary history, Gilbert and Gubar expound on the loneliness and alienation experienced by female artists, and discuss the 'secret sisterhood of their literary subculture'.

As J. Hillis Miller[1] himself also notes, the first and foremost student of such literary psychohistory has been Harold Bloom[2]. Applying Freudian structures to literary genealogies, Bloom has postulated that the dynamics of literary history arise from the artist's 'anxiety of influence', his fear that he is not his own creator and that the works of his predecessors, existing before and beyond him, assume essential priority over his own writings. In fact, as we pointed out in our discussion of the metaphor of literary paternity, Bloom's paradigm of the sequential historical relationship between literary artists is the relationship of father and son, specifically that relationship as it was defined by Freud. Thus Bloom explains that a 'strong poet' must engage in heroic warfare with his 'precursor', for, involved as he is in a literary Oedipal struggle, a man can only become a poet by somehow invalidating his poetic father.

Bloom's model of literary history is intensely (even exclusively) male, and necessarily patriarchal. For this reason it has seemed, and no doubt will continue to seem, offensively sexist to some feminist critics. Not only, after all, does Bloom describe literary history as the crucial warfare of fathers and sons, he sees Milton's fiercely masculine fallen Satan as *the* type of the poet in our culture, and he metaphorically defines the poetic process as a sexual encounter between a male poet and his female muse. Where, then, does the female poet fit in? Does she want to annihilate a 'forefather' or a 'foremother'? What if she can find no models, no precursors? Does she have a muse, and what is its sex? Such questions are inevitable in any female consideration of Bloomian poetics. And yet, from a feminist perspective, their inevitability may be just the point; it may, that is, call our attention not to what is wrong about Bloom's conceptualization of the dynamics of Western literary history, but to what is right (or at least suggestive) about his theory.

For Western literary history *is* overwhelmingly male – or, more accurately, patriarchal – and Bloom analyzes and explains this fact, while other theorists have ignored it, precisely, one supposes, because they assumed literature had to be male. Like Freud, whose psychoanalytic postulates permeate Bloom's literary psychoanalyses of the 'anxiety of influence', Bloom has defined processes of interaction that his predecessors did not bother to consider because, among other reasons, they were themselves so caught up in such processes. Like Freud, too, Bloom has insisted on bringing to consciousness assumptions readers and writers do not ordinarily examine. In doing so, he has clarified the implications of the psychosexual and sociosexual con-texts by which every literary text is surrounded, and thus the meanings of the 'guests' and 'ghosts' which inhabit texts themselves. Speaking of Freud, the feminist theorist Juliet Mitchell has remarked that 'psychoanalysis is not a recommendation *for* a patriarchal society, but an analysis of one'.[3] The same sort of statement could be made about Bloom's model of literary history, which is not a recommendation for but an analysis of the patriarchal poetics (and attendant anxieties) which underlie our culture's chief literary movements.

For our purposes here, however, Bloom's historical construct is useful not only because it helps identify and define the patriarchal psychosexual context in which so much Western literature was authored, but also because it can help us distinguish the anxieties and achievements of female writers from those of male writers. If we return to the question we asked earlier – where does a woman writer 'fit in' to the overwhelmingly and essentially male literary history Bloom describes? – we find we have to answer that a woman writer does *not* 'fit in'. At first glance, indeed, she seems to be anomalous, indefinable, alienated, a freakish outsider. Just as in Freud's theories of male and female psychosexual development there is no symmetry between a boy's growth and a girl's (with, say, the male 'Oedipus complex' balanced by a female 'Electra complex'), so Bloom's male-orientated theory of the 'anxiety of influence' cannot be simply reversed or inverted in order to account for the situation of the woman writer.

Certainly if we acquiesce in the patriarchal Bloomian model, we can be sure that the female poet does not experience the 'anxiety of influence' in the same way that her male counterpart would, for the simple reason that she must confront precursors who are almost exclusively male, and therefore significantly different from her. Not only do these precursors incarnate patriarchal authority (as our discussion of the metaphor of literary paternity argued), they attempt to enclose her in definitions of her person and her potential which, by reducing her to extreme stereotypes (angel, monster) drastically conflict with her own sense of her self – that is, of her subjectivity, her autonomy, her creativity. On the one hand, therefore, the woman writer's male precursors symbolize authority; on the other hand, despite their authority, they fail to define the ways in which she experiences her own identity as a writer. More, the masculine authority with which they construct their literary personae, as well as the fierce power struggles in which they engage in their efforts of self-creation, seem to the woman writer directly to contradict the terms of her own gender definition. Thus the 'anxiety of influence' that a male poet experiences is felt by a female poet as an even more primary 'anxiety of authorship' – a radical fear that she cannot create, that because she can never become a 'precursor' the act of writing will isolate or destroy her.

This anxiety is, of course, exacerbated by her fear that not only can she not fight a male precursor on 'his' terms and win, she cannot 'beget' art upon the (female) body of the muse. As Juliet Mitchell notes, in a concise summary of the implications Freud's theory of psychosexual development has for women, both a boy and a girl, 'as they learn to speak and live within society, want to take the father's [in Bloom's terminology the precursor's] place, and *only the boy will one day be allowed to do so*. Furthermore, both sexes are born into the desire of the mother, and as, through cultural heritage, what the mother desires is the phallus-turned-baby, *both* children desire to be the phallus for the mother. Again, *only the boy can fully recognize himself in his mother's desire*. Thus *both* sexes repudiate the implications of femininity,' but the girl learns (in relation to her father) 'that her subjugation to the law of the father entails her becoming the representative of "nature" and "sexuality", a chaos of spontaneous, intuitive creativity.'[4]

Unlike her male counterpart, then, the female artist must first struggle against the effects of a socialization which makes conflict with the will of her (male) precursors seem inexpressibly absurd, futile, or even – as in the case of the Queen in 'Little Snow White' – self-annihilating. And just as the male artist's struggle against his precursor takes the form of what Bloom calls revisionary swerves, flights, misreadings, so the female writer's battle for self-creation involves her in a revisionary process. Her battle, however, is not against her (male) precursor's reading of the world but against his reading of *her*. In order to define herself as an author she must redefine the terms of her socialization. Her revisionary struggle, therefore, often becomes a struggle for what Adrienne Rich has called 'Re-vision – the act of looking back, of seeing with fresh eyes, of entering an old text from a new critical direction ... an act of survival.'[5] Frequently, moreover, she can begin such a struggle only by actively seeking a *female* precursor who, far from representing a threatening force to be denied or killed, proves by example that a revolt against patriarchal literary authority is possible.

For this reason, as well as for the sound psychoanalytic reasons Mitchell and others give, it would be foolish to lock the woman artist into an Electra pattern matching the Oedipal structure Bloom proposes for male writers. The woman writer – and we shall see women doing this over and over again – searches for a female model not because she wants dutifully to comply with male definitions of her 'femininity' but because she must legitimize her own rebellious endeavors. At the same time, like most women in patriarchal society, the woman writer does experience her gender as a painful obstacle, or even a debilitating inadequacy: like most patriarchally conditioned women, in other words, she is victimized by what Mitchell calls 'the inferiorized and "alternative" (second sex) psychology of women under patriarchy'.[6] Thus the loneliness of the female artist, her feelings of alienation from male predecessors coupled with her need for sisterly precursors and successors, her urgent sense of her need for a female audience together with her fear of the antagonism of male readers, her culturally conditioned timidity about self-dramatization, her dread of the patriarchal authority of art, her anxiety about the impropriety of female invention – all these phenomena of 'inferiorization' mark the woman writer's struggle for artistic self-definition and differentiate her efforts as self-creation from those of her male counterpart.

As we shall see, such sociosexual differentiation means that, as Elaine Showalter has suggested, women writers participate in a quite different literary subculture from that inhabited by male writers, a subculture which has its own distinctive literary traditions, even – though it defines itself *in relation to* the 'main', male-dominated, literary culture – a distinctive history.[7] At best, the separateness of this female subculture has been exhilarating for women. In recent years, for instance, while male writers seem increasingly to have felt exhausted by the need for revisionism which Bloom's theory of the 'anxiety of influence' accurately describes, women writers have seen themselves as pioneers in a creativity so intense that their male counterparts have probably not experienced its analog since the Renaissance, or at least since the Romantic era.

The son of many fathers, today's male writer feels hopelessly belated; the daughter of too few mothers, today's female writer feels that she is helping to create a viable tradition which is at last definitively emerging.

There is a darker side of this female literary subculture, however, especially when women's struggles for literary self-creation are seen in the psychosexual context described by Bloom's Freudian theories of patrilineal literary inheritance. As we noted above, for an 'anxiety of influence' the woman writer substitutes what we have called an 'anxiety of authorship', an anxiety built from complex and often only barely conscious fears of that authority which seems to the female artist to be by definition inappropriate to her sex. Because it is based on the woman's socially determined sense of her own biology, this anxiety of authorship is quite distinct from the anxiety about creativity that could be traced in such male writers as Hawthorne or Dostoevsky. Indeed, to the extent that it forms one of the unique bonds that link women in what we might call the secret sisterhood of their literary subculture, such anxiety in itself constitutes a crucial mark of that subculture.

Notes

1. J. Hillis Miller, 'The limits of pluralism, III: The critic as host', *Critical Enquiry*, Spring (1977), p. 446.
2. See Harold Bloom, *The Anxiety of Influence*, New York: Oxford University Press, 1977.
3. J. Mitchell, *Psychoanalysis and Feminism*, New York: Vintage, 1975, p. xiii.
4. *Ibid.*, pp. 404–5.
5. A. Rich, 'When we dead awaken: writing as re-vision', in B. C. Gelpi and A. Gelpi (eds), *Adrienne Rich's Poetry*, New York: Norton, 1975, p. 90.
6. Mitchell, *Psychoanalysis and Feminism*, p. 402.
7. See E. Showalter, *A Literature of Their Own*, Princeton, NJ: Princeton University Press, 1977.

13.4 **On Lies, Secrets and Silences**
Adrienne Rich

In this Reading from notes first read at the Hatwick Women Writers' Workshop, New York, in 1975, Adrienne Rich argues for a new ethics for women which addresses the problems of speech and language and, in particular, what she regards as the 'negative power of the lie in relationships with women'.

I come back to the questions of women's honor. Truthfulness has not been considered important for women, as long as we have remained physically faithful to a man, or chaste.

We have been expected to lie with our bodies: to bleach, redden, unkink or curl our hair, pluck eyebrows, shave armpits, wear padding in various places or lace ourselves, take little steps, glaze finger and toe nails, wear clothes that emphasized our helplessness.

We have been required to tell different lies at different times, depending on what the men of the time needed to hear. The Victorian wife or the white southern lady, who were expected to have no sensuality, to 'lie still'; the twentieth-century 'free' woman who is expected to fake orgasms.

We have had the truth of our bodies withheld from us or distorted; we have been kept in ignorance of our most intimate places. Our instincts have been punished: clitoridectomies for 'lustful' nuns or for 'difficult' wives. It has been difficult, too, to know the lies of our complicity from the lies we believed.

The lie of the 'happy marriage', of domesticity – we have been complicit, have acted out the fiction of a well-lived life, until the day we testify in court of rapes, beatings, psychic cruelties, public and private humiliations.

Patriarchal lying has manipulated women both through falsehood and through silence. Facts we needed have been withheld from us. False witness has been borne against us.

And so we must take seriously the question of truthfulness between women, truthfulness among women. As we cease to lie with our bodies, as we cease to take on faith what men have said about us, is a truly womanly idea of honour in the making?

Women have been forced to lie, for survival, to men. How to unlearn this among other women?

'Women have always lied to each other.'
'Women have always whispered the truth to each other.'
Both of these axioms are true.

'Women have always been divided against each other.'
'Women have always been in secret collusion.'
Both of these axioms are true.

In the struggle for survival we tell lies. To bosses, to prison guards, the police, men who have power over us, who legally own us and our children, lovers who need us as proof of their manhood.

There is a danger run by all powerless people: that we forget we are lying, or that lying becomes a weapon we carry over into relationships with people who do not have power over us.

I want to reiterate that when we talk about women and honor, or women and lying, we speak within the context of male lying, the lies of the powerful, the lie as false source of power.

Women have to think whether we want, in our relationships with each other, the kind of power that can be obtained through lying.

Women have been driven mad, 'gaslighted', for centuries by the refutation of our experience and our instincts in a culture which validates only male experience. The truth of our bodies and our minds has been mystified to us. We therefore have a primary obligation to each other: not to undermine each other's sense of reality for the sake of expediency; not to gaslight each other.

Women have often felt insane when cleaving to the truth of our experience. Our future depends on the sanity of each of us, and we have a profound stake, beyond the personal, in the project of describing our reality as candidly and fully as we can to each other.

13.5 **Silences**
Tillie Olsen

In this short passage of autobiographical writing, Tillie Olsen documents those personal domestic and public responsibilities, those 'discontinuities', which are so much a part of women's lives, and cost her writing time and space until she was fifty.

As for myself, who did not publish a book until I was fifty, who raised children without household help or the help of the 'technological sublime' (the atom bomb was in manufacture before the first automatic washing machine); who worked outside the house on everyday jobs as well (as nearly half of all women do now, though a woman with a paid job, except as a maid or prostitute, is still rarest of any in literature); who could not kill the essential angel (there was no one else to do her work); would not – if I could – have killed the caring part of the Woolf angel; as distant from the world of literature most of my life as literature is distant (in content too) from my world:

The years when I should have been writing, my hands and being were at other (inescapable) tasks. Now, lightened as they are, when I must do those tasks into which most of my life went, like the old mother, grandmother in my *Tell Me a Riddle* who could not make herself touch a baby, I pay a psychic cost: 'the sweat beads, the long shudder begins'. The habits of a lifetime when everything else had to come before writing are not easily broken, even when circumstances now often make it possible for writing to be first; habits of years – response to others, distractibility, responsibility for daily matters – stay with you, mark you, become you. The cost of 'discontinuity' (that pattern still imposed on women) is such a weight of things unsaid, an accumulation of material so great, that everything starts up something else in me; what should take weeks takes me sometimes months to write; what should take months takes years.

I speak of myself to bring here the sense of those others to whom this is in the process of happening (unnecessarily happening, for it need not, must not continue to be) and to remind us of those (I so nearly was one) who never come to writing at all.

We must not speak of women writers in our century (as we cannot speak of women in any area of recognized human achievement) without speaking also of the invisible, the as-innately-capable: the born to the wrong circumstances – diminished, excluded, foundered, silenced.

We who write are survivors, *'only's'*.[1] *One-out-of-twelve.*

Author's note

1. For myself, 'survivor' contains its other meaning: one who must bear witness for those who foundered; try to tell how and why it was that they, also worthy of life, did *not* survive. And pass on ways of surviving; and tell our chancy luck, our special circumstances.

    'Only's' is an expression out of the 1950s Civil Rights time: the young Ralph Abernathy reporting to his Birmingham Church congregation on his trip up north for support:

    > I go to Seattle and they tell me, 'Brother, you got to meet so an so, why he's the only Negro Federal Circuit Judge in the Northwest'; I go to Chicago and they tell me, 'Brother, you've got to meet so and so, why he's the only full black professor of Sociology there is'; I go to Albany and they tell me, 'Brother, you *got* to meet so and so, why he's the only black senator in the state legislature ...' [long dramatic pause] ... WE DON'T WANT NO ONLY'S.

    Only's are used to rebuke ('to be models'); to imply the unrealistic, 'see, it can be done, all you need is capacity and will'. Accepting a situation of 'only's' means: 'let inequality of circumstance continue to prevail'.

13.6 **A Literature of Their Own**
Elaine Showalter

Elaine Showalter exposes the inaccuracy which has characterised critical discussion of women writers on two important counts: the 'Great Tradition' and 'the projection of culturally imposed notions of femininity'.

There are many reasons why discussion of women writers has been so inaccurate, fragmented, and partisan. First, women's literary history has suffered from an extreme form of what John Gross calls 'residual Great Traditionalism',[1] which has reduced and condensed the extraordinary range and diversity of English women novelists to a tiny band of the 'great', and derived all theories from them. In practice, the concept of greatness for women novelists often turns out to mean four or five writers – Jane Austen, the Brontës,

George Eliot, and Virginia Woolf – and even theoretical studies of 'the woman novelist' turn out to be endless recyclings and recombinations of insights about 'indispensable Jane and George'.[2] Criticism of women novelists, while focusing on these happy few, has ignored those who are not 'great', and left them out of anthologies, histories, textbooks, and theories. Having lost sight of the minor novelists, who were the links in the chain that bound one generation to the next, we have not had a very clear understanding of the continuities in women's writing, nor any reliable information about the relationships between the writers' lives and the changes in the legal, economic, and social status of women.

Second, it has been difficult for critics to consider women novelists and women's literature theoretically because of their tendency to project and expand their own culture-bound stereotypes of femininity, and to see in women's writing an eternal opposition of biological and aesthetic creativity. The Victorians expected women's novels to reflect the feminine values they exalted, although obviously the woman novelist herself had outgrown the constraining feminine role. 'Come what will,' Charlotte Brontë wrote to Lewes, 'I cannot, when I write, think always of myself and what is elegant and charming in femininity; it is not on these terms, or with such ideas, that I ever took pen in hand.'[3] Even if we ignore the excesses of what Mary Ellmann calls 'phallic criticism' and what Cynthia Ozick calls the 'ovarian theory of literature', much contemporary criticism of women writers is still prescriptive and circumscribed.[4] Given the difficulties of steering a precarious course between the Scylla of insufficient information and the Charybdis of abundant prejudice, it is not surprising that formalist-structuralist critics have evaded the issue of sexual identity entirely, or dismissed it as irrelevant and subjective. Finding it difficult to think intelligently about women writers, academic criticism has often overcompensated by desexing them.

Yet since the 1960s, and especially since the re-emergence of a Women's Liberation Movement in England and in America around 1968, there has been renewed enthusiasm for the idea that 'a special female self-awareness emerges through literature in every period'.[5] The interest in establishing a more reliable critical vocabulary and a more accurate and systematic literary history for women writers is part of a larger interdisciplinary effort by psychologists, sociologists, social historians, and art historians to reconstruct the political, social, and cultural experience of women.

Scholarship generated by the contemporary feminist movement has increased our sensitivity to the problems of sexual bias or projection in literary history, and has also begun to provide us with the information we need to understand the evolution of a female literary tradition. One of the most significant contributions has been the unearthing and reinterpretation of 'lost' works by women writers, and the documentation of their lives and careers.

In the past, investigations have been distorted by the emphasis on an elite group, not only because it has excluded from our attention great stretches of literary activity between, for example, George Eliot and Virginia Woolf, but also because it has rendered invisible the daily lives, the physical experiences, the personal strategies and conflicts of ordinary women. If we want to define the ways in which 'female self-awareness' has expressed itself in the English novel, we need to see the woman novelist against the backdrop of the women of her time, as well as in relation to other writers in history. Virginia Woolf recognized that need:

> The extraordinary woman depends on the ordinary woman. It is only when we know what were the conditions of the average woman's life – the number of her children, whether she had money of her own, if she had a room to herself, whether she had help in bringing up her family, if she had servants, whether part of the housework was her task – it is only when we can measure the way of life and the experience of life made possible to the ordinary woman that we can account for the success or failure of the extraordinary woman as writer.[6]

Notes

1. *The Rise and Fall of the Man of Letters*, London, 1969, p. 304.
2. C. Ozick, 'Women and creativity', in *Woman in Sexist Society*, ed. V. Gornick and B. K. Moran, New York, 1971, p. 436.
3. Letter of November 1849, in C. Shorter, *The Brontës: Life and letters*, 11, London, 1908, p. 80.
4. M. Ellmann, *Thinking About Women*, New York, 1968, pp. 28–54; Ozick, 'Women and creativity', p. 436.
5. P. M. Spacks, *The Female Imagination*, New York, 1975, p. 3.
6. 'Women and fiction', *Collected Essays*, London, 1967, p. 142.

13.7 Archetypal Patterns in Women's Fiction
Annis Pratt

So much women's fiction of the last hundred and fifty years has been – and continues to be – dominated by considerations of romance and marriage. Here Annis Pratt writes of marriage as archetypal enclosure in fictional texts.

While women have achieved a measure of marital and reproductive freedom in the twentieth century, the clash between social norms and individual desires persistently underlies archetypal narrative patterns and images in women's fiction. These archetypes remain intact because the alienation in which they originate still exists. The modern novel of marriage continues to picture a patriarchy that controls economic and political activities, a wife as subordinate to husband, and feminine sexuality as a target of fear and loathing.

Walter Houghton, speaking of Victorian novels, agrees with Stone that novels promulgating affectional relationships were not mere day-dreams but, instead, were pleas for a greater acceptance of passionate feelings between men and women and 'a bitter arraignment' of the system that ignored these feelings.[1] Authors developed fictional strategies that encouraged affectional marriage while fully aware of the difficulties that *any* marriage entailed for women. Jane Austen, for example, was concerned with the debilitating effects of bearing many babies. 'Anna has not a chance of escape', she wrote of a woman she knew.

> Her husband called here the other day, and said she was *pretty* well but not *equal* to so long a walk; she *must come in her Donkey Carriage*. Poor animal, she will be worn out before she is thirty. I am very sorry for her. Mrs Clement too is in that way again. I am quite tired of so many Children – Mrs Benn has a 13th. ... Good Mrs Deedes! – I hope she will get the better of this Marianne, and then I would recommend to her and Mr D. the simple regimen of separate rooms.[2]

Reviewers soundly condemned Charlotte Brontë for allowing Jane Eyre to take the initiative with Mr Rochester. After *Jane Eyre* (1847) was published Brontë wrote to a friend that 'no young lady should fall in love until the offer has been made, accepted, the marriage ceremony performed, and the first half-year of wedded life has passed away. A woman may then begin to love, but with great precaution, very coolly, very moderately, very rationally. If she ever loves so much that a harsh word or a cold look cuts her to the heart, she is a fool.'[3] Whereas Austen was concerned with the physical strain of marriage, Brontë's fears, here, relate to the emotional vulnerability of a woman who has placed her well-being in the hands of a husband. In an authorial comment couched in a tangle of negative constructions in an alternative ending to *Middlemarch* (1871–2) George Eliot wrote:

> It was never said in the neighborhood of Middlemarch that such mistakes [Dorothea's marriage to Casaubon] could not have happened if the society into which she was born had not smiled on propositions of marriage from a sickly man to a girl less than half his own age.[4]

This desire for equity in marriage accounts for the rebellion underlying much of women's fiction.

Twentieth-century authors have been equally perturbed by the dichotomy between love and marriage. Contemporary novelist Katherine Anne Porter calls herself a 'Western romantic', finds the idea of love within marriage a 'charming work of the human imagination', but wonders how 'Romantic Love got into marriage at last, where it was most certainly never intended to be'.[5] Like a number of other modern authors – Elizabeth Bowen, Doris Lessing, Fay Weldon, Jean Rhys, for example – Porter's fiction consists of an intrepid but perennially frustrated quest for a relationship in which a hero can achieve equity, authenticity, and Eros.

The nineteenth-century author's desire for affectional marriages and the twentieth-century author's desire for romantic and erotic ones inevitably lead them to create textual constructions and narrative strategies that emphasize these themes. Although in-depth textual studies of works by major authors are beyond the scope of this book, it will be useful to note the techniques employed by writers like Austen and Eliot. Austin's fiction is uniquely concerned with the question of marriage for money: 'All of Jane Austen's opening paragraphs, and the best of her first sentences, have money in them', remarks Ellen Moers.[6] Austen approaches marriage by balancing critique with acceptance, using wit, humor, and satire to spoof the worst marital abuses and then to proffer an affectionate *and* financially prudent model husband. Another Austen plot strategy matches a minor character in an undesirable marriage while the dismayed hero looks on and strives to do otherwise. 'Mr Collins, to be sure, was neither sensible or agreeable,' reflects the girl who has decided upon a prudent marriage in *Pride and Prejudice* (1813):

> His society was irksome, and his attachment to her must be imaginary. But still he would be her husband. Without thinking highly either of men or of matrimony, marriage had always been her object; it was the only honourable provision for well-educated young women of small fortune, and however uncertain of giving happiness, must be her pleasant preservative from want.[7]

A similar plot strategy, which involves a comparison of undesirable unions with desirable ones, characterizes Eliot's *Middlemarch* as well as a great number of nineteenth-century and turn-of-the-century novels. In the 'double-marriage plot' an unsuitable alliance is proffered or consummated but, fortunately, terminated by either jilting or death so that a more equal norm may be achieved. This second marriage or engagement, however, is rarely depicted; picturing it as the festive goal of the denouement, the author rarely details its actual dimensions. Using comic conventions, many authors spoof the foibles of married life so soundly as to make marriage a target of satire. This is true of such humourists as Nancy Mitford and Angela Thirkell, who carry on in a minor vein many of the turns of wit and satire developed by Austen and Eliot.

Not all marital plotting is comic, however; many women authors develop so bitter a portrait of matrimony that their heroes are destroyed by it, worn down by society's pressure for non-affectional, economically viable marriages, or turned outcast because they demand more of the institution than the patriarchy can permit. Tragic plots characterize the novels of not only Edith Wharton, Charlotte Perkins Gilman, and Elizabeth Stuart Phelps but also a number of more recent women writers, like Jean Rhys and Joan Didion. Finally, as in the case of the *Bildungsroman*, many women develop extended metaphors of insanity, likening effects of matrimony to madness and incarceration.

Marriage as archetypal enclosure

Since *Bildung*, true maturation, is as rare for the married hero as for the adolescent one, many of the archetypal images and patterns characteristic of the novel of development persist in the novel of marriage, the perspective differing only in the sense that the heroes are now *within* the wedded circle. Each attribute of authenticity meets with its opposite: freedom to come and go is abrogated; early, ideal lovers are banished, to be replaced by a husband who resembles the gothic villain; erotic freedom is severely limited; intelligence becomes a curse, and, correspondingly, too much consciousness of one's situation leads to punishment or madness. Defined as 'normality', mental abnormality shapes an archetype antithetical to the virgin goddess – the mad wife. Authors describe the golden circle of marriage, symbolizing an eternity of mutual love, as a tarnished enclosure. I touch here upon some typical examples of these novels. Once again, I will principally deal with minor novelists, although similar themes and images can be found in the works of more recognized authors.

Freedom to come and go, which involves the right to make decisions about one's own time, work, and other activities, is a basic element of authenticity. The irony that permeates so much of women's fiction results from a recognition of the discrepancy between premarital dreams of authenticity and marital realities. During courtship, in the novel of marriage, the quest for mutuality often leads men to promise more freedom to their fiancées than traditional patriarchal marriage permits. This disappointment of expectations characterizes Elizabeth Stuart Phelps's *The Story of Avis* (1877), in which the hero takes long, happy walks over the fields, fosters her ambition as an artist, and falls in love with a man who promises that he will hamper neither her freedom nor the development of her talents. Her doubts produce a frightening proposal scene: '"I suffer because I love you"', she remarks. '"It is like – death"'.[8] The young husband quickly limits Avis's freedom, and her health atrophies as she realizes her decorative function within the enclosure of marriage.

Notes

1. W. E. Houghton, *The Victorian Frame of Mind*, Yale University Press, 1957, p. 117.
2. Jane Austen, letter quoted in M. Wilson, *Jane Austen and Some Contemporaries*, Crescet, 1938, p. 37.
3. Charlotte Brontë, letter to Ellen Nussey, quoted in M. Sinclair, *The Brontë Sisters*, Kennikat, 1967, p. 76.
4. Alternative ending (first edition) to George Eliot's *Middlemarch*, quoted from B. W. Harvey, 'Criticism of the novel', by critic Barbara Hardy (ed.), *Middlemarch: Critical approaches to the novel*, Oxford University Press, 1967, p. 133
5. Katherine Anne Porter, 'The necessary enemy', *The Collected Essays and Occasional Writings of Katherine Anne Porter*, Delta, 1973, pp. 184–5.

6. E. Moers, *Literary Women*, New York: Doubleday, 1976, p 108.
7. Jane Austen, *Pride and Prejudice*, New York: Random House, 1950, p. 104.
8. E. S. Phelps, *The Story of Avis*, 1877, p. 192.

13.8 **Writing the Body: towards an understanding of** *l'écriture féminine*

Ann Rosalind Jones

Ann Rosalind Jones introduces three significant French theoreticians – Julia Kristeva, Luce Irigaray, and Hélène Cixous – whose work in challenging phallocentric definitions of female sexuality has greatly influenced feminist literary discourse.

Julia Kristeva, a founding member of the semiotic-Marxist journal *Tel Quel*, and the author of several books on avant-garde writers, language, and philosophy, finds in psychoanalysis the concept of the bodily drives that survive cultural pressures toward sublimation and surface in what she calls 'semiotic discourse': the gestural, rhythmic, prereferential language of such writers as Joyce, Mallarmé, and Artaud. These men, rather than giving up their blissful infantile fusion with their mothers, their orality and anality, re-experience such *jouissances* subconsciously and set them into play by constructing texts against the rules and regularities of conventional language. How do women fit into this scheme of semiotic liberation? Indirectly, as mothers, because they are the first love objects from which the child is typically separated and turned away in the course of initiation into society. In fact, Kristeva sees semiotic discourse as an incestuous challenge to the symbolic order, asserting as it does the writer's return to the pleasures of his preverbal identification with his mother and his refusal to identify with his father and the logic of paternal discourse. Women, for Kristeva, also speak and write as 'hysterics', as outsiders to male-dominated discourse, for two reasons: the predominance in them of drives related to anality and childbirth, and their marginal position *vis-à-vis* masculine culture. Their semiotic style is likely to involve repetitive, spasmodic separations from the dominating discourse, which, more often, they are forced to imitate.[1]

Kristeva doubts, however, whether women should aim to work out alternative discourses. She sees certain liberatory potentials in their marginal position, which is (admirably) unlikely to produce a fixed, authority-claiming subject/speaker or language: 'In social, sexual and symbolic experiences, being a woman has always provided a means to another end, to becoming something else: a subject-in-the-making, a subject on trial.' Rather than formulating a new discourse, women should persist in challenging the discourses that stand: 'If women have a role to play ... it is only in assuming a *negative* function: reject everything finite, definite, structured, loaded with meaning, in the existing state of society. Such an attitude places women on the side of the explosion of social

codes: with revolutionary movements.'[2] In fact, 'woman' to Kristeva represents
not so much a sex as an attitude, any resistance to conventional culture and
language; men, too, have access to the *jouissance* that opposes phallogocentrism:

> A feminist practice can only be ... at odds with what already exists so that we may
> say 'that's not it' and 'that's still not it'. By 'woman' I mean that which cannot be
> represented, what is not said, what remains above and beyond nomenclatures and
> ideologies. There are certain 'men' who are familiar with this phenomenon.[3]

For Luce Irigaray, on the contrary, women have a specificity that distinguishes
them sharply from men. A psychoanalyst and former member of l'École
freudienne at the University of Paris (Vincennes), she was fired from her
teaching position in the fall of 1974, three weeks after the publication of her
study of the phallocentric bias in Freud. *Speculum de l'autre femme* is this study,
a profound and wittily sarcastic demonstration of the ways in which Plato and
Freud define woman: as irrational and invisible, as imperfect (castrated) man.
In later essays she continues her argument that women, because they have been
caught in a world structured by male-centred concepts, have had no way of
knowing or representing themselves. But she offers as the starting point for a
female self-consciousness the facts of women's bodies and women's sexual
pleasure, precisely because they have been so absent or so misrepresented in
male discourse. Women, she says, experience a diffuse sexuality arising, for
example, from the 'two lips' of the vulva, and a multiplicity of libidinal energies
that cannot be expressed or understood within the identity-claiming
assumptions of phallocentric discourse ('I am a unified, coherent being, and
what is significant in the world reflects my male image').[4] Irigaray argues further
that female sexuality explains women's problematic relationship to (masculine)
logic and language:

> *Woman has sex organs just about everywhere.* She experiences pleasure almost
> everywhere. ... The geography of her pleasure is much more diversified, more
> multiple in its differences, more complex, more subtle, than is imagined – in an
> imaginary [system] centered a bit too much on one and the same.
>   'She' is infinitely other in herself. That is undoubtedly the reason she is called
> temperamental, incomprehensible, perturbed, capricious – not to mention her
> language in which 'she' goes off in all directions and in which 'he' is unable to
> discern the coherence of any meaning. Contradictory words seem a little crazy to
> the logic of reason, and inaudible for him who listens with ready-made grids, a
> code prepared in advance. In her statements – at least when she dares to speak out
> – woman retouches herself constantly.[5]

Irigaray concedes that women's discovery of their autoeroticism will not, by
itself, arrive automatically or enable them to transform the existing order: 'For
a woman to arrive at the point where she can enjoy her pleasure as a woman,
a long detour by the analysis of the various systems that oppress her is certainly

necessary.'[6] Irigaray herself writes essays using Marxist categories to analyze men's use and exchange of women, and in others she uses female physiology as a source of critical metaphors and counterconcepts (against physics, pornography, Nietzsche's misogyny, myth),[7] rather than literally. Yet her focus on the physical bases for the difference between male and physical sexuality remains the same: women must recognize and assert their *jouissance* if they are to subvert phallocentric oppression at its deepest levels.

Since 1975, when she founded women's studies at Vincennes, Hélène Cixous has been a spokeswoman for the group Psychanalyse et politique and a prolific writer of texts for their publishing house, des femmes. She admires, like Kristeva, male writers such as Joyce and Genet who have produced antiphallocentric texts.[8] But she is convinced that women's unconscious is totally different from men's, and that it is their psychosexual specificity that will empower women to overthrow masculinist ideologies and to create new female discourses. Of her own writing she says, 'Je suis là où ça parle' ('I am there where it/id/the female unconscious speaks').[9] She has produced a series of analyses of women's suffering under the laws of male sexuality (the first-person narrative *Angst*, the play *Portrait de Dora*, the libretto for the opera *Le Nom d'Oedipe*) and a growing collection of demonstrations of what id-liberated female discourses might be: *La, Ananké,* and *Illa*. In her recent *Vivre l'orange* (1979), she celebrates the Brazilian writer Clarice Lispector for what she sees as a peculiarly female attentiveness to objects, the ability to perceive and represent them in a nurturing rather than dominating way. She believes that this empathetic attentiveness, and literary modes to which it gives rise, arise from libidinal rather than sociocultural sources: the 'typically feminine gesture, not culturally but libidinally, [is] to produce in order to bring about life, pleasure, not in order to accumulate'.[10]

Cixous criticizes psychoanalysis for its 'thesis of a "natural" anatomical determination of sexual difference–opposition', focusing on physical drives rather than body parts for her definition of male–female contrasts: 'It is at the level of sexual pleasure in my opinion that the difference makes itself most clearly apparent in as far as woman's libidinal economy is neither identifiable by a man nor referrable to the masculine economy.'[11] In her manifesto for *l'écriture féminine*, 'The laugh of the Medusa' (1975), her comparisons and lyricism suggest that she admires in women a sexuality that is remarkably constant and almost mystically superior to the phallic single-mindedness it transcends:

> Though masculine sexuality gravitates around the penis, engendering that centralized body (in political anatomy) under the dictatorship of its parts, woman does not bring about the same regionalization which serves the couple head/genitals and which is inscribed only within boundaries. Her libido is cosmic, just as her unconscious is worldwide.

She goes on immediately, in terms close to Irigaray's, to link women's diffuse sexuality to women's language – written language, in this case:

> Her writing can only keep going, without ever inscribing or discerning contours.
> ... She lets the other language speak – the language of 1,000 tongues which knows
> neither enclosure nor death. ... Her language does not contain, it carries; it does
> not hold back, it makes possible.

The passage ends with her invocation of other bodily drives (*pulsions* in the French) in a continuum with women's self-expression:

> Oral drive, anal drive, vocal drive – these drives are our strengths, and among
> them is the gestation drive – just like the desire to write: a desire to live self from
> within, a desire for the swollen belly, for language, for blood. [12]

In her theoretical and imaginative writing alike (*La Jeune Née*, 1975, typically combines the two) Cixous insists on the primacy of multiple, specifically female libidinal impulses in women's unconscious and in the writing of the liberatory female discourses of the future.

What Kristeva, Irigaray, and Cixous do in common, then, is to oppose women's bodily experience (or, in Kristeva's case, women's bodily effect as mothers) to the phallic-symbolic patterns embedded in Western thought. Although Kristeva does not privilege women as the only possessors of prephallocentric discourse, Irigaray and Cixous go further: if women are to discover and express who they are, to bring to the surface what masculine history has repressed in them, they must begin with their sexuality. And their sexuality begins with their bodies, with their genital and libidinal difference from men.

For various reasons, this is a powerful argument. We have seen versions of it in the radical feminism of the United States, too. In the French context, it offers an island of hope in the void left by the deconstruction of humanism, which has been revealed as an ideologically suspect invention by men. If men are responsible for the reigning binary system of meaning – identity/other, man/nature, reason/chaos, man/woman – women, relegated to the negative and passive pole of this hierarchy, are not implicated in the creation of its myths. (Certainly, they are no longer impressed by them!) And the immediacy with which the body, the id, *jouissance*, are supposedly experienced promises a clarity of perception and a vitality that can bring down mountains of phallocentric delusion. Finally, to the extent that the female body is seen as a direct source of female writing, a powerful alternative discourse seems possible: to write from the body is to re-create the world.

But *féminité* and *écriture féminine* are problematic as well as powerful concepts. They have been criticized as idealist and essentialist, bound up in the very system they claim to undermine; they have been attacked as theoretically fuzzy and as fatal to constructive political action. I think all these objections are worth making. What's more, they must be made if American women are to sift out and use the positive elements in French thinking about *féminité*.

Notes

1. Kristeva, 'Le Sujet en procès', in *Polylogue,* Paris: Éditions du Seuil, 1977, p. 77.
2. 'Oscillation du "pouvoir" au "refus"', interview by Xavière Gauthier in *Tel Quel,* no. 58 (1975), transl. in *New French Feminisms,* E. Marks and I. de Courtivron (eds), Hemel Hempstead: Harvester Wheatsheaf, 1981, p. 166.
3. Kristeva, 'La Femme, ce n'est jamais ca', interview in *Tel Quel,* no. 58 (1975), transl. in *New French Feminisms,* pp. 134–8.
4. Luce Irigaray, in an interview, 'Women's exile', *Ideology and Consciousness,* no. 1 (1977), pp. 66–7; transl. and intro. D. Adlam and C. Venn.
5. Irigaray, *Ce Sexe qui n'est pas un,* Paris: Éditions de Minuit, 1977, transl. in *New French Feminisms,* p. 103.
6. *New French Feminisms,* p. 105.
7. Irigaray discusses the historical position of women in Marxist terms in 'Le Marche aux femmes', in *Ce Sexe.* Her responses to Nietzsche are in *Amante marine.*
8. Hélène Cixous's studies of male writers include her doctoral thesis, *L'Exil de Joyce ou l'art du remplacement,* Paris: Grasset, 1968; *Prenoms de personne (sur Hoffman, Kleist, Poe, Joyce),* Paris: Éditions du Seuil, 1974; and introductions to James Joyce and Lewis Carroll for Aubier. Since 1975 all her books have been published by Des Femmes.
9. Cixous, 'Entretien avec Françoise van Rossum-Guyon', *Revue des sciences humaine,* 168 (December 1977)', p. 488; 'Ça parle' is a Lacanian formula, but elsewhere (in her fiction/essay *Partie,* Paris, Des Femmes, 1976, for example) she mocks what she sees as the Father/phallus obsession of recent psychoanalysis.
10. Cixous, 'Entretien', p. 487.
11. Cixous, 'Sorties', *La Jeune Née,* Paris: Union Générale d'Éditions, 1975, transl. in *New French Feminisms,* p. 98.
12. *New French Feminisms,* pp. 259–60.

13.9 **Toward a Black Feminist Criticism**
Barbara Smith

Here Barbara Smith argues the necessity for a black feminist approach which embodies the politics of sex as well as of race and class.

In her introduction to 'A bibliography of works written by American black women' Ora Williams quotes some of the reactions of her colleagues toward her efforts to do research on black women. She writes:

> Others have reacted negatively with such statements as, 'I really don't think you are going to find very much written.' 'Have "they" written anything that is any good?' and 'I would't go overboard with this woman's lib thing.' When discussions

touched on the possibility of teaching a course in which emphasis would be on the literature by black women, one response was, 'Ha, ha. That will certainly be the most nothing course ever offered!'[1]

A remark by Alice Walker capsulizes what all the preceding examples indicate about the position of black women writers and the reasons for the damaging criticism about them. In response to her interviewer's question 'Why do you think that the black woman writer has been so ignored in America? Does she have even more difficulty than the black male writer, who perhaps has just begun to gain recognition?' Walker replies:

> There are two reasons why the black woman writer is not taken as seriously as the black male writer. One is that she's a woman. Critics seem unusually ill-equipped to intelligently discuss and analyze the works of black women. Generally, they do not even make the attempt; they prefer, rather, to talk about the lives of black women writers, not about what they write. And, since black women writers are not – it would seem – very likeable – until recently they were the least willing worshippers of male supremacy – comments about them tend to be cruel.[2]

A convincing case for black feminist criticism can obviously be built solely upon the basis of the negativity of what already exists. It is far more gratifying, however, to demonstrate its necessity by showing how it can serve to reveal for the first time the profound subtleties of this particular body of literature.

Before suggesting how a black feminist approach might be used to examine a specific work, I will outline some of the principles that I think a black feminist critic could use. Beginning with a primary commitment to exploring how both sexual and racial politics and black and female identity are inextricable elements in black women's writings, she would also work from the assumption that black women writers constitute an identifiable literary tradition. The breadth of her familiarity with these writers would have shown her that not only is theirs a verifiable historical tradition that parallels in time the tradition of black men and white women writing in this country, but that thematically, stylistically, aesthetically and conceptually black women writers manifest common approaches to the act of creating literature as a direct result of the specific political, social and economic experience they have been obliged to share. The way, for example, that Zora Neale Hurston, Margaret Walker, Toni Morrison and Alice Walker incorporate the traditional black female activities of rootworking, herbal medicine, conjure and midwifery into the fabric of their stories is not mere coincidence, nor is their use of specifically black female language to express their own and their characters' thoughts accidental. The use of black women's language and cultural experience in books *by* black women *about* black women results in a miraculously rich coalescing of form and content and also takes their writing far beyond the confines of white/male literary structures. The black feminist critic would find innumerable commonalities in works by black women.

Another principle which grows out of the concept of a tradition and which would also help to strengthen this tradition would be for the critic to look first for precedents and insights in interpretation within the works of other black women. In other words she would think and write out of her own identity and not try to graft the ideas or methodology of white/male literary thought upon the precious materials of black women's art. Black feminist criticism would by definition be highly innovative, embodying the daring spirit of the works themselves. The black feminist critic would be constantly aware of the political implications of her work and would assert the connections between it and the political situation of all black women. Logically developed, black feminist criticism would owe its existence to a black feminist movement while at the same time contributing ideas that women in the movement could use.

Black feminist criticism applied to a particular work can overturn previous assumptions about it and expose for the first time its actual dimensions. At the 'Lesbians and literature' discussion at the 1976 Modern Language Association convention Bertha Harris suggested that if in a woman writer's work a sentence refuses to do what it is supposed to do, if there are strong images of women and if there is a refusal to be linear, the result is innately lesbian literature. As usual, I wanted to see if these ideas might be applied to the black women writers that I know and quickly realized that many of their works were, in Harris's sense, lesbian. Not because women are lovers, but because they are the central figures, are positively portrayed and have pivotal relationships with one another. The form and language of these works are also nothing like what white patriarchal culture requires or expects.

I was particularly struck by the way in which Toni Morrison's novels *The Bluest Eyes* and *Sula* could be explored from this new perspective.[3] In both works the relationships between girls and women are essential, yet at the same time physical sexuality is overtly expressed only between men and women. Despite the apparent heterosexuality of the female characters, I discovered in rereading *Sula* that it works as a lesbian novel not only because of the passionate friendship between Sula and Nel, but because of Morrison's consistently critical stance toward the heterosexual institutions of male/female relationships, marriage and the family. Consciously or not, Morrison's work poses both lesbian and feminist questions about black women's autonomy and their impact upon each other's lives.

Sula is an exceedingly lesbian novel in the emotions expressed, in the definition of female character, and in the way that the politics of heterosexuality are portrayed. The very meaning of lesbianism is being expanded in literature, just as it is being redefined through politics. The confusion that many readers have felt about *Sula* may well have a lesbian explanation. If one sees Sula's inexplicable 'evil' and nonconformity as the evil of not being male-identified, many elements in the novel become clear. The work might be clearer still if Morrison had approached her subject with the consciousness that a lesbian relationship was at least a possibility for her characters. Obviously Morrison did not *intend* the reader to perceive Sula and Nel's relationship as inherently lesbian. However, this lack of intention only shows the way in which heterosexist assumptions can veil what may logically be expected to occur in a work. What I have tried to do here is not to prove that Morrison wrote something that she did not, but to point out how a black feminist critical perspective at least allows consideration of this level of the novel's meaning.

In her interview in *Conditions:One* Adrienne Rich talks about unconsummated relationships and the need to re-evaluate the meaning of intense yet supposedly non-erotic connections between women. She asserts: 'We need a lot more documentation about what actually happened: I think we can also imagine it, because we know it happened – we know it out of our own lives.' Black women are still in the position of having to 'imagine', discover and verify black lesbian literature because so little has been written from an avowedly lesbian perspective. The near non-existence of black lesbian literature which other black lesbians and I so deeply feel has everything to do with the politics of our lives, the total suppression of identity that all black women, lesbian or not, must face. This literary silence is again intensified by the unavailability of an autonomous black feminist movement through which we could fight our oppression and also begin to name ourselves.

In a speech, 'The autonomy of Black lesbian women', Wilmette Brown comments upon the connection between our political reality and the literature we must invent:

> Because the isolation of Black lesbian women, given that we are super-freaks, given that our lesbianism defies both the sexual identity that capital gives us and the racial identity that capital gives us, the isolation of Black lesbian women from heterosexual Black women is very profound. Very profound. I have searched throughout Black history, Black literature, whatever, looking for some women that I could see were somehow lesbian. Now I know that in a certain sense they were all lesbian. But that was a very painful search.[4]

Heterosexual privilege is usually the only privilege that black women have. None of us have racial or sexual privilege, almost none of us have class privilege, maintaining 'straightness' is our last resort. Being out, particularly out in print, is the final renunciation of any claim to the crumbs of tolerance that non-threatening ladylike black women are sometimes fed. I am convinced that it is our lack of privilege and power in every other sphere that allows so few black women to make the leap that many white women, particularly writers, have been able to make in this decade, not merely because they are white or have economic leverage, but because they have had the strength and support of a movement behind them.

Notes

1, O. Williams, 'A bibliography of work written by American black women', *College Language Association Journal*, vol. 15, no. 3 (1972), p. 355.
2. J. O'Brien (ed.), *Interviews with Black Writers*, New York: Liveright, 1973, p. 201.
3. T. Morrison, *The Bluest Eyes* [1970], New York: Pocket Books, 1972; *Sula*, New York: Alfred A. Knopf, 1974.
4. W. Brown, 'The autonomy of Black lesbian women', MS of speech delivered 24 July, 1976, Toronto, Canada, p. 7.

13.10 **Feminist Criticism**
Maggie Humm

Maggie Humm engages with the central desire to establish an alternative literary canon which validates black and lesbian literary history and explores ways in which both black and lesbian criticism challenge and imaginatively expand the parameters of feminist literary theory.

Like all movements, the feminist arguments of the 1960s and early 1970s led to generalisation. Gayle Rubin invented a general term, 'sex/gender system', to try to define the oppression of women separately from other social divisions of class or country. But the problem with large definitions of this kind is that they can lead to artificial universalism. To assume that all women irrespective of background have more in common with each other than with men, as feminists did in the 1960s, leads many to generalise from the limitations of their own white experience and ignore the richness of Black or lesbian lives.

Black women and lesbians needed to speak out about *their* own experiences and to point to some of the differences that could make for a distinctive perspective on the meaning of feminist criticism. On the other hand, of course, no critic could posit the notion of a definitive or *exclusive* Black or lesbian criticism. The regional, national or class differences within each cultural tradition are immense. For example, the experience of the American lesbian Adrienne Rich is not at all the experience of Toni Cade Bambara. Each critic's style, themes and mode of address is insistently and recognisably her own. Rich is imagistic, Bambara aggressively direct. But the criticism and writing of Black women and lesbians have features in common which are very different from white feminism. Indeed, they cannot be considered separately since the lives and politics of both are often found in the one person. Because many important critics, such as Audre Lorde or Barbara Smith, are both Black *and* gay, it would be ludicrous not to consider the commonalities rather than differences of culture. Perhaps the most convincing case for writing in tandem about Black and lesbian feminist criticism is that together they demonstrate subtle and innovative techniques for the future of all feminist criticism.

Some of the patterns of Black and lesbian writing derive inextricably from their positions outside mainstream criticism. Both Blacks and lesbians start by establishing identifiable and separate literary traditions. For both, the critical text in a curious way calls a culture into existence. For example, the controversy among some Black Americans about Ntozake Shange's choreo poem *For Colored Girls* shows how much the Black community wants to read literature as sexual politics.[1] Without understanding the tradition of lesbian oppression, for example, criticism cannot deal adequately with a literary theme such as lesbian obliqueness. Both begin from a primary commitment to the political over cultural implications of their writing and the connections between the artistic and the political situations of their communities. In America lesbian discourse has been strongly influenced by the visibility of the Black movement of the mid 1960s as much as by the women's movement in which lesbian feminists now represent an avant-garde. The flowering of lesbian poetry in the 1960s came as much from lesbian involvement in Black civil rights as from involvement in white anti-war movements.

Conceptually, both Black and lesbian critics have in common certain critical themes which are a direct result of the kind of political and social experience both share. The way, for example, that both Adrienne Rich and Alice Walker focus on women as victims not just of physical violence but of a kind of psychic violence is not a simple coincidence, nor is their use of a sexual terminology to express profound cultural motifs accidental. The intimidation of colour or sexuality is part of the collective and historical oppression of Blacks and the suppression of lesbian women. Most important, the language and ideas of these critics is nothing like what white patriarchal criticism demands and teaches. This is why it seems to me that for feminist criticism to grow into a full body of work all feminist critics – white, lesbian and Black – must overcome fears of intrusion or of writing as 'outsiders' and provide overviews of, and access to, all outstanding feminist writing, most of which is now firmly located in Black and lesbian studies. Just as when reading Black women authors those of us who are white have to make an imaginative engagement with a different culture, we need to be similarly clear about reading Black writing and what specific pleasures or lessons it can teach us. As a white critic I am making a political gesture when reading Black writing. There are satisfying analogies between Black and white women's oppression. There is a way in which Black writing focuses the problem of estrangement for all women now. But I also have to emphasise the notion of difference without showing that difference as exotic. Just as one of the dangers of anthropology is the way it invites voyeurism, so it is too easy to use Eurocentric models or definitions. In other words, the central motifs of Black and lesbian criticism need to become pivotal to feminist criticism rather than the other way around.

Note

1. B. Smith, *House Girls*, New York: Kitchen Table Press, 1983, p. 290.

13.11 **Feminine Fictions: revisiting the postmodern**
Patricia Waugh

Patricia Waugh debates the relationship between feminist criticism and postmodernist theory, noting particularly their concern with a sense of alienation resulting from the loss or dislocation of subject-identity.

My contention in this book is that feminism and postmodernism clearly *do* share many concerns as they each develop from the 1960s onwards. Both are concerned to disrupt traditional boundaries: between 'art' and 'life', masculine and feminine, high and popular culture, the dominant and the marginal. Both examine the cultural consequences of the decline of a consensus aesthetics, of an effective 'literary' voice, or the absence of a strong sense of stable subjectivity. Each expresses concern about the extension of relationships of alienation within a consumer society and the expansion of technological and scientific modes of knowledge which cannot be contained within traditional moral paradigms. In each case, too, there is a close relationship between theory and practice leading to an unprecedented aesthetic self-consciousness and awareness of the problematic situation of the contemporary writer in relation to historical actuality and fictional tradition.

Clearly, the reasons for the *absence* of women writers from postmodernist debates from the 1960s to the 1980s is similarly multiple and complex, overdetermined by economic, social, psychological, political, and aesthetic factors. *One* reason, in particular, however, is advanced here and will become the focus of the argument in this book. At the moment when postmodernism is forging its identity through articulating the exhaustion of the existential belief in self-presence and self-fulfilment and through the dispersal of the universal subject of liberalism, *feminism* (ostensibly, at any rate) is assembling *its* cultural identity in what appears to be the opposite direction. During the 1960s, as Vonnegut waves a fond goodbye to character in fiction, women writers are beginning, *for the first time in history*, to construct an identity out of the recognition that women need to discover, and must fight for, a sense of unified selfhood, a rational, coherent, effective identity. As male writers lament its demise, women writers have not yet experienced that subjectivity which will give them a sense of personal autonomy, continuous identity, a history and agency in the world.

Subjectivity, femininity, and the postmodern person

There have been numerous attempts to define both postmodernism and feminism, and clearly neither constitutes a homogeneous category – nor should they. However, there is a striking set of opposed – yet complementary – issues around the questions of subjectivity and authority which occur again and again in separate discussions of each movement. The philosophical transition from a Hegelian or Marxian understanding of the subject in history to a structuralist or post-structuralist one is a shift fundamentally from consciousness to language. Postmodernism situates itself epistemologically at the point where the epistemic subject characterized in terms of historical experience, interiority, and consciousness has given way to the 'decentred' subject identified through the public, impersonal signifying practices of other similarly 'decentred' subjects. It may even situate itself at a point where there is no 'subject' and no history in the old sense at all. There is only a system of linguistic structures, a textual construction, a play of differences in the Derridean sense. 'Identity' is simply the illusion produced through the manipulation of irreconcilable and contradictory language games. In Raymond Federman's postmodernist fiction *Double or Nothing*,[1] for example, 'narrators', 'characters', and implied 'readers' dissolve into the categorizations of grammar, where the play of proper names ridicules our nostalgia for stable identity:

FIRST PERSON

or

THIRD PERSON

FIRST PERSON is more restrictive more subjective more personal harder
THIRD PERSON is more objective more impersonal more encompassing easier

I could try both ways:
I was standing on the upper deck next to a girl called Mary …
No Peggy
He was standing on the upper deck next to a girl called Mary …
No Peggy.
(Comes out the same).

(p. 99)

One detects through the ridicule that nostalgia for the full subject also present in Vonnegut and Barth. The play with pronouns reminds the initiated (post-structuralist-informed) reader of Benveniste's analysis of the relationship between language and subjectivity: that the subject of the enunciation always exceeds the subject of the utterance, the 'I' can never be fully present in what it says of itself. Postmodernism's rejection of representation is premised on an acknowledgment of the necessary gap between subjectivities (grammatical and existential), yet for most postmodernist writers there is still a longing, a nostalgia for the discovery of an identity behind signification, a desire to close the gap and locate the 'self' in pure consciousness. Several commentators on postmodern art have drawn attention to this. As Hal Foster argues:

> To speak of a fragmented subject is to presuppose a prior moment or model in which the subject is whole and complete, not split in relation to desire or decentred in relation to language; such a concept, whether heuristic or historical, is problematic. On the Right this tendency is manifest in a nostalgic insistence on the good strong self, pragmatic, patriarchal, and ideological in the extreme. Yet the Left positions on the subject are only somewhat less troublesome. Diagnoses of our culture as regressive, one dimensional, schizophrenic ... often preserve this bourgeois subject, if only in opposition, if only by default. [2]

Women writers clearly occupy a rather different position in relation to such covert postmodernist nostalgia. Subjectivity, historically constructed and expressed through the phenomenological equation self/other, necessarily rests masculine 'selfhood' upon feminine 'otherness'. The subjective centre of socially dominant discourses (from Descartes's philosophical, rational 'I' to Lacan's psychoanalytic phallic/symbolic) in terms of power, agency, autonomy has been a 'universal' subject which has established its identity through the invisible marginalization or exclusion of what it has also defined as 'femininity' (whether this is the non-rational, the body, the emotions, or the pre-symbolic). The 'feminine' thus becomes that which cannot be expressed because it exists outside the realm of symbolic signification. Constituted through a male gaze and thus endowed with the mysteriousness of one whose *objective* status is seen as absolute and definitive,

> One is not born, but becomes a woman. No biological, psychological or economic fate determines the figure that the human female presents in society: it is civilisation as a whole that produces this creature, intermediate between male and eunuch, which is described as 'feminine'. [3]

In the dialectical relationship between traditional humanism and the postmodern anti-humanism emerging in the 1960s, women continue to be displaced. How can they long for, reject, or synthesize a new mode of being from a thesis which has never contained or expressed what they have felt their historical experience to be? Feminist theory at this time thus focused less on deconstructing the discursive formations which position the subject than on analysing the socially constructed differences between the sexes as the chief source of women's oppression, and on examining sex roles as a mode of social control. Its emergent aesthetics drew not on structuralism or anti-humanist discourses but on humanist Marxism, liberal theories of inalienable rights, sociological role and social learning theory, and on theories of psychology which emphasized the need to 'actualize' and 'strengthen' the self-in-the-world. In particular, it emphasized the ideological production of 'femininity' as the 'other' of patriarchy and the need, therefore, for women to become 'real' subjects and to discover their 'true' selves. Thus, with a search for a *coherent and unified feminine subject*, began the deconstruction of the myth of woman as absolute Other and its exposure as a position within masculine discourse.

The practice of consciousness-raising, which aimed precisely at the forging of an individual and collective sense of identity and subjecthood in these terms, epitomizes the distance separating feminism from postmodernism. Postmodernism expresses nostalgia for but loss of belief in the concept of the human subject as an agent effectively intervening in history, through its fragmentation of discourses, language games, and decentring of subjectivity. Feminism seeks a subjective identity, a sense of effective agency and history for women which has hitherto been denied them by the dominant culture. Postmodernist writers express the disintegration of the potency of that 'individual vision' mediated through the 'unique' style of modernism and stress the inability of the contemporary subject to locate 'himself' historically. Ultimately, what has been lost is faith in the historically representative and ordering power of narrative itself and in the unified subject who believes 'he' is producing the world in producing a representation of it. Feminist writers, in the meantime, *appear* to be pursuing the sort of definition of identity and relationship to history which postmodernists have rejected. For many women there can be no prior subject or self whose fragmentation becomes a political necessity, source of nostalgic regret, or hedonistic *jouissance*.

In fact, and for this reason, I would argue that women's writing, whether feminist or not, has largely existed in a highly contradictory relationship to both the dominant liberal conception of subjectivity and writing and to the classic 'postmodernist' deconstruction of this liberal trajectory. Much women's writing can, in fact, be seen as an attempt not to define an isolated individual ego but to discover a collective concept of subjectivity which foregrounds the construction of identity in *relationship*. Historically, such a concept of self appears strongly in women's writing well before 'postmodernism', though I shall argue that its emphasis has shifted more recently as the lessons of post-structuralism have been absorbed. This concept grows out of women's particular history and out of the collective politics of the women's movement. It appears in Virginia Woolf's writing, for example, where the exploration of a dispersed/relational/collective concept of identity becomes a weapon in the killing of the 'Angel in the House'. Woolf seeks to become aware of the paralysing and alienating determinations of the myth of Woman, but equally to avoid embracing an identity articulated through an ideal of contained, coherent, 'proportioned' subjectivity which for her expressed the dominant cultural norm of masculinity.

Woolf desired that a woman writer should write *as a woman*, but as one who has forgotten this fact. To ask 'Who am I?' is to articulate a question which usually assumes an *a priori* belief in an ultimate unity and fixity of being, a search for a rational, coherent, essential 'self' which can speak and know itself. For

Woolf, like many women writers positioned in a patriarchal society, a more appropriate question would be 'What represents me?' This question carries an implicit and necessary recognition of alienation: the phenomenological perception that 'I' am never at one with myself because always and ever already constituted by others according to whom, and yet outside of what, I take myself to be. For the woman writer, the further implication is that, if the 'I' is spoken or positioned in a discourse where subjectivity, the norm of human-ness, is male, then 'I' is doubly displaced, 'I' can never in any material or metaphysical sense be at one with myself. If 'I' can accept this, however, then I may be able to see the possibility of shifting from an identity defined necessarily through alienation to one defined potentially through relationship in a more equal society.

Woolf writes in *The Waves*:

> And now I ask, who am I? I have been talking of Bernard, Neville, Jinny, Susan, Rhoda and Louis. Am I all of them? Am I one and distinct? I do not know. We sat here together. But now Percival is dead, and Rhoda is dead; we are divided; we are not here. Yet I cannot find any obstacle separating us. There is no division between me and them. As I talked I felt 'I am you'. This difference we make so much out of, this identity we so fervently cherish was overcome.[4]

It is the relational connection of being not simply an 'I' but also a 'you' in the eyes of others which stabilizes the shifter, the indexical deictic 'I', which thus *reassures* Bernard of his identity and rescues him from the feeling that he is 'a man without a self' (p. 245). Woolf has accepted and fictionally embodied the recognition that differentiation is not necessarily separateness, distance, and alienation from others, but a form of *connection* to others. [...]

In my view, many twentieth-century women writers (whether consciously feminists or not) have sought alternative conceptions of subjectivity, expressing a definition of self in relationship which does not make identity dependent axiomatically upon the maintenance of boundaries and distance, nor upon the subjugation of the other. However, for the most part, the institution of literary criticism has ensured, through the marginalization or misinterpretation of their works (in the terms of the dominant aesthetic theories), that this potentially radical aspect of their work is silenced through its non-representation. This is as true of Virginia Woolf as of more recent writers like Anita Brookner or Grace Paley:

> Both in theory and practice our culture knows only one form of individuality: the male stance of over-differentiation, of splitting off and denying the tendencies towards sameness and reciprocal responsiveness. In this 'false differentiation' the other subject remains an object rather than emerging as a person in her/his right. This way of establishing and protecting individuality dovetails with the dualistic, objective posturing of western rationality. To be a woman is to be excluded from this rational individualism, to be either an object of it or a threat to it. To be a man

is not merely to assert one's side of the duality, the supremacy of the rational subject. It is also to insist that the dualism, splitting and boundaries between the male and female postures are upheld.[5]

Notes

1. R. Tederman, *Double or Nothing*, New York: Swallow Press, 1971.
2. H. Foster, '(Post)modern polemics', *New German Critique*, vol. 33, p. 77.
3. S. de Beauvoir, *The Second Sex*, transl. H. M. Parshley, Harmondsworth: Penguin, 1972, p. 249.
4. V. Woolf, *The Waves*, Harmondsworth: Penguin, 1972.
5. J. Benjamin, 'The bonds of love: rational violence and erotic domination', in H. Eisenstein and A. Jardine (eds), *The Future of Difference*, Boston: G. K. Hall, 1980, pp. 46–7.

Further Reading

Abel, E. (ed.) (1982), *Writing and Sexual Difference*, Sussex: Harvester.

Armstrong, I. (ed.) (1992), *New Feminist Discourses*, London: Routledge.

Belsey, C. and Moore, K. (eds) (1989), *The Feminist Reader*, London: Methuen.

Cameron, D. (ed.) (1990), *The Feminist Critique of Language*, London: Routledge.

Coward, R. (1984), *Female Desires*, London: Paladin.

Ellmann, M. (1979), *Thinking About Women*, London: Virago.

Figes, E. (1982), *Sex and Subterfuge*, London: Macmillan.

Green, G. and Kahn, C. (eds) (1985), *Making a Difference*, London: Routledge.

Jacobus, M. (ed.) (1982), *Women Writing and Writing about Women*, Sussex: Harvester.

Kenyon, O. (1988), *Women Novelists Today*, Hemel Hempstead: Harvester Wheatsheaf.

Marks, E. and de Courtivron, I. (eds) (1981), *New French Feminisms*, Hemel Hempstead: Harvester Wheatsheaf.

Moi, T. (1985), *Feminist Literary Theory*, London: Methuen.

Spender, D. (1980), *Man Made Language*, London: Routledge.

Weedon, C. (1987), *Feminist Practice and Poststructuralist Theory* London: Methuen.

Wolff, J. (1990), *Feminine Sentences*, Cambridge: Polity.

Woolf, V. (1967), *A Room of One's Own*, London: Hogarth.

14 REPRESENTATIONS OF WOMEN IN THE MEDIA

Edited and Introduced by Michele Ryan

INTRODUCTION

Discussions around the representation of women in the media usually fall into two broad camps. One argues that under the political economy of a capitalist patriarchy all representations of women are likely to be negative. It incorporates an analysis of the text and the way it works ideologically on the spectator/viewer, as well as a notion that she can do very little to resist these dominant and oppressive representations except by a revolution. The other camp would argue that despite these negative representations, women – or members of any other subordinated section of society – bring their own subjectivities and cultural competence with them when they consume the media; and that far from being a passive experience it is in fact a complex, interactive one which enables apparently subordinated groups to resist dominant representations. Here there is a concern to move away from a purely academic analysis of texts studied out of contexts and to argue for the cultural analysis of audiences/consumers as they interact with those texts; and for a historical and class analysis so that knowledge is not frozen into the abstract and ahistorical.

Most of the feminist theories of the media deal with how we make sense of the pleasures we get from consuming the media when the representations we receive from them are often stereotyped and demeaning to women. If the regimes of representation are based on patriarchy, is it inevitable that women are positioned as objects and men as subjects? As we undoubtedly derive great pleasure from our consumption of the media, does this mean that we willingly accept the way patriarchy defines us either as objects of desire or as threats to masculinity that have to be controlled? Can we form new and more diverse representations of women that more clearly reflect the complexity and diversity of their lives? Is it possible that a 'female gaze' can be part of our cultural life? Since the early 1970s feminists have been asking these questions in film and media studies.

Much of this feminist discourse took as its starting point Laura Mulvey's theory about the male gaze.[1] Mulvey entered into a pyschoanalytic and semiotic debate which dominated cinema studies in the early 1970s, arguing that the pleasure we receive from watching mainstream Hollywood films is a masculine one derived from the structure of the gaze, which is involved with the concepts of voyeurism, scopophilia and fetishism. Her critique, with its strong textual emphasis, was part of what has loosely been defined as 'screen' theory, and whilst it was influential – particularly her deconstruction of narrative – it did appear to leave women with access to only two positions: either the assumption of a masculine position or the assumption of a passive or masochistic position through identification with a female character. What her critique did stress was the importance of creating an alternative feminist film practice as a way of producing an alternative representation to the dominant monolithic male gaze. Such a practice would enable women to experiment with new forms to create a filmic language in which woman would occupy the subject position, thereby creating a female spectatorship.

The debate over whether there can be a female gaze and a female spectatorship is still going on, but now it draws on other academic disciplines as well as on semiotics and psychoanalysis. Of particular note is the cultural studies critique which can be broadly associated with the Birmingham University Centre for Contemporary and Cultural Studies [CCCS] department. Writers like Angela McRobbie, Dorothy Hobson, Christine Geraghty and Christine Brunsdon have been concerned with aspects of mainstream/popular culture, and their work has contributed significantly to empowering women as cultural consumers of the media. In the last few years, further feminist research on television genres and gender has offered some of the most interesting insights into women and the media. Much of this feminist work in television studies draws on the context as well as the text, the ethnographic as well as the theoretical, to try to understand the way women use and interact with the media – and, like Mulvey in her early work, its aim is to empower women. An excellent book on feminist cultural television criticism is *Television and Women's Culture* (see Reading 14.7). It covers nearly all the areas this Section addresses and deals with a range of both genres and subject positions.

The first three Readings give a clear and accessible account of discussions around representation in relation to cinema, romantic literature and pornography. Each Reading is concerned with how we understand the process of constructing gendered representation, and how we intervene in the regime of representations so that we can change them. Reading 14.1 gives a useful summary of the various feminist theories in relation to cinema studies, particularly around the text – spectator relationship and feminist film-makers' problems in dealing with mainstream and alternative practices. *Female Spectators* provides a good overview of current debates in film and television. In Reading 14.2 Janice Radway discusses why she combined ethnographic and psychoanalytic approaches in her study of the reading practices of women and romantic fiction. In the process she argues brilliantly against the prevailing view of women's consumption of romantic fiction – that it is a totally escapist activity from the drudgery of their lives – and argues that women use it to achieve a new sense of strength and independence. Reading 14.3 offers a different perspective on representation – Susanne Kappeler argues that pornography is only the logical extension of existing representational regimes, and it is therefore vitally important for women to participate actively in all areas of cultural practice in order to transform the structure of representation, the conventions of viewing and the conception of creativity. It would then become 'a practice in the interest of communication, not representation'.[2]

The remaining Readings highlight key areas of discussion in film and TV, and reflect the dominant concerns of feminist cultural theory in relation to the media: incorporating class, ethnicity and other social contexts in examining gender relations. As Annette Kuhn has argued in an earlier book,[3] an important aspect of feminist theoretical practice must be the effort to make accessible some of the difficult theoretical arguments relating to film and representation in order to facilitate 'oppositional' intellectual and cultural work. This concern is also evident in most of these Readings, and Reading 14.6 has been chosen because it raises a still neglected area of media studies: women's role in media production.

Finally, it is soap opera that has been the object of some of the most interesting feminist cultural studies critiques within media studies, and the work of Ien Ang, Dorothy Hobson, Tania Modleski and Charlotte Brundson has helped to raise the status of this kind of media critique, and thereby the status of women in general.[4] Christine Geraghty's book (see Reading 14.9) represents the best of this feminist critical work, and does not flinch from addressing some difficult questions.

Notes

1. See L. Mulvey's 'Visual pleasure and narrative cinema', *Screen*, vol. 16, no. 3 (1975). P. Cook (ed.), *The Cinema Book*, London: British Film Institute, 1985, provides a useful summary of the various theoretical approaches to film and cinema and the feminist contribution to these theories.
2. See S. Kappeler's conclusion to *The Pornography of Representation*, which argues for a feminist cultural practice.
3. A. Kuhn, *Women's Pictures: Feminism and cinema*, London: Routledge & Kegan Paul, 1982.
4. I. Ang, *Watching Dallas*, London: Methuen, 1982; D. Hobson, *Crossroads: The drama of a soap opera*, London: Methuen, 1982; T. Modleski, *Loving with a Vengeance: Mass produced fantasies for women*, London: Methuen, 1982; *Feminism Without Women*, London: Routledge & Kegan Paul, 1991; C. Brunsdon, 'Crossroads: notes on a soap opera', *Screen*, vol. 22, no. 4 (1981), pp. 32–7.

14.1 **Female Spectators**
E. Deidre Pribram

This Introduction to Female Spectators *gives a concise account of the major feminist debates in film studies and argues for more work to be done in incorporating film-making practice, spectatorship and textual analysis. All the contributors to this book share a concern to 'emphasise women's presence in, rather than absence from, the "cinematic experience"'.*

How have we come to perceive all forms of filmic gaze as male when women have always taken up their proportionate share of seats in the cinema? How have we come to understand cinematic pleasure (narrative, erotic, and so on) as pleasurable to the male viewer, but not the female? Why have we failed to see our own presence in the audience when women have always watched – and loved – film? Questions of pleasure and spectatorship, as they relate to women, arise out of recent work in feminist film theory. Or rather, they arise as omissions in these theoretical analyses. All too frequently, women's participation in the 'cinematic experience' has been neglected or entirely overlooked.

In the early and mid 1970s, many feminist film-makers and film theorists began to discuss women's historical and cultural position as one of absence from, or marginalization to, dominant cultural forms. Using psychoanalytic and semiotic models,[1] they theorized that women have been defined in masculine culture as lack and as Other. Woman is not a subject in her own right but the object by which the patriarchal subject can define himself. Mainstream cinema's contradictory/complementary representations of women as either idealized objects of desire or as threatening forces to be 'tamed' are not attempts to establish female subjectivity but rather reflect the search for male self-definition. Popular forms of filmic discourse, therefore, are said to 'belong' to the patriarchy; women are silent, without language or voice. Filmic gaze, in terms of both gender representation and gender address, also 'belongs' to the male, leaving the female audience to identify with either the male-as-subject or the female-as-object. In this analysis women are left with no active spectatorial position at all. Any pleasure the female spectator derives from classic realist cinema is false because it is based on woman as object of someone else's desire.

In the 1970s and into the early 1980s, feminist film-makers and theorists, seeking to create new forms outside and beyond those historically known to us, worked towards denying traditional pleasure in film. The resulting work was an attempt to create an alternative cinema in which women were engendered as subjects, and which thus made possible a female spectatorial position. While still indebted to the work of this feminist avant-garde, however, more recent feminist analysis and production have found that these earlier models pose considerable problems.

Freudian and Lacanian psychoanalytic theories have been central to cinema studies in recent years because they have helped forge a link between cultural forms of representation, such as film, and the acquisition of subject identity in social beings.[2] Feminist appropriations of these psychoanalytic models, which connect dominant ideology with bourgeois patriarchy – the individualized male

subject formed and reaffirmed through the playing out of the Oedipal drama –
have aided our understanding of the existing cultural order. However, they
have proven less helpful in subverting, or creating alternatives to, that order.
One weakness lies in the fact that many versions of psychoanalysis hypothesize
a development pattern for language and subject identity which occurs across all
time and across all cultural groups, a pattern established initially in infancy
within the nuclear family unit. That is to say, 'self-image' is regarded as acquired
in uniform manner for members of each gender based upon their respective
roles in the Oedipal struggle. Thus while psychoanalytic theories may succeed
in recognizing gender as a primary cause of subject formation and social
division, they simultaneously fail to address the formation and operation of
other variables or differences amongst individuals, such as race and class.

In addition, the transhistorical nature of psychoanalytic models – the
presumption that they apply equally across all time and instances – leaves them
open to justifiable charges of inaccuracy and inflexibility. When psychoanalysis
is applied to film, the potential for theorizing alternative readings or
interpretations within any given text is inhibited by a denial of viewing *contexts*:
no place is allowed for shifts in textual meaning related to shifts in viewing
situation. As a result, varying social groups – white women or women of colour,
lower-, middle- or upper-class women – are readily assumed to have the same
viewing experience. At the same time, audiences of differing historical periods
and circumstances – a contemporary audience viewing a contemporary work,
a contemporary audience viewing a past work, a past audience viewing a work
of its own time – are all assumed to be positioned by, and therefore to interpret,
a text in the same manner.

Following the psychoanalytic–semiotic argument, then, classic realist cinema
– by addressing woman as non-subject – eliminates the possibility of an
'authentic' female spectator. And further, by repressing the fact that women are
historically and socially constituted (and therefore differing) subjects, the
argument also precludes the possibility of diversity *among* women as female
spectators.

Feminist appropriations of psychoanalytic models are useful, however, to the
extent that their application is in keeping with the goals of a feminist agenda.
In a society which has formalized, as its centrepiece, the white bourgeois male,
feminist efforts have focused on the need to open up sociocultural spaces to
include previously excluded or marginalized subgroups. The concept of sexual
difference which describes a binary structure of subject/object, in which object
function produces subject validation, has seemed an accurate model of what is
– for those excluded from it – a dysfunctional system. And it has also pointed
the way to the necessity for a more flexible system in which a multiplicity of
subjects can operate in a simultaneous and mutually satisfactory manner. But
while the concept of sexual difference seems to account for what has appeared
to be, throughout historical memory, the systematic exclusion of women
(amongst others) from the political, economic and cultural life of Western

society, the theories within which the concept is formulated restrict the means to envision alternatives. For if, as some psychoanalytic theories appear to suggest, social subjects are determined, through family relations and language acquisition, *prior* to the introduction of other considerations, including race, class, personal background or historical moment, the social construct thus described is a closed system unamenable to other subject formations. And indeed, feminist applications of psychoanalytic theory have described the ideology of bourgeois patriarchy as not only dominant, but 'monolithic'. A notion of ideology which implies dominance to, and therefore co-existence with, other ideologies leaves open the possibility of inroads by alternative or minority groups: but the concept of monolithic ideology suggests a unified and unyielding structure. The meanings of a filmic text, which can be said to reflect/remake the ideologies of the culture from which it springs, are also seen as closed, fixed in the playing out of the Oedipal drama over all time and in all instances, unavailable to alternative, variable or multiple readings.

While feminist theory generally accepted the notion of a 'monolithic' ideology, no distinction was made between the social constructs described by the theory and the theoretical constructs which were doing the describing; and doing so in such a way as to preclude the possibility of cultural debate or change. Psychoanalysis, which seemed able to explain existing social – or at least psychic – structures, could do so only in terms that implied their very inevitability. No matter what the specifics, women are relegated to playing out 'the same old story', living out the same gender relations.

This may have been a factor in the decision by many feminist film-makers not to participate in dominant cultural forms. The closed system/closed text formulated by theoretical arguments based in psychoanalytic theory left few points of entry for alternative representations of women. The ability to critique was not met by an equal ability to create. The logical extension of arguments surrounding women's exclusion from popular cinema was that filmic gaze, discourse and pleasure belonged inevitably to the male. The only answer was to establish an alternative to this patriarchal cinema.

But women's participation in popular culture on the basis of these theoretical arguments embodies an impossible contradiction. For instance, women have long critiqued our exclusion from the centres of cultural production. Except in rare instances, women have not been involved as directors, producers, technicians, or in any other capacity of significant decision-making in the production of mainstream film. To define popular cultural activity as belonging to the patriarchy is to suggest therefore that women who do participate in mainstream production are being co-opted by dominant ideology. Yet, if women do not seek to be included at the centre of cultural production, we only reinforce our exclusion from it, in opposition to many of feminism's political aims.

Theoretical work of recent years has emphasized the crucial role played by cultural texts in subject formation: subjectivity is produced and affirmed, and ideology disseminated, through spectatorial identification with characters, narrative meaning and supporting aesthetic codes. The function of a text is to position the spectator to receive certain favoured – and restricted – meanings which the text 'manages' for the viewing subject in keeping with dominant ideology. In this model the spectator is not an active part of the production of textual meaning but the passive side of a unidirectional relationship in which the text disperses meanings while the spectator-subject receives them. The spectator can only interpret (be interpreted by) a text in terms preformulated by gender difference. There is no possibility of a mutually informing relationship between spectator and text, and therefore no accumulative building of textual meaning. As a result, psychoanalytic–semiotic theories do not distinguish the subject formulated by the text from the spectator-subject viewing the text. The intention of the text and the reception of textual meaning are defined as one and the same.

The assumption that the text positions the spectator to receive its intended meanings has led to a foregrounding of textual analysis as a methodology for the study of film, since the text is regarded as both container and disseminater of ideology. Ideology, in turn, is mediated through a medium's aesthetic and technical codes. These codes, through repetition in time, cultural familiarity, context of use, and so on, are themselves presumed to be infused with ideology. If this is so, the question remains: how does one utilize the formal aspects of film to convey alternative ideologies without, in the process, conveying dominant ideology as well? For many feminist film-makers this has seemed an irreconcilable position, and has resulted in a rejection of aesthetic and technical practices associated with mainstream cinema. But again, this view needs to be measured against feminism's political agenda, its intent to alter public consciousness about gender roles and relations. Spectatorship in this sense also involves a consideration of film's widespread appeal and influence: its accessibility, and its availability, to large audiences. The aesthetic and technical codes of mainstream cinema have served traditionally as a common language and meeting ground between those who make and those who watch films. In an analysis which presumes that a text imposes ideology on a fixed spectatorship in a fixed manner, the aesthetic and technical codes of dominant ideology can impose only dominant ideology. But a method of analysis which argues that the viewing process includes the active participation of spectators means that film's codes can be implemented, by both producer and consumer, to allow for alternative usage.

Notes

1. These theories are too complex to be provided for in a brief summary. For an indepth examination, see E. A. Kaplan, *Women and Film: Both sides of the camera*, London and New York: Methuen, 1983; and A. Kuhn, *Women's Pictures: Feminism and Cinema*, Boston, MA. and London: Routledge & Kegan Paul, 1982.
2. While references here are specifically to psychoanalytic theories, their application is inseparable from a semiotic methodology of textual analysis.

14.2 **Reading the Romance**
Janice Radway

Janice Radway, in her Introduction, explains her process of thought in deciding on a set of theoretical approaches to her own study of representation in romantic fiction. She outlines her concern to treat the readers as actively contributing to the complex social event of reading, and is ambitious in the areas she explores.

I would ... now want to agree with Angela McRobbie when she states flatly that 'representations are interpretations'.[1] As she goes on to say, they can never be pure mirror images of some objective reality but exist always as the result of 'a whole set of selective devices, such as highlighting, editing, cutting, transcribing and inflecting'. Consequently, I no longer feel that ethnographies of reading should *replace* textual interpretation completely because of their greater adequacy to the task of revealing an objective cultural reality. Rather, I think they should become an essential and necessary component of a multiply focused approach that attempts to do justice to the ways historical subjects understand and partially control their own behavior while recognizing at the same time that such behavior and self-understanding are limited, if not in crucial ways complexly determined, by the social formation within which those subjects find themselves. [...]

... it was the women readers' construction of the act of romance reading as a 'declaration of independence' that surprised me into the realization that the meaning of their media-use was multiply determined and internally contradictory, and that to get at its complexity it would be helpful to distinguish analytically between the significance of the *event* of reading and the meaning of the *text* constructed as its consequence. Although I did not then formulate it in so many words, this notion of the event of reading directed me towards a series of questions about the uses 'to which a particular text is put, its function within a particular conjuncture, in particular institutional spaces, and in relation to particular audiences'.[2] [...]

   Although *Reading the Romance* does not use Morley's terms,[3] it does work toward a kind of genre theory as he conceives it. To begin with, it attempts to understand how the Smithton women's social and material situation prepares them to find the act of reading attractive and even necessary. Secondly, through detailed questioning of the women about their own definition of romance and their criteria for distinguishing between ideal and failed versions of the genre, the study attempts to characterize the structure of the particular narrative the women have chosen to engage because they find it especially enjoyable. Finally, through its use of psychoanalytic theory, the book attempts to explain how and why such a structured 'story' might be experienced as pleasurable by those women as a consequence of their socialization within a particular family unit. [...]

Turning from the particular processes impinging on production which create the conditions of possibility for regular romance purchases, *Reading the Romance* then attempts a parallel look at the conditions organizing women's private lives which likewise contribute to the possibility of regular romance reading. It is in this context that I distinguish analytically between the event of reading and the text encountered through the process. I found it necessary to do so, the reader will discover, because the Smithton women so insistently and articulately explained that their reading was a way of temporarily refusing the demands associated with their social role as wives and mothers. As they observed, it functioned as a 'declaration of independence', as a way of securing privacy while at the same time providing companionship and conversation. [...] I have therefore tried to take seriously the dual implications of the word escape, that is, its reference to conditions left behind and its intentional projection of a utopian future.

It is this move, I think, that specifically relates *Reading the Romance* to Hobson's 'Crossroads' work, to her work on housewives, and to McRobbie's work on the culture of working-class girls.[4] [...]

I try to make a case for seeing romance reading as a form of individual resistance to a situation predicated on the assumption that it is women alone who are responsible for the care and emotional nurturance of others. Romance reading buys time and privacy for women even as it addresses the corollary consequence of their situation, the physical exhaustion and emotional depletion brought about by the fact that no one within the patriarchal family is charged with *their* care. Given the Smithton women's highly specific reference to such costs, I found it impossible to ignore their equally fervent insistence that romance reading creates a feeling of hope, provides emotional sustenance and produces a fully visceral sense of well-being.

It was the effort to account for the ability of romance reading to address the women's longing for emotional replenishment that subsequently directed my attention to the cultural conditions that had prepared the women to choose romances from among all the other books available to them. Thus I found myself wondering how, given the particular 'needs' the event of reading seemed to address for the Smithton women, the romance story itself figured in this conjuncture. I began to wonder what it was about the romance heroine's experience that fostered the readers' ability to see her story as interesting and accounted for their willingness to seek their own pleasure through hers precisely at the moment when they were most directly confronting their dissatisfaction with traditionally structured heterosexual relationships. What contribution did the narration of a romance make to their experience of pleasure? Why didn't the Smithton women choose to read detective stories, westerns or bestsellers in their precious private moments?

In thus searching for a way to link a specific desire with a particularly chosen route to the fulfilment of that desire, I turned to psychoanalytic theory in general and to Nancy Chodorow's feminist revision of Freud in particular.[5] [...]

Reading the Romance turns to Chodorow's revision of psychoanalytic theory in order to explain the construction of the particular desires that seem to be met by the *act* of romance reading. However, it additionally uses that theory to explore the psychological resonance of the romantic *narrative* itself for readers so constructed and engendered, a narrative which is itself precisely about the process by which female subjectivity is brought into being within the patriarchal family. Psychoanalysis is thus used also to explain why the story hails these readers, why they believe it possible to pursue their own pleasure by serving as witness to the romantic heroine's achievement of hers. What the psychoanalytically based interpretation reveals is the deep irony hidden in the fact that women who are experiencing the consequences of patriarchal marriage's failure to address their needs turn to a story which ritually recites the history of the process by which those needs are constituted. They do so, it appears, because the fantasy resolution of the tale ensures the heroine's achievement of the very pleasure the readers endlessly long for. In thus reading the story of a woman who is granted adult autonomy, a secure social position, and the completion produced by maternal nurturance, all in the person of the romantic hero, the Smithton women are repetitively asserting to be true what their still-unfulfilled desire demonstrates to be false, that is, that heterosexuality can create a fully coherent, fully satisfied, female subjectivity.[6]

Notes

1. See A. McRobbie, 'The politics of feminist research', *Feminist Review*, 12 (1982), p. 51.
2. D. Morley, *The 'Nationwide' Audience*, London: British Film Institute, 1980, p. 18.
3. D. Morley, 'The "Nationwide" audience: a critical postscript', *Screen Education*, 39 (1981), pp. 3–14.
4. See D. Hobson, 'Housewives: isolation as repression', in Centre for Contemporary Cultural Studies, Women's Studies Group (ed.), *Women Take Issue: Aspects of women's subordination*, London: Hutchinson, 1978; D. Hobson, *Crossroads: The drama of a soap opera*, London: Methuen, 1982. A. McRobbie, 'Working class girls and the culture of femininity', in *Women Take Issue*, 96–108; 'Settling accounts with subcultures: a feminist critique, *Screen*, 34 (1980), pp. 30–49; and '*Jackie*: an ideology of adolescent femininity', in *Popular Culture: Past and present*, ed. B. Waites *et al.*, London: Croom Helm, 1982.
5. N. Chodorow, *The Reproduction of Mothering: Psychoanalysis and the sociology of gender*, Berkeley, CA: University of California Press, 1978.
6. Cora Kaplan has recently advanced an argument which suggests that readers do not identify only with the romantic heroine but in fact identify in multiple and wandering fashion with the seducer, the seduced and the process of seduction itself. See '*The Thorn Birds*: fiction, fantasy, femininity', in *Sea Changes: Feminism and culture*, London: Verso, 1986, pp. 117–46. Although I found little evidence of this kind of multiple identification in the group I interviewed (at least at a conscious level), I have been told by many romance writers that the act of writing a romance is especially enjoyable because it gives them the opportunity to imagine themselves as the hero. It is also interesting to note that several American publishers of romances have recently

permitted writers to experiment with the writing of a romance entirely from the hero's point of view. Thus it might be possible that this sort of multiple identification actually varies from reader to reader and therefore can be increased by cultural or personal changes.

14.3 **The Pornography of Representation**
Susanne Kappeler

In this Reading Susanne Kappeler provides an interesting synopsis of why we should consider pornography as a form of representation, and argues that we should move away from a concern with content towards an analysis of representational practices.

Pornography is not a special case of sexuality; it is a form of representation. Representation, therefore, not 'real-life sex', should be the wider context in which we analyse this special case of representation: pornography. The traditional debate has focused on 'porn' at the expense of 'graphy', an emphasis duly reflected in the customary abbreviation to 'porn'. 'Porn', in this slippage, has gradually come to mean 'obscene sex' or 'violent sex' – forms of sexuality we disapprove of. We do not like them (or would not like them) in real life, therefore we do not want them represented.

The object of this study is pornography, that is representations, word- or image-based, or, to be more precise representational practices, rather than sexual practices. The fact of representation needs to be foregrounded: we are not just dealing with 'contents'. Sex or sexual practices do not just exist out there, waiting to be represented; rather, there is a dialectical relationship between representational practices which construct sexuality, and actual sexual practices, each informing the other.

Forms of representation have their own histories, yet we have become so accustomed to representations in many media that the media and their conventions have become naturalized, 'transparent', apparently giving a key-hole view on make-believe reality, reflections of reality. Literature and the visual arts are the expert domains of representation, and they embody the history of the naturalization of the medium. Their concepts of realism have fostered our commonsense attitude of dividing representations into form and content, medium and represented reality. The aim of realism is to obliterate our awareness of the medium and its conventions and to make us take what is represented for a reflection of a natural reality. Realism sees itself as holding up a mirror to life. The mirror, if not transparent, reflects, and it is above all 'faithful'. The question should never arise as to who is holding the mirror, for whose benefit, and from what angle; at least it should not arise in terms which would make this concept of the mirror – and hence of reality – problematical.

Within the disciplines of the study of art and literature, cinema and photography, the analysis of realism and of the relationship between form and content has long significantly advanced beyond this simple sketch. Yet the notions of 'realism' and of 'form and content' still have a firm hold upon our commonsense responses. They are at the bottom of the content orientation towards pornography (the focus on sex). They are at the bottom of our easy division into fact and fiction. And they are at the bottom of official newspaper policy, of professional organisations of editors and journalists claiming to produce neutral, unbiased, objective or transparent reporting – to hold up the mirror of events to the reading public. It is for this reason that a more elaborate analysis of representation needs to be brought to bear in a feminist analysis of pornography.

Representations are not just a matter of mirrors, reflections, key-holes. Somebody is making them, and somebody is looking at them, through a complex array of means and conventions. Nor do representations simply exist on canvas, in books, on photographic paper or on screens: they have a continued existence in reality as objects of exchange; they have a genesis in material production. They are more 'real' than the reality they are said to represent or reflect. All of these factors somehow straddle the commonsense divide between fiction and fact, fantasy and reality.

So a first shift of ground, for a feminist critique of pornography, involves moving from a content orientation to an analysis of representation. This move, however, takes us out of the comfortable seclusion of the Arts – the storehouses of (respectable) representations – and leads us to look at the functions of representations in society. Crucial factors of representation are the author and the perceiver: agents who are not like characters firmly placed within the representation as content. They are roles taken up by social beings in a context. This context is political: a question of class, race, gender. This context is cultural: a question of the relationship of representations to a generalized concept of culture (and 'reality'). And this context is economic: a question of the relationships of cultural production and exchange. None of these questions, of course, is independent of the others, which poses a problem of how to present them.

14.4 The Power of the Image
Annette Kuhn

Annette Kuhn is another author who combines semiotics, psychoanalysis, cultural studies and historical approaches to investigate how meanings are circulated between representation, spectatorship and social formations particularly in relation to the cinematic image.

Since the early 1970s, the study of images, particularly of cinematic images, as signifying systems has taken up and developed these 'prefeminist' concerns, bringing to the fore the issue of the spectator as subject addressed, positioned, even formed, by representations. To semiotic and structuralist approaches to representation has been added psychoanalysis, whose object is precisely the processes by which human subjectivity is formed.[1] In work on the image, the cinematic image particularly, an emphasis on subjectivity has foregrounded the question of spectatorship in new ways. [...]

What relation, for instance, does spectatorship have to representations of women? What sort of activity is looking? What does looking have to do with sexuality? With masculinity and femininity? With power? With knowledge? How do images of women, in particular, 'speak to' the spectator? Is the spectator addressed as male/female, masculine/feminine? Is femininity constructed in specific ways through representation? Why are images of women's bodies so prevalent in our society? Such questions may sometimes be answered by looking at and analysing actual images. But although such analysis must be regarded as necessary to an understanding of the relationship between representation and sexuality, it is not always sufficient. For, in practice, images are always seen in context: they always have a specific use value in the particular time and place of their consumption. This, together with their formal characteristics, conditions and limits the meanings available from them at any one moment. But if representations always have use value, then more often than not they also have exchange value: they circulate as commodities in a social/economic system. This further conditions, or overdetermines, the meanings available from representations.

Meanings do not reside in images, then: they are circulated between representation, spectator and social formation. [...]

But why spend time and effort analysing images of a kind often considered questionable, even objectionable, by feminists? Why not try instead to create alternatives to culturally dominant representations? As I have argued, politics and knowledge are interdependent: the women's movement is not, I believe, faced here with a choice between two mutually exclusive alternatives, though individual feminists – if only because one person's life is too short to encompass everything – often experience their own politics in such a way. Theory and practice inform one another. At one level, analysing and deconstructing dominant representations may be regarded as a strategic practice. It produces understanding, and understanding is necessary to action.

It may also be considered an act of resistance in itself. Politics is often thought of as one of life's more serious undertakings, allowing little room for pleasure. At the same time, feminists may feel secretly guilty about their enjoyment of images they are convinced ought to be rejected as politically unsound. In analysing such images, though, it is possible, indeed necessary, to acknowledge their pleasurable qualities, precisely because pleasure is an area of analysis in its own right. 'Naive' pleasure, then, becomes admissible. And the acts of analysis,

of reconstruction and of reading 'against the grain' offer an additional pleasure
– the pleasure of resistance, of saying 'no': not to 'unsophisticated' enjoyment,
by ourselves and others, of culturally dominant images, but to the structures of
power which ask us to consume them uncritically and in highly circumscribed
ways.

Note

1. These developments are traced in R. Coward and J. Ellis, *Language and Materialism*,
   London: Routledge & Kegan Paul, 1978.

14.5 'A Question of Silence'
Jeanette Murphy

These first two pages from Jeanette Murphy's article provide an interesting critique of a
film which appears to conform to mainstream practices whilst at the same time offering
the possibility of a 'female gaze'. It also problematises the male viewer.

In this piece I want to explore the extent to which *A Question of Silence* as a
feminist text succeeds in presenting a coherent and integrated challenge to a
certain set of patriarchal assumptions and taken-for-granted notions of how the
world operates and has to be – namely notions and assumptions relating to
heterosexuality, power relations between men and women, women's visibility
and status, violence, and that curious entity, (male) 'logic'. However, while the
film expresses and examines these conflicts and women's position within
patriarchy, *A Question of Silence* articulates these around women's violence,
anger and silence. An examination of the negotiation of these issues within the
particular, woman-orientated perspective constructed by the film and the
feminist politic which motivates it must necessarily expose some of the
dilemmas and contradictions inherent in feminism itself. *A Question of Silence*,
I would argue, presents separatism as feminism taken to its logical and
inevitable conclusion.[1] It reveals women's anger as a problematic, the
negotiation of which profoundly affects all women's lives, and which feminism
itself has failed to resolve.

A challenge to patriarchal presumption

An outstanding aspect of *A Question of Silence* is its creation and assertion, its
apparent naturalisation, of a woman-orientated and identified perspective – a
woman's logic and world-view. This is established through a combination of the
different ways in which women and men respond to the events and characters
within the film. The women protagonists' responses are represented as

reasonable and rational; they make sense in terms of the filmic events themselves, they are represented sympathetically, space is allowed for our identification – but not an identification associated with most mainstream (classical narrative, realist) films where the camera, camera movement, editing, lighting, etc., serve to absorb us willy-nilly into the film and its characters and plot. While *A Question of Silence* uses a realist *mise-en-scène* and story-line and a more or less conventional way of filming, it also sparingly uses and refers to modernist and avant-garde filming techniques. There are few close-ups. The camera is almost always at a distance from the characters and events and it is often still. Tracking shots – used to follow Christine to the boutique and in the boutique itself – are kept some distance from the characters themselves. The camera is often placed at a lower or higher level to the person(s) it films. The only point-of-view shots in the film (and I could find only two) are those bearing the look of a woman – that of the therapist. The difficulty in identifying point-of-view shots, and their rarity – even were I to have missed a few – is significant. Although we identify through the therapist, this identification is mainly established through her central role in and her progressive enlightenment within the course of the narrative. Thus throughout the film we are consistently kept at a distance – allowing the viewer to think and assess the meaning of events and characters' responses and make a more active and thoughtful, a more 'intelligent' identification. Inevitably, in terms of the politics underpinning the film, this identification is woman-orientated.

In contrast, the men's responses in the film are shown to be irrational, complacent and overbearing – only explicable within a structure where men thoughtlessly oppress women. In the film's narrative men are the butt of jokes – those of the film and of the women in the film. Andrea, the secretary, allows a 'respectable' man to mistake and hire her as a prostitute. An, in response to a grossly sexist statement by one of the café clientèle, tells him to throw his hat in the canal and crawl under it. Christine's husband reveals to the therapist his lack of insight or concern when he speaks of his wife's silence and withdrawal as being symptomatic only of a particular kind of woman (the 'quiet type'), denying her role in providing his home comforts and child-care (glaringly lacking now) by saying: 'I work hard ... she didn't have anything to do all day.' All these jokes demonstrate to the viewer the nature of male presumption and power, but the film conveys this in a way which dismisses this patriarchal way-of-being as inconsequential and inappropriate. In this way constructed as 'other', lacking in authenticity, men arrogantly assume a knowledge and understanding of matters which, as the film convincingly demonstrates they have no right or reason to do. The therapist's husband ignores her specialist knowledge in psychology and confidently asserts the three women's madness ... because within *his* framework of knowledge their action makes no possible sense. This attitude is echoed by all the relevant male characters in the film. In perhaps the most painful and resonant (flashback) scene, the secretary's capabilities, competence and knowledge are – in one male sleight of hand –

simultaneously dismissed and denied *and* appropriated by her 'boss' in the board meeting.

Crucially, men are shown to have no insight into their structural power, or their use and abuse of it, and since the project of the film is the therapist's (and our, the viewers') realisation of this, men – already constructed as 'other' (those with power-over and alien perception) – are structured out of the rationale of the film. Thus, patriarchal discourse, the (male) language of dominance, is disrupted on the level of representation (because films are not normally like this) and on the level of ideology (because our preconceptions about a male perspective being the 'truth' are challenged).

Note

1. Arguments for and against separatism are dispersed over time and through various publications. For an accessible account of the debate, see *Love Your Enemy! The debate between heterosexual feminism and political lesbianism*, London: Onlywomen Press, 1981. See also L. Valeska, 'The future of female separatism', and C. Bunch, 'Not for lesbians only', in *Building Feminist Theory: Essays from Quest*, New York: Longman, 1981.

14.6 The Status of Women Working in Film and Television
Anne Ross Muir

This Reading documents the appalling lack of women in the film and TV industries, and the dominance of men in all the popular genres of TV. This is a situation which makes it difficult to assess what differences would be made if there were more women employed, but implies that a female gaze might be realisable.

Recent feminist debates have used psychoanalytic theory to explore why the 'male gaze' is dominant in mainstream cinema. But there may be a more concrete (if related) explanation: that the masculine point of view is prevalent simply because men control the industry.

One has only to watch the credits roll by at the end of a film or television programme to realise that women are sadly under-represented in the worlds of cinema and broadcasting. One major reason for this state of affairs is that women have been discriminated against, and have been barred from many jobs in the film and television industry. It is a depressing picture. Over the years a large number of very talented women have tried to break down those barriers – and failed. Pessimists point out that such discrimination is so entrenched and longstanding that it could take generations to wipe out. It is not surprising, therefore, that many women don't even try to enter the industry. They are defeated before they begin.

Yet it is because of this attitude that women are in danger of losing an unprecedented opportunity to sweep aside the barriers which have kept them out of key jobs in film and television. The conditions for change are right. For example, many of the major broadcasting organisations have now agreed, in principle, that women should have an equal opportunity for careers alongside men.

It is, however, a fragile opportunity. If past experience is anything to go by, such policies may make little difference unless women take them at their word and make things happen. It's up to us.

There is no doubt that the present situation is desperately in need of improvement. In 1975 the results of an enquiry into the status of women in the film and television industry conducted for the ACTT (Association of Cinematograph, Television and Allied Technicians) showed that the position of women had not improved since the Second World War and had, in fact, deteriorated.[1] In the 1950s women worked in a wide variety of grades and represented 18 per cent of the labour force within the industry. By 1975 they constituted only 15 per cent and had been buried in ghetto jobs, that is, in jobs held almost exclusively by women, which are often lower paid and which are given little status.

By 1986 the situation was hardly better. The figures for employment provided by the ITCA (Independent Television Companies Association) showed that of 306 camera operators, only 12 were women; there were only 8 female sound technicians compared to 269 male ones; while of 1,395 engineers, 19 were women. On the other hand, none of the production assistants or secretaries was male.

A survey of the situation of women within the BBC conducted by Monica Simms and released in 1985 reached similar conclusions.[2] In the BBC's top grade of personnel, there were 159 men and only 6 women, while only 8 per cent of staff in the category which includes heads of department, senior producers and correspondents were female. When I interviewed Michael Grade, then Controller of BBC1, he admitted that, at his level of decision-making, there were no women involved.

The film industry is, if anything, worse. It's true that the National Film School has now increased its intake of female students from 1 out of 25 when it opened in 1971 to around 30 per cent in the last few years. Yet although qualifications from the NFS have been a passport to success for a number of male graduates, it has not helped many women to break into mainstream film-making. Sir Richard Attenborough can be moved to tears at the racial discrimination suffered by Gandhi, yet women (black and white) are more likely to be scrubbing studio floors than directing movies, and that doesn't seem to worry anyone. [...]

Whenever women have been given the opportunity, they have proved themselves as competent as their male counterparts and, in many cases, far outshone them. Their exclusion is not only unfair to women, but represents a great loss of talent to the film and television industry.

The lack of female representation in the media also has wider implications. It affects us all – not just those women who would like careers in film and television. The EEC has targeted the media as being instrumental in any campaign against sex discrimination, recognising that television, which is heavily viewed by children and is the main source of news for adults, can shape social attitudes. If a film or television company is a mini sexist society, with women congregated in the lower-paid service and support jobs, how can we expect the image of women produced by it to be anything but sexist? [...]

To sum up, the exclusion of women from many of the key jobs in film and television means that we are denied opportunities for work which is not only challenging, creative and well paid, but which can influence the ways in which women are perceived and view themselves in our society. We are also being shut out from an important means of self-expression and a form of communication which could link women across this and other countries. As it is, children are being shown a one-sided (basically male) view of the part that women play in our society. Women themselves are presented with role models which are very far from reality, which make individuals feel isolated and aberrant when they do not conform to the stereotypes, and which tend to inhibit, rather than stimulate, women's belief in their own strength and capabilities. [...]

So the situation is in the balance. The potential for overcoming discrimination against women in film and television is there. And only when we have complete access to these important media for self-expression and mass communication, when we really share control of the means of production, can we fully establish a 'female gaze' within popular culture and present women's point of view in all its fascinating multiplicity.

Notes

1. S. Benton, 'Patterns of discrimination against women in the film and television industries', *Film and Television Technician*, March 1975.
2. M. Simms, *Women in BBC Management*, London: BBC, 1985.

14.7 **Women Audiences and the Workplace**
Dorothy Hobson

This is a small study, based on a telephone sales office, but it provides another perspective on conceptualising the female audience, and looks at the way women integrate their television viewing with their personal and working relationships.

Television is a part of the everyday life of its audience. The way that women manage their time to fit their viewing into their domestic work has been discussed in many texts, but there is much less information about the way that television comes into discussions outside the home, and particularly in the workplace. This chapter begins to look at the way that a group of women talked about television in their general conversation at work. But it tells much more than that, for in talking about television these women reveal the way that their discussions are wide-ranging and the whole question of the way that women bring their feminine characteristics to their work situation, to augment their jobs, is revealed in their accounts of how they work and at the same time talk about everything. The thesis of this chapter is that women use television programs as part of their general discourse on their own lives, the lives of their families and friends, and to add interest to their working lives. It adds to the critique of audiences as passive viewers by putting forward the hypothesis that it is the discussion after television programs have been viewed which completes the process of communication and locates television programs as part of popular culture.

The article is based on an account which one young woman – Jacqui, who worked as a telephone sales manager for an internationally known pharmaceutical and feminine hygiene company – gave of the way that the women in her office spent their working day, selling, talking and as she terms it 'putting the world to rights'. The women are graphically described in the following comment by Jacqui:

> The eldest was Audrey who was 56, two children, both gone to university, husband has a good job, staying there till she retires, quite quiet, just talks about curtains and things like that, but will contribute to discussions. The youngest person, who is the office junior, is little Tracey, who gets a black eye from her boyfriend every 5 weeks or whatever – 17 and very young in her ways. And then you've got all the ages in between and all the different marital statuses and all the different backgrounds, different cultures and classes which were just mingled together. Which was so nice because it was so different but they all came together in one unit and discussed openly different issues and topics, which were sometimes, but not necessarily triggered off by television.

Although this chapter is based on the account of one telephone sales office, it is part of a larger study of the way that women talk about television in the workplace. Although the amount of talking which can be done differs according to the occupation, there are general features which are similar in many of the accounts which women have given. [...]

It would seem that a documentary did not have to have been seen by everyone for it to become the topic of conversation in the office. One interested viewer could spread the information which would provide the trigger for the whole conversation. The program would work in conjunction with any knowledge or experience other people in the office had about its subject and they would impart their knowledge to the others and the whole subject would become a topic for open discussion and debate. These accounts disprove the theory that watching television is a mindless, passive event in the lives of the viewers. On the contrary, the events and subjects covered in television programs often acted as the catalyst for wide-ranging and open discussions. The communication was extended far beyond the moment of viewing. [...]

It became clear during the course of this interview and our discussions that this working group had used television to its and their best advantage, to advance their understanding of themselves and the world in which they lived. The myth that people who watch television are not using their time to the full is demolished by the range of views which these women expressed and explored through their use of television. The office seemed never to be silent and conversation was the dynamism which fuelled their work and social intercourse. [...]

It is the interweaving of the narratives of fiction with the narratives of their reality that formed the basis for sharing their experiences and opinions and creating their own culture within their workplace.

14.8 Women and Television: an overview
Gillian Dyer

In this Reading Gillian Dyer looks at the growth of feminist television criticism, and at how it can also provide insights into the beliefs and assumptions about women in our society.

Feminist television criticism is an emerging body of work which examines the representation of women on television, women's readings and spectatorship of television and related issues of employment and feminist production practices. It is concerned too with exploring the notion of feminine discourse and feminine pleasures in relation to television. It is being developed by women working within academic disciplines such as Media, Film and Cultural Studies, and by the women's movement and feminist media practitioners. That television is an important source of insights into the beliefs and assumptions about women and their sexuality in contemporary society is axiomatic to this critique. Television provides entertainment and information, and as a discursive practice and producer of cultural meanings it is a major force in the production of dominant images of women. In addition, market research indicates that overall the majority of TV viewers in Western cultures are women.

From its beginnings in the 1960s, the Women's Liberation Movement identified the basic pattern of power that exists in the mass media. Men own and control the media and it is their ideas, viewpoints and values which dominate the systems of production and representation in broadcasting, the press and advertising. This power has not gone unchallenged. Women have reacted against the traditional representations which centre on women's domestic and sexual roles because they are limited and limiting; they undermine the way women think about themselves and also constrain how others think of them. Television, of all the media, seems to offer the most 'real' images, They are readily available, for the initial layout of the cost of a television set and a licence fee – often they appear to be 'live', conforming to 'real time' and are, for the most part, consumed within the domestic environment. But this 'reality' is deceptive. Television does not present innocent, neutral pictures of the world; rather its views are selective, schematic and constructed. The women's movement understands the extent to which our consciousness is shaped by powerful, simplified images and has exerted some pressure on the media, in order to combat cultural stereotyping of women and their experience. Over the past two decades, feminist activity in media practice and in media studies has increased. There have been calls for equal opportunities in employment and a challenge mounted to discredit sexist content. Alternative images have been created which develop and expand women's consciousness of themselves instead of limiting it. The media has had to recognise the criticisms and demands of women. In some cases they have accommodated a women's perspective and women's issues; they have also seen the commercial and ideological potential of creating a new cultural stereotype: the 'new woman'. The 'new woman' has become the new media cliché overtaking the traditional domestic image of the 1950s. [...]

It is perhaps easy to be pessimistic about the representations of women in mainstream television and to wish for a greater and more rapid involvement of women in the industry's creative and decision-making areas. Certainly, the women's movement has exerted pressure from within and without television, so that there is a more conscious and concerted effort to tackle inequality of opportunity and a greater willingness to include women's issues in programmes. Equally important arc those television narratives, some of which embody a feminist critique, which allow some play with conventions and meanings and open up the possibility of feminist readings. Critical writing on soap operas has also shown the polysemic possibilities of women's readings of television, and while the genre is still 'rubbished' (and sneakily watched) by men, the recognition is there that it is an important aspect of women's culture. The rapid expansion in the use of the home video recorder also opens up interesting possibilities for women. The context of viewing is changing and there is potentially a greater choice of texts available. While these have their negative aspects, and by and large women's use of video is circumscribed by the family context, there are possibilities for women to negotiate viewing and control the reception of video. However, the gains in terms of increased recruitment into television and a greater equality and wider variety of representations of women on television must be set against the drawbacks: the spectre of more privatised broadcasting systems and an increasingly timid and retrenched public broadcasting service.

14.9 **Women and Soap Opera**
Christine Geraghty

Christine Geraghty's conclusion offers a summary of the arguments made in this pioneering book. In particular she examines the transformations in prime-time American and British soaps in the last decade, and argues that those changes do offer the possibility of promoting change and influencing attitudes in that they can question gender divisions whilst simultaneously providing pleasure.

These soaps offer a space for women in the TV schedules which not only acknowledges their existence but demonstrates their skills and supports their point of view. At one level, soaps do not treat women homogeneously; they present different aspects of female experience in a way which allows the woman viewer to identify with the emotional dilemmas of female characters who are rarely all good or all bad but who struggle with the demands of their families and communities and with their own high expectations of the value of personal relationships. On the other hand, prime-time soaps, like their daytime counterparts, do present a version of a universal 'female condition' which cuts across age, race and class and allows women to recognise each other across the barriers. It is this essentialism which is both a source of pleasure and a problem in soaps. It allows for reassurance, support, recognition of common problems to be experienced by the woman viewer and provides a challenge to an ideology, expressed on television as elsewhere, which accords women's work in the personal sphere lavish praise but no value. It is also clear, however, that soap's pleasures are based on highly conventional notions of women's skills, their role in the family or community and the notion that they should look for fulfilment, albeit often unsuccessfully, in the personal sphere.

This book has also been concerned to explore the way in which this classical soap position has been subject to change in the eighties, both in terms of the issues which are now being taken up and the way in which they are presented. Prime-time soaps have quite consciously picked up on 'new' issues and centred their stories on women at work, for instance, and on the new-found assertiveness which was deemed to characterise women in the eighties. Such stories set women characters against the grain of more traditional soap concerns and fitted uneasily into the rhythms of the narrative. In addition, issues which could not be labelled as specifically of concern to women such as class, race and age began to provide an impetus for narrative action and programmes as different as *Brookside* and *Dynasty*, at opposite ends of the soap spectrum in terms of aesthetic values, shared a common concern to use class and sexual orientation as the mainspring for key characters and story lines. If I have been critical of the way in which these 'new' issues have been handled, it is because I believe that soap operas have the potential to accommodate change, to make it interesting, acceptable or even desirable, which they have not always used bravely or well. Issues around class, sexuality and race threaten the cosier constructions of the soap community and have therefore been problematic. In addition, the move away from the concentrated examination of the personal sphere has been attempted through the adoption of more conventionally male story lines and generic codes. The breaching of the women's space which soaps provided has let in relatively little fresh air to recompense for the loss of the pleasures traditionally offered to women in the prime-time soaps.

In referring to these pleasures, I have been careful to suggest that they are *offered* to women and that individual viewers may reject the possibilities which others take up and enjoy. In marking a change in the experience of writing about *Coronation Street* in the mid-seventies and in writing about soap opera now, I am conscious of my own ambiguities about the project. What then was a desire to re-evaluate a cultural form which was denigrated, at least in part, because it was associated with women, now runs the risk of celebrating an illusion – the assertion of a common sensibility between women and a set of values sustaining us simply because we are women. In this context even to write 'we' rather than 'they' becomes problematic in its assumptions and smacks of a community of interest which needs to be constructed rather than asserted. As Lynne Segal puts it: 'there has always been a danger that in revaluing our notions of the female and appealing to the experiences of women, we are reinforcing the ideas of sexual polarity which feminism originally aimed to challenge.'[1] It is tempting to read off the essentialism which lurks in the programmes I have been discussing onto the female audience which is assumed 'naturally' to share the values of the personal which soaps endorse. In this context, it is not merely a question of arguing for understanding womanhood as a construction but stressing the importance of understanding that it is a construction which is inhabited differently in ways that are to do with race, class, age and experience as well as gender. The female viewer may welcome the valuing of her competencies and experiences which soaps offer but she may feel uneasy at what she perceives to be her own inadequacies in the personal sphere; she may reject the programmes as too restrictive and limiting or she may relish their more disruptive elements when the traces are broken and women like Sue Ellen, Alexis or Angie refuse to take up their domestic and familial responsibilities. The guilt which women feel about 'their' programmes may be as much to do with their own ambiguity towards the terrain which soaps map out as fear of male mockery.

The space offered women by soaps is thus a contradictory one. It allows 'women's issues' to be worked through and valued but endorses a female viewpoint only because it is so firmly based on the domestic and the personal; it allows its audience actively to enjoy the trials of the patriarch but reasserts the importance of familial relationships as a model for other kinds of love. It is not surprising, then, that the space offered by soaps is often perceived as a ghetto in which poor production values and bad acting give visible proof of the low esteem in which women's programmes are held. This question, 'space or ghetto?', has run through many debates in the women's movement and is central to the notion of revaluing those things which have traditionally been a source of enjoyment for women. Do we accept male judgments on the Mills and Boon romances which so many women enjoy reading, for instance, or do we resist being fobbed off with what is considered second-best, formulaic writing? Are soap operas a space in which women viewers can relax and enjoy their superiority or are they a pen into which women are corralled even if they know they want something better? Such questions are not confined to the cultural arena. In debates on employment, for instance, women have been asking whether women's work is undervalued simply because it is done by women or because it is tedious, boring, hard? Soaps, perhaps more than any other fictional form available to women, stress the relationship between text and reader; their constructions are dependent on the audience to fulfil their possibilities. In the end, then, the programmes cannot answer the questions posed because they are potentially both a space and a ghetto. Soaps' capacity both to engage and distance the viewer, to involve us in a story and allow us to stand back and make judgments on its implications, means that the pleasure and use got from them depends on the viewer. The position of women is endorsed in the programmes but the space also allows for it to be dissected, exposed, celebrated, disrupted and escaped from in a neverending set of narrative puzzles. In these possibilities lie soaps' strengths. It will be up to the reader to judge whether they survive into the nineties.

Note

1. L. Segal, *Is The Future Female?: Troubled thoughts on contemporary feminism*, London: Virago, 1987, p. xii.

Further Reading

Chester, G. and Dickey J. (1988), *Feminism and Censorship: The current debate*, London: Prism Press.

Chapman, R. and Rutherford, J. (eds), (1988), *Male Order: Unwrapping masculinity*, London: Lawrence & Wishart.

Dyer, R. (1986), *Heavenly Bodies*, London: British Film Institute/Macmillan.

Ecker, G. (ed.) (1985), *Feminist Aesthetics*, London: The Women' Press.

Gledhill, C. (ed.) (1987), *Home is Where the Heart Is: Studies in melodrama and the woman's film*, London: British Film Institute.

Holdsworth, A. (1988), *Out of the Doll's House: The Story of Women in the Twentieth Century*, London: BBC Books.

hooks, b. (1981), *Ain't I a Woman?: Black women and feminism*, London: Pluto.

Kaplan, E. A. (1983), *Women and Film: Both sides of the camera*, London and New York: Methuen.

Mattelart, M. (1986), *Women, Media, Crisis: Femininity and disorder*, London: Comedia.

Murphy, G. (1987), 'Media influence on the socialization of teenage girls', in J. Curran *et al.*, *Impacts and Influences: Essays on media power in the twentieth century*, London: Methuen.

Root, J. (1984), *Pictures of Women: Sexuality*, London: Pandora.

Segal, L. (1990), *Slow Motion: Changing masculinities, changing men*, London: Virago.

NOTES ON CONTRIBUTORS

All the editors have taught at the University of Glamorgan and contributed to the planning of the University's BA in Women's Studies.

Stevi Jackson was Principal Lecturer in Sociology at the University of Glamorgan until December 1992, when she took up her present post as Lecturer in Sociology and co-ordinator of the M.Litt Women's Studies at the University of Strathclyde. She is the author of *Childhood and Sexuality* (Blackwell, 1982) and *Family Lives: A feminist sociology* (Blackwell, forthcoming). She is co-author, with Deirdre Beddoe and Pauline Young, of *Imagined Freedoms: Women and popular fiction in the twentieth century*, to be published by Harvester Wheatsheaf. She is also working on a book on Christine Delphy, to be published in the Sage series 'Women of Ideas'.

Karen Atkinson has taught sociolinguistics at Roehampton Institute, at Carmarthen Institute and at the University of Glamorgan. She is writing a book on Language, Women and Old Age to be published by Longman, and is also conducting research on the language of friendship.

Deirdre Beddoe is Professor of Women's History at the University of Glamorgan. Her books include *Welsh Convict Women* (Stewart Williams, 1979), *Discovering Women's History*, and *Back to Home and Duty: Women between the wars*, both published by Pandora. She is co-editor, with Leigh Verrill-Rhys, of *Parachutes and Petticoats: Welsh women writing on the Second World War* (Honno, 1992) and co-author, with Stevi Jackson and Pauline Young, of *Imagined Freedoms*.

Teri Brewer is Senior Lecturer in Anthropology at the University of Glamorgan. She has just completed research on the May Day rites in Oxford, and is co-editing for publication, with J. Baillie, the diary of George Pawley, eighteenth-century emissary to the Cherokee.

Sue Faulkner is Lecturer in Psychology at the University of Glamorgan. Her research interests include stress and illness, women's health and motherhood.

Anthea Hucklesby is a Research Assistant in the Department of Law and Finance at the University of Glamorgan, working on remand decisions in magistrates' courts. Her other research interests are women and crime, and the criminal justice system.

Rose Pearson is Senior Lecturer in Sociology at the University of Glamorgan. Her main research interests are in sociolegal studies, and she has published a number of papers on women and magistrates' courts. She has also been conducting research on the social consequences of nuclear power.

Helen Power is Senior Lecturer in Law at the University of Glamorgan. She has published papers on corporate crime, and on the 1984–5 miners' strike.

Jane Prince is Senior Lecturer in Psychology at the University of Glamorgan. She is currently researching the experience of women working in male-gendered occupations, and is co-authoring, with Steve Hammett, a book on the ideological context and content of mainstream psychology.

Michele Ryan until recently taught Media and Gender Studies at the University of Glamorgan. She was a founder member of 'Red Flannel', the Welsh women's film collective, and is now a freelance TV director/producer. Her films include *Mary Shelley, Maker of Monsters*; *Milena Jesenska, The Art of Standing Still*; *Thursday's Child*; *Mam*; *Women Have No Country*. She is co-author with Helen Baehr of *Shut Up and Listen! Women and Local Radio* (Comedia, 1985).

Pauline Young is Senior Lecturer in Women's Studies at the University of Glamorgan, where she is course leader of the Women's Studies degree. She also teaches English and Theatre Studies and has published a number of papers and articles on women's writing. She is co-author, with Deirdre Beddoe and Steri Jackson, of *Imagined Freedoms*.

LIST OF SOURCES

The Readings are taken from the following sources:

Section 1   Feminist Social Theory

1.1   from Shulamith Firestone (1972) *The Dialectic of Sex*, London: Paladin, pp. 16–17, 19–20.
1.2   from Juliet Mitchell (1976) *Psychoanalysis and Feminism*, Harmondsworth: Pelican, pp. 372–3, 403, 408–9, 414.
1.3   from Michèle Barrett (1980/1988) *Women's Oppression Today*, London: Verso, pp. 248–51; p. xiii (1988 edn).
1.4   from Heidi Hartmann et al. (1981) *The Unhappy Marriage of Marxism and Feminism*, London: Pluto, pp. 10–11, 18–19, 22–3, 25.
1.5   from Christine Delphy (1984) *Close to Home*, London: Hutchinson, pp. 25–6.
1.6   from Sylvia Walby (1990) *Theorizing Patriarchy*, Oxford: Basil Blackwell, pp. 23–4.
1.7   from Parveen Adams, Rosalind Coward and Elizabeth Cowie (1987), Editorial, *m/f*, no. 1, p. 5.
1.8   from Jane Flax (1987) 'Postmodernism and gender relations in feminist theory', *Signs*, vol. 12, no. 4, pp. 623, 630–1; reprinted in L. Nicholson (ed.) (1990) *Feminism/Postmodernism*, London: Routledge, pp. 40–1, 48–9.
1.9   from Luce Irigaray (1991) 'Women: equal or different?', in M. Whitford (ed.), *The Irigaray Reader*, Oxford: Basil Blackwell, pp. 32–3.
1.10 from Monique Wittig (1992) 'One is not born a woman', in *The Straight Mind and Other Essays*, Hemel Hempstead: Harvester Wheatsheaf, pp. 11–12, 13, 14, 15–16, 20.
1.11 from Hazel Carby (1982) 'White woman listen! Black feminism and the boundaries of sisterhood', in Centre for Contemporary Studies, *The Empire Strikes Back: Race and racism in 70s Britain*, London: Hutchinson, pp. 212–15, 232–3.

1.12 from Denise Riley (1988) *Am I That Name?*, London: Macmillan, pp. 1–2.
1.13 from Tania Modleski (1991) *Feminism Without Women*, London: Routledge, 1991, pp. 20–2.
1.14 from Liz Stanley (1990) 'Recovering "women" in history from historical deconstructionism', *Women's Studies International Forum*, vol. 13, nos 1/2, pp. 153–5.
1.15 from Avtar Brah (1992) 'Questions of difference and international feminism', in J. Aaron and S. Walby (eds), *Out of the Margins*, London: Falmer, pp. 168–76.

Section 2   Women's Minds

2.1   from Jean Grimshaw (1988) 'Autonomy and identity in feminist thinking', in M. Griffiths and M. Whitford (eds), *Feminist Perspectives in Philosophy*, London: Macmillan, pp. 98–101.
2.2   from Wendy Hollway (1989) *Subjectivity and Method in Psychology*, London: Sage, pp. 111–18.
2.3   from Corinne Squire (1989) *Significant Differences: Feminism in psychology*, London: Routledge, pp. 80–3.
2.4   from Valerie Walkerdine (1990) 'Femininity as performance', in *Schoolgirl Fictions*, London: Verso, pp. 134–9.
2.5   from Nancy Chodorow (1974) 'Family structure and feminine personality', in M. Z. Rosaldo and L. Lamphere (eds), *Women, Culture and Society*, Stanford, CA: Stanford University Press, pp. 49–66.
2.6   from Kate Millett (1971) *Sexual Politics*, London: Rupert Hart-Davis, pp. 177–8, 179–81, 187.
2.7   from Juliet Mitchell (1974) *Psychoanalysis and Feminism*, London: Allen Lane, pp. 8–13.
2.8   from Jacqueline Rose (1982) 'Introduction II' to J. Mitchell and J. Rose (eds), *Feminine Sexuality: Jacques Lacan and the École Freudienne*, London: Macmillan, pp. 44–9.
2.9   from David Macey (1988) *Lacan in Contexts*, London: Verso, pp. 12–13.

Section 3   Cross-Cultural Perspectives on Women's Lives

3.1   from Margaret Mead (1949) 'Human fatherhood is a social invention', in *Male and Female*, New York: William Morrow, pp. 177–8.
3.2   from Edward Evans-Pritchard (1965) 'The position of women in primitive societies and in our own', in *The Position of Women in Primitive Societies and Other Essays in Social Anthropology*, London: Faber & Faber, pp. 37–57.
3.3   from Sherry Ortner (1974) 'Is female to male as nature is to culture?', in M. Z. Rosaldo and L. Lamphere (eds), *Women, Culture and Society*, Stanford, CA: Stanford University Press, pp. 67–87.

3.4   from Carol McCormick (1980) 'Nature, culture and gender: a critique', in C. McCormick and M. Strathern, *Nature, Culture and Gender*, Cambridge: Cambridge University Press, pp. 16–21.

3.5   from Peggy Reeves Sanday (1981) *Female Power and Male Dominance: On the origins of sexual inequality*, Cambridge: Cambridge University Press, pp. 163–83.

3.6   from Michelle Rosaldo (1980) 'The use and abuse of anthropology: reflections on feminism and cross-cultural understanding', *Signs*, vol. 5, no. 3, pp. 389–417.

3.7   from Henrietta Moore (1988) *Feminism and Anthropology*, Cambridge: Polity, pp. 192–5.

3.8   from Akemi Kikumura (1981) 'Childhood (1904–1922)', in *Through Harsh Winters: The life of a Japanese immigrant woman*, Novato, CA: Chandler & Sharp, pp. 15–19.

3.9   from Barbara Myerhoff (1978) 'Jewish comes up in you from the roots', in *Number Our Days*, New York: E. P. Dutton, pp. 240–5.

3.10 from Lila Abu-Lughod (1990) 'The romance of resistance: tracing transformations of power through Bedouin women', in P. Sanday and R. Goodenough (eds), *Beyond the Second Sex: New directions in the anthropology of gender'*, Pittsburgh, PA: University of Pennsylvania Press, pp. 313–31.

Section 4   Historical Perspectives on Women's Lives

4.1   from Ivy Pinchbeck (1930/1981) *Women Workers and the Industrial Revolution 1750–1850*, London: Virago, pp. 8–10.

4.2   from Catherine Hall (1981) 'Gender divisions and class formation in the Birmingham middle class, 1780–1850', in R. Samuel (ed.), *People's History and Socialist Theory*, London: Routledge & Kegan Paul, pp. 168–70.

4.3   from Sheila Rowbotham (1973) *Hidden from History: Three hundred years of women's oppression and the fight against it*, London: Pluto, pp. 55–6.

4.4   from Angela V. John (1980) *By the Sweat of their Brow: Women workers at Victorian coal mines*, London: Croom Helm, pp. 85–6.

4.5   from Anna Davin (1979) '"Mind that you do as you are told": reading books for Board School girls, 1870–1902', *Feminist Review*, no. 3, pp. 89–92.

4.6   from Margery Spring-Rice (1939/1981) *Working-Class Wives*, London: Virago, pp. 96–100.

4.7   from Jane Lewis (1980) *The Politics of Motherhood: Child and maternal welfare in England, 1900–1939*, London: Croom Helm, pp. 15–16.

4.8   from Deirdre Beddoe (1989) *Back to Home and Duty: Women between the wars 1918–1939*, London: Pandora, pp. 50–2.

4.9   from Ray Strachey (1928/1984) *The Cause*, London: Virago, pp. 307–11.

4.10 from Sylvia Pankhurst (1931/1984) *The Suffragette Movement*, London: Virago, pp. 607–8.

4.11 from Sheila Jeffreys (1985) *The Spinster and Her Enemies: Feminism and sexuality 1880–1930*, London: Pandora, pp. 105–6.

Section 5   Women, Education and Work

5.1   from Veronica Beechey (1987) *Unequal Work*, London: Verso, pp. 139–43.
5.2   from Michèle Barrett (1988) *Women's Oppression Today*, London: Verso, pp. 131–4.
5.3   from Lindsay German (1989) *Sex, Class and Socialism*, London: Bookmarks, pp. 70–5.
5.4   from Geoffrey de Ste Croix (1981) *The Class Struggle in the Ancient Greek World*, London: Duckworth, pp. 98–101.
5.5   from Valerie Walkerdine (1988) *The Mastery of Reason*, London: Routledge, pp. 56–9.
5.6   from Robert Hodge and Gunther Kress (1988) *Social Semiotics*, Oxford: Polity, pp. 245–9.
5.7   from John McCauley (1987) 'Academics', in D. Podmore and A. Spencer (eds), *In a Man's World*, London: Tavistock, pp. 165–70.
5.8   from Judi Marshall (1984) *Women Managers: Travellers in a male world*, Chichester: Wiley, pp. 211, 220–1.
5.9   from Nigel Fielding (1988) *Joining Forces*, London: Routledge, pp. 161–5.
5.10 from Marny Hall (1989) 'Private experiences in the public domain: lesbians in organizations', in J. Hearn *et al.*, *The Sexuality of Organizations*, London: Sage, pp. 129–32, 135–8.
5.11 from Heidi Mirza (1992) *Young, Female and Black*, London: Routledge, pp. 160–5.

Section 6   Marriage and Motherhood

6.1   from Sallie Westwood (1984) *All Day, Every Day: Factory and family in women's lives*, London: Pluto, pp. 163-9.
6.2   from Sylvia Walby (1992) *Patriarchy at Work*, Oxford: Polity, pp. 52–4.
6.3   from Nickie Charles and Marion Kerr (1989) *Women, Food and Families*, Manchester: Manchester University Press, pp. 68–76.
6.4   from Penny Mansfield and Jean Collard (1988) *The Beginning of the Rest of Your Life: A portrait of newlywed marriage*, London: Macmillan, pp. 172–9, 191–2.
6.5   from Haleh Afshar (1989) 'Gender rules and the "moral economy of kin" among Pakistani women in West Yorkshire', *New Community*, vol. 15, no. 2, pp. 216–17.

6.6 from Michele Bograd (1988) 'What are feminist perspectives on wife abuse?', from Introduction to K. Ÿllö and M. Bograd (eds), *Feminist Perspectives on Wife Abuse*, Beverly Hills, CA: Sage, pp. 13–15.

6.7 from Ann Oakley (1979) *Becoming a Mother*, Oxford: Martin Robertson, pp. 10–12, 59–62.

6.8 from Ann Oakley (1984) *Taking It Like a Woman*, London: Fontana, pp. 67–9, 72.

6.9 from Sheila Rowbotham (1981) 'To be or not to be: the dilemma of mothering', *Feminist Review*, no. 39, pp. 82–91.

6.10 from Julia Brannen and Peter Moss (1991) *Managing Mothers: Dual earner households after maternity leave*, London: Unwin Hyman, pp. 92–4, 97, 101, 107, 109, 111.

6.11 from Ann Phoenix (1988) 'Narrow definitions of culture: the case of early motherhood', in S. Westwood and P. Bachu (eds), *Enterprising Women*, London: Routledge, pp. 158–60, 162–3, 164–5, 169.

6.12 from Julia Berryman (1991) 'Perspectives on later motherhood', in A. Phoenix, A. Woollet and E. Lloyd (eds), *Motherhood: Meanings, practices and ideologies*, London: Sage, pp. 117–19.

6.13 from Anne Woollet and Ann Phoenix (1991) 'Afterword', in A. Phoenix, A. Woollet and E. Lloyd (eds), *Motherhood: Meanings, practices and ideologies*, London: Sage, pp. 216–17, 226.

6.14 from Lynne Harne (1984) 'Lesbian custody and the new myth of the father', *Trouble and Strife*, no. 3, pp. 12–14.

6.15 from Gemma Tang Nain (1991) 'Black women, sexism and racism: black or anti-racist feminism', *Feminist Review*, no. 37, pp. 9–10.

Section 7 Sexuality

7.1 from Sandra Bartky (1990) 'Foucault, femininity and the modernisation of patriarchal power', in *Femininity and Domination*, London: Routledge, pp. 72–81.

7.2 from Luce Irigaray (1985) *This Sex Which Is Not One*, Ithaca, NY: Cornell University Press, p. 23.

7.3 from Diane Richardson (1989) 'The challenge of AIDS', in *Women and the AIDS Crisis*, London: Pandora, pp. 174–9.

7.4 from Diane Scully (1990) *Understanding Sexual Violence. A study of convicted rapists*, London: Unwin Hyman, pp. 142–50.

7.5 from Patricia Collins (1990) *Black Feminist Thought*, London: Unwin Hyman, pp. 168–73.

7.6 from Rosemary Pringle (1989) 'Bureaucracy, rationality and sexuality: the case of secretaries', in J. Hearn *et al.*, *The Sexuality of Organizations*, London: Sage, pp. 164–77.

7.7 from Susan Ardill and Sue O'Sullivan (1986) 'Upsetting an applecart: difference, desire and sadomasochism', *Feminist Review*, no. 23, pp. 40–1, 52–3.

7.8 from Sheila Jeffreys (1991) *Anticlimax*, London: The Women's Press, pp. 299, 301, 312–16.

7.9 from bell hooks (1984) 'Ending female sexual oppression', in *Feminist Theory: From margin to centre*, Boston, MA: South End Press, p. 152.

7.10 from Deborah Cameron (1990) 'Ten years on: compulsory heterosexuality and lesbian existence', *Women: A Cultural Review*, vol. 1, no. 1, pp. 35–7.

Section 8   Women and the Law

8.1 from Albie Sachs and Joan Hoff Wilson (1978) *Sexism and the Law*, Oxford: Martin Robertson, pp. 40–53.

8.2 from Susan Edwards (1981) *Female Sexuality and the Law*, Oxford: Martin Robertson, pp. 17–18, 172–4.

8.3 from Katherine O'Donovan (1985) *Sexual Divisions in Law*, London: Weidenfeld & Nicolson, 1985, pp. 2–20.

8.4 from Catharine MacKinnon (1987) 'On collaboration' in *Feminism Unmodified: Discussions on life and law*, Cambridge, MA: Harvard University Press, 1987, pp. 198–205.

8.5 from Wendy Moore (1988) 'There should be a law against it … shouldn't there?', in *Feminism and Censorship*, Dorset: Prism Press, pp. 141–3; 148–50.

8.6 from Gillian Rodgers and Elizabeth Wilson (eds) (1991) *Pornography and Feminism: The case against censorship*, London: Lawrence & Wishart, pp. 9–10, 25–9.

8.7 from Carol Smart (1989) *Feminism and the Power of Law*, London: Routledge, pp. 20–5, 80–9.

Section 9   Women, Crime and Deviance

9.1 from Frances Heidensohn (1989) *Crime and Society*, London: Macmillan, pp. 87–8.

9.2 from Frances Heidensohn (1985) *Women and Crime*, London: Macmillan, pp. 141–4.

9.3 from Pat Carlen (1990) 'Women, crime, feminism and reason', *Social Justice*, vol. 17, no. 4, pp. 107–8.

9.4 from Jeanne Gregory (1986) 'Sex, class and crime', in R. Matthews and J. Young (eds), *Confronting Crime*, London: Sage, pp. 57–8.

9.5 from Pat Carlen (1992) 'Criminal women and criminal justice: the limits to, and potential of, feminist and left realist perspectives', in R. Matthews and J. Young (eds), *Issues in Realist Criminology*, London: Sage, pp. 53–4.

9.6 from Jeanne Gregory (1986) 'Sex, class and crime', in R. Matthews and J. Young (eds), *Confronting Crime*, London: Sage, pp. 65–6.

9.7   From Kathryn Chadwick and Catherine Little (1987) 'The criminalization of women', in P. Scraton (ed.), *Law, Order and the Authoritarian State*, Milton Keynes: Open University Press, pp. 255–60, 271–2.

9.8   from Frances Heidensohn (1985) *Women and Crime*, London: Macmillan, pp. 194–200.

9.9   from Pat Carlen (1992) 'Criminal women and criminal justice: the limits to, and potential of, feminist and left realist perspectives', in R. Matthews and J. Young (eds), *Issues in Realist Criminology*, London: Sage, pp. 55–8.

9.10   from Jeanne Gregory (1986) 'Sex, class and crime', in R. Matthews and J. Young (eds), *Confronting Crime*, Milton Keynes: Open University Press, pp. 66–8.

Section 10   Public/Private

10.1   from Margaret Stacey and Marion Price (1981) 'Given the odds, a great advance', in *Women, Power and Politics*, London: Tavistock, pp. 187–9.

10.2   from Susan Edwards (1989) 'Policing: the under-representation of women's interests', in *Policing 'Domestic' Violence: women, the law and the state*, London: Sage, pp. 31–3.

10.3   from Margery Wolf (1985) 'The birth limitation program: family vs state', in *Revolution Postponed: Women in contemporary China*, London: Methuen, pp. 257–9.

10.4   from Peter Squires (1990) *Anti-Social Policy: Welfare, ideology and the disciplinary state*, Hemel Hempstead: Harvester Wheatsheaf, pp. 162–4.

10.5   from Jill Evans, Clare Hudson and Penny Smith (1985) 'Women and the strike: it's a whole way of life', in B. Fine and R. Millar (eds), *Policing the Miners' Strike*, London: Lawrence & Wishart, pp. 188–92.

10.6   from Alison Young (1990) *Femininity in Dissent*, London: Routledge, pp. 34–40.

Section 11   Science, Medicine and Reproductive Technology

11.1   from Anne Fausto-Sterling (1989) 'Life in the XY Corral', *Women's Studies International Forum*, vol. 12, no. 3, pp. 319–31 (pp. 326, 327–9).

11.2   from Ruth Herschberger (1948/1970) 'Society writes biology', in *Adam's Rib*, New York: Harper & Row, pp. 71–2, 79–83, 84–7.

11.3   from Ludmilla Jordanova (1989) 'Natural facts: an historical perspective on science and sexuality', in *Sexual Visions: Images of gender in science and medicine between the eighteenth and twentieth centuries*, Hemel Hempstead: Harvester Wheatsheaf, pp. 19–20, 21–2, 23–4, 41–2.

11.4   from Elaine Showalter (1987) 'Managing female minds', in *The Female Malady*, London: Virago, pp. 81–4.

11.5   from Emily Martin (1989) *The Woman in the Body*, Milton Keynes: Open University Press, pp. 35, 40–1.

11.6   from Sophie Laws (1985) 'Who needs PMT?', in S. Laws, V. Hey and A. Egan, *Seeing Red: The politics of premenstrual tension*, London: Hutchinson, pp. 18, 19, 20, 22–3, 24, 57, 58.

11.7   from Frances Evans (1985) 'Managers and labourers: women's attitudes to reproductive technology', in W. Faulkner and E. Arnold (eds), *Smothered by Invention: technology in women's lives*, London: Pluto, pp. 110, 111, 112–13, 119, 120.

11.8   from Gena Corea (1985) 'The reproductive brothel', in G. Corea *et al.*, *Man-Made Women: How new reproductive technologies affect women*, London: Hutchinson, pp. 45–9.

11.9   from Jana Sawicki (1991) 'Disciplining mothers: feminism and the new reproductive technologies', in *Disciplining Foucault*, London: Routledge, pp. 83–5.

11.10 from Christine Delphy (1992) 'New reproductive technologies', in 'Mothers' union', *Trouble and Strife*, no. 24, pp. 13–15.

Section 12   Language and Gender

12.1   from Dale Spender (1985) 'Language and reality: who made the world?', in *Man Made Language*, London: Routledge & Kegan Paul, pp. 138–62.

12.2   from Susan Ehrlich and Ruth King (1992) 'Gender-based language reform and the social construction of meaning', *Discourse and Society*, vol. 3, no. 2, pp. 151–7.

12.3   from Robin Lakoff (1975) *Language and Woman's Place*, New York: Harper Colophon, pp. 7, 14–17, 53–4.

12.4   from Nancy M. Henley and Cheris Kramarae (1991) 'Gender, power and miscommunication', in N. Coupland, H. Giles and J. Wiemann (eds), *Miscommunication and Problematic Talk*, Newbury Park, CA: Sage, pp. 21–3.

12.5   from Deborah Cameron, Fiona McAlinden and Kathy O'Leary (1989) 'Lakoff in context: the social and linguistic functions of tag questions', in J. Coates and D. Cameron (eds), *Women in Their Speech Communities*, New York: Longman, pp. 80–6.

12.6   from Jennifer Coates (1989) 'Gossip revisited', in J. Coates and D. Cameron (eds), *Women in Their Speech Communities*, New York: Longman, pp. 113–19.

Section 13   Feminist Literary Criticism

13.1   from Simone de Beauvoir (1953/1972) *The Second Sex*, Harmondsworth: Penguin, pp. 15–16.

13.2   from Kate Millett (1970) *Sexual Politics*, London: Virago, pp. 127–9.

13.3   from Sandra Gilbert and Susan Gubar (1979) *The Madwoman in the Attic*, New Haven, CT: Yale University Press, pp. 46–51.

13.4   from Adrienne Rich (1979) *On Lies, Secrets and Silences*, New York: W. W. Norton, pp. 188–90.

13.5   from Tillie Olsen (1980) *Silences*, London: Virago, pp. 38–9.

13.6   from Elaine Showalter (1978) *A Literature of Their Own*, London: Virago, 1978, pp. 6–9.

13.7   from Annis Pratt (1982) *Archetypal Patterns in Women's Fiction*, Sussex: Harvester, pp. 42–6.

13.8   from Ann Rosalind Jones (1986) 'Writing the body: towards an understanding of *l'écriture féminine*', in E. Showalter (ed.), *The New Feminist Criticism: Essays on women, literature and theory*, London: Virago, pp. 362–7.

13.9   from Barbara Smith (1985) 'Toward a black feminist criticism', in J. Newton and D. Rosenfelt (eds), *Feminism and Social Change*, London: Methuen, pp. 8–15.

13.10   from Maggie Humm (1990) *Feminist Criticism*, Hemel Hempstead: Harvester Wheatsheaf, pp. 105–6.

13.11   from Patricia Waugh (1989) *Feminine Fictions: Revisiting the postmodern*, London: Routledge, pp. 6–22.

Section 14   Representations of Women in the Media

14.1   from E. Deidre Pribram (1988) *Female Spectators*, London: Verso, pp. 1–5.

14.2   from Janice Radway (1987) *Reading the Romance*, London: Verso, pp. 5–14.

14.3   from Susanne Kappeler (1986) The Pornography of *Representation*, Cambridge: Polity, pp. 2–4.

14.4   from Annette Kuhn (1985) 'The big sleep', in *The Power of the Image*, London: Routledge & Kegan Paul, pp. 2–8.

14.5   from Jeanette Murphy (1986) '"A Question of Silence"', in C. Brunsdon (ed.), *Films for Women*, London: British Film Institute, pp. 99–101.

14.6   from Anne Ross Muir (1988) 'The status of women working in film and television', in L. Gannon and M. Marshment (eds), *The Female Gaze*, London: The Women's Press, pp. 143–52.

14.7   from Dorothy Hobson (1990) 'Women audiences and the workplace', in M. E. Brown (ed.), *Television and Women's Culture*, London: Sage, pp. 61–71.

14.8   from Gillian Dyer (1987) 'Women and television', in H. Baehr and G. Dyer (eds), *Boxed In: Women and television*, London: Pandora, pp. 6–15.

14.9   from Christine Geraghty (1991) *Women and Soap Opera*, Cambridge: Polity, pp. 195–8.

ACKNOWLEDGEMENTS

The editors and publishers acknowledge with thanks permission granted to reproduce in this volume the following material previously published elsewhere. Every effort has been made to trace copyright holders, but if any have been inadvertently overlooked the publishers will be pleased to make the necessary arrangement at the first opportunity.

From Shulamith Firestone, *The Dialectic of Sex*, Jonathan Cape and William Morrow Co., Inc. Copyright © 1970 by Shulamith Firestone. By permission of Laurence Pollinger Ltd and William Morrow Co., Inc. From Juliet Mitchell, *Psychoanalysis and Feminism*. Copyright © 1974 by Juliet Mitchell. Reprinted by permission of Penguin Books Ltd. and Pantheon Books, a division of Random House, Inc. From Michèle Barrett, *Women's Oppression Today* (Verso/NLB, London and New York, 1988). Reprinted by permission of Verso. From Heidi Hartmann, *The Unhappy Marriage of Marxism and Feminism* (1981). By permission of the author. From Christine Delphy, 'Sex classes', in *Close to Home* (1984). By permission of Hutchinson. From Sylvia Walby, 'Forms and Degrees of Patriarchy', in *Theorizing Patriarchy* (1990). By permission of Blackwell Publishers. From Parveen Adams, Rosalind Coward and Elizabeth Cowie, Editorial, *m/f*, (Verso, NLB, London and New York, 1987) no. 1, p. 5. Reprinted by permission of the authors and Verso. From Jane Flax, 'Postmodernism and gender relations in feminist theory', in *Signs*, vol. 12, no. 4 (1987). Reprinted by permission of the author and the University of Chicago Press. From Luce Irigaray, 'Women: equal or different', translated by David Macey, in M. Whitford (ed.), *The Irigaray Reader*. Copyright © 1991 by David Macey, and reprinted by kind permission. From Monique Wittig, 'One is not born a woman', in *The Straight Mind and Other Essays* (1992), Harvester Wheatsheaf and Beacon Press. From Hazel Carby, 'White Woman listen! Black feminism and the boundaries of sisterhood,' in Centre for Contemporary Cultural Studies, *The Empire Strikes Back: Race and racism in 70s Britain* (1982). Reprinted by permission of Hutchinson. From Denise Riley, *Am I That Name?* (1988). Reprinted by permission of the Macmillan Press Ltd., and the University of Minnesota Press. Extract from *Feminism Without Women* by Tania Modleski, 1991, appears by courtesy of the publisher, Routledge, New York, and the author. From Liz Stanley, 'Recovering 'women' in history from historical deconstructionism', in *Women's Studies International Forum* (1990). By permission of Pergamon Press. From Avtar Brah, 'Questions of difference and international feminism', in J. Aaron and S. Walby (eds), *Out of the Margins* (1992). Reprinted by kind permission of the author, editors and Falmer Press Ltd. From Jean Grimshaw, 'Autonomy and identity in feminist thinking', in M. Griffiths and M. Whitford (eds) *Feminist Perspectives in Philosophy* (1988). By permission of the Macmillan Press Ltd. and Indiana University Press. Reprinted with permission from Wendy Hollway, 'Male mind and female nature', in *Subjectivity and Method in Psychology* (1989), Sage Publications Ltd. From Corinne Squire, *Significant Differences: Feminism in psychology* (1989). By permission of Routledge. From Valerie Walkerdine, 'Femininity as performance', in *Schoolgirl Fictions* (Verso/NLB, London and New York, 1990) pp. 134–9. By permission of Verso. From Nancy Chodorow, 'Family structure and feminine personality', and from Sherry Ortner, 'Is female to male as nature is to culture?', excerpted from *Woman, Culture and Society*, edited by Michelle Zimbalist Rosaldo and Louise Lamphere with the permission of the publishers, Stanford University Press. © 1974 by the Board of Trustees of the Leland Stanford Junior University. From *Sexual Politics* by Kate Millett. Copyright © 1969, 1970, 1990 by Kate Millett. Reprinted by permission of Georges Borchardt, Inc. for the author. From Jacqueline Rose, 'Introduction II' to *Feminine Sexuality: Jacques Lacan and the Ecole Freudienne* (1982), edited by Juliet Mitchell and Jacqueline Rose and translated by Jacqueline Rose. Reprinted by permission of the Macmillan Press Ltd. and Pantheon Books, a division of Random House, Inc. From David Macey, *Lacan in Contexts* (Verso/NLB, London and New York, 1988). By permission of Verso. From Margaret Mead, *Male and Female*. Copyright © 1946, 1967 by Margaret Mead. By permission of William Morrow & Company, Inc. From Edward Evans-Pritchard, *The Position of Women in Primitive Societies and Other Essays in Social Anthropology* (1965). By permission of Faber and Faber Ltd. From Carol McCormick, 'Nature, culture and gender: a critique', in C. McCormick and M. Strathern, *Nature, Culture and Gender* (1980). By permission of Cambridge University Press. From Peggy Reeves Sanday, *Female Power and Male Dominance: On the origins of sexual inequality* (1981). By permission of Cambridge University Press. From Michelle Rosaldo, 'The use and abuse of anthropology: reflections on feminism and cross-cultural understanding', in *Signs*, vol. 5, no. 3 (1980). By permission of the University of Chicago Press. From Henrietta Moore, *Feminism and Anthropology* (1988). By permission of Blackwell Publishers. Reprinted by permission of the publisher from *Through Harsh Winters: The Life of a Japanese Immigrant Woman* by Akemi Kikumura. Copyright © 1981 by Chandler & Sharp Publishers, Novato, CA, USA. All rights reserved. From *Number our Days* by Barbara Myerhoff. Copyright © 1978 by Barbara Myerhoff. Used by permission of the publisher, Dutton, an imprint of New American Library, a division of Penguin Books USA Inc. From Lila Abu-Lughod 'The romance of resistance: tracing transformations of power through Bedouin women'. Reproduced by permission of the American Anthropological Association from *American Ethnologist*, 17:1, February 1990. Not for further reproduction. From Ivy Pinchbeck, *Women Workers and the Industrial Revolution, 1750–1850* (1930/1981). From Catherine Hall, 'Gender Divisions and class formation in the Birmingham middle class, 1780–1850', in R. Samuel (ed.), *People's History and Socialist Theory* (1981). By permission of Routledge. From Sheila Rowbotham, *Hidden from History: 300 years of women's oppression and the fight against it* (1973). By permission of Pluto Press. From Angela V. John, *By the Sweat of their Brow* (1980). By permission of Croom Helm. From Anna Davin, '"Mind that you do as you are told": reading books for board school girls, 1870–1902', *Feminist Review*, no. 3, (1979). By permission of the author. From Margery Spring-Rice, *Working-Class Wives* (1939/1981). By permission of Virago Press and the author. From Jane Lewis, *The Politics of Motherhood: Child and maternal welfare in England, 1900–1939* (1980). By permission of Croom Helm. From Deirdre Beddoe, *Back to Home and Duty: Women between the Wars 1918–1939* (1989). By permission of Pandora, an imprint of HarperCollins Publishers Limited. From Ray Strachey, *The Cause* (1928/1984). By permission of Virago Press and the estate of Ray Strachey. From Sylvia Pankhurst, *The Suffragette Movement* (1931/1984). By permission of Virago Press. From Sheila Jeffreys, *The Spinster and her Enemies* (1985). By permission of Pandora, an imprint of HarperCollins Publishers Limited. From Veronica Beechey, *Unequal Work* (Verso/NLB, London and New York, 1987) pp. 139–43. By permission of Verso. From Lindsay German, *Sex, Class and Socialism* (1989). By permission of Bookmarks. From Geoffrey de Ste. Croix, *The Class Struggle in the Ancient Greek World* (1981). By permission of Duckworth. From Valerie Walkerdine, *The Mastery of Reason* (1988). By permission of Routledge. From Robert Hodge and Gunther Kress, *Social Semiotics* (1988). By permission of Blackwell Publishers. From John McCauley, 'Academics', in D. Podmore and A. Spencer (eds), *In a Man's World* (1987). By permission of Tavistock Publications. From Judi Marshall, *Women Managers: Travellers in a male world*. Copyright © 1984 by Judi Marshall. Reproduced by permission of John Wiley and Sons Limited. From Nigel Fielding, *Joining Forces* (1988). By permission of Routledge. Reprinted with permission from Marny Hall, 'Private experiences in the public domain: lesbians in organizations', in J. Hearn *et al.*, *The Sexuality of Organizations* (1989), Sage Publications Ltd. From Heidi Mirza, *Young, Female and Black* (1992). By permission of Routledge. From Sallie Westwood, 'Domestic labourers, or stand by your man – while he sits down and has a cup of tea', in *All Day, Every Day: Factory and Family in women's lives* (1984). By permission of Pluto Press. From Sylvia Walby, 'The elements of the patriarchal mode of production', in *Patriarchy at Work* (1992). By permission of Blackwell Publishers. From Nickie Charles and Marion Kerr, *Women, Food and Families* (1989). By permission of Manchester University Press. From Mansfield, Penny and Collard, Jean, *The Beginning of the Rest of your Life?: A portrait of newlywed marriage*, Basingstoke and London: Macmillan; New York: Sheridan House, 1988. From Haleh Afshar, 'Gender rules and the "moral economy of kin" among Pakistani Women in West Yorkshire', *New Community*, vol. 15, no. 2, (1989), pp. 216–17.

By permission of New Community. From Michele Bograd, 'What are feminist perspectives on wife abuse?' from Introduction to K. Ylló and M. Bograd (eds) *Feminist Perspectives on Wife Abuse* (1988). By permission of Sage Publications Ltd. From Ann Oakley, *Becoming a Mother* (1979). By permission of Blackwell Publishers. From Ann Oakley, *Taking it like a Woman* (1984). By permission of Jonathan Cape Ltd. From Sheila Rowbotham, 'To be or not to be: the dilemma of mothering', in *The Past is Before Us* (Penguin Books, 1990). Copyright © Sheila Rowbotham, 1989. From Julia Brannen and Peter Moss, *Managing Mothers: Dual earner households after maternity leave* (1991). By permission of Unwin Hyman. From Ann Phoenix, 'Narrow definitions of culture: the case of early motherhood', in S. Westwood and P. Bachu (eds), *Enterprising Women* (1988). By permission of Routledge. From Julia Berryman, 'Perspectives on later motherhood', in A. Phoenix, A. Wollett and E. Lloyd (eds), *Motherhood: Meanings, practices and ideologies* (1991). By permission of Sage Publications Ltd. From Anne Woollet and Ann Phoenix, 'Afterword', in A. Phoenix, A. Wollett and E. Lloyd (eds), *Motherhood: Meanings, practices and ideologies* (1991). By permission of Sage Publications Ltd. From Lynne Harne, 'Lesbian custody and the new myth of the father', in *Trouble and Strife* (1984), PO Box 8, Diss, Norfolk IP22 3XG. Copyright © 1984 by Lynne Harne. By permission of the author. From Gemma Tang Nain, 'Black women, sexism and racism: black or anti-racist feminism', in *Feminist Review*, no. 37, pp. 9–10 (1991). By permission of the author and *Feminist Review*. Extract from *Femininity and Domination* by Sandra Lee Bartky, 1990, appears by courtesy of the publisher, Routledge, New York, and the author. From Luce Irigaray, *This Sex Which Is Not One* (1985). By permission of Cornell University Press. From Diane Richardson, 'The challenge of AIDS', in *Women and the AIDS Crisis* (1989). By permission of Pandora, an imprint of HarperCollins Publishers Limited, and Methuen Inc., New York. Extract from *Understanding Sexual Violence: a study of convicted rapists* by Diane Scully, 1990, appears by courtesy of the publisher, Routledge, New York and the author. Extract from *Black Feminist Thought* by Patricia Hill Collins, 1990, appears by courtesy of the publisher, Routledge, New York and the author. Reprinted with permission from Rosemary Pringle, 'Bureaucracy, rationality and sexuality: The case of secretaries' in J. Hearn *et al.*, *The Sexuality of Organizations* (1989), Sage Publications Ltd. From Susan Ardill and Sue O'Sullivan, 'Upsetting an Applecart' from *Feminist Review*, no. 23 (1986). By permission of the authors. The extract from *Anticlimax* by Sheila Jeffreys, first published by The Women's Press, 1990, 34 Great Sutton Street, London EC1V 0DX, reprinted on pages 243–44, is used by permission of The Women's Press Ltd. From bell hooks, 'Ending female sexual oppression', in *Feminist Theory: From margin to centre* (1984). By permission of South End Press. From Deborah Cameron, 'Ten years on: compulsory heterosexuality and lesbian existence', in *Women: A Cultural Review*, vol. 1, no. 1 (1990). By permission of Oxford University Press. From Albie Sachs and Joan Hoff Wilson, *Sexism and the Law* (1978). By permission of Blackwell Publishers. From Susan Edwards, *Female Sexuality and the Law* (1981). By permission of Blackwell Publishers. From Katherine O'Donovan, *Sexual Divisions in Law* (1985). By permission of George Weidenfeld & Nicolson Limited. For permission to photocopy this selection, please contact Harvard University Press. Reprinted by permission of the publishers from *Feminism Unmodified* by Catharine MacKinnon, Cambridge, Mass.: Harvard University Press, Copyright © 1987 by the President and Fellows of Harvard College. From Wendy Moore, 'There should be a law against it ... shouldn't there?', in *Feminism and Censorship* (1988), Prism Press Book Publishers Ltd., 2 South Street, Bridport, Dorset DT6 3NQ. By permission of the author and the editor, Gail Chester. Reprinted with permission from *Pornography and Feminism: The case against censorship*, edited by Gillian Rodgerson and Elizabeth Wilson, Lawrence & Wishart Ltd., London 1991. From Carol Smart, *Feminism and the Power of Law* (1989). By permission of Routledge. From Frances Heidensohn, *Crime and Society* (1989). By permission of the Macmillan Press Ltd. and New York University Press. From Frances Heidensohn, *Women and Crime* (1985). By permission of the Macmillan Press Ltd. and New York University Press. From Pat Carlen, 'Women, crime, feminism and reason', in *Social Justice*, vol. 17, no. 4, Winter 1990. By permission of *Social Justice*. From Jeanne Gregory, 'Sex Class and Crime', in R. Matthews and J. Young (eds), *Confronting Crime* (1986). By permission of Sage Publications Ltd. From Pat Carlen, 'Criminal women and criminal justice: the limits to, and potential of, feminist and left realist perspectives', in R. Matthews and J. Young (eds), *Issues in Realist Criminology* (1992). By permission of Sage Publications Ltd. From Kathryn Chadwick and Catherine Little, 'The criminalization of women', in P. Scraton (ed.), *Law, Order and the Authoritarian State* (1987). By permission of the Open University Press. From Margaret Stacey and Marion Price, 'Given the odds, a great advance. How to go further?', in *Women, Power and Politics* (1981). By permission of Tavistock Publications. From Susan Edwards, 'Policing: the under-representation of women's interests', in *Policing 'Domestic' Violence: women, the law and the state*

(1989). By permission of Sage Publications Ltd. From Margery Wolf, 'The birth limitation program: family vs state', in *Revolution Postponed: Women in contemporary China* (1985). By permission of Methuen & Co. From Peter Squires, 'Policing the Family', in *Anti-Social Policy: Welfare, ideology and the disciplinary state* (1990), Harvester Wheatsheaf, Hemel Hempstead. From Jill Evans, Clare Hudson and Penny Smith, 'Women and the strike: it's a whole way of life', reprinted with permission from *Policing the Miners' Strike*, edited by Bob Fine and Robert Millar, Lawrence & Wishart Ltd., London 1985, and by permission of the authors. From Alison Young, 'Body/politics: our bodies triumphed', in *Femininity in Dissent* (1990). By permission of Routledge. Reprinted with permission from Anne Fausto-Sterling, 'Life in the XY Corral', in *Women's Studies International Forum*, vol. 12, no. 3, Copyright 1989, Pergamon Press Ltd. From Ruth Herschberger, 'Society writes biology', in *Adam's Rib*, Harper & Row. Copyright © 1948, 1970 by Ruth Herschberger. By permission of the author. From Ludmilla Jordanova, 'Natural facts: an historical perspective on science and sexuality', in *Sexual Visions: Images of gender in science and medicine between the eighteenth and twentieth centuries* (1989), Harvester Wheatsheaf, Hemel Hempstead. By permission of the author. From Elaine Showalter, 'Managing female minds', in *The Female Malady* (1987). By permission of Virago Press and Pantheon Books, a division of Random House, Inc. From *The Woman in the Body* by Emily Martin. Copyright © 1987 by Emily Martin. Reprinted by permission of the Open University Press and Beacon Press. From Sophie Laws, 'Who needs PMT?', in S. Laws, V. Hey and A. Egan, *Seeing Red: the Politics of premenstrual tension* (1985). By permission of the author and Hutchinson. From Frances Evans 'Managers and labourers: women's attitudes to reproductive technology', in W. Faulkner and E. Arnold (eds) *Smothered by Invention: technology in women's lives* (1985). By permission of Pluto Press. From Gena Corea, 'The reproductive brothel', in G. Corea *et al.*, *Man-Made Women: How new reproductive technologies affect women* (1985). By permission of Hutchinson. Extract from *Disciplining Foucault* by Jana Sawicki, 1991, appears by courtesy of the publisher, Routledge, New York and the author. From Christine Delphy, 'New reproductive technologies', in 'Mothers' Union', *Trouble and Strife*, no. 24, 1992, PO Box 8, Diss, Norfolk, IP22 3XG. By permission of the author. First published in French in *Nouvelles Questions Féministes*, nos. 16–17–18, 1991. From Dale Spender, 'Language and reality: who made the world?', in *Man Made Language* (1985). By permission of Pandora, an imprint of HarperCollins Publishers Limited. From Susan Ehrlich and Ruth King, 'Gender-based language reform and the social construction of meaning', in *Discourse and Society*, vol. 3, no. 2, 1992. By permission of Sage Publications Ltd. Excerpts from *Language and Woman's Place* by Robin Lakoff. Copyright © 1975 by Robin Lakoff. Reprinted by permission of HarperCollins Publishers. From Nancy M. Henley and Cheris Kramarae, 'Gender, power and miscommunication', in N. Coupland, H. Giles and J. Wiemann (eds), *Miscommunication and Problematic Talk* (1991). By permission of Sage Publications Ltd. From Deborah Cameron, Fiona McAlinden and Kathy O'Leary, 'Lakoff in context: the social and linguistic functions of tag questions', in J. Coates and D. Cameron (eds), *Women in Their Speech Communities* (1989). By permission of Longman Group UK Ltd. From Jennifer Coates, 'Gossip revisited', in J. Coates and D. Cameron (eds), *Women in Their Speech Communities* (1989). By permission of Longman Group UK Ltd. From Simone de Beauvoir, *The Second Sex* (1953/1972). By permission of the Estate of the author and Random House UK Limited. From Sandra Gilbert and Susan Gubar, *The Madwoman in the Attic* (1979). By permission of Yale University Press. From Adrienne Rich, *On Lies, Secrets and Silences* (1979). By permission of W.W. Norton & Company Inc., New York. From *Silences* by Tillie Olsen. Copyright © 1965, 1972, 1978 by Tillie Olsen. Used by permission of Virago Press and Delacorte Press/Seymour Lawrence, a division of Bantam Doubleday Dell Publishing Group, Inc. From Showalter, Elaine, A Literature of Their Own. Copyright © 1977 by Princeton University Press. Reprinted by permission of Princeton University Press. From Annis Pratt, *Archtypal Patterns in Women's Fiction* (1986). Harvester Press, Brighton. From Ann Rosalind Jones, 'Writing the body: towards an understanding of *l'écriture féminine*', in E. Showalter (ed.) *The New Feminist Criticism: Essays on women, literature and theory* (1986). By permission of Virago Press. From Barbara Smith, 'Toward a black feminist criticism', in J. Newton and D. Rosenfelt (eds), *Feminism and Social Change* (1985). By permission of Methuen & Co. From Maggie Humm, *Feminist Criticism* (1990). Harvester Wheatsheaf, Hemel Hempstead. By permission of the author. From Patricia Waugh, 'Feminine Fictions: Revisiting the postmodern' in *Postmodernism and Feminism* (1989). By permission of Routledge. From E. Deirdre Pribram, *Female Spectators* (Verso/NLB, London and New York, 1988). By permission of Verso. From Janice Radway, *Reading the Romance* (Verso/NLB, London and New York, 1987). By permission of Verso. From Susanne Kappeler, *The Pornography of Representation* (1986). By permission of Blackwell Publishers. From Annette Kuhn, 'The big sleep' in *The Power of the Image* (1985). By permission of Routledge. From Jeanette Murphy,

'"A Question of Silence"', in C. Bransdon (ed.), *Films for Women* (1986). By permission of the British Film Institute. From Anne Ross Muir, 'The status of women working in film and television', in L. Gannon and M. Marshment, *The Female Gaze* (1988). By permission of the author. From Dorothy Hobson, 'Women audiences and the workplace', in M.E. Brown (ed.), *Television and Women's Culture* (1990). By permission of Sage Publications Ltd. From Gillian Dyer, 'Women and television', in H. Baehr and G. Dyer (eds), *Boxed In: Women and television* (1987). By permission of Pandora, an imprint of HarperCollins Publishers Limited. From Christine Geraghty, *Women and soap opera* (1991). By permission of Blackwell Publishers.

INDEX

abortion, 320, 366
absence, 41, 70, 369, 464
academics, 135, 155–60
African women, 236–8
AIDS, 226, 231–4
androcentrism, 133–4, 414
androgyny, 40, 336
anthropology, 78–82, 90–6, 99–102
anti-essentialism, 5, 20–4, 26–9
anti-feminism, 60–4, 82, 128, 221, 252,
    257, 259, 283–91
Artificial Insemination by Donor, 366
Austen, Jane, 448, 451–2
autonomy (and identity), 42–4

Bachofen, J.J., 77–8, 81
Barrett, M., 4, 11–13, 139–41, 326
Beauvoir, Simone de, 7, 79, 82, 84, 433,
    438–9
Bedouin women, 102–3
Bem Sex Role Inventory, 40
Beveridge Report, 325, 343, 349
bilingualism, 420
biological: determinism, 39, 60–4, 90–2,
    206, 325, 336, 371–4; differences, 5,
    12–13, 19, 21–2, 29–34, 297–9, 336–7;
    family, 7–9; reductionism, 84, 85–6
biologism, 3–4, 7–9
Birmingham study, 112–14
birth control, 7–8, 348–9, 366

black women, 220–1, 236–8; literary
    criticism, 458–63; social theory, 5–6,
    25–34; at work, 173–7
Bloom, Harold, 442–5
Board Schools, 117–18
body, 227–30; control of, 3–4, 7–9,
    380–7; disciplinary technologies,
    394–6; politics, 354–9; see also
    pornography; reproductive technology
bos–ssecretary relations, 239–40
bourgeois feminists, 319–20
bourgeois women, 134, 139–40
Brontë family, 448, 449, 451

Cameron, D., 246, 404–5, 421–5
capitalism, 94, 114–15, 345–6; and class,
    134, 140–5; crime and, 320, 323, 326–7;
    marriage and, 181, 199–200, 220–1;
    social theory and, 3–4, 9–16, 18–19
Carlen, P., 308–9, 314–15, 317–19, 333–5
castration, 41, 58, 62, 63, 65, 69
censorship, 252–3, 276–91
children, 92, 121, 143, 183; Japan study,
    96–9; lesbian custody, 217–20;
    maintenance, 349–51; 'quality time',
    210, 211; see also education;
    motherhood
China, 83, 348–9
Chodorow, Nancy, 41, 58–60, 91, 481
Cixous, Hélène, 435–6, 456–7

class: consciousness, 137, 145; and crime, 316, 319–21, 336–7; historical perspective, 112–20, 122–4; sex class, 7–9, 17–18, 24; struggle, 3, 134, 146–8; women's oppression and, 134, 139–46
co-operativity, 406, 424, 427
coal mines, 115–16, 351–4
colonialism, 30–1, 94–5, 226
commodity production, 142, 143
common law, 256–7, 258, 262
community care, 326, 343–4
conscious, 64–5, 263, 466
consciousness-raising, 162, 467
control: of female reproduction, 3–4, 7–9; maintenance system, 349–51; menstruation as metaphor, 380–7; theories, 330–2; *see also* social control
conversation, 416–18, 422–5
crime, 307; control theory, 330–2; criminalisation, 321–8; feminist criminology, 319–21; gender and, 312–15; left realism, 317–19, 333–5; liberation thesis, 308, 316; non-sexist, 336–7; society and (statistics), 309–11
cross-cultural perspectives, 77–8; anthropology, 90–6, 99–102; childhood in Japan, 96–9; fatherhood, 79–80; nature and gender, 84–6; resistance (Bedouin women), 102–3; sexual inequality (origin), 86–9; status of women, 80–4
culture: difference, 29–34; early motherhood, 211–14; enculturation (social semiotics), 151–5; femininity construction, 53–7, 177; kinship, 9–11, 195–6; –nature opposition, 82–6, 91–2, 374–7; patterning, 86–9; *see also* cross-cultural perspectives
custody, 217–20

deconstructionism, 5, 21, 26–9, 301, 318–19, 334, 457
deficit theory, 416–20
dependence relations, 11–13

depression, 199–200, 202–4
Dialectic of Sex, The, 3–4, 7–9
difference, 49–50, 93–6, 297–9; *see also* sexual difference
disciplinary practices, 227–30
disciplinary technologies, 394–6
division of labour, 9, 12, 16, 136, 140, 145–6, 184–7, 239, 271, 336
divorce, 219
domestic: labour theory, 141–6; mode of production, 4, 11–13, 16–19, 181–2, 187–8; service, 122–4
domesticity, 116–20, 122–4, 264
dominant ideologies, 207–13, 476–9
domination, 16–18, 86–9, 408–10
Dworkin, Andrea, 23, 252, 276–83, 286, 287, 290, 367

education: laws, 121; Marxist feminism and, 139–41; mastery of reason, 134–5, 148–51; performance in school, 53–7; preschool, 151–5; working class, 116–18
Electra complex, 443, 444
Eliot, George, 449, 450, 451–2
embryology, 372–4
employment: academics, 155–60; black women, 173–7; crime and, 325–7; in film/television, 488–90; historical perspective, 109–16, 122–4; lesbian corporate experience, 167–73; Marxist feminist view, 139–41; patriarchal structure, 4, 18–19; professions, 254–64, 364–5; relationships, TV viewing and, 490–2; sexuality in workplace, 238–40; women's dual role, 184–7; women managers, 160–3; women's oppression (class context), 141–8; work consciousness, 136–9
English women, 80–2
Enlightenment, 374–7
epistemic modality, 406, 416–18, 426–7
epistemological approach, 45–50, 299, 376

Equal Pay Act, 287, 326
equality, 21–2, 199, 243–4, 297–9, 320
essentialism, 5, 21–4, 26–9, 32–3, 39,
    50–3, 133, 135, 155–60, 318, 436, 494,
    495
ethnocentrism, 25–7, 84, 95–6
ethnography, 78–9, 82, 95, 99–102
Eurocentrism, 177, 220–1, 463
exogamy, 9–10, 11

family, 17, 80, 94, 134, 145; in Ancient
    Greece, 146–8; food, 188–91, 352–4;
    household, 220; nuclear, 11, 183, 198,
    200, 322, 324–5; privacy, 269–71;
    problem-solving, 191–4; as social
    institution, 197–8; structure, 58–60;
    unregulated, 272–3; wage, 15–16, 144,
    326; *see also* children; fatherhood;
    marriage; motherhood; wives
fantasy, 42–3, 68–70, 235, 240, 243, 441,
    482
farmers' wives, 110–11
fatherhood, 58, 79–80, 211, 442; lesbian
    custody and, 217–20
Fawcett, Millicent, 81, 125
feelings, shared, 191–4
female: embryology, 372, 374; gaze, 473,
    486–90; nature, 45–50; power, 86–9;
    sexuality, *see* sexuality
femicide, 366–7
feminism: pornography and, 288–91;
    power of law and, 291–302; *see also*
    Marxist feminism; radical feminism
feminist criminology, *see* crime
feminist jurisprudence, 295–7, 302, 315
feminist literary criticism, 433–7; alienation
    (Freudian model), 441–5; archetypal
    patterns, 450–3; black/lesbian
    challenge, 462–3; black criticism,
    458–61; inaccuracies in critical
    discussion, 448–50; phallocentrism
    challenged, 454–8; postmodernism,
    464–9; sexual revolution, 439–41;
    silence, 445–8; woman defined, 438

feminist social theory, 3–6;
    difference/international feminism,
    29–34; feminism without women,
    27–8; *m/f 1* (Editorial), 19–20;
    patriarchy, 11–16, 18–19;
    postmodernism, 20–1; psychoanalysis
    and, 9–11; racism challenged, 25–6;
    sex class, 7–9, 16–18; sex equality,
    21–2; woman (myth and definition),
    22–4; women (historical
    reconstruction), 26–7; women in
    history, 28–9
femininty, 58–61, 177, 225–6, 300, 336–7,
    344, 437; as performance, 41, 53–7;
    sexualised ideal, 227–30; subjectivity
    and, 40, 45, 51, 225, 465–9, 485
films, 473–9, 484–90
Finer Report (1974), 351
FINNRAGE, 367, 389, 394
Firestone, S., 3–4, 7–9, 16, 366
food, 188–91, 352–4
Foucault, M., 21, 56, 103, 227–30
Franchise Act (1867), 117, 125
Frankfurt School, 16
French critics, 435–7, 454–8
Freudian theory, 8, 10–11, 39–41, 43,
    58–67, 69, 369, 436, 441–3, 445, 455,
    476, 481
Friedan, Betty, 163, 221
frigidity, 374
functionalism, 140, 142

gender, 4, 17–18, 39–40, 58–9, 240;
    -based language reform, 410–15; crime
    and, 312–14, 336–7; cultural category,
    9–11, 19–20, 148–51, 225, 239;
    language and, *see* language (and
    gender); nature–culture theory, 84–6;
    power and, 86–9, 148–51, 197–8;
    psychological theories, 50–3; relations,
    5, 20–1; roles (Pakistani women),
    195–6; sexual difference, 5, 12–13, 19,
    21–2, 29–34, 49–50, 477; specific
    semiosis, 151–5; *see also* men; women

genetic engineering, 366–7, 389–93
gossip, 426–7
government employment policy, 122–4
Greece, Ancient, 146–8
Greenham Common, 162, 323, 328, 354–9
Griffiths Report (1988), 343

Hartmann, H., 4, 13–16, 141, 144–5
health, 44, 118–20, 121
Heidensohn, Frances, 308–14, 330–2
heterosexuality, 24, 59, 66, 109, 243–5;
   compulsory, 226, 239, 246
Hidden from History, 107, 114–15
hierarchical relations, 14–15
higher education, 155–60
historical reconstruction, 26–9
historical perspectives, 107–8; domestic
   service, 122–4; education for working
   class, 116–18; gender divisions,
   112–14; Industrial Revolution, 109–11;
   motherhood, 121; spinsters, 127–8;
   suffrage, 124–7; working class wives,
   118–20; working class women, 114
historical specificity, 32–3
homosexuality, 66, 128, 265, 271–2; *see
   also* lesbian women
hooks, bell, 245
household, 11–13, 18–19, 109–11, 220–1,
   326; *see also* domesticity
humanism, 42, 457, 466
hysteria, 64–5, 260, 363, 386, 454

identity (and autonomy), 12–4
ideologies, 85–6, 263–4, 267–8, 275, 320,
   323; dominant, 207–13, 476, 478–9;
   patriarchal, 9–11, 327–8
images, 44, 47, 157, 206–7, 210, 229–30,
   344, 377, 484–6, 493
impotence, 374
in vitro fertilisation, 366, 390–2
incest, 9–10, 11, 64–5
industrial action, 323, 351–4
Industrial Revolution, 108–11, 115, 134,
   357

international feminism, 29–34
Irigaray, Luce, 5, 21–2, 231, 436, 455–6,
   457

Japanese women, 96–9
Jeffreys, S., 108–9, 127–8, 226, 243
Jewish tradition, 99–102
jouissance, 70, 436, 454–7, 467
judicial neutrality, 251, 254–64

Kikumura, Akemi, 79, 96–9
kinship, 9–11, 68, 77, 195–6, 398
knowledge, 20–1, 45–50, 56, 300–1, 376
Kristeva, Julia, 436–7, 454–7

labour-power, 4, 11–15, 140, 142–5, 147,
   187–8
Labov, W., 412
Lacan, J., 41, 49, 67–72, 476
Lakoff, R., 405–6, 416–18, 421–5
language, 457, 459, 465–6; Lacan's view,
   41, 67–70, 72
language (and gender), 403–6; gossip,
   426–7; miscommunication, 418–20;
   reality, 407–10; reform, 410–15;
   womans place, 416–18; *see also*
   poststructuralism
law, 251–3; female sexuality and, 265–8;
   pornography, 276–91; power of,
   291–302; sexism and, 254–64; sexual
   divisions, 269–76
left realism, 317–19, 333–5
lesbian women, 53, 244; compulsory
   heterosexuality, 246–7; custody rights,
   217–20; literature, 460–3; in
   organisations, 167–73; political
   lesbianism, 226–7, 241, 245;
   sadomasochism, 241–2; scientific
   category, 127–8; woman role (refusal
   of), 5, 22–4
Levi-Strauss, C., 68, 84–5
LEXIS, 279
'liable relative' policy, 349–51
liberalism, 252, 269–75, 437

liberation thesis, 308, 316
libertarian sexual politics, 243–4
lies (negative power), 445–7
linguistic sexism, 403–4, 407–15
literature, *see* feminist literary criticism
love, 68, 70, 182, 202–3, 209, 451–3
lunacy/madness, 378–80

m/f (journal), 19–20
MacKinnon, C.A., 234–5, 252–3, 276–83, 295–7, 299
madness/lunacy, 378–80
males, *see* men
management careers, 160–3, 240
marriage, 181–3; archetypal enclosure, 450–3; black women's, 220–1; division of labour, 184–7; food, 188–91; gender role (Pakistani), 195–6; laws, 9–10, 147; patriarchal mode of production, 187–8; problem-solving, 191–4; wife abuse, 197–8; *see also* fatherhood; motherhood; wives
Marxist feminism: *m/f* editorial, 19–20; oppression at work (class context), 141–8; patriarchy, 3, 4, 12–16, 320; psychoanalysis, 64–7; work consciousness, 134, 136–9
masculinity, 40–1, 45, 48, 58–60, 177, 225–6, 300–1, 336–7, 467, 485
masochism, 40, 61, 240–4
materialist feminism, 4–5, 19, 22–4, 26–8, 181–2
maternity care, 388–99
mathematics education, 54, 55
matriarchal society, 372–4
meaning, 45, 82–6, 375, 410–15
media, 473–4; female spectators, 475–9; images, 484–6; pornography, 483–4; *A Question of Silence*, 486–8; reading romantic fiction, 480–2; soap operas, 494–6; status of women in, 488–90; television (feminist criticism), 492–3; women audiences (and workplace), 490–2

medicine, 267; *see also* science and medicine
men: domestic labour debate, 143–6; male dominance, 86–9, 408–10; male embryology, 372–4; male gaze, 473–4, 488; male mind, 45–50; male model of literary history, 441–5; male monopoly cases, 256–7, 259–62; nature–culture opposition, 82–6, 91–2; positional identity, 58–60; relationships with (in management), 161–3; violent, *see* violence; woman defined relative to, 438–9; *see also* fatherhood; gender
menstruation, 380–4; PMT, 336–7, 363–4, 385–7
mental health, 199–200
metanarratives, 5, 20
middle-class women, 112–14
midwifery, 364, 365
Millett, Kate, 60–4, 434, 439–41
miscommunication, 418–20
Mitchell, J., 4, 9–11, 39, 64–7, 442, 443–4
Morrison, Toni, 459, 460–1
mortality rates, 121
Mossman, M.J., 292, 293–4, 295
mother-blaming, 183, 216–17
motherhood, 41, 77, 121; in black families, 220–1; changing perspectives, 204–7; dominant ideology, 207–11; lesbian, 217–20; older, 214–16; postnatal depression, 202–4; professionalisation, 183, 216–17; relational identity, 58–60; surrogate, 396–7; transition to (impact), 198–202; young, 211–14; *see also* reproduction technology
Mundurucu women, 87, 88
mutual support (couples), 193–4

narcissism, 40, 61, 63, 240
National Assistance Board, 350
National Federation of Women workers, 122, 123
National Film School, 489

National Health Service, 343
National Insurance scheme, 343
National Union of Women's Suffrage,
   109, 124–6
Nationality Act (1986), 196
nature, 7–8; –culture opposition, 82–6,
   91–2, 374–7; –nurture debate, 79–80,
   86–9; significance, 45–50
non-sexist terms, 336–7, 410–15; *see also*
   language (gender)
novels/novelists, 440–1, 448–53, 460–1,
   480–2
nuclear family, 11, 183, 198, 200, 322,
   324–5

Oakley, Ann, 4, 182, 198–204, 312
object-relations theory, 41, 58–60
objectivity, 46, 48, 49, 408
Oedipus complex, 10–11, 41, 46–7, 58–9,
   65, 69, 442–4, 477, 478
otherness, 363, 365, 436, 439, 466
out-of-work donation, 122–4

Pakistani women, 195–6
Pankhurst family, 109, 127, 255, 260, 261
panopticism (Foucault), 227–8, 230
part-time work, 200, 326
passivity, 40, 55, 57, 61, 197, 435
paternalism, 165, 166
patriarchy: a historical concept, 4, 11–13;
   crime and, 317, 320, 322–7, cultural
   origins, 4, 9–11; domestic labour
   theory, 143–6, 187–8; dominance, 3–4,
   7–9; forms and degree, 18–19;
   language and, 403, 408, 410–15; law
   and, 252, 289, 301–2; literature and,
   433–7, 440, 442–4; Marxist feminism
   and, 3–4, 13–16, 139–41; media and,
   473, 476, 478, 486–8; scientific
   discourse challenged, 371–4; sex
   classes, 17–18; sexuality and, 226–30,
   246–7; state and, 341–59
penis envy, 40, 59, 61–3, 64, 231
performance, 41, 53–7

personality, feminine, 58–60
'persons cases', 251, 254–5, 257, 261,
   262, 264
phallic case, 69, 70, 71–2
phallocentrism, 41, 225–6, 231, 435–7,
   455
phallogocentrism, 300, 435–6, 454–8
phantasy, 65, 71
Plowden Report, 57
PMT, 336–7, 363–4, 385–7
poetry, 440–3 *passim*, 463
police work, 163–7
policing violence, 346–8
political: activities, 259–60, 351–9;
   lesbianism, 226–7, 241, 245; power, *see*
   state and politics
politics, 162, 274; of identification, 33–4
pornography, 236–7, 347–8; and
   censorship, 252–3, 276–91; of
   representation, 483–4
positioning concept, 56–7
postmodernism, 354–9; and feminist
   literary criticism, 437, 464–9; gender
   relations, 5, 20–1
postnatal depression, 202–4
poststructuralism, 20, 40, 55, 354–9, 465
power, 21, 45, 56; eroticization of, 226,
   243–4; gender and, 86–9, 148–51,
   197–8; of image, 484–6; of law,
   291–302; male dominance, 86–9;
   miscommunication and, 418–20;
   patriarchal, 227–30; political/traditional,
   344–6; relations, 190, 238–40, 321–8,
   345; resistance, 102–3, 151–5, and
   sadomasochism, 241–2; sexuality in
   workplace, 238–40; transformation of,
   102–3
pre-menstrual tension, 336–7, 363–4,
   385–7
pre-school education, 151–5
pregnancy, 146, 202–4, 211–16, 297,
   365–6, 388–9, 395; *see also* birth
   control; motherhood
primitive societies, 77–8, 80–2, 90–3

privacy, 252, 269–71
private: patriarchy and, 4, 18–19; and
  public (politics), *see* state and politics;
  and public (sexual divisions in law),
  269–76
problem-solving (families), 191–4
professionalisation: of medicine, 364–5;
  of motherhood, 183, 216–17
property rights, 147–8
prostitution, 237–8, 270–2, 292, 314,
  347–8, 440
psychoanalysis, 13, 19; antifeminist,
  60–4; feminism and, 9–11, 64–7;
  Lacan, 67–72; literary psychohistory,
  441–5; media and, 476–82
psychoanalytic theory, 39–41;
  autonomy/identity, 42–4; family
  structure, 58–60; feminism in
  psychology, 50–3; feminity as
  performance, 53–7; Freud, 60–7;
  Lacan's influence, 67–72; male
  mind/female nature, 45–50
psychology, 39–41; feminism in, 50–3;
  see also psychoanalysis; psychoanalytic
  theory
public: patriarchy and, 4, 18–19; and
  private (politics), *see* state and politics;
  and private (sexual divisions in law),
  269–76; rights, 257, 261

'quality time', 210, 211
Question of Silence, A (film), 486–8

race/racism, 5–6, 23, 25–6, 34, 94–5,
  285–6; *see also* black women
radical feminism, 3, 7–9, 133, 320, 437,
  457; eroticization of equality, 243–4;
  materialist, 4, 5, 22–4, 26–8
rape, 232, 234–6, 238, 265–6, 277,
  289–90, 292–3, 301, 347
reading romantic novels, 480–2, 496
realism, 483–4; left, 317–19, 333–5
reality, language and, 407–10
Rehabilitation of Offenders Act, 285

relationality, 133
religion, 77, 99–102, 441
reproduction, 146, 267, 363–4, 371–4;
  female (metaphors), 381–4; male
  control, 3–4, 7–9; *see also* motherhood;
  pregnancy
'reproductive brothel', 367, 389–93
reproductive technology, 366; disciplinary
  technologies, 394–6; genetic
  engineering, 389–93; new (critiques),
  396–9; women's attitudes, 388–9
'residence order', 217–20
resistance, 102–3, 151–5
revisionist/pro-family feminism, 221
Rich, Adrienne, 226, 239, 246–7, 434,
  444–7, 461, 462–3
romantic fiction, 43, 480–2, 496
Rowbotham, Sheila, 107–8, 114–15,
  204–7, 345
Royal Family, 43–4

sadomasochism, 240, 241–2, 243–4
science and medicine, 363–7; lunacy,
  378–80; menstruation, 380–7;
  nature/culture, 374–7; patriarchal
  discourse challenged, 371–4;
  reproductive technology, 388–99; sex
  determination/differentiation, 368–71
Second Sex, The, 82, 438–9
self, 20, 42–4, 191–4, 199, 227–30, 466–8
separatism, 160, 162–3, 437, 486
sex classes, 7–9, 17–18, 24
sex differentiation/differentiation, 368–71
Sex Discrimination Act (1975), 287, 297,
  326
sexism, law and, 254–64
sexist terminology, 403–4, 407–15
sexual: difference, 5, 12–13, 19, 21–2,
  29–34, 49–50, 477; division of labour, 9,
  12, 16, 136–7, 140, 145–6, 184–7, 239,
  271–2, 336; divisions in law, 269–76;
  equality, 21–2, 199, 226, 243–4, 297–9;
  harassment, 238–40, 277, 324;
  inequality (origins), 86–9; perversion,

sexual (*continued*)
65–6; politics, 60–4, 243–4, 246–7, 439–41, 463

Sexual Politics, 60–4, 439–41

sexual revolution, 61, 103; in literature, 439–41

sexuality, 68–9, 225–6; AIDS, 231–4; black feminism, 236–8; compulsory heterosexuality, 246–7; eroticization of equality, 243–4; law and, 265–8; patriarchal power, 227–30; phallocentrism, 231; political lesbianism, 245; sadomasochism, 241–2; science and, 374–7; violence, 234–6; in workplace, 238–40

Showalter, Elaine, 378–80, 434–5, 444, 448–50

silences, 445–8

single parents, 183, 219, 343, 349–51

Smart, Carol, 252–3, 291–302, 307, 316, 318–19, 322, 324

Smith, Barbara, 245, 437, 458–61

Smith, Dorothy, 292, 322, 408

soap operas, 43 493 494–6

social class, *see* class

social construction of meaning, 410–15

social control, 60, 134, 466; crime and, 308, 322–5, 330–2, 337

social domination, 16–18

social institutions, 77

social learning theory, 466

social security, 342–3, 350, 351

social semiotics, 151–5

social status of women, 80–4

social theory, *see* feminist social theory

socialism, 8–9, 11, 134, 141–6, 241, 260, 320–1, 345–6

society, 309–11, 371–4

spectatorship, 475–9

Spender, Dale, 41, 403–4, 407–10

spinsters, 127–8, 357

state, 18–19, 323–5

state and politics: birth limitation (China), 348–9; Greenham Common,

354–9; maintenance payments, 349–51; patriarchal forms, 341–4; pit strike, 351–4; policing violence, 346–8; political and traditional power, 344–6

strikes, 323, 351–4

structuralism, 39, 82–6, 466, 485

subjectivity, 40, 44–9, 51, 57, 68, 408, 476, 478–9, 485; fictions, 433, 437–8, 464–9, 482; gendered, 9–11, 148–51, 225, 239

suffrage movement, 78, 109, 117, 124–7, 259–62, 344

superego, 40, 63

surplus value, 142, 143

symbolic meanings, 82–6, 375

symbolism, 41, 49, 62, 64, 67–70, 408–10, 436–7, 454

tag questions, 405–6, 416–18, 420–5

teaching, women in, 155–60

television, 488–96

trade unions, 144, 145, 256, 352–4

trades (women's businesses), 112–14

truth, 20, 21

Truth, Sojourner, 26, 27–8

unconscious, 64–5, 67, 69–70, 72, 457

unemployment, 122–4, 174, 214, 327

universalist, 32–3, 92, 462

use values 142–3, 485

violence: rape, 232, 234–6, 238, 347; sadomasochism, 240, 241–2, 243–4; suffrage campaign, 125–7, 259–60, 262; under-policed, 346–8; wife abuse, 197–8, 347

wages, 11–12, 14–16, 18, 114–15, 123–4, 142–5, 188, 326

Walby, Sylvia, 4, 18–19, 181, 187–8, 343

Walker, Alice, 459, 463

war work, 122–4

welfare state, 325–6, 343–4

Williams Committee, 290

Wittig, Monique, 5, 22–4, 226
wives: of farmers, 110–11; violence against, 197–8, 347; working class, 118–20; *see also* marriage; motherhood
Wolfenden Report (1957), 271–2
women: definitions, 22–4, 438–9; development, 161–3; differences, 93–6; education, *see* education; female embryology, 372, 374; female gaze, 473, 486–90; female nature, 45–50; female power, 86–9; feminism without, 27–8; historical reconstruction, 26–9; nature–culture opposition, 82–6, 91–2; history, 107–28; language of, *see* language (and gender); law and, *see* law; minds of, *see* psychoanalytic theory; representation, *see* media; unifying category, 29–34; at work, *see* employment; writers, *see* feminist literary criticism; *see also* black women; gender; motherhood; wives
Women's Freedom League, 126

Women's Health Inquiry, 118–20
Women's Liberation Movement, 25, 79, 162–3, 204–7, 345, 388, 449, 492
Women's Oppression Today, 11–13
Women's Social and Political Union, 126, 127
women's subordination: capitalism and, 3–4, 13–16, 134; cultural construction, 4, 9–11; education and work, 139–41; marxist feminism, 19–20; post modernism and, 5, 20–1; sex classes, 17–18; sexual differences as product, 5, 22–4; sexuality and, 243–5; working-class, 114–15
women's talk, 404–6, 416–27
Woolf, Virginia, 449, 450, 467–8
work, *see* employment
working class, 3, 114–20, 122–4, 144–5, 326, 333, 337, 345

young mothers, 211–14
Younger Report (1972), 270